THE FRANCO-PRUSSIAN WAR 1870–71

VOLUME 2

After Sedan: Helmuth von Moltke and the Defeat of the Government of National Defence

Quintin Barry

Helion & Company

To Sarah, Jo and John

Helion & Company Limited
Unit 8 Amherst Business Centre
Budbrooke Road
Warwick
CV34 5WE
England
Tel. 01926 499619
Email: info@helion.co.uk
Website: www.helion.co.uk
X (formerly Twitter): @Helionbooks
Facebook: @HelionBooks
Visit our blog at https://helionbooks.wordpress.com/

Published by Helion & Company 2007. This paperback edition 2025
Designed and typeset by Helion & Company
Cover designed by Paul Hewitt, Battlefield Design (www.battlefield-design.co.uk)

ISBN 978-1-806721-05-4

British Library Cataloguing-in-Publication Data.
A catalogue record for this book is available from the British Library.

In this concluding volume of his acclaimed study, Quintin Barry continues the story of the Franco-Prussian War from the collapse of Napoleon III's empire to the proclamation of the German Empire at Versailles and the uneasy peace that followed.

After Sedan, Helmuth von Moltke faced a new and uncertain struggle. The war against the self-proclaimed Government of National Defence was no longer a conventional campaign between professional armies but a test of endurance against hastily raised forces, popular resistance, and the political passions of a nation in revolt.

Barry traces the German advance on Paris and the long siege that followed, alongside simultaneous operations across France — at Strasbourg, Metz, Orleans, Amiens, the Loire, Belfort, and the North. Drawing deeply on contemporary German and French sources, he reconstructs the major battles — Coulmiers, Beaune-la-Rolande, Loigny-Poupry, Le Mans, and St Quentin — and shows how Moltke's command structure adapted to new challenges of logistics, winter campaigning and dispersed warfare.

The narrative captures both the strategic and the human dimensions: Gambetta's desperate mobilisation efforts, the rise of the Francs-Tireurs, and the strains within the German high command as the war dragged into 1871. The culmination comes with the fall of Paris, the armistice, and the emergence of a united Germany — the moment when modern European history was reshaped.

Illustrated with detailed maps, period engravings, and comprehensive orders of battle, this volume stands as an indispensable companion to Volume 1, completing one of the most thorough English-language studies of the war that ended an empire and created another.

Quintin Barry was a retired solicitor and employment judge who had a distinguished career in both the public and private sectors, including roles within the NHS and local radio. A lifelong history enthusiast, he was the author of numerous well-regarded books on military and naval history. His notable works include a two-volume history of the Franco-Prussian War of 1870–1871, a history of the Austro-Prussian War of 1866, and the first modern account of the Russo-Turkish War of 1877–1878. Barry was particularly known for his in-depth study of the life and career of Helmuth von Moltke. Barry's work is highly regarded by historians and enthusiasts of military and naval affairs. Sadly, Quintin passed away in early 2025.

Helmuth von Moltke (Scheibert)

Contents

Appendices

List of Illustrations

Key to Sources

Bork *Deutschlands große Jahre 1870/71 geschildert in Liedern* (Munich, 1889)
Hohenlohe-Ingelfingen *Aus meinem Leben* (Berlin, 1897–1908)
Illustrierte Kriegs-Chronik 1870–1871 (Leipzig, 1871)
Klein *Fröschweiler Chronik* (Munich, no date)
Lindner *Der Krieg gegen Frankreich 1870–71* (Berlin, 1895)
Pflug-Harttung *Krieg und Sieg 1870–71, ein Gedenkbuch* (Berlin, 1895)
Rousset *Histoire Générale de la Guerre Franco-Allemande (1870–1871)* (Paris, no date)
Rousset *Les Combattants de 1870–71* (Paris, 1895)
Scheibert *Der Krieg 1870–71* (Berlin, 1914)

List of Maps and Plans

Acknowledgements

The writing of this book stretched over a long period of time, in the course of which I received both inspiration and practical help from many people.

I should particularly like to record my gratitude to Professor Michael Foot, who long ago encouraged me to start; to the late Colonel Philip Howes, who read the manuscript and made a number of valuable suggestions; to Lindsay Cadle and Jean Hawkes whose efforts finally put volumes 1 and 2 respectively into an acceptable state of readiness after they had bravely undertaken the painful task of deciphering my appalling handwriting; to Michael Embree and Bruce Weigle for providing the orders of battle; to Nigel Vichi for his work in preparing the maps; to Duncan Rogers of Helion & Company for all his help with the illustrations and in preparing the book for publication; and of course to my wife and family, who endured without complaint my frequent and prolonged absences of mind when I was engrossed in the events of 1870–71.

In addition, the publishers wish to acknowledge the following:

Birlinn Ltd for permission to reprint an excerpt from *A Day of Battle: Mars-la-Tour, 16 August 1870* by David Ascoli, p. 339, published Birlinn (www.birlinn.co.uk), 2001.

Cambridge University Press for permission to reprint an excerpt from "Remarks on the preconditions to waging war in Prussia-Germany, 1866–1871" by Wilhelm Deist, appearing on p. 325, *On the Road to Total War* by (eds.) Stig Förster & Jörg Nagler, Cambridge University Press, 1997.

Harvard University Press for permission to reprint an excerpt from *Napoleon III and the German Crisis 1865–1866* by E.A. Pottinger, pp. 193–194, Cambridge, Mass.: Harvard University Press, Copyright © 1966 by the President and Fellows of Harvard College. (Harvard Historical Studies, 75)

Thomson for permission to reprint three excerpts from *The Franco-Prussian War: The German Invasion of France 1870–1871* by Michael Howard, pp. 24, 267 and 423, published London: Rupert Hart-Davis, 1961.

1

The Road to Paris

The strategical situation that confronted Moltke after the capitulation of the Army of Châlons at Sedan was extremely complex. The political context of the problem complicated it still further, since there was no clear precedent with which it could be compared. The comprehensive defeat of the armies of the French Empire ought, in normal circumstances, to mean the end of the war. But the Empire itself had, as Moltke had expected, collapsed under the blows of the military disasters it had suffered; and while any rational government might, in such a military situation, see the sense of negotiating an early peace, this did not necessarily apply to the Government of National Defence, given the political circumstances of its formation. In fact, although he could not have realised it at that time, Moltke was about to conduct an entirely different war, altogether distinct from that which had ended at Sedan, and of a quite dissimilar character. The new opponents he would face were to succeed in raising an army both enormous in size and possessing considerable resources, although lacking almost completely in training and experience. This new war would be fought in quite different conditions and would raise entirely novel

King William of Prussia, painting by von Angeli (Rousset/*Histoire*)

problems of both strategy and logistics, and it would make enormous demands on Moltke and those responsible for its conduct. All of this lay in the future; for the moment, Moltke could, not unreasonably, believe in his heart that there would be a speedy end to the fighting. In the meantime, however, he was obliged to proceed on the basis that this would not prove to be the case.

This required a number of consequent decisions, the first and most important of which was whether to march on Paris, and besiege the city, or to stand on the defensive in Eastern France, while pursuing the various sieges of Metz, Strasbourg and the other fortified places around which the advancing German tide had lapped. In military terms the decision to advance on Paris was not hard to take; standing fast would have given the French time to recruit and reorganise their armies, and to fight again when ready to do so on their own terms. Politically, the issue was more complex. Bismarck, musing on whether the Republic established in Paris would last, famously speculated in a letter to his son Herbert, that perhaps the best course 'would be to let the people stew in their own juice, and that we make ourselves at home in the conquered departments until we can go forward', adding that if the Germans advanced too soon it would prevent the French quarrelling among themselves.[1] But this was hardly a serious suggestion on Bismarck's part; even in political terms, it was not a practicable option, since it would leave the war continuing indefinitely, thereby increasing the risk of foreign intervention, while the siege and capture of Paris must necessarily speed its ending. Much later, reflecting on the unexpectedly long and arduous struggle which followed the battle of Sedan, Moltke was still in no doubt about the correct course: 'If, with the experience we have now, we were again placed in the position we were in after Sedan, I should have nothing better to propose to the King than what we have done, viz. to advance on Paris'.[2] The speed with which new French armies were put into the field was to demonstrate conclusively that Moltke was right. If Bismarck's recipe had been followed, the opportunity to expand and more importantly to train those armies would have immeasurably increased the magnitude of Moltke's task. Moltke, therefore, had wasted no time in issuing orders for the resumption of the march on Paris, and as early as noon on September 3 instructions had gone out from Vendresse which took account of the positions of the armies after Sedan. 'The operations of the last few days have led to the shifting of the army, in such wise that the troops of HRH the Crown Prince of Saxony will be on the left of the Third Army during the further advance upon Paris ... which is now to be commenced on a broader front.'[3] Two corps of the Third Army, the XI Corps and the I Bavarian Corps, were to be left for the moment at Sedan, to deal with the arrangements for the French prisoners, while the remainder of the Third Army, and the Army of the Meuse, moved off at once, preceded by the cavalry well in advance.

The only organised body of French troops between the German armies and the capital was Vinoy's 13th Corps, which hastily abandoned Mézières. In the course of his retreat, Vinoy headed at first for Rethel, but hearing that the Germans had got there before him, made for Laon. From there, in response to an urgent message from the capital, his corps was despatched by rail to Paris.

On September 4 Moltke moved his headquarters from Vendresse to Rethel and then, next day, to Reims. There, he revised the plans for the further advance on Paris, ordering the Army of the Meuse to move out to the right and come in on the

Moltke in Reims, painting by Braun (Rousset/*Histoire*)

north of Paris, while the Third Army took the more direct route to take up a position along the south front of the capital. The rapid lengthening of the German lines of communication, however, was already beginning to cause problems, not least because they were exposed to the possibility of attacks from the franc-tireurs, which were already showing signs of becoming more active.

On September 9 Duke William of Mecklenburg-Schwerin, with the 6th Cavalry Division, entered Laon; he was just taking possession of the citadel when it blew up, causing enormous damage and many casualties. Forty-two Prussians were killed and seventy-two wounded, including Duke William and some of his senior officers; while three hundred French troops were killed or wounded. Subsequent enquires revealed that the explosion was caused by a French NCO named Henriot who blew up himself and the powder magazine. In general, however, the German troops advanced towards Paris with little or no interruption.

As they did so, it became increasingly clear that the French intended to defend the capital. Moltke, who moved his headquarters from Reims to Chateau Thierry on September 14, held a conference there next day with the Chiefs of Staff of the Third Army and the Army of the Meuse, Blumenthal and Schlotheim, to discuss the arrangements for the investment of Paris. He concluded that it was unlikely that there would be any forward movement from the troops in Paris to interrupt the process, so that the two armies should be able to undertake their movement into the designated positions independently. The intention was to complete the investment by September 19; the investing troops were ordered at once to carry out defensive works around the perimeter, and to close down all road, rail and telegraphic communication. The only prospect of interference might come from the direction of the Loire; in that case the investment of the city must be committed

Prussians on the march towards Paris, by Speyer (Bork)

temporarily to weak detachments, and the Third Army will move with its main forces to meet the advancing foe, but at the most one or two marches, in order to defeat him and then once more resume a close and well prepared investment.[4]

The unopposed advance of the Germans towards Paris was a military spectacle which, to independent observers, was as remarkable as it was unexpected. The *Daily News* correspondent reported on September 12:

> all through this fertile province of Champagne, down the straight chaussées, with their lines of poplar trees, and among the pleasant villages on the vine covered slopes, the Prussians have advanced towards Paris ... To travel up from the rear to the front of the invading army gives a better notion of the vast scale of the operations against Paris than any one sight along the front. These whole districts occupied by foreign troops, these different corps scattered over the country, far and wide, are deeply suggestive.[5]

The same correspondent noted a few days later the lack of rancour that, at this stage of the war at any rate, was apparent on the part of the French population, which was enduring the consequences of military defeat with 'patient logic.' As a result, there was no need for the level of security that would manifest itself later. 'It is only a few days ago that I saw General von Moltke driving into Reims late in the day, quite alone in a carriage, with no escort of any kind. At another time I saw one Prussian soldier on foot calmly halting in a village full of Frenchmen, to light his pipe at the inn-door.'[6] Most of the war correspondents covering the march towards Paris noted the discipline of the German troops and how little damage they had done during their passage across France. After some of the spartan conditions endured by the senior commanders and staff during the hectic month of August as battle followed battle, they now found themselves billeted in decidedly more comfortable quarters. As a result, their diaries and correspondence began to take on the form of travel writing. Blumenthal, on September 10, noted: 'The sojourn in this princely and romantic Castle of Boursault is very pleasant. After dinner the whole of the company assembles in the reception rooms and makes life go very merrily, in spite of the momentous events in hand.'[7] Even Moltke, unwinding after the acute stress of the preceding six weeks, could be seen to be enjoying himself. Verdy accompanied him on his journey on September 14 from Reims to Château Thierry.

> On the way we had a few hours' rest at a delightful small chateau ... Moltke took his coffee with us in a small tastefully furnished turret-room, which so took his fancy that he was loath to leave it again; nor were we at all eager. We were in the best of spirits, and so the resting-place became the birthplace of innumerable plans. Scarcely had we arrived at Château Thierry – our limbs being still stiff from our long drive – when we saw our honoured chief already surveying the country from a weather-beaten old tower. It was too dark to see much, but it is a habit of Moltke wherever there is some point from which a wide view can be obtained, to immediately climb up to it.[8]

As the German armies continued their advance they were inconvenienced, although sometimes only to a limited extent, by the destruction wrought by the retreating enemy. On his way to the next location of the Royal Headquarters at Meaux, Verdy saw that a large railway bridge had been blown up;

> Likewise the bridges over the Ourcq Canal and several others besides. This will cost them much money, and the only damage they do is to themselves. In such acts of destruction there is no sense, except where the river line in question is to be held, or if the river is so large that the bridging will cost the enemy some considerable time, neither of which was the case here.[9]

From Meaux on September 16 Moltke wrote to his sister Augusta. He remained hopeful that the war might be entering its closing stages.

> Not withstanding all the successes already achieved, the anxieties of one day after the other weigh heavily on our minds. The responsibility is too great and the continual suspense a galling one ... I look forward, however, to an early peace without further great shedding of blood. The bravado of the Parisian leaders only testifies to their weakness. Much will soon have to be settled.[10]

Royal Headquarters took up residence at the vast and imposing palace of Baron de Rothschild at Ferrières on September 19. The château itself left Busch cold. 'It is a square building, of two stories, and at each of the four corners comes a three – storied tower, with a rather flat roof. The style is a mixture of different schools of the Renaissance, which do not produce a very effective whole.' The contents, however, were spectacular. The walls were

> hung with Gobelin tapestry, and among the pictures of this gorgeously furnished room there is an equestrian portrait by Velazquez. Amid so many beautiful objects, the eye wanders first to one and then to another, but the whole gives one the impression that the possessor thought less of beauty or comfort than of bringing together the costliest articles.

The grounds, however, seemed to Busch to be worthy of the highest praise.[11]

Baron de Rothschild's steward at first greatly annoyed Bismarck by refusing to sell any of the seventeen thousand bottles of wine in the cellars of the palace, although after a stormy interview with the Chancellor he was prevailed upon to change his mind. Bismarck, a previous visitor to Ferrières some fourteen years earlier, was amused to see the entry in the gamebook recording that with the Marquis de Gallifet, who had led the cavalry charge at Floing on September 1, he had been out shooting on the estate. Meanwhile the Crown Prince reached Montmirail on September 12 and took up residence in the château of the Duke de la Rochefoucauld; Prussian helmets and Prussian uniforms were now to be seen in what the *Daily News* correspondent described as 'the very richest parts of la Belle France.' The château itself was 'one of the best quarters that His Royal Highness has had since the beginning of the war. There is a large park – like garden with well grown timber, and with a beautiful view across the neighbouring valley.'[12] It was to Montmirail that W.H. Russell, who had paid a flying visit to London after Sedan, now returned. Blumenthal was disturbed to learn that the French newspapers were discussing the possibility of peace negotiations. His view of the position, as he repeatedly expressed it in his diary, was brutally simple.

> The enemy must first of all be trodden under foot and annihilated else we shall never have rest. We ought not to remain outside Paris, as we did before Vienna. We ought to make a triumphal entry into Paris, even if the whole city be undermined. What we need is Blücher, with his splendid hatred of the French.[13]

Blumenthal was accordingly outraged to learn a few days later of the visit of Jules Favre, the Foreign Minister, of the self appointed Government of National Defence, to Ferrières, to see Bismarck where he had been 'very graciously received ... I felt boiling with indignation, and am sure that I could not have brought myself to discuss affairs with such a rank democrat who had made himself Minister; at the most, I should have sent my servants to interview him.'[14]

Bismarck himself had approached the discussion with Favre in a rather dubious state of mind. The first approaches for a meeting had been made through the agency of the British government, and Lord Granville, the Foreign Secretary, had sent a note demanding that Bismarck respond. Bismarck was profoundly unimpressed: 'There is no hurry to answer this rubbish,' he told his staff.[15] As far as he was concerned, the Empire was still the only regime that he recognised. It was impossible to say what authority might now clothe Jules Favre and his self appointed colleagues in Paris, and Bismarck, although he wanted to bring the war to a conclusion as soon as possible, needed above all a stable government with which to deal.

Favre's defiant circular of September 6 to French diplomatic representatives setting out the refusal of the government of National Defence to contemplate any territorial adjustment- 'we will not yield an inch of our country nor a stone of our fortresses'- was also not calculated to improve the chances of a successful resolution at Ferrières. Favre hoped at least to get Bismarck to agree to an armistice of sufficient length to enable elections to take place. This would at least have legitimised the French representatives at any peace negotiation; but it would have meant the abandonment of at least part of the German military advantage with no guarantee that anything useful would come of it, and Bismarck would accept an armistice

Bismarck, painting by Lenbach (Rousset/*Histoire*)

only if Toul, Strasbourg and one of the Paris forts were given up at once. He demanded, as his minimum terms for peace, the cession of Alsace and part of Lorraine. Favre should not have felt any surprise at this; such territorial demands had, after all, been extensively canvassed in the German press since the outbreak of war. As it was, he became extremely emotional, saying tearfully: 'you want to destroy France!' It was, he said miserably, a mistake for him to come to Ferrières; and he returned to Paris empty handed with the prospect of an indefinite war stretching before him. Count d'Herisson, who was serving on Trochu's staff, described the 'singular impression' that the account of the meeting between Bismarck and Favre made upon him. 'The report produced some such sensation as one would experience on seeing a poor old goat trembling between a lion's paws.'[16]

Bismarck told his staff, and also the Crown Prince, that he did not expect Favre to come again, which at least left those of the military of the same mind as Blumenthal well pleased.[17] On September 21 Bismarck's expectations of the outcome of his meetings with Jules Favre were confirmed, when the latter wrote to him formally to restate that the French government could not accept the conditions that Bismarck had laid down for an armistice. However predictable the French response, it left Bismarck with a problem that would increase in its complexity as the war went on. The longer it continued the greater would be the demand, not only from the military, for severe terms to be imposed on France as the price of peace, and his object was to get an overall settlement that would endure. And the longer the war went on, the greater was the danger of foreign interference.

Two particular difficulties confronted Moltke as he embarked on the second phase of the war. The first was the lack of firm intelligence about the forces opposed to him, and the second was the problem of maintaining large armies at the end of very lengthy and inadequate lines of communication, exposed all the time to interruption by French irregular units.

During the first phase of the war, Moltke's staff had had the benefit of a detailed and largely accurate knowledge of the French order of battle. On this Moltke could base his own plans with some confidence. Now, however, with the capture or investment of practically the whole of the Imperial regular army, information about the enemy was almost completely lacking. Vinoy's 13th Corps had, it was known, succeeded in escaping its pursuers and was in Paris. Within the city there were also a number of other units out of which there was soon formed the 14th Corps. But of the forces outside the capital little or nothing was known as the German armies bore down on the city, and it was these other forces that were or might be in the process of assembly which would provide the challenge to the investing armies and their covering units.

Although large numbers of French soldiers were now prisoners of war, or were shut up in Metz, there still remained an enormous available potential in manpower. Apart from the 626,114 men which, it has been calculated were in August liable for service in the regular army, there were 623,458 men liable for service with the Garde Mobile. There were about 40,000 marines available, together with other men under arms with the customs service, gendarmerie and so forth. These impressive numbers were swollen by the potential recruitment on a nationwide basis of the Garde Nationale, which it has been calculated could provide up to 788,800 men. Lastly, there were the franc-tireurs, whose usefulness varied widely from unit to unit, but who added a further 40,000 or so men to the total available to the Government of National Defence.

Moltke's staff had naturally been able to calculate the theoretical potential manpower on which the enemy could call; but in translating these statistics into informed predictions of the likely number of men that would actually serve with the new French armies in the field, they decidedly understated the strength of their opponents. Even more importantly, however, they had at first very little to go on as to where the fresh units would be formed or the strategy that they would follow. Clearly they would be employed directly or indirectly in an attempt to raise the investment of Paris, but it was a matter of guesswork as to the direction they would take. Ultimately a clear picture could only emerge by actual contact with the French forces in the field. Unless and until the French themselves advanced to the attack, the only way to establish their size and whereabouts was for the Germans to advance and seek them out. The enormous size of the country, of which they presently controlled only a relatively small part, made this a particularly difficult task.

The other huge problem with which Moltke had to deal was that of logistics. Each of the German armies was responsible for the establishment and maintenance of the lines of communication on which it depended, and there were attached to each of the armies 'Etappen' units for the protection of these lines. Although the occupied territories of Alsace and Lorraine were made subject to the administration of Governors General appointed on August 14, questions of security remained the province of the army commanders and their respective Etappen units. The first task of the latter was to restore, as far as possible, the rail links which they now controlled. This task was severely hampered by a number of fortresses which remained in French hands, and which it was, in general, Moltke's policy to observe or invest rather than assault or besiege.

Toul, however, was a fortress which Moltke was particularly anxious to reduce as soon as possible. The crucial line from Weissenburg through Nancy, over which supplies ran to the Third Army and the Army of the Meuse, was closed west of Nancy by French possession of the fortress of Toul, and on August 16 an attempt was made to seize it by coup de main. When this failed, the place was invested by a force drawn from the II Bavarian Corps, reinforced by an infantry regiment on August 22, together with the corps artillery of the VI Corps. A bombardment of the fortress next day was also ineffective, and for the moment this important military line remained closed. One of Moltke's first decisions after Sedan was to order the commencement of siege operations against the place. He kept a constant eye on the situation there, on September 7 sending an urgent telegram to Colonel Hippel, commanding the troops before the fortress, calling for news and asking if he could count on its capture soon.[18] North west of Toul the fortress of Verdun was also strongly held, and an attempt to seize it by coup de main on August 24 was also unsuccessful. For a while after this, the place was merely observed by cavalry; but after the garrison had made a nuisance of itself by a series of sorties which threatened the easy transit of supplies past the fortress, it was invested at the end of August by a strong force under General von Bothmer, who reported initially to Frederick Charles. The Second Army was also responsible for masking the fortresses of Thionville and Longwy.

The fortresses of Phalsbourg and Bitsche, close to the frontier, also still held out; but these did not directly affect the German lines of communication, and Moltke was content that these should merely be observed. Phalsbourg in fact fell on December 12, while Bitsche held out to the end of the war.

The extent to which formal operations against the fortresses held by the French would be necessary was not at first generally appreciated. Immediately after the battle of Sedan, the Army of the Meuse had advanced on Montmédy, the garrison of which was believed to consist solely of Gardes Mobiles. Moltke ordered that an attempt be made on the fortress on September 4, and the task was given to Prince Hohenlohe, the commander of the Guard Corps Artillery. Opening at 9.30am, the bombardment continued for two hours, after which the mayor of a neighbouring town, Thonnelle, was sent into the fortress to negotiate its surrender. When he failed to return, the bombardment resumed, but without much effect, and after another hour of this Hohenlohe gave up, and set off after the rest of the Guard Corps which had moved to Mouzon.[19]

After Sedan, as the German armies moved westwards and their lines of communication steadily lengthened, an increasing number of troops were involved in their security. The Württemberg Division was held back from the advance on Paris in order to reinforce the Etappen troops in protecting the supply convoys that followed the advancing armies.[20] Moltke was therefore obliged on September 8 to give the responsibility of clearing the country between Metz and Paris to the newly formed XIII Corps under the Grand Duke of Mecklenburg-Schwerin. This Corps consisted of the 17th Infantry Division and the 2nd Landwehr Division; the

Grand Duke was ordered to use one division to capture Toul as quickly as possible, while the other moved on Châlons and Reims. Later in September an increasing part of the responsibility for the protection of lines of communication was transferred from the field armies to the Governors General of Alsace (von Bismarck-Bohlen) and Lorraine (von Bonin) to whom were transferred a large part of the Etappen troops. The Grand Duke acquired an additional responsibility when on September 16 he was named as Governor General of all those territories that were not covered by the Governors General of Alsace and Lorraine.

Toul was a fortress well protected by inundation of the low lying ground around the fortress, but was vulnerable to artillery attack from the heights. Major Huck, the commandant, had some 2,300 men, and 70 fortress guns and had thus far been able to hold out against the German assaults. The appearance of the Grand Duke of Mecklenburg-Schwerin with the 17th Division, the 17th Cavalry Brigade and three batteries, followed by three batteries of fortress artillery, meant that Huck's defences would be more seriously tested.[21] In fact, the Grand Duke soon realised that he had more troops before Toul than he needed, and on September 19 he sent off to Châlons the 33rd Infantry Brigade, and some cavalry and artillery, leaving Lieutenant General Schimmelmann to conduct the siege with the remaining troops. By September 23 the siege guns were ready to open their bombardment of the fortress; at 3.30 the white flag was hoisted, and Huck agreed to capitulate. Next day the Grand Duke had the satisfaction of leading the German troops into the town, which had cost him only some 30 casualties. The capture of Toul was extremely important, since the railway line was now open all the way from Weissenburg to Nanteuil sur Marne; there, however, it ended, because two tunnels and three bridges had been blown up by the retreating French, and it was a long time before the break in the line there could be restored.

This line served the Third Army; but it was urgently necessary to put at least one more line into working order to supply the Army of the Meuse on the north side of Paris, which at the moment depended on a railway line that effectively ended at Château Thierry. For this, operations must be undertaken to open the lines from Châlons and Reims through Soissons and Laon-La Fère respectively. This would require the reduction of the fortresses of Soissons and La Fère. Moltke therefore ordered the Grand Duke to move the units which had taken Toul on Soissons.

A brief attempt on this fortress had been made on September 14 by the IV Corps in the course of its march towards Paris; but it was soon apparent that the strength of the fortress was sufficient to resist a bombardment by field artillery, and the troops concerned at once resumed their march. Soissons had a garrison of 4,800 with 128 guns under Lieutenant Colonel de Noue; by October 1 these were opposed by eight battalions from squadrons, two field batteries and two pioneer companies under Major General von Selchow.[22] A close investment now became possible, and by October 11 thirty six siege guns were in position. An intensive bombardment ensued, in the course of which heavy damage was inflicted on the defences of the fortress. By 8 p.m on October 15 the defenders had had enough and de Noue surrendered. Next day the garrison, 'for the most part intoxicated and in a more or less disorganised state,' marched out and the Grand Duke led his troops into the fortress.[23]

The capture of Soissons meant that the terminus to which supplies for the Army of the Meuse arrived could be moved there from Château Thierry, but another month elapsed before the clearance of a blocked tunnel at Vierzy, ten miles to the south west of Soissons, enabled the line to be cleared to Mitry, just outside Paris. While not all the destruction of bridges and tunnels carried out by the retreating French armies had been effective, the steps taken to wreck the railways at key points had in some instances seriously hampered the Germans, whose dependence on the railways increased in proportion to their advance deeper into France. This in turn heavily increased the burden of maintaining the security of the railway lines against the operations of the franc-tireurs; their activity was bitterly resented at Royal Headquarters, not least by Bismarck, whose conversation with his staff from the outset of the second phase of the war often contained bloodcurdling demands for reprisals against unofficial actions.[24]

2

Investment

Once Moltke had completed the investment of Paris by the Army of the Meuse and the Third Army, he would thereby have defined the total resources available to Trochu for the defence of the city. There were two organised army corps composed of regular troops, the 13th Corps of General Vinoy that had successfully made its way back from Mézières, and the 14th Corps that had been assembling in the capital itself, under the command of General Renault. Each of these corps consisted of about 25,000 men. Vinoy's divisional commanders were Maud'huy, Blanchard and Exéa, while Renault's were Bechon de Caussade, d'Hugues and de Maussion. There was a Zouave Regiment de Marche organised from about 2,000 Zouaves who had escaped from Sedan; 14,000 sailors were organised into a division under the command of Vice Admiral de la Roncière, and these were probably just about the most effective troops in the city. There were also about 8,000 customs officers, gendarmes and other officials. In addition to these more or less reliable units, there were 115,000 Gardes Mobiles, who were most decidedly unreliable, although they had had the benefit of some training.

Finally, there was the Garde Nationale. This had, prior to the outbreak of war consisted of 40,000 men, organised in sixty battalions. Immediately after war was declared, it was ordered that the force be increased by a further sixty battalions each of which was to consist of 1,500 men. Subsequently, all able bodied men between the ages of 25 and 35 were called up, and by this measure the total number of Garde Nationale battalions in Paris by September 14 had increased to one hundred and thirty. By the end of the war the Garde Nationale had recruited some 350,000 men; but as Trochu grimly remarked, 'we have many men but few soldiers'. Only the original Garde Nationale battalions had received any military training at all.[1] As the pincers of the investing army closed around the city, Trochu therefore had nominally about 300,000 men under arms immediately available to him. These included a cavalry division under General Champéron, composed of those cavalry units of the 13th and 14th Corps that had not been sent out of the city to join the Army of the Loire. There was also a separate cavalry brigade under Bernis. Throughout the siege, the total number of the cavalry included in the defending forces did not exceed 5,000.

The strength of the field artillery was rapidly developed. At first there were available only the regular batteries attached to the 13th and 14th Corps, but by the employment of marines, and discharged artillery men, it quickly became possible to take advantage of the large amount of available equipment to form new batteries. By the end of the siege their number had risen to 124, of which sixteen were manned by marines and fifteen by Gardes Mobiles.[2] Trochu himself was in overall command; his chief of staff was General Schmitz. Originally Vinoy and Renault, the two corps commanders, had reported direct to Trochu. However, when Ducrot, who had escaped from the French army taken captive at Sedan (and who, according to the Germans had done so in breach of his parole) arrived in

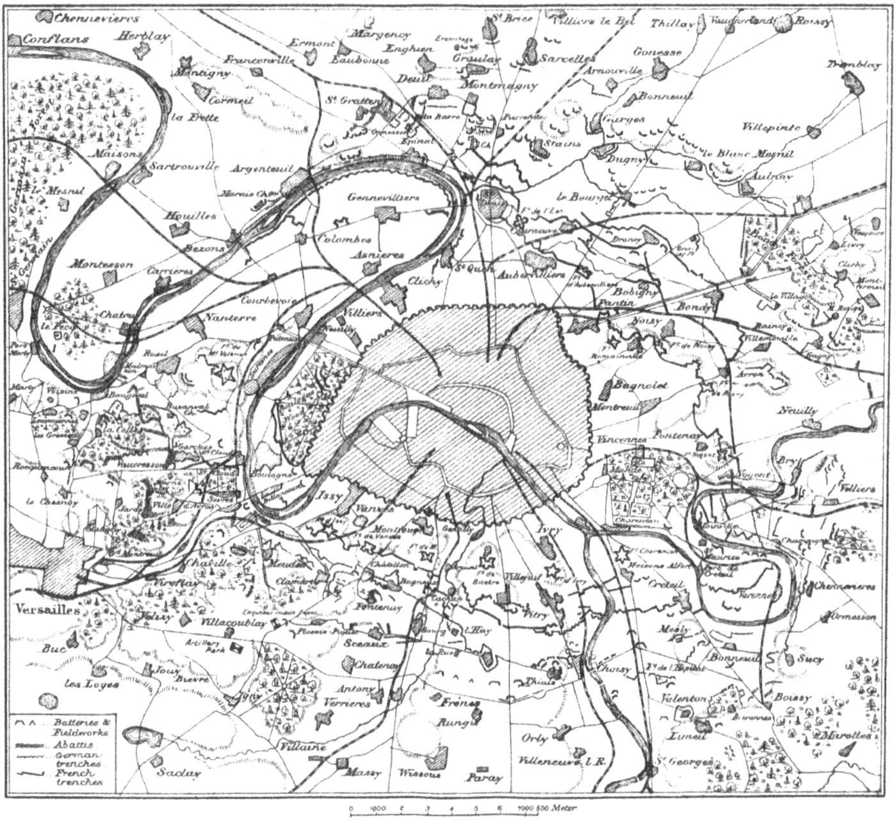

Paris and its environs

Paris, Trochu gave him responsibility for the two corps, to the great indignation of Vinoy in particular. Ducrot had been perhaps the most effective, and certainly the most energetic, of the Imperial corps commanders, and had of course briefly succeeded MacMahon in command of the Army of Châlons on September 1. His arrival represented a valuable reinforcement for Trochu, although the effect of his appointment was to add another tier to the command structure of the forces defending Paris.

It was however Trochu himself who was in every sense at the heart of the defence of the city, as well as presiding over the Government of National Defence. Aged fifty five, he had been always mistrusted by the previous regime, both because he was an Orleanist and because he was an outspoken military thinker. He commanded enormous support among the general public, however, and had been an obvious choice to lead the new government. He had insisted, before joining it, on a pledge from its members that they would respect God, the family, and property. After obtaining this, he went on to insist that he must be president of the new government, and have unlimited authority over the army. His new colleagues were in no mood to resist; as d'Herisson put it, 'he might have made them recognise the Syllabus, the Infallibility of the Pope, and the Immaculate Conception, had he so chosen. They accepted everything, and said Amen to everything!'[3] He was also apt to express himself at inordinate length in discussions, as d'Herisson also recorded: 'Each time the door opened to let a member in or out, we heard the voice of the Governor. The General spoke incessantly and well. The others only listened'. In fact, however, Trochu did not lack competition; many of the members of the government were also extremely talkative. The despatch of Crémieux and Glais-Bizoin to Tours to represent the government outside Paris, just before the completion of the investment, removed two of the most loquacious. One other member of the government went to Tours at this time; this was the elderly Admiral Fourichon, the Minister of Marine, who also discharged the office of Minister of War at Tours, where he resigned on October 3, after a dispute with his two equally elderly colleagues.

Trochu was by nature a pessimist. His professional assessment of the situation had been one of despair since MacMahon departed on his ill fated march to relieve Bazaine, and nothing that had happened since had increased his confidence that Paris could be successfully defended. Unless Moltke could somehow be induced to court disaster by launching an all out assault on the fixed defences around Paris, Trochu did not see how ultimate defeat could be avoided. Between such views, and those of the optimists, d'Herisson from the outset saw a 'terrible antagonism – the complete history of the siege – between those who believed in victory and those whose knowledge of warfare compelled them even to foresee defeat'.[4] But even the realistic d'Herisson, however, felt on watching Trochu's grand review of the army on September 14, which he thought the finest he had ever seen, that there 'are times when one need be of iron not to feel a thrill of hope'. Trochu himself was deeply moved by the experience which he described as a 'delirium'. He issued an Order of the Day to his troops: 'Never has any general had before his eyes such a spectacle as you have just given me'.[5]

The defences to be manned by Trochu's enormous army were themselves extremely strong. Paris lies in a valley basin partly through which and partly around the edge of which runs a double loop of the River Seine. Around the valley rise heights which to the north and east projected into the city, while to the south east they are about seven miles from the enceinte wall and moat which surrounded the city proper. Further out, the hills rise to a height of about five hundred feet. The course of the Seine made an attack on Paris extremely difficult. Below the city, the winding river effectively precluded a direct assault; there were few bridges above the city for the use of an attacking force. The Marne, which shielded the city to the east, and the Ourcq and St Denis Canals also presented considerable obstacles to an attacker.

These natural advantages had been strengthened by the construction of powerful fortifications. Around the city ran the enceinte wall, some thirty feet high, which was protected in front by a ten-foot moat. Behind the wall ran a circular railway for the rapid movement of troops. In front of the wall there had been erected, between 1840 and 1845, a chain of sixteen powerful forts, each containing between fifty and seventy pieces of heavy artillery, and each was within range of its neighbour to ensure support. The most powerful of these forts was Mont Valérien to the west of the city, situated on a hill five hundred feet above the loop of the Seine to the north of St Cloud. By 19 September there were 2,627 fortress and siege guns in the city, of which 1,380 were required for the forts, and the remainder for the other fixed defences. This left a reserve of several hundred heavy guns that could swiftly be moved to any threatened point. There was a flotilla of armoured batteries and gunboats operating on the Seine to protect the

A view of Châtillon, Meudon, St Cloud and Mont Valérien (Pflugk-Harttung)

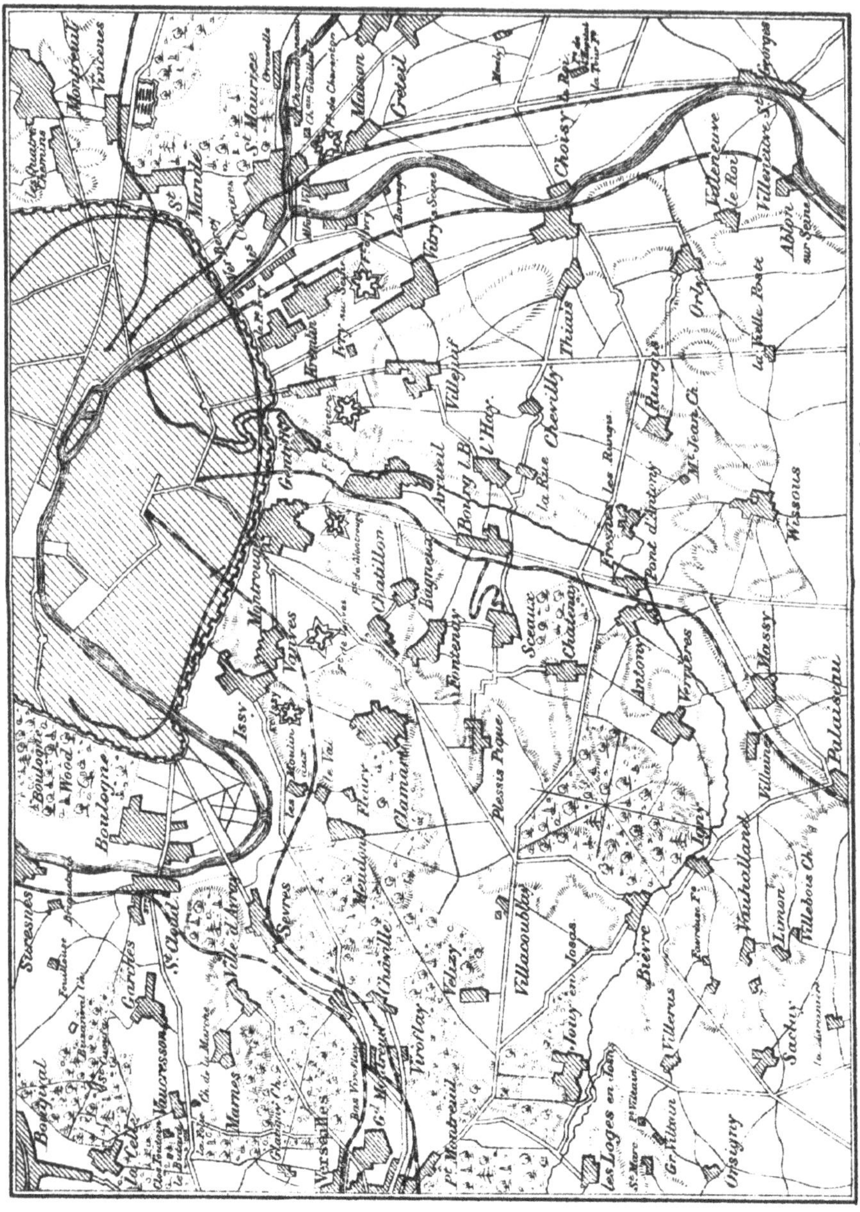

Southeast portion of the investment of Paris

dams, the bridges and the points where the river crossed the line of the enceinte. Immense supplies of ammunition had been brought into the city.[6] This chain of forts, which formed a perimeter some forty miles long, kept any investing army at arm's length from the city, and meant that the line of works which the Germans must erect and defend was itself some fifty miles in length. Work started on the construction of these positions as soon as the German armies arrived outside Paris, but it was a considerable task to create a line of investment which would be proof against any sortie from Paris of even a part of Trochu's huge army. Even though Moltke had decided merely on a close investment of the city, and was neither going to launch an assault nor embark on formal siege operations, he was still setting his armies a formidable task. The forces available in the Army of the Meuse and the Third Army amounted in all to about 150,000 men with 620 guns; this force had not only to maintain the investment, but also to provide troops to undertake any field operations against any French force that might attempt to raise the siege.

The forward movements to give effect to the plans agreed at the meeting at Château Thierry on September 15 proceeded largely without incident. The advance of the Army of the Meuse was led by the 5th and 6th Cavalry Divisions, commanded by von Rheinbaben and Duke William of Mecklenburg- Schwerin respectively. The intention was that once the investment had been completed they were both to pass under the command of the Third Army. Their orders were to cross the Seine below Paris and to cover the movement of the Army of the Meuse into its designated positions on the north side of the city. The 12th Cavalry Division (Graf zur Lippe) would remain with the Army of the Meuse to cover the rear of the investing forces.

Preparations for the defence of Paris, by Pallandre (Rousset/Combattants)

Of the Third Army's cavalry, the 2nd Cavalry Division (Stolberg) was to push on ahead and establish contact with the Army of the Meuse on the far side of the city, while the 4th Cavalry Division (Prince Albrecht) had orders to cross the Seine at Fontainebleau and to reconnoitre in the direction of the Loire.

The Army of the Meuse would have three army corps in positions covering the semicircle between the Seine and the Marne. The most westerly of these was the IV Corps, commanded by Gustav von Alvensleben. The IV Corps had enjoyed a successful baptism of fire at Beaumont before being present at Sedan. The sector it was to occupy stretched from Croissy, opposite Malmaison in a loop of the Seine, all the way through Argenteuil to Pierrefitte. Before taking up in position, the corps had first to dislodge weak French detachments in the villages on its line of march, driving them back into the fortifications of St Denis.[7] On the left, the Guard Corps (Prince August of Württemberg) took up a position on the line Arnouville-Gauges-Le Blanc-Mesnil-Aulnay. This corps had suffered heavy casualties at St Privat, where it had not been particularly well led, before later taking part in the battle of Sedan. Its most forward units were in an outpost at Le Bourget. Finally, at the eastern end of the line, the XII (Saxon) Corps, led by Prince George of Saxony since the formation of the Army of the Meuse, and which had had a lively time of it during the Sedan campaign, extended the line from Aulnay to the Marne. The Crown Prince of Saxony, of whom Moltke had held a high opinion since the Kōniggrätz campaign in 1866, in which the Crown Prince had commanded the Saxon contingent extremely competently, continued in command of the Army of the Meuse. His advance on August 17–19 went smoothly enough, and his troops at once set about fortifying the positions taken up, throwing up earthworks and repairing or building internal communication links such as roads, bridges and telegraphs. The supply line for the army ended for the moment at Château Thierry, after which convoys were obliged to come on by road.

South of the city, however, the Crown Prince's Third Army was to encounter rather stiffer opposition as it moved forward. Blumenthal for once had found no occasion to grumble about Moltke's plans for the investment, noting in his diary after the Château Thierry conference that he 'was quite in accord with Moltke, and am pleased that it is to take place as I had previously planned, and as I had laid down to my Staff officers as the plan I should adopt'.[8] The leading corps of the Third Army was the V Corps, which was to connect on its left with the right wing of the Army of the Meuse, taking up a position on the line from Bougival to Sèvres, opposite St Cloud and covering Versailles. The corps was commanded by the able and experienced Lieutenant General von Kirchbach, and had played a prominent part in the victory at Sedan. The commander of its 9th Division, Major General von Sandrart, was to gain a particular reputation for the skill he showed in developing his defensive positions, and the consequent thoroughness of the devastation of woods and villages which these called for. They became known as the 'Sandrartschen Verschönerungsverein,' and Sandrart was nicknamed satirically the 'Director of the Society for the Embellishment of the Country'.[9] During September 17 the pioneers of the V Corps built a pontoon bridge over the Seine at Villeneuve St Georges. While this work was going on a sharp encounter occurred at Mont Mesly, which Vinoy had occupied with Daudel's brigade and two batteries. After an exchange of artillery fire, two battalions of the 17th Brigade from

General Trochu, President of the Government of National Defence (Rousset/*Histoire*)

Sandrart's division moved forward to the attack, and the French retreated to Créteil on another of Vinoy's brigades in position there. At 4.00pm the French launched a three battalion counter attack which broke down in the face of the concentrated rifle fire of the 59th Regiment. The French fell back through Créteil, pursued by the 58th Regiment towards Fort Charenton.

The V Corps was followed by the II Bavarian Corps, whose commander was the elderly but energetic von Hartmann, who had been heavily engaged in most of the battles in which the Third Army had been involved. After crossing the Seine at Corbeil and Ris on September 17, the corps was to take up a position from Meudon to Bagneux, occupying the Châtillon plateau. Before it could do so, however, there occurred the first serious engagement of the investment of Paris.

Ducrot had posted the 14th Corps on the plateau between Meudon and Châtillon in defensive positions; but as the German troops moved past the temptation to take them in flank proved irresistible, and he applied for permission to launch a major assault on the German troops crossing his front. Trochu was sceptical and gave only a very grudging consent to the projected attack, saying to Ducrot that he could probe the German flank, but only with the greatest circumspection. Ducrot was furious, but although he continued to press Trochu to allow an all out attack, in the end he had to content himself with a compromise plan with more limited objectives.

During September 18 the most advanced units of the 14th Corps were in contact with the picquets of the V Corps as it marched westwards, and all day there were skirmishes along the plateau. On September 19 Ducrot launched two divisions in an assault towards the road to Versailles along which Kirchbach's troops were marching, directing Caussade's Division on Villacoublay and Hugues' Division on Petit Bicêtre, with Maussion's Division in reserve at Bagneux.[10]

On the right of Kirchbach's corps as it made its way towards Versailles, the 18th Brigade had on September 18 come into contact with the advanced French troops around Villacoublay, and overnight its 47th Regiment had taken up a position at the farm of Petit Bicêtre on the main road to Versailles. At 6.45 on September 19, before the early morning mists had cleared, Ducrot launched his troops in heavy columns towards the road, supported by a strong force of field artillery and by batteries in and to the south of the Châtillon Redoubt. This key position on the edge of the plateau, which threatened the forts of Issy, Vanves and Montrouge, was the principal reason for Ducrot's concern to hold on to the plateau if at all possible. The oncoming French troops suffered heavily from the 47th Regiment's rifle fire, but the only German artillery, a light battery to the west of Petit Bicêtre, suffered heavy damage from the French guns. Sandrart, however, sent up artillery reinforcements, which enabled the battery to be withdrawn. Under the sustained French barrage, the Germans pulled out of Petit Bicêtre which had been set on fire, but the French infantry, which had reached the road to the west of the village, could make no further progress.

Meanwhile Hartmann's II Bavarian Corps had been marching north towards the Châtillon plateau. His left wing encountered units of the V Corps as they moved north-westwards out of Bievre towards the Versailles road. The sound of heavy gunfire was audible, and on hearing from a Prussian officer of the French advance, Colonel von Diehl, at the head of the Bavarian columns, directed his men forward from the Abbaye du Bois towards Petit Bicêtre. These reinforcements soon turned the tide of battle, and the French were thrown back to Pavé Blanc. To the left, Sandrart had sent up further reinforcements to strengthen Villacoublay, which was just as well, because at 8.30 the French launched a further assault towards the Versailles road; this, however, broke up in the face of heavy rifle fire, and in spite of all his efforts, Ducrot could not get his inexperienced troops to advance further. A regiment of Zouaves at the farm of Trivaux panicked under artillery attack, and fled northwards up the road to Paris.

On the right the Bavarians pushed the French back from Pavé Blanc to the village of Plessis Piquet, and at 10am threw back a counter attack. Diehl now swung to his right to prepare an advance on the park of the Château Plessis, while on the far left of the German line the fusilier battalion and the 1st Battalion of the 7th Grenadier Regiment advanced into the Bois de Meudon, picking up scores of Zouaves as prisoners. Kirchbach had interrupted his march towards Versailles to be ready if necessary to deploy the whole of his corps to meet the attack, and by 10.00am he was concentrated around Villacoublay, where he had himself been with the Corps artillery for the past hour. It was soon clear, however, that with the French recoiling behind Plessis Piquet in the direction of the Châtillon Redoubt the Bavarians could handle the situation by themselves and at noon Kirchbach resumed his march towards Versailles.[11]

On the Bavarian right, Hartmann was deploying the 5th and 7th Brigades, the former being directed on Sceaux and the latter through L'Hay towards Fontenoy. Cavalry patrols soon identified Maussion's Division near Fontenoy, while the

French heavy artillery in the Hautes Bruyères Redoubt also opened fire on the advancing Bavarians.

To the west von Walther, the commander of the 3rd Bavarian Division, now brought up the rest of his forces and launched an assault from Pavé Blanc and Malabry on the French troops holding Plessis Piquet. By about noon the farmhouse of Plessis Moulin was in his hands; soon afterwards the southern wall of the park, which had been holding up the advancing Bavarians, was breached by artillery fire. The 7th and 15th Regiments passed through and began clearing the defenders from the main street of the village. In spite of heavy gunfire from the Châtillon Redoubt, they pushed on towards it.

Caussade's Division, which had been the first to crack, had meanwhile retreated beyond Châtillon to take up a position behind the Fort d'Issy and Fort de Vanves. Part of Hugues' Division had also fallen back towards Fort de Montrouge while Maussion, due to a misuderstanding, had abandoned his forward position based on the Bagneux Redoubt. Ducrot realised that there was nothing more he could do, and ordered his troops back off the plateau, under cover of heavy artillery fire. At 3.00 p.m. a party led by Captain von Imhoff dashed into the Châtillon Redoubt to find it already abandoned by the enemy, and Walther took immediate steps to secure the position, bringing up strong reinforcements to the redoubt and to the heights immediately to the south.[12] Thus, as night fell, the whole of the plateau was in German hands, and the Bavarians could look down into the city of Paris itself. The battle had cost then some 443 casualties; on the French side, the total losses were a little short of 1000.

The French had however also suffered a serious blow to their morale as a result of the manner of their defeats. Many troops had abandoned their units and fled back into the city. Ernest Vizetelly watched their return.

> Pitiful was the spectacle presented by the disbanded soldiers as they rushed down the Chaussée du Maine. Many had flung away their weapons. Some went on dejectedly; others burst into wineshops, demanded drink with threats, and presently emerged swearing, cursing and shouting 'Nous sommes trahis!' The whole scene was an evil augury for the defence of Paris.[13]

While this had been going on the remaining units of the Third Army had moved into their designated positions, although not without some difficulties, as Blumenthal recorded. 'The second portion of the march was wrongly marked out, and there was endless confusion. The Crown Prince was very much displeased'.[14] By 3.00 pm, however, Kirchbach was in possession of Versailles, while beyond to the west his cavalry had made contact with the Army of the Meuse. On the right of the II Bavarian Corps, the dependable von Tümpling had brought his VI Corps into position at Chevilly and on either side of the Seine at Choisy-le-Roi. In the late afternoon he had to face a rather half-hearted attack by Maud'huy's Division which advanced towards Chevilly; but this was soon stopped by the 22nd Regiment, supported by two batteries of artillery, and when Tümpling's infantry advanced, the French fell quickly back to their fortifications. Finally, on the far right of the Third Army's position the Württemburg Division prolonged the line to the Marne, in contact there with the Army of the Meuse. The two other corps of the Third Army, the XI Corps under von Bose and the I Bavarian Corps under von der Tann, were coming up behind, covered by cavalry, to remain for the moment in reserve.

In this way Moltke completed the investment of Paris. The Crown Prince had watched the battle of Châtillon from just south of Croix de Bernis, and derived considerable satisfaction from the close co-operation of his troops. 'I could not today make out with any clearness who had most to do with it, whether Prussians or Bavarians; but this much was certain, that both sections had afforded one another mutual assistance.'[15] Next day he and Blumenthal visited Hartmann and then went on to inspect the captured Châtillon Redoubt, on their way narrowly escaping injury from stray shells from the Paris fortifications. But on reaching the redoubt, he found his ride well worthwhile. 'A noble prospect here lay before us; Paris lay directly under our very feet, shining clear in the sunshine with its sea of houses, the richly gilded dome of the Invalides and the numerous forts.'' Later that day the Crown Prince rode on to Versailles, where the headquarters of the Third Army was now established. On the terrace of the palace, he recalled his visit there in 1867 with his father and Tsar Alexander as guests of Napoleon and Eugénie, 'who did the honours with an amiable courtesy that charmed us. How swiftly has the star of that Imperial pair faded! Now Prussian uniforms enliven this superb scene of French pomp and pride!'[16]

The generals of the Government of National Defence, fragment of a panorama by Stevens and Gervex. They include, from left to right: Charette, Gougeard, de Sonis, Jauréguiberry, Chanzy, Crémieux, de Freycinet, d'Aurelle de Paladines, Gambetta, Carrey de Bellemare, Clinchant and Faidherbe (Rousset/*Histoire*)

3

Battle to the Last

Now that the investment had been completed, there was much speculation as to how long it might take to enforce the city's surrender. Moltke wistfully wrote to his brother Adolph on September 21: 'I cherish a private hope that I may be shooting hares at Creisau by the end of October.'[1] Estimates of the supplies within Paris varied widely. On the day after Châtillon the Crown Prince encountered an Englishman who had recently left the city, and who told him that 'Paris was fully prepared to make a stand of certainly three months.'[2] Other reports reaching the staff indicated that there were provisions for six weeks.[3] But not everyone was so optimistic. From the outset Bismarck, perpetually anxious about the possibility of foreign intervention, wanted to see steps taken to hasten the end; while Roon had gloomily written on September 6: 'whether, old as I am, I shall live to see the end of the war is indeed a matter of indifference, but I doubt it.'[4] And both the King and Frederick Charles were inclined to believe it would be a very long haul indeed

Whatever might be the outcome of the investment, Moltke was as always bringing a coolly dispassionate view to the task in hand, remarking: 'We enter upon a venture which the world will judge according to its success.'[5] On one aspect of the problem he was absolutely determined; there could be no question of an assault on the city. The huge risk of the completely unacceptable casualties which the Germans would face ruled that out completely. Although, as he wrote to Adolph, 'the superiority of the German troops had been shown in all the battles, even in those in which they were opposed to greater numbers, as, for example, was the case on the 16 August, and here in front of Paris,'[6] the disparity in numbers – he assumed that the French probably already had 300,000 men under arms in the city – and the difficulties of the house to house fighting that would be necessary were very much in his mind. Nor was he in the least enthusiastic about carrying out a formal siege of the city or undertaking a thorough bombardment. He had, it is true, ordered up the siege train but, as he noted in the same letter to Adolph, it would be a long time before that could be in position and in the meantime the investing troops could do little to respond to the fire from the fortress artillery opposing them.

> We are placed at present in the awkward position of having to submit to being fired at without being able to answer in like manner, for our four-pounders cannot possible compete with the 74-pounders in the forts. The siege train, which is conveying over one hundred thousand hundredweights of ammunition cannot be brought on very quickly, there being but a single line of rails.

For the present, he had no doubt that even if he was wrong about an early capitulation, a patient strategy was called for: 'The process of starving out is, as Metz has shown, a very slow one, but it finally accomplishes its work ... It is a hard trial of patience for the investing troops, and a harder one still for those invested.'[7]

Verdy was expressing the view which Moltke continued to hold throughout the investment when he noted in December that 'It will only be when the hope of relief from the provinces vanishes that a bombardment may possibly produce an effect.'[8]

For the moment, therefore, all that Moltke could do was to watch and wait. On September 23 he accompanied Verdy and Bronsart to the outpost line of the Württemberg Division, going on foot beyond it to

> a kind of garden pavilion, standing high on the slope which descends steeply to the Marne. The little building had been put in a state of defence, and we had a good view of the neighbouring forts through the loopholes. We could see plainly some Gardes Mobiles on the ramparts and we overlooked that part of the town lying between the forts and Mont Valérien.[9]

That even the Chief of the General Staff was exposed to serious risk was demonstrated when Verdy recorded two days later that the little houses had been demolished by French shells.

Inside Paris, questions similar to those being considered at the Royal Headquarters were also being asked. The first of these might reasonably have been to ask why Paris was being defended at all, rather than simply being declared an open city. It had of course always been intended that, if the need arose, Paris should be defended and there had been considerable investment in building up its fixed defences. Given the overall situation of the war, with the bulk of the Imperial army effectively off the board, the most important reason for defending the city was to give time for fresh forces to be raised in the provinces with which to continue the war. This, of course, then provided the strategic focus for all of the French operations thereafter, since it was inconceivable that Paris could be allowed to fall without efforts being made for its relief. A second reason for defending the city was to pin down a very large part of the German forces remaining mobile at Moltke's disposal, bearing in mind that Frederick Charles was engaged indefinitely at Metz. As a historian of the second phase of the war has pointed out, the loss of mobility of an invading army is extremely dangerous: 'Not merely is time afforded to the invaded for fresh preparations for defence, but the prestige inherent in the continued offensive is lost; the invaded have time to recover their self possession and morale.'[10]

In spite of the strategic effect of the need to make efforts to relieve Paris, which meant that the true target, the German armies, was to a large extent lost sight of, the defence of Paris was probable justified. Its abandonment would have had a fearful effect on national morale, and all the time it held out it offered a beacon of hope that France was undefeated, which was crucially important in terms of political negotiations. But it is worth speculating what might have been the outcome if the capital had been abandoned, and the troops available for its defence had been withdrawn deeper into provincial France to serve as the nucleus for the formation of a new army. Moltke's available force was not so large that he could lunge in every direction; the huge distances over which he could be made to operate would render the task of coming to grips with an elusive opponent very difficult. Ultimately, no doubt, German determination would no doubt have outlasted that of the French, but it might have been a very different kind of war.

A French outpost sights German troops approaching the outskirts of Paris, painting by Dujardin-Beaumetz (Rousset/ *Histoire*)

As it was no serious consideration was given to abandoning Paris, which had produced the new Government of National Defence, not least because that government did not anticipate the speed and effectiveness of Moltke's steps to invest the city.[11] However, the rapid removal of the embassies of the other Great Powers soon made it necessary to send out of Paris some effective representation of the new government. It was in this way that there came into being the delegation, which established a subsidiary government at Tours. Led first by the seventy four year old Isaac Crémieux, the new Minister of Justice, who was sent to Tours after a prolonged discussion throughout September 11 with a team of officials from other ministries, the delegation was soon reinforced by the despatch of Glais-Bizoin, the Minister of Posts and Telegraphs and by Admiral Fourichon, the Mminister of Marine who was also to act as the delegate of the Minister of War, General Le Flô. It was not a very charismatic group, as has been graphically pointed out.

> The old Jewish lawyer Crémieux, the old parliamentary wit Glais-Bizoin, and the elderly, obscure, routine-loving Admiral Fourichon, were no men to stir a country to enthusiasm; the high sounding proclamations in which they sought to echo the fiery calls to action of the great Revolutionaries were merely ludicrous.[12]

Even if the delegation had been composed of more effective individuals (and the key officials that accompanied it were certainly men of ability) the functions which it was intended to perform were those of communication rather than management.

It was from Paris that the real direction of the war effort was intended to come. Gambetta's message to the préfets of the eighty nine departments spelt out clearly the way in which it was to be managed. 'Our new Republic is a Government of National Defence, a Republic of battle to the last against the intruders. Gather around you citizens who, like yourselves, are animated by the lasting desire to save the country, and are prepared not to shrink from any sacrifices.'[13] The urgency of the task of mobilising an entirely new French army was apparent to all. The process was hampered by the lack of any overall direction, but nonetheless it got under way with considerable speed. Fourichon seems to have begun his task in the belief that France should aim to fight an essentially partisan war, recommending that the Gardes Mobiles be employed not in regular formations but in small units

> whose role is less to fight than to harass the enemy ... To obstruct him in his requisitions ... Above all to carry out coups de main and pointes, to capture convoys, cut roads and railways, destroy bridges ... These troops must wage real partisan war, and for that they will need vigour, dash, intelligence and above all a great deal of cunning.[14]

There were plenty of other voices raised in support of putting the first emphasis on waging a merciless guerrilla war against the invaders, of whom Gambetta at first was one. But the need to relieve Paris soon made it clear that properly organised troops, given such training as time allowed, and equipped with whatever arms were immediately available, must be put into the field as soon as possible. Of men at least there were plenty; those called to the colours were at once subjected to intensive basic training, but their equipment was in many respects unsatisfactory. The diary of Roger de Mauni reflects the experience which he shared with many of the newly enrolled troops.

> We begin our target-shooting today, and it is to be continued tomorrow. A great number of our mobiles have been sportsmen, and take a much better aim than one would expect. Our muskets are detestable, and it is aggravating to hear them spoken of as being so excellent. As we cannot be convinced on this point, they talk of giving us others. It looks as if they were trying to amuse us; if so, the attempt is not very successful.[15]

The largest concentration of troops outside Paris was, as Moltke already knew, to be found on the Loire. Here, under the command of General de la Motte-Rouge, had assembled the 15th Corps, which by the end of September had attained a total strength of 60,000 men, albeit in a state of some considerable disorganisation. De la Motte Rouge had only three regular regiments of the line; the remaining units consisted of two thirds Regiments du Marche, and one third Gardes Mobiles. In the north west, General Fiereck was assembling a scattered force which never attained the same level of concentration. It was based on seven regular battalions and two marine battalions, and apart from these consisted of various units of franc-tireurs, Gardes Mobiles, Gardes Nationales and groups of the local population under arms. As the 'Army of the West,' this shadowy force was to exert an influence on German strategic thinking far beyond its real strength.

French officials view dispatches delivered by pigeon post, painting by Guiaud and Didier (Rousset/*Histoire*)

Further east, around Rouen and Elboeuf, a force of about 14,000 men had been put together under General Gudin, while a small force of about 4,000 men at Vernon and Dreux connected with the Army of the Loire, and covered the crucial rail links from Rouen to the south. Far away in the south east, at Besancon, a corps was being collected by General Cambriels to cover Lyon. It was here, in the Vosges mountains, that the operations of the franc-tireurs had caused particular problems. As early as September 9 Moltke had ordered von Werder to detach from the troops besieging Strasbourg a number of flying columns to deal with them, and he formed a force of four battalions, eight and a half squadrons and three batteries under Major General Keller to deal with the problem. After a sharp encounter at Horburg on September 14, Keller marched on Mulhouse, which he occupied on September 16.[16] Other flying columns operated through Blamont and Celles, and from Mûtzig on Heiligenberg and Schirmeck.

The lack of any hard intelligence about French formations continued to give Moltke considerable difficulty in the deployment of the relatively few troops available to him to deal with them, but the first indications which he received as to their number and effectiveness did not dispel the general optimism at Royal Headquarters. Typical of the attitude of the staff was that of von Podbielski, the Quarter Master General, who was Moltke's number two, and who has been described as 'a bluff, outspoken man, one of that invaluable class of men who, though they may see the darker side of affairs, express themselves in optimistic language and treat difficulties with contemptuous speech.'[17] Podbielski dismissed the French troops now being organised as 'ragamuffins;' given the problems of training and equipping large masses of men, under the circumstances his arrogance is not surprising.

As one French officer remarked, it was difficult to teach things one did not know oneself.

Meanwhile, behind its forts and entrenchments at Metz, France's only remaining professional army was closely invested by Frederick Charles with the First and Second Armies. The abortive attempt at a breakout on August 31 and September 1 had been followed by a lull in operations, which gave Frederick Charles the opportunity to redeploy his forces, strengthening his positions on the south side of the fortress. The VIII corps (von Goeben) and the VII corps (von Zastrow) were shifted to their right, occupying a position between Jussy and St Thiebaut. Beyond them, the newly formed XIII corps under the Grand Duke of Mecklenburg Schwerin extended to Colombey, until it was pulled out of the line in mid September to operate against Toul and Soissons, which necessitated a further rearrangement of the positions it had occupied. Beyond it stood von Manteuffel's I corps, while next came the IX corps (von Manstein), pushed south to Gravelotte. Next stood Konstantin von Alvensleben's III corps, based on Verneville, connecting in its turn with the X corps of von Voigts- Rhetz. Von Fransecky's II Corps was in reserve at Rezonville and between Gorze and Novéant. When the XIII corps left the investment, its line was taken over partly by the I Corps shuffling to its right, and partly by Kummer's Division.[18]

With the benefit of hindsight, it is easy to see that the forces at Frederick Charles' disposal were a good deal stronger than was actually needed to keep Bazaine penned in. But in fact, if proper use had been made of them, the troops comprising the Army of the Rhine still constituted an extremely powerful force, only slightly less in numbers than the forces surrounding it. In total Bazaine disposed of 154,481 men organised in five corps. Among its leaders were some of the most famous and accomplished names in the military history of the Second Empire; General Frossard commanded the 2nd corps, Marshal Leboeuf the 3rd corps, General Ladmirault the 4th Corps, Marshal Canrobert the 6th Corps and General Bourbaki the Imperial Guard. But Bazaine himself, worn down by defeat and by the responsibilities that had been thrust upon him, was decidedly equivocal as to the correct course to be followed now that his army was completely invested. This was the case even before the appalling news of Sedan reached the defenders of Metz. The painful details of the defeat and capture of the Army of Châlons became available when Frederick Charles helpfully exchanged on September 6 some hundred or so soldiers taken prisoner at Sedan. This was done in the hope of inducing Bazaine to enter into negotiations; to hammer the point home, Frederick Charles commenced a heavy bombardment of the fortress at 7 pm on September 9 from nineteen batteries to the south west and north. In pouring rain, and with darkness falling, it was impossible to see the physical effect and the bombardment ceased after an hour. It appeared not immediately to have had the desired moral effect on Bazaine, either; he merely issued a proclamation on September 16 to his army announcing the defeat of Sedan and the fall of the Empire, reminding the troops that the Army of the Rhine's duties were unchanged, and concluding 'Let us continue, therefore, to serve it with devotion, and with equal energy defend its territory from the stranger, and social order against evil passions.'[19] The last phrase no doubt indicated his considerable reserve about the establishment of the Government of National Defence. At the same time he did send a note to Frederick

Charles seeking further information about the state of things in France; but the response did not prompt any negotiations.

Moltke had written on September 5 to von Stiehle, Frederick Charles' Chief of Staff, to set out his own views on the future conduct of operations before Metz.

> Now that every prospect of relief has been taken away from the army in Metz, the important thing is to make its stay there still more disagreeable, and for that purpose one means is to disturb it every night. I think this can be done as well with field guns as with 12-pounders and is possible at very great ranges if only you can see the enemy's camps or find their distance exactly. Even against the town – a target you cannot miss – the 6-pounder with the same charge and loading as the 12-pounder will do. Perhaps also with pick and spade you can increase the difficulty for the enemy of breaking through in face of the advantage of the defensive on which you lay stress. But you should allow an officer from the fortress to look round at Sedan in order to convince himself of the helplessness of the position.[20]

On September 13 Moltke at last rid himself of the wilful and insubordinate Steinmetz, the Commander of the First Army, who was posted as Governor-General of Posen. He did not for the moment replace him, leaving the First Army under the direct command of Frederick Charles. As his letter to Stiehle demonstrated, as in the case of Paris, Moltke had no intention of incurring heavy casualties in an assault on the fortress of Metz. He had no doubt that a lack of supplies would cause it to fall in due course and for the moment he was prepared to wait, useful as the forces surrounding the city would nonetheless be to him as the overall theatre of operations steadily widened. For the present, all that was required of Frederick Charles was that he should strengthen his lines of defence and ensure that the investment was totally secure. However, additional resources with which to reduce the fortress were gradually becoming available. Heavy artillery had now arrived from Germany, enabling five batteries, each of ten guns, to be established on commanding heights around the fortress respectively at Jussy, north of Serrécourt, southwest of Amanvillers, west of Augny and on the Château Salins road.[21]

The investing force was not without its own problems of supply. The principal railway line in use was the line from Saarbrücken to Pont à Mousson, and this bore a heavy traffic. Food supplies were short, as a cattle plague had broken out in Germany, and meat had to be bought in Holland and Belgium. The appalling weather meant that considerable efforts had to be made to construct cover for the troops and although this work was carried forward, the colder weather later led to the spread of much sickness, especially dysentery. But for the troops inside the fortress, the position was of course much worse, and the need to do something about it led to a decision by Bazaine to undertake a series of sorties in order to lay hands on the supplies it was hoped to find in the villages between the lines and inside the German outpost line.

The first of these sorties was directed against villages in the front of the I Corps and the VII Corps. Under cover of a heavy artillery bombardment, strong parties of infantry from the 3rd Corps moved forward on September 23. They succeeded in occupying all or part of the villages of Nouilly, Lanvallier, Colombey, Villers L'Orme, Mercy la Haut and Peltre, from which the German outposts retired on their main positions. As a result the French were able to carry off a quantity of garden supplies in wagons brought forward for the purpose. Emboldened by this success, the French made a similar sortie on the following day, one division of the 3rd Corps advancing on Vary and Chieulles on the front of Kummer's Division while another moved on Nouilly and Villers L'Orme, on the right of the position occupied by the I Corps. Gradually, practically all the German artillery on this part of the front was drawn into the contest; meanwhile a French advance on Rupigny broke down in the force of heavy rifle fire. After about an hour the attack was called off, no further supplies having been obtained. Abortive advances were also made against the lines of the VII Corps and the X Corps, which were driven back when the defenders brought troops up to the outpost line. During the operations of September 22 & 23 the French suffered 183 casualties: the German losses amounted to 108 men killed and wounded.[22]

Following these raids, Bazaine decided to embark on a larger scale operation with the same objective. On September 27 sorties were undertaken on the northern front against the lines of the X Corps, and on the south-east against the VII Corps. The latter thrust was directed on Peltre and Mercy le Haut, beginning with a heavy bombardment of the German positions from Fort Queuleu and the du Pate Redoubt at about 9.00 am, following which Duplessis' Brigade moved on Peltre and that of Lapasset on Mercy le Haut. These movements were largely successful, and in Peltre the French succeeded in cutting off and taking prisoner a large part of a company of the 55th Regiment which was trapped in the village. On the right of the position attacked, the German outposts withdrew from the village of La Grange aux Bois, but after strong forces of the 13th Division had moved forward, the French settled for what they had got, and advanced no further, removing all the supplies to be found in the occupied villages before, at about 11.30 am, abandoning them. Further north, the French also succeeded in occupying Colombey and removing stores found there, before retreating under a heavy artillery fire, which set the village ablaze by about noon.[23]

A little before this, a similar thrust had been made against the villages in the front of the 40th Brigade. This also succeeded in its object, the villages of Bellevue and Franclanchamp and the farm of St Agathe being occupied, and stores removed, before the French retreated under heavy gunfire from the Serrécourt heights and from the field artillery of the X Corps and Kummer's Division. By 3 pm the firing died down, and the German outposts reoccupied their former positions.

The engagements on September 27 cost the Germans total casualties of 355 killed wounded and captured; of these, 141 prisoners fell into French hands. The French losses were not recorded. Frederick Charles now took immediate steps to ensure that no such further attempts could succeed by removing all the supplies collected in villages vulnerable to a French attack, and destroying a number of farms and villages that might offer a tempting target. With the end of this series of engagements, operations around Metz drew for the time being to a close.

4

The Key of our House

The city of Strasbourg, the capital of Alsace, had held huge symbolism for Germany ever since on September 30 1681 it had been seized by France. It had grown in commercial and industrial significance over the years, and had from the moment of the French occupation served as one of the most important fortified places on the French frontier. Vauban, who accompanied the occupying forces in 1681, had within six weeks prepared an elaborate portfolio of memoranda and plans, on the basis of which there were constructed works there which made it in its time one of the strongest fortresses in Europe, and its location on the left bank of the Rhine made its possession vital to the national security of both France and Germany. By 1870 the population had risen to about 85,000. Of its many fine buildings, the most notable was the cathedral, which had been begun in 1015 although it was not completed for another four hundred years. Its northern tower was 492 feet high, making it at the time the highest building in Europe. Bismarck, in his conversation with Favre at Ferrières, succinctly described Strasbourg as being 'the key of our house.'[1]

However, the vastly increased range of modern rifled artillery meant that by 1870 it was no longer the impregnable fortress which it had once been. The whole of the city and the works surrounding it were now within range of German artillery on the right bank of the Rhine, and the immensely complex system of fortifications was no longer proof against heavy bombardment by modern guns, although improvements had been planned to start in 1871. Nor had the fortress as a whole yet been uprated to meet modern conditions by the construction of proper bomb-proof shelters. On the other hand the strength and complexity of the fortifications, which were supported by the powerful citadel on the east of the city, were such that they were defensible against all but the most determined attacks; and the system of rivers and canals that flowed through the city meant that the whole of its southern flank could be protected by extensible inundations. With the Rhine and its offshoot the Little Rhine (which formed Sporen Island) covering the eastern flank, and further inundations along the north face of the fortifications, it was apparent to both sides that the natural front of attack was the northwest section of the defences.[2]

The bastions at this point were numbered 7 to 12; the French engineers had recognised that the sharp angle at Bastion No 12 was the weakest point of the whole of the northwest front and had strengthened it by the construction of four lunettes, and by the Finkmatt hornwork on the right of Bastion No 12, projecting northwards. A further weakness had been the urban sprawl of the city on its west and northern sides, by the building of the suburbs of Kriegshoffen, Kronenbourg and Schiltigheim.

On the outbreak of war the sixty eight year old General Uhrich was brought out of retirement and appointed Governor of Strasbourg and the military district of Alsace; he took up his duties on July 21. His first act was to seek permission to demolish all the buildings and plantations within artillery range of the fortress, but his request was for the moment denied.[3] Accordingly he got on with the task of putting the fortress in a state of defence. As at August 4, the garrison consisted of the 87th Line Regiment (Colonel Blot), two other infantry battalions with their depôts, the depôt of the 6th Lancers, eleven companies of the 16th Artillery Regiment under Colonel Fiévet, and the depôts of two other artillery regiments. There were also a number of other associated fortress troops, gendarmes and frontier guards at his disposal, and in addition Uhrich called out the Garde Mobile. MacMahon's 1st Corps had based its initial assembly on Strasbourg before moving north to take part in the initial battles of the campaign. By the afternoon of August 6 civilians began to reach the town with news of the defeat at Wörth, and by nightfall wounded and stragglers began to reach the city from the battle field. MacMahon at once telegraphed news of the battle to Uhrich, and next day larger bodies of his defeated army arrived, together with one infantry battalion that had never reached Conseil-Dumesnil's Division. Out of the troops reaching him in this way, Uhrich formed a Regiment du Marche of five battalions, together with a cavalry regiment. The Garde Mobile was by August 19 some 3,000 strong, and a similar number of Gardes Nationales had joined the colours. Together with some sailors available as the result of an abortive attempt to construct a river flotilla of ironclads, under the command of Rear Admiral Exelmans, Uhrich's total force had, by the second half of August, reached a total of 23,000 men with 1,200 guns.[4] He organised the defence of the city in four districts, each under a separate commander, and prepared for the inevitable attack.

He did not have long to wait. On August 10 Moltke sent an order to Lient General Carl von Werder, the commander of the Baden Division, instructing him that 'any approach of enemy troops and materiel towards Strasbourg, especially from the south, if possible to be prevented. Best would be complete investment, for which troops are on the way.'[5] Werder, who was born in 1808, had had a distinguished career, including a spell with the Russian army during the Caucasus campaign of 1842–3; he had fought with distinction as a divisional commander at Königgrätz. When he received his orders, Werder was at Brumath about twenty miles north of the city; he moved off next day, and by nightfall on the following day had thrown a screen of outposts around Strasbourg. The importance attached to Strasbourg at Royal Headquarters can be gauged by the fact that although he was now heavily occupied with the operations around Metz, Moltke found time on August 12 to despatch a telegram to Werder demanding to know what measures the latter had taken. Werder's division was strong enough for a distant blockade, but it was already clear to Moltke that a larger force would be necessary to invest or besiege the city, and on August 14 he ordered the formation of a siege corps to undertake the necessary operations. In addition to the Baden Division, it was to comprise the 34th Fusilier Regiment, the 30th Infantry Division (both coming from Karlsruhe) and three reserve batteries of field artillery. A siege train including 200 guns was to be brought up by rail, while the Grand Duke of Baden also set off for Karlsruhe to join his troops in the field. On August 13 Werder began to close up to the fortress, driving back the French troops outside the enceinte, and opening fire on the military station and the suburbs of Kronenbourg. He also took the precaution of removing all food supplies that might be in reach of the garrison.

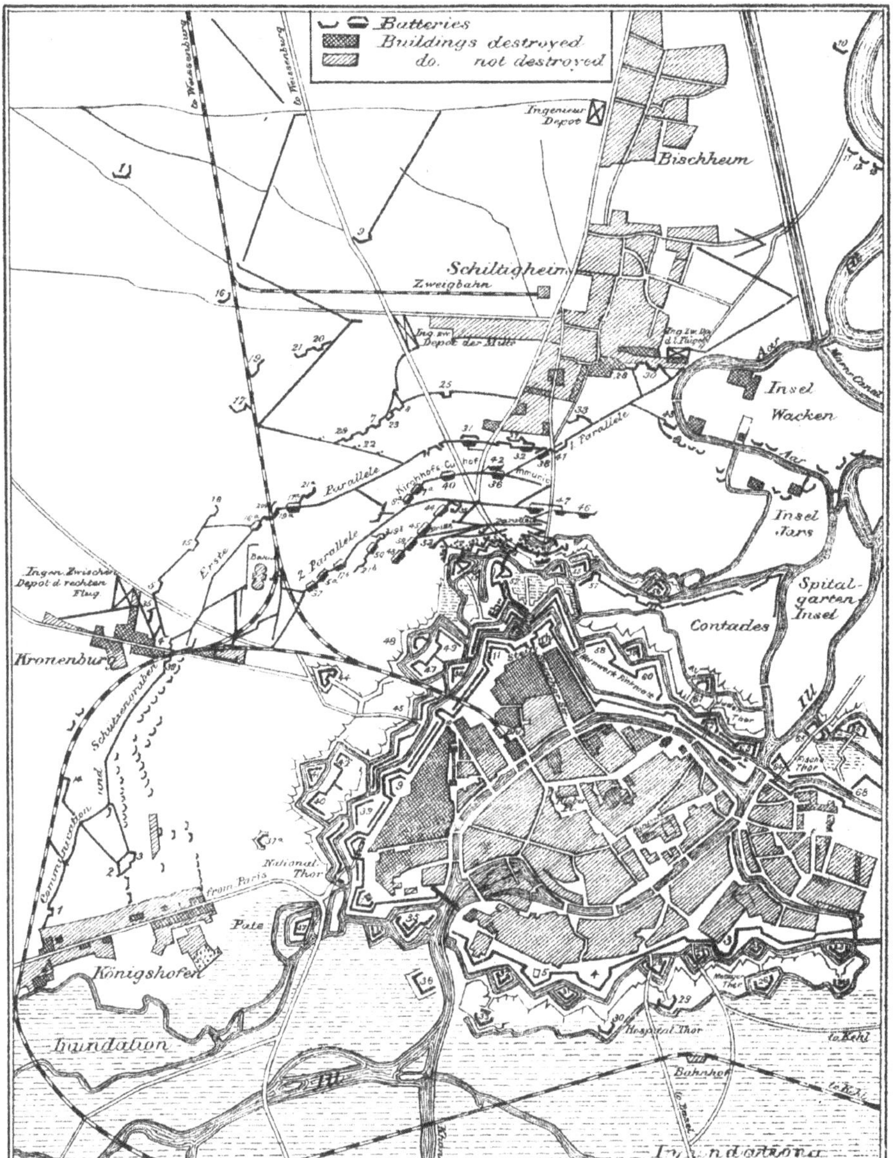

Siege of Strasbourg

Lieutenant Colonel von Leszcynski, his chief of staff, together with the chief of his engineers reconnoitred the position, and concluded that Schiltigheim and the ground towards the Rhine must be occupied before embarking on siege works against the northwest of the fortress, and steps were taken to build the necessary bridges. Some of the promised reinforcements now began to arrive from Hagenau, and on August 15 troops were sent forward to occupy Schiltigheim and the Rhine-Ill Canal, while the erection of batteries of artillery got under way. A series of skirmishes ensued as the French tried unsuccessfully to hold up the German advance into the forward positions designated.

On the south of the city, where the 3rd Baden Regiment was also moving forward, there was a more serious clash on August 16, when a French sortie under Colonel Fiévet, leading two battalions with 4 guns and 400 cavalry, was launched towards Illkirch. In the face of fierce rifle fire, the assault broke down, and Fiévet was killed; his troops retreated with the loss of three guns and 29 casualties. While he was turning over in his mind the best way to proceed to the reduction of the fortress, Werder was alarmed to receive a report from the headquarters of the Third Army that two divisions of de Failly's corps were said to be advancing to its relief from Charmes and Epinal. In the face of this threat, he was obliged to interrupt his preparations for the siege, and to concentrate a large part of his forces to the west of the city, leaving only small forces in position to watch its defenders, and withdrawing completely from the south side. Fortunately for him the French took no steps to mount a sortie. By the following day Werder's cavalry reports suggested that it was a false alarm, and his troops were ordered to return to their positions to continue the siege. It was as well they did, for on August 18 a sortie led by Colonel Blot advanced on Schiltigheim with a view to cutting down trees in the St Helena cemetery, opposite Lunettes Nos. 52 and 53, which obstructed the defenders' field of fire. The attackers were soon repulsed, having succeeded only in setting fire to a large brewery at the edge of the suburb.

Werder returned to his headquarters to consider whether a bombardment would be more effective than complex siege operations. Next day, however, occurred an incident which made up his mind for him. Three batteries had been established on the German bank of the Rhine at Kehl, and their commander, having jumped to the conclusion that Werder was expecting immediate artillery support from him, opened fire on the citadel on the morning of August 19. Not surprisingly, the fortress returned the fire, shelling the town of Kehl heavily until 5.00 pm, even though Werder had ordered the German guns to cease fire about noon. Werder protested to Uhrich about the devastation of Kehl. Correspondence between them was maintained with the greatest courtesy throughout the siege, and Uhrich at once responded: 'Kehl may, it is true, be no fortress, but at any rate it is a post surrounded by two forts, and therefore subject to all the perils of war; moreover, a fire has been directed from thence upon the citadel.'[6] There had developed meanwhile a sharp disagreement on Werder's staff as to the best way to proceed; Schulz was in favour of formal siege operations, while Leszcynski was all for bombardment. There were rumours of disaffection in the city, which suggested that the latter course would bring quick results.[7] On the other hand, the German artillery might be outmatched by the fortress artillery, and Schulz, with this in mind, prepared a plan for opening the siege proper.

German Siege Battery Föhrenbach (southern battery) at Kehl, during the Siege of Strasbourg, engraving after a contemporary photograph (Pflugk-Harttung)

Aware that Moltke was anxious to see Strasbourg reduced as quickly as possible both for its own sake and to release the besiegers for further operations, and with the example of Uhrich's bombardment of Kehl in his mind, Werder asked Royal Headquarters for permission to open fire on the city. Moltke passed the buck back to him in a curt telegram: 'Bombardment of Strasbourg from Kehl quite justified if by this means capitulation can be obtained, but that cannot be judged from here.'[8] Meanwhile Werder continued his correspondence with Uhrich, calling on him to surrender. Uhrich rejected the request, but asked that women, children and old people to be allowed to leave the city. Werder courteously refused, and gave notice on August 22 that the bombardment would be commenced. In taking this decision he had in mind a further letter just received from Moltke reiterating that Werder's task was to capture Strasbourg 'with the least possible delay.' Accordingly, on the evening of August 23 outpost battalions were pushed forward, to cover thirteen batteries comprising 54 heavy guns which were to carry out the bombardment from the northwestern side of the fortress; on either side of them, enfilade batteries and mortars at Königshoffen and Schiltigheim were to support the attack, while field artillery shelled the city from the south, and the batteries around Kehl fired on Sporen Island.[9]

The bombardment commenced on the evening of August 23 and continued, with brief pauses, in driving rain, both day and night until August 25. The French response was fitful; a sortie was made towards Königshoffen, but the fortress artillery was generally ineffective, although the fire directed at Kehl had caused further extensive damage to the town. On the afternoon of August 25 the Bishop of Strasbourg came out to the German lines to ask for a ceasefire, but lacking any power to negotiate, Werder was obliged to refuse his request. The damage inside the city had been very considerable; the art gallery, library and a new church were destroyed by fire, and the citadel badly damaged.[10] The bombardment was resumed that night until 4 am the following morning, causing widespread fires in the railway station, the cathedral and again the citadel. In the hope that all of this might have now weakened Uhrich's will to resist, or at least that of the inhabitants, Werder again wrote to summon him to surrender, warning him that the bombardment would recommence if he did not. The only immediate response came from

Lunette 52, Strasbourg (Pflugk-Harttung)

the fortress artillery, which continued to fire on the siege batteries, and Werder duly ordered his artillery to open fire again. Meanwhile, however, his staff had been taking stock of the position, both figuratively and literally, reaching the conclusion that the bombardment was proving ineffectual and that in any case ammunition was running short. Werder accepted this, and gave orders for formal operations to begin at once, only a moderate rate of fire being maintained until the completion of the first parallel. Siegecraft in its most formal sense had been continuously refined since the Middle Ages until as Professor Howard wrote, it had attained 'the precise rhythm almost of a dance.'[11] First one parallel, then a second with communicating trenches, and then a third would be dug, until the intended point of attack was reached; then the artillery would attempt to batter a breach in the defences wide enough for an infantry assault. Werder's engineers at once started the necessary preparatory work, extending shelter trenches, building connecting roads and cover for infantry outposts and generally strengthening the positions occupied by the besieging troops. A formal siege was not a hasty affair, but properly managed it could go remorselessly on until its object was attained.

Uhrich, meanwhile, had not been unmoved by Werder's efforts, reporting to the War Ministry on August 26:

> Continuous bombardment for the last six days. Many fires and much destruction. Numbers of people in Strasbourg without shelter or food. Cathedral considerably damaged. Citadel completely burnt down. Approaches commenced. Situation very serious and commences to be disquieting.[12]

And morale in the city was becoming seriously affected; both officially from the city council, and unofficially from a mass demonstration, Uhrich received demands to capitulate. With the fortress still defensible, he refused to contemplate this and his stern determination to resist appears to some extent to have restored the spirits of the civilian population. On the night of August 28–9 Werder had given orders for the occupation of Wachen Island, to cover the left flank of the parallel. That evening crowds of civilians surged out of the town, but were turned back by the German outposts. On the following night outposts were pushed forward to within four hundred metres of the glacis; behind them, working parties formed up to open the first parallel, about seven hundred metres from the glacis, and stretching from the Rhine-Marne Canal through the cemetery of St Helena across the Paris railway line to Kronenbourg. The German troops moved forward under cover of the stone houses of Schiltigheim, and through the maze of shelter trenches that had been dug. The work was under the direction of Major General von Mertens; the recently arrived commander of the artillery, von Decker, constructed eleven new siege artillery batteries, to bring the total on the left bank of the Rhine to twenty one, comprising in all eighty eight guns. The work went on undisturbed and by August 31 was largely complete. Meanwhile at Kehl additional mortar batteries were established, so that a total of thirty six guns was available to fire from there on the citadel.[13] Mertens had reached the same conclusion as the French engineers that the sector at which he should aim was between Bastion Nos. 11 and 12, and during the evening of August 31 he drove two approaches about three hundred meters beyond the first parallel to this point of the defences.

The rapid progress of the siege works enabled Werder on September 1 to move the second parallel to be opened within three hundred and fifty metres of the glacis; at this point, a substantial body of French troops briefly emerged from the Stone Gate, adjoining Bastion No 12, and for a while the besiegers were obliged to withdraw to the St Helena cemetery. But by 3am on September 2, the line of trenches was largely complete.

An hour or two later as dawn broke on that day, Uhrich launched a large scale sortie from various points along the enceinte, towards Königshoffen, Kronenbourg and Wachen Island. At Kronenbourg, six companies led by Colonel Blot dashed towards the village, seizing the farm buildings on its edge, before being halted at the east edge of the village. At Königshoffen the advance of five companies was less successful, being pinned down in front of the shelter trenches; while at Wachen, where three companies had advanced, an early advantage was quickly reversed when several companies of the 4th Pomeranian Landwehr Regiment came up and drove back the attackers. As the troops involved in the three sorties withdrew, an artillery duel opened in which the besiegers soon gained the upper hand. Each side had lost about 150 men during the sorties. Uhrich later reported candidly to the War Ministry: 'This morning a glorious sortie, but dearly purchased, and no other success than imposing respect on the enemy.'[14]

However, as the morning wore on, the Germans found that the lines taken in digging the new parallel had been miscalculated, the right hand section not being connected with the left; attempts were made throughout September 2 to connect it, but under heavy fire these efforts had to be abandoned, and it was not until the night of 2/3 September that it could be completed. The garrison made one further attempt to disrupt the works, when at 3.30 next morning another sortie burst out of the Sarenne and Stone Gates, but although at one point the advance reached the second parallel, it was soon driven back with the loss of 40 men. Thereafter, the point of attack being confirmed as the sector between Bastions No 11 and 12, the work on the second parallel continued, but was not extended as far as Königshoffen. The second parallel was finally completed on September 9.

Meanwhile, the news of Sedan had reached Werder; Moltke telegraphed him on September 4 to tell him of the victory and the defeat of Bazaine's attempt at a breakout from Metz, adding that he should again summon Strasbourg to surrender.[15] Werder at once did so; Uhrich again refused, and took pains to keep to himself the news of Sedan. Werder reported to Moltke that Uhrich had broken off discussions because of his refusal of an armistice, and because Werder could not accept as a basis for negotiation that the troops comprising the garrison should be allowed to leave with all their arms and baggage. In reply to his request for further instructions, Moltke telegraphed on September 6 that an officer could be sent under escort to the Royal Headquarters, but that meanwhile 'a rapid capitulation is certainly desirable. In the light of the actual situation, it is necessary that the garrison remain prisoners. The officers could be set free on giving their parole.'[16] Werder soon reported Uhrich's refusal of all discussion: and next day he suggested to Moltke that a further bombardment would certainly hasten the fall of Strasbourg. Moltke replied on September 8 that 'a serious bombardment of the city by all means is permissible, but it must be avoided if possible, and in any event advance warning should be given to the commandant.' He went on to tell Werder that two emissaries of the revolutionary government named Valentin and Engelhardt had apparently been sent to Alsace, and who were to be given short shrift; 'arrest them and treat them with the full rigour of the law,' he added.[17]

Meanwhile, at Strasbourg, Werder's guns continued to batter Uhrich's defences. By September 8 Lunette No 44 had been silenced, and the Finkmatt barracks destroyed. Unfortunately a few days later the theatre suffered the same fate by mistake; the bombardment had been intended for the artillery school. As a result of the damage to the defence works, only the concealed mortars responded to the German fire on the threatened front, although the flank defences were still actively counter firing. It was obvious to Uhrich that his situation was deteriorating; in response to his reports, the War Ministry instructed him to hold out as long as he could and then, before the end, to attempt a breakout over the Rhine, where the German lines were at their weakest. For his part Werder now resolved to press on with his attack on the sector between Bastions Nos. 11 and 12. Steps were accordingly taken to reduce the water level in the ditches of the fortress by destroying the dams which held the water in place; and while efforts were made to render harmless the French mining works at Lunette No 53, a resourceful captain of engineers named Ledebour lowered himself into the water filled ditch to remove the charges. Work began on the third parallel on September 9 and on the following night two approach trenches were driven forward. By the night of September 11–12 a trench line over seven hundred metres long was dug only a few metres from the glacis. On September 11, a Swiss delegation had been allowed by Werder to enter the fortress to negotiate the release of about 2000 women and children. The delegation brought with them the news, which quickly spread, of the battle of Sedan, which put further pressure from the civilian population upon Uhrich for a capitulation. He remained adamant however that resistance must continue, and morale again rose when the redoubtable Valentin, who had tried to get into the fortress first from the south side and then from the right bank of the Rhine, succeeded in evading the German outposts and entering the city by swimming across the river Aar and one of the water filled ditches.[18]

At Kehl, the siege batteries had been reinforced; they had been able to concentrate on the citadel since the abandonment by the French on September 2 of Sporen Island. On the night of September 13–14 Werder seized the opportunity to send troops over the Rhine to hold a small bridgehead there, covering the road bridge over the river. Uhrich was stung into an immediate response, opening a heavy bombardment on the German troops, followed by a powerful infantry assault on the bridgehead. After a sharp struggle Uhrich's force withdrew, and the German troops entrenched their position. This was just as well, because on September 17 Uhrich launched another violent though unsuccessful assault on the bridgehead.

Rumours had reached Werder on September 5 of an impending sortie from the south front of the fortress, necessitating the urgent throwing up of defensive works to meet it. No sortie came, however, and on the night of September 11–12 Werder moved troops up to the line of the railway embankment which ran round the south side, from which they were driven by an assault on September 13. The French held the line of the embankment until the following day before withdrawing, but in the belief that this might yet be the direction taken by the expected sortie, Werder reinforced his position there. There was, however, no major attack in this sector, although on September 25 the French again moved out briefly to the railway line.

During September, as has been seen, Werder was obliged to detach part of his force to operate against franc tireur and other threatened military activity in Upper Alsace. In spite of the successful operations of Keller's flying columns, the whole area of Southern Alsace remained one of considerable danger for small German detachments covering lines of communications and carrying out reconnaissances in this area. Werder was called upon, therefore, frequently to detach troops from the siege to operate against small groups of French troops and franc tireurs over a wide area.

This problem was of considerable concern to Moltke; but he was even more anxious that Strasbourg should be reduced without delay, and it was with unmistakable irritation that he telegraphed Werder on September 21: 'Since the 15th of this month I have received no news from you. I beg that you send me, each day, a complete report by telegraph.'[19] To this, Werder plaintively replied that he had been reporting regularly; and in fact the missing telegrams turned up next day. On that day, Werder asked what powers he had to negotiate a capitulation, if the situation arose. Moltke responded on September on September 24 setting out the terms on which he should insist. The garrison must be made prisoner; subject to this, the honours of war should be accorded them; the officers could go home on giving their parole for the rest of the war.[20]

Meanwhile the besiegers were getting closer to the crucial assault on the fortress. After crowning the glacis, part of the ditch wall opposite Lunette No 53 was brought down on September 19; Major Bayer sent troops over the ditch in a boat, and the displaced wall and earth was used to make a dam, which was completed by 4pm. Lieutenant Frobenius dashed into the lunette, to find it abandoned; it was promptly occupied and the six guns there were spiked. On September 21 after NCO Freitag had swum across over the ditch around Lunette No 53 to measure its width, a bridge was thrown over that night. When entered,

A French artillery battery during the siege of Strasbourg, by Röchling (Lindner)

this lunette, too, was found to be abandoned. The occupation of the lunette by a company of the 34th Regiment appears at first not to have been noticed by the French, but when reinforcements came up a heavy fire was poured upon the German troops there. By September 25 access to the captured lunettes had been strengthened to the point at which mortars could be brought into them. The courageous Ledebour reached the basin behind the lunettes by swimming, in order to reconnoitre the next positions to be assaulted, as a result of which the front of the attack was widened.[21]

On the night of September 22–23, the advance commenced; siege batteries in the captured lunettes, together with a heavy concentration of artillery brought up close to the enceinte, battered the enceinte walls to the east of Bastion No11 and the west of Bastion No 12. Under heavy fire, the French abandoned the counterguard. By noon on September 24 the wall at Bastion No 11 was destroyed; but it was not until the morning of September 26, after a lengthy battering, that the wall at Bastion No 12 finally collapsed along a length of thirty six feet.

On the French side the breach was inspected by Colonels Sabattier and Maritz, who next day reported that the breach was practicable, and that the position would no longer be defensible in the face of an assault that was obviously imminent. Uhrich recognised that no more could be done. The attempt to break out, recommended from Paris, was almost certainly not feasible; his force, or that part of it that could be readied for such a hazardous attempt, would almost certainly have quickly disintegrated. 'At 5 pm a white flag was seen to float over the cathedral tower; shortly after, similar signs were visible upon the other churches and buildings, and lastly at the northern works … joyful songs of victory shortly echoed around Strasbourg.'[22]

Contact was made between the respective headquarters after a few hours; that night, at Königshoffen, Leszczynski negotiated the capitulation. The regular troops and the gardes mobiles, some 17,500 strong, were made prisoner; the officers were paroled. The Germans took possession of 1,200 guns, 800 carriages, 200,000 rifles and a huge supply of ammunition, as well as the gold bullion of the Government bank.

Next morning the French garrison marched out, led by Uhrich and his senior commanders on foot. Werder and the Grand Duke of Baden, chivalrous as always, dismounted to receive them. As had been the case throughout the siege, the capitulation was conducted with scrupulous propriety and Uhrich was greeted with a friendly courtesy. Unfortunately not all Uhrich's soldiers behaved as well; many were drunk, and disobeyed their officers, smashing their rifles and throwing them into the ditch.

Werder deferred his own entrance into the battered city, choosing September 30 to do so; it was one hundred and eighty nine years to the day that the French had seized Strasbourg. By then, he had been rewarded for his successful conduct of the siege by his promotion on September 27 to the rank of General of Infantry. Werder, who was one of the relatively unsung heroes of the Franco-Prussian war, certainly deserved this promotion. There were, however, still greater responsibilities for him yet to discharge, and a lot more fighting in front of him, before the war was to draw to its close. He had little time to reflect on his triumph, and its symbolic significance; on the day he entered the city, fresh orders arrived from Moltke.

5

Chevilly

Back at Versailles, Blumenthal had on September 29 received an unpleasant surprise, with the news that the whole of the Royal Headquarters was to be transferred there.

> We shall, I suppose, have to move out of our beautiful palace and seek some humbler abode. I do not mind that so much, but the close propinquity of the King's Headquarters has its drawbacks, especially for me, as I have not always sufficient command over myself to return the diplomatic or evasive answer to all the unnecessary questions and unsolicited conundrums set to solve. I am afraid I shall become again somewhat caustic or brusque without wishing to be so, and shall get myself disliked.[1]

Apart from Blumenthal's characteristic impatience, a more serious point arose; with Moltke located so close to the headquarters of one of his armies in particular, there was always the risk of some distortion in his own strategic thinking, as well as offering the temptation to interfere too directly in Third Army operations matters. And a couple of weeks later Blumenthal's gloomy forebodings seemed to be confirmed: 'The presence of the King's Headquarters in my neighbourhood means interruptions without end. Reports are required about everything.'[2]

Meanwhile, inside Paris, Trochu and Ducrot were confirmed after Châtillon in their view that the only way of achieving a result against the encircling German armies was by being able to fight a major defensive battle in which they could, from the undeniably strong positions which they occupied, inflict a serious defeat on the Germans by smashing an assault on the city. This, however, Moltke had no intention of launching; as he explained to Scheller, his financial adviser, on September 29: 'we must now wait to see how long matters will remain as they are. The condition of France meanwhile can only become worse, if the other powers do not interpose, which they would scarcely do in favour of the Republic ... We must let the volcano burn out by itself.'[3] As time passed, it became increasingly evident to Trochu that this was indeed Moltke's strategy, and as a result he became more inclined to yield to the pressure, both from his subordinate commanders and from the Paris newspapers, for some action on the part of the substantial forces at his disposal to disrupt the remorseless strengthening of the German positions opposed to him.

During the last days of September both sides were engaged in completing their entrenchments, throwing up artillery emplacements and exchanging sporadic gunfire. On the German side of the lines one immediate task was the finding of quarters for the troops; fortunately, the large number of abandoned villages around the capital amply filled this need, and for the rest of the siege the German troops were in the main well housed. More of a problem was supplying the army; the inhabitants who had fled from the villages had from the most part removed or destroyed food stores (apart from the wine vaults which according to the official history 'appeared to conceal inexhaustible supplies'). The problem could only be overcome by restoring the railway lines, which remained a high priority. As to communications, the Germans soon installed a comprehensive telegraph system, and built a large number of bridges over the Seine and the Marne to ensure that reinforcements could be quickly moved to any part of the front.[4]

About a mile and a half north of the powerful position of St Denis, the IV Corps had occupied Pierrefitte; on September 23 the 28th Regiment de Marche under General Bellemare attacked the village, held by a battalion of the 93rd Regiment. For a while, the assault made progress into the centre of the village, until taken in flank by a battalion of the 31st Regiment, after which the attackers fell back into St Denis. A simultaneous attack on positions held by the Guard Corps was also repelled, the two engagements costing each side about 100 casualties. South east of Stains the Guard occupied an advanced position at Le Bourget, although due to constant shelling the village itself was held only by one company.

Behind its line of outposts, the main defensive position of the Army of the Meuse was about seven miles from the enceinte of Paris, extending from Orgemont, north of Argenteuil to the Marne. It was based on a line of strongly fortified villages: in these, and in many of the gaps between them, an extensive system of earth works had been thrown up. The position was strengthened by inundations, caused by the diversion of the Ourcq Canal, along the line of the Morée brook, which ran in an arc behind Le Bourget, through Dugny and Le Blanc Mesnil. The road crossings over the flooded area were heavily defended. In the sector covering the loop of the Marne, held by the Württemberg Division, the main defence line was based on the villages of Noisy, Villers and Coeuilly, covered by strong outpost positions at Le Plant, Champigny, Chennevières and Ormesson, connected by a complex trench system. To the left of this position Bose's XI Corps had come up into line, on either side of the Troyes road, its outposts facing Creteil and extending the line as far as the Seine through Bonneuil and Mesly. Further west, Tümpling did not attempt to hold Villejuif, as being too much exposed to attack from the line of the forts; on September 22 he ordered the destruction of the Hautes Bruyères Redoubt, and pushed troops forward to Villejuif to cover this operation. These collided with troops of Maud'huy's Division, which had come forward to try to reoccupy the positions abandoned on September 19, and the Germans retreated on Chevilly, although during the night pioneers succeeded in returning to the redoubt and extensively damaging the works there. Major General von Hoffman, not realising that his troops had pulled out of Villejuif, had intended to reinforce the village. Discovering the true position, he probed forward next morning towards the village and into the Hautes Bruyères Redoubt, but the strength of the French forces on the Villejuif heights was such that he gave up, and pulled his troops back to their original positions, leaving the French in possession of Villejuif and the redoubt, which they proceeded to restore, defending it with mitrailleuses and heavy artillery.[5] These engagements did something to restore morale in the French army, so badly dented after Châtillon. The VI Corps now settled itself down in a position along the road west from Choisy Le Roi to Frenes le Rungis, with outposts at L'Hay, Chevilly and Thiais.

Hartmann's II Bavarian Corps remained in the positions it had occupied after the action of September 19, strengthening these by close parallel lines of entrenchments, and fortifying the farms and villages in its front. Infantry redoubts were constructed on the Villacoublay plateau, and a powerful artillery position was established east of Croix de Bernis. The Châtillon redoubt was rebuilt to front on Paris, and was supported by a reserve at Plessis Picquet consisting of units of the 3rd Division. The western end of the Third Army's front was defended by Kirchbach's V Corps; the strong positions occupied by Sandrart's 9th Division covered Versailles, the front line running from Meudon to Sevres and Ville d'Avray, while von Schmidt's 10th Division occupied a network of fortified villages and chateaux on the Rocquencourt plateau, including Bougival, the Villa Metternich with its park, La Celle St Cloud and Garches. The chateau of St Cloud was lightly held by a small outpost. The left of the corps position rested on the Seine near Croissy.[6]

The rear of the Third Army was covered by the 2nd, 5th and 6th Cavalry divisions, which were already sending patrols deep into enemy territory to collect supplies of food for the army. Already, however, they were beginning to encounter resistance from franc tireurs, and by the end of the month required infantry support for some of their raiding expeditions. This was provided by von der Tann's I Bavarian Corps, which had reached Longjumeau by September 22, and was soon obliged to push some units forward in the direction of Pithiviers in support of the cavalry scouting towards Orleans. Reviewing in particular the positions taken up by the Third Army, Blumenthal was realistic in his assessment. Properly conducted, it was his view that a French assault would enjoy at least temporary success. 'Our lines are so weakly held that, if the enemy should attack at one point with the whole of his force concentrated, we must be beaten back and have our line cut through. Fortunately, he does not understand his business and wastes his strength, striking out blindly in all directions.'[7] On the other hand, as d'Herisson pointed out, 'if the blockade had unfortunately been forced, the victorious troops, without provisions, without convoys or ammunition, would have fallen to the last man in the fatal grasp of the Germans, who would have fallen back and surrounded them in the impassable and devastated zone they occupied round Paris.'[8]

Vinoy, whose 13th Corps contained most of the regular troops in Paris, and who had with other troops a total of 42,000 men under his command, was impatient to try his hand at an assault himself, and Trochu gave his approval, giving him precise instructions as to his objectives. These included the destruction of a bridge believed to have been built at Choisy Le Roi. On September 30 at 6.00 am Vinoy launched three brigades, with another in reserve, in separate attacks towards Thiais, Chevilly, and L'Hay under cover of a lengthy preparatory bombardment from the forts of Montrouge, Bicêtre, Ivry and Charenton, and from the redoubts of Hautes Bruyères and Moulin Saquet. Simultaneous diversionary attacks by three other brigades were aimed at Clamart and Carrefour Pompadour, although these were not pressed home in the face of German artillery fire. On Vinoy's right, Blaise's Brigade deployed in front of Thiais and Choisy, with the object of outflanking and cutting off Thiais. Immediately the French artillery preparation began, the 22nd Regiment under Colonel von Quistorp moved up to Choisy supported by the 6th Heavy Battery, with the 62nd Regiment in support. The heavy rifle fire of the defenders soon beat off the attack. At Thiais, the 62nd Regiment occupied the village in order to thwart the French enveloping movement; it was deprived of immediate artillery support when swarms of French tirailleurs charged forward between the two villages, and obliged the two batteries which had come up in support to fall back. The French reached the village, but after a fierce struggle at close quarters the attack was repulsed, and Blaise retreated behind Villejuif.

In the centre, Guilhem's Brigade was directed on Chevilly, held by a battalion of the 23rd Regiment. Guilhem's men forced their way into the village, temporarily isolating a party of German troops in a building at its north eastern edge; these broke out after fierce hand to hand fighting, but as the struggle continued the French occupied more and more of the village. Guilhem now led two battalions forward to complete his success, but fell mortally wounded; disheartened, his troops retreated in disorder.

Tümpling, watching the battle from a couple of miles back towards Orly, ordered von Gordon's 11th Division up in support. Meanwhile, however, Fabeck's 24th Brigade was getting the better of the struggle around Chevilly, and by 8am the French retreated from the village, although holding on to the farm buildings at its north eastern edge. Hoffmann, the commander of the 12th Division, who had taken over the direct conduct of the battle from Fabeck, his brigade commander, ordered a fresh assault to clear the farm, with the support of part of the 11th Brigade, which had come up. This attack succeeded in overcoming the resistance of the French who fell back behind the Hautes Bruyères redoubt, taking with them a cavalry brigade which had advanced to their support.

The return of the corpse of General Guilhem, killed at Chevilly, by Pallandre (Rousset/ *Combattants*)

Dumoulin's brigade was directed on L'Hay, reaching the outskirts of the village before a determined counter attack by the 23rd Regiment under Colonel von Briesen threw it back, with the aid of a flank attack by the men of one company which had worked round the French right. These charged with a loud cheer, and the French quickly disintegrated, falling back in a chaotic stream behind Hautes Bruyères. In spite of all Vinoy could do there to revive his assault, his troops had had enough; by 10.00 am the guns fell silent.[9]

During the morning's struggle, the Germans suffered a total of 441 casualties; the French losses were much greater, being of the order of 2,500. The damage to French morale was equally great, compounded by the loss of Guilhem. D'Herisson went out under flag of truce with the mournful duty of recovering the body.

> The Prussians gave it up with all the solemnity possible under the circumstances. Eight soldiers carried the bier, covered with flowers and foliage, on Uhlan lances; and, as they passed onwards, the various guards and isolated sentries presented arms, the officers saluting with their swords. It was a more striking sight, in the midst of the ravaged and desolated country, than the most gorgeous funeral procession that ever approached the Invalides.[10]

Trochu, who had not expected a great deal from the attack, put the best face he could on its outcome, issuing a communique to the Paris population.

> Our troops successively occupied Chevilly and L'Hay, and advanced as far as Thiais and Choisy Le Roi. All these positions were strongly occupied, the latter with cannon. After a sharp artillery and musketry engagement our troops fell back to their positions with remarkable order and calm. The Gardes Mobiles were very firm. All in all, a very honourable day. Our losses have been heavy, the enemy's losses probably no less heavy.[11]

Although the French attacks had been defeated comprehensively enough, they certainly caused disquiet at the Royal Headquarters. Blumenthal, on hearing the bombardment that preceded Chevilly, confessed to being 'anxious,' and there is no doubt that the Germans saw their situation as a little more precarious than it actually was. Von Hindersin, the Inspector- General of Artillery, had reached the conclusion that a bombardment by itself would not lead to the fall of Paris, and recommended that consideration be given to formal siege operations against Forts Issy and Vannes, and thereafter against the enceinte itself. This would not be possible until sufficient siege guns were in place. The sites for their location on the Châtillon plateau were identified, and the preliminary planning for an attack was put in hand.[12] Moltke approved the outlines of Hindersin's scheme on October 2.[14] On October 6 Blumenthal was told at a meeting with Podbielski that the Third Army would be responsible for an assault if it became necessary, and next day he met with Major General Schulz, the commander of his engineers, and Colonel Rieff to discuss the preliminary arrangements. Later in the day he was greatly annoyed to discover that he was not now to be responsible.

> I fancy that there are several who want to have their way in the matter, and this they would not have were it put into my hands. It is really most extraordinary that, in spite of the fact that Moltke and I continually come to an agreement on

certain points, there invariably steps in between us some third person, so that matters are eventually arranged quite otherwise than I expected.[15]

On October 10, when after all his responsibility for any bombardment was confirmed, Blumenthal was surly about the prospect: 'I only hope it will not be as it was at Düppel and Alsen, where I had to do all the work and others reaped all the fruit. I have no great yearning for the job, but if it is to be done, and the affair entrusted to me, I do not wish, neither shall I permit, others to put in their oars.'[16]

The hopes of a very early end to the war by now were quickly evaporating. As late as October 7 Moltke still seems to have been of the view that the war might indeed be as good as over, remarking hopefully to Waldersee: 'The war is at an end; these things are only its last gasps. There is no more question of big operations.'[17] A few days later, however even the steadfast and implacable Moltke was beginning to exhibit signs of battle weariness, writing to Adolph on October 12: 'Frequently do I long for the quiet retirement of the Kapellenberge. The news which I get from my peaceful home are like sun-rays amidst the restless turmoil and the exciting state of expectancy in which we are living here.'[18] Moltke had by now moved with the rest of the Royal Headquarters to Versailles, where they arrived on October 5. The enormous convoy that brought them struck even the Crown Prince as excessive.

> The mass of conveyances the Royal train requires is beyond belief, as Count Bismarck, General von Moltke, War Minister von Roon, as well as the Inspectors of Artillery and of the Pioneers, together with their bureaux, all belong to it, and even Councillor Schneider and Police Commissioner Stieber have their special carriages- not to forget Prince Karl and Prince Adalbert, as also the Grand Duke of Saxe-Weimar and Prince Luitpold of Bavaria![19]

The palace of St Cloud, overlooking the Seine, was only lightly held, and was subject to constant sniper fire from the French side of the river. On September 27 the Crown Prince went to have a look at a palace he had in times of peace visited more than once. Colonel von Bothmer, whose 17th Brigade covered this sector, forbade the Crown Prince to go into the building, but he succeeded in evading his minders, and wandered fascinated among its spacious rooms, pausing to study a painting of the visit of his mother in law, Queen Victoria, to the palace in 1855, before examining the Imperial apartments. He had a narrow escape; as he slipped away from the palace, the French snipers opened fire.[20] A fortnight later, French artillery fire from Fort Valérien set the palace on fire; in a strong wind, the flames spread rapidly, and few of the works of art could be saved.

Trochu had not completely abandoned in his mind the possibility that Moltke might still launch a major attack on Paris, and the movement of troops on the front of the Third Army seemed to confirm that something might be in the wind. On the other hand, reports of German activity in the direction of Orleans suggested that part of the investing army might have been withdrawn, so he ordered Vinoy to carry out a reconnaissance in force to ascertain what was going on. Vinoy concentrated some 25,000 men and eighty guns for the attack, to be directed on Bagneux and Châtillon, against Hartmann's positions there. The latter's outposts reported at 8.00am on October 13 that the enemy were moving up, evidently intending an assault; an hour later, the forts of Montrouge, Vanves and Issy began a preparatory bombardment, and columns of infantry from the brigade formerly led by Guilhem

Scene from the fierce fighting for possession of Bagneux, during the Battle of Chevilly, by Pallandre (Rousset/*Combattants*)

and now commanded by Mariouse, advanced on Bagneux. They were supported by Dumoulin's Brigade. Pushing into the village, three battalions of Gardes Mobiles soon reached the crossroads, while a fourth advanced to the east. By 11.00am they had driven the Bavarians out of the village but, pinned down by cross fire from Châtillon, could make no further progress.

At 1.30pm Lieutenant General von Bothmer, the commander of the 4th Bavarian Division, now brought up the 5th Regiment, which he sent forward from Sceaux; after a violent struggle, the Bavarians forced their way back into Bagneux. Meanwhile, to the west, Susbielle's Brigade advanced on Châtillon, bringing up field guns into the streets of the village, in which there was fierce hand to hand fighting in the course of which the French succeeded in occupying most of the place. Another assault took Clamart. The lightly held forward posts of the Bavarians having been overrun, it was some time before the reinforcements brought up could make their presence felt, handicapped as they were by the difficulties the artillery experienced in supporting them; but by 3pm it was evident to Vinoy that there were now substantial forces in his front, and he broke off the action, retreating in good order behind Forts Vanves and Montrouge, taking with him some 200 prisoners. Including these, the total losses on each side were about 400; but it had been an action which did something to restore morale among the defenders of Paris, even if not much useful information had been elicited.[21]

Blumenthal, meanwhile, had been discussing with Rieff the precautionary arrangements for a bombardment, as a result of which he could see that there was bound to be a considerable delay in bringing up the necessary siege guns and ammunition, due principally to the restricted railway availability.

> When once we commence firing, we must not – like inconstant children – break off our task unfinished. We must have the means of making success a certainty, otherwise a bombardment of the forts will damage us as much as them. It will, however, be very difficult to satisfy the inquiries of the ignorant and put a stop to idle talk.[22]

He remained profoundly unconvinced of the effectiveness of the siege artillery, noting on October 16: 'This should be our keynote, namely, to lay stress upon starvation, rather than bombardment, as the actual means for reducing the garrison.' It was a view shared by Moltke's staff, Verdy noting: 'A regular siege of Paris is entirely out of the question, and I only hope that we shall never attempt such a thing. If only we wait till hunger compels the town to surrender, we shall lose fewer men and make it more certain that we shall attain our end.'[23] Still brooding on the practical difficulties, Blumenthal reflected a few days later that the fortress could not be stormed before January, by which time the investment should already have led to its fall. Persuading the Crown Prince to his opinion, he decided to put down a marker with his views. 'I then drove across to see Moltke about it. He agreed with me entirely, and considered that it would never come to a question of bombardment, as the French would be starved out long before that could arise.'[25] Moltke himself was extremely disappointed by the delay in opening the railway, pointing out on October 6 to Itzenplitz, the Minister responsible for railways, that nine days after the taking of Toul the line was not yet in full operation: he called on him to use his influence to ensure that it was able to carry from twelve to fifteen trains a day in each direction which, as he pointed out, was not much for a double track line.[26] He kept up the pressure, writing again to Itzenplitz on October 21 with a detailed account of the continued shortcomings of the railway system.

Bismarck, however, took an entirely different view from the military leaders of the correct strategy to pursue, and was becoming extremely impatient with them. He related to Busch on October 14 a particularly frustrating meeting he had had with Moltke and Roon. Roon had agreed with him; but Moltke appeared not to have paid any attention to Bismarck's view, which annoyed the Chancellor very much. Although describing Moltke as 'an exceedingly able man,' he added bitterly that 'for years past he has devoted himself to one single subject, and he has come to have no head and no interest for anything else. It put me in a temper to find I had been talking to deaf ears.'[27]

As time went by, it became increasingly obvious to the French that Moltke did not intend to launch the all out attack on the capital which Trochu had seen as giving him his only chance to inflict a major defeat on the Germans. Moltke himself made it clear that he was not going to be tempted to an assault in a letter to Stiehle on October 9, observing that since they had been immobile in front of Paris, he could understand Stiehle's groans over the general lack of enterprise. 'Everyone, more or less, feels that the campaign is reaching its end, and desires accordingly to avoid the smallest losses. On the other hand, it is true that nothing bores the Parisians more than to see that we do not attack their forts.'[28] The natural instinct of the commander of a large army is to do something with it (although Bazaine was proving an exception to this rule) and Trochu now began to study the possibility of a break out. The difficulty was, as d'Herisson had pointed out, that even a successful force had to have somewhere to go, and had to have the resources, in the form of ammunition and supplies, to get there. The problem was to find a point in the lines of investment where they could be broken which coincided with worthwhile objectives to aim at, which must of course include contact with the armies outside Paris. Another aspect of the matter was that unless in the course of the breakout an absolutely crippling defeat was inflicted on the German armies, the size of the attacking force had to be limited by the need to leave a strong enough garrison to hold the city. A number of sectors appeared to offer possible opportunities for a breakthrough; these included on the south, the Villejuif plateau, on the east from Joinville, on the north from St Denis towards the plain northwest of the city, and on the west from the Gennevilliers peninsula. The first two were ruled out because once through the German lines extraordinary difficulties would have to be surmounted before any safe destination could be reached. The other two offered the French the chance to fight their way through to Normandy, where they could be supplied by sea and reinforced by troops from the Loire. Of these Ducrot, entrusted with the planning of the operation, thought Gennevilliers the better bet; an assault would fall where the besieging armies met, always a more vulnerable point, and the German defences here looked weaker than around St Denis.[29] Finally, an advance here had the advantage of being supported by the powerful position on Mont Valérien. As it happened, Moltke had ordered the Army of the Meuse to occupy the Gennevilliers peninsula but had been persuaded by Schlotheim, its chief of staff, that to do so would be too costly, and for the moment he suspended the instruction. Ducrot decided to launch a preparatory attack to push back Kirchbach's V Corps, to enable him to strengthen his positions on the west of Mont Valérien. After thorough reconnaissance, he prepared a force of 10,000 men with 120 guns for the purpose. At 8.30am on October 21 the guns of Fort Valérien opened a heavy bombardment of the positions to be assaulted, in which the field artillery joined at 1.00pm. For another two hours they pounded the German positions before the assault went in at 3.00pm. On the right Berthaut advanced on Rueil and the park of Malmaison; north of Buzenval Wood, Noel moved from the east of the Cucufa ravine, while Cholleton advanced on the Château of Buzenval. Another column reached Briqueterie. The preparations for the attack had not gone unnoticed by Kirchbach's outposts, and he deployed to meet it. In his front line the 19th Brigade was between Celle St Cloud and La Jonchère, with the left wing reaching Villa Metternich, east of Bougival.

In the face of a determined assault through Rueil, the Prussian outposts retreated to a defensive line which Lieutenant General Schmidt, the commander of the 10th Division, formed from the Seine to the Cucufa ravine. The French, however, came on, well supported by artillery, advancing on Bougival and on their left into the park of Malmaison. One company of Zouaves reached a wooden summerhouse on the slope below La Jonchère. By now the 19th Brigade was fully extended, and Schmidt brought up the 50th Regiment in support. A brisk counter attack into the Malmaison Park and over the walls of the Château itself, coupled with fierce rifle fire all along this point of the front, finally turned the tide, and the French were driven back.[30]

Further south, the counter attack of the 50th Regiment captured two guns before occupying Château Buzenval, and Ducrot now pulled back all his troops to their jumping off positions. Under a sporadic fire from Fort Valérien, the Prussians reoccupied their previous entrenchments. Moltke, who had been out for a drive in the opposite direction, rode with Verdy to the scene of the fighting. As the Prussians began to gain the upper hand, the King arrived, and with a large group of princely observers accompanied Moltke and Verdy to a water tower at Marly to watch the progress of the battle.

> The French artillery were deployed in a long line halfway down the long and steep slope of Mont Valérien; they were covered by strong bodies of infantry, especially numerous behind the right wing, the battalions there extending right up to the crest of the hill slope, along which further back, the dark masses of their reserves were visible ... Suddenly flashes of fire were seen on the opposite back of the Seine; they came from batteries that had just come up, having been sent forward from the IV Corps, and which were now brought into action. The extreme right of the enemy being right in their line of fire, now hastily beat a retreat, followed gradually by the other troops. Night was now coming on, and the flames blazing up from Buzancy showed out brightly.[31]

Ducrot's reconnaissance had cost him casualties of about 620 in all, the Prussians losing about 400 men. He was not, however discouraged; this sector still seemed to be the best at which to aim the breakout, and he and Trochu settled down to work on its further preparation. The secrecy of their work however was not wholly effective, and rumours soon spread through the city about 'Le Plan Trochu', which would bring salvation.

On October 26 Moltke celebrated his seventieth birthday, which brought numerous visitors through the heavy rain to his headquarters to congratulate him. One of these was Blumenthal, who took the opportunity to discuss the general position with him and to talk about the course of future operations, 'and found him of the same mind as myself.' Dinner was taken that day at the Hotel des Reservoirs, to which the Crown Prince was a surprise visitor, as was the Crown Prince of Saxony; and the evening finished, as was so often the case, with Moltke's favourite leisure pursuit, a game of whist. Next day, Moltke wrote to Adolph, reflecting on the physical and material costs of the investment.

> The sallies have hitherto been baffled by our outposts. Nowhere were they successful in their efforts to break through our lines. But any pursuit on our part is utterly impossible, and we are daily losing men by the fire of the forts, which continue their tremendous expenditure of ammunition ... each shot costs six thalers, while one of the large steel shells of the navy costs as much as ninety three thalers.

As to the immediate future, he added: 'There is nothing else left for us to do, so long as no really supreme authority, one, too, duly acknowledged by the nation, is constituted in France, except to spread the devastation of war to an even greater extent.'[32] And by now, events outside Paris, particularly to the south and west of the city, were beginning to occupy his attention.

6

The Fall of Orleans

Although the reports sent in by the German cavalry operating south and west of Paris could not give in any way a complete picture of what was going on on the Loire, there were by the end of September unmistakeable indications that a substantial force was being assembled. In fact this was largely concentrating behind the Loire, but a force of Gardes Mobiles, with a cavalry division under General Reyau covering the assembly, had been posted in the Orleans area; behind this, the 15th Corps was forming at Nevers, Bourges and Vierzon. Patrols from Rheinbaben's 5th Cavalry Division operating westwards from St Germain en Laye had encountered resistance at Les Alluets, and with the support of two battalions from the I Bavarian Corps cleared the place. The infantry moved on to occupy Marle, the French retiring to Vernon. The cavalry, under the command of von Bredow, the hero of Mars La Tour, pushed on to the line of the Eure after breaking the railway at Mantes. Fresh contact was made on October 9 at the village of Chevisy, which was briefly seized by a small detachment before stronger French forces compelled it to retire. Next day Bredow moved on the village with his whole force, driving out a regiment of Gardes Mobiles. Further reconnaissance found the French in strength at Dreux and Evreux.

The 6th Cavalry Division was now commanded by von Schmidt in succession to Duke William of Mecklenburg-Schwerin, who had not fully recovered from wounds sustained at Laon. Moving outwards from Paris in a south westerly direction and also supported by the end of September by Bavarian infantry, it had collided on October 2 with French troops based on Epernon; two days later the 15th Cavalry Brigade (von Alvensleben), with two companies of Bavarian infantry moved through Rambouillet and after a brisk action drove the French out of Epernon in the direction of Hauches, after inflicting 75 casualties on them.

It was in the front of the 4th Cavalry Division (Prince Albrecht the elder) that more substantial contacts were made. A brief skirmish on September 25, after which the German cavalry advanced through Artenay, was followed by a cavalry encounter south of the town on the following day. When the 10th Uhlan Regiment followed up its initial success, it met with strong infantry resistance, suffering many casualties, and was forced to go back to Artenay. Further reconnaissance found strong French forces all along the northern edge of the Forest of Orleans, and Prince Albrecht withdrew to Toury, which he held with two brigades, with another at Pithiviers.[1]

The German cavalry activity had led the French to reinforce the garrison of Orleans by strong forces from the newly formed 15th Corps, and this advance guard was placed under Reyau. On being appointed Motte-Rouge had been to Tours to get instructions; as he left, it is reported that one of the members of the Delegation said to him, 'For God's sake do something or other as soon as you possibly can. Public opinion insists on it.'[2] Motte-Rouge now brought up his 2nd and 3rd Divisions to Orleans, and his 3rd Division from Nevers to Gien. On

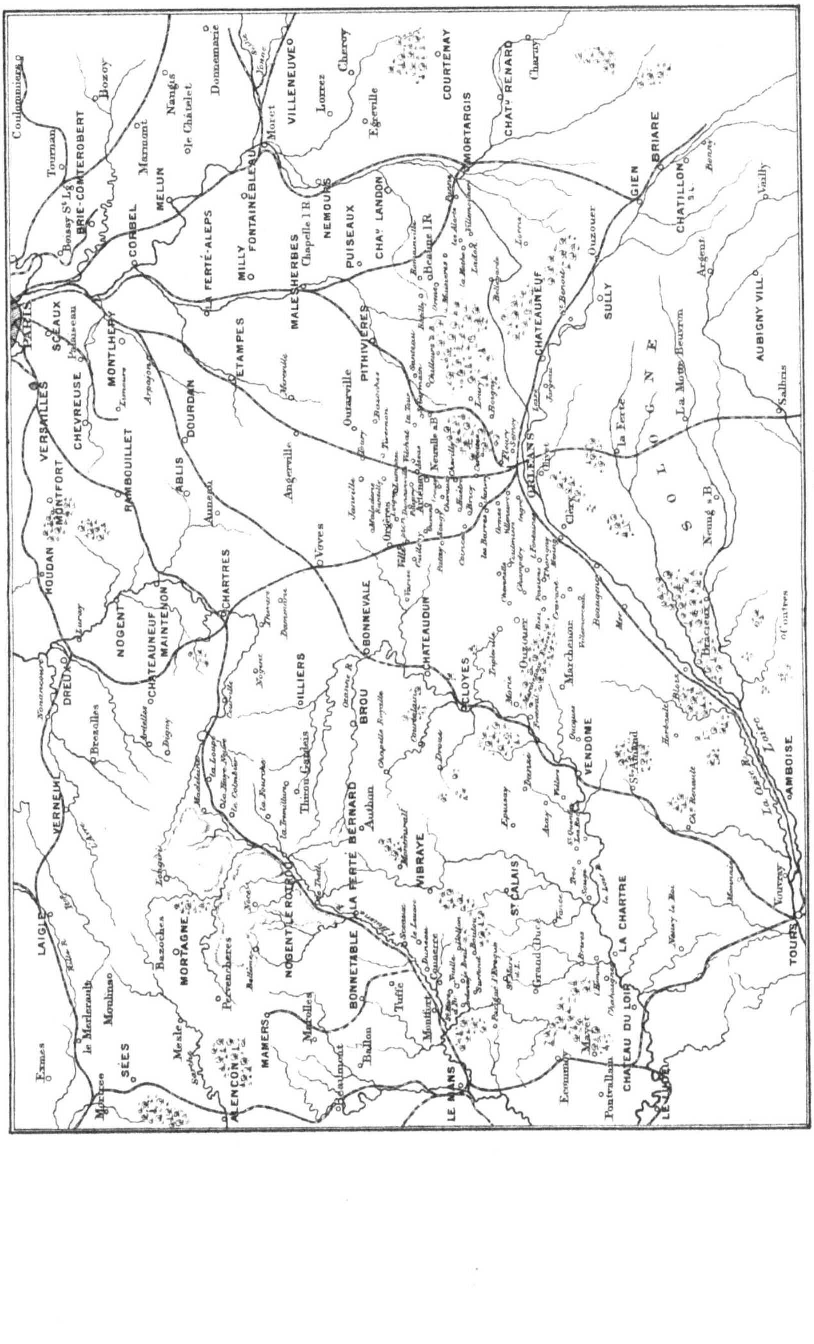

The Western theatre of war - Orleans and Le Mans

October 5 Reyau moved through Artenay towards Toury, behind which he encountered the two brigades of Prince Albrecht. After gaining some initial success, the Prussian cavalry was obliged to withdraw, at first to Angerville and next day to Étampes, where it was joined by the rest of the division from Pithiviers.

News of Reyau's advance concentrated Moltke's mind on the growing threat from the Loire, and next morning he and Blumenthal met to consider what to do. Moltke jotted down the outline of a plan for von der Tann to take his I Bavarian Corps, with Wittich's 22nd Division, and with the 2nd Cavalry Division (Stolberg) in addition to the two cavalry divisions already operating against the troops of Motte-Rouge, to deal with the situation.[3] That afternoon the I Bavarian Corps concentrated at Arpajon while Wittich reached Montlhéry late that night. Next day von der Tann continued to occupy his defensive position at Arpajon awaiting an attack which the French had no intention of making. His front was covered by Stolberg's cavalry and his right flank by units from Schmidt's division. Late that night at Ablis the division suffered a set back when a squadron of hussars was overwhelmed by a party of franc tireurs and a large part of it taken prisoner; the Bavarian company which had accompanied it managed to get away to Rambouillet. The infuriated Schmidt at once brought up both his brigades, but failed to catch the franc tireurs and had to be content with burning the village, on the grounds that its inhabitants had participated in the attack.

During October 7 von der Tann had remained at Arpajon, reporting that he would remain there until ordered to advance, much to Blumenthal's annoyance when he learned of this from Major von Hahnke, who had been sent down from Versailles to hurry him up.[4] Detailed orders for von der Tann arrived that night; his instructions were to clear the enemy westwards as far as Chartres, and southwards to Orleans. After taking the city he was to move on Tours. On October 8 von der Tann accordingly moved forward to Etampes, followed by Wittich who reached Etréchy. Scouting ahead, Stolberg had a brush with French troops near Saclay, which he drove back before bivouacking for the night at Marolles.

Motte-Rouge, meanwhile, had been back to Tours to receive further orders from the Delegation, and when he got back on October 8 he found that the situation had very much changed. Instead of prodding continuously at a distant enemy, he now had to deal with a fully fledged offensive in the direction of Orleans. Accordingly he pushed forward a strong force to Artenay on the great high road to support the scattered units which had been sporadically engaged with the German cavalry screen. During October 9 the Bavarians brushed aside these advanced units which were encountered at Angerville and in the Juine valley; patrols also reported the existence of strong French forces at Pithiviers. Moltke, in one of his regular letters to Stiehle at Metz, reported on October 9 to him Reyau's advance of October 5 and the measures taken to deal with the growing menace of the army of the Loire, adding that if it 'did not retreat of its own accord there will be a decisive battle in the outskirts of Angerville. Truth to tell, in front of Paris, we are for the moment without reserves.'[5] Pushing south down the high road at 6.00am on October 10, the 1st Bavarian Brigade encountered French troops around Dambron, and the brigade commander, von Dietl, deployed four battalions to deal with it; but the enemy soon withdrew towards Artenay, although still holding Assas and Vilchat on the east of the road. Von Stephan, the commander of the 1st

Bavarian Division, brought up his 2nd Brigade at 11.00am to deal with this. Von der Tann, who had accompanied his leading troops, expected to have to fight a major action at Artenay, and built up a gun line in an arc around the north of the town as far as Poupry, behind which the 2nd Bavarian Division, followed by Wittich's 22nd Division, were held in reserve.

Meanwhile, however, Prince Albrecht, reconnoitring further to the west, had heard the sound of gunfire and swung back towards the Paris road. Arriving at Ouvans, about three miles to the west of Artenay, his horse artillery opened fire on French troops in Autroches and Chateau Auvilliers. By 3.00pm this unexpected attack on his flank decided Motte-Rouge that his defensive position at Artenay was in fact indefensible, and he gave orders for an immediate retreat, which soon disintegrated into a rout. East of the road, a French battery at Arblay Farm, in flight from the advancing Bavarians, was caught in the open by three squadrons of hussars from the 10th Cavalry Brigade, and broken up with the loss of 250 prisoners. Worse was to follow. About 600 French infantry had taken refuge in the village of La Croix Briquet on the main road, were surrounded there, and quickly surrendered. Motte-Rouge fell back into the Forest of Orleans in considerable disorder. Von der Tann's victory had cost him some 200 casualties; the total French loss, which included some 1,500 prisoners and which must have been considerable, is not recorded.[6]

Blumenthal, who had the previous day been expressing the hope that von der Tann would 'put a goodly fear in their hearts' because he was 'certain that nothing will convince the French sooner of our power than the knowledge that we can prevent the formation on their part of new armies' was somewhat prematurely delighted by the news of Artenay. 'I had so much difficulty in getting this expedition sanctioned, and am naturally rejoiced it should be turning out so well.'[7]

Next day von der Tann pushed on towards Orleans, with his main force astride the high road, and with Wittich on his right at Les Barres. His cavalry was ordered to move far out towards the west. Motte-Rouge, however, dispirited by the swift collapse of his troops at Artenay, had already decided that he must retreat behind the Loire, and by October 11 his troops had begun to cross the river, covered by a rearguard in position between Ormes and the main road. By 9.15am von der Tann's artillery, which had moved up in close support of Wittich's division, compelled the evacuation of Les Barres on the Chateaudun road, and Wittich moved directly on Ormes. Here, much stiffer resistance was encountered, and Wittich was obliged to develop his attack on his right, a move which gradually forced the French to retreat, following which the 83rd Regiment, under Colonel Marschall von Bierberstein, stormed the village, which fell at 2.00pm. South east of the village the retreating French were broken up by the advancing 43rd Brigade, which took some 80 prisoners. As the German advance continued, it was held up by the French, who fiercely contested the numerous villages, gardens and vineyards which lay between Wittich and Orleans, and which prevented the easy movement of the German cavalry. Von der Tann, who was with the 22nd Division, had pushed forward the1st Bavarian Brigade from Chevilly in support of the advance on Ormes, linking with the main body of the I Bavarian Corps coming down astride the high road from Paris.[8]

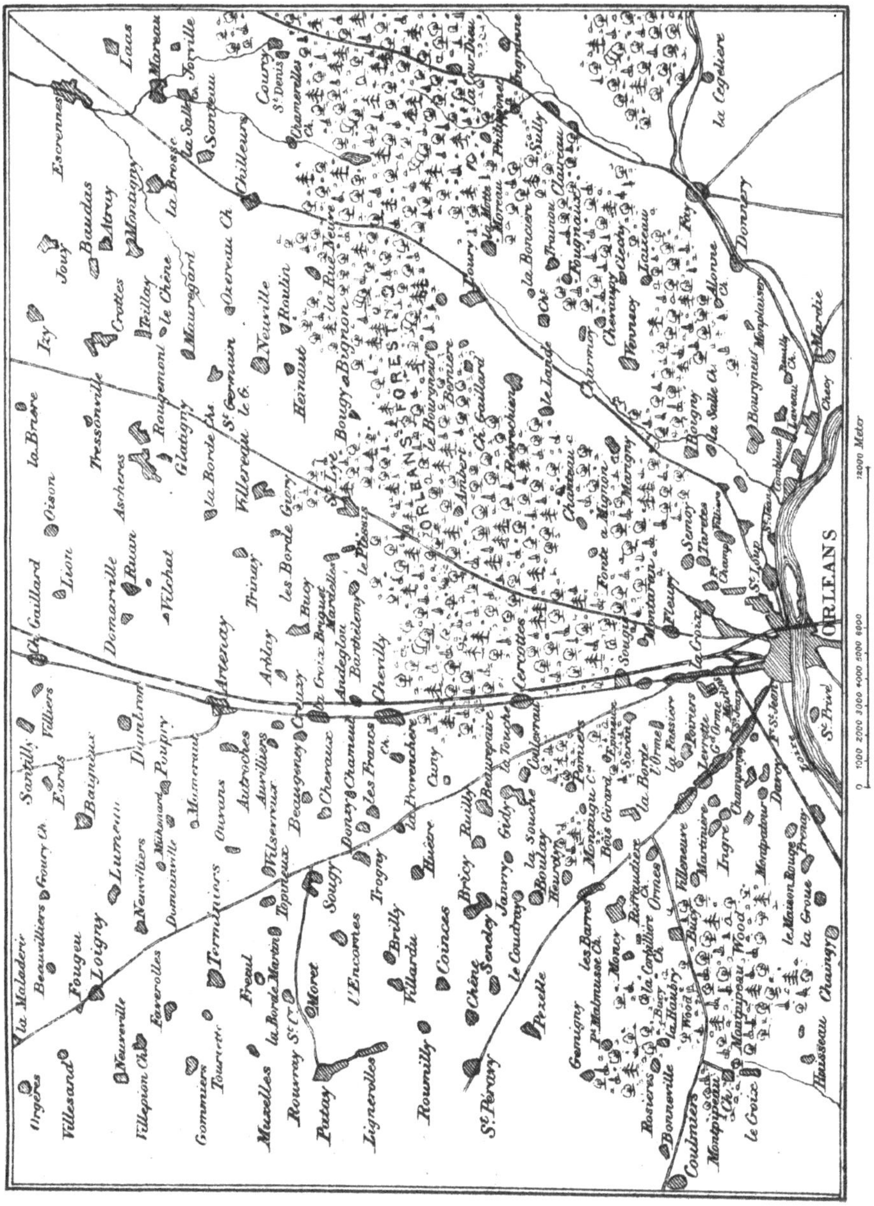

The Battle of Orleans, October 10, 1870

As the leading troops on the right of the advance approached Saran, it ran into stiff opposition from French troops who occupied this village and the woods and farms to its west, and from which they launched a series of attacks on the lead troops of the advancing Bavarians. It was not until 1.30pm that the position was finally cleared, and the advance on Orleans could be resumed. On the main road, the advance of the 3rd Bavarian Brigade (Schumacher) encountered less resistance until entering the northern part of the built up area around Orleans at the suburbs of Bel Air. Here, the French put up a vigorous struggle in defence of the vineyards and houses, and for some time Schumacher could make little progress, even after committing all his reserves. It was not until the 4th Bavarian Brigade arrived, coming up on his right and advancing towards Les Aides, that the French were obliged to abandon their position at Bel Air, and the struggle for Les Aides continued for a long time before the village was finally taken. East of the main road, more rapid progress was made at first through the station at Les Aubrays and further south to the gas works, which was stormed by Colonel Narciss at the head of six companies of infantry; but the French were still not done with, and counter attacked in considerable force, compelling Narciss to retreat to Les Aubrays, which he held in the face of repeated charges by the attacking French infantry.

Von der Tann, who had not expected to meet such a fierce resistance in his advance on Orleans, was determined to take the city by nightfall, and ordered Dietl and the 1st Brigade to come up on the right flank of the 4th Brigade to take Le Grand Orme. Then as night fell, and led by Lieutenant Colonel Heinleth, von der Tann's Chief of Staff, the 1st Bavarian Regiment charged forward through the suburbs of St Jean. Held up briefly by rifle fire and hand grenades at a toll gate, the regiment soon charged on, driving the French through the streets of Orleans until it reached the Place du Martroi in the centre of the city at 7.00pm. The 43rd Brigade pushed forward in close support through Bannier, the French retreating rapidly towards the bridges over the Loire. Von der Tann and Wittich, riding into the centre of Orleans, feared that in the darkness confusion could result from any attempt to pursue them, and ordered instead the occupation of the city. Ordered to advance to the Mairie, one battalion of the Body Guards

> advanced through the dark and silent streets with bands playing and drums beating, and was greeted at La Place Martroi by the ringing cheers of the 1st Regiment. The flames of the bivouac fires, which had been hastily kindled, lit up the martial groups, and the outlines of the gigantic statue of the Maid of Orleans, which towered over the foreign soldiers, as they exulted in their victory.[9]

Von der Tann's total casualties in what had turned out to be a suprisingly tough struggle amounted to 1,190 in all. French losses were severe, including over 1,800 prisoners.[10] The first part of his task appeared to have been convincingly completed.

Events meanwhile were occurring which were to change altogether the nature of the struggle against the Government of National Defence. In Paris there had been considerable discussion as to how the Delegation should be strengthened. The first man to volunteer to leave the beleaguered city by balloon had been Ducrot, who was much disappointed by Trochu's refusal to entertain the idea.

Leon Gambetta (Scheibert)

Gambetta had at first declined the suggestion that he should go, and on October 3 it was suggested that Jules Favre should leave the city, on the not unreasonable ground that the Minister for Foreign Affairs should be in a position freely to deal with foreign governments. The idea did not appeal to him, however, and it was decided that it must be Gambetta who proceeded to Tours. At 11.00am Gambetta, accompanied only by the pilot and his secretary Eugene Spuller, rose into the air in the balloon 'Armand Barbés.' Gambetta, although understandably pale and nervous, had the presence of mind to wave a tricolor as they left. His mind was full of the huge task ahead of him; he told Favre that 'I shall return with an army, and if I have the glory of delivering Paris I shall ask nothing more of destiny.'[12] Crossing the German lines at 2,000 feet, and surviving a fusillade of rifle fire, the battalion made two abortive descents into what turned out to be German occupied territory, before finally landing at Montdidier.

Gambetta hastened to Tours, where he arrived soon after midday on October 9. There, he found that the office of acting Minister of War was vacant, Fourichon having for the second and final time resigned on October 3, although continuing as a member of the Delegation as Minister of Marine. Gambetta wasted no time in meeting the Delegation and announcing the wide powers invested in him (including a casting vote); Fourichon's first reaction was to resign altogether because, as he later wrote 'he saw the dawn of dictatorship,' but after Gambetta and the others begged him to stay in office, he relented. As to the War Ministry, Gambetta did not hesitate to seize the unexpected opportunity to propose that he should take over. Both Crémieux and Glais-Bizoin opposed this; but Fourichon supported Gambetta, and the other two, 'neither daring nor wishful to protest by

General von der Tann, commander of the Bavarian I Corps (Scheibert)

resignation, bowed before the possessor of the casting vote.'[13] On October 10 Gambetta announced his assumption of the office of War Minister in a circular to the préfets; in an address to the army he made it clear that there would be changes made. 'I have determined to quit the usual paths. I wish to give you young and active chiefs capable by their intelligence and their energy of renewing the prodigies of 1792. Therefore I have no hesitation in breaking with the old administrative conditions.'[14] It was all too much for Colonel Lefort, who had been managing the War Ministry since the investment of Paris, and he resigned, observing that 'we would go no faster by departing from routine.' In a stirring general proclamation Gambetta called for a supreme effort to mobilise the untapped resources of the country. 'It is impossible that the genius of France should be veiled forever, that the great nation should be deprived of its place in the world by an invasion of 500,000 men. Let us rise up, then, en masse, and die rather than undergo the humiliation of dismemberment.'[15]

The news of Motte-Rouge's difficulties at Orleans, which Gambetta received even before the battle was ended, called forth immediately one of the snap decisions that were characteristic of him; he immediately dismissed Motte-Rouge and was only with reluctance persuaded to abandon his demand for a court martial. In his place, however, he had no 'young and active chief' to put, and the command of the Army of the Loire was given to the highly experienced General d'Aurelle de Paladines. An extremely competent if somewhat cautious soldier, who had led a division in the Crimea, d'Aurelle was also a firm disciplinarian and a capable organiser who inspired confidence in his troops. Behind the Loire he took charge

General view of Orleans (Rousset/ *Combattants*)

not only of the battered 15th Corps, which he pulled back southwards to cover Vierzon and Bourges, but also of the partly formed 16th Corps.Additional men and resources were still arriving, and d'Aurelle was soon successful in turning the huge number of 'ragamuffins' into the semblance of an effective army.

At Tours, Gambetta made another appointment that was to prove immensely important, choosing as his 'Delegate of the Minister for the War Department,' to be responsible for its administration, a little known engineer, the 42 year old Charles de Freycinet, who thereafter operated as Gambetta's right hand. They worked extremely well together, Freycinet being an excellent foil to the passionate Gambetta; his 'frigid, methodical, cautious and calculating nature' not being disguised by what one observer described as his 'smiling courtesy and exquisite manners.'[16] Although playing for safety in his appointment of d'Aurelle, Gambetta meant what he said about finding younger leaders for the army, writing to the government in Paris soon after his arrival at Tours: 'The retired generals of division are targets for intense public anger which is only too well justified by their feebleness and incapacity.'[17] A German writer, the extremely influential Colmar von der Goltz, later appraised Gambetta's success in bringing about the revival of French military power to the point where it offered a major threat to the German armies.

> The part he played has been great enough for his name to live in history for all time ... By the energy of his will he succeeded in animating a country without arms and already tired of resistance, and in drawing it into a struggle which for several months kept the German forces occupied ... To him sufficed a few

> weeks to form, out of the chaos of armed men he found available, a well-equipped army of hundreds of thousands.[18]

Immediately after the loss of Orleans, the Army of the Loire disposed of about 40,000 regular troops, with about 10,000 Gardes Mobiles and about 100 guns. Fiereck's mixed force of about 30,000 regulars, Gardes Mobiles and Gardes Nationales stretched on an arc from Chartres to Evreux under the high sounding name of the Army of the West. Elsewhere there was a small nucleus of troops in Normandy, and the partly organised forces of Cambriels in the east. The statistics which support von der Goltz's judgment tell their own story of Gambetta's success; within four months the French

> had put into the field 230,000 infantry of the line, 32,400 cavalry, and 1,400 guns, and could also dispose of 111,600 militia, a second reserve of 180,000, and 30,000 franc tireurs. The force was divided into twelve army corps, most of them well armed, and the great bulk of them well clad and well shod.[19]

At Versailles in mid October, Moltke can be forgiven for not foreseeing the ultimate extent of Gambetta's success in creating so quickly such a huge army from such unpromising beginnings; but he was clear in his mind as to the bases on which the French might attempt tot build such a revival, and he set out his thoughts to Blumenthal on October 12.

> The greatest difficulty which confronts the enemy in the formation of new army corps is the lack of artillery and trains. The centre of the organisation of the

Bavarian infantry during the Battle for Orleans, 11 October 1870, after a painting by Becker (Lindner)

> Army of the Loire's artillery is at Bourges. It is there that have been directed several artillery depôts and their workshops. There is to be found there the principal cannon foundry, explosive workshop, cartridge factory and large stores of powder. At Châteauroux is the only train still available. It will perhaps suffice, after the rapid success at Artenay, to push only a little beyond Orleans for the government at Tours to decide against lifting the siege from the south. However, there would be no more decisive step we could take to prevent the establishment of an army behind the Loire than a surprise attack by our forces to Bourges and Châteauroux, a surprise which would result in the total destruction of the establishments and stores to be found in these two towns.

He went on to make clear that, although it would be for the Third Army to decide how to proceed, it might be best if such an operation began at once.[20] After receipt of this, Blumenthal dutifully passed on instructions to von der Tann to operate towards Tours and Bourges, although it was left to von der Tann, as the man on the spot, to decide how to proceed. The objectives indicated to him were undeniably important; the commander of the 3rd Cavalry Brigade noted in his diary of the war: 'Had the German army been able to gain possession of Vierzon and Bourges, the vital nerve of the National Defence would have been cut through.'[21]

Moltke's assessment of the importance of Bourges as an objective was clearly strategically correct; but from where von der Tann was placed at Orleans, the task looked a lot less practicable. Reduced by detachments and by casualties his total force included no more than 19,000 infantry, although he was well provided with cavalry and artillery. On the western flank of his lines of communications, Chartres and Châteaudun were still in French hands, which meant that he would have to leave behind any southward advance a strong force in Orleans. Bourges, and the other target offered him at Tours, lay in very different directions. It would take him at least five days to reach Bourges, and the country through which he must advance was much less suited to cavalry operations than had been the case north of Orleans. 'In this labyrinth of lakes, woods, and numerous brooks, the French could offer a most obstinate resistance without well trained troops; all that was needed was large numbers, even if only half trained, and of these the French had more than enough.'[23] At Bourges itself it was known that field works had been thrown up and armed with heavy guns, while reinforcements could readily be brought up by the French from the west and south. 'The expedition against Bourges might possibly succeed, but in our situation it would have been rash to risk all on one move, and tempting as the prize was, it hardly seemed adequate to the stakes.'[24] In the face of these considerations, von der Tann concluded that a further advance into the Sologne was too risky and decided to content himself with holding the line of the Loire. When news of this reached him on October 14, Blumenthal was disappointed, although not disposed to give any more peremptory instructions, noting: 'I should have pressed forward, nevertheless. Perhaps, though, he is right.'[25] Certainly, if Moltke's suggestion had been acted upon, the rest of the campaign against the Army of the Loire would have taken a very different form, and perhaps risking the loss of the Bavarian I Corps would have been justified. This, though, is to apply hindsight; and in any case it is clear that even the taking of Bourges would not have prevented Gambetta from assembling enough troops with which to mount some sort of campaign towards the relief of Paris.

Von der Tann's decision meant that the 22nd Division and the 4th Cavalry Division were available for use first to clear the western flank of the lines of communication, and then to return to Paris, and on October 17 Blumenthal sent Wittich the necessary orders. Pointing out that the Gardes Mobiles and franc tireurs at Châteaudun and Chartres were continually threatening the rear of the Third Army, he gave him the duty of clearing the enemy from this district, ordering him to form flying columns for the purpose.'You have perfect freedom to halt when you please, and complete liberty in your choice of action. You can even go some miles further west if you consider it is desirable to do so. The essential thing is to clear this district entirely of the enemy.'[26]

The garrison of Châteaudun had, by the transfer of troops to Blois, been reduced to a force of 1,200 franc tireurs and Gardes Nationales under Colonel Lipowski. When Wittich's advanced patrols arrived there on October 18, it found that these had taken up position in entrenchments around the town, from which the cavalry by itself was unable to dislodge them. Bringing up infantry and artillery, Wittich moved on the town at about 1.00pm, but as the afternoon wore on his progress was held up by the stout resistance of the defence. After a heavy bombardment, his infantry attacked the town from three sides as darkness fell. 'The barricades at the entrances to the town were captured; but in the interior the French held out with the stubbornness of despair, so that house after house had to be stormed, and in the course of the struggle which lasted far into the night a great part of the place became a prey to the flames.'[27] At 8.00am next day the French retreated in disorder, leaving 150 prisoners; on each side the killed and wounded amounted to about 100 men. It was estimated that 235 houses had been destroyed by fire during the struggle. Wittich's division spent the rest of the next day in and around the smoking ruins of the town, while his cavalry probed in the direction of Chartres, towards which he advanced on October 20.

His patrols reported that the main road was blocked south of the city, and that there were between 6,000 and 10,000 French troops there. Wittich decided to attack from the southeast. Next day his advanced guard pushed forward to Thivars, and succeeded in clearing the road, to the right of which moved the main body of the division. A force of Marines and Gardes Mobiles moved out of the city to meet it, but was driven back by artillery fire. Further right, and around to the northeast, the German cavalry closed in on Chartres, while other cavalry cut the railway westwards towards Le Mans. Wittich now met the Curé of Morancez, three miles outside Chartres, with the mayors of the surrounding villages. He warned them of his intentions. 'To the Curé, who was interceding for the city of Chartres, I said that I must enter it today, either by force of arms or amicably. If it was defended it must expect the fate of Châteaudun.'[28] Shortly after this, the Préfet of the department and the Mayor of Chartres came out and after some debate, agreed upon the city's surrender. Wittich was a commander who stood no nonsense, and was taking no chances; he deployed for the attack and brought up his artillery, giving the Préfet until 3.00 to give up possession of the city. In his war journal, Wittich laconically noted:

> The appearance of a battery of guns made a considerable impression, and the capitulation was agreed; but I declared that I would consider it null and void if a single shot was fired at my troops inside or outside the town ... After the convention was agreed, the town was able to feed the troops and satisfy the requisitions arising from military needs.[29]

The strength of the resistance which Wittich had encountered suggested strongly to the Third Army headquarters that the threat from the west had hitherto been underestimated, and Blumenthal ordered him to remain at Chartres, and to send out a flying column in the direction of Dreux.[30] Blumenthal was already speculating that the French intended an advance from the west in conjunction with a sortie from Paris, and believed that the best way to meet it would be to organise flying columns to hinder the formation of new armies. He would have liked, he noted in his diary, to send two corps to Tours to break up the forces assembling there. By October 23 he was proposing to Moltke that Wittich and von der Tann should combine in such an operation.[31]

At Tours, Adolphe Thiers had returned from his abortive journey around the capitals of the other Great Powers. Neither at St Petersburg nor Vienna nor Florence did he hear anything to lift his spirits, while in London the best that Lord Granville could do was to make an offer to help mediate an armistice. Discouraged by the failure of his efforts, and by what he saw of the state of the Army of the Loire, he sent a letter through von der Tann's outposts on October 25 asking for a safe conduct to Paris. In response to von der Tann's request for instructions, Moltke telegraphed him next day that he should tell Thiers that he could have a safe conduct, escorted by a German and not a French officer, only if it was used to report to the Royal Headquarters, where the time and place of his entry to Paris would be decided. He reiterated two days later that this was the only basis on which Thiers could be allowed to proceed. Next day Moltke, anxious to ensure that proper account be taken of military considerations, set out in a detailed memorandum to Bismarck the terms on which he submitted that any armistice should be negotiated.[32] He was determined not to let slip his position of advantage, but rather to strengthen it, calling for the occupation of most of Northern France and the surrender of those fortresses still holding out.

Meanwhile, at Orleans, von der Tann was already getting edgy about his position. As early as October 19 he was reporting to Blumenthal that 'he thinks he cannot remain longer in Orleans, as a very strong force of the enemy is collecting at Gien on the Loire.' Blumenthal was unimpressed, and advised him to stay put.[33] But it was a further contribution to the growing unease at Versailles about the resurgence of French activity all around the circumference of the circle of troops covering the investment of Paris. South of the city there were repeated incursions by parties of franc tireurs, necessitating an operation by the Württemberg Division through Montereau towards Nogent to drive them back. After a sharp encounter there, where stiff resistance in the town was encountered, the French were driven back with losses of 600 men, retreating in the direction of Troyes. The Württembergers lost 50 men in killed and wounded. It was particularly difficult for the German cavalry patrols to get a handle on the real points of French concentration. Operating over a very wide sweep of countryside, they were frequently held up by points of resistance, which might for a while be stoutly defended. 'The cavalry could report what places and woods were held by the French within a semicircle of three quarters to one and a half day's march radius; but what they could not find out was where the main body of the enemy was, whether there was any main body, or what this ever active army was intending to do. This restless enemy seemed ubiquitous.'[34]

North of Paris, in the rear of the Army of the Meuse, a similar situation obtained. By mid October, cavalry operations under Prince Albrecht the younger, based on Beaumont, had largely pacified the districts adjacent to the lines of investment, and as far as Clermont and Beauvais, and towards Pontoise and Luzarches. 'But beyond this district under their immediate control the German patrols nearly everywhere encountered armed resistance; moreover there were increased indications of the assembly of large bodies of troops in Picardy and Normandy.'[35]

On October 12, after reports of a French concentration at Breteuil and Montdidier, Count Lippe, the commander of the 12th Cavalry Division, sent forward a force of infantry cavalry and artillery in a successful attack on Breteuil; on October 17 he attacked and took Montdidier. Further to the west the Guard Cavalry Division, operating out of Gisors, pushed its line of patrols further to the northwest. Towards the end of the month further activity on the part of the French was observed in the area of the Andelle, and reinforcements were sent to the German troops holding an outpost line along the River Epte, along which there were frequent engagements with parties of franc tireurs.

On October 25 cavalry reports indicated the concentration of stronger French forces on the railway line between Amiens and Rouen, and a mixed force under Major General Senfft von Pilsach marched northwest on October 27 in the direction of Formerie. Encountering opposition there, the German forced their way into the town, only to be driven back to its outskirts by the arrival of French reinforcements. A fresh attack by the Germans was making progress when a much larger French force, arriving by rail from Amiens, seriously threatened Senfft's line of retreat, and he decided to break off the engagement, and withdrew to Beauvais with only slight losses. It was, however, a clear indication that in the north as elsewhere more substantial French forces were in cause of formation.

That this was so was largely due to the efforts of two men. Doctor Testelin, who had been appointed by the Delegation as 'Commissaire' of the north, had after encountering a pronounced lack of encouragement from the local commander, employed the able and energetic Colonel Farre, the Director of Fortifications at Lille, in the task of organising an effective force in the region. After the sluggish start, great strides were made in assembling forces strong enough to provide a serious threat to the rear of the Army of the Meuse.

As October drew to a close, therefore, Moltke was beginning to feel that his forces covering the investment of Paris were being stretched uncomfortably thin. For most of the month, though, his eyes had been fixed on Metz, the capitulation of which would release large forces which he was coming to realise would be urgently needed.

7

Metz

It rained a lot in Metz that autumn, and for its defenders the gloomy course of events matched the weather. With the hope of relief gone, it became increasingly evident that the ordeal of Bazaine's beleaguered army could be ended only by political developments or by a breakout, and the morale of the population as well as the troops began slowly to ebb away. There was a finite quantity of supplies in the city which must itself set a term to the siege, and Bazaine's commanders increasingly began to ask what he proposed to do about the situation. For his part, he gave little away. 'His callers found the Marshal uncommunicative. But what was there to say? Their situation was embarrassingly simple; and if Bazaine was a sphinx, he was a sphinx without a secret.'[1] To enquiries from Jarras, his chief of staff, about his plans, he snapped that in the present situation of the army he took advice from no one. His headquarters were in the suburb of Ban St Martin and there for the most part he stayed, brooding on the impossibility of effective action.

The Army of the Rhine remained a large and effective fighting force. It was surrounded by an adversary not significantly stronger, apart from the important exception of its belief in eventual victory. The functioning of the army as an organisation remained unchanged.

> The entire raison d'etre of the army in Metz may have collapsed, but life within its ranks could go on much as usual; for in this, as in all other human organisations, the object of its existence could be easily forgotten in the time-filling routine of merely existing … It seemed to some observers that Bazaine now deliberately emphasised questions of routine and administration so as to divert the minds of his subordinates from more dangerous speculations.[2]

In the confused political situation that followed the collapse of the Second Empire, it seemed in the first weeks after Sedan that the solution was more likely to be found by political rather than military action. The first and the most remarkable indication of this came with the strange episode of Edouard Regnier.

Regnier was a private individual who had no official authority to speak for anyone, let alone the government, any government, of France. But he was a loyal supporter of the Empire, and he resolved to do something by himself to assist its restoration. He wrote, therefore, an unsolicited letter to Eugenie in exile at Hastings with some extravagant proposals as to how she might act in reassuming the authority to govern France; rebuffed by the Empress, he contrived to meet the Prince Imperial there, and got him to write a few words to his father on the back of a postcard, which he proceeded to use as a passport to gain access to Bismarck before travelling on to see Napoleon at Wilhelmshöhe. Bismarck was already addressing the complex political situation in discussions with Jules Favre at Ferrières, and saw in Regnier's unlikely mission a possible counterweight that he could use at least as a threat to coerce the Republic. The legitimacy of Favre's authority to speak for France was questionable; the possibility that the Germans

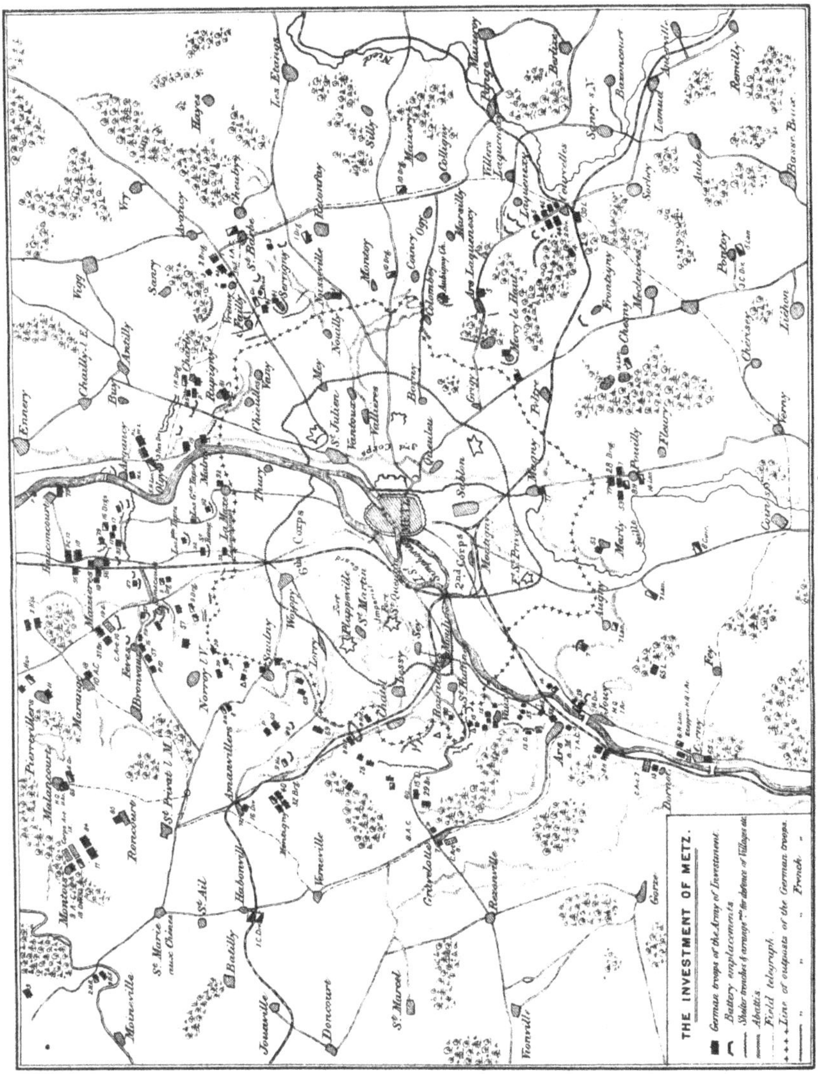

The investment of Metz

Prince Frederick Charles, commander of the German Second Army (Rousset/*Histoire*)

might do a deal with Napoleon might well unsettle him, and in any event Bismarck could lose nothing by keeping alive the possibility of a settlement with the Empire to which Bazaine, at any rate, was prepared to remain loyal. Regnier was accordingly allowed on September 23 to enter Metz, where Bazaine was persuaded by him that he should send a senior officer to Eugenie to put forward his scheme. Of the two suggested, Canrobert would have none of it, so the choice fell on Bourbaki, who was allowed out on September 25 to go to England. When he got there, Eugenie flatly refused to have anything to do with Regnier's proposals, and although its author then made an abortive attempt to get an interview with Napoleon, his initiative had evaporated.

Moltke, as well as Frederick Charles and Stiehle, was strongly of the view that political shenanigans of this kind should not be allowed to spoil the Prussian military triumph, and expressed this to Stiehle on September 27.

> In my opinion, it is only after a capitulation, or better still a peace with a government we can trust, that Marshal Bazaine's army can get out of its present situation ... In any case, the operations of our army at Metz have cost us too much to lead to a result which, from the military point of view, would be absolutely negative.[3]

When Bourbaki returned to Metz after his abortive mission, Frederick Charles' reaction was to take an entirely legalistic point as to his passport, and refused to let him back into the fortress, as a result of which Bourbaki went off to join the forces of the republican government. It was an incident that greatly annoyed Bismarck, and he wrote to Stiehle in the strongest terms to protest at what he saw as direct military interference in a purely political question. He went on to point out the effect of this on the conduct of his own policy.

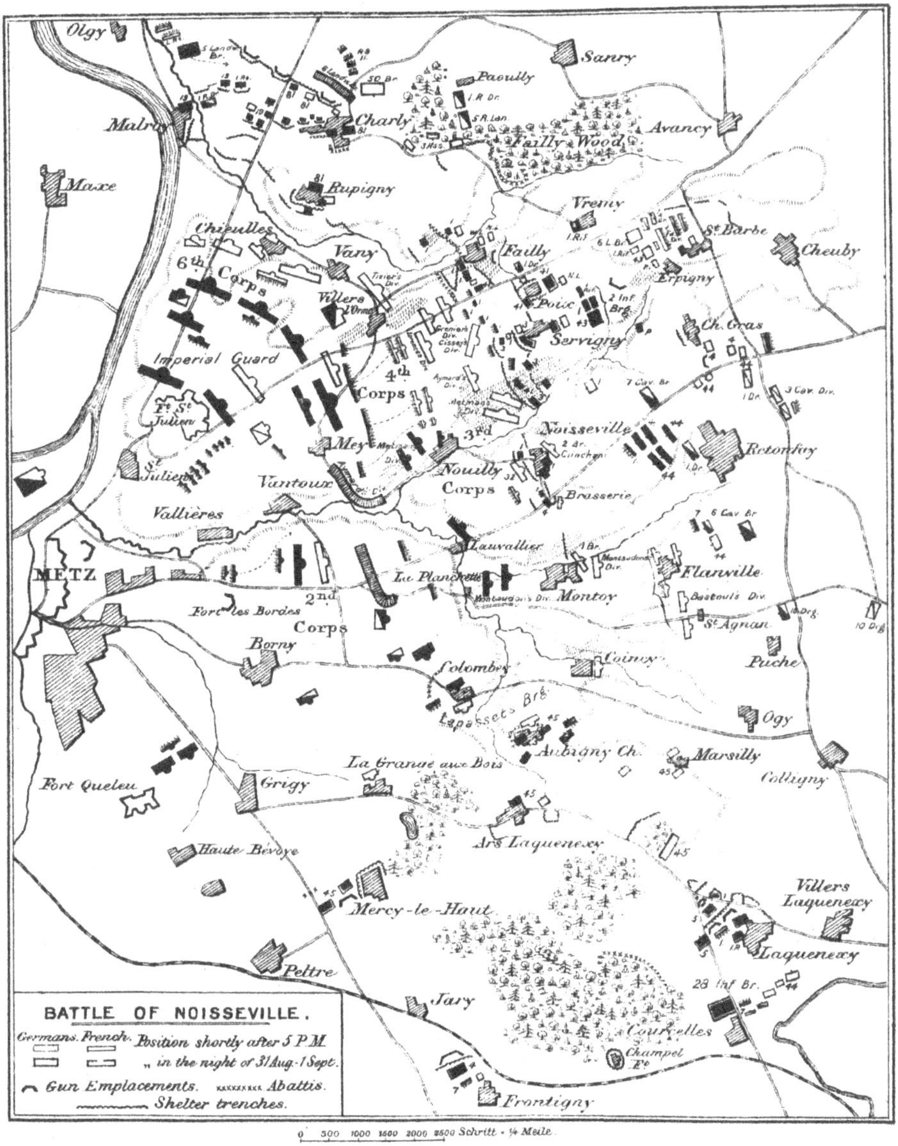

The Battle of Noisseville, August 31 - September 1

> I appeal to your Excellency's clear judgement and to your own perception, so that you will understand how discouraging it must be for me when, through this kind of failure to execute explicit royal orders, the danger arises that in the whole constellation of political calculations one single cog, which is necessary in its place, will refuse to do its work. How can I have the courage to proceed with my work if I cannot count on royal orders … being faithfully executed?[4]

Inside Metz, dwindling supplies had led to the increasing consumption of horseflesh, and on September 20 the army rations of bread had been substantially reduced. The failure of the foraging expeditions of late September, and the steps taken by the investing army to ensure that they would not easily be repeated, meant that with the lack of any political solution in sight a serious look must now be taken at the possibility of a break out. Although the investment pinned down a large army of which Moltke could make good use elsewhere, this factor was obviously time limited. As at Paris, the problem was not only to find a weak point in the German lines at which to direct an assault, but also to devise some effective strategy to pursue once the army got out.

To Bazaine's staff, reviewing the options, the best bet seemed to be a breakout from the north eastern side of the fortress, in the direction of Thionville. This fortress, close to the border with Luxembourg, had been only imperfectly watched by a weak corps of observation, and the garrison had succeeded in making a considerable nuisance of itself by raids into German held territory. The French succeeded in putting the railway line into Luxembourg into working order, and on the night of September 24/25 brought a train of 80 wagons into the fortress.[5] There were indications from within Metz which convinced the watching Germans that something might be attempted in the direction of Thionville; a bridge had been built on September 29 over the Moselle west of Fort St Julien, and on the following night a considerable increase was noted in the light signals exchanged between Metz and Thionville. Unusually heavy artillery fire from the forts of Plappeville and St Quentin also suggested that preparations for a sortie were under way. This appeared to receive confirmation from reports reaching Moltke that large quantities of supplies had been collected in France, with the intention that they be transported to Thionville via the Belgian railways, and Moltke reported this to the Second Army headquarters.[6] With the fall of Strasbourg, which might otherwise have been a reasonable point at which a breakout might be aimed, Thionville certainly seemed the likeliest possibility.

Frederick Charles, therefore, took immediate steps to strengthen his positions in the threatened area, moving Voigts-Rhetz's X Corps into the entrenchments previously occupied by Kummer's Division, which took over the X Corps position and was placed under the command of Voigts Rhetz. On the west side of the fortress he shuffled the I Corps (Manteuffel), VII Corps (Zastrow) and VIII Corps (Goeben) northwards, so that the three corps now occupied the positions previously held by the first two, and extended the front of the II Corps (Fransecky) to fill the gap. The III Corps and IX Corps remained in their existing positions. Steps were also taken to reinforce the troops watching Thionville. The French, meanwhile, now prepared for the breakout by occupying more forward positions. On October 1, on the front of the XI Corps, the French pushed troops forward into the village of Lessy and to Chalet Billandel, and immediately entrenched them in order to protect the western flank of the planned move to the north. During the night of October 1/2 a successful attack was made on the German outpost line at Ladonchamps, and the Landwehr battalion there was driven back to St Rémy, abandoning as it did so the village of St Agathe. German counter attacks to retake the position failed; on the other hand the French attempt to develop the initial success by advancing to St Rémy also broke down, and the two sides settled down to a prolonged exchange of rifle and artillery fire.[7]

Next day the French under cover of a heavy bombardment set about entrenching the positions they had gained, pushing their outposts further forward to cover these. The German artillery replied, and the guns of the forts joined in, and for the next few days the artillery exchanges continued. On October 4 Bazaine convened a meeting of his senior commanders, and announced to them the plan for a breakout towards Thionville, along both banks of the Moselle. However, although preparations for the advance were at once put in hand, Bazaine's new found resolution soon began to waver. Coffinières, the commandant of the fortress, was no great help. A British correspondent in Metz wrote of him that 'He was a large-built, kindly-hearted man of nearly sixty years of age; but, like many large-built kindly-hearted men, he had no great strength of mind.'[8] Coffinières now pointed out that there were already 25,000 sick and wounded men in the fortress, and that the assault might cost a further 15,000 wounded. If the army was to move north, the fortress could no longer be held unless a garrison of at least 20,000 men was left behind to defend the place. Easily discouraged, Bazaine cancelled a foraging expedition planned for October 5 southeastwards to Courcelles sur Nied, and convened another council of war on October 6 to review the planned assault; proving once again the old adage that a council of war never fights, the decision was taken to call off the operation and to substitute instead a large scale raid to bring into the fortress supplies of food believed to have been harvested and stored in the farms in the direction of the proposed advance.[9] The army was disappointed, but not surprised; one cynical officer remarked cheerfully to Robinson, the English war correspondent, that he should wait a day or two for the offensive – 'Prince Frederick Charles has sent word to say he is not quite ready yet.'[10]

Although the more ambitious objectives had been abandoned, the operation launched on October 7 was nonetheless substantial, on a front nearly four miles long. It was to be undertaken by Canrobert's 6th Corps and the Voltigeur Division of the Guard. On its left, the advance was to be supported by an attack of Ladmirault's 4th Corps from the woods northwest of Woippy, while on its right Leboeuf was to push his 3rd Corps up the right bank of the Moselle towards Malroy. 400 wagons were brought up to carry off the stores to be seized. However delays in the issue of orders meant that the attack did not get under way until 1pm, under the cover of heavy gunfire from Fort St Julien.

On the left bank of the Moselle, the attack fell at first on Kummer's Division, in position either side of the railway line, occupying Bellevue, St Rémy and the farms of Les Petites Tapes and Les Grandes Tapes, supported by a strong artillery position at Serrecourt. The strength of the assault was such that first Les Grandes Tapes, with a large part of its defenders, was taken by the French and, by 2.30pm, Les Petites Tapes and most of its garrison as well. Advancing from Ladonchamps, the 2nd Voltigeur Brigade took St Remy. On the other side of the railway, Bellevue was set on fire and abandoned by its garrison, which retreated northwards in the face of enveloping infantry attacks; these were finally halted half way to Serrecourt. In the woods to the west there was a bitter struggle, in the course of which the French were held up by the 10th Rifle Battalion. Throughout their advance, the French were pounded by the German batteries at Serrecourt and around the Amelange Farm, on the left bank of the Moselle, which succeeded in silencing the French field artillery which had deployed around St Agathe.[11]

Further to the west, Stülpnagel's 5th Division moved forward through Norroy and Plenois into the woods to the south, with orders to support Kummer in any way that the situation demanded. A brick kiln to the east of Villers Les Plenois now became the focal point of the French advance, which broke down in the face of a brisk counter attack by the 48th Regiment from Point du Jour. The 9th Brigade commander, Colonel von Conta, now launched a strong attack, driving the French back into the Bois de Woippy, and by 4.00pm the struggle on this part of the battlefield came to an end.

On the other side of the Moselle, the French advance had been led by Aymard's Division of the 3rd Corps, moving off from under the guns of Fort St Julien, but it was soon pinned down by the fire of the German artillery. Sensing that this was no more than a feint, Voigts-Rhetz ordered his 38th Brigade over the river at Argancy, east of Amelange, in support of Kummer's troops which had retreated there. The Landwehr had, however, already embarked on a counter attack, although this was held up by the French occupants of Les Grandes Tapes, Les Petites Tapes and Franclonchamp, and Kummer was grateful to receive the reinforcements sent to him. Meanwhile, charging forward across the open ground south of Amelange, the attack of the 57th Regiment also stalled in front of the positions taken up by the French. Further strengthened by the 16th Regiment, a fresh assault was made on Franclonchamp, from which the French were already now in retreat; by 5.00pm the village, and the farm of Les Grandes Tapes were in German hands, and soon after Les Petites Tapes was abandoned by the French rear guard.[12]

Some time after 5.00pm Kummer advanced to retake Bellevue, supported by units of Stülpnagel's Division, moving forward under a heavy artillery barrage, and attacking the village on its west and north sides, while further to the west troops of the 9th Brigade from La Forêt and the Bois de Woippy also moved to the attack. After delaying the German advance briefly with concentrated chassepôt fire, the French pulled back, abandoning St Remy at the same time, so that by 6.00pm they were back on their start line.

Meanwhile, on the eastern side of the Moselle, Leboeuf had during the course of the afternoon launched Metman's Division against Manteuffel's positions between Lauvallier and Noisseville. Manteuffel was unworried by this threat, and aware that the spearhead of the attack was on the other side of the river, he ordered his 2nd Brigade to move towards Charly to support the defenders there. By 4.00pm the diversionary attacks of both Ladmirault and Leboeuf came to an end, and the French withdrew towards their entrenchments. An attempt to follow them up, however, was held by reinforcements in the Bois de Grimont, and the French then, for no very obvious reason, launched a further series of assaults along the line of Manteuffel's outposts. These enjoyed some brief success before in their turn they were halted by heavy fire from the corps artillery at Poix, Servigny and Noisseville. At about 6.30pm Leboeuf broke off the engagement at all points and pulled his troops back to the fortress.

The battle was, however, not yet over. Having regained the positions with which he had begun, Voigts-Rhetz decided to seize the opportunity to recapture the areas occupied by the French since their preliminary advances on October 1 and 2. By now darkness had fallen, so no artillery support was available. A total of twelve companies from various regiments took part in the advance on Ladonchamps, which was stoutly defended. After a fierce engagement Voigts-Rhetz brought the action to an end at about 8pm. For five hours the struggle had swayed back and forth over the battlefield, only for the two sides to finish where they had started; the French attempt to seize the stores of food at which their advance was aimed had been wholly unsuccessful. On the other hand the Germans had lost heavily in the course of the day; including some 500 prisoners brought back by the French into Metz, their total casualties were of the order of 1,700. French sources suggest that their losses were somewhat less, a figure of 1257 being reported.[13]

The stiff resistance put up at Ladonchamps suggested that the French might well be contemplating a renewal of the offensive on the following day, and Frederick Charles ordered all the German units engaged to remain closed up behind the outpost lines to meet a further attack. Although French infantry columns were seen moving towards their front line, and there were throughout October 8 some brisk exchanges of fire between the German batteries and the guns of the forts, in fact nothing transpired. During the following days, heavy rain limited the prospects for any advance by the infantry, and on all fronts it was the artillery alone that was in action.

Since there was no longer any hope of being relieved, and he was aware that no political solution was likely to be devised in time to save his army, Bazaine set out the position starkly in a circular letter to his senior commanders on October 7. He told them that the time was approaching when the Army of the Rhine would find itself in perhaps the most difficult position a French army had ever had to endure; and he went on to say that it was the duty of a commander in chief to seek the opinions of his corps commanders.[14] The first response that he received was from Coffinières on October 8. It discouraged Bazaine still further. The commandant's estimate was that provisions would be exhausted by October 19. The various corps commanders took the opportunity of discussing the question with their divisional commanders. Each wrote a detailed and in some cases a very verbose reply to Bazaine's circular, carefully reviewing the situation. Le Boeuf recommended that the army should engage in a decisive struggle, making 'a new and great effort, towards a well defined objective;' but he unhelpfully concluded that it was for the commander in chief to decide what the objective should be. The others, to a greater or lesser extent, pointed to the problems attendant on any further offensive operations and were accordingly resigned to the need to open negotiations with Frederick Charles.[15] With these replies to hand, Bazaine convened another council of war for October 10. A full minute of its proceedings was made by General Boyer who recorded the conclusions reached.

> First, that Metz should be held as long as possible. Secondly, that there should be no further operations, the objective of which being so improbable. Thirdly, that negotiations start with the enemy after forty-eight hours, with the aim of concluding an honourable military convention. Fourthly, in the event of the enemy wishing to impose conditions incompatible with our honour and our military duty, a breakout "les armes à la main" will be attempted.[16]

General Boyer was accordingly entrusted with a mission to Versailles to open discussions, but the news of this led to a sharp difference of opinion at the Royal Headquarters as to how this approach should be received. Frederick Charles himself was, as the Crown Prince noted in his diary on October 13, 'against receiving the French intermediary, for he is rightly enough afraid that the capitulation will come to be signed at Versailles instead of before Metz, and he, after being detained there for months, will only be a looker on.' The Crown Prince also recorded other opinions. Frederick Charles' view of the matter was supported by Moltke and Roon, who wished Bazaine 'to act only on the basis of the Sedan Convention, that no interference is to be allowed, and therefore no intermediary to be received here provisionally;' their fear was that the French army would seek to negotiate its release from Metz to be free to act in the interests of the Imperial regime. Bismarck, on the other hand, wished to hear what Boyer had to say. 'Generals von Moltke and von Roon on the one side, Count Bismarck on the other, are often at loggerheads, the gist of their mutual reproaches being that the departments are kept separated by too hard and fast a line and not enough reciprocal exchange of information practised.'[17]

The continuing dispute over the basis of any discussion with Bazaine was important in itself, since it materially affected the way in which Bismarck was able to pursue his policy for ending the war. But it was even more important as another outward indication of the submerged tensions that existed between Bismarck and the army, and which were destined to become even more serious as the war continued. Moltke, like all his military colleagues, was capable of taking an entirely simplistic and traditional view of the external forms of any capitulation of the Army in Metz, entirely sharing the views expressed by Frederick Charles and Stiehle that the army must be allowed to enjoy the satisfaction of receiving the formal surrender on its own terms. To an even greater extent, though, Moltke saw in Bismarck's insistence on his position a readiness to interfere in matters which the Chief of Staff regarded as exclusively within the military sphere; Bismarck had done it before, during the war of 1866, and Moltke was determined that he should not do so again. This led to Bismarck being deprived of information in particular as to Moltke's intentions, which he and his senior staff jealously guarded.

Bismarck got his way, and Boyer was allowed to visit Versailles. He brought with him a letter from Bazaine setting out his views on the situation, acknowledging the defeat of his army but suggesting that if kept together 'it would establish order and protect society whose interests are common with those of Europe.'[18] In this way peace might be made with a stable French government. Bismarck, anxious to bring the war to a speedy end, still had some hopes of the Imperial regime; Moltke, on the other hand, still insisted that the capitulation of Metz should be treated solely as a military question, to be settled by the responsible military leaders. The upshot of this was that Boyer, after a number of exceedingly frank

The French Army of the Rhine surrenders at Metz, by Speyer (Bork)

conversations with Bismarck, was sent back to Metz, the Chancellor having made clear to him that any deal such as Bazaine was proposing must depend on Eugénie's willingness to back it, and upon the army declaring in favour of her regency, and forthwith surrendering Metz. When Boyer got back, yet another council of war was convened to receive his full report; at the end of the discussion, Boyer was sent off to England to see Eugénie who was now at Chislehurst. The Empress was unclear exactly what terms she was being asked to endorse but she certainly did not intend to sell France short; temporising, she sent Boyer back to Versailles with a letter to the King, asking for a fortnight's armistice and for Metz to be reprovisioned. At Versailles, such a request was seen as entirely unacceptable, and the King's response was to the effect that he desired peace with all his heart, but that the uncertainty as to whether any proposals would be supported either by the Army of the Rhine or by France as a whole meant that negotiations on these lines could not continue.

On October 24 another council of war met in Metz to consider the position following the receipt of Bismarck's formal response rejecting Bazaine's proposals. Bismarck recorded that the proposals which had been received from London were absolutely unacceptable, and that there was no longer any prospect of a political settlement. Bazaine asked the council, in the light of the fourth condition laid down by the council of war of October 10, to consider where the final breakout should be attempted. Desvaux, the acting commander of the Guard, suggested an operation in the direction of Amanvilliers and St Privat which he believed offered the best chance of success; but although agreeing with the proposed point of attack, none of the others believed it had any hope of breaking through the German lines. As Bazaine put it, it would be truly suicidal, and would simply give the Germans an easy victory over an exhausted army. The council of war concluded with a resolution that the enemy should be asked to allow the army to go free or if not, for Metz and the army to be neutralised pending elections for an assembly. At the very least, Frossard proposed, if Metz and the army were to be surrendered, the officers should keep their swords and personal effects, and the soldiers their haversacks.[19]

But when Changarnier as Bazaine's emissary presented himself at the Third Army headquarters, Frederick Charles was absolutely firm. He would not go beyond the terms granted to Wimpffen at Sedan; and these the council of war held on October 26 recognised that Bazaine had no choice but to accept. The Army of the Rhine was declared prisoner of war and Metz was to be surrendered with all its public property. Moltke, on October 27, authorised Frederick Charles to allow the officers to keep their arms.[20] Jarras and Stiehle, the chiefs of staff, met at Frescaty and on the evening of October 27 agreed the formal terms of the capitulation, which was to take effect on October 29.

Next day, the King celebrated the event by promoting both Frederick Charles and the Crown Prince to the rank of Field Marshal, and by granting Moltke the title of Count. The Crown Prince first heard of his elevation next day when he got a telegram from Frederick Charles: 'Congratulate my worshipful General Field Marshal,' which he thought at first was a joke, before getting his father's formal letter of appointment an hour and a half later.[21] Frederick Charles thought his own promotion long overdue; characteristically showing rather more generosity of spirit, the Crown Prince thought that Moltke 'before all others should have been made Field Marshal.' The King wrote a charming letter to Moltke, to the effect that he could give him no reward, which he would find in his own conscience, but for the brilliant way in which he had conducted the operation he owed him before the world some outward recompense.[22] Moltke was evidently pleased by his elevation; Waldersee was surprised 'to find that old Moltke, whom I had thought above any such things, has been as happy as a child over being made a Count.'[23]

On October 29 the Army of the Rhine marched out, minus its senior commanders whom Frederick Charles allowed to remain Metz for the moment; Bazaine, after the surrender was complete, went off to Kassel to join his Emperor at Wilhelmshöhe. A total of 173,000 men surrendered, with a huge quantity of arms and ammunition of all kinds. It was the sort of victory to gladden even the heart of the proud and ambitious Frederick Charles, but he had little time to savour it; even as the capitulation took effect, Moltke was determining as a matter of urgency the redeployment of the units of the investing army. Indeed, he had begun this task even before the negotiations for the surrender, preparing on October 23 a plan for the possible reconfiguration of the forces of Frederick Charles immediately the fortress fell. Manteuffel was to command the First Army; leaving Zastrow's VII Corps to hold Metz and to besiege Thionville, he was to march with the I and VIII Corps into northern France, on Rouen and Amiens. Frederick Charles, with the Second Army, comprising the II, III, IX & X Corps, was to march via Chaumont and Auxerre on Bourges. Kummer's Division was to deal with the transport and security of the prisoners. One division was to be detached from the Second Army to fill them in for a reserve for the armies investing Paris. Finally, the Grand Duke

The surrender of Metz, painting by Freyberg (Scheibert)

of Mecklenburg-Schwerin would take command of a force comprising the Württemberg and 17th Divisions, and the I Bavarian Corps.[24] The fall of Metz was not a moment too soon, and came as an enormous relief to Moltke; now, perhaps, he could make a speedy end to the armies springing up all around the circumference of his forces investing Paris.

While the investment of Metz had been slowly grinding to a conclusion, Moltke had been keeping an eye on some of the other fortresses in the frontier areas that were still holding out. As early as September 21 he had appointed Major General von Schmeling, then the Director of the Military Economy Department in the War Ministry, to command the 4th Reserve Division, which was assembling at Freiburg. His task was to link with Werder, invest Neu-Brisach and Schlettstadt and observe Belfort, reporting directly to Moltke.[25] Following the fall of Strasbourg, Moltke wrote to Schmeling on October 1 to tell him that his task was not only to invest the fortresses, but also to seize them. Attaching a senior engineer officer, Lieutenant Colonel von Scheliha, to Schmeling's staff, he left it to Schmeling to decide for himself whether he could besiege both Neu-Brisach and Schlettstadt, as well as maintaining the occupation of Central Alsace.[26] Crossing the Rhine from Neuenburg, Schmeling had first to pacify the area around Mulhouse, clearing away some large groups of franc tireurs that were active before moving on the two fortresses. Schmeling now concluded that in fact he did not have a large enough force to besiege them simultaneously, and he decided for the moment to confine himself to an investment until he was in a position to judge which should be his first target. To Neu-Brisach he sent first two Landwehr regiments with a regiment of Uhlans and five batteries; the investment of the fortress was completed on October 6 and next day he opened fire upon it before summoning it to surrender. The French commander, Lieutenant Colonel Lostie de Kerhor, whose garrison, consisting of two regular battalions, with Garde

Mobiles and Garde Nationales, amounted to 5,500 men in all, rejected the summons on October 8. Schmeling then went off to reconnoitre Schlettstadt, leaving Major General von Tresckow in command of the troops investing Neu-Brisach.

Schlettstadt, which at that time had a population of about 10,000, lies on the left bank of the River Ill. Its south and east sides were protected by extensive inundations. It was, however, by no means a modern fortress, and like Strasbourg lacked bombproof shelters for its garrison. But it was well sited, and on its north side the attackers would be hampered by the Giesen brook, a broad stream carrying water down from the mountains. Only on its west side could it be easily approached, where vineyards and hedges, and the railway embankment that ran north-south, offered some protection to the besiegers. The garrison was small, consisting of some 1,200 Gardes Mobiles and 700 gunners, with 120 guns.[27] It seemed to Schmeling, after a preliminary bombardment on October 11 following which his summons to surrender was rejected, that Schlettstadt offered an easier target than Neu-Brisach, and after being reinforced by fortress artillery and engineer troops released by the fall of Strabourg, he settled down to commence formal siege operations.

The first gun emplacements were in position by the night of October 19/20, and next day the German guns began to pound the defences of the fortress. The French made a vigorous response. That night the German outposts were established about 400 yards from the fortress, the first parallel following the line of the railway. The efforts of the French artillery failed to obstruct the progress of the German engineers, their guns being sighted to hit targets well to the rear of the siege works. By the morning of October 23 these had been completed in readiness for an assault. As dawn broke, the French opened a heavy fire on the lines of trenches. The German siege batteries responded, seriously damaging the French artillery, and the southern part of the town itself. Throughout the day the artillery duel continued, but as night fell and a heavy storm blew up, the French gunfire gradually ceased. By 7.30am on October 24 the garrison had had enough, and white flags were seen. A capitulation was speedily negotiated, providing for the Germans to enter the town at 3pm. Within the fortress, however, the bonds of discipline had completely snapped; 'the greatest disorder already prevailed inside the town; the mob and drunken soldiers were plundering or firing the public buildings and had even blown up a powder magazine.'[28] As a result, the commandant asked Schmeling to come in at once, and order was restored by three German battalions, although it took them until the following day to get the fires still raging in the city under control. The siege had been conducted with remarkably few casualties, the total German losses being only 23.

Neu-Brisach is situated just over two miles from the Rhine in the low-lying ground to the west of the river. It is and was an important road junction. On the level ground, its designers had been able to build a well-organised octagonal fortress, which was well protected against enfilade fire and with bombproof shelters against artillery. Its defence was strengthened by the construction on the banks of the Rhine of Fort Mortier, north east of the fortress and opposite the town of Alt-Brisach, from the heights above which the fort was overlooked.[29] Following the completion of the investment, there had been little activity until October 15, when a sortie of about 1,500 men was launched under the cover of thick morning mist from the west side of the fortress, one column being directed on Wolfganzen to the northwest, and one on Weckolsheim to the southwest. Both advances were initially successful in driving back the German outposts, but were forced back into the fortress as reinforcements came up, and it was all over by 7.00am. Another sortie on October 22, again towards Weckolsheim, met with little success.

Because troops had been drawn off to take part in the siege of Schlettstadt, the southern side of the fortress had been watched only by a small force, and the lines of investment were not fully complete until October 27, when Schmeling returned to take over the operation. In anticipation of the long awaited fall of Metz, Moltke had written to Schmeling on October 23 placing him under Werder's orders for the future, although he was instructed to continue to report any major developments directly to Moltke.[30] With the arrival of the siege train from Schlettstadt by the end of the month, Schmeling wasted no time in embarking on siege operations against Neu-Brisach, resolving to attack the northwest sector of the defences. For this, he located his principal batteries well back at Wolfganzen, firing at long range on the fortress: Fort Mortier was to be neutralised by batteries thrown up on the heights on the east of the Rhine.[31]

The siege works were completed without interference from the garrison, and the bombardment commenced on November 2, causing damage to the northern entrances of the fortress. The guns firing on Fort Mortier at first achieved little success. Next day, the shelling continued, the centre of the town being heavily damaged, while Fort Mortier was pounded into silence. An attempted coup de main against the fort failed; but on November 6 advancing German patrols found the drawbridge lowered, and the fort's commander surrendered with 220 men. By November 8 the artillery bombardment of Neu-Brisach had done its work; at 1.30pm Lostie de Kerhor hoisted the white flag over the battered town. The total losses sustained by Schmeling's forces during the siege were again very light, amounting in all to seventy-five casualties.[32] Schmeling, from whose force three battalions, four squadrons and a couple of batteries had previously been detached to operate towards Belfort, was now free to join Werder in his operations over a wide area of the south east, and Moltke wrote to Werder on November 11 to tell him that Schmeling was now at his disposal.[33] The siege train was made available for operations against the fortress of Belfort.

The fortress of Verdun was a much more serious obstacle to the German road and rail communications. The town, which in 1870 had a population of about 14,000, lies on both sides of the Meuse. The ancient fortifications were modernised by Vauban towards the end of the seventeenth century and had been kept in good order. On the west of the town stood the powerful citadel, while on the southeast the Victor hornwork projected towards Mont Constantin. The fortress was also protected by inundations in the Meuse valley, which blocked any assault from the southwest. The vine clad heights which commanded the town, and particularly the Côte St Michel to the north, completely overlooked the defences. The fortress was equipped with 140 guns, and was commanded by General Guerin de Waldersbach. The garrison had at first been only small, but the arrival of escaped prisoners of war, Gardes Nationales and franc tireurs had by the end of September increased it to about 6,000 men.[34]

The lack of German troops available to reduce the fortress had meant that for some time after the unsuccessful attempt to seize it on August 24, Moltke had had to be content with arranging merely observing it by cavalry patrols. However on September 7 troops under General von Bothmer arrived to invest it. Sorties from the fortress on September 15 and 18 were driven back without great loss, but the investment was not completed until September 23, when German reinforcements arrived. Most of the investing troops were in positions on the right bank of the Meuse, on the heights of Côte St Michel through the farm of La Blancharderie, and on the heights of La Grimoine. West of the river the Germans occupied Belleray, and the heights of St Barthelemy and the Côte de Blamont and Côte des Hayvaux, extending north to Villers les Moines. On September 24 Guerin tested the German outpost lines by an attempted advance through Thieville northwest to Villers les Moines, meanwhile rejecting summonses to surrender. On September 26 a prolonged exchange of artillery fire began.

In October Guerin launched a series of sorties for the improbable purpose of allowing the grape harvest to be brought in, advancing on October 2 and 3 and briefly driving back the German picket lines. By October 5 Bothmer had brought up sufficient siege artillery for him to plan a continuous bombardment of the north of the town and more particularly the citadel; but on October 9 he was promoted to command the 13th Division, and the siege was now taken over by Major General von Gayl. On the evening of October 11, in preparation for the bombardment, Gayl pushed the 65th Regiment forward under a bright moon to occupy the villages of Thieville, Belleville and Reguet; next day the regiment moved up closer occupying Glorieux and La Jardin Fontaine. The German front line was now only 600 yards from the fortress itself, and work began on the construction of batteries to the west and on Côte St Michel. On October 13 the bombardment commenced; the fortress replied with vigorous counter battery fire, which silenced two German batteries on the Côte des Hayvaux. The artillery exchanges continued for two days, both sides suffering considerable damage to their batteries, before Gayl decided that regular siege operations would be required in order to reduce the fortress.[35] While he waited for a full siege train to come up, and for fresh stocks of ammunition, he pulled the 65th Regiment back from its most advanced positions.

Emboldened by this, Guerin launched a successful raid on the night of October 19/20 on the batteries situated on the Côte des Hayvaux, the attackers spiking the guns before withdrawing. On the morning of October 28 he launched a more substantial sortie northwards up both banks of the Meuse. On the east side of the river, the attackers took and smashed up the entrenchments on the Côte St Michel, before advancing into the Bois Lecourbier. Another attack drove the Germans out of Belleville. However, further progress by the French was halted by a counter attack which retook the Côte St Michel, although the French were able to retain possession of Belleville against infantry advancing through the vineyards. West of the Meuse, the French were held up by a battalion of the 65th Regiment in Thieville, but further south their advance on Côte des Hayvaux was undetected, and this height was occupied and twelve guns in the German batteries there were spiked. On the other side of the little River Scance, an attack from Glorieux southwards was frustrated, and the engagement died down, with the French still in possession of Belleville and Glorieux.[36]

By now, however, reinforcements were reaching the besiegers from the First Army following the fall of Metz. Moltke wished to put paid to Verdun without further delay, and on October 31 he put the operations against the fortress under Manteuffel's control.[37] The 60th Regiment, with a jäger battalion and two pioneer companies, arrived by the end of October, together with a number of siege guns and a quantity of field artillery. It was now entirely plain to Guerin that there was no worthwhile prospect of prolonging the siege; after an armistice of two days had been agreed on November 5, negotiations began for the capitulation of the fortress. This took place on November 9, when the Prussian troops marched in to see for themselves the evidence of the prolonged bombardment apparent in the badly damaged buildings of the town.

8

Coulmiers

On the northern front of Paris the Crown Prince of Saxony had been particularly anxious to maintain the advanced position which he held at Le Bourget. The French troops in the St Denis sector were commanded by the vainglorious General Carrey de Bellemare, who thought that the exposed position of Le Bourget made it an inviting target, and on October 27 he resolved to attack it, throwing up entrenchments about 800 yards from the German lines that evening in preparation. It was entirely unauthorised; Bellemare was on the other hand entirely conscious of the public relations aspect of the attack, for it was a volunteer unit known as the 'Franctireurs of the Press' which at 5.00 am next morning he led to the assault.[1] Le Bourget was held at that moment by one company of the Queen's Regiment of the Guard, and it was taken entirely by surprise when the franc tireurs surged forward out of the darkness supported by heavy rifle fire. The Guards were driven back to the north end of the village; as day broke the French, who had now brought up in support two line battalions and a battalion of Gardes Mobiles, soon occupied the whole of Le Bourget, and at once put in hand the work of fortifying it against any Prussian attempt to retake it. Its erstwhile defenders fell back to Le Blanc Mesnil and Pont Iblon.[2] French artillery deploying to the west of Le Bourget shelled Pont Iblon until reduced to silence by the batteries of the Guard which took up a position there; in their turn, however, these were forced to break off the action under heavy fire from St Denis.

Bellemare reported his success personally to Trochu, who was furious, considering that 'this is increasing the death roll for nothing at all.' For the moment, however, he did not make his views public. Much later he recorded his opinion of Bellemare's performance, which was summarised by his biographer, who wrote that after announcing a great victory Bellemare at once 'left his troops, and at the very moment that the Germans were preparing to pay us out for this absurd demonstration, he appeared twice before the governor to demand – a promotion!'[3] Meanwhile, however, the news of Le Bourget spread rapidly throughout Paris, and kindled enormous enthusiasm everywhere. Back at Le Bourget, that evening, a strengthened battalion of the Prussian Guard made a reconnaissance in force to test the strength of the French forces there, but was driven off by close range rifle fire from the village which was by now heavily fortified. Next day the Prussians turned to the artillery to drive out the invaders, which shelled the village for several hours from a gun line behind Pont Iblon without result.[4]

The Crown Prince of Saxony was determined to recover Le Bourget, stressing the importance of this in his orders to the Guard Corps on the afternoon of October 28. But at the Royal Headquarters Moltke was of a very different view. After the failure of the artillery attack on October 29, he pointed out that even if it was recaptured, Le Bourget would always be difficult to hold, situated as it was under the guns of St Denis. He advised, therefore, that there should be no attempt to retake it. But in spite of this the Crown Prince stubbornly held to his view, and insisted on an immediate attack, to be led by Lieut General von Budritzki, the commander of the 2nd Guard Division.[5] For this operation Budritzki was given nine battalions, supported by two batteries of field artillery and three batteries of horse artillery; he was to launch an enveloping attack from Dugny, Pont Iblon and Le Blanc Mesnil. Strong forces were brought up in reserve to meet any forward movement the French might make on either side of Le Bourget.

The German artillery opened up at 8.00am; half an hour later, the centre of Budritzki's attacking force advanced from Pont Iblon in widely spaced lines over the open fields that surrounded the village, a tactic which materially reduced losses from the fierce rifle fire which greeted them. By 9.00am they were into the northern end of the village, where a bitter house to house conflict developed. Extending to their right, the Prussians linked up with the troops advancing into the west of the village from Dugny. These stormed the barricade erected across the road, and went on to take the church after a savage struggle at close range. In the farms on the east side of the village, their defenders had the benefit of fighting from buildings with high and strong walls. In spite of this, the Prussians forced their way forward into the side streets of the village, albeit with heavy losses; Colonel Georg von Waldersee was among the casualties, killed at the head of his troops.

By 10.00 am that part of the village north of the Mollette Brook was largely in Prussian hands, although parties of French soldiers held out in isolated houses and the French remained in possession of farm buildings to the west of the village. Crossing the brook, the attackers next came on the sheep farm at the south end of the village, where another barricade had been built. The sheep farm was quickly surrounded on all sides and captured in a general assault, and the attack surged on down the road. Meanwhile the Prussian left, working around the east side of Le Bourget, had taken the station and gas works south of the village, trapping the French troops retreating down the road, who surrendered. The Guards now turned their attention to the large farm on the west side of the village still held by the French, and stormed the place at the point of the bayonet. Although the main body of the French troops had been driven out or captured by 11.00am, mopping up operations in individual houses of the village continued for another two hours.[6] Budritzki, whose total casualties were about 500, had taken 1,200 prisoners. The unrecorded French losses were extremely high. In view of the heavy shelling from the adjacent forts, Budritzki pulled the bulk of his victorious troops out of the village, leaving only two battalions as a garrison.

Thus, after all, the enormous enthusiasm aroused in Paris by the initial success at Le Bourget came to nothing. D'Herisson thought that this was the reason for the German counter attack. After October 28, he suggested:

> What ought to have been done was to send battalion after battalion, battery after battery, to Bourget. That is precisely what the Prussians did. They probably attached no more importance to Bourget than we ourselves did. They had no more need of it than we had. But it did not suit them to lose any conquered ground whatever. Above all, it did not suit them to see any revival of spirit among the inhabitants of Paris, even though it was due to a success more apparent than real.[7]

If that had been the Crown Prince's motive in so obstinately seeking the recapture of Le Bourget, he was soon justified. The news of the defeat on October 30 spread as quickly as had the news of the original victory, and caused consternation which rapidly turned to anger when the Parisians read next day in the 'Journal Officiel' not only the news of Le Bourget, but also of the opening of negotiations and, worst of all, of the fall of Metz. That morning large crowds gathered in the Place de la Concorde, and from there marched on the Hôtel de Ville, where the Government of National Defence was meeting. Ominously, the protesters were joined by some units of the Garde Nationale. At the Hôtel de Ville, they forced their way in. In an effort to appease them, the government agreed to hold the municipal elections which had been consistently called for by the Left. It was not enough; insurgent troops of the Garde Nationale seized the ministers and announced that the government was deposed. Without effective leadership, however, the insurgents hesitated. A loyal Garde Nationale unit got Trochu and other ministers safely out of the Hôtel de Ville, and he went to the Louvre where, soon after, Ducrot arrived at the head of his troops. Trochu, however, retaining his usual sang froid, forbade Ducrot from taking immediate action against the revolutionaries, to the latter's profound disappointment. The army, he said 'must not on any pretext abandon their positions in the face of the enemy';[8] and he ordered that loyal units of the Garde Nationale should stand by to take action under the leadership of Jules Ferry, the Préfet of the Department of the Seine. Backed by these, but mindful of the safety of the ministers still held by the insurgents, Ferry began a prolonged negotiation with them, which ultimately led to their dispersal the following morning. The rising had fizzled out; but it left Thiers, in the city to try to negotiate peace terms, profoundly depressed, and did nothing to strengthen the extremely weak hand he was playing. Bismarck was quite aware of Thiers' position and of the situation that had arisen in Paris; and in the course of their discussions, which were doomed to failure, he hardened his position. Reporting to Favre and Ducrot at a meeting in no man's land at Sèvres, Thiers found no readiness at all on the part of the Government of National Defence to entertain Bismarck's terms. Ducrot was particularly dismissive of the proposals, and his attitude was endorsed by Trochu and the rest of the government when he and Favre returned to the city. For his part, Moltke expected nothing from the talks with Thiers, writing to Tümpling on November 3:' 'The present negotiations with M. Thiers cannot lead to any result. These haughty, infatuated Frenchmen must be humiliated much more before they will listen to reason. There are means enough and more than enough since the fall of Metz, but time is needed for them to take effect.'[9]

For the moment, therefore, Moltke's principal task was deciding upon the most effective redeployment of the troops at Metz. Manteuffel had, as previously planned, been ordered north with the First Army, with the responsibility also for the siege of Mézières. It was the movement of the Second Army with which Moltke was particularly concerned. It had begun to leave Metz on October 28, moving west on a broad front in the direction of Troyes and Chaumont. On the right, the IX Corps and the 1st Cavalry Division crossed the Meuse at St Mihiel on November 2. The III Corps crossed at Commercy. Finally, somewhat behind the other corps, the X Corps left Metz on November 2. The II Corps was for the moment earmarked to act as a general reserve for the armies investing Paris. Moltke wrote a long letter to Stiehle on the operations to be conducted by the Second Army, giving him an up to date appreciation of the enemy's forces in the light of the latest available intelligence. Best estimates of their total strength put this at about 126,000 men, of which perhaps 30,000 were in the north concentrating at Lille under Bourbaki, about 16,000 covering Rouen and Le Havre, up to 60,000 with d'Aurelle on the line Bourges-Amboise and in the south about 35,000 under Cambriels at Besancon, covering the road to Lyon. In addition, an unknown number of Gardes Mobiles and Gardes Nationales, formed into brigades in each of the departments of France, might be encountered in the course of the Second Army's advance.

The actual tasks of the Second Army would depend on the course of events, but Moltke thought it unlikely that Werder, in a defensive position Vesoul- Gray-Dijon, would need support. He had not lost sight of the key targets that provided the French with their essential resources. 'On the other hand, on your left wing are three points at which the most serious injuries can be inflicted on French military capability, Chalons sur Saone, Nevers and above all Bourges where there are the major cannon foundries and cartridge manufacturers etc.' In Moltke's view, it seemed unnecessary for the Second Army to keep together; one corps should be enough to break the enemy at each point.[10] Given what was known about the French forces, this assessment was in general pretty accurate. Having regard to the very considerable distances between the possible objectives, it did however significantly underestimate the powers of resistance of which the emerging French armies might be capable. On the basis of this appreciation, though, the lines of advance of the various units of the Second Army remained entirely appropriate and the army continued its march. It soon began to recover from the ill effects of its unhealthy sojourn at Metz, as the Official History noted: 'Through good diet, the prevalence of better weather, and less fatiguing marches along well made roads, the health of the troops visibly improved.'[11]

There were however a number of clashes with small bodies of the enemy, which from time to time held up the advance, especially on its southern flank. Moltke was alive to the possibility that the breakdown of the talks between Bismarck and Thiers, coupled with the fall of Metz, might lead to serious military developments. He wrote to Frederick Charles on November 7 to report the negative outcome of the discussions, adding that the French 'might make a serious attempt to lift the investment of Paris.'[12] The Second Army should therefore accelerate its march, directing its right towards Fontainebleau. By November 9 the X Corps, marching from Toul, reached Andelot; the III Corps was at Doulevant and Bar sur Aube, while the leading units of the IX Corps and the 1st Cavalry Division had reached Troyes. Behind them, the Etappen troops covered their lines of communication, while engineers repaired facilities destroyed by the French, in particular three important railway bridges over the Marne near Villers. The importance attached to this process was shown by Moltke's request to Stiehle on November 6 for a daily report on the damage encountered in the course of the advance.[13] The advance of the Second Army was therefore well up to schedule; but on the following day news reached Stiehle and Frederick Charles at Piney that necessitated an immediate revision of their plans.

On October 15 Gambetta had left Tours for a short visit to Besancon, to pull together the operations in the east. Apart from sorting out the disorganisation of the troops retreating before Werder's advance, he also considered the situation in the Upper Saône valley. He concluded that this would provide suitable employment for Garibaldi, who was put in command of a large force of volunteers to cover this sector.[14]

Inspired by this success, and unaware that the situation was about to be radically changed by the fall of Metz, Gambetta returned to Tours to organise a forward move by the Army of the Loire. The available forces had been considerably strengthened by the formation of the 16th Corps, the leading units of which had been pushed forward to Blois to block any German advance towards Tours. This threat, of course, did not materialise, and by October 24 at a conference at d'Aurelle's headquarters at Salbris, Freycinet was pressing for the Army of the Loire to undertake an advance on von der Tann. D'Aurelle recorded the conclusions that were reached: 'The idea of recapturing Orleans, by marching from Blois on this city, prevailed and, for the moment there was no other objective. This was the only programme decided on; there was no discussion of the possibility of marching on Paris.'[15] It was agreed that before any order was given, the plan required the approval of Gambetta and next day a further meeting was held at Tours at which Gambetta confirmed that there must be immediate action. D'Aurelle was decidedly reluctant, complaining that his troops were 'still too young, too little used to fatigue, too badly equipped' to go into action, and that in any case the poor condition of the roads due to the appalling weather made it impossible to advance. Gambetta would have none of it, and it was agreed that the Army of the Loire should begin a forward movement on October 27, with the aim of reaching Orleans by November 1. D'Aurelle returned with Borel, his chief of staff, to Salbris and that night issued the necessary orders.

On October 28, however, d'Aurelle began to experience further doubts. After a visit to Blois that day, where the local commander pointed out the problems of the troops bivouacked there due to the bad weather, he received further discouraging information. From his artillery commander he received a report of the 'difficulty of reorganising his batteries due to the dispersal of part of his equipment, loaded too hastily when departing from Vierzon.' In addition, d'Aurelle recorded,

> the cavalry were not in the best of condition. No preparation had been made by railway staff to unload their horses, which were obliged to remain the station for half a day, because there had not been provided the loading ramps and platforms, equipment that was always needed for this operation.[16]

Because of this, d'Aurelle believed he must defer any movement on Orleans, and he telegraphed this opinion at once to Tours. The response from Tours was immediate. Gambetta reluctantly acquiesced in the delay, but followed up a telegram to this effect with a letter from Freycinet ordering d'Aurelle to assemble five divisions around Blois. Pourcet was relieved of command of the 16th Corps, which was to pass to General Chanzy. 'As soon as you feel you are in a state to march toward the Prussians, you will tell us. Meanwhile, remain vigilant, fortify your positions and keep an eye on the area between Blois and Salbris, to prevent an advance by the enemy towards Tours and Vierzon.'[17] The letter crossed with one from d'Aurelle reciting in gloomy detail how 'everything has turned against us'- the weather, the roads, and the lack of supplies and ammunition; he feared too that 'the secrecy on which we counted is not secure.'

At Versailles Moltke was becoming increasingly discontented with the lack of any activity on the part of von der Tann, and he wrote to Blumenthal on November 2 that it was

> inadmissible that General von der Tann should remain any longer in an entirely passive attitude; His Majesty wishes, on the contrary that this officer and also General Wittich use the troops available to take the offensive and seek to prevent the movements which the enemy appear to be carrying out completely undisturbed.[18]

Blumenthal was disturbed by this:

> I cannot say that I at all approve this idea, for it throws to the winds my plan, which has hitherto been followed, of remaining quiet until all should be ready for a big stroke. It may easily lay us open to defeats in detail. I drove over to Moltke at once, and we came to terms as soon as he had heard what I had to say. He now desires nothing more than that they should make reconnaissances in force, which they are both doing.[19]

Blumenthal was now of the view that the main French thrust would come not from the south through Orleans, but from the west. He correctly put the 16th Corps at Blois, but had got fixed in his mind that the rest of the Army of the Loire was at Le Mans. On November 3 he telegraphed his fears to Wittich: 'According to information, fairly reliable and just received, the hostile army at Le Mans is 60,000 strong. I advise you to be very careful. I cannot get good intelligence agents.'[20] Believing that it was 'high time that these impudent folk should have their corns trodden upon,' Blumenthal asked the Crown Prince on November 4 to get the King to agree to Wittich being supported by the 4th Division, which had just arrived from Metz, in a joint operation with von der Tann. 'It was all in vain, as the King fancies our own position in front of Paris to be extremely hazardous, and will not sanction any troops being sent away. We shall have to wait another day.'[21]

Blumenthal continued to press the point, on November 5 sending Bronsart over to Moltke to advocate an advance towards Le Mans. Moltke was not convinced, recording in a letter to both the Third Army and the Army of the Meuse his opinion that 'the situation of the enemy indicates less an inclination to energetic offensive than plans for local defence. Certainly it may become abruptly necessary to organise a large expedition, but that moment does not appear yet to have arrived.' Meanwhile the arrival of the 3rd Division would provide the resources for an offensive operation should that prove necessary.[22] Blumenthal was extremely disgruntled at a decision which appeared to leave the initiative to the French.

> They will hoodwink us, and keep us occupied here, then suddenly make a big sortie and march away to the west. If, however, we destroy their Army of the Loire, now at Le Mans, all fear of this contingency is past, and they can no longer trouble us. It seems to me to be as clear as daylight.[23]

Two days later however, Moltke was prepared to change his mind about the need for immediate action, in the light of the latest information received at the Royal Headquarters. Noting that 'the French Army of the Loire is likely soon to be upwards of 80,000 strong,' Verdy thought that 'there may be fresh fighting to be done against the latter presently, as it appears that those divisions which are already formed have crossed the Loire at Tours and will advance against us from the west, along the right bank of the river.'[24] Blumenthal on the other hand saw no immediate danger: 'This afternoon we received information from von der Tann that he is expecting to be attacked. I do not anticipate any such thing, as the enemy cannot be ready for it yet.'[25] The Crown Prince, perhaps expressing a fashionable view at Versailles, commented rather unfairly of the Bavarians that 'they seem to be in a state of nervousness there, knowing no Prussian helmets to be any longer in the immediate neighbourhood.'[26] Moltke's response on November 7 to the reports coming in of increasing French activity was, as has been seen, to accelerate the march of the Second Army, and to form a 'Detachment' under the command of the Grand Duke of Mecklenburg-Schwerin to be responsible for operations against the enemy forces south and west of Paris. The Detachment was to consist of the troops already operating there, comprising von der Tann's I Bavarian Corps, still at Orleans, Wittich's 22nd Division at Chartres, and the 2nd, 4th and 6th Cavalry Divisions; in addition however the Grand Duke was to have von Tresckow's 17th Division, which would be pulled out of the lines of investment around Paris and replaced there for the moment by the 3rd Division. The Detachment was to operate under the orders of the Third Army.[27]

The Crown Prince thought the selection of the 17th Division an unfortunate one, because it 'was under the command of Lieutenant-General Schimmelman, a man who provokes serious anxiety by reason of his excitable temper.'[28] Blumenthal was delighted with Moltke's decision and saw the Grand Duke next morning, who evidently agreed with everything he said. 'He seemed particularly pleased at his appointment, and was so smart and quick in apprehending his task that I have the greatest hopes of him. It may be, however, that the operations will be more difficult than we think, owing to the delay that has taken place.'[29] The task which Blumenthal communicated to the Grand Duke was based entirely on his own inaccurate assessment of the position of the French forces and was, with the benefit of hindsight, well beyond the power of the Detachment as constituted to carry out. It was to

> break up the Army of the Loire now in process of formation, and to compel it to retreat by Le Mans. If the 15th and 16th Army Corps are to be found north at Blois and Le Mans, they may perhaps be driven apart, and their reunion rendered impossible. A further (subsidiary) object would be the destruction of the hostile communications between Tours and Rouen, as well as the utilisation of the occupied territory for the supply of the army. In order to make the communication with the superior command better and quicker, the capture of one or two locomotives would be beneficial.

The Grand Duke was ordered to report regularly on the situation.[30]

Later that day came confirmation that events were indeed moving swiftly, with news from von der Tann of the advance of strong French forces, and a request from Wittich to know if he should march to support the Bavarians. Blumenthal could not resist a sanctimonious if somewhat inaccurate comment on all this in his diary that night. 'All my prayers and entreaties have been in vain, and now people will not be surprised that it should have made me ill. My conscience is, however, clear. I did all I could, and never hesitated, and God will show who was right.'[31]

For some days the uneasiness that von der Tann was feeling at Orleans had been steadily mounting. As early as October 25 there had been a sharp little engagement at Binas, west of Ouzouer Le Marché, with a party of franc tireurs who were driven back into the Forest of Marchenoir, while on October 31 a strong French force again emerged from the forest to advance on Ouzouer Le Marché. They succeeded in driving back a foraging party of Bavarian cuirassiers, but in their turn retreated when cavalry reinforcements arrived. Further east, parties of franc tireurs were active in the Forest of Orleans and south of the Loire. In the first days of November the German outposts west of Orleans were picking up increasingly strong indications that large French forces were coming forward on a wide front. One of von der Tann's staff, sent to the French outposts with a private message for Madame Thiers, noted the construction of barricades and trenches on the road between Beaugency and Mer, and substantial bodies of regular troops coming up from Mer.[32] To the north, patrols found that Châteaudun had been reoccupied, while there was a stiffening resistance experienced by patrols down the north bank of the Loire.

On November 7 von der Tann pushed Stolberg's 2nd Cavalry Division forward to test French strength beyond Baccon and Ouzouer le Marché, supported by one and a half battalions of infantry. The French outposts withdrew into the forest of Marchenoir and Stolberg decided to pursue them to find out just how large a force was sheltering there. Concentrating at Marolles, he advanced westwards, soon encountering strong French forces sent forward by Chanzy from St Laurent and Autainville. Stolberg put his infantry in defensive positions between Marolles and Vallière, where they were at once attacked by forces which greatly outnumbered them. After an hour Stolberg, who had learned that French cavalry advancing to the north of Vallière threatened his line of retreat, broke off the action and fell back towards Baccon under cover of the gunfire of a horse artillery battery south east of Chantôme. Apart from the very large numbers of French troops engaged, the Bavarians observed of the enemy that 'in the bearing, as well as the handling of his troops there was a marked improvement over all the detachments, with which we had come into collision at the outposts since the occupation of Orleans.'[33] Stolberg had achieved his object, but not without substantial loss, losing 28 killed, 51 wounded and 64 men taken prisoner.

Von der Tann was now in no doubt of the enemy's intention to advance to the attack. Not only had he Stolberg's report of the strength of French forces in and around the Forest of Marchenoir, but he had also learned that d'Aurelle's headquarters were now at Mer, which confirmed the probability that an offensive was about to be launched. Von der Tann accordingly put his corps on standby to move at a moment's notice, meanwhile sending out further patrols on November 8. All along the line of outposts facing west there were signs of enemy movement; particularly significant were reports of large bodies of French cavalry in the area of Prenouvellon, and of artillery and infantry near Charsonville to the south of that place. Strong French forces were reported as moving on Baccon, while still further to the south Le Bardon was occupied by them. As a precaution against an immediate assault von der Tann concentrated the 3rd Bavarian Brigade between Huisseau and the Loire at St Ay, and sat down to ponder his position.

Summarising this, the Bavarian Official History noted that 'to remain in the town of Orleans would have been a strategical and tactical absurdity. The army was weak in infantry, but comparatively powerful in cavalry and artillery.' It was not an easy decision that von der Tann had to make.

> In reflecting on the measures to be taken in the course of the next few hours, one idea was constantly present in General von der Tann's mind, viz. to follow the orders from Versailles, and not to give up Orleans without a struggle, or without proving the superiority of the enemy's forces.

This ruled out an immediate retreat to a place of safety such as Chartres and Tours, notwithstanding all the indications which he had already received that he was heavily outnumbered.[34] Von der Tann in fact had immediately available a total of 14,543 infantry, 4,450 cavalry and 110 guns. Opposed to him the two corps of d'Aurelle's army had between 70–75,000 men, with one hundred and sixty guns.

Looking at the country west and northwest of Orleans, von der Tann had to choose between two positions, each of which covered his line of retreat if that should become necessary. One, to the north around St Péravy, was far enough back from Orleans for the French to secure Orleans without a serious engagement, if that was what they wanted to do, so instead he decided to take up a position around the village of Coulmiers which would compel the French to attack him before moving into the city. During the night of October 8/9 the Bavarian troops began to pull out of Orleans, and moved north to take up defensive positions in front of the woods of Buisson and Montpipeau. News, however, that the French appeared to have pulled back from Charsonville, and that Wittich was marching south from Chartres to his support, induced von der Tann to leave the Bodyguard Regiment in Orleans to garrison the city and protect the sick and wounded in hospital there.[35] For the moment, von der Tann protected his left flank by the detachment of two battalions covering Baccon, La Rénardière, Huisseau and Château Prefort, while a squadron of cavalry remained at St Ay to watch the road from Meung.

Further north, where the main body was assembling, Schumacher's 2nd Bavarian Division was in the front line, and he quickly saw that it would be necessary to push forward from the two woods in front of which he was to take up a position, and to occupy Coulmiers itself. The Bavarian Offical History described the place:

> Coulmiers, which lies on the road to Ouzouer le Marché, consists, like all the villages of La Beauce, of stone houses, and has a massive castle with an extensive park. This park, which lies at the south western extremity of the village and is surrounded by a thick quickset hedge and a ditch, was the key to the defence of Coulmiers.[36]

It was also clear to Schumacher that he must extend his defensive position north of the village to Carrières-les-Crottes and Ormeteau. Into this triangle he put the 4th Bavarian Brigade, commanded by Rudolph von der Tann. The weather was cold and dark; as the sun came up, the early mist dispersed. At Huisseau at 8.00am von der Tann senior reviewed the reports of the French advance which for the moment seemed to be coming from the area of Meung. To meet this he at once moved the 1st Bavarian Brigade from Descures to a more forward position at La

Rénardière, pushing the 3rd Bavarian Brigade towards Château Prefort. The 2nd Bavarian Brigade was held in reserve with the Corps artillery at Bonneville.[37]

Seven miles to the west of von der Tann at Huisseau, d'Aurelle had himself ridden forward to reconnoitre, and brought up four batteries to an ideal artillery position near Champdry: he directed them to open fire on Baccon. Behind Baccon the leading troops of the 1st Bavarian Brigade moved up to La Rivière supported by artillery to the north of La Rénardière. French infantry now began to move forward south of Champdry though Les Barchats, under the fire of horse artillery batteries at Baccon. These were soon, however, overpowered by the French guns at Champdry. Further south the 3rd Bavarian Brigade had reached Château Prefort, and took up a position along the bank of the little River Mauve; as the morning progressed without an attack by the French in this sector von der Tann, who was by now himself at Coulmiers, at about noon pulled them back through Huisseau to reinforce La Rénardière, where the main French thrust was developing, although the distance the brigade had to cover meant that for two critical hours it could not influence the crisis of the battle. Its presence at Château Prefort had, however discouraged the French from attempting to turn the Bavarian left. Chanzy's advance was led by Barry's Division; this, advancing through Champdry, was held up for a while by the Prussian battery north of Baccon. To its left the division led by the redoubtable Admiral Jauréguiberry advanced through Charsonville on Cheminiers, immediately north of Schumacher's positions around Coulmiers. Seeing the risk of being outflanked on his right, Schumacher posted one battalion and the 5th Cavalry Brigade at Vaurichard, while beyond this the 2nd Bavarian Brigade (von Orff), hitherto in reserve at Bonneville, was ordered by von Stephan, the divisional commander, to move north towards Champs, supported by the 4th Cavalry Brigade from St Sigismond.

Chanzy's corps now began a general advance, Barry advancing south of Saintry towards Coulmiers, while on the other side of the main road Jauréguiberry pushed forward on Ormeteau, where it was held up by fierce rifle fire. Behind them, on either side of the main road, Chanzy concentrated a line of guns to support an attack on the Bavarian positions.[38] Meanwhile, on the far left of the French advance there were a series of encounters between Reyau's cavalry and the Bavarian Cuirassier Brigade at Renneville and around La Vallée. By about noon, all along the northern part of the front there were intensive artillery exchanges; but further south things were not going well for the Bavarians. Peytavin's Division had taken Baccon, and brought up artillery on either side of the village, which poured a heavy fire on the defenders of La Rivière; by now this village was in flames, and its defenders pulled back to the castle and part of La Rénardière, prepared to resist the next assault. Dietl, the commander of the 1st Bavarian Brigade, held on there as long as he could; but, driven out of the farm of La Grande Motte on the left of the village, he was finally obliged to pull back, at first to the Clos Farm north east of the village, where he was supported by the 3rd Cavalry Brigade at La Motte aux Taurins. Further French advances east of La Rénardière compelled Dietl to fall back on the Bois de Montpipeau, where he maintained his position for the rest of the day. By now, at about 3.00 pm the 3rd Bavarian Brigade had completed its march from Château Prefort, and came up in support on Dietl's right, also sending

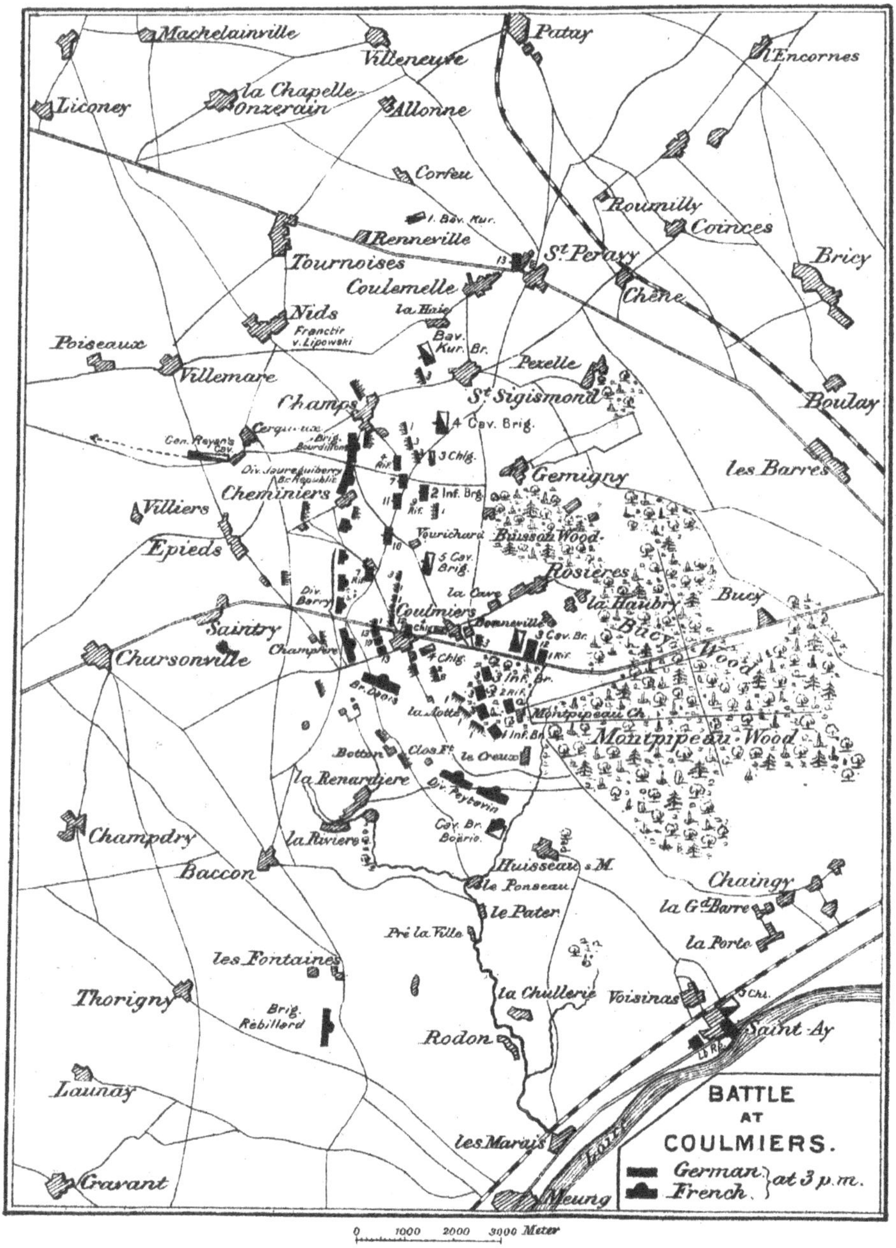

The Battle of Coulmiers, November 9 1870

forward two batteries and an infantry battalion to support the 4th Bavarian Brigade.

North of Coulmiers, the defenders of the quarries of Carrières les Crottes were overwhelmed by the attacks which had been launched by Barry's division as it advanced along the main road from Saintry. Here repeated French assaults were resisted at the point of the bayonet and they retreated to the park at Coulmiers. South of the park, French artillery firing from Le Grand Lus drove back a Bavarian battery, which retreated half a mile to the east. Barry's attempts to outflank Coulmiers on its northern side, however, were defeated by gunfire from three batteries to the north of the village, and by spirited charges by the 5th Cavalry Brigade on the advancing French infantry. To their left, Deplanque's Brigade from Jauréguiberry's Division had occupied Cheminiers and Champs. Orff deployed the 2nd Infantry Brigade on the right of a strong artillery position east of Champs and from there overwhelmed the French artillery supporting Deplanque's advance. After some confused fighting east of Champs, Deplanque fell back from the village at about 2.00 pm, and Orff, although enormously outnumbered, launched a vigorous attack on Cheminiers under the close support of his artillery. Here, however Jauréguiberry put up a fierce defence, and on learning that the position at Coulmiers was deteriorating, Orff broke off his attack and took up a defensive position to cover any northward retreat.

It was by now becoming clear to von der Tann that he had two choices-either to hold on to his position until nightfall, or to retreat while Orff's Brigade securely held the right wing. The risk of the heavy losses which maintaining his position would entail, and the need to commit his last reserves to do so decided him in favour of breaking off the action, and retreating on Artenay. He determined first to pull back his left wing, in front of the Bois de Montpipeau. Accordingly at 4.00 pm he issued orders for the retreat.[39]

Meanwhile in the centre the struggle for Coulmiers park reached a climax. French infantry, in fierce hand to hand fighting, had broken in again on the north western side, while four battalions threatened it from the southwest. Colonel von Ysenburg, commanding the 13th Bavarian Regiment, gave orders for a gradual retreat; houses in the village were defended until the last minute to cover the withdrawal. Further north Ormeteau was also abandoned, the retreat being covered by sustained artillery fire; the French made no attempt to pursue. Ysenburg collected up all the men he could find, from whatever unit, and formed a skirmish line behind which the retreat of the whole corps was gradually effected.[40] D'Aurelle made his headquarters at Le Grand Lus, while his army settled down to put the captured villages in a state of defence. There was every expectation that the Germans would counter attack next day, and no attempt was made to pursue them. D'Aurelle, addressing in his memoirs the point that 'many people have asked why General d'Aurelle did not pursue the enemy after the battle of Coulmiers', set out his reasons for not doing so: 'the battle had not finished until nightfall: the cavalry which, launched on the enemy's line of retreat, would have been able to begin the pursuit and bring good results, had returned to its cantonments at Prénouvellon.' In addition, fearing that his advance might be turned from the north, Chanzy had refused his left flank.[41] But if there had been no pursuit the French could at least claim to have won a victory. The recapture of Orleans was a

French infantry assault the park at Coulmiers, by Knötel (Pflugk-Harttung)

major symbol of the determination and ability of the Government of National Defence to carry on the war. Gambetta made the most of it, of course: but

> unfortunately the military importance of the success was negligible in comparison with its moral effect ... the actual achievement was from a military point of view more a matter for regrets than congratulations, since the opportunity to surround the whole Bavarian force had had been lost, and the inexperienced French troops were in no condition to follow up their advantage.[42]

The total losses sustained by von der Tann during the battle amounted to 1,308, of which several hundred were prisoners; French losses appear to have been about 1,500, most of which had been suffered by Chanzy's corps. While the French remained on the battlefield digging in against any counter attack, von der Tann retreated northward along roads that were almost impassable as a result of the heavy rain and snow that began to fall in the early evening. The 1st Bavarian Division and the 4th Cavalry Brigade reached Artenay by midnight. The western flank of the retreat was covered by the 3rd Cavalry Brigade and the Bavarian Cuirassier Brigade, while the rearguard was composed of the 3rd Bavarian Brigade and the 5th Cavalry Brigade; it took up a position for the night between Gémigny and St Sigismund, quite close enough to the battlefield for the French to attack it if they were disposed to do so. Meanwhile the Bodyguard Regiment, which had originally remained in Orleans, was, before setting out towards St Ay during the battle, informed by a Bavarian cavalry patrol of the state of affairs and was able to make its way safely to rejoin the main body, although it arrived at Cercottes at 1.00 am next morning in a state of complete exhaustion.

On November 10 von der Tann continued his retreat to Toury, and took up a defensive position astride the main road. He began a further retreat on Angerville on reports that the French were advancing on Artenay; but in fact no serious attempt was made to follow the Bavarians, although one of Jaureguiberry's staff

The château at Coulmiers (Rousset/*Histoire*)

officers leading a cavalry patrol beyond St Péravy came upon the ammunition column of the 2nd Bavarian Division which had, due to a misunderstanding become separated from the main body, and was captured intact at Lignerolles. Learning that the French were not after all advancing von der Tann returned to his defensive position at Toury.[43] When he reached there he learned of the formation of the Detachment, and that he was thereafter to operate as part of the Grand Duke's command.

At Versailles Moltke, who always held that nothing is certain war, received the news of von der Tann's defeat calmly, sending a telegram to Stiehle to speed his advance: 'Strong enemy forces advancing from the Loire close to Orleans. It is necessary to hasten the march of the Second Army. The IX Corps cannot have a rest day on November 11 and must reach Fontainebleau by November 14.'[44] He followed this with a letter which he had begun a day or two earlier, in which he mused that if, contrary to expectations, the Army of the Loire advanced further, they might have to reckon with a general sortie from Paris. He was not, however, to be panicked into rash decisions. 'In a few days we will be able to judge if the left wing of the army may not be more useful on the left bank of the Loire than in the area between that river and Paris.'[45] For the moment the Grand Duke was ordered to Angerville to await events; the 17th Division was on its way there, and completed its concentration there on November 12. The assembly of the Detachment was screened by the cavalry, operating on a wide arc to the south and west.

That evening Blumenthal was glad to receive a visit from Moltke. 'We discussed the situation, being both of the same mind. He also told me that Prince Frederick Charles would arrive in Fontainebleau on the 14th instant with the IX Army Corps. We shall then be able to take the offensive in earnest, and place the Army of the Loire in a very uncomfortable position.'[46] There was some way to go before this result could be achieved; for the moment, as the Crown Prince commented, the strategy of the Detachment would call for 'calmness, coolness, determination, and admitting of no looking on the dark side of things.'[47]

9

The March of the Detachment

With the benefit of hindsight, it can be seen that the next three weeks were to determine the outcome of the second phase of the Franco Prussian war. The assembly and deployment of the very large and well equipped, though under-trained, Army of the Loire, coinciding with the preparations by the garrison of Paris for a major sortie, gave the Government of National Defence its only serious chance of turning the war around. To achieve this it was going to need a lot of luck, no mistakes on the part of its commanders and a substantial failure of Moltke's nerve or that of his widely scattered troops. Still applying hindsight, it is clear that the odds against the French were just too great to be overcome; but it did not look like that at the time, either at Tours or at Versailles. The events of the campaign on the Loire, and elsewhere, during the period from November 12 until December 4, were to confront Moltke and his army with their sternest test. Moltke, of course, had to manage the campaign from Versailles, where he was assailed every day by the minutiae unavoidable in the conduct of a great war over a huge area, as well as by the complex political situation which increasingly affected his strategy. The onset of winter meant that the demands made of his troops would be greater than ever; the rapid growth of the new armies of the Government of National Defence, and the many different areas of their concentration, meant that the gathering of reliable intelligence about them was essential to Moltke's strategic decisions. And it was a crucial lack of intelligence that profoundly affected the decisions to be made in the earliest stages of a campaign which faced Moltke with a series of enormously intricate problems.

Almost at once after assuming command of the Detachment the Grand Duke and Colonel von Krenski, his chief of staff, were faced with an immediate and very puzzling lack of information as to their enemy's intentions. After Coulmiers, and not for the last time in the course of the Loire campaign, each of the adversaries had expected the other on the day after the battle to advance to the attack. Pending the concentration of the Detachment, of course, Moltke had no intention of taking any offensive action against the Army of the Loire on the Paris-Orleans road; and it gradually became apparent that the French had no aggressive intention either. In the course of a meeting after Coulmiers with Gambetta and Freycinet, attended by d'Aurelle, his chief of staff, and des Pallières, it was agreed to follow the previously determined plan to establish an entrenched camp around Orleans before making the next move.[1] Later, Freycinet was to claim in his own extremely tendentious account of the second phase of the war that 'after the taking of Orleans, if we had marched on Paris at once, it seems clear that we would have succeeded;[2] but, as d'Aurelle pointed out, this was not what had been intended, and 'in spite of all the courage of which it had given such proof, to march on Paris after Coulmiers was a senseless and rash attack, exposing the army to certain destruction.'[3] In this view d'Aurelle was undoubtedly correct; his great concern was with the oncoming

The Grand Duke of Mecklenburg-Schwerin (Scheibert)

troops of Frederick Charles from Metz and he was certain that these must be destroyed before he could contemplate moving directly to the relief of the capital.

Thus it was that although on November 11 the report of the German cavalry that they had identified strong forces moving north towards Pithiviers had led to von der Tann's retreat towards Angerville, by the afternoon of that day they were reporting that the French had withdrawn; and next day 'no French troops showed themselves to the north of the Forest of Orleans; some detachments pushed forward by way of Patay to Orgères, as speedily withdrew before the advance of the 5th Cuirassiers.'[4] The apparent disappearance of the enemy from immediately in front of the Detachment led the Grand Duke and Krenski to jump to the altogether erroneous conclusion on November 12 that d'Aurelle 'had moved away to the left, and, in concert with the French troops on the Lower Eure and Seine, intended to attack the army investing Paris.'[5] It was decided that notwithstanding its originally defensive mission, the Detachment must at once wheel to its right, and next day, covered by the 2nd and 4th Cavalry Divisions, it moved off north-west towards Chartres. His report of this intention got Blumenthal into a lot of trouble at Versailles, as he recounted.

> In the afternoon a telegram arrived from the Grand Duke, saying that tomorrow he will march to Chartres. I forgot to send it to the King, and when the Crown Prince returned in the evening from St Germain it was very unpleasant for him ... There is a very decided tendency here to dictate every move to the Grand Duke, and this ought to be resisted. If I were in his place, I should report nothing, but just cut the telegraph-wire.[6]

General von Blumenthal, Chief of Staff of the German Third Army (Rousset/*Histoire*)

It does seem more than a little surprising that neither Moltke, nor Blumenthal, nor above all the Grand Duke insisted on greater reconnaissance efforts being made to determine exactly where the French were, and the extent to which they might be found, as was in fact the case, to be still around Orleans.

The news of the Grand Duke's march towards Chartres was not well received at the Royal Headquarters. The Crown Prince, at a meeting with Moltke and the King, was told to tell the Grand Duke

> that his Majesty does not wish your Detachment to take the offensive unless very special reasons not known here should make it necessary. The IX Corps, under General von Manstein, has, with special view to this, been so directed that its advance guard arrives at Fontainebleau in the 14th, crosses the Seine on the 15th, and can connect with you on the 16th. Success seems to be the more certain thereby, as General von Manstein will perhaps be able to act on the flank of the enemy, who does not expect him.[7]

This order demonstrates that Moltke was not yet at any rate a complete convert to the theory that the French were planning a long left hook to come in on the west of Paris. The terms of this instruction, which reached the Detachment during its march on November 13, required that the staff issue new orders for the next day; these provided that the Detachment halt in its present positions, with the exception of the 22nd Division which was to continue its march on Chartres. Discontent with the Grand Duke was already becoming apparent at Versailles, although Blumenthal stuck to his policy of leaving the man on the spot to get on with it.

> The advance of the Grand Duke on Chartres appears here not to be understood, though at the time I said to the Crown Prince and to others that they could not be judges of everything that was happening; that no doubt the Grand Duke had good reasons for his action, and if he did not happen to report every detail he was quite right and a wise man. This was not at all appreciated at Headquarters!

He went on to record a meeting with Moltke the outcome of which was, as was usual in Blumenthal's mind although by no means so often in reality, Moltke's agreement with Blumenthal's views. He did concede, though that 'Moltke was annoyed that the Grand Duke should from the outset have divided his forces too much. He is right there, but we do not know what were the Duke's reasons for so doing.'[8] In fact what happened was that at Moltke's request a further warning was sent in the name of the Crown Prince to the Grand Duke, reminding him that Manstein could be at Etampes by November 16, and that in the meanwhile 'the road from Orleans to Paris must not be left open, if the enemy advances by Artenay.'[9] The Grand Duke's response was to suggest that Manstein should be placed under his orders. In the light of Moltke's mounting concern, it is hardly surprising that Verdy, observing that 'we can make nothing of the operations of the Grand Duke,' added that 'one of us will probably have to go there.'[10] It had not taken very long for confidence in the Detachment and in its commander to be seriously eroded.

Moltke's regular letters to Stiehle reflecting on the current state of the war and his own future intentions provide a valuable and continuous record of his strategic thinking in a constantly changing situation. On November 14 he wrote a long letter reviewing the current position. Noting the power of the new French army which faced the Germans, he estimated the Army of the Loire as being at least 60,000 strong. 'It seems to be seeking to turn by the west the positions we occupy, which it does not dare to attack. For this march it would be able to join the new units of which the centre is at Nogent-le-Rotrou; perhaps even with the 30–40,000 gardes nationales which, under the command of Generals Briant and Bourbaki, have for a long time checked our forces on the line Pacy-Vernon-Les Andelys and as far as Gournay.' An attack from the west, Moltke thought, would be just as dangerous as one from the south. He did not rule out the possibility that the French were still at Orleans; but there was, however, no news from Stolberg at Toury.

> It is possible that the Army of the Loire is limiting itself to the passive defence of Orleans and the left bank of the river, but it is unlikely, since Gambetta knows for certain that Paris cannot hold out without being relieved. If therefore the Army of the Loire does take a northern direction the Grand Duke must keep in touch with it until he has the opportunity of a decisive attack.

Moltke reiterated that the key military objective was the destruction of Bourges and the key political objective was to drive the French government from Tours. Moltke was grateful for the rapid approach of the Second Army which had, he wrote, helped 'to overcome a kind of crisis.'[11] He had, of course, had his eye on these objectives for some time; what he was now finding was that the extent of the

French recovery, and the assembly of significant forces over a very wide area, was making it increasingly difficult to discern a point at which a decisive blow could be struck.

On November 14 the Detachment picked up further indications that the French might be shifting round to the west, when both the 5th and 6th Cavalry Divisions reported enemy activity in their front, apparently centering on Dreux. At Bu, six miles north east of Dreux, cavalry patrols encountered unexpectedly strong opposition and were later driven back from the village by a force of two companies of marines and three battalions of Gardes Mobiles, with artillery support. On the basis of this encounter, and information from local residents, the reports to headquarters indicated a total of 12,000 French infantry, with eight squadrons and eight batteries, as being in the area.[12] Moltke, on receipt of this news, that night decided to support the cavalry, which had taken up a position at Houdan, by withdrawing five battalions of the Guard Landwehr Brigade and a heavy battery of artillery from the Argenteuil peninsula and sending them to Neauphle. In considering Moltke's immediate response, it must be borne in mind that Bu is only twenty six miles from Versailles and, apart from cavalry, there were not many German troops between the French and the lines of investment. Although he believed that the French movement was only a blind, Blumenthal was pleased with the reinforcements that he thus acquired.[13] Next day, Moltke issued an order to the Third Army, expressly releasing the Detachment from its duty of covering the Orleans-Paris road, giving it instead the exclusive task of covering the investment from the west; responsibility for any threat from the south was to be assigned to the Second Army. Moltke concluded by recommending that the Detachment should 'concentrate immediately and take the offensive against the enemy forces reported to be marching from the area of Dreux and Chartres. The Royal Headquarters has sent no communication on this subject to HRH the Grand Duke.' [14]Simultaneously, Moltke sent orders direct to Manstein, who was now thirteen miles east of the Orleans – Paris road, at Milly, to the effect that he should now cover that road, and telling him that as the Detachment was now moving somewhat towards the west, he should watch the roads from Dreux and Chartres. In copying the order to the Second Army, Moltke emphasised that it was desirable that as soon as circumstances allowed, the army should take the offensive towards Orleans and beyond.[15]

The Grand Duke did not receive a copy of Moltke's order releasing him from the protection of the Orleans-Paris road until November 16, but he was already taking active steps to meet the possible threat from the west, based on the enemy's apparent intention 'either to make a long turning movement against Versailles, or to advance against Chartres and to turn our right flank.'[16] For November 15, the 17th Division was to move to Rambouillet, and thence towards Manstein, while von der Tann was on the road between Ablis and Chartres. These dispositions would mean that the Detachment could concentrate to meet any French advance from Chateauneuf en Thymerais, a dozen miles northwest of Chartres, which was seen as the centre of the French concentration. The Grand Duke himself took his headquarters to Nogent le Roi, which represented the right wing of the 17th Division. This division, no doubt to the relief of the Crown Prince, was now under the command of von Tresckow, Schimmelmann having been relieved on grounds of ill health.[17] In Versailles, Moltke was still discontented with the Detachment's performance, as Blumenthal unsympathetically noted.

> Moltke came to me today, and complained that the Grand Duke reported so little, and said that I ought to order him to take the offensive. That is not at all necessary. The Duke will do that of his own accord, and up to now it seems to me that he has done perfectly right. He remains concentrated, as it appears, between Chartres and Maintenon.[18]

Although the operations of the Detachment had thus far been conducted without undue difficulty, the Bavarian official historian noting that 'the march of November 15 furnished a fresh instance of the ease with which the various large bodies of troops were handled,'[19] the Grand Duke was about to embark on a much more difficult venture.

> With 52 battalions, 110 squadrons, 220 guns and unwieldy and huge trains, he stood on the edge of a tract of broken, close and wooded country, totally unsuitable for guns or cavalry, seamed with cross roads and lanes, and into which his cavalry scouts could scarcely penetrate; into this he was to enter and strike a decisive blow on an enemy moving unseen within, an enemy of whose strength, organisation and whereabouts he had not the faintest idea.[20]

While the Detachment was thus prepared to counter the largely illusory threat from the west, the various units of the Second Army continued to hasten westwards to take up their intended positions covering the investment of Paris against interruption from the south. Manstein's IX Corps was the most advanced, and he continued his march from Milly to Angerville, on the Orleans-Paris road. There, ten miles back from Toury, he was fifteen miles from the key road junction of Pithiviers, to which Alvensleben's III Corps was marching, and about forty miles from Montargis, which was the intended destination of the X Corps. As the Second Army moved forward, it had been frequently pestered by franc tireurs; on November 13 Voigts- Rhetz had had to issue orders to take account of this: 'attitude of the inhabitants of Châtillon hostile; the place evacuated only early this morning by French troops; armed parties in the neighbouring wood. Casualties must not be left behind, but must be brought up in wagons.'[21] The III Corps encountered serious resistance in the area of Chateau Landon around Nancray before taking up its position on November 20 at Pithiviers. Behind it and to the south, the X Corps continued to meet stubborn opposition, such as at Joigny, on November 18, where 'all three arms had to be brought into action before the enemy found it necessary to retreat upon Auxerre, a principal rallying-point of the national armament in that neighbourhood,'[22] Both these difficulties, and the delay by franc-tireurs of the staff officer with his orders held up Voigts- Rhetz so that it was not in fact until November 21 that his leading troops reached his destination of Montargis.

On November 16 Stiehle responded to Moltke's letter of November 14, reporting on the position and intentions of the Second Army, in the light of the priorities that Moltke had set out. Frederick Charles had evidently already decided on the capture of Orleans, rather than the destruction of the Army of the Loire, as his immediate objective; Stiehle wrote that

> By the capture of Orleans his Royal Highness believes he can best carry out the duty assigned to him ... Afterwards, according to circumstances, his Royal Highness intends to move down the Loire by Blois on Tours, the IX Army Corps on the right bank, the III Army Corps on the left bank of the river.

The X Corps could reach the Loire in two marches from Montargis, 'and eventually operate against Bourges, render it of no further military importance, and then, perhaps, advance down the Cher against Tours.' Thereafter, Poitiers might be the next target.[23] It was a hugely ambitious programme and, as Stiehle was shortly to discover, far beyond the forces he had at his disposal. These forces, it appeared, no longer conveyed to the increasingly hostile inhabitants of the villages through which they marched an air of invincibility, as a German historian observed:

> Already it had become known through the outspoken remarks of the population which eyed, with a certain amount of contempt, the weak marching columns of the advancing Second Army that, on the Loire, was assembling an army numbering hundreds of thousands, well equipped, and animated by the highest spirit. The expression "La belle Armée de la Loire" was heard here and there. On the German side, this was at first regarded as mere rodomontade, as an exaggeration due to the constitutionally excitable temperament.[24]

As the Second Army marched, it picked up increasing indications that a stern test lay ahead of it; newspaper reports put the Army of the Loire variously as being between 100,000 and 300,000 strong, and there were suggestions that it was being reinforced from the east. What was very clear to Frederick Charles and to Stiehle was that reliable intelligence was essential, and on November 18 Manstein was given specific orders that the 1st and 2nd Cavalry Divisions for the moment under his command should make thorough reconnaissances of the enemy's position. Frederick Charles was also concerned to know what was going on beyond the IX Corps; he required that Manstein should 'send an officer every day (by midday) to my headquarters with the information obtained about the enemy, and anything that may have taken place on Your Excellency's right flank.'[25] Moltke's reply to Stiehle's letter was sent off on November 18; it was already becoming evident to Moltke that, much as he would like to see a thrust at Bourges, it might not for the present be practicable.

> It does not yet appear possible to decide on the despatch of the X Corps to Bourges, since one cannot yet judge the eventual necessity of employing all the forces of the Second Army against Orleans and Châteaudun ... The reconnaissance of the next few days will show whether the principal forces of the Army of the Loire are still near Orleans or perhaps a little to the west towards Châteaudun. Information as to this will be sent as soon as possible.[26]

Clearly Moltke was no longer acting on the basis that the Army of the Loire had slipped away to the west; but, as he emphasised, the immediate question of how the Second Army was actually to be deployed would depend in particular on the advance of the Detachment which he expected to begin that day.

Following receipt of the orders freeing him from responsibility for the Orleans-Paris road, the Grand Duke decided to aim his advance at Dreux, which he took to be the centre of the French troops facing him. On hearing the news of the Grand Duke's intention to attack the enemy at Dreux, Blumenthal readily accepted the importance of the movement; 'God grant that he may defeat him, for that will soon bring the war to an end.'[27] On November 17 Tresckow moved directly on Dreux, encountering some resistance first at Luray on the Eure and then at Nuisement; but by the afternoon he was able to enter Dreux, and to push forward outposts west of the River Blaise. To the south, Wittich's 22nd Division advanced towards Châteauneuf from Chartres, reaching Boullay and Marville les Bois before nightfall. It too had encountered opposition en route, which slowed its progress. Although Dreux had been identified as the principal point of concentration of the enemy, there was still some lingering doubt, and the deployment of the Bavarian Corps reflected this; apart from acting as a reserve, it was also to be used if necessary on the left flank 'where as yet we were in uncertainty as to the strength and intentions of the enemy.'[28] Von der Tann moved up the Chartres- Dreux road in support, without incident apart from the discovery that the chateau selected from the map for von der Tann's headquarters proved not to exist. The events of November 17 appeared to demonstrate pretty clearly that wherever the French had gone, it was not in the region of the Eure. Krenski and the Grand Duke accordingly had to think again; their first thrust had turned out to be a blow in the air.

At Versailles the Crown Prince faithfully reflected Blumenthal's view of the Grand Duke's proceedings: 'it is not quite easy to see what his criss-cross movements mean, but I am convinced he is only acting as a result of inquiries made and is going where he conjectures the main force of the enemy to be concentrated.'[29] Moltke, meanwhile, remaining decidedly anxious about the Detachment's movements, sat down to write a letter to Krenski intended to serve as a general policy statement for the future operations of the Detachment. Reiterating that its only duty was 'to prevent all enemy movements directed by roads from the west towards the left bank of the Seine,' he spelt out the importance of not letting the force get too scattered:

> there is no question that you should attempt to defend each of these roads by a separate force; on the contrary, I count on you attacking on the road on which the strongest enemy column advances. Your success on a single road will prevent all movement of the enemy on the others. You will certainly achieve this if you keep your forces closely together. Generally speaking, His Royal Highness' Detachment has as its mission not to occupy territory but to carry out a war of movement, which is also the only way in which the troops can be kept supplied.[30]

Krenski did not in fact get this wise advice until November 20 by which time he had already in his movements of November 17 been acting substantially in breach of its central principle.

The conclusion reached by Krenski and the Grand Duke was that the main body of the enemy was well to the south west and that the most effective way of achieving the Detachment's objectives was to set off in that direction, marching first on Nogent Le Rotrou and thence towards Le Mans, before turning south towards Tours. The movement to the south west meant that the Detachment must wheel to its left, pivoting on Châteauneuf. The marches which this involved, in the much more difficult country of the Perche, and on a short foggy November day, would make considerable demands of the troops and their leaders, and would require highly efficient staff work. This, on what turned out to be a really dreadful day, Krenski's team entirely failed to provide, as Colonel Hale points out: 'as a warning, as a really profitable example of thoroughly bad leading and bad staff work, the movements of the 18th are worthy of consideration in detail.'[31] Tresckow's division, marching west from Dreux to Brezolles, got only as far as Laons, about five miles short of his objective, 'as the roar of artillery resounding from the south had caused it to halt for a considerable time and send out reconnoitring detachments.'[32] Wittich, heading from Châteauneuf to La Loupe, also failed to reach his destination, being repeatedly held up by stubborn resistance at various points. First of all he found parties of enemy troops obstructing his departure from the area around Châteauneuf, and the 44th Brigade had to move north to deal with them; in the time taken to clear these away, the Bavarians, who were to follow Wittich when they had moved through Châteauneuf came up to the rear of the 22nd Division. The Grand Duke refused to allow Wittich to halt to let the Bavarians pass across his division, with the result that when the Bavarians arrived they were obliged to pass through the 22nd Division, part of which, the 42nd Brigade, was after all obliged to stop and was unable to get beyond Châteauneuf. Meanwhile the most advanced unit of the division, the 43rd Brigade, had got no more than five miles out of the town towards La Loupe, having run into fierce resistance at Digny. Wittich applied for support from Rudolph von der Tann's 4th Bavarian Brigade, which set off at once to Digny. During the Bavarians' march

> darkness had set in and was rendered more intense by the thick fog, which had lain over the country ever since the morning; not a shot could be heard from Digny; all was quiet, and it appeared probable that the Prussians had meanwhile occupied the village, but, as soon as the column had reached the first houses of Digny, it was received with several volleys. The village was still in the hands of the enemy.[33]

In the prevailing conditions von der Tann wisely forbore to launch a night attack. Farther south, the 4th Cavalry Division, advancing towards Illiers and Bonneval, was held up at Illiers and obliged to withdraw for the night to a position about six miles south west of Chartres.

The Detachment's troubles were not yet over. Many of the troops

> had been on the march since the morning, and even during the frequent halts had obtained no real rest, and were now obliged to seek their cantonments amid the darkness, which owing to the mist, had set in at 4pm, only to find them either occupied by the enemy or in flames, and were obliged to drive the enemy out of their quarters or to bivouack in the cold without fires. Dropping shots were heard till late at night in the neighbouring woods, and created a certain feeling of insecurity, which compelled some of the troops to place outposts even on every side.[34]

Not unreasonably, the Grand Duke ordered that November 19 should be a rest day, to enable the Detachment to disentangle itself. Krenski, announcing this in a general order, put the best face on it that he could;

> In today's advance the army encountered opposition at almost all points. This, and more especially the victorious action in which Wittich's Division was engaged, have enabled us to accomplish our object of ascertaining the strength and position of the enemy. It appears that our enemy belongs to the Army of the West (General Fiereck) and is based upon Le Mans.[35]

The order was, to say the least, thoroughly disingenuous; the Detachment was still none the wiser about the enemy it was pursuing or even the direction it was taking.

Still, there were some indications on November 19 that it was to the south west that the Detachment should march. 'The reports received during the day pointed conclusively to a general withdrawal in that direction by the enemy, and also to a strong occupation of Nogent Le Rotrou,' and it was towards that town that the Detachment moved on November 20.[36] The 17th Division accordingly marched to Senonches, and the 22nd Division to La Loupe. The two Bavarian divisions had been ordered to concentrate at Ardelles and Favières, south and southwest of Châteauneuf; however, at 8.00am, while von der Tann was meeting Krenski and the Grand Duke at the Detachment's headquarters at Digny, news came from the 4th Cavalry Division that the French were advancing from Bonneval and Illiers towards Chartres. Accordingly the I Bavarian Corps was ordered to move in a more southerly direction, the 1st Division getting as far as the village of Champrond en Gatine, which it found strongly held by the French, and the 2nd Division to Conville. The 6th Cavalry Division bivouacked at St Denis des Puits. Once again, night had fallen before the corps could reach all its objectives; as their historian noted, the Bavarians were still further handicapped by the fact 'that the movements of the Detachment had led them into territory not covered by the maps already issued' and 'the rapidity with which the war was carried on rendered it impossible to keep up a regular supply of the necessary maps. The maps often arrived after we had marched into another "sheet".'[37]

The Detachment was now operating in country which made it even more difficult to gain a clear idea of the strength and intentions of the enemy, and hampered the rapid deployment of troops against them when they were located. The Perche is noted for 'irregular but continuous chains of hills, with more or less steep inclines, and often with precipitous ravines at the base, and ... was covered with thick woods and crossed by a number of small brooks, both of which formed natural obstacles, well fitted for an obstinate resistance.'[38] Convincing evidence that the enemy intended to make a serious stand at Nogent Le Rotrou came when Wittich's 22nd Division ran into stiff resistance on the heights of Le Colombier and around the Bretoncelles railway station, which was finally broken at about 1.00pm: 'the retreat of the adversary, which took place in a west and southwest direction towards the L'Huisne Valley, degenerated shortly into a disorderly flight under the fire of the German artillery.'[39] To the rear of the 22nd Division, Tresckow's 17th Division also encountered opposition in La Madeleine before driving the French back in a westerly direction.

The Bavarians meanwhile were moving towards Nogent Le Rotrou from the east. Stephan, with the 1st Division, met the enemy east of La Fourche in what appeared to be a strong position. It was, however, overlooked by a hill some two miles east, on which Stephan posted the divisional artillery, which commenced a steady bombardment of the French positions, before Dietl's 1st Brigade launched an outflanking attack on La Fourche from the west and north. By 4pm the French were in retreat to the south and west. Meanwhile the 2nd Division had made a long march from Courville to Thiron Gardais in front of which brief resistance was offered before its defenders fell back towards Nogent le Rotrou.

The events of November 21 appeared to confirm that the French indeed intended to fight for Nogent le Rotrou; they had put up resistance all along the wide front – some thirty six miles – over which the Detachment had been advancing, and it seemed to the Grand Duke 'probable that we had already come into collision with a considerable part of the Army of the Loire, the position of which it was our task to reconnoitre.'[40] For the next day, therefore, it was decided to attack Nogent le Rotrou from both the west and east sides. Wittich was to move around and attack from the right back of the Huisne, while von der Tann moved directly from the east. Tresckow was held back in reserve at Regmalard.

However, during November 21 the Grand Duke had received a telegram from Moltke reporting the occupation of Toury by the Second Army, and that the French were in position along a front of thirty five miles between Orgères and Beaune la Rolande; the 4th Cavalry Division was ordered directly to make contact with the Second Army, and reconnoitre the Chartres-Chateaudun road. The Grand Duke was severely criticised by Hönig for not drawing the conclusion from the orders sent to the 4th Cavalry division that a different view was now taken of the situation, and that Moltke's telegram 'was a weighty and clear strategical indication, and had been sent by wire in order that the Detachment might, by proper preparations, be ready for other possibilities that might occur.'[41] Hönig conceded that in order to recognise the somewhat enigmatic indication that Moltke's telegram contained, 'the penetration and intuition of a leader far seeing and of clear judgement were necessary.' The Grand Duke and Krenski, evidently lacking these qualities, were quite unaffected by it. At noon next day therefore, the Detachment advanced upon its prey in Nogent le Rotrou only to find that during the night the bird had flown. 'So it had happened that the Grand Duke had to suffer a second time the mortification of dealing a blow en l'air, even less hurtful to the enemy than he had delivered at Dreux.'[42] The direction taken by the retreating French appeared to be towards Le Mans, and in ordering his troops to press on beyond Nogent le Rotrou, the Grand Duke had it in mind that it might be at Le Mans, thirty five miles further on, that the decisive battle would be fought. By nightfall on November 22 the leading Bavarian unit, the 3rd Brigade, had reached La Ferté Bernard, having marched some thirty miles during the day. Its entrance into the town was briefly contested by several hundred Gardes Nationales and franc tireurs, the majority of whom appeared to be drunk. Certainly it must have appeared to the Grand Duke that he was on the right lines in aiming for Le Mans, since at 7.00am on November 22 a letter had come from Frederick Charles to the effect that he expected to attack the enemy in his front in four or five days, and suggesting that the Detachment should cooperate by advancing through Le Mans on Tours. With evident satisfaction the Grand Duke responded by telegram: 'Cooperation in the direction of Le Mans, with the projected further advance on Tours, already prepared for by my departure from the Paris-Orleans road. Advance today for concentrated attack on Nogent Le Rotrou.'[43]

However Blumenthal, to whose army the Detachment reported, had something else to suggest, writing a most surprisingly tentative letter to the Grand Duke which the latter also received on November 22. Blumenthal explained that he had not written previously, as 'our information is so indefinite, that I have always been afraid of saying something that was incorrect. And even now things are so little clear, that I must restrict my remarks to the following matters.' And after an inaccurate survey of Frederick Charles' position he went on that in view of the possible strength of the enemy in the Detachment's front, 'it would be desirable not to advance too quickly on Le Mans, but rather to defer the attack for a few days, till you know with certainty about the advance of Prince Frederick Charles.'[44] The diffidence of this advice was such that it exerted no restraint at all on the Grand Duke's determination to pursue his elusive quarry; and the orders from November 23 which he issued to the Detachment were to push all units forward towards Le Mans. Tresckow was to march on St Cosme, Wittich was now to form the right flank and to concentrate at Belleve, and von der Tann to concentrate the whole of his corps around La Ferté Bernard. The 6th Cavalry Division was to move south on Vibraye, while the 4th Cavalry Division was to operate against the Chateaudun-Tours railway line. It might scarcely exist as a fighting force; but the 'Army of the West' had done a remarkably good job in luring the Detachment off the board during the crucial time of preparation by the Army of the Loire for its next move.

10

Stosch

While the Detachment had been engaged in its energetic tour of first the Beauce and then the Perche country, the Second Army had been continuing its movement westward. It provided Frederick Charles with an opportunity to see for himself the nature of the campaign on which his army was to embark, which had already been marked by a significant change in the attitude of the civilian population. Riding towards Pithiviers on November 20, where his headquarters was to be established, he was forcibly struck both by this and by the nature of the countryside, which would give the French a major advantage.

> During the ride, the farms and villages were found deserted; in the fields bodies of armed men were visible; bullets fell all around irregularly; prisoners, some of them priests with gloomy faces, came before the Prince; the roads were in many places cut through and destroyed, the sign posts carried away; and the bells of the churches signalled from church tower to church tower the march of the invaders. By this gloomy November picture the Prince was so deeply impressed that he repeatedly made remarks to those around him about the rising of the Spanish nation against Napoleon 1.[1]

All the signs were that a critical point in the second phase of the war was about to be reached; 'numerous watch-fires at Artenay, Creuzy and Chevilly revealed more particularly the presence of larger bodies of troops on the road from Orleans to Paris.'[2] On the evening of November 20 the Second Army reported to Moltke its news that the Army of the Loire was concentrated in its front. 'Headquarters and III Army Corps have arrived here; the advanced parties drove the enemy today out of Nancray and Beaune la Rolande. No news of the X Army Corps since the 17th, but no ground for anxiety; its arrival at Montargis is awaited. Our impression is that after the fight at Coulmiers none of the enemy moved away to the North West.'[3]

Voigts-Rhetz's X Corps had in fact been continuing to encounter difficulties in its westward march, and there had been a lengthy delay in the orders that he should be at Montargis by November 20 actually reaching him. The officer sent by Stiehle with these orders, who had an escort of infantry carried in carts, only got to Voigts-Rhetz after brushes with a number of groups of franc tireurs who had to be cleared out of his way by detachments of the III Corps.[4] The leading troops of the X Corps finally reached Montargis on November 21.

Meanwhile Alvensleben's III Corps, in position at Pithiviers and Boynes, had been pushing forward outposts towards the Forest of Orleans, while Manstein, with the IX Corps, remained at Angerville. The intelligence reaching the Second Army made it clear that it would be imprudent to make any forward move until all three corps were concentrated, and probably not before November 26. Stiehle set out his concerns in a letter to Moltke of November 21. 'From every place even not occupied by troops, fire opens on the approach of our troops. If we send strong

Crown Prince Frederick William, commander of the German Third Army (Rousset/*Histoire*)

detachments the enemy falls back to the next place and repeats the same game. This is facilitated by the close cultivation.' He went on to identify the principal French forces as being the 16th Corps south of Artenay and the 15th Corps at St Lyé, adding that 'for the present, in view of the presumable strength of the enemy, it would be unwise, before the X Army Corps has joined the Second Army, to appeal to a decision of arms, which will influence the whole course of affairs in France.' When the army was ready to attack, the object would be 'to drive the enemy towards Tours,' which would fit nicely with the advance proposed for the Grand Duke.[5] It was with this intention in mind that Frederick Charles had suggested to the Grand Duke that he should move on Le Mans with a view to threatening Tours, and in this way compel the French to detach troops from the forces facing the Second Army, as well as preparing the way for a concentric advance on Tours. In readiness for the advance on Orleans, the right wing of the Second Army was on November 22 shifted westwards, Manstein occupying a position on the Toury-Allaines road, covered in his front by the 2nd Cavalry Division; meanwhile the 6th Division moved to Bazoches les Gallerandes and the 5th Division was strung out between Pithiviers and Boynes. Alvensleben's Corps was covered by the 1st Cavalry Division.

During the day Voigts-Rhetz closed up on Montargis. Patrols continued to report enemy activity over a wide area. When, on the following day, Voigts-Rhetz pushed forward to Beaune la Rolande, his cavalry reported that Bellegarde, six miles to the south, was strongly held by French infantry. Statements by civilians suggested that there were large enemy forces at Lorris, and that as many as 80,000 men were marching from Gien towards Montargis. On the other hand, reconnaissance pushed forward on the Second Army's right wing suggested that there were substantial movements of French troops across their front westwards.

Stiehle's letter of November 21 reinforced the evidence reaching Moltke, which was getting stronger by the hour, that the crisis of the Orleans campaign was approaching. A further strong pointer to the likelihood that the French were themselves planning a big push came with a report from Werder in the south east that 'the Corps of General Michel (two divisions) left Autun on 16 and 17 November by forty trains in a westerly direction.'[6] This reached Moltke on November 22, and that evening he made up his mind; the Grand Duke's march must be arrested immediately and his line of advance switched back in a south easterly direction to cooperate directly with the Second Army. Moltke went to see the King; and at 8.45pm Blumenthal received the necessary orders.

> As we have not succeeded at Nogent le Rotrou in inflicting a decisive defeat on the French Army of the West, the pursuit in the direction of Le Mans will only be carried out for the moment by cavalry reinforced by weak detachments of infantry, and His Majesty wishes that the Grand Duke, with the rest of his army be put immediately en route towards the Loire. The Detachment must be able to reach Beaugency or Blois by November 26 or a little after.[7]

A copy of this went next day to Stiehle, to whom Moltke had already conveyed a warning about the possible arrival in his front of Michel's corps. Moltke was by now in no doubt of the extent of the threat posed by the Army of the Loire to the Second Army. But if it was a threat, it was also an opportunity. There clearly existed a splendid chance to strike a decisive blow at the resurgent French armies, which appeared to be concentrating around Orleans, and a movement by the Detachment towards the Loire between Beaugency and Blois would enable the Germans to fall on d'Aurelle's left flank. If the Army of the Loire could be driven over the river, it might well be possible to break it up altogether. Blumenthal at once saw the point, commenting on Moltke's orders that it was 'a most excellent move, and will effect a junction with Prince Frederick Charles on the 26th about Orleans. A victory here will be certain, and the French will be not only cut off from a retreat on Tours, but also from a junction with the troops at Le Mans.'[8] Forwarding the order to Krenski, he stressed the importance of capturing intact one of the bridges over the Loire. The unimaginative Frederick Charles, however, had his eyes fixed solely on the capture of Orleans, after which he planned only to push the Army of the Loire towards Tours.

As he entered one of the most complex and difficult periods of his entire career, Moltke found time to write on November 23 to his brother Adolph reflecting on the situation.

> When one is compelled to follow out but one idea day and night for months, it becomes almost a torture, and yet it is difficult to tear one's mind away from it. After Sedan and Metz, it appeared, no doubt, in Berlin as if all was at an end. We have had since, however, to pass through a most anxious time … the only way, however, to bring about a final decision now is by the exercise of unmerciful strictness … Nobody could wish for peace more heartily than I do, but

General von Wittich (Pflugk-Harttung)

> never could I bring myself to vote for a peace which did not secure to Germany the existence which she has obtained through such great sacrifices.[9]

But if Moltke was beginning to feel the strain, it did not show to those around him. That day, the Crown Prince graphically recorded the scene at Royal Headquarters.

> We are at a crisis of the most exciting and interesting strategical combinations. Day by day Count Moltke expounds the situation of affairs with the utmost clearness, nay, to some extent with overmuch sobriety; he has always thought out and calculated everything and invariably hits the nail on the head. War Minister von Roon, who has an asthmatic cough, spits copiously, and is fond of shrugging his shoulders if any piece of news sounds strange; this sort of pantomime, joined to the Olympian calm and confidence that Lieutenant General von Podbielski shows under all circumstances, often makes more impression on the King's now highly nervous temperament than Count Moltke's admirable clarity.[10]

On November 24 the Second Army carried out a series of reconnaissances to gather some reliable intelligence as to the strength and dispositions of the Army of the Loire. One of these was launched by the III Corps, early in the morning and was led by Colonel von Flatow.

This was to be a reconnaissance in force, involving four battalions, two squadrons and two batteries advancing through Teillay St Benoit southwards towards the Forest of Orleans. Neither Alvensleben nor his Chief of Staff, Colonel von Voigts-Rhetz approved of the operation, which Stiehle none the less persuaded Frederick Charles should be carried out. Flatow, advancing over rain sodden ground, at first entered St Germain, which he found had been abandoned by the French, and then drove back detachments of French infantry into Neuville aux Bois. Here, however, there were strong French reinforcements, and in spite of an advance under cover of heavy artillery fire that got to within one hundred yards of the village, no further progress could be made. Flatow broke off the action and fell back to his original positions about noon, having sustained 171 casualties and failed to take a single prisoner. Frederick Charles, when the failure of the operation was reported to him, was far from pleased with Stiehle, whose relationship with the staff of the III Corps was also not improved by the debâcle. Further west, advancing down the main Paris-Orleans road, the IX Corps pushed forward the 11th Regiment, with two batteries of horse artillery and the 3rd Cavalry Brigade in support, The force was led by Colonel von Falkenhausen, and he briefly occupied first Assas and then Ártenay, and then sent cavalry forward as far as La Croix Briquet before falling back in the face of strong forces advancing from Chevilly. Nothing much, therefore had been achieved by this reconnaissance either. Blumenthal on learning of these setbacks, was derisive, observing that Frederick Charles 'cannot dispense with that absurd reconnoitring-in-force, a form of tactics whereby the Austrians always spoil their battles. He forgets that one exposes one's position just as much as one uncloaks that of the enemy.'[11]

On the left, however, in the front of the X Corps, some rather more successful operations had been carried out, which taken together were in due course to provide the chief of staff of the corps, the astute Colonel von Caprivi, with enormously valuable information. The three reconnaissance forces sent forward in the direction of the Forest of Orleans involved a total of two battalions and two squadrons. Two of the three returned empty handed, having encountered strong enemy forces, and having taken no prisoners. On the other hand, the third, reconnoitring towards Boiscommun under the command of Major von Schöler, was more fortunate. The force was accompanied by Captain Seebeck, from Caprivi's staff, who emphasised the vital necessity of taking prisoners. As it approached Boiscommun, the leading cavalry unit encountered and drove back into the village some dismounted French lancers. Following up the enemy, the German cavalry rode into an ambush, from which they extricated themselves with some difficulty. However, at the south end of the village, the commander of the French Lancers, Colonel de Brasserie, was just entering with the main body of his regiment. His leading squadron rode without orders in pursuit of the retreating German cavalry; de Brasserie went after them to recall them; his horse bolted, and as he came up with his advancing troops, they ran into the main body of the German cavalry coming south. In the ensuing engagement, the French were driven back, leaving de Brasserie, who had been wounded, a prisoner. Interrogated, he said he was from Polignac's Corps, and had come from Besancon, which was only partly true; Polignac was a divisional commander in the 20th Corps, formerly commanded by Michel but now under Crouzat. Seebeck duly reported all this to Caprivi, who thus gained some valuable intelligence as to the forces in his front.[12]

During November 24, while these reconnaissances were being undertaken, that part of the X Corps which was still at Montargis moved to join the rest of the Corps at Beaune la Rolande.

The 37th Infantry Brigade, marching during the morning along the road to Ladon, met strong detachments of French troops which necessitated first two, and then two more battalions deploying into line before the enemy could be cleared out of the way. When the brigade moved on Ladon, the French troops there fell back to Bellegarde. The brigade set off again, only to be interrupted once again its march by the sound of heavy gunfire from Maizières. Here, the 39th Brigade had also encountered stiff resistance, which was only overcome when artillery came up to join the lead battalions. Finally, both brigades were able to make their way to Beaune la Rolande and thus complete the concentration there of the X Corps.

During the fighting near Ladon, a trumpeter of the 9th Dragoons had picked up a pocket book belonging to a Captain Ogilvy, a Englishman serving with the French, who was killed there. It contained three papers. One was an order for the march on November 24 of an unidentified army corps. Another was a letter of introduction from Gambetta, describing Captain Ogilvy as attached to the staff of the 18th Corps, but temporarily detached from it, and referring to Gien as 'the key of our position on the Loire' which was 'safe in the brave hands of General Crouzat.' The third was an order of battle of an army corps, which would have been very valuable if it had had a heading to it.[13] All this information was, naturally, passed to the headquarters of the Second Army, where the reference to Gien made a considerable impression. It seemed to indicate clearly an intention on the part of d'Aurelle to advance with the right wing of his army, and the Second Army orders for November 25 were issued with the expectation that the army would have to meet an attack from this direction. The responsibility for covering the left flank of the army was naturally assigned to Voigts- Rhetz, whose troops were put on alert for an offensive that for the moment did not materialise.

At Versailles, meanwhile, the sense of impending crisis on the Loire front had deepened. Brooding on this, the King decided to despatch an emissary of his own to the headquarters of the Second Army, to enable him to find out for himself exactly what was going on. Sending for Alfred von Waldersee, his aide de camp, on November 25 he told him: 'We are at a critical moment of the campaign. The French Army of the Loire has gradually become greatly strengthened. I saw that coming, but these gentlemen always know everything better than I and have been declaring that the war is at an end.' Waldersee noted in his diary that 'King William is referring principally to General Podbielski, who annoyed him by habitual over confidence. As the King's tendency is towards pessimism it is a good thing that there should be someone to take the opposite point of view.' Looking very much on the black side, the King went on to review the situation, remarking that if Frederick Charles was beaten, the investment of Paris must be abandoned and the campaign would be lost. He gave Waldersee a letter to the Prince setting out his views, and told Waldersee to pass on to him that in his hands lay the fate of the campaign, but that he had 'the fullest confidence in his leading and war-experience.' Instructing Waldersee to report to him every day, the King shook his hand, saying 'Don't be foolhardy; I want you to come back unhurt. You have rendered me excellent services and I want to make much more use of you.'[14]On his way to

Pithiviers, Waldersee reflected that Frederick Charles might well be far from pleased to see him, and resolved to be especially tactful. After he arrived on November 26, and Frederick Charles had read the King's letter 'very slowly,' Waldersee took an early opportunity to flatter the Prince by paying some compliments about his gifts as an army leader-recording sardonically that he 'knew that one could safely go to great lengths in this kind of thing'-and then mendaciously assured him that in his reports to the King he would write nothing but what the Prince wished. For his part Frederick Charles complained bitterly to Waldersee about the directions he was receiving from Versailles.

During November 25 there had been little military activity in the front of the Second Army, but at the headquarters of the X Corps Caprivi had had a stroke of luck. Colonel de Brasserie, the wounded prisoner who had been captured at Boiscommun, wrote a letter to his wife, in which he had stated that his unit was part of the 20th corps under Crouzat. Read by the German censors, the letter gave Caprivi the information he needed about the identity of one at least of the French corps opposed to him, and also made sense of the order of battle found in Captain Ogilvy's pocket book. It was Caprivi's view that there was more than one French Corps on the front of the X Corps, and he reported this to Stiehle at Pithiviers. There, the examination of a number of French prisoners taken at Ladon appeared to confirm this, indicating that both the 18th and 20th Corps were opposite the German left; but Frederick Charles was unconvinced, still believing that Voigts-Rhetz faced only one corps.

The Detachment, meanwhile, had begun its movement southeastwards to the right of the Second Army. The order to march on Beaugency which had been received at 11.00am on November 23 had come too late to affect the march arrangements for that day, but next day the widely spread units of the Detachment wearily got into position to change direction. The Grand Duke, on receiving the order to move to Beaugency, had asked to be allowed November 24 as a rest day, but this was firmly denied by Blumenthal, acting on Moltke's instructions. He noted in his diary that 'this cannot be dreamt of; every effort must be made to press forward, or the enemy will escape us, a contingency of which there is every possibility.'[15] All the Detachment's commanders had supported the request for a day's rest for their men.

> The troops, and more especially the infantry, were much fatigued by the last marches of from 21 to 24 English miles daily, in continuous rain, along bad roads and with irregular supplies. The troops frequently did not reach their quarters before nightfall, and were obliged to start again before daylight. Their equipment suffered considerably under these circumstances.[16]

On November 25 the Detachment continued its march, and by nightfall the I Bavarian Corps had reached the area Mondoubleau-Savigny-St Calais. Behind it, the 17th Division was on the road between Berfoy and Vibraye while the 22nd Division was still further to the rear at Authon. The 6th Cavalry Division covered the front of the Bavarians at Epuisay, while the 4th Cavalry Division covered the flank at La Bazoche Gouet patrolling towards Bonneval and Châteaudun. At Versailles, the progress of the Detachment was regarded with a good deal of dissatisfaction. Moltke emphatically shared Blumenthal's view that 'the Grand Duke unfortunately marches very slowly, and Prince Frederick Charles will have to put off his attack until the 28th or 29th. That this pretty stroke is being carried out so haltingly is sad, but we must wait.'[17]

Blumenthal sent off at 9.55am a hurry up telegram: 'It is of the utmost importance that the Detachment should move forward.'[18] But mere exhortation seemed insufficient. To Moltke it appeared that perhaps one way to speed up the Detachment's movements might be to change its reporting structure and to place it under the orders of the Second Army, which was out in the field and with which the Grand Duke was intended to cooperate, rather than the Third Army, the headquarters of which were at Versailles, and which was principally concerned with the investment of Paris. Accordingly, a telegram went off at 1.10pm to the Grand Duke, putting the Detachment under the orders of Frederick Charles until further notice. Moltke added a further reminder: 'the Detachment will direct itself at once by forced marches to Beaugency; its cavalry, supported by detachments of infantry, will observe the roads from Tours and Le Mans to Paris; its march tables will be sent to Pithiviers and to Royal Headquarters.'[19] The instruction that it was still to Beaugency that the Detachment must direct its march was confirmed in the letter which Moltke wrote that afternoon to the Grand Duke and which he copied to both the Second and Third Army headquarters. During the day, Moltke also raised the possibility that someone reliable might have to be sent to supersede Krenski as the Grand Duke's Chief of Staff; the discussions at Royal Headquarters pointed to either Podbielski or Stosch as being the most suitable. It was an opportunity that Stosch was determined not to miss. Walking back to his quarters with Verdy that afternoon, Stosch said to him: 'I would be ready to assume this difficult post, and, if the conversation returns to it, you can mention me as a candidate.'[20]

The movement of the Detachment's combat troops on November 25 had in fact been largely uneventful, but unexpectedly the baggage train and ammunition columns marching south from Authon and Brou had come under attack. This action appeared to have been mounted by troops advancing from Bonneval to Brou and although the escort with the help of the 4th Cavalry Division succeeded in rescuing the convoy, the French remained in Brou. Reports reaching the Grand Duke's headquarters suggested that the French had at least eight battalions there, which meant a most serious threat to the flank and rear of the Detachment. It was stretched over thirty six miles, from its advanced guard just south of Sarigny to its rear which was still around Nogent le Rotrou, and although the possibility of a threat to its right from Le Mans had been taken into account, the arrival of a strong French force on its left rear came as a complete surprise.

This should not have been the case. The Grand Duke had known since November 23 of a French force at Châteaudun although he did nothing about reporting this to Versailles.[21]

It seemed clear to the Grand Duke that this French advance against his line of communications required immediate action to retake Brou, and the orders for November 26 involved the line of march of the Detachment being swung round ninety degrees, to the north east. His intention was to concentrate the Detachment in the position Brou-La Bazoche Gouet-Arville, but his orders required more of his troops than was reasonable. Von der Tann was ordered to concentrate his corps at Arville by 10am, which as the Bavarian official historian pointed out was absolutely

General von Stosch (author's collection)

impossible, since only the 2nd Division in Mondoubleau could reach the rendezvous by the appointed time.[22] Nonetheless, the various units of the Detachment marched off during November 26 towards their new positions until, at 3pm, news came that the enemy against which they were marching appeared to have vanished. General de Sonis, whose 17th Corps had launched the advance on Brou, had been alarmed by reports that the Germans were closing in on him, and had retired precipitately during the morning of November 26 to Châteaudun. When the Germans re-entered Brou, the information that they received suggested that some 14,000 French troops had been there.[23] Thus the Detachment and the 17th Corps had each momentarily been greatly alarmed by a threat to their communications, and each had reacted defensively to that threat. If the Grand Duke had been bolder, and had pushed on to the south east, he might have left de Sonis very much exposed, while avoiding the delay caused by his change of direction; on the other hand if de Sonis had not lost his nerve, he might have imposed still further loss of time on the Detachment.

As it was, however, Moltke's discontent with the leadership of the Detachment had reached a point where he felt the need to take decisive action. On the morning of November 26, being according to Blumenthal 'very much vexed' with the dilatory proceedings of the Grand Duke, he learned from Verdy of Stosch's willingness to go down to the Loire. He asked Roon, as Stosch's superior, for his agreement which, while saying that Stosch could not be spared for very long, the War Minister readily gave. Moltke went off to the King and obtained his immediate approval; and Stosch set off the same day to take up his duties.[24]

Moltke's decision to appoint Stosch demonstrated his determination to get a firm grip on the situation. He

> knew that he had now on the Loire two obstinate personalities, over whom he had voluntarily given up control. Stosch was an excellent soldier, a large-minded man, but in view of the situation he was a good deal more. Owing to his high position on the supreme staff of the German forces, and his close personal connection with Moltke, the chief staff officer of those forces, he was, on the Loire, little less than Moltke present by proxy. The Grand Duke must now be aware that if he rebelled against his new Chief Staff Officer he would be rebelling against Moltke, while the Prince knew similarly, that ... there was present only a few miles away from him, Moltke's personal representative endeavouring to hold him in check.[25]

The order announcing Stosch's appointment went off at once to the Grand Duke, who cannot have received it with pleasure. It was decidedly unusual for an army commander not to have a say in the choice of his Chief of Staff, and this was a rule particularly followed in the case of royal personages. The blow to his pride must have been considerable. Stosch himself arrived at the Detachment's headquarters on November 27, handing the Grand Duke his letter of appointment and saying that he 'would remain until a military decision took place.' The Grand Duke's reception of him was frosty in the extreme, and Stosch was under no illusion as to the delicate task which lay ahead of him.[26] On his way, Stosch had encountered units of the 4th Cavalry Division and of the 22nd Division to the north of Bonneval, and saw for himself the condition of the Detachment. The reality was very different from the position as it was understood at Versailles. 'The whole Detachment, including its staff, was in a state of moral depression. As the officers he met told him, this depression was not due to the mere physical exertions ... these trials and discomforts would not have told on the men if only there had been some tangible result, one battle, one real encounter.'[27] When he reached headquarters, he found that the staff work was in a thoroughly unsatisfactory state; 'there was no Field Bureau, the records were in disorder, précis of information received were not forth coming, there was no proper subdivision and distribution of staff duties.'[28] All of these problems owed much, no doubt, to the fact that the Detachment had been hurriedly assembled and sent off on its mission without the advantage of any permanent or established staff. Stosch at once set about the reform of the staff and its methods of operations.

During November 26 the Second Army had issued orders to the Detachment which confirmed the instructions previously given that only the right wing of the Detachment was to make for Beaugency, while the left headed for Janville to effect the junction with the Second Army. So far as the Grand Duke could tell, the enemy were on the Loir between Bonneval and Châteaudun, and the orders he issued for November 27 were based on this. During the day the Bavarians in particular, marching in one column down poor cross country roads, made only slow progress; but news soon came in that de Sonis had retreated. In fact, in moving not towards Orleans but due south towards the Forest of Marchenoir his inexperienced troops had become seriously disorganised in the face of brief encounters with the leading German cavalry units, and the 17th Corps accordingly offered no threat to the continued advance of the Detachment. By nightfall on November 27 the

Bavarians were on the Loir between Marboué and Châteaudun, while the 17th Division was to the north at St Maunie and the 22nd Division in Bonneval. Having seen the condition of his troops, Stosch was in no doubt of the need for a rest day on November 28, and his request for this was readily granted, although the 4th Bavarian Brigade in Châteaudun was unable to take advantage of it, being considerably harassed by French cavalry patrols.

The Second Army, meanwhile, had continued to seek intelligence as to the strength and intentions of its adversary. The views held at the headquarters of the Second Army by no means accorded with Moltke's strategic intention. Stiehle, writing to Moltke on November 26, displayed no aggressive intentions, explaining that any advance must await the arrival of the Detachment. He also offered a summary of the intelligence reports which had been received, although still not accepting Caprivi's view as to the strength of the French left; the information he gave was extremely wide of the mark. Frederick Charles, meanwhile, wrote privately to the King in reply to the letter which Waldersee had brought. Complaining about his lack of reliable information about the situation of the French main body, he added: 'I hope I shall know more about the enemy when the Grand Duke arrives, whom, under the existing circumstances, I must employ tactically, not strategically, against the Army of the Loire.'[29] It seemed to Frederick Charles that the enemy wanted him to attack. Furthermore, the options open to him to do so were limited by the duty to cover the road to Paris, and in any case the French had had the chance to prepare the ground in front of Orleans for defence. It was a very pessimistic letter that can have done little to cheer up the King; it was scant comfort that Frederick Charles promised to do his 'best for both, to hold the enemy as far from Paris as possible, or to wrest Orleans from him.'

Meanwhile the expected forward movement against the X Corps did not occur, and apart from clashes between patrols there was little activity along the entire front of the army. On the morning of November 27 the 35th Infantry Brigade and the 3rd Cavalry Brigade, supported by four batteries, moved forward from Allaines towards Orgères and Loigny, in readiness for the junction with the Detachment. No opposition was encountered, and patrols found that the French pickets were pulling back behind the Conie. On the other hand, at the eastern end of the Second Army's front there were reports that some 25,000 troops were encamped south of Montargis, while there was activity beyond the Orleans Canal. These movements appeared to confirm the likelihood of a French advance directed towards Fontainebleau, and the 5th Division was brought up from Pithiviers to Boynes and Barville to support the X Corps; while the orders to the Detachment were, after its rest day on November 28, now to aim to reach the Orleans-Paris road at Toury with its leading units.[30] This marked the complete abandonment by Frederick Charles of any concentric advance against the Army of the Loire, as had been Moltke's intention in directing the Detachment on Beaugency.

Ever since the French victory at Coulmiers, the commander of the Army of the Loire had been facing considerably stronger pressure for swift action than had his opponents. D'Aurelle had not been particularly enthusiastic about the decision to make Orleans into a fortified camp as a base for further operations. But having accepted this he was still determined that the plans for the future operations of the Army should be based on its actual military capability. To Gambetta and Freycinet, d'Aurelle's passive attitude was wholly unacceptable. The clock was ticking loudly for the relief of Paris, and the rapid assembly of very substantial forces on the Loire demanded immediate action. Freycinet wrote to d'Aurelle on November 19 to express the Delegation's position. He ordered d'Aurelle to study with his generals the best line of operations for his army, which he estimated to be 250,000 strong. 'We cannot remain forever at Orleans. Paris is hungry and calls on us. Study, therefore, the line of march to be taken to enable us to join hands with Trochu, who will march to meet us with 150,000 men.'[31] D'Aurelle's response, next day, was to say that before planning to link up with Trochu, he must be kept informed as to the latter's intentions. Gambetta at once responded to reiterate that d'Aurelle had 250,000 men; he must plan at once an operation that had Paris as its objective, and he should put the best troops on the flank. D'Aurelle's only reply, on November 23, was a vague reassurance as to his absolute devotion to the cause.

Frustrated at d'Aurelle's apparent unwillingness to do anything positive, Freycinet began to prepare his own scheme. As far as the Delegation knew, Trochu's sortie was planned for November 26 so there was very little time. In view of the probable move by Trochu towards Melun, it was decided to make Fontainebleau the objective for the Army of the Loire, with the advance being directed on Pithiviers in the first instance. On November 22 Freycinet sent the necessary orders for d'Aurelle to pass on to his corps commanders, which he did, while raising a protest to Freycinet. The latter responded at once, saying that

> if you brought me a better plan than mine, or even any plan at all, I would give up mine and revoke my orders. But during the twelve days you have been at Orleans, you have not, in spite of repeated invitations from M. Gambetta and myself proposed any kind of plan ... We must do something and this means leaving Orleans. As M. Gambetta and I have explained to you, Paris is hungry and wants to be helped.[32]

With this, Freycinet effectively took control of the Army of the Loire, which now prepared to move on his orders.

Although it was not quite as large as Freycinet had claimed in his correspondence, it had nevertheless grown to an impressive strength, comprising over 200,000 men organised in six corps, five of which were more or less complete and one, the 21st Corps, still incomplete; this was the one time Army of the West and was forming around Le Mans. As combat formations, much the best were the 15th and 16th Corps, the latter being led by the able and energetic Gereral Chanzy. The army was in position around the fortified camp of Orleans, and its right wing consisted, as Caprivi had divined, of two corps. These were the 20th Corps under Crouzat, lately arrived from the eastern theatre and now based at Gien, and the 18th Corps, partly at Gien and for a while partly at Nevers, which was presently led by its Chief of Staff, General Billot, while waiting for Bourbaki to arrive and take up the command. In the centre, to the east of the Paris-Orleans road, was the 30,000 strong 1st Division of the 15th Corps (des Pallières); its other two divisions were west of the road. To the left of these was Chanzy's 16th Corps, which continued the French line to the Conie. Finally, apart from the 21st Corps at Le Mans, on the extreme left of the line was de Sonis, with the 17th Corps, which had

Charles-Louis de Freycinet (Rousset/*Histoire*)

already demonstrated that its dashing commander could not make up for its lack of training and combat experience.

The orders issued by Freycinet, against which d'Aurelle had protested, had called for an advance by des Pallières on Chilleurs aux Bois on November 23, moving next day on Pithiviers. In the face of d'Aurelle's protests, the plan was modified, and des Pallières moved only as far as Chilleurs aux Bois, while Crouzat moved up to Boiscommun and Bellegarde. It was these moves which had led to the contacts at Ladon and Maizieres on November 24; after these, the French remained in the positions they had taken up. Meanwhile the 18th Corps, for the moment placed under the orders of Crouzat, had moved up to Ladon and Montargis. Crouzat's instructions were to move forward with his two Corps on November 28 to Pithiviers, supported as far as was necessary by the 15th Corps. He chose as his lines of attack Maizières and Juranville for the 18th Corps, and Boiscommun and Montbarois for the 20th Corps; these intentions meant that his attack would fall on Voigts-Rhetz as, for some days, had been expected.[33] The decisive phase of the Loire campaign was about to begin.

11

Dead or Victorious

Inside Paris, the events on the Loire had had a profound effect. After the collapse of the attempted revolution of October 31, and the failure of the Thiers-Bismarck negotiations over the following days, work had continued on the plan for a great sortie. It was by now abundantly clear that Moltke was not going to oblige Trochu by launching an attack himself. The French assault of October 21, which had been intended to probe the enemy defences in the sector chosen for the sortie, had given Ducrot sufficient encouragement to believe that the planned breakout in a westerly direction should be persevered with. Preparations continued for an attack which it was hoped to launch during the third week of November. These included a complete reorganisation of all the forces under Trochu's command. The Garde Mobile regiments and the provisional infantry regiments which had been formed were brigaded together. From each Garde Nationale battalion were drawn four 'compagnies de marche' which were formed into 'battalions de marche,' about 500 strong, and which were intended to take over garrison duties in the fixed defences from the Garde Mobile. The available forces were reformed into three armies. The 1st Army, under Thomas, which consisted of 266 Garde Nationale battalions including the new battalions de marche, together with a cavalry and an artillery legion, comprised about 130,000 men; its task would be to garrison the

General Ducrot, commander of the Second Army of Paris (Rousset/*Histoire*)

Garde Mobiles from (l to r) Seine-et-Oise, Brittany, Montpellier and Normandy, by Knötel (Pflugk-Harttung)

city's defensive positions. Ducrot himself commanded the 2nd Army, about 100,000 strong, which comprised the picked troops intended to carry out the intended sorties. These included the troops of the former 13th and 14th Corps, and were organised in three corps of eight infantry divisions each of two brigades together with a cavalry division. Vinoy commanded the 3rd Army, which consisted of six infantry divisions of Gardes Mobiles and a cavalry division and was 70,000 strong. Its task, when the sortie was launched, would be to carry out diversionary attacks to confuse the investing troops, and for this purpose was to be reinforced by Maud'huy's Division from the 2nd Army. In addition, the forts and other advanced fortifications contained about 80,000 Gardes Mobiles, while in the works around St Denis there were 35,000 men under the command of Vice Admiral de la Roncière le Noury. The total strength of the Paris Army was about 400,000, which was a huge force for the investing armies to keep penned in.[1]

The work of preparing for the assault, and the assembly of the necessary materiel to carry it out, continued through the first half of November, although by no means as quickly as Ducrot had hoped. It was substantially behind schedule when the electrifying news of the victory at Coulmiers reached the capital on November 14. This news, coupled with previous suggestions that he should be aiming at co-operation with d'Aurelle by attacking down the Orleans road, led Trochu reluctantly to the conclusion that he might have to abandon his plan and look instead at ways to break out to the south.[2] Four days later arrived a second message from Gambetta, sent after the meeting with d'Aurelle which had decided that the Army of the Loire should take up a position in a fortified camp around Orleans. Gambetta had previously received details of

Trochu's plan for a breakout to the west, but in view of the plans that the Army of the Loire should advance north towards Paris, he now repeated his suggestions that Trochu should instead aim to break out to the south to meet them. However, he accepted that a sortie to the west would still be valuable, suggesting an attempt at 'a vigorous break-out towards Normandy which will let you get out of Paris, hitherto impregnable, 200,000 men who are not necessary to her defence and who, holding out in the open country, will act as a counterweight to the forces which Prince Frederick Charles is bringing from Metz.'[3] Although Trochu was thus left a choice, on the following day in the face of popular pressure for direct co-operation with the forces coming from the Loire to relieve Paris, the Government of National Defence confirmed that the breakout to the west must be abandoned, and an attack launched to the south. To Gambetta, Favre wrote that although there was food enough till January, December 15 should be regarded as the deadline for the relief of the city, and it was this message that had prompted Freycinet to take into his own hands the planning of a forward movement by the Army of the Loire.

Trochu and Ducrot were appalled at the decision. A biographer of Trochu wrote that 'it was the substitution, for a plan that was risky but achievable, of a plan that was absolutely fanciful, and it necessitated overturning completely in less than twelve days the immense preparations that had been made.'[4] It involved Ducrot and his staff in the enormous logistical exercise of shifting four hundred heavy guns, fifty four pontoon bridges and eighty thousand men, with all their field artillery transport and ammunition from one side of Paris to the other. The choice of a point at which to launch an attack with a view to breaking out towards the Army of the Loire was extremely limited, as the Official History noted:

> As a reconnaissance demonstrated that the German positions at Mesly, Thiais and Chevilly, so often attacked on previous occasions, had had their powers of resistance materially augmented, the French resolved first to cross the Marne between Joinville and Neuilly, and take up a firm position on the plateau lying to the eastward.[5]

To coincide with the main assault, Ducrot planned diversionary attacks to the southwest towards Buzenval, southwards towards L'Hay and in the north from St Denis in the direction of Epinay.

It would have been in any case difficult to conceal the preparations for an assault on the scale that was contemplated; the revised arrangements inevitably drew the attention of the Germans to what was in the wind. As early as November 19, the Crown Prince noted that there were many indications that a sortie was imminent.[6] His Chief of Staff was on the other hand a good deal more sceptical, commenting five days later that 'a deserter has said that in the next few days we are to have a sortie. I do not believe it.'[7] Moltke however, in one of his regular letters to Stiehle on November 27, drew the correct conclusion.

> Numerous troop movements and reports from our agents show us that a sortie is imminent, perhaps the last; but it is difficult to guess at the principal direction of the attack; and one cannot understand the object aimed at unless one of the new armies from the provinces succeeds in getting in the vicinity.[8]

For some reason Trochu deferred sending any message to Gambetta about the change of plan until November 24. His letter betrayed his resentment at Gambetta's criticisms.

> What you call my persistent inactivity is the inevitable result of the enormous and complicated efforts I have had to make. I have had to organise 100,000 men, provide them with artillery, remove them from the fifteen leagues of positions which they occupied, and replace them with untrained troops and soldiers from the National Guard. And these well-nigh incredible efforts have had to be made in contradiction of a plan already being executed, which consisted of breaking out to the west, in the direction of Rouen. The news from the Army of the Loire naturally decided one to break out towards the south and go to meet it whatever the cost[9]

Trochu went on to summarise the plans for Ducrot's breakout, and committed the letter to a balloon. This, however, unluckily miscarried, being swept in a northeasterly direction, and out over the North Sea, before finally coming to earth in the centre of Norway. En route, the aeronauts had been obliged to jettison the sacks of despatches they carried, including Trochu's letter; amazingly, these were picked up and brought in by a fishing boat, and despatched to France by the French Consul. In the event it did not make a great deal of difference; Gambetta's determination on positive action by the Army of the Loire meant that operations were already under way, and the Army of the Loire was becoming engaged with the Second Army and the Detachment in its bid to relieve Paris.

Monitoring the preparations being made by Ducrot for the forthcoming offensive, Moltke put in place his own arrangements to defeat it. On November 16 he had ordered that for the time being the responsibility of the Third Army was to be limited to the left bank of the Seine, and that Fransecky's II Corps should be brought over from the right bank to stand as the army's reserve. To strengthen the Army of the Meuse, he transferred to it the Württemberg Division, which was put in to cover the position between Brie and the Seine. On its right, the XII Corps occupied the northeastern sector of the investment lines, while the Guard Corps remained along the northern front.

Moltke's redeployment, of course, in this way correctly anticipated Ducrot's intentions for the sortie. By November 27 it was obvious even to Blumenthal that the assault was imminent, when news reached him from Tümpling's VI Corps that the French had thrown a bridge over the river near Joinville, opposite the positions of the Württemberg Division.[10] This coincided with a marked increase in the artillery fire from the forts in this sector, while along the southern front there was an intensification of outpost activity. Elsewhere, there were also clear signs that the moment had arrived for the great sortie, with considerable additions to the French batteries all along the line of investment, particularly on Mont Valérien.

The date selected for the sortie was November 29. Inside Paris, as preparations intensified, an air of expectation gripped the population. The effect was striking. Edwin Washburne, the American Minister, noted on November 27 that 'Paris has never been so tranquil and never before has there been so little crime. You do not hear of a murder, robbery, theft or even a row, anywhere.'[11] Trochu, the Government and Ducrot all drew up proclamations to be published on the night before the assault. Ducrot, dining with the great engineer Ferdinand de Lesseps, showed

The defence of the plaster works at Champigny, by Pallandre (Rousset/*Combattants*)

him the proofs of the message he had written for the inspiration of his inexperienced troops. Taking up his pencil, de Lesseps suggested that Ducrot should add that as far as he was concerned he would only return dead or victorious. Ducrot hesitated for a moment, and then added the phrase that was to become one of the most memorable utterances of the war. 'I swear this before you – before the entire nation. I will only re enter Paris dead or victorious. You may see me fall but you shall not see me retreat. Then do not falter, but avenge me. Forward then! Forward! And may God protect us!'[12]

In the sector chosen for the assault, the Marne describes a double loop. The main defence position occupied by the Württembergers, about four miles long, ran along the top of a plateau to the east of the river, from Noisy le Grand in the north to Chennevières in the south; the key points of this defensive line were the heavily fortified villages of Villiers and Coeuilly. In front of them an outpost line reached the river at each of the lightly held villages of Brie and Champigny. Ducrot planned that the main assault should take the form of an advance by the 1st and 2nd Corps from Joinville on Champigny, while to the left of this Bellemare, from Exéa's 3rd Corps, who by now had obtained the promotion which he coveted, was to direct his division on Brie. To the north, crossing the river between Nogent and Neuilly, the attack was to be supported by the rest of Exéa's 3rd Corps. The offensive was to be preceded by a heavy bombardment of the German positions from the forts and from new artillery positions thrown up on Mont Avron to the north. The intention was that once a breakthrough had been achieved, the army should swing to its right, marching southwards towards the Forest of Fontainebleau with the intention of meeting there the advancing Army of the Loire. Coinciding with the main assault, Vinoy was to launch his diversionary attacks along the southern front while simultaneously assaults were also undertaken in the north.

On the night of November 28, however, disaster struck, when the Marne flooded and it was found that the pontoon bridges that had been brought up for the use of the advancing columns were now too short to span the river. There was nothing for it but to put off the assault for twenty four hours to enable the necessary material to be assembled. With this delay went the last hope of achieving any surprise for an attack which the Germans had been expecting for ten days. The preparations for a sortie were plainly visible to the defenders, securely dug in their strong positions. The news of the advance by the Army of the Loire on Beaune la Rolande in any case demonstrated clearly where the assault would come, and at 9.45 on November 29 Moltke informed the Crown Prince of Saxony that 'as a result of the news received from the Second Army, a serious attack on the Württemberg Division is very probable ... you should support it as soon as possible with all the forces available and eventually with a division of the Guard Corps.'[13] In response to this instruction, the Army of the Meuse brought the 2nd Guard Division up to Sevran.

Even worse for the French, the news of the delay came too late to halt Vinoy's Corps, which was already committed to its attacks towards L'Hay and Choisy le Roi. Maud'huy's Division was already in position behind Les Hautes Bruyères, and Tümpling had ordered the 12th Division to move up to meet the threatened attack. By 6.00 am French skirmishers had got into L'Hay and Bievre Mill, and in spite of immediate local counter attacks held on there and in the neighbouring vineyards. A fresh assault at about 8.30 was however thrown back, and the Prussians, supported by units of the II Bavarian Corps, advanced to retake their outpost positions, the French falling back to their start line at Villejuif. To the left, meanwhile, Rear Admiral Pothuau's marines had been directed on Choisy le Roi, seizing Gare aux Boeufs Farm at 6.30 and capturing the outpost troops there. Since it seemed to Tümpling that the French intended to try to hold the ground won, he ordered a bayonet charge to retake the position before the French could consolidate. Before this was launched, however, Vinoy heard of the postponement of the main attack, and pulled back his troops to Vitry under cover of heavy shellfire from the forts. These pointless operations had cost him about a thousand men killed and wounded, together with three hundred prisoners; Tümpling's losses were about one hundred and forty men in all.[14] The only other operation on November 29 was on the west of the investment lines at Malmaison, where an assault after heavy artillery preparation on the positions of the V Corps at about 8.00 am was soon driven back. After a day of 'great excitement' at headquarters of the Third Army, Blumenthal rather prematurely assumed that 'now we shall have rest at the hands of the Parisians. They did not attack with the same élan as of old, and they seemed to see that they can do us no harm.' His airy confidence was not shared by the King, with whom he had lunch; 'His Majesty's face, however, betrayed great anxiety.'[15]

In support of the main assault on November 30, there were to be further diversionary attacks. On the southern front, south west of the principal Württemberg position to be attacked, General Susbielle's Division crossed the Marne at Port de Créteil, and at 6.00 am commenced a heavy bombardment of the Württemberg positions in Bonneuil and Mesly, and on Mont Mesly, before the barrage lifted at 9.00 and the infantry advanced to the assault. Occupying Mesly, Susbielle pushed on to take Mont Mesly, and a fierce struggle ensued for the possession of Bonneuil. By 11.00 the German artillery checked the French advance; a counter attack launched by three and half Prussian battalions caused Susbielle to retreat, and a charge by the Württemberg cavalry broke up the retiring columns, taking a considerable number of prisoners. By 1.30 Susbielle had retreated into Créteil under cover of heavy fire from the forts; he had incurred casualties of about 1,200 men, compared to the German losses of 350. Unaware of Susbielle's advance Vinoy, who it had been intended should support it by yet another attack in the direction of Choisy le Roi, did not come into action until Susbielle's attack had been driven back; as on the previous day, he was able to take the German outpost position at Gare aux Boeufs, but in spite of supporting fire from gunboats and from armoured trains an attempted advance on Choisy le Roi soon broke down, and Vinoy retreated on Vitry and Villejuif after suffering a further 100 casualties.[16] It was on the northern front, however, where another diversionary attack was launched which indirectly was of much greater consequence. From St Denis, Admiral de la Roncière le Noury launched a brigade of marines under Hanrion in an assault on the village of Epinay, supported by a floating battery on the Seine. The attackers succeeded in occupying the village and maintaining their position there for two hours before Major General von Kessler concentrated troops of his 15th Brigade and, under the fire of seven batteries on the heights overlooking the village, retook it after savage street fighting. The engagement lost each side some 300 casualties. Its effect, however, was to be considerable; the news of the taking of Epinay was sent by balloon out of the city to the delegation at Tours, where Gambetta, when he finally received it, was entirely to mistake its import.

In the Brie-Champigny sector the main assault was timed for 9.00 am. Before dawn the French artillery commenced a violent bombardment of the Württemberg positions from Fort Nogent and Mont Avron. At 6.30, in freezing cold, the French infantry of the 1st and 2nd Corps began to cross the Marne over five pontoon bridges at Joinville and two more at Nogent. By 8.30 they were assembled in their jumping off position on the left bank of the river. Of the 1st Corps, commanded by Blanchard, Faron's division, on the extreme right, was directed on Champigny; immediately on his left was Malroy's division, and Maussion's division from Renault's 2nd Corps. To the left rear of these came Berthaut's division of the 2nd Corps, while further north Exéa's 3rd Corps was preparing to throw pontoon bridges over the Marne at Neuilly, led by Bellemare's Division. The attack went in at 9.00, falling on the line of outposts which had been taken over by the Saxon 107th Regiment. Maussion soon evicted the outpost at Le Plant; pushing forward, his advanced troops next compelled the abandonment of the outpost position at Brie. As Berthaut and Malroy came up, the limekilns on the Brie-Champigny road were taken without difficulty, but on the right, meanwhile, Faron had been suffering heavy casualties as he struggled towards Champigny. By 10.00, however, the defenders of that village had been compelled to fall back on the main defensive line to the east. The first part of Ducrot's advance had gone according to plan, and his troops now stood at the foot of the plateau, and were ready to attack the main Villiers-Coeuilly position.

A scene from the Battle of Champigny, by Pallandre (Rousset/*Combattants*)

In the face of heavy artillery and rifle fire from the Württembergers' prepared positions, the attackers were pinned down, and Ducrot now discovered that Exéa, who was due to come in on the left of Villiers at Noisy le Grand, had still not crossed the Marne. His intention had been to defer his assault on the plateau until Exéa's advance got under way, but under the galling fire of the defenders his troops were suffering heavy losses, and it was clear to him that in his exposed position he could wait no longer. He at once launched a general assault.

On his right Faron, after clearing the barricades in Champigny, moved up the slopes towards Coeuilly. Behind him his artillery experienced difficulty in getting through the streets of the village, and the first two batteries to deploy on the plateau were forced back by the German artillery. Other guns deployed at the limekilns, while his infantry also moved down the Marne towards the left of the Württemberg position at the Jägerhof. Here they could make no impression on the defenders, supported by additional artillery which had come into position on the heights, and von Reitzenstein, the commander of the 1st Württemberg Brigade, attempted a counter attack towards Champigny. This, however, soon ran into difficulties in the face of further advancing columns of Faron's division, and Colonel von Beyer, the commander of the 1st Württemberg Regiment, was killed. In its turn however Faron's advance broke down, and he fell back towards Champigny having sustained heavy losses. For the moment, the fighting died down on this part of the battlefield.[17]

On Faron's right Berthaut had reached the edge of the plateau on either side of the railway line from Villiers to Nogent, but was held up by three companies of

Württemberg infantry firing from gravel pits by the railway embankment. He was finally able to get forward and take the gravel pits before a counter attack by a battalion of the Saxon 104th Regiment, under the cover of heavy artillery fire, drove the French out again. Berthaut could make no further progress and with his attack in the centre stalled like that of Faron on the right, Ducrot discontinued his assault for the day, strengthening his hold on the ground he had gained by the deployment of eighteen batteries across the centre of his position.[18] Since the Germans, too, were concerned for the moment only with consolidation, it seemed by 2.00 pm that the fighting had come to an end.

However, at this point Exéa had belatedly woken up to the need to advance. His artillery compelled the Germans to pull back from their advanced positions north of the river, while he got Bellemare's division over the Marne by two bridges thrown over the river southwest of Neuilly. Bellemare deployed opposite Villiers, extending his right to link with Maussion. Opposite him, Lieutenant General Nehrhoff von Holdenberg, the commander of the Saxon 24th Division, who had taken charge of this sector of the defences, pulled back his advanced troops into prepared positions around the west and north of Villiers, and reinforced Noisy le Grand, while strengthening his gun line on the heights by batteries brought over from the right bank of the Marne. Bellemare's first assault, up the sunken road from Brie, was broken up by the fire of the German artillery, a Zouave regiment losing all its officers and half its men killed and wounded;[19] but Ducrot ordered Bellemare to make a further attack in the direction of Villiers, which he supported by fresh attempts to advance by Faron and Berthaut. All three attacks broke down, however, with heavy loss, and as darkness fell firing ceased all along the line. Between the outpost lines that were now established on both sides lay the carnage of a battlefield that had exacted a fearful toll of the attackers.

Throughout the day Moltke had kept in close touch with events on the battlefield, exchanging a stream of telegrams with the headquarters of the Army of the Meuse, and with Fransecky, Tümpling and Prince George, the commanders of the II, VI and XII Corps, and with the Württemberg Division. He was also kept closely informed by Captain Zingler, of his staff, who was on the battlefield, and from whom he received regular reports. When the Crown Prince of Saxony reported that he could not provide support for the left wing of the Württemberg Division, Moltke replied that it would be reinforced by troops from the VI Corps and if necessary from the II Corps.[20] After the fighting had died down on November 30, but still concerned as to what more should be done to strengthen the defences against any resumption by Ducrot of his offensive next day, Moltke telegraphed the XII Corps: 'Have the German troops retaken all their original positions, and has the enemy been thrown back over the Marne? And if so, is it necessary to have recourse to the II Corps, which has crossed the Seine at Villeneuve St Georges?'[21] This crossed with a report from the XII Corps that in spite of heavy losses it had successfully held its ground between Villiers and Noisy le Grand, but that the enemy were still on the left bank, probably in force, and that it was 'absolutely necessary for it to be supported on the following day at dawn.' In view of this, late that night, Moltke telegraphed both Prince George and Crown Prince Albert to tell them that the Third Army had been asked to provide substantial reinforcements.

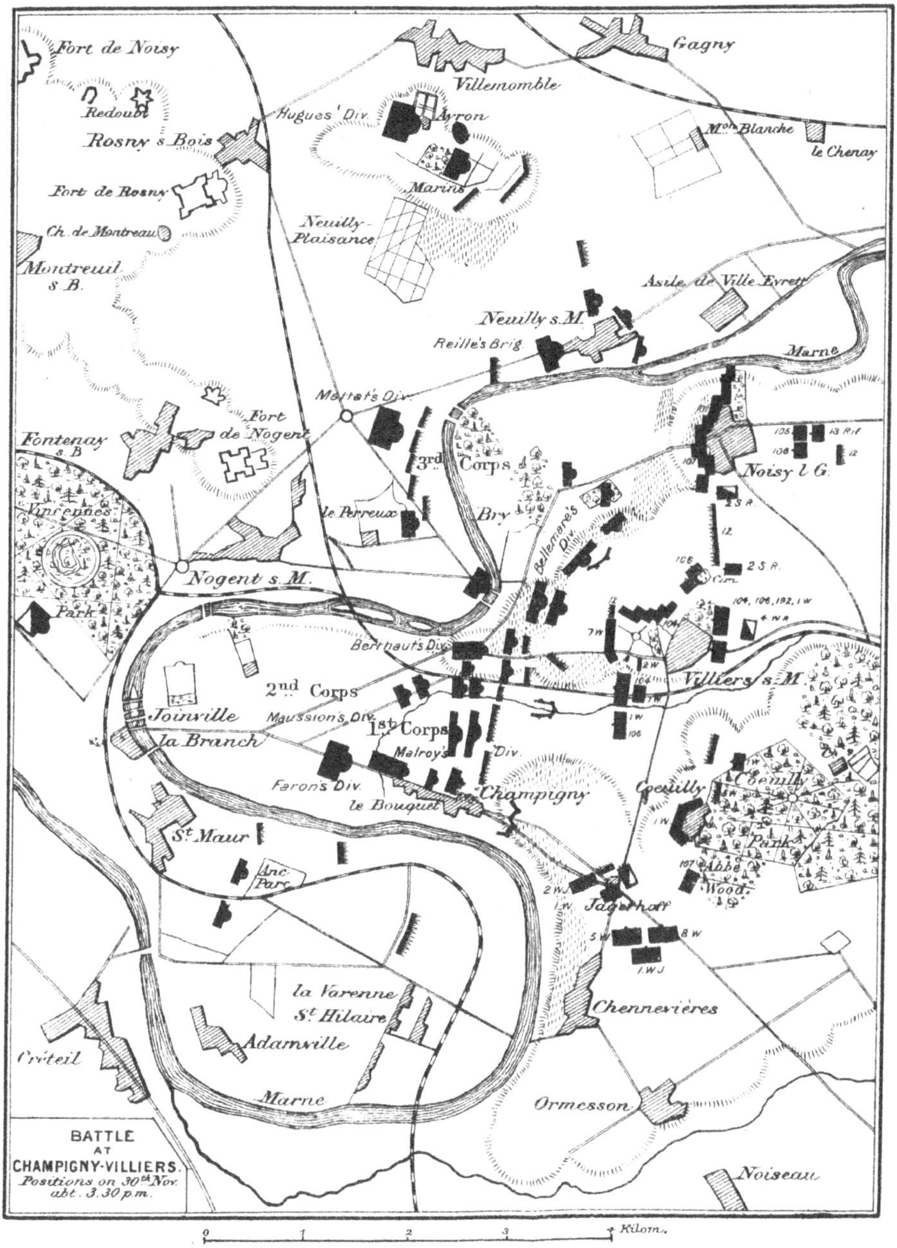

The Battle of Champigny, November 30 1870

Moltke then learned, to his dismay, that Fransecky's II Corps had, after the end of the day's fighting, returned to its original position some ten miles to the rear, and after some discussion with Verdy sent the latter to see Fransecky to sort things out. It was clearly necessary to get his corps back on the battlefield without delay, and Verdy set off at once after going over to the headquarters of the Third Army to tell the Crown Prince of his mission. The discussion took place at Blumenthal's bedside, the Chief of Staff having retired for the night. Pausing on his way to see Tümpling, Verdy was relieved to find that the latter had brought up a brigade to fill the gap left by the II Corps; he then continued on his mission, passing long columns of infantry marching up to the front in the darkness. Soon after Verdy got to the headquarters of von Obernitz, the Württemberg commander, he was relieved to hear Fransecky and his staff riding up. The latter, perhaps somewhat touchy at being peremptorily recalled, asked Verdy what orders he had brought. Verdy had brought none; but showing the initiative expected of an officer of the Prussian General Staff, did not hesitate.

> I therefore requested Captain Zingler, who accompanied me, to take down carefully in writing every word that I was going to say, and then explained to the General as follows: "The enemy is still on the right bank of the Seine and on the left of the Marne, outside his works, and it is in accordance with the intentions of His Majesty for your Excellency, as soon as your corps is assembled, to advance to the attack and drive the enemy back again behind the line of his forts.'[22]

On his way back to the Royal Headquarters, Verdy stopped again to visit Tümpling; he could not spare the time to dine with the staff there, but while his horses were being changed was served with some fricassee. A few days later he heard from the King that the VI Corps had reported to the Crown Prince that two carrier pigeons had been caught; the Crown Prince had ordered that they be forwarded at once to Versailles, only to receive a report that 'Lieutenant Colonel von Verdy has just eaten them up.'[23]

While Verdy had been thus engaged, Moltke had been pondering the situation. Since Ducrot's assault had been directed at the junction between the Army of the Meuse and the Third Army, which was always the most vulnerable point, he concluded that fresh command arrangements should be made, and issued on order putting Fransecky in command for the time being of all operations between the Seine and the Marne. Fransecky was ordered to report promptly and directly to the Royal Headquarters, although he would be technically under the command of the Army of the Meuse.[24]

As it turned out, Moltke's immediate anxieties were unjustified. After the terrible hammering his forces had taken, at the end of which they were only hanging on desperately to the ground they had won in the first couple of hours, Ducrot was in no doubt that the attack had failed, and that a resumption of the assault next day would be pointless. Casualties had been heavy; among them was Renault, who received a wound from which he died a few days later. On the other hand, to fall back at once into the city would be to acknowledge the magnitude of the defeat, with all sorts of possible consequences for the Government and the maintenance of public order. Ducrot decided for the moment to hold his ground. For each side, therefore, December 1 was a day of recuperation and the consolidation of the defensive positions they occupied, and as the day wore on a formal truce was agreed to enable burial parties from both sides to go between the lines to clear the battlefield of its dead. Most of the German troops had the benefit of reasonable quarters in which to rest; upon the French, on the other hand, largely out in the open, the intense cold imposed fearful hardships. The Crown Prince of Saxony, meanwhile, had concluded that, as at Le Bourget, steps should be taken at once to recover the lost ground. Fransecky demurred; the positions occupied by the French posed no great threat to the investment lines, which had successfully repelled all the assaults on November 30, and as Blumenthal noted, 'the villages lie within the range of heavy artillery and are untenable.'[25] The Crown Prince, however, was insistent, and he ordered Fransecky to mount an assault early on December 2 to seize Brie and Champigny, with all his available troops. This was, in fact, at odds with an order Moltke had sent to Fransecky late on December 1, to the effect that he should keep one of his divisions back, covering the position between the Marne and the Seine; Fransecky, however, did not get this order until 3am on December 2, and in the face of the direct orders he had received from the Crown Prince, and with preparations for the assault well advanced, he felt obliged to go through with it as planned.[26]

The attack was launched at 7,00am, when Nehrhoff launched three Saxon battalions from Noisy le Grand towards Brie. The assault was at first successful, one battalion driving back the French outposts and seizing a barricade in the middle of the village. Fresh French troops came up at once, however, and the Saxons became involved in a bitter house to house struggle for the village; in spite of heavy losses, and facing a heavy numerical superiority, they managed for the time being to retain their hold on the houses at the north end of Brie. Meanwhile, to the south, the 1st Württemberg Brigade advanced from Belair towards Champigny. Here, too, they gained some initial success before Faron brought up his reserves to bar their further progress.

Ducrot, who was himself at Champigny, ordered at 8.30 a general counter attack under the cover of a strong line of French batteries around the limekilns. The gravel pits were taken by Malroy's division, and then lost to a fresh attack by the 49th Regiment, before again being occupied by strong columns of French infantry advancing in the centre from Le Plant. Fransecky now committed part of his reserve, the 1st Division under Major General von Hartmann bringing up the 6th Brigade from Sucy to Chennevières and the 5th Brigade to Coeuilly. After a long struggle, Hartmann's men again reoccupied the gravel pits, taking 160 prisoners there. The fusilier battalion of the 49th Regiment which had got as far as Champigny church hung on there, while to the north of the village the heights were held, but no further progress was made.[27]

At Brie, the Saxons launched further attacks with the assistance of reinforcements pushed forward by Prince George, and succeeded in spite of further losses in driving back the enemy towards the eastern side of Brie. By noon, however, Ducrot had attained such a measure of numerical superiority that the Saxons were obliged to fall back towards Villiers, which in turn meant giving up their tenuous hold on the northern side of the village. The troops there retreated towards their jumping off positions in front of Noisy le Grand. In the centre, Ducrot now launched the divisions of Susbielle and Bellemare; but their attempt to move forward on Villiers was frustrated when they were taken in flank by Hartmann's artillery which he brought up from the Jägerhof at the gallop, and which poured a devastating fire into the French right. As darkness fell to end the short November day, the French assaults on Villiers and to the south petered out, and both sides pulled back their main forces, leaving the outpost lines in close contact.

Throughout the day Trochu and Ducrot had been in the thick of the fighting, exposing themselves with almost suicidal courage. D'Herisson, who spent a large part of the day looking for Trochu with a message from Schmitz, his Chief of Staff, that a carrier pigeon had arrived with news that the Army of the Loire hoped to be in the Forest of Fontainebleau by December 6, wondered if Trochu was deliberately seeking death. And one of Ducrot's staff officers said to him:

'You should see Ducrot! He is absolutely mad. All today he has been riding a horse as white as snow, and he is continually galloping in front of the Prussians. I would like to have as many francs – not income but capital – as he has had shots, from rifles and ordnance, fired directly at him today. Would you believe that he charged the Saxons single-handed? He cut one down with his small sword as if he had a regulation weapon in his hand. He is perfectly mad.'[28]

In view of the news of the advance of the Army of the Loire in the direction of Fontainebleau, Ducrot decided that night that in spite of the sufferings of his troops, they must remain on the left bank of the Marne in order to pin down the German forces facing them. Accordingly, during the night, fresh supplies of ammunition were brought up, and the batteries moved into position at Le Plant, Brie and on the edge of the plateau. From there, before dawn, they opened fire on the German positions, causing Fransecky to take up a position to meet an expected advance. In fact, this never materialised, although throughout December 3 there were skirmish engagements all along the front. As night fell, the Germans pulled back into their relatively comfortable quarters; the French continued to bivouack in the open.[29]

That night, the Saxon Crown Prince wrote a pessimistic report to Moltke on the condition of his troops. They were, he said, exhausted; there could be no question of pulling troops out of the sector between the Seine and the Marne. On the contrary, they should be reinforced. A gloomy conference with the King followed, as a result of which Moltke ordered Blumenthal to send all the available reinforcements he could to Fransecky, since it was to be expected that on the following day the whole of Ducrot's army would launch a sortie towards Noisy le Grand. The King, much moved, wrote an angry note on the back of the Saxon Crown Prince's report which, he thought, 'gives no confidence in the issue of a battle tomorrow, if the enemy debouches from five bridges and turns Brie.'[30]

Later still that evening, Moltke patiently if perhaps a little wearily, wrote a reassuring note to the King:

> In reply to the question which Your Majesty deigned to address to me this evening, I have the honour to set out respectfully the total number of troops established today on the line Noisy-le –Grand – Villeneuve St Georges:
>
> 24th Division 13 battalions
> Württemberg Division 15 battalions
> All the II Corps 24 battalions
> A brigade of the VI Corps 6 battalions
>
> Total 58 battalions
>
> and more than 200 guns

> The Third Army and the Army of the Meuse have received the order to have, tomorrow morning, other reinforcements ready to march.[31]

The King was unconvinced, noting on this that the 58 battalions were only the equivalent of 30.

So pessimistic had been the Crown Prince of Saxony's report, and so evidently upsetting to the King, that on the morning of December 4 Moltke sat down to write a memorandum setting out the steps to be taken in the event of the French succeeding that day in breaking through at Villiers. It might, he thought, be necessary to raise the investment on the north of Paris until Manteuffel's First Army could be pulled back from Rouen to reoccupy the lines, and for the Guard Corps and the IV Corps to be pulled out and brought round to deal with the enemy, while the XII Corps and the Württemberg Division regrouped and followed the enemy's movements. To the south, Fransecky would concentrate at Ormesson. If the French marched east, it would be necessary to hang on to them to prevent them damaging the vital German rail links. But Moltke cannot have thought that this plan was remotely likely to be required; more probably, it was an exercise designed to calm William's nerves. Moltke was accustomed to this kind of thing, since the King was invariably jumpy when the enemy appeared to pose any sort of a threat.[32]

In fact the exercise was unnecessary. That night there was a hard frost and it started to snow, and it was clear to Ducrot that his troops could do no more. He described them as 'crouched on the frozen ground, exhausted and shivering, their bodies and souls enfeebled by weariness, suffering and lack of food.'[33] For his part, he feared that a fresh German assault might result in his whole army being thrown back to the Marne, and he gave the necessary orders for its retreat across the river. On the morning of December 4, the German patrols found Brie, Champigny and the French positions on the edge of the Villiers plateau to have been abandoned. Under cover of a thick fog the whole of the French army succeeded in recrossing the Marne, Ducrot reassuring his troops that the retreat was solely to enable them to recover their fighting energies. With this, the investing forces once more realigned themselves into the positions occupied before the battle, and the great sortie was over.

Although the Crown Prince of Saxony's ill judged insistence on the assault of December 2, which had cost 3,500 men, had enabled the French to show that, in defence, they were still a force to be reckoned with, Ducrot's attack had been an expensive failure. Total French casualties exceeded 12,000; the Germans lost nearly 6,200. The moral effect of the defeat was even greater than its military consequence. Edmond Goncourt wrote mournfully of this in his diary: 'The heights and depths of hope; this is what kills you. One believes oneself saved. Then one realises one is lost … Today the recrossing of the Marne by Ducrot has thrown us back into the darkness of failure and despair.'[34]

12

Werder

Moltke's further orders to the newly promoted General von Werder, sent immediately after the fall of Strasbourg and which had reached him on September 30, placed him in command of a new formation, the XIV Corps. This was intended to comprise the Baden Division, the Guard Landwehr Division, the combined infantry brigade under Major General von Boswell and the combined cavalry brigade led by Major General von Nidda. The Guard Landwehr Division was not, however, immediately available, being almost at once earmarked for operations around Paris, and Werder was obliged to set off on his new mission without it. His immediate task was to advance to the Upper Seine towards Chatillon and Troyes, clearing the area of hostile troops, and to endeavour to put the railway from Blainville via Epinal to Chaumont in running order. Moltke suggested that a coup de main might be attempted against Langres, at which point the line was blocked. Bearing in mind the extensive franc tireur activity in the area, Moltke emphasised to Werder that he was responsible for the security of his own lines of communication.[1] Werder was, however, already very sensitive to the problem; even before receiving Moltke's order, he had on September 29 reported a concentration of franc tireurs at Raon-l'Etape, and asked permission to despatch one brigade to deal with them; Moltke the same day telegraphed his authorisation for this mission.[2]

It was the first in a series of operations which, responding to a variety of enemy threats, were to pull Werder's forces in many different directions during the months to come. His immediate adversary was General Cambriels, who had briefly been commandant of Belfort, before being appointed as commander of all the French troops in the Eastern region. Cambriels had commanded a brigade in the cavalry division of the 7th Corps and had suffered a head wound at Sedan so severe that the Germans had released him. He had a rather mixed bag of troops at his disposal, although they had been stiffened by the despatch of a regular infantry brigade that was intended to serve as the nucleus of a new 'Army of the Vosges.' Apart from this his troops consisted of Gardes Mobiles from Belfort, part of the garrison of Besancon and troops drawn from the 'Army of Lyon' which was in course of assembly at that city.[3]

Cambriels at least enjoyed the advantages of geography. The area over which his forces were expected to operate was protected by a series of mountainous districts in which the north-south communications were very poor, while those running from west to east offered a number of defensive positions along the Saône, the Ognon and the Doubs. The heavily wooded mountains rise gradually until in the east they reach the massif of the Upper Vosges and the Jura, and in the west the Langres plateau. The most advanced positions held by the French, and upon which, when they were strong enough to move, any advance must be based, were the fortresses of Langres and the important road and rail junction at Epinal. South of Langres, the key communications centre was Dijon, beyond which lay the entrance to the Rhône valley. The principal base for Cambriels was the strong fortress of Besancon on the River Doubs.

It was a huge area for Cambriels to cover, but its size gave him considerable opportunities to surprise an enemy who, like himself, had far too few troops with which to carry out the operations that were soon to be expected of him.

Werder acted with impressive speed to put together a force to disperse the threat identified at Raon-l'Etape. Without waiting for his troops to sort themselves out after the ending of the siege of Strasbourg, he put together on October 1 a mixed detachment under Major General von Degenfeld, the commander of the 2nd Baden Brigade. This force included six battalions, two squadrons and two batteries, and was ordered to march in two columns converging on October 5 south of Raon l'Etape on the road to Etival. Degenfeld set off next day, finding that on his route 'the passes were much obstructed by barricades, erected by the inhabitants under the direction of engineer officers on a very large scale (in some places there were abatis 1,000 paces long) whose removal was a work of great labour.'[4] In spite of this, Degenfeld's two columns reached Raon l'Etape on time and occupied the town after chasing a few hundred Gardes Mobiles and franc tireurs out of the defensive positions that had been prepared around it.

Meanwhile Werder had been putting the rest of his corps in order for a movement that would initially be towards the south. He organised it for the moment into three further detachments, intending that Degenfeld should operate as the advanced guard. His aim was to advance on Epinal, which he intended to approach from an easterly direction after he had marched through Raon l'Etape and St Dié;

A view of Dijon (Pflugk-Harttung)

Degenfeld's next mission would be to seize the latter town, which intelligence reports suggested was the centre of organisation of the French forces in the vicinity and which, it was reported, had been prepared for an extended defence. This information was substantially correct. Cambriels, anticipating a German advance, had collected some 15,000 troops under General Dupré, and had concentrated them in St Die, Nompatelize and La Voivre, with the intention of preventing any German advance down the Meurthe valley. Degenfeld faced, therefore, an even tougher assignment than he realised.

His orders for October 6 provided that he should also cover the western exits from the passes over the Vosges to his left, and to assemble supplies at Raon l'Etape and Etival. He left behind two battalions and one squadron to carry out these tasks, and advanced south down the valley with the rest of his force on both sides of the river. His leading troops soon ran into opposition at La Voivre and Nompatelize, but the strength of the enemy could not for the moment be ascertained, due to the heavy morning mist which lay in the valley; but by 9.00 am Degenfeld was able to push forward one battalion towards the height of Nompatelize and another on Biarville. They soon collided with the enemy, themselves advancing to the attack, and fierce fighting took place as the Germans entered Nompatelize and Les Feignes to the south east. To the east of the river, less resistance had been encountered, the French being pushed back through La Voivre to Marzelay, and Degenfeld, in view of the size of the enemy forces decided to bring all his troops across the river, and to bring up the troops left at Raon l'Etape and Etival.[5]

The need for reinforcements was becoming very evident. By noon, French counter attacks had recovered about half of the village of Nompatelize, the rest of which was still held by half a battalion of the 6th Regiment. The right of the German line was seriously threatened by strong French forces in St Remy, and Degenfeld launched a battalion of the 1st Grenadier Regiment under Major Betz in a successful attack on the village from which the French retreated before, in their turn, launching a counter attack which recaptured the south eastern part of the village. Further south, the Germans took the farmhouse of Le Han.

By one o'clock Dupré had brought up the whole of his force, and advanced to a general assault supported by his artillery. In general, the attack was successfully resisted, although the French recaptured the burning farmhouse of Le Han and began to build up large forces on Degenfeld's right which appeared to indicate an attempt to outflank him there. Degenfeld's position was now extremely exposed; if his line gave way, the considerable numerical superiority of the French and the difficult terrain meant that his force would be completely destroyed. At 2.00pm, however, the last remains of the foraging party at Raon l'Etape reached the battlefield, and with loud shouts stormed first the centre of the French position at La Salle and then the Bois de Jumelles. In the face of this, and a further advance by Betz at St Remy, the French line collapsed, and a general retreat, in mounting disorder, took place towards Bruyères and Rambervillers.

Degenfeld's victory had been dearly bought; his total losses were 403, or about ten per cent of the force he had engaged. Dupré, who had himself been wounded during the battle, lost a total of about 1,400 men, and had his force thoroughly broken up and disorganised.[6] Degenfeld did not think it wise to attempt a pursuit with his exhausted troops; night was beginning to fall, the terrain was extremely

General von Werder, commander of the German XIV Corps (Scheibert)

difficult, and the interrogation of prisoners suggested that fresh French troops were approaching. Accordingly, he bivouacked on the battlefield; his communications had, for the moment, been cut by the hostile inhabitants and he was only able to get news of his victory to Werder by sending a fusilier, disguised as a franc tireur, on a hazardous journey over the mountains.[7]

Meanwhile Werder had been advancing with the main body of the XIV Corps. By October 8 it had reached St Dié, which was found to have been precipitately abandoned by the French. For a few days after the battle of Etival, Werder's reconnaissance patrols had found little trace of the French, but on October 9 resistance was encountered on the roads leading south from St Dié and La Bourgonce, and on the road through the Mortagne valley to the west towards Rambervillers. Lieutenant Colonel Nachtigal, commanding the 2nd battalion of the 30th Prussian Regiment, learned that the French intended to concentrate at Rambervillers, and launched an immediate attack to frustrate this. By nightfall, in spite of stiff resistance inside the town from behind barricades and fortified houses, Nachtigal had captured about half the place; fighting was broken off with the intention of renewing the assault next day, but it was found at dawn that the French had pulled out.[8]

Cambriels now concentrated the bulk of his troops at Bruyères to cover Epinal, taking up a strong entrenched position to the south of that town between Beaumenil and Laval. But on October 10 his advanced positions north and north east of Bruyères were briskly assailed by Werder's leading troop advancing from St Dié, and by 2.30pm Colonel Beyer, who was temporarily commanding the 1st

Baden Brigade, was in a position to move to the attack of Bruyeres itself. By 4.30 pm he had captured the town, while his advanced patrols advanced as far as Laval before being driven back by substantial French reinforcements. Cambriels, however, had already had enough; the morale of his troops was rapidly deteriorating and during the course of the following day he retreated first to a position between Chaudry and Faucompierre and then to Remiremont and Gerardmer, thereby uncovering Epinal. The further he retreated, the worse became the disintegration of his force which finally reached Besancon on October 14 in a state of collapse.

The news of his setback caused dismay in Besancon where the authorities demanded of Gambetta to know of Cambriels:' Is he mad? Is he incompetent, or a traitor?'[9] Gambetta, who had probably asked himself much the same questions, resolved to go to the east to find out for himself the situation there. One of his biographers recorded the outcome of his trip. 'He stayed two days at Besancon, where he showed for the first time his marvellous power of rallying dispirited troops. In those two days he formed a disorganised mass of men into a field force covering the main approach to Lyon.'[10] He also took the opportunity to interview Cambriels, whose exposition of the true situation of the troops under his command was very much like that given by d'Aurelle on the Loire: 'If you are counting on this Army of the East, which is at present in an embryonic condition, you must give it time to acquire a proper organisation, clothes, shoes and above all to learn discipline.'[11] It was advice that Gambetta was for the moment prepared to accept, and satisfied with the results of his visit he returned westwards.

Werder, meanwhile, had a problem. There was no difficulty in occupying Epinal, of course; although when Krug's column approached it on October 13 the town had seemed to be strongly held, as soon as the advanced guard moved forward to test the strength of the defences, the opposition melted away. The Germans marched in, and Werder established himself in the Préfecture; the population of Epinal seemed not at all hostile. Werder's problem, however, was what he should now do about Cambriels. The historian of the XIV Corps noted the conflict between taking any decisive action against the Army of the Vosges and carrying out the original orders given by Moltke. 'An energetic pursuit of the enemy, who was not only disinclined for fighting, but even avoided every chance of an important battle, did not seem to be justified, taking into consideration the trifling results to be expected.'[12] Although Werder would have attacked Cambriels if the latter stood and fought, 'he and his staff had to consider how far they would be justified in departing from their general directions of September 30, without further permission from the Royal Headquarters;'[13] it was certain that any pursuit southwards would draw the XIV Corps away from the line originally prescribed in the direction of Troyes. Uncertain as to the right course to follow, Werder reported his position to Moltke on October 14, pointing out that the next step in his movement had been intended to be southwest from Epinal towards Jussey; with Cambriels having some 20,000 men around Remiremont, and hence on the flank of his march he reckoned that this would be imprudent, and he suggested that he could better attain the objectives originally set for him by marching to Neufchâteau and thence along the railway to Chaumont. Werder concluded by adding: 'I may remark that on the departure of the Corps, hostile pressure will most likely be felt at Lunéville and I therefore request further instructions.'[14] This was not at all well received at the Royal Headquarters, where it was generally felt that the strength of Cambriels' force had been overestimated; it should, thought Moltke, be perfectly possible for this to be speedily broken up and dispersed. His telegram in reply to Werder contained a touch of asperity: 'His Majesty orders that the enemy be attacked without any other consideration. His forces can only comprise depot troops and gardes mobiles and in particular a maximum of 36 guns. A base, and railway lines, are not essential. Acknowledge.'[15]This telegram went off at 9.15am on October 15; before he received it, however, Werder had himself sent another telegram to Moltke reporting the further retreat of Cambriels to Rupt, as a result of which he would himself try to reach Vesoul. He estimated the enemy to have between sixteen and twenty thousand bad troops. Moltke's reply to this next morning was curt. Noting that he had had no acknowledgement of his previous telegram, which he repeated, Moltke wrote that the views previously expressed still held good. 'Accordingly, do not take the town of Vesoul as the objective of your advance, but only the position of the enemy.'[16] This did not reach Werder until October 17.

The arrival of Moltke's previous telegram had in the meanwhile prompted a rather defensive response from Werder. 'For eight days, I have directed all my efforts to attacking the enemy, but he has never stood. In accordance with your order, I am going immediately to march on Luxeuil and Lure, points on which he must retire.' He went on to repeat his request to know if he should follow the enemy or pursue his original line of march towards the Upper Seine.[17] To this, Moltke replied by giving an extremely succinct summary of the objectives now to be pursued by the XIV Corps, which Werder received during the night of October 18: 'You may push your offensive against the enemy corps as far as Besancon. Then resume the westward march through Dijon on Bourges.'[18] This at least dispelled all further doubt in Werder's mind; as the XIV Corps historian remarked, 'the order was a distinct one; it admitted of no modification, and the preparations for the necessary movements were set about at once.'[19] What it also did was to confer a degree of additional independence on the corps, which need not, for the moment at any rate, be concerned with events in the west. This pronounced change of emphasis derived from von der Tann's success in occupying Orleans.

The XIV Corps, still disposed in four columns, had in the meantime continued its march to the south in pursuit of its elusive quarry. Encountering no opposition, Keller's column, reached Luxeuil on October 17; Werder himself, riding with Krug's column, got as far as St Loup that day. On the following day the column led by Prince William of Baden entered Vesoul, to find it unoccupied. Degenfeld pushed out reconnaissances from his column towards Lure and Belfort, but no contact with the enemy was made. All the intelligence reaching Werder's headquarters now appeared to confirm that Cambriels had gone all the way back to Besancon. If so, and the French were to be found only under the guns of the fortress, it would make it extremely difficult for Werder to launch any attack on his enemy that would bring the kind of decisive result which Moltke was impatiently awaiting. Werder was on the point of abandoning his pursuit of Cambriels when, on October 19, he received intelligence suggesting that the French were intending to make a stand along the line of the Ognon some seven miles north of Besancon.

Given the length of his lines of communication, the deteriorating weather conditions, the uncertainty as to the numbers or intentions of the French, and the strength of the Besancon position, Werder might well feel dubious about advancing to the assault; but in the light of Moltke's very firm instructions he had no choice but to seize the opportunity of meeting Cambriels' force in the open field. In suppressing any doubts he might have, Werder's general frame of mind was expressed very clearly in the words of Löhlein, the XIV Corps historian:

> The task set to the Corps contained many difficulties; it was hardly possible to weigh them all, the only thing to do was to resolve to advance firmly, and as fast as possible, leaving behind ... all the train, and to carry out the distinct order from the Royal Army Chiefs without asking any more questions.[20]

Acting in the spirit of this resolve, Werder reported to Moltke on October 20 that he intended, while holding Vesoul firmly, to march by three roads on Besancon, and to send his cavalry towards Dijon. He was careful to add, however, that it did not appear to him that it would be possible to remain directly before Besancon, which was a powerful fortress and strongly held; he would therefore retire in due course into the Saône valley and act in the light of subsequent events. Moltke, for his part, was pleased to see this determination to get on with the job, and approved Werder's plans on October 24, noting that 'Vesoul and Dijon must be occupied by garrisons. Offensive desirable, if there is a chance of success. Only march westward if this will result in contact with the enemy.' He added that a feldjäger was coming with further instructions.[21]

These instructions formed part of the general reworking of Moltke's plans arising from the imminent fall of Metz, and gave Werder a general responsibility for all operations in the south castern theatre. The XIV Corps, from which the Guard Landwehr Division would remain detached, would take over the command of the 1st Reserve Division (Schmeling) and the 4th Reserve Division (Tresckow). It was charged with conducting first the investment and then the sieges of Schlettstadt, Neu Brisach and Belfort, as well as covering Alsace and the left flank of the Second Army, while immobilising any enemy forces in its front. Werder was to make Vesoul his base for observing the enemy at Besancon. He was also to be responsible for protecting the railways and putting them into working order. But Moltke also judged it necessary to remind Werder of his responsibility to maintain the pressure on the enemy:

> Your Excellency must not hesitate to take the offensive against weak detachments of the enemy. In particular, until the investment of Belfort by the 1st Reserve Division which can scarcely be in line before 6 November, you must exercise the strictest surveillance of that fortress and prevent any organisation from there of a guerrilla war in the Vosges and Upper Alsace.[22]

Werder, who was required to report regularly not only to Moltke but also to the Second Army and the Governor General of Alsace, was left in no doubt that a great deal was expected of him; these instructions did not, however, reach him until the night of October 28/29.

Long before this, however, Werder had already been in action, marching south towards the Ognon, in the direction of Pin and Voray, on October 21. For the next day, he aimed only to seize the crossings over the river, until he could form some clearer idea of the position of the French. First reports from his right, where Prince William of Baden had just under five battalions with one squadron and 9 guns at Autoreille with his advanced guard in Pin, suggested that there was no substantial opposition along the river there. In the centre, Degenfeld with four battalions, two squadrons and 12 guns, was moving on Etuz with his advanced guard, and reported significant enemy activity. On the left, there was no report at first from Keller, who was marching on Voray and Buttier with three battalions, two squadrons and 12 guns; when news did come from Keller, it was that there were strong French forces in his front, and that he wanted reinforcements. The news cheered Werder, with his headquarters at Oiselay, who planned to turn the enemy's right with Prince William's column, while the rest of his force held the enemy in position. Issuing the necessary orders, Werder rode off to Bonnevent, determined not to commit any part of his reserve on the left.[23]

Almost at once, however, things started to go wrong. After Degenfeld had been engaged for some time in a prolonged exchange of rifle fire, Werder strengthened the centre with two Prussian battalions from Krug's column, which he was employing as the reserve; and this apparently prudent step proved unwise because it enabled Degenfeld to push too far forwards too soon, clearing Etuz and the line of the Ognon of enemy troops by 1.30pm before continuing the struggle with the French troops at Cussey. When the latter finally retreated over the bridge there, they were closely followed up by the 2nd Baden Brigade, which soon forced them back through the woods south of Cussey in the direction of Upper and Lower Auxon. Meanwhile, the two battalions from Krug's column had crossed the river at Bussières, and moved to the attack of the heights above Gerenville.[24]

By now, the effect of Prince William's turning movement should have been felt. Unfortunately, the direction of the wind was such that, stationary at Autoreille with his main body, he heard nothing of the engagements to the east, and remained there until he received Werder's orders at 2.00pm. Hurriedly crossing the river, he turned eastwards at 3.30pm through Emagny and Montcley in the direction of the Bois de Cussey, but by the time he emerged from the woods he found that the battle was all over, the enemy having retreated southwards through Lower Auzon before Degenfeld's advance and the movement of Keller's column from Voray. What had promised the chance of cutting off a significant part of the enemy force dissolved therefore into a series of frontal assaults in the face of which the enemy was able to fall back towards the fortress of Besancon. Werder, fully conscious of the strength of the enemy positions there, had no intention of following them, at 5.00pm ordering his troops back to the line of the Ognon for the night. The engagements had cost him a total of 120 casualties; so far as could be ascertained, the total French losses were about 350, of which 200 were taken prisoner.[25]

Next day Werder reconnoitred the French positions around Besancon, finding them quite as strong as he had expected; and he was in no doubt that he should now move off towards Gray and Dijon via the Saône valley in pursuance of his previous orders to march westwards. On October 24, therefore, Krug moved westwards to seize the crossings of the Saône north east of Gray, encountering continuous delays from obstructions on the roads thrown up by the inhabitants. By October 26 the whole corps was around Gray; to the northwest of that town cavalry probing forward to the Vingeanne encountered French troops advancing from Dijon. The weather was appalling; the continuous heavy rain was followed on October 26 by a fierce storm which made reconnaissance almost impossible.[26] Later in the day, however, in a series of successful engagements, detachments of French troops under the command of Lavalle were thrown back. In one case after the head of a French column had been attacked, a large part of the column, finding itself surrounded in the open field near Talmay, surrendered, and 496 prisoners were taken.

Although the French had made a number of ineffectual advances on October 26, it was difficult for Werder to assess their strength with any accuracy, or indeed their intentions. So far as he could tell, they seemed to be moving from Dijon and Pontailler with the object of retaking Gray, so he prepared for October 28 an attack on these based on another right hook, intending to drive them into the Saône. Once again, however, he was cheated of his prey. The French, destroying the bridges at Pontailler and La Marche, had already retreated in a state of chaotic disorganisation mostly towards Dijon, although a smaller body had retreated south to Auxonne. Close pursuit was extremely difficult:

> the land on each side of the roads had become so soft from the continued rain, that it could not be marched on, and the removal of the barricades on roads and bridges, some of which were skilfully constructed, the filling up of the cuttings and the clearing away of the abatis, took an extraordinarily long time owing to the slushy state of the ground.[27]

Nonetheless, Werder pushed on; he intended to continue his advance on the following day when early on the morning of October 29 he finally received Moltke's instructions for the future course of the campaign.

Pondering these, Werder came to the conclusion that perhaps he should defer his occupation of Dijon for the time being. He

> considered it impossible, in the present condition of affairs, and with his corps so split up as it would have to be, to carry out simultaneously all that still remained to be done. He therefore determined, as the best way of gradually executing it, to concentrate the main strength of his corps about Vesoul, to watch Belfort from thence and to confine its garrison.

He would also hold Gray, and cover Besancon from there and Vesoul.[28] Orders at once went out therefore to the marching columns, halting them with a view to retracing their steps on the following day; and this was the position until 5.00pm on October 29, when a report came in from Prince William that a cavalry patrol pushed towards Dijon had found the roads entirely clear of the enemy. Information from the inhabitants suggested that the local authorities had decided that city was not to be defended. It seemed to be too good an opportunity to miss; Dijon was itself an important centre, and its possession would seriously hamper future French operations by threatening the roads running southwards from the city. It was also of considerable political and historical significance, being the ancient capital of Burgundy. On the other hand, given the extended responsibilities of the corps, both the operation to occupy Dijon, and the drain on resources of providing a garrison for it thereafter meant that the decision to take the city was by no means risk free. In the hope that the defeats recently inflicted on the French might keep them quiet for a fortnight or so Werder, after a lengthy discussion with

Beyer at Reneve l'Eglise on the morning of October 30, finally ordered him to advance with two brigades and to occupy Dijon that day. Werder emphasised to Beyer, however, that he was not to allow himself to be drawn into any serious engagement except under the most favourable circumstances.[29] If Dijon should, after all, be found to be occupied, Beyer was to halt on the Tille, seven miles east of the city.

News of the local authority's intention to give up Dijon without a fight had spread rapidly in the city, providing angry public protests; and the decision was reversed. During the night of October 29/30 reinforcements poured into the city until Lavalle's successor Colonel Fauconnet, commanding the defences, could dispose of three line battalions, up to eight battalions of Gardes Mobiles, and a chasseur company, as well as some Gardes Nationales. This gave him a total of some 10,000 men; he had, however, been obliged to promise that he would fight the battle outside the city, and he had therefore pushed forward his leading units towards the line of the Tille, at Orgeux, Arcelot and Arc sur Tille.

It did not, however, take long for Prince William's advanced guards, which had deployed in front of Arcelot and Arc sur Tille, to force back the French outposts, which retreated to St Apollinaire. After a short engagement, the leading troops of the 1st Baden Brigade forced their way into the village, where Prince William concentrated the rest of his brigade before advancing towards St Nicolas the northeastern suburb of Dijon. In the fighting around St Apollinaire, Fauconnet was himself mortally wounded. As the French fell back towards the city, it was clear that their positions on its eastern edge, based on a series of large farms and vineyards, were strongly based and supported by a huge barricade on the Gray road. Beyer ordered Keller's 3rd Brigade to hasten its advance and to send its artillery forward to support the attack on the city, which presented an impressive spectacle from the St Apollinaire ridge.

> A rare gleam of sunshine at this moment lit up the proud old capital of Burgundy which lay beneath; darkly rose behind it the lofty conical peaks of Talant and Fontaine, while north and south the white villages stood out from the dark background formed by the vine clad slope of the Cote d'Or as in a picture.[30]

Picturesque it may have been, but for Beyer's troops there was stiff fighting ahead. Keller's three batteries had, by 3.00pm, arrived on the battlefield to reinforce the three batteries which Prince William already had in action on either side of the main road to Gray at St Apollinaire, giving the Germans a total of 34 guns to support the attack. North of the road, a barricade at the Montmusard Park was successfully stormed, and the Baden troops pushed on, taking many prisoners in the outlying farmsteads. To the south, the French launched a counter attack on Prince William's left towards Mirande, which was only thrown back after fierce fighting. The advance into Dijon itself began at about 3.00 pm and immediately ran into stiff resistance which led to savage house to house fighting. Before his troops advanced any further, Beyer realised that his gun line on the St Apollinaire heights effectively put Dijon at his mercy; but mindful of Werder's wish to spare the city as much as possible, and concerned about his ammunition supply, he desisted from a bombardment that would have been extremely effective.[31]

By 4.30pm it was growing dark. Keller's infantry was now on the scene, having hurried down the main road from Gray, advancing through Quetigny. But the onset of darkness, and the continuing ferocity of the street fighting, caused him mounting anxiety, and he decided to pull back his troops to positions outside the city, and resume the attack next day. His infantry fell back under cover of a heavy bombardment from St Apollinaire, although suffering not inconsiderable losses from the French. Prince William's brigade took up positions for the night in St Apollinaire and Varois, while Keller found quarters in Quetigny and Couternon. During the night detachments of Keller's brigade advanced through a large park south of the city to complete the work of destroying the railway at its junction near Maison Bernard.[32] News of the fighting at Dijon only reached Werder, who was at Gray, at about 10.00pm, and caused him considerable anxiety. He sent off Major Grolmann of his staff to tell Beyer that he had a free hand to decide for himself how to take Dijon subject to the overriding consideration that he should avoid street fighting and should only continue the assault if he could do so without heavy loss. If this was impossible, Beyer was to fall back on Mirebeau, to which place Werder sent off some artillery and cavalry to cover any retreat should it be necessary.[33]

Werder's anxieties, however, proved needless. At 3.45am on October 31, a deputation from the city arrived at Beyer's headquarters at Varois to negotiate a convention for the surrender of Dijon. The terms that were agreed provided for the deposit of half a million francs as guarantee of the inhabitants' peaceable conduct, the return of German prisoners, the removal of barricades and provisions for 20,000 men.[34] Next day, Beyer rode into the city and established his headquarters in the Préfecture; the French defenders of Dijon had during the night retreated southwards towards Lyon and southwest towards Auxonne. It was an important victory, but it had not been achieved without loss; Beyer's total casualties in killed and wounded amounted to 268. French losses were harder to ascertain; the total of killed was of the order of 200, while 103 prisoners were taken, many of whom were found to be extremely drunk. On October 31 the funeral of Colonel Fauconnet took place, with full military honours; the officers of the Garde Nationale in the city attended in uniform.

Moltke, meanwhile, unaware of the most recent events in the south eastern theatre, had been considering the threat posed by Belfort, and on October 28 he sent a telegram on the subject to the Governor General of Alsace, emphasising the importance of completing the investment of Belfort as soon as possible. Tresckow would take command of this operation, to which the Governor General was ordered to give as much support as he could. Moltke sent a similar telegram to Werder, adding the by now familiar injunction that 'it is desirable that, on your part, you should display enterprise.'[35] In fact, Werder did not get this further prompt until November 3, by which time, of course he was able to point to the occupation of Dijon as a demonstration of his vigorous compliance with Moltke's wishes. Werder was entitled to feel some satisfaction at the taking of Dijon, which had a considerable propaganda value, even if it created further operational difficulties for him. The XIV Corps historian recorded this:

> The capture of Dijon had a great moral effect in France. It frustrated the concentration of the strong bodies of the enemy intended to close on the embracing entrenchments already begun. Once taken, Dijon had to be held, in

spite of the forces of the XIV Corps being split up and disseminated over a great extent of country.[36]

On November 3 Moltke notified Werder of the progress of the Second Army, telling him that it would reach the Seine at Chatillon and Troyes by November 8. As usual, he took the opportunity to add a further prompt, since he was also able to confirm that Tresckow had set out with the 1st Reserve Division from Colmar to Belfort, as a result of which, he told Werder, 'you can now pursue your offensive towards Dôle and the rail junction at Arc en Senans. You can also push from Dijon towards Châlon sur Saône and observe Besancon.'[37] This further direct instruction from Moltke gave Werder no choice but to prepare an advance towards Dôle, but first he must ascertain what French forces might await him. Unknown to him as well as to Moltke, these had reached a considerable strength. At Besancon Michel, who had taken over from Cambriels on October 29, had 45,000 men and 42 guns. Garibaldi, who following Gambetta's visit in October had set about assembling his forces around Dôle, now had some 12,000 men with six guns. At Nevers a corps of some 18,000 men with three batteries had been assembled. At Langres, about 12,000 Gardes Mobiles and Garde Nationales offered a permanent threat to Werder's communications, while the garrison of Belfort would also be a constant menace until the investment was complete.[38] In Werder's favour, however, was the fact that there was no overall commander of these forces which so heavily outnumbered him; the lack of any co-ordination between them gave him the chance to defeat them in detail, or at least to avoid defeat himself.

Werder had been at Vesoul since November 2, and in the days following his arrival there the intelligence gathered by his patrols began to indicate that the forces opposed to him were rapidly strengthening. He was particularly concerned to protect his communications with Tresckow, whose force was now assembling to complete the investment of Belfort, and detached a flying column eastwards for the purpose. Reconnaissance towards Besancon found little enemy activity; on the other hand, in front of Gray, the German outposts noted a good deal of activity on the Dôle and Besancon road, and Werder concluded that Michel aimed to effect a junction with Garibaldi.[39] Further west, French activity south of Dijon had considerably increased, suggesting that Beyer might be increasingly at risk in his exposed position there. With only eleven battalions, eight squadrons and six batteries, totalling 10,500 men with 36 guns, Beyer had to hold down a potentially hostile population of 46,000 in the city, while preparing to face an assault from the evidently rapidly increasing forces around him.[40] Apart from the troops investing the fortresses, the rest of Werder's forces totalled only 21,500 men and 72 guns, and with this he had to cover his line of communication from Vesoul to Dijon, some 54 miles long, as well as the lines of communication to Epinal and Belfort. To carry out Moltke's desired operation against Dôle might require the abandonment for the moment of Dijon, after which he could move the whole of his force to a central position between Besancon and Dôle, thus preventing any junction between Garibaldi and Michel. As a first step, he had planned an advance by Beyer against Auxonne; but what seemed to be the growing likelihood of an advance against Gray led him to defer it for the moment.

In fact, the movements of the French were defensive rather than offensive in character. It seemed to them that there was a serious risk of a German advance due south from Dijon towards Chagny, and it was to this place that Michel was heading on November 8 when he set off from Besancon leaving a garrison there of 15,000 men. Michel was shortly afterwards succeeded by Crouzat, a sound artillery general, when the extreme pessimism of Michel's opinions – he believed it would be necessary to fall back from Chagny all the way to Lyon – led to his removal from command. It was soon evident that Garibaldi, too was on the move, pulling out of Dôle on the same date and setting off for Autun, leaving one brigade behind as a rearguard. By November 10, having concentrated all his available forces at Vesoul, Werder also began a westward march, which was intended to take him to the line of the Ognon by November 13. Writing to Beyer on that day reporting his planned movements, he left it to him to decide whether to hang on to Dijon or to pull out all of his forces in co-operating with Werder's planned movement against Dôle. Considering the size of the forces available to the enemy, the operations on which Werder was about to embark would, but for the extremely timorous policy followed by the French command, have been somewhat hazardous. The news of the fall of Neu Brisach on November 10, which Moltke circulated to Werder, Tresckow and the Governor General of Alsace on the following day, meant that Tresckow could now embark on formal siege operations against Belfort; but it would have no bearing on Werder's immediate task of catching, pinning down and defeating Crouzat and Garibaldi.[41] In fact Crouzat was to be available to Werder as a potential quarry for only a few days. The need to concentrate all their available forces for a decisive thrust to relieve Paris led Gambetta and Freycinet to the conclusion that Crouzat's troops would best be employed as part of the Army of the Loire, and he was accordingly ordered to transfer his entire force, now designated the 20th Corps, to Gien. The movement began on November 17 and was completed three days later. Crouzat now found himself in command of the right wing of d'Aurelle's army, the 18th Corps also being placed under his command for the forthcoming operation.

13

Beaune La Rolande

It was upon Crouzat that was to fall the responsibility of fighting the first battle in the campaign brought about by the Army of the Loire's attempt to advance to the relief of Paris. Crouzat's orders came, to d'Aurelle's very great annoyance, direct from Freycinet, who had lost all patience with the commander of the Army of the Loire as a result of his negative attitude in the course of an increasingly acrimonious correspondence. What upset d'Aurelle particularly were the instructions repeated in each set of orders sent direct to the corps commanders that further orders would follow. D'Aurelle, who regarded this process as both unjustified and unprecedented, and destructive of the corps commander's freedom of action, contemptuously noted the consequences: 'This succession of movements, sometimes forward and sometimes back, these pauses automatically executed after orders were sent each day by telegraph, and issued far away from the scene, is this a skilful conduct of war as we understand it?'[1] Nonetheless, there was nothing he could do about it unless he was prepared directly to overrule Freycinet, so Crouzat was left to do the best he could. His orders were by nightfall on November 28 to occupy Beaune la Rolande, Juranville and Maizières, and to dig in that position pending further instructions. Crouzat's connection with the main body of the Army of the Loire to his left was covered by Cathelineau's franc-tireurs on the edge of the Forest of Orleans; behind this stood the 1st Division, which was available to support Crouzat's advance if necessary.

Crouzat might have some reason to be dubious about prompt support from des Pallières, who had a day or two before hijacked a supply convoy carrying rations destined for the 20th Corps and diverted them to his own troops, obliging d'Aurelle to intervene on Crouzat's behalf. Even without support however, Crouzat disposed of some 60,000 troops and 138 guns with which to attack the positions occupied by Voigts-Rhetz initially with some 11,000 men and 70 guns. The outpost line of the X Corps was nearly ten miles in length but the main body of the corps was well established on the heights on either side of Beaune and on the Long Cour ridge in a series of solidly built farmhouses. The key to the position was Beaune la Rolande itself, which had been carefully prepared for a prolonged defence based on the thick stone walls of the town which stood twelve feet high. Crouzat ordered his own corps to advance towards the right of the German position, the 1st Division (de Polignac) advancing from Boiscommun, and the 2nd Division (Thornton) from Montbarrois and St Loup directly on Beaune, with the 3rd Division (Ségard) held in reserve at St Loup. The 18th Corps was temporarily under the command of Colonel Billot, its chief of staff; it was intended that Bourbaki should command the corps but he had not yet arrived to take up the post. Crouzat's orders to Billot were to advance through Maizières and Juranville.[2]

Beaune la Rolande was held by the 38th Brigade (von Wedell), while to the east the position of the 39th Brigade (von Valentini) was based on Les Cotelles, south of Long Cour ridge. In support, the 37th Brigade (Lehmann) and the Corps

General von Voigts-Rhetz, commander of the German X Corps (Rousset/*Histoire*)

artillery were moving up from Egny to Marcilly, partly since Voigts-Rhetz and Caprivi felt that the 39th Brigade was in the more exposed position and partly because of reports of French activity in the Loing valley north of Montargis, which if true suggested that the French might be taking that line in an advance towards Fontainebleau. Voigts-Rhetz had been promised the support on his right of Stülpnagel's 5th Division from Alvensleben's III Corps in the event of a substantial French advance, to which all the indications pointed as being highly probable. Although heavily outnumbered, Voigts-Rhetz could count on the reliable and very experienced Hanoverian troops of the X Corps to put up a stout defence in the positions that had been carefully chosen and which they had had time to prepare. He also had available Hartmann's 1st Cavalry Division, which was held in reserve around Boynes.

The battle was opened by Crouzat's artillery, at about 8.00 am, firing into Beaune la Rolande from positions around St Loup. One of the first shells to fall hit the building housing the headquarters of Voigts-Rhetz. All along the front line of the X Corps the German outposts were soon driven back. On the right of the French advance, Robert's Brigade of the 18th Corps pushed forward into Juranville, the German garrison of the villages retreating on the main position at Les Cotelles. Meanwhile, on the extreme right Bonnet's Brigade moved through Lorcy, its defenders falling back to the line of the railway embankment just west of Corbeilles. Billot was encountering much stiffer opposition than he had expected; when Crouzat drew up his plan he was relying on reports, which were correct at the time, that this part of the position was only lightly held. However, Voigts-Rhetz's decision to bring the 37th Brigade up to Marcilly meant that it was immediately able to support Valentini's troops around Les Cotelles. Prolonged fighting ensued around Juranville, as Valentini attempted to counter attack from the direction of Venonville. It was not until approaching noon that, supported by a battalion from Lehmann's 37th Brigade, he was able to reoccupy Juranville; but he was able to hold on to the village for only a short while before Bonnet's advance on the far right into Corbeilles threatened to out flank him, as a result of which he fell back again on Venonville and Long Cour.[3] It was on the Long Cour ridge that Voigts-Rhetz now concentrated the bulk of his corps, leaving Beaune to be defended by Wedell's brigade and the corps' horse artillery. Billot now assembled the main body of his corps for an immediate assault on the ridge, without waiting for any artillery preparation. Advancing in dense columns, over open ground to the east of Les Cotelles the French infantry came under heavy fire from the German gun line north of the Moulin des Hommes Libres, and broke in disorder.[4] The French enjoyed more success in front of Les Cotelles; their first assault at about 2pm was thrown back, but a further attack half an hour later compelled the Prussian fusilier battalion holding the village to fall back towards the mill on the heights to the north. Realising that this was as much progress as he could make, Billot broke off his attack, and contented himself with digging in at Les Cotelles, while holding himself ready to support the 20th Corps in its attacks on Beaune la Rolande.

Crouzat's leading troops had run into the German outposts at about 9.00am; as the latter fell back, Crouzat ordered Thornton to move with the 2nd Division against the southeast side of the town while Polignac tried with the 1st Division to work his way around Wedell's right flank by advancing eastwards from Batilly. This was broken up by the heavy German artillery fire, and it was not until Crouzat committed part of Ségard's Division that the French could make any further headway to the west of Beaune. By 12.30pm, however, the pressure began to tell, and the Germans fell back along the line of the Roman road known as the Chemin de César. This French advance put Crouzat's leading troops well around the northeastern edge of the town, and Crouzat could begin to hope that he might soon surround it completely, since on the east side of the town his troops had begun to move up the heights of Les Roches, from which the two German battalions there fell back to the north of the town at La Rue Boussier. The threat posed by the French advance along the Roman road was serious; Voigts-Rhetz was however able to counter it by bringing forward the 1st Cavalry Division. The division had stood to arms as soon as the battle began, and at noon Voigts-Rhetz had brought it south east to the Butte de L'Ormeteau. From there its horse artillery opened fire on Polignac's troops as they moved eastwards along the Roman road, causing them to halt, and to deploy along the Fosse des Près. An attempt by two cuirassier regiments to charge the French infantry failed, however, in the rain sodden ground. Although the French advance around the north of Beaune was held up in this way, by 1.00 pm Crouzat had practically succeeded in encircling the town, and was able to concentrate all his artillery fire on it.[5] Wedell's brigade was now effectively divided into two parts. Lieutenant Colonel Sannow, with the 16th Regiment, occupied Beaune, while the bulk of Colonel von Cranach's 57th Regiment stood at La Rue Boussier. Sannow deployed the 1st Battalion on the southwest side of the town and in the cemetery to the west with the fusilier battalion on the south and the 2nd Battalion on the east. Sannow also had a couple of companies from the 57th Regiment, which held the wall on the northwest. The first French assault, from the west, was launched soon after 1.00 pm; it was thrown back, as was a further assault, after which the French kept up a heavy rifle and artillery fire on the German positions. Some houses in the town caught fire, and breaches were made in the walls of the cemetery. Ammunition was running low, and by 2.00 pm it was beginning to look as if the town could not be held. In receipt of an erroneous report that the French were in Beaune, and fearing that his troops would be heavily defeated if the corps did not pull back, Voigts-Rhetz now gave the order for a general retreat.

Caprivi, however, aware that the leading troops of the 5th Division were by now close enough to save the day, dissuaded him from issuing the order. The 5th Division had been assembled early in the day at Dadonville, just outside Pithiviers, and had set off down the road to Boynes as the sound of gunfire reached the Second Army headquarters. When he heard the roar of artillery, Waldersee hastily abandoned the letter he was writing, and rode off towards Beaune, noticing as he went that the inhabitants were clearly greatly excited at what seemed to be the start of the long awaited and decisive battle.[6] Frederick Charles remained at Pithiviers, monitoring the reports as they came in. As well as reporting on the developing situation at Beaune, there were others, by no means all accurate, which appeared to confirm the earlier indications that the French might be preparing an advance in the Loing valley, and these persuaded Frederick Charles that he must shift the Second Army

Alfred von Waldersee (author's collection)

to the east. In spite of the constant reports from Voigts-Rhetz, whose corps was fighting for its life at Beaune, Frederick Charles all day paid more regard to the supposed need to move troops into the Loing valley, and ordered Voigts- Rhetz to detach a brigade for the purpose; he had formed a fixed belief that it was the 18th Corps that was advancing north from Montargis. To be fair to Frederick Charles, the possibility that the assault on Beaune might be intended to mask just such a movement had not left the mind of Voigts-Rhetz either, as he confirmed in a telegram to the Second Army headquarters at 11.45 am.[7]

In spite of the mounting evidence that a major battle was in progress, Frederick Charles remained at Pithiviers until gone noon; he then made slow progress towards the battlefield because of his preference to ride only at a trot. He was south of Boynes when the leading troops of the 5th Division arrived there, and ordered them to march south east towards the fighting; he also sent orders to Alvensleben that the 6th Division and the corps artillery should follow. Before leaving Pithiviers with the Prince, Stiehle had at 11.00 am sent a report to Moltke of the situation as it was now seen at the Second Army headquarters. Repeating the erroneous information about French activity in the Loing valley, he told Moltke of the intention to deploy the X Corps in the district between the Loing and the Yonne, to place the III Corps on the line Beaumont-Chateau Landon and to concentrate the IX Corps at Pithiviers. 'Obviously, this state of affairs upsets, for the time, all plans for crossing the Loire below Orleans … I suggest to your Excellency whether, from the troops before Paris a strong occupation of Fontainebleau and Monet could not be carried out'.[8] Even after reaching the German right flank, Stiehle and Frederick

A scene from the Battle of Beaune La Rolande, by Pallandre (Rousset/*Combattants*)

Charles seem not to have grasped the extent of the battle in which Voigts-Rhetz was engaged, and made no attempt to contact him as, from the Long Cour ridge, he continued to direct the defence of his hard pressed position.

On the right flank, the advanced guard of the 5th Division under Colonel von Wulffen had deployed on the south side of the Butte de l'Ormeteau and towards Arconville; thereafter, the French made no further very determined attempts to advance in this sector. Further south, the advancing troops of the 5th Division came up in support of the 1st Cavalry Division, and ejected the French from the woods at La Pierre Percée, while Wulffen, crossing the Roman road, occupied the Bois de la Leu.[9]

It was however around the battered walls of Beaune la Rolande itself that the struggle continued. All day Crouzat had been waiting for units from the 18th Corps to come up and join the assaults on the town; but it was only as night fell that Billot's troops came forward to support the attack on the eastern side of the town. In spite of desperate fighting against heavy odds and at close range, Sannow's men resisted these last assaults, led by Crouzat in person, and the French fell back through Montbarrois and Jarrisoy under a hail of artillery fire from the eight batteries which the Germans brought up either side of Beaune. Crouzat led his corps back to the positions it had occupied before the battle at Bellegarde and Boiscommun, while Billot remained in possession of Venonville, Juranville and Maizières. Out on the far left of the French position, Cathelineau's franc tireurs retreated from Courcelles and disappeared again into the Foret d'Orleans. Behind them the 1st Division of the 15th Corps, which had made no move to support Crouzat, remained where it was at Chambon. The X Corps remained in Beaune and along the Long Cour ridge, while the 5th Division bivouacked for the night behind it at La Pierre Percée and Marcilly. The 6th Division had in the meanwhile reached Boynes. The battle had cost the Germans a total of 898 casualties; the bulk of these, naturally, had come from the X Corps, which suffered losses of 758 killed wounded and missing. Crouzat had lost a total of about 3100 men, of whom 1800 were prisoners.[10]

It was a crucially important victory for the Germans, and had administered what might prove a fatal check to an advance by the Army of the Loire upon Paris. Moreover, its effects were so considerable that they were to be felt elsewhere. As Colonel Hale noted:

> Rarely has an attacking force been so completely overthrown and rendered so thoroughly incapable for either defence or offence: rarely has the demoralisation resulting from a single defeat in one theatre of war so greatly influenced the course of a subsequent renewal of the struggle in another theatre of war. Beaune la Rolande made itself felt on the Lisaine.[11]

But curiously the extent of the victory was not apparent to the Germans:

> The Headquarters staff of the Second Army was unable, on the evening of the 28th November, to grasp to its full extent the importance of the victory which had been gained. As it was rather expected on the following day that the enemy would renew his attack ... General von Manstein received instructions to move off with two brigades very early next morning to Boynes and Bazoches les Gallerandes.[12]

French infantry on the assault during Beaune La Rolande, by Pallandre (Rousset/ *Combattants*)

Not everyone on the German side was mistaken about what had been achieved; Waldersee, who had been all day on the battlefield, came up to Frederick Charles at about 5.30 pm, as the Prince was about to ride back to Pithiviers, to urge him to exploit the victory. 'A complete victory has been won,' said Waldersee; 'it will be a Rossbach for the French if there is a vigorous pursuit.' In making this oblique comment, Waldersee was being tactful; Hartmann's cavalry was available to pursue the retreating enemy, but had made no move to do so in the absence of orders, apparently due to the heavy ground.[13] Frederick Charles showed no marked enthusiasm, merely telling Stiehle to inform Alvensleben and Voigts-Rhetz of his wishes, which included again a requirement that Voigts-Rhetz send a brigade to the Loing valley. After this, Frederick Charles and Waldersee rode back to Pithiviers. In spite of the comprehensive account which Waldersee gave him, the Prince's report that night to the Royal Headquarters was laconic and did scant justice to all that had been achieved. Stiehle, meanwhile, had found Alvensleben, and appears to have accepted from him that he had no forces immediately available for a pursuit; he then went to look for Voigts-Rhetz. Not locating him, he left written orders about the transfer of a brigade to the Loing valley, with no mention of any pursuit; and Voigts-Rhetz, when he read these, refused to send off one of his exhausted brigades to the Loing that night. In this manner an opportunity to smash Crouzat was completely lost.

Crouzat himself was under no illusion as to the outcome of the battle, reporting to d'Aurelle that night his retreat to his previous positions, and noting

General von Stiehle, Chief of Staff of the German Second Army (Rousset/*Histoire*)

with relief that he had not been followed. When he sat down three days later to give a comprehensive report to the War Ministry at Tours as to the state of his corps after the battle, he listed their urgent needs: 'twenty thousand haversacks, ten thousand pairs of shoes, ten thousand pairs of gaiters, and tents for ten thousand men. Let me have several days of rest to recover. The morale of my men is good, but they lack too much for the cold and wet weather.'[14] This greatly annoyed Freycinet, who immediately dashed off a response which Aurelle described as 'hard, brutal, unjust' to a brave and loyal soldier. Freycinet wrote:

> It seems to me that you are very quickly discouraged, and you do not face the enemy with the solidity without which success is impossible … It is necessary to march and to march quickly … If the attitude of this corps continues to appear so uncertain, I will consider you as personally responsible, and you will have to account to the government for the consequences of the situation.

When he read this, d'Aurelle was furious, saying to General Borel that he refused to transmit such a message, which was a 'moral assassination;' Borel, however, pointed out to him that he had a copy for information only, and that the message had gone direct to Crouzat.[15] For his part Crouzat was hurt and bewildered; giving an account of the immediate state of his corps had seemed to him no more than his simple duty. In the meantime, however, his initial report of the outcome of Beaune la Rolande had brought in response instructions not to pursue any further attack, so on November 29 he pulled back the units of the 18th Corps

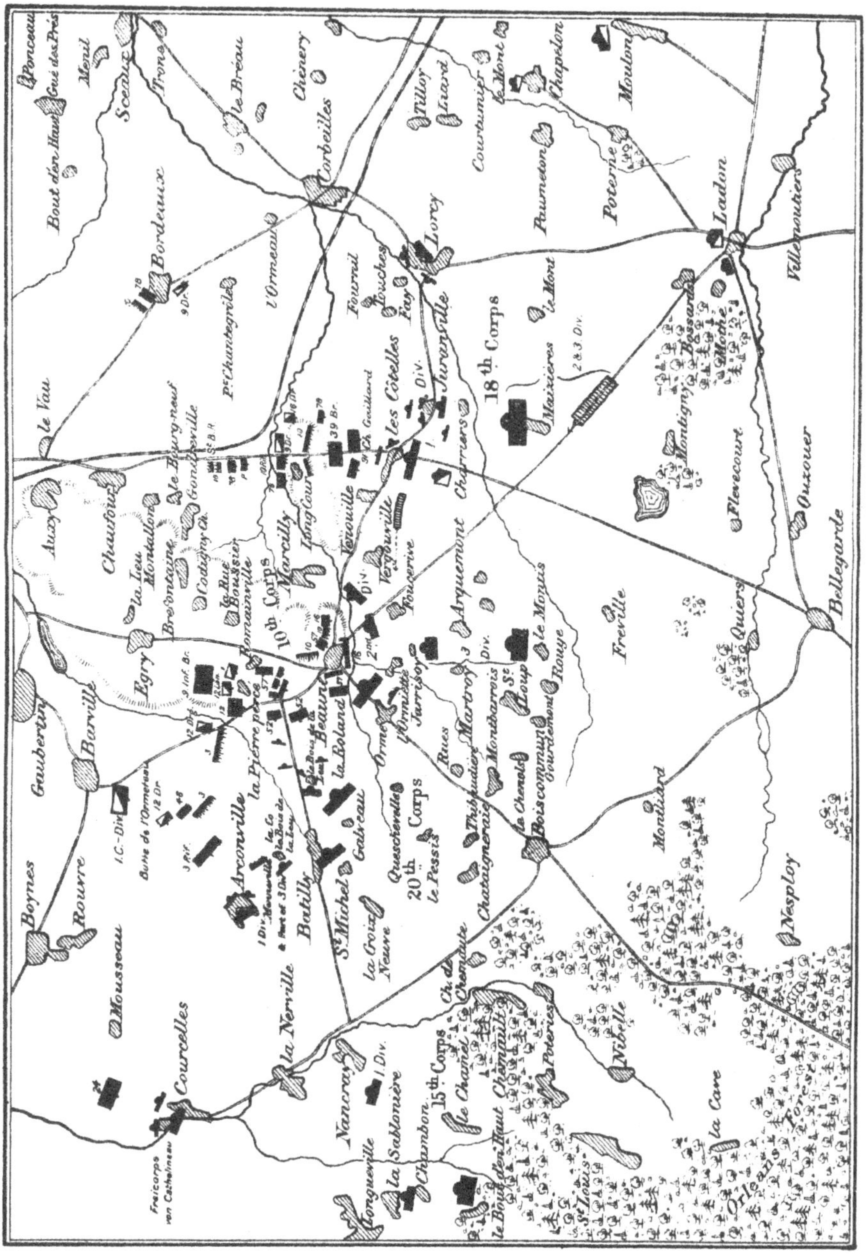

The Battle of Beaune La Rolande, November 28 1870

which had remained in position around Venonville and Juranville in the direction of Ladon.

The Detachment had on November 28 at last enjoyed a rest day in the positions it had reached on the Loir. It was not before time. The official historian of the Bavarian Army described the condition of von der Tann's Corps:

> The troops were much exhausted, their clothing and equipment were very defective, the horses were tired and low in condition, and the general tone was far from cheerful. The incessant and forced marches of the last fortnight, under most unfavourable conditions of weather and ground, as well as the fatiguing outpost and patrol duty in face of an enemy whom we could never grasp, and yet whose existence continually made itself felt, had exhausted the physical strength of the soldiers.[16]

While his troops recruited their strength, Stosch pondered how best to execute the general spirit of Moltke's instructions. Looking at the opportunities presented by what was known of the position of the French, he prepared and sent to the Second Army a message outlining a plan for the Detachment to move next day in an arrowhead formation, the point being aimed at Villamblain on the main road from Châteaudun, seventeen miles from Orleans. This scheme, however, which would give the Detachment the chance to operate strategically against d'Aurelle's left flank, Stosch was obliged to adandon. During the day he received instructions from Stiehle to move towards Janville-Toury, to take up the duty of covering the Orleans-Paris road so that the Second Army would be free to move to its left to deal with the imaginary threat in the Loing valley. Accordingly, Stosch sent a revised march plan which would put the Detachment next day in a position facing south and standing immediately to the right of the Second Army. It was not what Stosch wanted, nor did he suppose that it would be what Moltke wanted, and he was careful to report it all by telegram to Versailles.[17]

The immediate aftermath of the battle of Beaune la Rolande was shaped by the failure of Frederick Charles and his staff to understand the true position, being 'unable, on the evening of November 28, to grasp to its full extent the importance of the victory which had been gained'.[18] It was only on the following day, when staff officers of the headquarters of the Second Army visited the battlefield that the extent of the success of the X Corps began to be appreciated. Kretschmann, writing to his wife that day, recorded his impressions of the heavy losses that the attackers had suffered.

> The X Corps has sent back 700 prisoners; we have nearly 900 more unwounded. Most of them were soldiers of the line and Zouaves. The French brought against us their best troops. The 1st Zouaves has been particularly hard hit; around Beaune la Rolande alone, among the dead, there are nearly 300 Zouaves. The men fought extremely well; in fact there were corpses all round our position within two yards; in one place three officers together.[19]

Frederick Charles himself did not leave Pithiviers, which was a pity, because he might have felt more disposed to follow up the victory by launching an attack on the beaten French. As it was, the Germans spent November 29 dug in around Beaune la Rolande and on the Long Cour ridge, awaiting an attack that Crouzat had seen clearly was out of the question. When he pulled back during the day, the Germans were able to stand down and go into quarters.

At Pithiviers, Stiehle had on the morning of November 29 received Moltke's letter of two days earlier, reporting on the imminence of the expected sortie from Paris, and confirming Stosch's departure to take over as Chief of Staff of the Detachment. In his letter, Moltke also analysed the overall position of the German armies. He drew attention to the threat to the communications system from the south, where Werder did not have sufficient resources to cover the whole of the line between Montbéliard and Chatillon, as a result of which he was moving the 13th Division by rail to Troyes. But the main point of his letter was to emphasise the crucial role of the Second Army.

> It is the struggle which you are going to engage in against the only real army that France can put into the field that has a truly decisive importance. If (and I sincerely hope this does not happen) you lose the battle, my plan will be to lift the blockade of Paris without regard to the loss of our siege equipment. The Crown Prince of Saxony would operate with General Manteuffel against the concentrations in the north, and the Crown Prince of Prussia with you against the Army of the Loire. In this way, our decisive superiority will bring us victory, and we shall return to Paris which because of the broken rail lines will not have been able to be revictualled, and after the surrender of which we will recover our guns.[20]

It was an emphatic statement of the need to take the offensive, but Stiehle and Frederick Charles had got themselves into a mind set that meant that Moltke's encouragement had little effect on their conviction that the Second Army must await the expected attack from an enemy that hugely outnumbered it. Stiehle was, however, sufficiently struck by the obvious difference of view between Moltke and the Second Army to fix a meeting for the following day with Stosch at Bazoches les Gallerandes, evidently feeling that he had better hear at first hand from the Detachment's new Chief of Staff the current state of opinion at Versailles.[21]

For the moment, the orders from Second Army issued at noon on November 29 merely provided for concentration against a French advance. Voigts-Rhetz was relieved from any further responsibility from the Loing Valley, since the arrival of the 40th Brigade (von Kraatz) would enable that section to be covered, and ordered to concentrate east of Beaune; the III Corps would stand on its right, while the IX Corps was behind at Pithiviers. Meanwhile the Detachment had been making good progress in its eastward move. The troops, back in the Beauce country, were not sorry to be back in familiar ground.

> After nearly three weeks of exhausting marches, the monotonous and undulating plain appeared like an old acquaintance, whom we did not exactly regard with affection, but whose good qualities absence had taught us to esteem. The cavalry and artillery felt a sense of security, when they debouched from the valley of the Loir brook on to the wide open plain of La Beauce, leaving behind them the ground so ill adapted to their arms.[22]

The march of the Detachment, however, was not without incident. Its path, from which de Sonis had so abruptly recoiled when he retreated from Châteaudun on November 26, took it into the flank of Chanzy's 16th Corps, and this led to a sharp encounter at Varize, on the River Conie, where a force of Lipowski's franc tireurs had been posted to hold up the Detachment's advance from the main road from Châteaudun to Orgères on November 29.

Von der Tann's scouts had early that morning located French troops occupying Nobleville and Civy on the flank of the Bavarians. The batteries of Rudolph von der Tann's 4th Brigade, which formed the advanced guard, at once came into action; and a brisk advance by seven companies of infantry sufficed to clear the villages of the French troops. These now retreated to a strong position in a park to the west of Varize. This position had been well prepared for defence, and there was a stiff fight before two companies of the 10th Regiment, advancing from Civy, forced their way into the park. The French troops remaining there now found themselves attacked on all sides, and at 11.00 am surrendered. 'Extremely indignant at the bad leadership of Lieutenant Colonel Lipowski, who in order to save himself and the rest, had left them in the lurch,' the prisoners asked von der Tann to publicise Lipowski's cowardice, which however he declined to do.[23] To the south, meanwhile, the 6th Cavalry Brigade had been active, clearing the right flank of the Detachment's advance by driving back Digard's Cavalry Brigade which it encountered near Tournoisis on the road to Orleans. Further north, the 4th Cavalry Division had by the end of the day reached the Paris – Orleans high road at Toury, while the 22nd Division was at Allaines and Ymonville, and the 17th Division's advanced guard was at Bazoches les Hautes. The 1st Bavarian Division had stopped short of its intended destination around Terminiers, as reports indicated that the place was still occupied; the 2nd Bavarian Division, however, took up its position south of Orgères. Von der Tann had suggested hopefully that in order to give his corps some rest it might take up a position in which it was covered by one of the cavalry divisions, and thus not have to bivouack in direct contact with the enemy; but the request was firmly denied.

Stosch and the Grand Duke established the Detachment's headquarters for the night at Viabon, about five miles north of Orgères, and there received Frederick Charles' orders for the following day's operations. Announcing the projected exchange of cavalry divisions, the Prince ordered the Detachment to take up a position extending from Orgères to Bazoches Les Gallerandes, a front of over sixteen miles covering the main road north from Orleans. The position of the Second Army was similarly extended, so that all told the forces at Frederick Charles' disposal were spread over forty miles. The defensive nature of his intentions was unmistakable. That evening, the report from the Second Army to the Royal Headquarters was still extremely cautious, noting that not much could happen for the moment, not least because the position in the Loing Valley had not been conclusively resolved, and because the extent of the victory of the X Corps had not become known until late in the day. For the next day, advanced guards were to follow up the retreating French towards Montargis and Bellegarde.[24] In taking such a limited view of what was practicable, Frederick Charles appears to have been swayed by Alvensleben, whose reception of a tentative suggestion that the III Corps should advance on its own towards Orleans had been unenthusiastic.

Next morning came telegrams with news that the sortie from Paris had finally begun, which supported the expectation at the headquarters of the Second Army that the Army of the Loire would advance to the attack. Frederick Charles rode south from Pithiviers to watch the advance of the troops which had been pushed forward to reconnoitre the French positions. All along the line to the south of Beaune la Rolande the advancing Germans encountered resistance, which also appeared to confirm the view that the French were getting ready to advance. This was partly true; orders sent direct by Freycinet to Crouzat were to the effect that the 18th and 20th Corps should shift to their left behind the cover of some modest advances northward, which produced the series of collisions with the German reconnaissance in force. One of these led to an attack at day break on the German outposts in some farmhouses on the northern edge of Montbarrois; by noon, however, the French had been cleared from the village with the loss of a hundred prisoners. Another advance, north from St Loup, was soon abandoned when it encountered a company of German infantry supported by artillery. The orders given by Voigts-Rhetz for the operations of the X Corps pushed the 39th Brigade towards St Loup, Maizières and Lorcy, while the 38th Brigade remained on the Long Cour ridge. The 37th Brigade was to advance on Montargis. It was the 39th Brigade which was first in action, advancing to the attack of Maizières, which was found to be strongly held by French infantry, supported by artillery. Even after a half hour bombardment of Maizières by ten guns, the German infantry could make no headway, and Valentini, commanding the advance guard of the 39th Brigade, broke off the action and fell back. These signs of the enemy strength in his immediate front led Voigts-Rhetz to conclude that a general attack might be imminent, and he also halted the march of the 37th Brigade to Montargis, pulling it back from Mignerette to the Long Cour ridge to await the assault.

Meanwhile, in response to a request for support from the 39th Brigade, Stülpnagel had sent forward the 52nd Regiment with a squadron of cavalry and a light artillery battery in the direction of Maizières. When they arrived in front of the village, at about 4.00pm, the 39th Brigade had already broken off the action; but seeing that the enemy were resuming their advance, the German artillery opened a heavy fire on the French infantry and silenced the artillery, as a result of which they fell back into Maizières, while the Germans returned to Beaune.

All of this had led Frederick Charles to believe that he must reinforce his front line, and he ordered Manstein to advance to Boynes in support; when the leading troops of IX Corps reached there, they were pushed forward to Courcelles against an advance from the French towards Nancray from Boiscommun. By nightfall, the fighting had died down, and Manstein's troops went back to Pithiviers. Meanwhile Kraatz had on November 30 finally reached the valley of the Loing, so that although patrols reported, inaccurately, that Montargis was still held in force, there was no longer any need to divert Voigts-Rhetz from attending to the enemy in his immediate front.[25] It had been an inconclusive day, demonstrating again the usual pointlessness of so called reconnaissances in force. Little had been learned, and no significant damage had been inflicted on the enemy. Something of this seems to have communicated itself to Frederick Charles, who encountered Waldersee as he was preparing to return to Pithiviers. Inviting him to travel back with him in his carriage, the Prince mused on the outcome of the battle of November 28. 'The battlefield reminds me of St Privat. Yesterday great results might have been obtained, for this corps (Crouzat's 20th Corps) could not possibly be fit for a fight, and also is not now. Today a strong offensive might have reaped its reward, but -.'

At this point, he broke off, and changed the subject, but he later returned to it, saying firmly: 'The favourable moment for the offensive is gone; the information leads to the conclusion that the French have been reinforced on the line Boiscommun-Bellegarde; what is going on behind the Forest of Orleans is out of sight ... Now I am reduced to a waiting attitude.' He went on to speculate gloomily that 'a soldier's good fortune seldom comes back to him with the same favour;' and put his situation down to the difficulty of collecting intelligence in the face of a hostile population in difficult terrain. Clearly, whatever excuses he night make, he had become aware of the opportunity he had missed.[26]

Some idea of the continuing discontent at Versailles can be gained from the Crown Prince's diary. He was not, of course, an entirely dispassionate observer, missing few chances to criticise his royal cousin; on November 29 he noted: 'Today our prospects are once again quite favourable, and if only Prince Frederick Charles could make up his mind to face Orleans, the Parisians would have to abandon for good their hopes of relief.'[27] Next day, however, and more significantly, he recorded Moltke's own feelings about the lack of progress of the Second Army. 'Every day came reports from the "Prince Field Marshal," as he calls himself, with fresh reasons why the attack cannot be made, so that General Count Moltke is by this time quite beside himself at the dilatoriness displayed there.'[28]

Meanwhile Frederick Charles' Chief of Staff had gone off to his conference with Stosch at Bazoches les Gallerandes. Stiehle should really have been in no doubt as to Moltke's wishes, or the importance that was attached to the Loire campaign, and it may well have been partly with the object of self justification that he went to meet the man who constituted Moltke's virtual presence on the Loire. Stiehle did not, however, go in a state of mind ready to accept a new strategy; for him, the first essential was to cover directly the main road from Orleans to Paris, and he was not at all persuaded by Stosch's insistence that the time had come to take the offensive and to operate against Aurelle's left flank and his westward line of communication.[29] Stiehle maintained that the proper course was to await the enemy's attack, and from this view he would not be budged, believing that the Army of the Loire had moved decisively eastwards with the intention of marching on Fontainebleau. When he got back to Pithiviers, and reported to Frederick Charles, it seemed to them both that Stosch's offensive propensities were such that the situation should be spelt out in a formal order to the Detachment. This was accordingly done; the instructions went out that night. These, which were based on a comprehensive misreading of the situation, were intended to get a firm grip on the future operations of the Detachment, even to the extent of ordering that the 22nd Division should move eastward to relieve the brigade of Manstein's IX Corps that stood at Bazoches les Gallerandes. The object of this was to ensure that Wittich's division would be available to act as a reserve for the Second Army. The order concluded with a pompous assertion of Frederick Charles' authority. 'Until the situation on the enemy's side is clearer, I must reserve to myself the communication to your Royal Highness of my further plans for driving the enemy out of Orleans.'[30] For Stosch, these orders provided further confirmation that the Second Army had completely lost sight of what Moltke required should be its principal objective, which was the destruction of the Army of the Loire and not the recapture of Orleans.

At Tours, Gambetta and Freycinet were already extremely impatient with d'Aurelle and his failure to move forward. They had been further provoked by despatches from Favre estimating that the deadline for relieving Paris was now December 15, three weeks sooner than had been supposed. In this state of mind they were still more aroused by the need for haste by the arrival on November 30 of the much travelled and long delayed message from Trochu to the effect that the sortie would begin on November 29. Freycinet went off at once, carrying with him an order for the supersession of d'Aurelle if he refused to carry out Freycinet's instructions for an immediate advance.[31] By the time he met d'Aurelle and his generals at the headquarters of the Army of the Loire on the night of November 30, they all knew the Army of Paris would have been in action for two days. At this conference, Freycinet flatly stated that the army must march at once on Paris, beginning with an immediate advance to Pithiviers; protests by d'Aurelle, Chanzy and Borel that to do so before the 15th and 16th Corps had been concentrated was extremely hazardous were brushed aside, as d'Aurelle recorded. 'M. de Freycinet obstinately maintained that Chanzy's Corps was more than sufficient to beat the Grand Duke, and he finished by declaring that the plan he had described had been irrevocably approved by the Government at Tours.' D'Aurelle tried again, pointing out that if Chanzy moved on his own he would be at risk of being crushed. But Freycinet would have none of it; and the orders went out accordingly. Freycinet later claimed that the generals accepted as correct the general principles of the plan, an assertion that especially aroused d'Aurelle's indignation. The movement involved a change of front to the right, with the advance of Chanzy's 16th Corps, pivoting on des Pallières' 1st Division at Chilleurs, and the 18th and 20th Corps coming up behind the 15th Corps from the right wing.[32] When the conference broke up, the generals hurried off to get their orders out; only when he got to his headquarters did Chanzy realise that before the general advance he must first do something about the Detachment, which would threaten his left flank, so he applied for and got d'Aurelle's permission to advance next day to clear it out of the way, supported if necessary by de Sonis and the 17th Corps at Coulmiers. The immediate target must be von der Tann, whose corps stood between Orgères and Terminiers.

For December 1 Stosch intended no significant movement for the 1st Bavarian Corps, although he stressed that 'The general situation of the war necessitates great activity in patrolling, in order to maintain the touch of the enemy, and to make him believe that an attack is pending.'[33] His ability to undertake offensive reconnaissance operations had, however, been diminished by the exchange of cavalry divisions which had begun on November 30 when the leading units of the 6th Cavalry Division set off on a long ride for the night around the rear of the Detachment in order to join the Second Army; the 4th Cavalry Division had arrived to take its place, but was a poor substitute, being extremely worn out and far less familiar with the terrain. Schmidt, the commander of the 6th Cavalry Division, rode into Stosch's headquarters at Janville at 1.30 on December 1 to take his leave of the Grand Duke before having a final conference with Stosch. The latter remarked that it was very unfortunate that he should be leaving the Detachment at this time. 'And I also lament it,' exclaimed Schmidt. 'I do not grudge to any of my comrades the laurels which undoubtedly are immediately at hand for them, but after I have gone through the Perche country without any satisfaction, I am obliged at this very moment to take a ride in rear of the army, when I could reap all the fruit of my previous hard work.' He added that the enemy was on the point of attacking, and that what Stosch needed just then was an enterprising body of cavalry. Stosch asked him if he thought that part of the Army of the Loire had moved eastwards with a view to an advance on Fontainebleau. Certainly not, replied Schmidt. 'The whole lot are still round the salient point, Orleans, but if you do not look out they will be on the top of you here.' And he went on at Stosch's request to give chapter and verse for his belief that the Detachment was threatened by at least 50,000 men; even when told that Stiehle believed that both the 15th and 16th Corps were on the line Boiscommun-Bellegarde, Schmidt stuck to his opinion.[34]

All of this left Stosch convinced that it was going to be the Detachment and not the Second Army that would strike the decisive blow, and he wasted no time in sitting down with the Grand Duke to get him to agree that on the following day steps should be taken to concentrate the Detachment with a view to taking the offensive. One problem was the fact that Frederick Charles had earmarked the 22nd Division as a reserve for the Second Army, so that it was vital to regain control of that division at once. It was essential, explained Stosch, that the Detachment should not be tied to a position astride the Orleans-Paris road; 'the Detachment would accomplish the duty assigned to it if at the right time it brought up all its troops, even to the very last man, and beat the enemy. That would be the best protection of the roads. "Anyhow, we shall have," he added, "freedom of choice for the concentration in the favourable position from Loigny to Lumeau. It answers best for the attack and the defence according to the circumstances."'[35] The Grand Duke was immediately convinced, and eagerly told Stosch that he should give orders for an attack next day, which went a bit further than Stosch had intended. Even after getting the Grand Duke's agreement, he still had his problems; what he was proposing was not only to overturn the strategy of Stiehle and Frederick Charles, but to take control of the decisive operations out of their hands. Although he might be Moltke's representative in this theatre, he needed to carry Stiehle with him, and at 6.00pm he sent a carefully worded letter to the headquarters of the Second Army explaining what he intended to do, adding that although on December 2 he could manage with only the 17th Division, on December 3 at any rate he would need to employ the 22nd Division. Not surprisingly, the Prince, when he came to read the letter, was not best pleased, and at first not inclined to agree. News, however, that the French had pulled out of Boiscommun reassured him as to his left flank, and at 9.37pm Stiehle was able to send a telegram giving Stosch the necessary permission, although this did not arrive until midnight. Stosch had written his letter without having received up to date reports from von der Tann; he was soon to discover, however, that a lot had been happening to the south of Orgères.

On December 1, after the occupation of Terminiers, the 1st Bavarian Brigade had taken up a position to the west of the village fronting south along the line Guillonville-Gommiers. In posting Dietl's brigade there, von der Tann wished it to cover the concentration of the rest of his corps around La Maladerie, at the important cross roads a mile east of Orgères. At the time, he did not feel undue concern about the forward position of the 1st Brigade, because as late as 1.00 pm cavalry patrols were reporting, incorrectly, that the enemy had not moved beyond Patay.[36] Dietl's flanks were covered by cavalry; on the left, the Bavarian Cuirassier Brigade stood near Tourette Farm, while the right flank was covered by the 9th Prussian Cavalry Brigade. As the day wore on, however strong French columns were seen moving forward, covered by cavalry on both flanks. Chanzy had launched his 2nd and 3rd Division towards Sougy and Jauréguiberry's 1st Division towards Gommiers and Guillonville.[37] The French left was covered by Michel's strong cavalry division and the advance of this force soon compelled the heavily outnumbered 9th Cavalry Brigade to fall back on Cormainville, uncovering Dietl's right flank at Guillonville. In his very exposed position, he had no option but to retreat, and at 3.00pm he fell back to Villepion. The park walls, which had not been prepared for defence, were too high, so he put two battalions into the chateau and the other buildings on the east side of the park, with another battalion on the west of it, supported by one battery. On his left, on the road to Faverolles, he posted one battalion and a rifle company, with two batteries; and he covered his right with two companies in the open country south west of Nonneville. Considering the strength of the forces opposed to him, it was not terribly impressive, especially since his troops were separated by the indefensible park walls, but it was the best that Dietl could do.[38]

News of the French advance brought reinforcements helter skelter southwards; the first to arrive was Orff, with the 2nd Brigade, who deployed his troops under very heavy fire to the west of Nonneville. They were opposed by Deplanque's Brigade, which moved forward to the attack under the cover of an intensive artillery barrage. The Bavarian batteries, moving with difficulty in the heavy ground, responded; one of them was compelled to retreat almost at once, abandoning one gun when all the horses were killed. Manful attempts by two companies of infantry failed to rescue it, and it was only when Lieutenant von Stengel rode up with a gun limber and, under heavy fire, harnessed it, that it could be brought to safety.[39] All along the front the Bavarians were taking heavy casualties, and von der Tann gave orders to commit the rest of the corps. The 3rd Brigade, however, was in cantonments well to the rear while the 4th Brigade, which was much closer at Loigny, had heard nothing of the battle. When it moved, it came up on the left of the position on the Faverolles road.

One of the casualties was Stephan, the commander of the 1st Division, who was seriously wounded when he was hit simultaneously by a shell splinter and a bullet while with the front line of the 2nd Brigade. In spite of his vigorous protests, he was carried to the rear, and the command devolved upon Dietl. His 1st Brigade was by now coming under increasing pressure on the east side of Villepion, where as dusk fell Jauréguiberry personally led three battalions of Bourdillon's Brigade in an attack which succeeded, in fierce hand to hand fighting, in forcing its way into the farm buildings around the chateau. Dietl realised that the position was no longer defensible, and pulled his own brigade out towards Loigny. On the right Orff was able to hold his position until the French ceased firing, and he then retreated to Orgères, where he was joined by the 3rd Brigade. The 4th Brigade had also retreated to Loigny, while to the west the 4th Cavalry Division went into quarters to the north of the Conie. Chanzy remained where he was at the end of the engagement, holding Villepion, Terminiers and Sougy, while behind him de Sonis was at St Péravy and Patay. It was a success for the French, accomplished largely as a result of substantial numerical superiority; but the success was limited by the inability of the victors to pursue. Total German casualties amounted to 939, while the French losses were about 1100.[40] That night was bitterly cold; 'the troops had no shelter, and, being compelled to bivouack on account of the vicinity of the enemy's outposts, suffered greatly. In addition, the commissariat wagons were unable to find several detachments in the darkness; and the latter, being thrown upon the small contents of their haversacks, passed the night in cold and hunger upon the frozen ground.'[41]

Information about the fighting at Villepion only reached Stosch at about 9.00pm; half an hour later he sent a telegram reporting on these events to Stiehle, which he amplified about three hours later. The news confirmed the opinion which Stosch had expressed as to the whereabouts of the French, so that at Pithiviers the doubts that may have been held there about the imminent attack of the French were entirely dispelled. Colonel Hale recorded Stosch's assumption of responsibility: 'And now the Grand Duke, at Stosch's instigation, took a very bold step; he felt that necessity knows no law, and therefore, in his latest orders, he drew into his own fighting line the last reserve of the Second Army, the 22nd Infantry Division.'[42]

News of the success at Villepion reached Gambetta and Freycinet soon after the arrival of the latest news from Paris. The balloon bringing the despatch had been swept across France, finally and luckily coming to earth at Belle Isle, and the news it brought seemed stunning. Describing the events of the first day's fighting during the great sortie, the despatch announced the capture of Epinay. Gambetta jumped to the conclusion that, rather than the village of Epinay sur Seine near St Denis, taken in the diversionary attack, the attackers had reached Epinay sur Orge, twelve miles south of Paris. This being so, the lines of investment must have been broken through at Longjumeau; and Gambetta was at once moved to characteristic flights of oratory, announcing that 'The genius of France, for the moment veiled, is appearing anew! The Prussians can now judge the difference between a despot who fights to satisfy his whims and a People in Arms determined not to perish.'[43] The orders to d'Aurelle for December 2 were appropriately ambitious. Cathelineau was to advance with his franc tireurs into the Forest of Fontainebleau; Chanzy was to advance to Allaines, Janville and Toury with the 17th Corps in support, while the 15th Corps was to advance on Santilly. Even discounting the momentary euphoria engendered by the misreading of Trochu's despatch it was clear to all that the next encounter was likely to be extremely significant; as it turned out, the events of December 2 were to prove the decisive point of the Loire campaign.

14

Loigny Poupry

Loigny is today, as it was in 1870, a quiet little town at the junction of a number of roads, lying in a plain so flat that its spire can be taken as a point of reference for some distance in all directions. Surrounding it were a number of walled farms that, in that open countryside, were not surprisingly to become key strong points during the battle. For Chanzy, marching north east in what he intended as an advance directly towards Pithiviers, it was essential to get through Loigny and on towards Bazoches les Hautes with as little delay as possible. For Stosch, intent on marching south to attack what he correctly believed to be the whole of the left wing of the Army of the Loire, Loigny served as the first point to be seized, and was the line to be taken by the right wing of the Detachment.

It had been Stosch's original intention that the I Bavarian Corps, which was the force nearest to the advancing French, should stand to at 8.00am on December 2 in the vicinity of Loigny. As the full position became clearer after the fighting at Villepion, he revised this to provide for von der Tann to concentrate his entire corps at La Maladerie at 6.30am. It was evident to Stosch that he must be ready to encounter a French advance early in the morning, and that he must for this

General d'Aurelle de Paladines, commander of the 1st Army of the Loire, painting by Jacquemart (Rousset/*Histoire*)

purpose unite his whole force to meet them. For this reason he included Wittich's 22nd Division in the orders which he issued for the concentration of the Detachment. Von der Tann was to move eastwards to take up a position to the north east of Loigny between Beauvilliers Farm and Château Goury, and to be prepared to hold it against Chanzy's advance until the 17th and 22nd Divisions arrived, which he expected would be about 11.00am. Tresckow, with the 17th Division was directed to move at once to Lumeau, while Wittich, with the 22nd Division and the 3rd Cavalry Brigade, was to advance to Baigneaux. The only units that Stosch directly assigned to cover the Orleans-Paris road were the remaining two brigades of Stolberg's 2nd Cavalry Division. Finally, the 4th Cavalry Division was, as on the previous day, to be responsible for covering the right flank.[1] With these orders duly issued, Stosch was able to report at 8.10 am to the Second Army that the Detachment was concentrating for the attack on a line between Tanon and Baigneaux.[2] He also reported to Moltke telling him of the events of December 1 and of his intention to advance against the Army of the Loire, which, when Moltke compared it to the Second Army's failure to move, exercised a considerable effect on his mind.[3]

The intense cold was accentuated by the severe wind chill factor caused by a biting northeast wind; but the day was fine, and movement was easier over the frozen ground.[4] The ground over which the battle was to be fought is generally level, broken only by gentle undulations. Although highly cultivated, it was generally unfenced, and offered little cover. The Bavarians moved off soon after receiving Stosch's orders at about 8.00am; as they did so French infantry and cavalry were already to be seen to the south towards Villerand and Loigny. These skirmishers were soon followed by strong columns directed upon Loigny and towards Lumeau, where they came into contact with an advanced guard of the 4th Bavarian Brigade which had passed the night there. This consisted of the 3rd Battalion of the 10th Regiment, commanded by Captain Wetzger, with three squadrons of light cavalry and a four pounder battery; it was at once clear to Rudolph von der Tann, commanding the 4th Brigade, that Château Goury was of crucial importance to the Bavarian position, and must be held at all costs. He ordered Wetzger to break off the action and to move at once at the double to occupy the château. It was as well that he did; Wetzger got there just before the French leading troops reached it. Wetzger deployed one company in the buildings of the château, with two in the grounds surrounding it, and one in reserve, and succeeded in repulsing the first assaults upon the position. Soon, the rest of the 4th Brigade came up. One battalion was left to hold Beauvilliers Farm, while another took up a position on the crest of the gentle ridge that ran from the farm towards Château Goury. The remaining troops were moved into the grounds of the château to reinforce Wetzger's garrison there, one battalion going into the château with the rest in reserve behind the park.[5]

Behind the 4th Brigade, the 3rd Brigade, now commanded by Colonel Roth, reached Beauvilliers at about 9.00am, with orders to occupy the farm and surrounding buildings, and to extend its position along the long ridge to link with Rudolph von der Tann in Château Goury. Its artillery almost at once came into action against strong French columns which were seen advancing from Loigny and Ecuillon along the whole line. The terrain was open, offering little cover to both

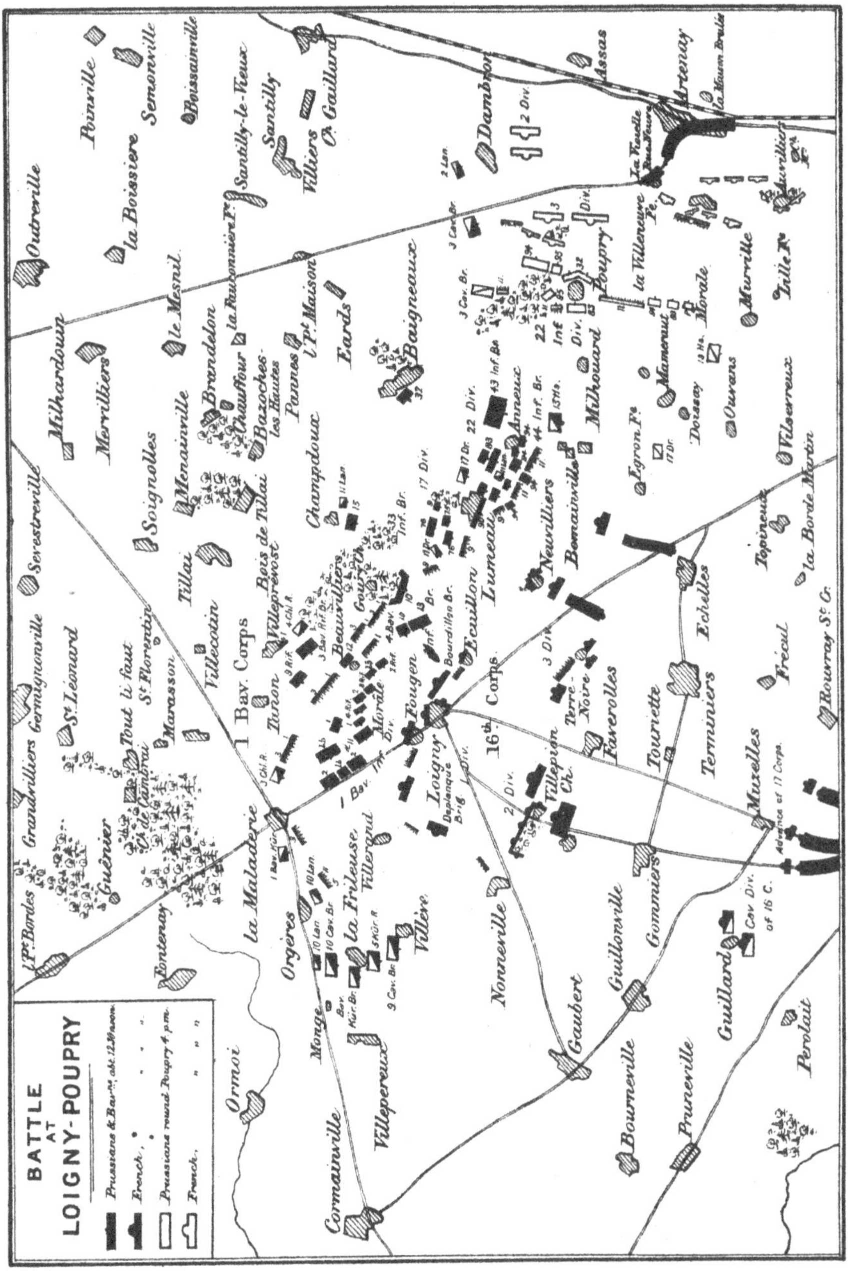

The Battle of Loigny Poupry, December 2 1870

attackers and defenders; and as the day wore on this had a telling effect as the casualties on both sides steadily mounted. The French were advancing down the slope of the low ridge from Loigny to Ecuillon which was very similar to that occupied by the Bavarians, and the heavy columns presented an easy target for both artillery and rifle fire. The Bavarians' position, however, presented one other disadvantage, as the official historian noted: 'Beauvilliers and Goury were exactly on the crest of the height, the north-east slope of which was sufficiently wooded to prevent our batteries from taking up a position on it. They were therefore obliged to take up positions in front of the line Beauvilliers-Goury, on the slope towards Loigny, completely exposed to the enemy's fire'.[6] In order to cover the artillery, the infantry had to be pushed forward down the slope, suffering severely from the superior range and power of the French chassepôts. Meanwhile, as the 2nd Bavarian Division got into position along the ridge, the 1st Division assembled behind it at Villeprevost, with the corps artillery.

The French attack through Loigny was made by the 2nd Division of Chanzy's Corps (Barry) while Maurandy's 3rd Division advanced on Lumeau. Jauréguiberry's 1st Division, which had so distinguished itself at Villepion the night before, was in reserve, following closely behind Barry's Division. By 9.00 am Barry's leading units had got close up to Beauvilliers when they were suddenly assailed by a counter attack down the slope from the farm by three battalions of the 3rd Regiment. This attack had been launched without the warning often given by artillery preparation, and succeeded in driving back the French attackers, who fell back quickly upon their main body. With the rest of the 3rd Brigade they pursued the retreating French with loud cheers, until halted in their turn by the troops of Bourdillon's Brigade from Jauréguiberry's Division which had been massing for an attack on the Bavarian position from Ecuillon, while Deplanque's Brigade to the left advanced towards Morâle Farm through Fougeu.[7]

By 10.30 the pressure of the heavy French numerical superiority was beginning to tell, and the Bavarians were gradually forced back up the slope to the position from which they had advanced, suffering heavy losses as they did so. Their sudden counter attack had, however, disrupted Barry's advance on the Beauvilliers position, and Chanzy was effectively on the back foot for the rest of the day. Meanwhile, Deplanque's Brigade had begun a fierce struggle in around Morâle Farm with the 1st Bavarian Division, of which von der Tann had deployed two battalions of Orff's 2nd Brigade in front of Tanon and the leading troops of the 1st Brigade (Tauffenbach) in front of Villeprevost, with its left in contact with the 3rd Brigade at Beauvilliers. Gradually the remaining units of the 1st Brigade were drawn into the action, battalions being fed into the firing line on either side of Beauvilliers, while the five batteries of corps artillery under Colonel Bronzetti moved up in close support. The French advance was halted in its tracks, and a hard fought struggle ensued, with neither side able to get the upper hand, although two companies of the Body Guard Regiment succeeded in re-entering the woods north of Morâle Farm which had been occupied by the leading battalions of Deplanque's Brigade.

At 11.30, however, the stalemate was broken by the advance on the extreme right of the 4th Cavalry Division and the rest of Orff's 2nd Brigade. Orff's artillery had been pounding Deplanque from the edge of the Tanon heights; the French now found themselves at risk of being completely outflanked when Prince Albrecht's cavalry, supported by the Bavarian Cuirassier Brigade, swung around the French left through Orgères and La Frileuse. The 4th Cavalry Division had something to prove after its rather ineffectual showing as flank guard during the previous day's fighting; now Prince Albrecht's troopers rode down the French infantry on the roads south to Villevé. The French troops scattered and broke, leaving 300 prisoners in German hands. Another party of Uhlans had a similar success near Villerand, and Jauréguiberry's flank was in danger of complete collapse, since Michel's Cavalry Division, which was supposed to be covering it, had gone all the way back to Muzelles, some four miles to the south. To meet the threat he posted a Garde Mobile regiment midway between Villerand and the Villepion Mill.[8]

Orff now launched a vigorous attack with all five battalions of the 2nd Brigade. Held up at first by French artillery fire and by the rifle fire of the defenders of Morâle Farm, he was soon aided by the artillery of the 4th Cavalry Division which, coming into action southwest of La Maladerie, took the French artillery in flank, and set on fire the buildings of Morâle Farm. After a long struggle, first the stables north of the farm, and then the farm itself, were taken at the point of the bayonet, and Deplanque's Brigade driven back off the road from La Maladerie to Loigny. In spite of a series of attempts by Deplanque's Brigade to regain the lost ground, Orff's men held their ground, and their success soon began to affect the fighting on their left.[9]

Colonel Tauffenbach's 1st Brigade, which had come up piecemeal to join the battle line, was mainly in position between Orff's left and the Beauvilliers Farm. When the second French attack on the centre of the Bavarian position came in a little before noon, Tauffenbach countered it by advancing southwards. This movement, however, did not produce any prolonged effect, in part because the individual battalions attacked independently, in part because ammunition was running low, but principally because of the continued French assaults around Beauvilliers Farm which threatened Tauffenbach's left. The struggle for Beauvilliers, which formed the centre of the Bavarian position, had continued all morning; by 12.30, however, in spite of a heavy bombardment, the Bavarians had gained ground towards Morâle Farm, compelling the French to fall back a little way, and enabling the battalion that occupied Beauvilliers to be relieved, having exhausted its ammunition.

Throughout the morning, the gunfire of the Bavarian artillery had proved crucially effective. Firing from a range that was at times less than four hundred yards, and completely exposed to rifle fire, the gunners had held their ground. So close were the enemy that at times various batteries had to fire in several directions at once. They sustained fearful casualties, not least among the horses; at times, the threat of losing guns to the enemy infantry was only narrowly averted. During the morning, von der Tann had been able to deploy a total of twelve batteries, of which seven were in position between Morâle Farm and Beauvilliers Farm, while five were posted between Beauvilliers and Château Goury.[10]

With the failure to take Beauvilliers, Chanzy now concentrated on Château Goury, whose defenders were running short of ammunition. The château is surrounded by high walls and every loophole and window was manned. At about

1.00pm Bourdillon's brigade, under cover of a heavy artillery barrage, advanced over the snow covered plain to the attack. A correspondent of *The Times* was present in Château Goury.

> Ascending one of the towers of the old chateau, I found myself in an admirable position for seeing the battle. The room was full of soldiers, who had loopholed the walls; but the enemy were not within range, or were not thought to be so, until suddenly a large body of infantry, which was supposed to be German for the first moment or so, unexpectedly opened a hot fire upon a regiment drawn up beneath the walls of the chateau. Then from every loophole and crevice in the towers and walls rolled an incessant fire of rifles, and the chassepôt balls seemed to rain upon the roofs and walls in reply, until by degrees the old castle became the centre of the fight, and, as it seemed to me, with every possible chance of being taken.[11]

The garrison had had orders to hold their fire until the last moment; when the signal was given, an annihilating file fire inflicted heavy losses. As the French wavered, the garrison charged out of the buildings in a counter attack. For a short while, the issue was in the balance; then, suddenly, the French were attacked in their flank, and fell back in disorder. The new arrivals were the leading troops of Tresckow's 17th Division, who had been marching from Santilly through Bazoches les Hautes to take up their position on the left of the Bavarians at Lumeau.

Earlier that morning, on hearing the gunfire from the southwest, Tresckow had sent on ahead at the gallop two batteries of horse artillery, escorted by three squadrons of dragoons, and these had since mid morning taken part in the defence of Château Goury. Their contribution had been invaluable; they had arrived in time to help the battered 3rd Brigade disengage itself and fall back, and throughout the day they were constantly in action, the two batteries which had ten guns between them firing a total of 1196 shells.[12] As he moved west and then south with his main body, Tresckow learned that strong enemy columns were advancing towards Lumeau and Baigneaux. He left a rifle battalion to hold Baigneaux until Wittich arrived with the 22nd Division, and himself hurried on to Lumeau. As his troops began to arrive there, they found that the leading units of Maurandy's division had already entered the village; but an immediate assault by a battalion of the 90th Regiment ejected them, and the French fell back towards Neuvilliers and Domainville. They also abandoned their advance on Baigneau, and for the moment confined themselves to a prolonged bombardment of Lumeau.[13]

After about half an hour of this, Maurandy made another attempt on Lumeau, throwing forward strong columns of infantry, preceded by skirmishers, who got close to the village before, under a hail of rifle and artillery fire, they were thrown back towards Domainville. By now Tresckow was being supported by the six leading batteries of Wittich's division which had been sent on ahead to take up a position north east of Lumeau. Behind them, marching flat out, came the leading unit of the 22nd Division, the 44th Brigade under Colonel Marschall von Bieberstein, with orders to follow up the retreating French by advancing through Anneux. Close range artillery fire accelerated the French retreat, in addition to which they were harried by the German cavalry, and they soon disappeared behind the hills south of Domainville, falling back towards Echelles and Terminiers in chaotic disorder.

In one remarkable exploit, Captain von Marschalck with a squadron of the 11th Uhlan Regiment had observed what he thought at first was a wagon train near Neuvillers. It was in fact a twelve pounder battery of the 16th Corps artillery. Marschalck, who had ridden on ahead of his squadron, prepared an ambush; when he realised it was a battery preparing to fire, 'the squadron rushed out suddenly upon their flank just as they were coming into action. So quickly and skilfully was the surprise effected, that not one single round was fired by the battery and the whole of it was captured ... one officer, 76 men, 77 horses, 6 guns and 8 wagons fell into the hands of the Germans without a shot being expended in self defence.'[14]

It was after ejecting the French from Lumeau that Tresckow had been able to swing to his right and deliver the decisive blow at Bourdillon's flank. The attack was delivered by two Hanseatic regiments of the 33rd Brigade under von Kottwitz, and fell upon Bourdillon's infantry as they were launched forward to the assault of Château Goury. Taken completely by surprise, the French panicked and fell back in great disorder towards Loigny; they tried to make a stand in the gravel pits just to the east of the town, but were driven out at bayonet point by a battalion of the 76th Regiment. Another battalion of the regiment forced its way into Loigny itself, while further companies charged on to Fougeu and took the village. An attempt to push on in the direction of Villepion was however checked. The Bavarians, who had defended Château Goury all morning under continuous shell fire and repeated infantry assaults, could not help some mixed feelings about the success of the Prussians, as their official historian recorded. 'We were, of course, delighted that the reinforcement was so effective; but, to prevent misconception, we must state that the defenders of Château Goury had no idea at that time of giving up. The capture of Goury, mentioned by General Chanzy, is an error, and probably intentional.'[15]

Although Tresckow's men had succeeded in gaining a footing in Loigny, Bourdillon still held the bulk of the village. Tresckow brought up four battalions from the 34th Brigade, which were in Lumeau, in an assault on the eastern side of Loigny, while a Bavarian battalion advancing from Château Goury swung around the north of the town. With the Germans gaining ground on all sides, Bourdillon had no choice but to retreat, falling back to Villepion. There remained, however, a small party which obstinately held on to possession of the churchyard on high ground at the western edge of the town. Loigny had fallen to sustained infantry assaults; for once the German artillery had played little part in the action, watching in frustration from close range as the infantry battled for possession of the houses in the town. As the artillery waited, about a mile outside Loigny, an enterprising group of French skirmishers moved forward to threaten them before they were ridden down by a squadron of the 17th Dragoon Regiment. Other squadrons of this regiment rode forward to Villepion, but were driven back by French artillery fire.[16]

Villepion, the scene of such fierce fighting on the previous day, was now the key point in Chanzy's line as he strove to prevent the complete disintegration of his corps. Quite apart from the defeat of the attacks by Deplanque and Bourdillon, he was becoming increasingly fearful about his left flank. The sight of strong German columns moving down from Tanon through La Maladerie, supported by large numbers of cavalry, told its own story. 'As soon as the enemy saw that our right wing was no longer to be feared, he embarked on a manoeuvre so often successful, and switching his order of battle, he moved en masse on our left with the intention of turning it.'[17] To meet the threat, Chanzy swung round part of Deplanque's brigade to take up a position south of Villerand, fronting the road to Nonneville, where it was supported by a battery of mitrailleuses. It seemed to Chanzy that he was facing an enemy that was considerably superior in numbers, an erroneous belief that reflected great credit on the efforts of the Detachment during the battle.[18]

With Bourdillon's retreat from Loigny, the German artillery moved forward from the defensive line it had occupied all day, and formed a gun line to the north of Loigny. From here it pounded the positions held by Deplanque and Bourdillon, north and east of Villepion. By 2.30 von der Tann felt able to move to the attack of Villepion, and ordered Dietl with the 1st Division to advance directly south from Villerand, the right wing opposite Nonneville and the left the chateau and park of Villepion. Under cover of a heavy bombardment of the French by some 80 guns of twelve batteries, Dietl's leading troops occupied a wood on the Loigny-Villepion road before being pinned down by heavy French rifle and mitrailleuse fire. On the right, Prince Albrecht's cavalry was continuing to advance, moving through Villevé towards Villepion; this advance was halted by the fire of the artillery of de Sonis' 17th Corps, which was now arriving on the battlefield, its leading brigade having moved at Chanzy's request to prop up his right flank at Faverolles. Three batteries of German horse artillery, however, remained around Nonneville, less than a mile from the park of Villepion, and continued to fire on Deplanque's Brigade. Michel's Cavalry Division had, in the meantime, moved rather diffidently forward again from Muzelles through Guillonville; but when Prince Albrecht switched his artillery in that direction, the French cavalry again abruptly left the field, falling back to the south until they were well out of harms way.[19] 'So headlong was their flight that the ten German cuirassier squadrons which had moved up to charge them could never catch them up. Finally, the French squadrons rallied behind their infantry at Gommiers, and the German pursuing horsemen had to let their prey escape.'[20]

De Sonis had begun his march forward at 4.00 am, although he hoped that his support would not immediately be required by Chanzy, due to the exhaustion of his troops. At 11.30 am, however, he received a message from Chanzy seeking his immediate help, and it was in response to this that he had sent a brigade on ahead to Faverolles, together with his corps artillery. The evident disintegration of the 16th Corps made him fearful for this detached force, and he hurried on with reinforcements. When he reached the front it was apparent that unless action was taken immediately, the advancing Germans would destroy Chanzy's Corps, and with it the 17th Corps as well, de Sonis ordered an immediate advance on Loigny. As darkness began to fall the two leading regiments of Gardes Mobiles crumbled under the fierce fire of the German infantry. Riding through them de Sonis cried 'Forward! Are you afraid? Miserable men! You will be our destruction!' But in spite of all he could do, the Gardes Mobiles fell back in disorder. In a last attempt to rally them, de Sonis personally led a charge of some three hundred Papal Zouaves, with five hundred other troops towards Villours. He had the satisfaction of seeing the

Charette's Papal Zouaves at Patay, painting by André (Rousset/*Histoire*)

German defenders pull back from Villours, and he pressed on. Outside the village, however, the charge was halted with heavy loss when it encountered Tresckow's last reserve, comprising two battalions of the 75th Regiment. Hundreds of French went down in the face of withering rifle fire; among them were de Sonis himself and the commander of the Zouaves, Colonel Charette, both of whom were badly wounded.[21]

Tresckow's men, retaking Villours, pushed on southwards towards Faverolles; the units of the 17th Corps opposed to them were scattered, and retreated in great disorder, leaving many prisoners and a mitrailleuse battery in the hands of the Germans. On the edge of Loigny, the beleaguered defenders of the churchyard finally laid down their arms. In front of Villepion, von der Tann reckoned that the fierce defence being put up by Jauréguiberry made it imprudent to attack again that night; he calculated, correctly, that the French would abandon the position during the night.[22]

With the collapse of the 17th Corps, Stosch had seen off two of the French corps opposed to him; but it was the appearance of a third, on his left flank, that presented the greatest threat of all to the Detachment. While Marschall, with the 44th Brigade, was engaged at about 1.00 pm in clearing Anneux, on the left flank of the 17th Division, Wittich, his divisional commander received an alarming message from Major General von Colomb, whose 3rd Cavalry Brigade was covering the left of the Detachment at Dambron. This was to the effect that heavy French columns appeared to be moving north through Artenay in the direction of Allaines and Toury. The only German units covering the main road were the 4th and 5th Cavalry Brigades and one of these, the 4th, was to the south of Pithiviers, leaving only von Baumbach's 5th Cavalry Brigade at Toury to hold up the French advance.[23]

The newcomers were the 2nd (Martineau) and 3rd (Peytavin) Divisions of the 15th Corps. The left wing of the advance of this corps, consisting of Peytavin's Division, had moved off with the intention of marching on Santilly. On its right,

Martineau was moving towards Ruan and Aschères, while the 1st Division was further to the east. At about noon, Peytavin's leading units had encountered Colomb's troopers at Dambron; under heavy artillery fire, and greatly outnumbered, Colomb was obliged to retire. Mindful of his responsibility for covering the Detachment's left, he moved down the road towards Poupry, and reported the position to Wittich. It was as well that he did; Peytavin, alerted by the sound of gunfire to the west, had abandoned his advance on Santilly and was turning to take the Detachment in flank.[24]

When he got the news, Wittich at once appreciated the danger. Although, as it happened, Stosch was just at that moment sending orders to him that he should move on Loigny, he at once swung his division round to face the threat. The troops nearest to the advancing French were the men of Colonel von Kontzki's 43rd Brigade; Wittich ordered Kontzki to lead the advance of the division from Anneux to Milhouard followed by the divisional artillery and then Marschall's 44th Brigade. The right flank of the advance was covered by the13th Hussars. Peytavin by now was moving westwards over the Chartres-Orleans road towards Poupry, and he and Kontzki sighted each other as the latter advanced to Milhouard. Realising that it was imperative to try to prevent the French from gaining possession of Poupry, Kontzki led forward his leading unit, the 95th Regiment, at the double. He collided with the first troops of Peytavin's Division in the middle of the village before driving them back and gaining control of the eastern edge of Poupry.[25] Poupry lies at the centre of a network of small roads; its loss would expose the left flank of the Detachment, but without it, Peytavin could make no progress in his march to the relief of Chanzy's Corps. For both sides, therefore, the struggle that ensued for possession of the village was of crucial importance. D'Aurelle had arrived at Chevilly, which he had designated as the location of his headquarters for the day, at about 10.30 am. Anxiously awaiting news of Chanzy, he was surprised to hear no gunfire; after a little while he ordered his staff to move forward to Artenay, where they would be nearer to the 15th Corps as well as to the 16th Corps. 'He arrived there about midday. A certain agitation reigned in the town. On the left, towards Loigny or Villepion, there was fighting; the guns were making themselves heard, but the sound did not indicate an engagement that was as serious as was really the case.'[26] Closer at hand, Peytavin was already in contact with the enemy; assuming direct command, d'Aurelle ordered up the corps artillery to take a position to the west of Autroches, while Martineau was ordered to deploy on the left of Peytavin's division.

Meanwhile, around Poupry things were hotting up. One battalion of the 95th Regiment had moved north of the village to occupy the copse that lay alongside the road to Eards, in order to prevent the occupants of Poupry from being outflanked. To the south, the six batteries of divisional artillery had arrived, and came into action along the road to Morâle. Kontzki's other regiment, the 32nd, was also now beginning to arrive and its battalions were brought into the firing line around the village as each of them came up.[27] Behind them, Marschall had succeeded in disengaging the 44th Brigade and this too had set off down the road towards Poupry. As his battalions arrived to join the battle line, Wittich sent the 94th Regiment (Lieutenant Colonel von Pallmenstein) into the copse to the north of the village, while the 83rd Regiment, now led by Major Schorlemmer, joined the 32nd Regiment in defence of the eastern edge of Poupry.

These reinforcements emboldened Wittich to make a forward move himself, and he ordered the 83rd and 32nd Regiments to advance against the French skirmish line. Although initially successful, the advance stalled when French reserves came up; as the Prussians retreated towards their original position around Poupry, they suffered heavy casualties. One of these was Kontzki, the 43rd Brigade commander, who was mortally wounded. The French did not, however, follow up their success, and Wittich took the opportunity to sort out the battalions of various regiments which had become thoroughly intermingled. In particular, he was concerned with his left wing, which was heavily involved in trying to clear the larger copse north of Poupry of French troops. By about 3.00 pm the 94th Regiment, together with part of the 95th Regiment, had reached the eastern edge of the copse when it was suddenly confronted by a large body of fresh troops advancing from the two small copses to the east, with the support of a battery which had unlimbered in the open ground between them. The French infantry charged forward to within two hundred yards of the German infantry in position along the edge of the large copse. 'But at this moment the case shot from the 5th Light Battery, unlimbered in front line, fell with such effect amid the ranks of the French, that the latter hurried back under cover of the woods, while for the same reason the guns posted in the intermediate space were also compelled to retire.'[28]

The battle continued to sway back and forth. A large body of French infantry moved forward over open ground against the German left. Seeing this, Colomb

General Chanzy, commander of the French 2nd Army of the Loire, painting by Henner (Rousset/*Histoire*)

with six squadrons of cavalry, trotted down the north eastern side of the copse; the spectacle of the advancing cavalry was too much for the French infantry, which hastily retreated, pursued by the shellfire of the 3rd Light Battery which had moved through the copse to its eastern edge.

Both on the north and south of Poupry the French had by now deployed a powerful gun line. D'Aurelle watched his artillery, which included ten mitrailleuses, in action on the south side of the village.

> Some Prussian batteries, rapidly brought up from Milhouard and Mamerant, replied to our fire, and a terrible artillery combat ensued. The superiority of our batteries of twelve pounders, and especially our mitrailleuses, inflicted heavy damage on the enemy; in less than three quarters of an hour, the Prussians guns were dismounted and reduced to silence.[29]

Having gained the upper hand in this artillery duel, Peytavin launched an attack by four battalions, supported by the mitrailleuses, which advanced from La Villeneuve and Autroches towards Wittich's right flank. All he had available to meet this attack were the five companies of infantry which had been assigned to protect the German artillery, which had been drawn up along the road leading south from Poupry. These companies deployed to the north of Morâle, supported by two pioneer companies, which were all that could be spared from the garrison of Poupry. Somehow, in spite of the heavy odds against them, the German infantry held on to their position; casualties were high, however and included Major von Lengerke, a battalion commander in the 83rd Regiment, who was killed as the French swept forward against the position at Morâle.[30]

Wittich was fighting in a very exposed position, with his back towards the troops of the 16th and 17th Corps. Fortunately for him, these were more concerned with getting away from the battlefield of Loigny than with any adventurous move eastward, where Wittich might have been caught between two enemies, as d'Aurelle observed: 'If Maurandy had been able to rally his division and bring it into action, the Prussians would have found the themselves between two fires. Their destruction at this point seemed certain. A prompt and bold decision would have brought good fortune and powerfully influenced the outcome of the day.'[31] All Wittich had available to cover his extreme right and rear were two regiments of cavalry operating in a wide screen to the south and southwest of Morâle and Mamerant.

By 4.00 d'Aurelle had the whole of Martineau's 2nd Division in hand, and a fresh attack was launched all along the line. Preceded by dense clouds of skirmishers, French columns advanced again towards Morâle; this attack was broken up by the rifle fire of the defenders. Other columns were launched against Poupry village, but these too were repulsed with heavy losses. On the German left, however, the French made more progress, pushing into the northern edge of the copse, and moving southwards, driving the Germans back towards Poupry. Fresh French troops came up to reinforce this success; a counter attack by a battalion of the 95th Regiment from Poupry failed to halt the French advance, and the Germans fell back into the village and to the Baigneaux road, giving up all but a narrow strip of woodland. Both sides sustained heavy losses during this fierce fighting; yet another senior German officer died fighting in the front line among his troops, when Pallmenstein, the commander of the 94th Regiment, was killed in the struggle for the copse.[32]

Inside the village, Colonel Marschall decided to commit his last reserve, the 83rd Regiment. Supported by detachments of the 94th and 95th Regiment, they charged northward into the copse. The French recoiled; as darkness fell, they were driven out of the copse altogether, and back across the open ground to the shelter of the two small copses to the east. In an attempt to capitalise on the situation, Colomb again trotted forward to pursue the retreating French infantry, but quickly broke off an attempt to charge them in the face of vigorous chassepôt fire from the copses. It was too dark for either side to do more. Wittich's men at first settled down for the night in the positions they had so strenuously defended; later, they pulled back to Anneux and Domainville, leaving only an outpost line facing the French. Behind them, Tresckow's 17th Division was quartered at Lumeau, with its outposts at Loigny and Fougeu, where part of the I Bavarian Corps was quartered. The rest of von der Tann's men were spread out between Villerand, Orgères, La Maladerie and Tanon. A cavalry screen to the south and west covered the exhausted troops, who 'either moved into confined cantonments, which they were often obliged to share with wounded friends and foes, or else bivouacked on the frozen fields. In the latter case, the bitter cold, the want of straw, and the very scanty nourishment prevented the soldiers from deriving much benefit from the repose.'[33]

Casualties on both sides had been high; the Germans had lost 771 men killed, 2,829 wounded and 544 missing, while French losses exceeded 6,500, of whom some 2,500 were unwounded prisoners. Although dearly bought, it was a stunning victory; and Stosch and the Grand Duke were entirely aware of it, as that night they prepared to exploit their situation on the following day, by a thrust towards the Loire in furtherance of Moltke's strategic objective of the destruction of d'Aurelle's army. It seemed to Stosch that the wisest course for the French was to fall back to the west, and in preparing orders for the Detachment for next day, he had in mind to cut off this escape route, and drive the enemy back into Orleans. Reporting laconically at the end of the battle to tell Frederick Charles of its outcome, he wrote that 'If the enemy is to be pursed tomorrow, it is absolutely necessary that the Second Army should attack Artenay, and undertake the protection of the Orleans-Paris road.'[34] This would free the Detachment for a decisive advance on the flank and rear of the Army of the Loire.

But the hopes of Stosch and the Grand Duke were soon to be seriously disappointed. All day, while the Detachment fought three French corps to a standstill, there had been a great deal of headquarters activity elsewhere. Frederick Charles had spent the early part of the day without any situation reports, either from the Detachment or from his own army. The first news he had from Stosch, at 10.00 am, was of the concentration of the Detachment for its advance southwards; in response to this, he gave orders to Manstein, whose IX Corps was around Pithiviers, to move westwards in support. Since he was some fifteen miles away from the Detachment, however, it was obvious that Manstein would not have any influence on events west of the main road until late in the afternoon. From the III and X Corps, engaged in reconnoitring French positions around Montargis and Bellegarde, Frederick Charles had no information. The next news he had, however, was unsettling. Waldersee had gone across to the west to witness events in the Detachment's front. En route, he became aware of the movement of Peytavin and Martineau northwards from Artenay, and at 10.35 am Frederick Charles received his telegram, written about 9.00 as Waldersee crossed the Orleans-Paris road, reporting that a large enemy force was advancing on Bazoches. At 11.30 am Manstein was ordered to move to protect the Paris road, on which Schmidt's 6th Cavalry Division, in the course of completing its transfer from the west, was also to halt. Stiehle, when speaking to Manstein, could not resist a jibe at the Detachment, remarking that, 'The Grand Duke is behaving somewhat in the same way as at a kriegspiel in peacetime.'[35]

At Versailles, Moltke's anxiety about events on the Loire had been deepening. None of the advice he had given seemed to have had any effect on Frederick Charles, whose failure to pursue an energetic offensive had caused extreme dissatisfaction. With matters on the line of investment around Paris more or less under control, Moltke turned his attack to getting some prompt action on the Loire, and with no further news from Stiehle, he went on the morning of December 2 to obtain the King's permission to give a direct order to Frederick Charles to move forward. William was uneasy; on the basis of the information he had received from Waldersee, it seemed that the bulk of the Army of the Loire was directly in the front of the Second Army. He raised with Moltke the possibility of the French turning the Second Army's left down the Loing valley. Since Moltke had not mentioned Stiehle's concerns on the point, he was surprised to find the King quoting Stiehle almost word for word. At any rate, he was able to reassure the King by pointing out that with the failure of Ducrot's sortie, there was little to fear from the Army of Paris, and he obtained the necessary permission for the advance of the Second Army. Soon afterwards though, the King heard of the report that there were 20,000 French troops in Montargis, causing him to write to Moltke with that report, remarking:

> From the annexed you will see that my opinion that the great Forest of Orleans keeps us in doubt as to what the enemy is doing (is correct), so that moving into the forest which is some twenty eight miles long involves at least two days fighting during which time the Second Army can be marched round on the flank and rear if there are 20,000 men in Montargis. I am doubtful whether our order of today is still advisable.[36]

Moltke, however, sent Verdy over to reassure the King, and his order went off to the Second Army at 1.10 pm. Its terms were peremptory.

> According to a report, the bulk of the Army of the Loire is now south of Artenay. The Grand Duke, on his own, is not in a state to meet an offensive from there upon Toury. His Majesty regards it as absolutely necessary that the Second Army moves without delay directly on Orleans for a decisive attack. This morning several advanced posts on the outpost line before Paris, which were lost yesterday, have been recovered.[37]

In sending such an order, Moltke demonstrated that he had despaired of getting Frederick Charles to do anything to achieve the strategic objective of destroying the Army of the Loire. Moltke's current state of information as to the location of the French was sketchy in the extreme. He knew that the Detachment was going into action that day; what had prompted the reference to d'Aurelle's main body being south of Artenay is unclear, but what is evident is that he had for the moment at any rate abandoned his plan of operating on the enemy's flank and rear. He was hoping instead that a frontal assault would not only result in the taking of Orleans but also in breaking up the Army of the Loire in the process. It was an uncharacteristic moment of weakness born of his mounting frustration and anxiety to achieve some kind of result without further delay.

The reaction of Frederick Charles to the order was sulky in the extreme. He sent back no fresh information to Moltke, even when he had received reports that might bear upon Moltke's decision. Moltke had issued the order without knowing anything more than Stosch's report that he was concentrating preparatory to a southward advance. Later in the day the King did get from Waldersee, between 5.00 and 6.00 pm, a telegram announcing the success of the Detachment; Waldersee recorded that

> on the evening of Beaune la Rolande, as well as that of Loigny, I telegraphed to the King William that a complete victory had been won. The order to Prince Frederick Charles of the 2nd December to commence the attack on Orleans was given by General von Moltke before he received tidings that a battle had begun on the west of the great Chaussée.[38]

The real mischief was of course in Moltke's reference to moving directly on Orleans. There was little strategic value in capturing the city; von der Tann had originally been sent in October to capture it in order to keep at a safe distance from Paris the activities of the franc tireurs, while for their part the French military saw no especial point in holding the city as a base for offensive operations. The problem was that, for both sides, its possession had taken on a symbolic value that was out of all proportion to its military significance, and Moltke may well have felt that because of this d'Aurelle would feel compelled to risk his army in fighting for its retention. At all events, those at Versailles welcomed Moltke's decision to give a direct instruction; when told by the Crown Prince, Blumenthal noted that 'the news came to me as a ray of sunshine, that the King had positively commanded Prince Frederick Charles to march and attack the Army of the Loire. It is impossible that he (Fabius Cunctator) can ignore such an order. He will have to go forwards at once.'[39]

The Crown Prince himself, meanwhile, reflected in his diary on the strategic demands of the situation and how Moltke faced them.

> In these times our military experiences from day to day are for all the world as they are laid down in the books. Combinations have to be made for three armies, quite separate and distinct, but still working in cooperation; successes alternate with reverses and surprises – in a word, the higher strategy and tactics are the order of the day. General Count Moltke in all this remains always his own calm, clear-headed, matter of fact self – a veritable worker of miracles; for me it is a pleasure of the rarest sort to hear him make his daily report.[40]

In deciding how to execute Moltke's instruction, Frederick Charles had the benefit of regular information from Stosch as to the progress of the battle. At 3.00 pm came news that the 17th and 22nd Divisions were advancing on Terminiers, while on the right the Bavarians were holding their position. At 5.00 pm another telegram arrived, reporting the capture of Loigny, and the advance of the 17th Division supported by the 1st Bavarian Corps in the direction of Nonneville – Orgères. It also gave important news from Poupry. '22nd Division advancing successfully on Artenay. Apparently the 15th Corps in front of it.'[41] 'Later in the evening, but still before the issue of operational orders for the following day, Frederick Charles heard from Waldersee, by now at the headquarters of the Detachment at Janville, with an outline of events. Waldersee added: 'I regard the battle as a brilliant victory.' Finally, just before the orders were distributed from the Second Army headquarters, there came Stosch's report with the proposal that the Second Army attack Artenay and cover the main road to enable the Detachment to strike southwest and then south.

None of this information made any impression on Frederick Charles and Stiehle. Still sulking, and resolved to do literally what they had been told, their orders began: 'The Second Army and the Detachment of HRH The Grand Duke of Mecklenburg are to advance tomorrow to the concentric attack against Orleans.' Manstein was to move on Artenay, Alvensleben on a wide front towards Chilleurs aux Bois and Voigts-Rhetz to a line between Villereau and Chilleurs aux Bois. The Detachment would 'according to its own dispositions, advance tomorrow west of the Artenay-Orleans road for a corresponding attack.'[42] Before receiving this, Stosch had transmitted to Stiehle the plans he had made for the Detachment's operations the next day, and followed this up by confirming that both the 16th and 17th Corps had opposed the Detachment on December 2. Hoping that all this would lead to some modification in the orders from Frederick Charles he waited until 4.00 am next day before issuing orders to his units; but no modification came, and he reluctantly acquiesced in what was required of him. Stiehle, in reporting to Moltke that night, unctuously offered an explanation of the orders issued for a concentric advance on Orleans.

> The offensive movement of the Detachment of HRH the Grand Duke had been so arranged with General von Stosch that an endeavour should be made to secure a crossing over the Loire below Orleans, but as today's telegram seems to make great haste necessary, the endeavour will be made to reach the objective Orleans by the direct road.[43]

15

The Second Battle of Orleans

During the night of December 2/3, d'Aurelle reviewed his position. He received detailed reports from Chanzy of the outcome of the fighting in front of Loigny, and of the condition not only of his own corps but also of the 17th Corps. The latter was clearly not in a state to face the enemy, as Chanzy reported at 4.00 am on the morning of December 3:

> The generals of the 17th Corps have just left here. They declared that their troops are in such a condition that it will be impossible for them to make any movement tomorrow. Many men are without shoes, no supplies have been distributed, all are exhausted. Not yet knowing your instructions, and wishing to be in the best to carry out your wishes, I told General Guépratte, commanding the 17th Corps in the absence of General de Sonis, who is wounded and has disappeared, to take steps to distribute provisions and to be ready in the morning.[1]

D'Aurelle had seen for himself the situation of the divisions of Martineau and Peytavin, and even before receiving Chanzy's account of the state of the 17th Corps had made up his mind to retreat. He wrote to Chanzy at 3.40 am: 'In the situation in which yesterday's battle puts us, it is impossible to carry out a march on Pithiviers, or any forward movement, and we must retreat to our former positions. I am too far from you to give you effective support, and I believe that the enemy have, during the night, been concentrating artillery on my right.'[2] To Pallières, he sent instructions that the 1st Division of the 15th Corps was to retreat early in the morning to Orleans to take up a position to defend the enceinte, leaving only a strong rearguard to cover his retreat. These instructions were entirely at odds with an order that Freycinet had issued over Gambetta's signature the previous afternoon at 4.00 pm, but which d'Aurelle did not receive until later on the morning of December 3.

> From today, and during the current operations, you will give your strategic orders directly to the 15th, 16th, 17th, 18th and 20th Corps. Until yesterday I have directed the 18th and 20th and for some time the 17th. From now on I leave this duty to you. From all the information received, I do not believe that you will find at Pithiviers or elsewhere prolonged resistance. In my opinion the enemy is only attempting to mask his movement to the north east, to meet Ducrot. The column which you encountered yesterday and perhaps today is no doubt an isolated detachment which seeks to delay us. But the main body must be, I repeat, making off towards Corbeil. At this moment we have reoccupied Châteaudun.[3]

Corbeil is on the Seine, fifteen miles from Paris; the ludicrous suggestion that the Detachment was engaged in a rearguard action while the Second Army was slinking away northward demonstrates that the ignorance of German movements

Bavarian Jäger skirmish during the Second Battle for Orleans, by Zimmer (Pflugk-Harttung)

prevailing at Tours was even greater than that at Versailles as to the precise whereabouts of the Army of the Loire. There had been one other event that day; Bourbaki had finally arrived, and took over command of the 18th Corps from Billot.[4]

In considering the overall situation as it appeared to them on the evening of December 2, Frederick Charles and Stiehle had not had to take account of any significant activity directly in the front of the Second Army during that day. Neither Pallières' 1st Division of the 15th Corps, nor the 18th and 20th Corps had made any important movement, and the French still had only a token presence at Montargis and in the Loing valley, rather than the large force which had so alarmed King William. Manstein had moved off at noon with the IX Corps in response to the order that he should take over from the Detachment the responsibility for covering the Orleans-Paris high road. By nightfall, Manstein was concentrated to the east of the road, well placed to advance to the attack by way of Artenay on the following morning, while Alvensleben around Pithiviers and Voigts-Rhetz at Boynes and Beaune la Rolande had also moved into their jumping off positions.[5] Schmidt, with the 6th Cavalry Division, would follow the right wing of the army from Chatillon le Roi, while out on the left the 1st Cavalry Division, reinforced by four infantry battalions and a battery taken from the X Corps, was to cover the country between the Yonne and the Loing. Having decided simply to carry out Moltke's order to the letter, it may have seemed immaterial to Frederick Charles that he had little intelligence on which he could rely about the situation of his adversary, but he was certainly not well informed.

> Rarely has any leader entered so completely blindfolded into a battle as did Prince Frederick Charles into the second battle of Orleans. Of even the general disposition of the enemy, he knew very little; of the position of even the larger hostile units, such as the Army Corps, he was equally in ignorance, and he refused to accept as correct the approximately correct information furnished to him by the Detachment.[6]

Nor was he in any hurry to find out things for himself; there was no reason why he should not have paid a visit to the headquarters of the Detachment, but 'possibly, the prospect of an interview with a royal Prince he personally disliked, and with a Chief Staff Officer who held views opposite to his own, was not specially attractive.'[7] Leading the advance in the centre of the Second Army, Alvensleben's task for December 3 was to advance down the Pithiviers-Orleans road, marching through Chilleurs aux Bois with Loury as his objective by the end of the day.

Although the Second Army did not have much information about d'Aurelle's position, it was the continuing belief at Pithiviers that a large part of the Army of the Loire was still to be found in position between Chilleurs and Bellegarde, which if correct meant that Alvensleben's mission was extremely hazardous. In fact, facing the III Corps, Pallières' division was spread out over nearly a dozen miles to cover the various entrances to the Forest of Orleans. At Neuville aux Bois General Minot had 8,400 infantry, with twelve guns, with a further 1,850 men and eight guns at Villereau. The main body of 8,500 men and thirty eight guns was with Pallières, at Chilleurs, fronting towards Santeau, while finally the right of the division, consisting of 2,070 men with six guns, covered the next road at Courcy aux Loges. Alvensleben himself was under no illusions about the difficulties of his task, which would increase the further south he went. It was clear to him that once in the forest, he would be severely hampered in the use of his artillery, while if the advance of the rest of the Second Army was checked he might be marooned in front of the fortifications of Orleans.

> I went, I was fully aware, into a den, of which the door closed of itself after my last man had passed Chilleurs. With every step forward diminished any chance of support, and also the possibility of withdrawing or of sending any news about myself, or of receiving news; and if I did fortunately succeed in arriving at the southern edge the situation of my corps before the city could become very unpleasant.[8]

Nonetheless, before dawn, the III Corps set off from its positions around Pithiviers, and by 9.30 am was pushing south down the road to Santeau. Pallières sent forward his main body to try to hold the III Corps there, some two miles north of the entrance to the forest. The advance of the III Corps was led by Buddenbrock's 6th Division; as soon as the French were encountered, the divisional artillery, which was moving just behind the leading infantry battalions, deployed at 10.30 am on either side of the road, with the 12th Brigade on its right. Behind these units came the corps artillery which as soon as it came up was assigned to the right of the gun line; by noon the Prussians had seventy eight guns in action. Movement of the artillery off the roads was here not so easy, as the severe weather had not hardened the ground as much as elsewhere. Colonel von Dresky, the commander of the corps artillery, recorded the difficulties. 'The batteries could move but very slowly. The soil of the meadows, being only slightly frozen, had no consistency, and the horses kept going through the crust, while the wheels sank half way up the spokes.'[9] Dresky soon found an admirable position between La Brosse and a small wood southwest of that village, giving his batteries the protection of the railway embankment. In the artillery duel that ensued the French were heavily outgunned, and their artillery so knocked about that Pallières withdrew his guns, ordering them back to Orleans down the Loury road while their retreat was covered by the infantry. Buddenbrock followed them, advancing to the west of La Brosse, over the line of the unfinished Orleans-Pithiviers railway, while on his left the 5th Division moved through Santeau down the main road, closely supported by the artillery. Alvensleben's men continued to push the French southwards. Soon, Chilleurs was abandoned, and Pallières fell back to the edge of the forest, where he had intended to make a stand; but the speed of the advance was such that he was quite unable to do so, and he fell back down the road into the forest. The retreating infantry were sped on their way by Dresky's artillery.

> When I saw the French infantry leave Chilleurs, I rode, after having given a general order that the fire was to be directed on them, up to the 4th Light Battery, whose leader, Captain Muller, had been through a course of instruction at the School of Gunnery, and had learnt to shoot on a good principle. I turned to his men and said, "For every shot which you throw directly into the enemy's infantry, I will give you three thalers." A gunner replied, "That will cost you a lot of money, Colonel; we shoot pretty well in this battery." The first shot went over, the second was short, then seven hit directly, which was, without doubt, the principal reason that the column broke up. I paid my 21 thalers in the midst of the cheers of the battery.[10]

Alvensleben gave his troops a short breathing space, while he reorganised the corps for its advance into the forest. Recognising the limited effectiveness of artillery there, he left outside the forest the six batteries of the corps artillery, and the four batteries of the 5th Division, protected by the 48th Regiment and two battalions of the 24th Regiment. With the rest of his force, which included the twenty four guns of the 6th Division, Alvensleben resumed his advance at about 3.00pm, The 5th Division, now led by Major General von Schwerin, took the line of a narrow track due south of La Rive du Bois, at the entrance to the forest; meanwhile to the west, the 6th Division marched down the road to Loury. Almost at once road blocks were encountered, which seriously delayed the advance; it took two hours to cover the first three miles. Alvensleben had realised that he could not hope to exercise effective control of the operation unless he was on the spot when any crisis developed, and rode with the leading units of the 6th Division. Apart from a brief word with his chief of staff, he kept his fears to himself; his troops, exhilarated by their success earlier in the day, pressed on through the gathering gloom in high spirits. The obstacles that were encountered meant that the advanced parties of the 6th Division did not reach the edge of the large clearing around Loury until 6.00 pm, by which time darkness had fallen. In the distance, the rattle of rifle fire had been heard from the direction of Neuville aux Bois, outside the forest, and to the right and the left of the corps Alvensleben posted a screen of infantry battalions as the rest of his troops settled down for the night in and around Loury.[11]

During the march through the forest nothing had been seen of Pallières and the main body of his division. This was because Pallières, acting on the orders he had previously received from d'Aurelle to retreat to Orleans, which reached him at 5.20 am, had led his troops as far south as the Avenue de Nibelle, one of the roads which criss-crossed the forest and which ran east-west. There, he turned off with his infantry in a westerly direction; the artillery had gone on down the road through Loury to Orleans. D'Aurelle had directed Pallières to retreat on St Lye and Chevilly, although at the time he gave this instruction he was of course quite unaware of the southward march of the III Corps. In fact, he remained unaware of it, since Pallières failed to report the outcome of the engagements at Santeau and Chilleurs, and chose to comply with the letter of his instructions, thereby opening the road southwards to Alvensleben's advance.

To the west, Manstein led the main body of the IX Corps directly down the Orleans-Paris high road. To cover his left flank he sent a detachment of three battalions, with one squadron of cavalry and a heavy battery under Colonel von Winckler, the commander of the 49th Brigade, in the direction of St Lye. As he approached the farm of La Tour, Winckler ran into strong columns of French infantry advancing between the farm and the village of Mauregard. Winckler deployed either side of the Roman road which runs north -south just to the west of the farm; for a while there was a stalemate, attacks from each side breaking down in the face of heavy rifle fire. By 4.00 however, the French fell back to St Germain, closely pursued by Winckler's men; it was, though, by now getting dark, and aware of the presence of stronger French forces to the south and south west, Winckler retreated in a heavy snow storm to a position behind La Tour.[12] The French troops he had encountered were those of Minot, who had been ordered to hold Neuville as long as he could, and then to fall back on St Lye; Pallières hoped in this way to cover his westward march along the Avenue de Nibelle.

Winckler's retreat for the night, however, did not mark the end of Minot's problems. The X Corps had been designated as the army reserve, and its operations for the day had involved it in a move westwards to a position in which it could support the advances of the III and IX Corps. By 3.00 pm Voigts-Rhetz's main body had reached Chilleurs; when, however, Kraatz, with the advance guard, heard of the engagement at La Tour, he decided to push on to Neuville, at which he launched a battalion in an attack which, deprived of artillery support by the fall of night, failed to force its way into the village. Kraatz therefore postponed any further assault until the following day. Meanwhile by about 4.00 pm Pallières had reached a point due south of Neuville, and he sent a message to Minot that instead of taking the road to St Lye, which he knew to be a bad one, and on which Minot might be attacked in flank, he could instead take the road to Rebrechien, by which he might gain the Loury-Orleans road before the Germans got there. Minot had already decided on this course, and set off on a night march through the forest. Reaching a fork in the road not far south of Neuville, Minot's column, led by his twelve guns, chose the wrong road, which led to Loury, rather than that to Rebrechien. As a result, at about 8.00 pm they ran into the outposts that Alvensleben had posted around his bivouacs at Loury. The sudden appearance of the French gave Kretschmann, who had been sent by Frederick Charles to accompany the III Corps on its march, a nasty shock when he was seeking quarters for the night.

> I was just in the process of finding a stable, when a salvo of shells burst in the village so close to me that I jumped into a house ... French troops had suddenly appeared close to our village; they ran into our outposts and there was a scattering of fire. The night gave me an ominous feeling; one could only hear the whistling of bullets and the crackle of rifle fire.[13]

Not surprisingly, there was confusion on both sides, but the better disciplined German troops soon recovered, while the French column disintegrated, the infantry fleeing in the direction of Orleans. The French gunners struggled heroically to save their artillery, but only managed to get seven of the guns away. Next morning, the III Corps patrols found the other five abandoned close to their positions.[14]

Manstein's task for December 3 was altogether more straightforward. His advanced guard moved off early from Chateau Gaillard down the main road in the direction of Artenay and soon encountered enemy resistance there and at Assas to the east of the road. These were troops from Martineau's division. Manstein spread out, sending the 85th Regiment west of the road towards Dambron and the 84th Regiment, with a horse artillery battery, to the east of the road to outflank the French at Assas, where a powerful force of artillery was firing on the high road at the main body of the IX Corps as it moved south. The German artillery clattered down the road and, deploying on either side of it, came at once into action, causing the French to pull back from Assas. The German artillery moved on south, and soon found fresh targets in the form of the rest of Martineau's artillery, which was posted to the north west of Artenay. They were quickly assisted by seven batteries of the 22nd Division and the 2nd Cavalry Division which opened fire at about 10.00 am from a position southeast of Poupry. The outposts of the 22nd Division had, before dawn that morning, fallen back towards Baigneaux in the face of a strong French reconnaissance towards the copse north of Poupry, but returned to the village before 9.00 am, and were joined there by the 2nd Cavalry Division.[15]

With 90 German guns pounding his troops in and around Artenay, Martineau could not be expected to hold on there very long; and he soon withdrew first his artillery and then his 1st Brigade down the road to La Croix Briquet, pulling back his 2nd Brigade, to the east of the road, to Arblay Farm. Quickly as the French infantry retreated, many of them were not quick enough, and a large number of stragglers were picked up in the streets of Artenay by the 11th Regiment, which had closely followed them down the high road, while on either side of the road the Germans also pushed southwards, taking Autroches and moving on Arblay Farm.[16] The Germans were now approaching, at Chevilly, the first of the prepared positions forming part of the fortified camp of Orleans. D'Aurelle had intended to meet the German advance there, but the speed of Manstein's movement southwards meant that Martineau could not avoid becoming engaged with the Germans further north.

After giving his men half an hour's break, Manstein resumed his advance at 12.30 pm, which was led by the 35th Brigade, heading for La Croix Briquet. On his right, Wittich moved forward with the 22nd Division past Murville and Lille

Farm, followed shortly by his artillery and the 2nd Cavalry Division. As his leading infantry approached La Croix Briquet, a heavy artillery barrage fell on them from the 15th Corps artillery, which had taken position on the heights to the north of the village. Martineau held both the Auvilliers Mill to the west of the road and Arblay Farm on the east, and the position was strong enough to warrant the postponement of any infantry assault until the German artillery had done its work. Manstein now deployed his guns on the slope south of Artenay, firing down the main road, on either side of which infantry units moved forward to La Grange Farm and the Chateau of Auvilliers. For a time, there was stalemate, as the respective gun lines sought to gain the upper hand in a prolonged artillery duel. Manstein's artillery commander, Major General von Puttkamer, was frustrated by the cover afforded to the French artillery by the trees in their front, until he brought four batteries around to the south west of the chateau. They were joined there by batteries from the 2nd Cavalry Division and soon after were also supported by the artillery of the 22nd Division from Lille Farm and Beaugency. Taken in enfilade, and overwhelmed by the now familiar concentration of German artillery fire, the French artillery ceased firing at about 2.pm. Without the protection of their gunners, the French infantry were quite unable to resist the ensuing assault by the 85th Regiment which stormed the Auvilliers Mill, and the 84th Regiment which forced its way into the burning buildings of Arblay Farm.[17]

With the capture of Auvilliers Mill, Manstein deployed five batteries there, and under their outflanking barrage the French defenders of La Croix Briquet fell back before the assault of the 11th Regiment. On their right flank the French infantry took up a strong position under the cover of some naval guns posted at Andeglou. Momentarily the French infantry were emboldened to counter attack before the arrival of four batteries of German artillery on the heights between Arblay Farm and the high road compelled them to retreat behind their own gun line, which for the time being prevented any further German advance. La Croix Briquet had fallen soon after 3.00 pm; by then Frederick Charles had already laid down the final objectives for the IX Corps for that day's operations, when at 2.45 pm he issued an order that called for a substantial further advance:

> I shall consider today's work finished when, after a thorough preparation by artillery, the village of Chevilly and the angle of the forest east of it are in possession of the IX Corps, and are, under all circumstances, held by them. The 17th and 22nd Infantry Divisions will similarly, after a bombardment, capture the Chevilly Chateau and the angle of the forest south of the village, and hold firmly on to them. If the day is not long enough the attacks must be continued after dark.[18]

This was a considerable requirement; the French had now reached the most advanced of the prepared positions that constituted the fortified camp of Orleans, and these were always going to be a tough nut to crack. To call for them to be taken in a night assault was asking a lot. As the afternoon wore on it became increasingly clear that this would be unavoidable if Frederick Charles' demands were to be met. In spite of a heavy bombardment by the German artillery, the French heavy artillery at Andeglou remained in action until after darkness had fallen; on the other hand, the German infantry succeeded in taking two farms to the east and south east of La Croix Briquet.[19]

On the western flank of the German advance, von der Tann had had the least demanding task for the day. His principal task was to cover the right against any attempt by Chanzy to renew his offensive of the previous day, but after the hammering taken by the 16th and 17th Corps this was unlikely. The French had hung on to Villepion overnight, but only to cover their retreat towards Patay. Bavarian patrols probed towards Villepion Faverolles and Echelles while the main body of the corps moved down to Lumeau to await further orders. At 11.00 am von der Tann was instructed that his 2nd Division should follow the 17th Division as a general reserve, while the rest of the corps was to march to Sougy.[20] The forward movements to comply with these orders led to no encounter with the enemy until after 3.00 pm, when the advanced patrols of the 1st Brigade found a substantial concentration of French troops in position north of Trogny. This body was however, forced to retire by heavy artillery fire from the batteries of the 1st Division and also of the 17th Division. Although the French halted and put up stiffer resistance in a prepared position to the south of Trogny, it was not long before they were chased out of the entrenchments there. There was also a short-lived advance from L'Encormes in the direction of Sougy. The French troops concerned in these operations were Barry's 2nd Division of Chanzy's Corps, and the movement was intended to cover the retreat of the main body southwards and to offer some support to the 15th Corps on the high road.

Chanzy's intention was that Barry should, by the effective use of his artillery, hold up any further German advance until nightfall.[21] By then, von der Tann's leading troops were in La Provenchère, with the rest echelonned back to Sougy, while the 2nd Division bivouacked at Chevaux.

Immediately to von der Tann's left, Tresckow and the 17th Division had also had a quiet day, marching southwards from Anneux through Murville to Chameul, where its artillery had come into action first against the French troops

Prince Leopold of Bavaria with his artillery at Villepion, by Knötel (Pflugk-Harttung)

falling back down the high road before Manstein's advance, and then in support of von der Tann's troops at Trogny. It was while his artillery was thus engaged that Tresckow received the orders from the Second Army that operations were to continue during the night if need be to occupy the chateau and village of Chevilly. Wittich, who received the same orders, had brought the 22nd Division southwards in rear of his artillery, which had also been in action against the French troops on the high road; as night fell he was deployed behind his guns on either side of the Chevaux- Chevilly road.[22] In these positions Tresckow and Wittich, like Manstein on their left, began preparations for the night attack ordered by Frederick Charles.

Stosch, meanwhile, who had been dismayed to receive this order, had resolved with the Grand Duke's permission to do something about it. Riding out from the headquarters of the Detachment, Stosch at about 5 pm found Frederick Charles with Stiehle and the staff of the Second Army at the village of Creuzy, a mile or so west of La Croix Briquet. It was not a confortable interview. Stosch reported on the positions occupied by the Detachment and of the French activity on his right flank, and made clear to the Prince his concerns about the risks of a night attack. He pointed out that on the previous day the Detachment had faced not only the 16th and 17th Corps, but a large part of the 15th Corps as well. Frederick Charles was unimpressed, telling Stosch that many prisoners taken in Artenay came from the 15th Corps: 'The Grand Duke has made a mistake, this Division cannot be opposite to him; he has nothing much opposed to him, and he has been deceived by a demonstration, and has again allowed himself to be drawn away from the real point of attack.' To a man who had just conducted the extremely successful battle of Loigny-Poupry, such a remark was thoroughly offensive, as well as ill informed; but whatever he felt Stosch was careful not to take offence, and repeated that the threat posed by Barry's Division might compel the Detachment to face west, rather than continue the march on Orleans. Frederick Charles was dismissive, saying pointedly: 'They are only franc tireurs and Gardes Mobiles. Orleans is the parole; the Detachment will advance against it tomorrow with all its forces.' Stosch again stifled his instinctive rejoinder, and returned again to danger of the proposed night attack. Confronted by this persistence, Frederick Charles, without further comment, turned to Stiehle and countermanded the attack; to Stosch, he sulkily observed that he had relied on the flanking movement of the whole of the Detachment. Stosch forbore to reply, and swung himself into his saddle. As he rode away, Frederick Charles called after him: 'But tomorrow we must be in Orleans,' to which Stosch replied, a little enigmatically, 'It will not be our fault if we are not.' As he rode back to his headquarters, he might have been entitled to congratulate himself on his considerable prudence in the face of much provocation; it had averted what might have been a serious error of judgment.[23] As it was, however, d'Aurelle had himself taken a hand in the events at Chevilly. He had gone there at 2.00 pm, to await the arrival of Pallières. By 4.30 pm no news had come from him. D'Aurelle now realised that he could no longer expect to hold on to Chevilly, so he departed, giving orders to Martineau that the village should be held until darkness fell, and that the troops occupying it and the adjoining heights should full back down the high road to Cercottes, the next prepared position some three miles to the south.[24] As it happened, therefore, the French pulled out just as the counter order reached Wittich, whose troops were getting ready to storm the village.[25] The counter order did not in fact reach Tresckow, whose men were advancing on Chevilly Château; after a brisk bombardment, his leading troops occupied it, while his main body remained at Chameul.[26]

Wittich, who had been directed by the counter order to remain in his existing positions, was reluctant to comply, as he later recorded.

> There was nothing for my men but the bare plain covered with wet snow, a bivouac without straw, wood water or food. My troops had been fighting during the whole of December 2; the leading troops had arrived at 10.00 pm that night, the last at one in the morning, in the icy bivouac at Anneux, where they had little to eat; they had fallen in before daybreak and had been in fighting formation all day.[27]

In the light of this, Wittich would have disobeyed the order, and gone all the way back to Poupry to seek shelter for his men; as it was, however, his cavalry patrols reported the French retreat, and his men passed a comfortable night in Chevilly.

D'Aurelle had finally left Chevilly at about 5.30, but it was not until 3.am the following day that he extablished his headquarters at Saran, some five miles north of Orleans; and there, he and Borel, his Chief of Staff reviewed the situation. On the road, he had passed large numbers of Martineau's troops falling back in disorder to Orleans, and when he got to Saran he finally got news of Pallières and of his retreat from his position at Chilleurs aux Bois. His right wing, consisting of the 18th and 20th Corps had, he knew, been badly shaken by its defeat at Beaune la Rolande, from which it had not recovered; Bourbaki, who was now in command of both Corps, had at 7.00 pm received orders to concentrate to his left to support Pallières, but so far as Aurelle knew these corps had not yet been able to take any part in the battle for Orleans.[28] As for his left wing under Chanzy, the 16th and 17th Corps, he was aware that it had been badly beaten the day before at Loigny-Poupry, and was in retreat; and he had seen with his own eyes the collapse of his centre on the high road. In the absence of any news of Pallières it seemed to d'Aurelle that he had no choice but to abandon Orleans, and to put the Loire between himself and his enemy. Borel emphatically agreed, telling him: 'Your troops will not hold, the demoralisation is too great, and, if you wait too long to order the evacuation of Orleans, you will expose yourself to a disaster much greater than the loss of this town.'[29] D'Aurelle believed that it was above all necessary to take a prompt decision, and there being still no information as to Pallières' division, at 4.am on December 4 he telegraphed Tours, announcing 'the sad and cruel necessity' of evacuating Orleans. After recounting the events of the last three days, he stated bluntly that he regarded the defence of Orleans as impossible. 'If we had time before us to reorganise and pull ourselves together, this could be attempted; but the enemy will be on us tomorrow and I must, sadly, but with a profound conviction, repeat to you that our troops, sorely tried and demoralised by the last two days, will not hold.' He went on to inform Gambetta that Chanzy's two corps would retreat by Beaugency and Blois and the 18th and 20th Corps, now both to be under Bourbaki, by Gien, while the 15th Corps would cross the Loire at Orleans; the army would thus retreat into the Sologne.[30]

Predictably, Gambetta and Freycinet were appalled to receive d'Aurelle's telegram. Freycinet despatched at 5.00 am an immediate response which d'Aurelle justly described as haughty and angry in tone:

> Your despatch of tonight has caused me a painful stupefaction. I can see, in the facts you recount, nothing which seems to justify the resolution of despair which you report ... You still have 200,000 men ready to fight if their leaders knew how, by their own example and the firmness of their attitude, to strengthen their courage and their patriotism. The evacuation of which you speak will be both for itself and beyond its military consequences an immense disaster.

It seemed to Freycinet that d'Aurelle should draw in the 18th and 20th Corps, while the other three corps closed up. [31]D'Aurelle was not putting up with lectures of this kind, replying crisply at 8.00 am: 'I am on the spot and better able to judge the situation. It is with no less pain than yours that I decided to take this extreme step.' He went on to add, in an echo of the advice given by Borel: 'In spite of all the efforts that we have been able to make, Orleans will inevitably fall into the enemy's hands tonight or tomorrow. It will be a great misfortune; but the only means of avoiding a still greater catastrophe is to have the courage to make a sacrifice while there is still time.'[32] Satisfying himself that his orders were being carried out d'Aurelle went off to Orleans.

At about 10.00 am he learned of the arrival of Pallières and his 1st Division. He was still unaware of the chaotic retreat from Chilleurs during the previous evening, and in the presence of Pallières and the strongest division of the army, his spirits rose. At 11.55 he telegraphed Gambetta anew: 'I am changing my plans; directing 16th and 17th Corps on Orleans, calling in the 18th and 20th, organising resistance, am on the spot in Orleans.'[33] This had crossed with a telegram from Freycinet grudgingly acknowledging d'Aurelle's decision to evacuate the city; when he got the news of d'Aurelle's change of heart, Freycinet sent a joyful response at 1.35 pm expressing 'complete faith that you will be able to put up an effective resistance behind your naval batteries,' and announcing that Gambetta himself would leave for Orleans in half an hour.

Frederick Charles had good reason to feel extremely satisfied with the operations of the Second Army and the Detachment on December 3, which had brought him within ten miles of Orleans. In the course of these operations his casualties had been extremely light, due largely to the tactical reliance which, wherever possible, had been placed upon the indefatigable German gunners. 'On nearly every occasion the adversary had abandoned the field directly after the deployment of the German artillery, and it was only at St Lye and Neuville aux Bois that he held out until evening.'[34] In issuing his orders for the next day, which he did at 9.00pm on December 3, Frederick Charles had firmly in his mind the intention to occupy Orleans that day. In the belief that Aurelle would be bound to put up fierce resistance in the Gidy-Cercottes position, Manstein was ordered to advance through Chevilly, extending eastward into the forest for an enveloping attack on Cercottes. The Detachment was to move on Gidy, to co-operate with this assault. The X Corps was to march south to act as a general reserve, arriving at Chevilly at 1 pm. With the position of all these units, Frederick Charles was more or less familiar; but he had heard nothing from Alvensleben since a message sent by the latter at 1 pm,

General Konstantin von Alvensleben, commander of the German III Corps (Rousset/*Histoire*)

which he only got at 7.00 pm because he had shifted his headquarters to Artenay. That message reported the retreat of Pallières' division from Chilleurs, where 'the wood is being attacked. One gun taken, 200 prisoners. Our loss small up to the present.'[35] That was all that Frederick Charles knew; his orders to Alvensleben, based on guesswork as to the position of the III Corps but even more on his desire to take Orleans that day, were that the Corps should 'advance along the Chilleurs-Loury road towards Orleans, covering itself on its left flank against any forces coming perhaps from Bellegarde, and has, as objective, to bring artillery into action as much as possible against the town of Orleans. The Corps will move off at 7.00 am.'[36]

The staff officer bearing this order got lost during the night due to a heavy snowstorm, and only arrived at Alvensleben's headquarters at 8.00 am on December 4. Fortunately, Alvensleben had put everything in hand for an advance, and he set off at 9.00 am. He was not, however, impressed by the orders he had received, describing them dismissively as 'armchair strategy.' Not having been made aware of Frederick Charles' determination to take Orleans that day, he was puzzled by the order to shell the city, although he entirely recognised the need to protect his left as he plunged on through the forest. The 6th Division marched down the Loury-Orleans road, after having first brought up the artillery which had been left overnight outside the forest at Chilleurs, while the 5th Division took the side road a little to the east through Vennecy, aiming to reach the Loire at Chécy. By noon the two divisions had halted in a position abreast of Boigny, having encountered no resistance although picking up numerous French stragglers en route. After a short break, they moved on, the 6th Division continuing on the road to Orleans, while the 5th Division headed for Bourgneuf.

When the leading troops of the 6th Division reached Vaumainbert at about 2.00, pm they ran into stiff opposition from troops of the 1st Division of the 15th Corps who had taken up defensive positions in a number of farm buildings covering the village. The close nature of the terrain precluded the use of artillery, so Buddenbrock had to rely solely on his infantry. One battalion of the 35th Regiment was launched in an assault on the east side of Vaumainbert, while the 20th Regiment came in on the north.[37] It took two hours fierce fighting before the enemy, which included marine units, were finally dislodged from the village. The Germans pushed on down the road towards the city, reaching St Loup as darkness begun to fall. Keen to be the first into Orleans, Kretschmann and the III Corps staff tried to persuade Alvensleben to continue the advance through the darkness; but it was obvious to him that to attempt more that night would be foolhardy.[38] However, mindful of the instructions he had received, and wishing to let Manstein, whom he presumed must by now be closing in on Orleans from the north, know how far he had got, he ordered Major General von Bulow, commanding his artillery, to find some way to throw some shells into the city.

> The sound of the guns would thus signal to the troops on the main road his arrival. So close was the country, that only with difficulty was found a place for a whole battery to come into action. At last, a grass plot in front of a villa was discovered; a heavy battery was unlimbered and twelve shells were fired, and then the battery limbered up just in time, for hardly had it gone, than eleven heavy shells, fired from Orleans, fell on the lawn.[39]

Meanwhile the expected threat from the east had materialised. The advanced guard of the 5th Division, under Lieutenant Colonel von L'Estocq, had reached the Loire at Chécy at about 2.00 pm, which was its objective for the day, when it received information of French troops advancing a westerly direction over the Orleans canal at Pont aux Moines. By 2.30 pm parties of skirmishers, followed by strong infantry columns, had appeared. L'Estocq deployed in front of Chécy, where he was soon reinforced by a battalion and a battery from the main body; after a short engagement, the attackers retreated to Port aux Moines. L'Estocq, who had by now received further reinforcements, advanced in pursuit; the French held the line of the Canal long enough to allow their main body to get away and then fell back to the east. L'Estocq, although unaware of it at the time, had been in the presence of overwhelming odds; the French troops he had encountered were Crouzat's 20th Corps which, in accordance with the orders which Bourbaki had received, was moving westwards in support of the 15th Corps. Crouzat had been aware of Alvensleben's advance, receiving regular reports from his scouts; at 11.00 one of these reported to him personally that 'we are in the midst of the Prussian Army.' As a result of this he had, when he arrived at Fay aux Loges, about five miles north east of Pont aux Moines, taken the precaution of sending his artillery and trains over the Loire at Jargeau while continuing along the right bank of the river towards Orleans with his infantry. Crouzat had not however realised just how much progress Alvensleben had made, and the encounter at Chécy caused him considerable anxiety; fearing to be trapped between the III Corps and the river, he

The French evacuate Orleans, by Pallandre (Rousset/*Combattants*)

retreated at once down the right bank towards the crossing at Jargeau where he was relieved to find that the bridge had been made passable by the inhabitants and over which his artillery had already made its way to safety. It was in this way that L'Estocq's boldness ensured that the III Corps 'escaped in a marvellous way being captured in the very den of the lion.'[40]

It was down the main road that Frederick Charles expected the decisive blow to be struck. Here, unlike the sector being traversed by the III Corps, his artillery would in the early stages of the advance be able to dominate operations, as it had done thus far. Manstein, whose advance was led by the 18th Division, moved out of La Croix Briquet at 8.30 am, pushing the 36th Brigade down the main road, followed by the corps artillery, while the 35th Brigade took the line of the railway to the left. The road and the railway ran only two to three hundred yards apart at this point; neither brigade encountered any resistance until they entered a wood to the south of Chevilly. Soon, however, the ubiquitous artillery came up to clear away the line of skirmishers and by 11.00 am the wood was cleared of French troops. Half a mile to the south was the fortified village of Cercottes, held by Martineau's 2nd Division, and connected by a line of entrenchments to Gidy, two miles to the west. Here, the French prepared to take a stand. The key to the French position was a height just to the west of Cercottes, and on this Manstein directed the fire of seven batteries of the 18th Division. Meanwhile at about 1.00 pm eight companies of infantry from the 35th Brigade had charged through the railway station at Cercottes and into the north eastern corner of the village, at which point the French hurriedly retreated.[41]

The retreat from Cercottes meant that the whole fortified position was no longer defensible, and the French pulled back all along their front; the German artillery, following close behind the advancing infantry, kept the retreating French under constant fire. Although small parties of infantry held out briefly in each defensible position in turn, there was really nowhere strong enough for them to hold up the German advance until they reached the railway station north of Orleans. Here, making skilful use of a deeply sunken road, troops of the 15th Corps had dug in, supported in their immediate rear by several naval guns. To deal with these, the Germans brought up a heavy battery, and in the ensuing duel the German gunners gradually got the upper hand. It was 5.30 pm however, by the time this stage was reached, and although his leading troops had taken the railway station at Les Aubrais, Manstein found the enemy still strongly posted immediately to the south. In an effort to shift them, he launched an attack by the 11th Regiment, which proved unsuccessful. It was by now entirely dark, and Manstein, like Alvensleben to the east, had no intention of taking unnecessary risks by launching a night attack on a determined enemy securely ensconced in the suburbs of Orleans. At 7.00 pm therefore he ordered his corps to break off the action, taking up a position for the night in the larger farm buildings either side of the main road, and in the railway station itself, whose defenders had to beat off a counter attack as late as 10.00 pm.[42] Behind the IX Corps the X Corps had reached Cercottes at 4.00 pm, and remained echelonned back along the main road as far north as Artenay. Held in reserve, Voigts-Rhetz was not called upon to undertake any operations during the day which, it seemed, was drawing to a close with the Second Army having failed in Frederick Charles' bid to take Orleans by nightfall.

To the west, the Detachment moved forward both to support Manstein's advance, and to cover the right flank. The 17th Division, to which a cavalry regiment was attached, was to be responsible for the main attack, marching south from Chateau Chevilly and Chameul towards Gidy. Wittich, with the 22nd Division, was to follow in reserve. Von der Tann, meanwhile, was to concentrate at La Provenchère before advancing on Janvry and thence towards Orleans. All the signs were that French morale was beginning to break up; during the bitterly cold night a number of hungry and frozen deserters arrived at the Bavarian outposts, reporting that the Army of the Loire was in retreat and had had enough.[43] This seemed to be confirmed next morning at 7.00 am when the naval guns at Gidy fired harmlessly only half a dozen rounds before being abandoned by their gunners later that morning.

The cavalry patrols leading Tresckow's advance had found, as expected, the entrenchments at Gidy to be strongly held; knowing that Manstein's advance, when it reached Cercottes, must threaten the French position at Gidy, Tresckow decided to hold his hand for a while, halting his main body at Cuny, two miles to the north. His judgement proved correct; and when the French pulled out of the Gidy position he was able to move through the enemy entrenchments without loss.[45]

Meanwhile Frederick Charles had at last paid a visit to the headquarters of the Detachment, where he had a brief, chilly, and uninformative interview with the Grand Duke. Unable to conceal his personal dislike, he confirmed his instructions for the day's operations, coldly rejecting the Grand Duke's opinion that the French in front of the Detachment were retreating over the Loire. No, said the Prince, they were retreating on Orleans, which must at all costs be occupied by nightfall. Having thus repeated his injunction to Stosch of the previous night, Frederick Charles brought the interview to an end, and rode slowly back to his own headquarters, having made little or no enquiry as to the actual events on the Detachment's front on the previous day, or the reason for the Grand Duke's belief about the direction of the enemy retreat.[46]

Certainly the indications reaching the Detachment's headquarters pointed firmly to the Grand Duke's opinion being correct. On the far left, the French continued to hold Patay; the troops holding that village beat off an attack by the flanking column of the Detachment led by Major General von Hontheim with considerable loss, causing it to retreat on Terminiers. In front of the main body of the I Bavarian Corps, the enemy were clearly preparing to make a stand in the earth works at Boulay, to cover the retreat of the French main body in a south and south westerly direction. Having been spared the necessity of storming the entrenchments at Gidy, Tresckow was now ordered to move to his right to support the Bavarians, while Wittich came up on his left to maintain contact with the IX Corps on the Paris road. By the time Tresckow reached Janvry at about 11.30 am, he found von der Tann deploying against the Boulay position and further west against a field work on the Châteaudun road. By noon, the Bavarian artillery had overpowered its opposition and the infantry moved forward. The demoralised French infantry had by now had enough, and as soon as the German advance began, they fell back southwards, once again abandoning their guns. The Grand Duke, who was up with his leading troops, saw his chance, and at once ordered Stolberg with the 2nd Cavalry Division to advance to the front in pursuit of the retreating enemy. There followed a series of cavalry operations which by themselves went a long way to sealing the fate of Orleans.

Stolberg's division came up at the trot, led by the 4th Hussar Regiment, which moved through the open space south of Gidy and then through the gap in the forest at Montaigne Farm. As they emerged from the shelter of the woods near Bois Girard, the hussars saw a party of French cavalry escorting a battery unlimbering on the Chateaudun road. The French gunners had no time to swing their guns round before the leading hussar squadron was on them; after the briefest of struggles, the whole battery of nine guns, with 79 men, was captured. Stolberg brought up his 4th Brigade to Bois Girard in support, while the 5th Brigade worked its way around the western edge of the woods through Heurdy. At about 1.00 pm the French attempted a counter attack, sending forward a large body of cavalry up the Châteaudun road from Ormes. The leading troops of the 4th Brigade were the Blücher Hussars; the nearest squadron, the 5th, wheeled to its left and, supported by two other squadrons moved forward along and to the north of the road towards the advancing French: then, they 'dashed at a rapid pace through the ranks of the French horsemen, and drove them back as far as Ingré, where further pursuit was stopped by infantry fire.'[47]

The advance had, however, carried them well to the south, where they made contact with the French troops falling back from the northwest towards the prepared positions just outside Orleans. These were troops of the 2nd and 3rd Divisions of the 15th Corps, and the unexpected arrival in their midst of German

General von Tresckow, commander of the German 17th Infantry Division (Rousset/*Histoire*)

cavalry caused panic which spread in all directions. 'The French now strove to stem Stolberg's advance by bringing artillery into action, but these were soon driven off by the German horse artillery, which was well to the front. The French in their wild flight completely broke up two of the gardes mobiles regiments, a marche regiment, and a battery.'[48] The effect on d'Aurelle's attempt to hold Orleans cannot be overstated. A French historian wrote:

> The retreat which commenced in great disaster is continued in the midst of ever increasing confusion. Demoralisation quickly assumes terrible proportions. There is no longer any command, any direction; isolated parties of infantry and entire bodies of troops are mixed up with trains and batteries. Some make for Orleans; most gain Meung, Beaugency, Mer or even Blois.[49]

While Stolberg was thus ripping a hole in the centre of the French defences, the Bavarians had experienced some difficulties to the north west, where Chanzy was once again attempting to hold up the German advancing by pushing forward into its right flank. For this, he employed Jauréguiberry's Division of the 16th Corps in an advance from Coinces, supported by the 17th Corps further south at Germigny. Von der Tann swung round his 3rd Brigade, with the Cuirassier Brigade and the corps artillery to block this advance, while von Bernhardi's 9th Cavalry Brigade moved west from Huêtre. At Coinces, the German cavalry ran into part of Jauréguiberry's Division, covered by a detachment of cavalry, at which Bernhardi at once launched a charge. At full stretch he jumped a shelter trench at the head of four squadrons, in the face of which the French cavalry beat a hasty retreat to St Péravy. Other squadrons followed them, and there ensued a confused struggle in which the French cavalry were only rescued by the fire of Jaureguiberry's infantry. The arrival of Hontheim with the 8th Cavalry Brigade at Patay, from which the French soon retreated, losing some ammunition wagons to the advancing German horsemen, convinced Chanzy that any further advance was doomed to failure, and he fell back behind the Bois de Montpipeau en route to the Loire.[50] It was, he wrote, 'no longer possible to imagine falling back on Orleans, the enemy already being master of a large part of the works which covered the city.'[51]

With this threat to his flank removed, the Grand Duke was able to continue his advance towards Orleans. Von der Tann was directed to take the Châteaudun road towards the city; having only one road for the whole corps necessarily slowed his advance, but French resistance was ebbing away. Even before Chanzy's retreat from Coinces, the main body of the I Bavarian Corps had been moving towards Ormes. For the Bavarians, it was a repeat of their experience in October, when they had first taken Orleans; but since then they had endured defeat at Coulmiers, as well as a long and exhausting campaign before once again finding themselves approaching their objective.

> The towers of the Cathedral of Orleans once more rose in the distance, and the houses of Ormes glittered in the sunshine, as they had done two months ago. Our goal was the same as on October 11, and neither officers nor men could restrain a feeling of proud satisfaction, when the trenches were once more stormed amid loud cheers, and the enemy was again seen in full flight.[52]

The leading troops gained an additional fillip to their morale, when a battalion of the 13th Regiment captured two guns, and two wagons, one containing a consignment of boots, which was gleefully shared out amongst the men of the battalion.[53]

The advance towards Orleans continued with little opposition; since the earlier successes of Stolberg's cavalry, there were no longer any organised bodies of French infantry on the Chateaudun road. But night was already beginning to fall as the short December day ended with the leading Bavarian troops having turned off the road to Ingré, while the 17th Division moved on to the Chateaudun road and marched down towards the gates of Orleans. After dislodging some French troops who tried to make a stand at St Jean de la Ruelle, Tresckow's leading troops reached the walls of the city at 6.pm.[54] The Grand Duke, who had spent most of the day with Tresckow, was of much the same opinion as Alvensleben and Manstein about the wisdom of launching a night attack on what might be a stubbornly defended city, and he too ordered a halt for the night. The main body of the 17th Division took up a position at the railway embankment about a mile from the city; Colonel von Manteuffel with the advanced guard pressed on, and by 6.00 pm was outside the entrance gate.

Back at the headquarters of the Second Army, Frederick Charles was becoming gloomily aware that his hope of taking Orleans that day was now gone, and at 6.45 pm he issued orders that all forces should cease fire and remain where they were, with a view to renewing the attack next day. Inside Orleans the situation had steadily deteriorated throughout the day, as demoralised French troops streamed back into the city. D'Aurelle's brief hope that he might after all be able to mount an effective defence flickered briefly but as the afternoon wore on it soon died. As d'Aurelle graphically described it: 'The illusion did not last long; the soldiers of the 1st Division of the 15th Corps were scattered over the various quarters of the town, in pubs, in private houses, or lying drunk in public places and beside the houses. The officers had abandoned their troops, and filled the hotels and cafés.'[55] By 4.00 pm it was abundantly clear to him that his situation was militarily impossible, and that he must revert to his previous decision to abandon the city at once if he was to save even part of the troops still remaining in its defences. An orderly officer sent to make contact with Chanzy was unable to get through. He gave the order to evacuate the city, reporting this to Tours an hour later. He was expecting Gambetta's arrival, but the latter's train ran into the leading units of German cavalry that had pressed on to the Loire. A horse artillery battery opened fire and it was only by the speed with which the drivers put the engine into reverse that it avoided falling into the enemy's hands. Had he got there, d'Aurelle wrote, Gambetta 'would have seen for himself ... the unavailing efforts made to restore a feeling of honour to the soldiers, for the moment distraught as a result of their suffering, exhaustion and demoralisation, and who refused to fight to their last bullet.'[56] While waiting for Gambetta with the Préfet, M. Pereira, d'Aurelle expressed himself bitterly about the position in which he had been put by the government at Tours. Pereira tried to cheer him up, telling him that their misfortune was not his fault, and that all France knew his energy and his courage; it was a reassurance that d'Aurelle particularly valued, since Pereira, whose health had been failing, died a few days later.

Manteuffel could see through the city gate French soldiers in the streets; when the guard refused his demand that the gate be opened, Manteuffel insisted that the commanding officer be sent for and notified this to Tresckow before riding back to report to the Grand Duke.

Pallières, given by d'Aurelle the task of covering the retreat, got Manteuffel's message at 7.00 pm. By then he was already aware that the French troops behind the walls of Orleans immediately facing the line of advance of the 17th Division had melted away, so he sent Captain Pendezec of his staff to find out what Manteuffel wanted, and moved up a battalion of infantry to frustrate any German attempt to seize the gate by a coup de main. Pendezec was taken to Tresckow, who told him that he had occupied the suburb of St Jean, while the Second Army was at the railway gate in the suburb of Bannier. Tresckow was firm, saying:

> If you wish I will have you taken there to convince yourself. I intend to occupy Orleans today, but would like to avoid a street fight, which will injure much both the city and the inhabitants; so for that reason I have halted here. Be so good as to convey to your commanding officer my summons that he evacuates the city by half past eleven. I shall then occupy the city as far as the Artenay road. If the commandant refuses, my batteries, which are now in position, will immediately open fire.

To emphasise his point, Tresckow asked that they synchronise watches.[57]

Tresckow was of course bluffing; but what Pallières knew, and he did not, was that there were scarcely any French troops left to resist a further German advance, and he sent Pendezec back to accept the terms. Soon after this, however, Pallières received an order from d'Aurelle to delay the evacuation, and he was obliged to send General d'Aries to Tresckow to ask for more time. They met on foot in the street outside the gate, and Tresckow extended the time by an hour; d'Aries accepted this and went back to d'Aurelle with the news. The Grand Duke, meanwhile, had deferred reporting to Frederick Charles until the situation had become clearer, but at 10.30 reported that he would occupy the city at 11.30. At 1.00 am he had the considerable satisfaction of riding into Orleans at the head of the 17th Division and the 2nd Bavarian Brigade. The news was not at all well received by Frederick Charles, as Waldersee noted: 'It was a thunderbolt. The Prince was beside himself. He had intended to make a formal entry into Orleans; his joy had vanished, and all owing to the Grand Duke, of whom he had an enduring dislike.'[58]

For Frederick Charles' injured feelings there would have been little sympathy at Versailles. There was, however, profound relief that Orleans had been recaptured. William, to whom the news first came in a telegram from the Grand Duke, responded promptly by awarding to him the Pour le Merité with oak leaves, and to Tresckow and Wittich the same decoration without oak leaves. The Crown Prince was overjoyed by the news, but confided sombrely to his diary that in spite of the victories at Paris and Orleans

> in a few weeks we shall have to fight again just the same, for in this war no single event is any longer decisive, in the same way as we have always hitherto found to be the case ... One cannot but think highly of the obstinate power of resistance shown by the French, for from it we clearly see what a united people can do when swayed by a great national ideal.

On the other hand, the completeness of the collapse of French morale was not unexpected. 'It is typical of the French how, so long as the struggle lasts, even when they are in the field against their will, they always fight bravely, but directly it is all over they throw to the winds, so to speak, all that is generally expected of soldiers.' He drew particular satisfaction, however, from Stosch's influence on the outcome; from the moment he arrived, 'all became clear and orderly, and we must thank him for the successes already reported.'[59]

Moltke was immediately concerned to exploit the victory to the greatest possible extent. With an eye to the effect on the morale of the Paris army, he sent a courteous note to Trochu to tell him of the defeat of the Army of the Loire near Orleans, and the occupation of the city, offering a safe conduct to one of Trochu's officers to enable him to check the position for himself, a proposition which Trochu politely declined.[60] More directly, he responded to the news with a telegram to Frederick Charles, to ensure that no time was lost in following up the victory. 'It is necessary vigorously to pursue the beaten enemy with the principal forces of the Second Army, without regard to events here.'[61] And he emphasised the point in a long letter to Stiehle of December 6, reviewing the new strategic situation. It was absolutely necessary, he wrote, to pursue the French vigorously and without respite, if they were not to be able, in a few days, to reassemble behind the Yèvre and then, due to their numerical strength, prove a fresh embarrassment. On the other hand, if they were pursued with sufficient forces the Army of the Loire might be completely broken up and dispersed. What was certain was that the Second Army must strike while the iron was hot. Once again, however, Frederick Charles' judgment let him down; he assigned the pursuit down the right back of the Loire to the Detachment, rather than the relatively fresh units of the Second Army which he had at his disposal; when Stosch pointed out the exhausted state of his troops, the Prince granted him a rest day, but still did not change his orders that it should be the Detachment which was to march on Beaugency.

However, Frederick Charles could claim that he had won a considerable victory. He had defeated an enemy army far larger than his own and split it into two parts, and had done so at the expense of relatively low casualties. His total losses amounted to 1,747 men, of which 353 were killed; French casualties exceeded 20,000 men, of whom about 18,000 were prisoners. The French had also lost 74 guns, and four gunboats left behind on the Loire. The moral effect of the loss of Orleans was quite as bad as Gambetta and Freycinet had feared; not only was the morale of the French troops badly damaged, but that of the German troops involved was greatly strengthened. The military effect of the campaign which culminated in the second capture of Orleans fell a long way short of Moltke's hopes for the complete destruction of the Army of the Loire; but its offensive power had been materially weakened, and there was no longer any realistic possibility of either part of the Army mounting a direct attempt to relieve Paris. Although it was evident to him that he must continue to keep Frederick Charles up to the mark, Moltke could at least turn to French activity on other points of the compass with the feeling that the most dangerous point of the war was now past.

16

Amiens

Bourbaki, denied re-entry to Metz by the obstinate obstructionism of Frederick Charles after his abortive mission to the Empress, had got tired of waiting at Luxembourg. He had offered his services to the Delegation, and Gambetta was delighted, suggesting to Bourbaki that he should take command of the Army of the Loire. This Bourbaki declined; as an alternative he put forward the proposal that he should take command in the North, with apparently some vague idea that he might from there be able to mount an operation for the relief of Metz. Gambetta accepted the idea, and on October 17 Bourbaki had set out for Lille, assuming command on October 22 of all the forces in Northern France. Sensibly, his first step was to appoint the dependable Farre as his chief of staff. However, his experiences of the war thus far had profoundly discouraged him, while his record of service to the previous regime did not inspire confidence in those he was to lead.

> Having just seen the destruction of magnificent armies he was unable to base much hope on a collection of recruits, escaped prisoners, poorly armed militia and complete novices. On the other hand, he was not favourably regarded because of his former close relationship to the Court, because of his command of the Imperial Guard at the outbreak of war, and above all because of his mysterious and romantic journey from Metz to London.[1]

The forces of which Bourbaki took command were not at that point very impressive. There were some troops of the line, consisting of the surplus that had been collected at regimental depots, and a large number of Gardes Mobiles, organised in battalions of up to 1,500 men, which were too unwieldy to be effectively managed. These latter he at once reorganised into units of five companies, each 150 strong with three officers. One of the problems that had immediately faced Bourbaki was the determination of the authorities, reckoning that the Loire was the most important theatre of war, to forward all new units there as soon as they were formed, and he was obliged to threaten resignation before this practice ceased. He also worked energetically to build up an effective artillery arm, based on guns and equipment brought from Mézières and La Fère. In one respect he was somewhat more fortunate than d'Aurelle on the Loire; a considerable number of experienced officers who had escaped from Sedan and Metz had made their way into north eastern France, where they were gratefully absorbed into the newly created 1st Division of the 22nd Corps. This consisted of two brigades, each 5,500 men strong; their first commanders were Colonel Lecointe, who had escaped from Metz, and the retired veteran Lieutenant Colonel Rittier, who had returned to the colours. Another escaper from Sedan, Commandant Charon, headed the artillery, of which four batteries had been formed and two more were assembling; these were to be manned by sailors hand picked from the naval battalions that had been organised. As for the cavalry, there were plenty of horses, but few men to ride them; two squadrons, designated the 7th Dragoon Regiment, were put together, reinforced by two other squadrons formed from gendarmes who were almost at once ready for action.[2]

As had been the case with other officers of the Imperial Army appointed to command the new Republican levies, Bourbaki was from the outset and remained extremely doubtful of their ability to face the Germans in the open field. This assessment of the battle worthiness of the new formations led him to advise Gambetta and Freycinet in the strongest possible terms that a suggested advance up the Seine valley by a force combining the Armies of the Loire and the North, marching to the relief of Paris, was utterly impracticable. Pessimistic opinions of this kind were extremely unwelcome to the Government of National Defence; the immediate necessity was to advance to the relief of Paris, and anyone who doubted the prospect of victory was no good to France. Under pressure, Bourbaki had agreed on November 14 to a forward movement against the advancing Germans. By this time he had still not yet completed the formation of the 2nd Division of the 22nd Corps, and the limited strength of the force at his disposal would make the operation extremely hazardous. His reluctant acquiescence in the plan was, however, insufficient to save him. With public opinion continuing to run strongly against Bourbaki, Freycinet felt compelled on November 19 to order him to give up his command, and to hand it over temporarily to General Farre.[3] Bourbaki, in accordance with his instructions, had then gone off to Tours, taking with him so many of his senior staff officers that Farre would have been left with no staff at all if he had not been able to recruit another officer who had escaped from Metz, Lieutenant Colonel Villenoisy, and a number of engineer officers.[4] It was not to be long before Farre was obliged to commit his newly assembled troops to serious operations.

The mounting indications in the reports reaching Moltke that in the north, as elsewhere, the Government of National Defence was putting together forces of significant strength, had further sharpened his anxiety to see the long drawn out siege of Metz reach its inevitable conclusion. However, he was not prepared to allow himself to be distracted from what he could see to be the proper military course. Goeben, of all his corps commanders the one for whom Moltke had the greatest respect, had written to him on October 9 to suggest that two corps might be detached from the army besieging Metz, to be employed either in strengthening the investment of Paris or in operations on the Loire. Moltke, while acknowledging that the lines of investment were painfully thin, and that he had been obliged to commit his only reserve, the I Bavarian Corps, against the nascent Army of the Loire, pointed out to Goeben that the Army of Metz was still by far the most dangerous enemy, and that it was at Metz that it was necessary to seek a result that would be decisive of the whole campaign. However attractive it might be to have more forces available elsewhere, the Army of Metz must be finished off first, and he did not want to delay that for an instant. Only after that, he told Goeben, it would be 'necessary to destroy rapidly the resistance which is being organised at Amiens and Rouen. It is of course true that these are improvised and unstable armies, but they must not be allowed to be used against the separated parts of our army.'[5]

By October 23 it was clear that the fall of Metz was imminent, and Moltke sat down to draft his scheme for the future employment of the armies that had conducted the siege. The Second Army was of course to march westwards; the First

General von Manteuffel, commander of the German I Corps, later the First Army (Rousset/*Histoire*)

Army would leave the VII Corps (Zastrow) to garrison Metz and besiege Thionville, while the rest of the army (I & VIII Corps) would march north, its objectives being Amiens and Rouen. It was his hope that both armies would be in a position to bring their forces to bear on the enemy by mid November.

The First Army had been without a commander since the obstreperous Steinmetz had been despatched to Posen as governor; Moltke now selected as his successor Edwin von Manteuffel, who had been an effective commander of the I Corps and had, in the war of 1866, conducted a very successful campaign in south Germany.[6] Manteuffel had, however sustained a serious injury on September 6 when falling with his horse. He had broken a bone in his foot, which had to be bandaged daily throughout the rest of the war. Colonel von Wartensleben, who was acting as Chief of Staff of the First Army in the absence of Sperling through illness, noted the consquence: 'The General was obliged to use a walking stick, and could not mount his horse without assistance. Nevertheless, although sixty three years of age, he performed almost all marches on horseback, long and fatiguing as many of them were.'[7] Keen though Moltke was to see the First Army operating against the newly raised enemy forces in Northern France, he had first a number of tasks for Manteuffel before he could advance there. The problems that the First Army had to overcome between the capitulation of Metz on October 27 and its attainment of its first objective on the line of the Oise on November 23 graphically illustrate the difficulties confronting Moltke in his conduct of the second phase of the war. The first of these tasks was the complex problem of dealing with the 173,000 prisoners taken at Metz. These were collected in six large camps, two to the west of the city, two to the north in the centre of the siege lines, and two to the east. The prisoners were moved in echelon through the camps from west to east, and from the eastern camps by rail and road to prisoner of war camps in Germany. The Second Army, based to the west of the city, was therefore freed to get away on its more urgent march to the west well before the First Army, which was held up at Metz for several days while the task was completed.[8]

The next task assigned to Manteuffel was the clearance of franc tireurs from the Argonne. It was desirable, wrote Moltke to him on October 29, to advance to Clermont en Argonne with as little delay as possible in order to destroy completely the partisan forces operating there.[9] The 3rd Cavalry Division (Count von der Groeben) was reinforced by the 33rd Regiment and two batteries, and sent off to carry out this mission. Two days later, Moltke despatched a telegram ordering Manteuffel to put at least one division of the I Corps in motion, to be available if the need arose for the reinforcement of the troops presently in front of Mézières; in the same order, Moltke reminded Manteuffel of his additional responsibility for the siege of Verdun.[10] Fortunately for the First Army, this latter task was soon disposed of by the capitulation of Verdun on November 8. By November 4 Manteuffel had more or less sorted out the various remaining problems at Metz, and was able to report to Moltke that he would be able to set off for the north on November 7. Mindful of the lack of any period of rest since the ending of the siege, he was concerned to advance on as broad a front as possible, so that his troops should be able to find good quarters.[11] In the orders he issued on November 5, Manteuffel estimated that the First Army should reach the line St Quentin-Compiègne by November 22. One further detachment was made from the army; on November 5 Moltke ordered that one brigade should be sent by rail to La Fère, to besiege the fortress there which was holding out, and which stood on the line of the First Army's march. Manteuffel assigned this task to the 4th Brigade, with a squadron of dragoons and a battery of heavy artillery.[12] Behind him at Metz Manteuffel left Zastrow, the commander of the VII Corps, with an overall responsibility for all military questions at and around the city and, when the troops escorting the prisoners returned, for the formation of an army reserve, and for the sieges of Thionville and Montmèdy.

As he made his way across France, moving with the advance guard of the army, Manteuffel was relieved to hear on November 8 of the capitulation of Verdun, which would release those troops of Goeben's VIII Corps which had been detached to support the siege, but on the same day he belatedly received a more detailed explanation of Moltke's order of October 31. This informed him that Landwehr troops were henceforth to be assigned to guard the increasingly exposed lines of communication and meant that the 1st Division (von Bentheim) must be ready to go to Mézières to relieve the Landwehr troops there.[13] On the other hand, Goeben was able to report that, after his passage across the Argonne, that district was free of any organised parties of franc tireurs, and he was accordingly able to rejoin the First Army when it caught up with him at St Ménéhould and Vienne le Château on November 12, after five days of very heavy marching. Manteuffel now had to turn his attention to the siege of Mézières, to which Moltke had ordered that the siege artillery and gunners, originally assembled for the reduction of Verdun, should be sent. These were however, still in transit, and would take some time to get in position, while the siege train originally intended for Mézières had been moved on to La Fère. The 1st Division, which had set off earlier in order to go Mézières if necessary, reached the lines of investment there on November 13, and relieved the force of Landwehr previously observing the fortress.

Back at Metz, Zastrow had been assembling the army reserve as instructed. This, under Major General Schuler von Senden was weaker in infantry, but stronger in cavalry. Since, until the siege guns from Verdun could arrive, a full blown siege of Mézières was out of the question, and it was necessary also to observe the fortresses of Rocroi and Givet, Manteuffel decided that Schuler should take over the responsibilities of the 1st Division at Mézières; Schuler was still to report to Zastrow, but was to march at once to Boulzicourt to take over from Bentheim.

Manteuffel was, however, adamant that the operations against Mézières were to be conducted prudently, and on November 15 issued especially strict orders for this. 'The siege of the fortress of Mézières must not be commenced until means sufficient to ensure success have arrived and can be brought to bear on it. Until this is the case I forbid any half measures, such as bombarding the town and the like, which only cause loss of life and destruction of property, without obtaining any military result.'[14] Bentheim, to whom these orders were issued, was firmly told to pass them on to his successor. It was necessary to be entirely clear about the policy for the sieges of the fortresses, since as he moved westward Manteuffel would be getting further and further away from the scene of these operations.

At La Fère, there had been an encouraging rumour that the fortress was about to capitulate; and in the hope of this, a detachment of troops under Colonel Kahlden had gone to reconnoitre. It was found however that the newly appointed commander of the garrison, the naval Captain Planche, was resolute in his determination to defend it, so von Zglinitzki's 4th Brigade was to be required to undertake the siege. Zglinitzki came up to La Fère on November 15, and the investment was completed next day. Although La Fère was only one of a series of fortresses that still held out, and which fell within Manteuffel's responsibility, it was by some way the most important. Although their reduction would be helpful in freeing important rail links, all the others, the frontier fortresses which lay on the right flank of Manteuffel's march, could, if necessary be masked; but La Fère stood right in his path, and its continued retention could seriously hamper the First Army's future operations. The German lines of communication were getting longer and more complex all the time; on November 9 Moltke had issued strict orders for the use of the available railway lines, apportioning them according to the size of the armies they were to serve. Stosch, in carrying out his duties as commissary general, was heavily dependent on keeping these lines running; for Manteuffel, Moltke's order was reassuring, assigning to the First Army the crucial main line Saarbrucken-Metz-Frouard-Epernay- Reims.[15]

As the army continued its march westwards, it entered country which was less secure, and in which operations by parties of franc tireurs were to be expected against detached German units. This was the area to the west and north of the line Reims-Rethel, and Manteuffel resolved to bring his troops into closer contact, narrowing the front on which it was intended that the army should reach the Oise by aiming at a position between Compiègne and Guiscard, rather than extending as far north as St Quentin. The changed conditions in which advanced patrols or isolated bodies of troops must now operate were graphically spelt out by Manteuffel in his orders to Goeben on November 18:

> We may be perhaps now in face of a less important enemy, but of one whose organisation is new, and, therefore, for the most part unknown to us, and whom experience will have taught to rival us in vigilance. We are, at the same time, in a country in the act of rising up in arms, where we must expect to find the peasant one movement standing with folded arms before us, and the next changing to a franc tireur behind us.[16]

The army's march continued. On November 19 Zglinitzki repulsed a sortie from La Fère, inflicting considerable loss on the enemy, and taking a number of prisoners. On the same day there came an important order from Moltke, setting out the immediate objective of the First Army, which was

> to continue beyond the line Noyon-Compiègne its march in the direction of Rouen. Whether the main body takes the road to Amiens will depend on the large body of the enemy (about 18,000 men) said to be assembling remaining there, or retreating before the advance of our troops. In any case Amiens is of itself a sufficiently important point for it to be permanently held by a strong detachment.[17]

As his leading units closed up to the Oise, Manteuffel was able to give them a breather. They had had a prolonged period of hard work in the Metz area before undertaking two weeks of hard marching, and were badly in need of rest. The 1st Division, relieved by the arrival of Schuler's detachment before Mézières, was able to start for Laon on November 21. By this time Goeben had been able to take up a position around Compiègne with the VIII Corps, and the leading troops of the I Corps had reached Noyon, while Manteuffel established his headquarters in the Imperial palace at Compiègne. The total strength of the First Army, as it prepared to move forward against the enemy, was 38,244 infantry, 4,433 cavalry and 180 guns; this included the 1st Division en route from Mézières and the 4th Brigade in front of La Fère.[18]

Ahead of the army, von der Groeben's cavalry patrols probed French positions all the way up to Amiens. All the indications which they reported to army headquarters were to the effect that the French had concentrated some 17,000 men in Amiens, a move which made a lot of sense, since Manteuffel could not move on Rouen with such a large force on his flank in a relatively strong position. There were political as well as military reasons why a blow at Amiens was called for; there was some concern at Versailles that the French victory at Coulmiers might have had a considerable effect on neutral opinion, and a quick victory was felt desirable to correct this impression. With this in his mind, Manteuffel decided not to wait for the complete concentration of the army on the Oise, but to push on on November 24 with a view to being on the line Montdidier- Roye by nightfall on November 25. The army's advance, with the VIII Corps on the left and the I Corps (of which Bentheim had now taken command) on the right, would be covered by the 3rd Cavalry Division scouting towards Amiens as well as northwards towards

Peronne and St Quentin. Wartensleben described in some detail the country which the army was now entering.

> The district between the Oise and the ocean, the Somme and the Epte- ancient Picardy- is a highly cultivated hilly country, crossed in all directions by good roads, and containing numerous towns, villages, and other localities. The woods mostly consist only of small patches. The sweeping undulations of the ground which intervene between the different streams, form in many cases broad open plateaus, easy to be overlooked. This is especially the case with the plateau of Sains and Dury, between the Noye and the Celle, in the immediate neighbourhood of Amiens, which town lies at the foot of the plateau, and is completely commanded by it.[19]

It was not long before the advanced parties of the 3rd Cavalry Division patrolling towards Amiens along the main road from Roye ran into significant opposition; on the morning of November 24, as they reached the line of the Luce, they were attacked by strong French forces and driven back several miles to Mézières, where with the aid of reinforcements they were able to make a stand. However, further French attacks exposed both flanks of the small detachment, which consisted of the 14th Uhlans, with a rifle company and two guns, under Colonel Lüderitz and it was obliged to fall back to Le Quesnel. Although the French pulled back at nightfall, they were found next day to be in force at Moreuil and to the south. Later on November 25 the leading troops of the VIII Corps came up from Montdidier, and drove the French back into Montreuil.[20] The first hand experiences of his leading units were confirmed by other intelligence reports reaching Manteuffel, which suggested that the French might have as many as 46,000 troops around Amiens, including 11,000 troops of the line with 42 guns. They also reported, correctly, that Bourbaki was no longer in command. It was now clear to Manteuffel that his march on Amiens was by no means a wild goose chase; indeed, it might well be that he had scarcely sufficient troops at his immediate disposal to deal with the enemy. On the face of it, the more prudent course might be to stand fast, and complete the concentration of his army. On the other hand, that would also give the French more time, and would also risk losing the initiative. Talking it over on the afternoon of November 25 with Wartensleben and with Goeben, who happened to be visiting headquarters, Manteuffel found both of them strongly in favour of an immediate advance; and that night he gave orders for an advance next day upon the city.[21]

As it turned out, there was little action on November 26, the French having pulled back towards Amiens, where Farre was hastily concentrating all his available forces to meet the German advance. Before his departure, Bourbaki had posted the bulk of his troops along the line of the Rouen-Amiens railway, with a view to his projected advance on Beauvais; but this was no position in which to meet a direct advance by Manteuffel upon Amiens.[22] Farre had available the three complete brigades of Lecointe, Derroja and Bessol, and the incomplete brigade of Rittier, together with 4 squadrons and 7 batteries. At Amiens itself he had available the garrison of 8,000 men with 12 heavy guns under General Paulze d'Ivoy, while three more battalions were brought forward from Lille and Arras, to the line of the Somme between Peronne and Corbie, together two heavy batteries from Douai and Brest. It seemed evident to Farre that if he contented himself with merely holding the line of the Somme there was no realistic chance of holding on to Amiens, and that to do so he must push forward to occupy the heights between the Somme and the Avre which commanded the city. The position he intended to hold ran from Bores through Gentelles and Cachy to Villers Bretonneux, while he pushed forward Paulze d'Ivoy to Dury to cover his western flank. All told he had, including the three battalions from Arras, something under 30,000 men at his disposal.[23]

By nightfall on November 26 the First Army had moved up to the Luce, its advanced units having crossed that river northwards. On the left, the 16th Division (von Barnekow) was at Essertaux and Ailly; of Kummer's 15th Division, the 29th Brigade (von Bock) was around Moreuil, with the 30th Brigade (von Strübberg) at Haille, Thennes and Domart. When Strübberg's leading troops moved north of the Luce, the French launched an attack from Gentelles, three battalions strong, in the direction of Domart, but this was driven back with considerable loss. Further to the right the leading troops of the I Corps were in Questel and Arvillers; when news came that Kummer was over the Luce, Bentheim was ordered to close up to the river, finding no opposition there at Démuin and Ignancourt. Cavalry patrols operating from Rosières rode up to and beyond the Somme, where they found that the bridges over the river at Sailly had been destroyed. All this pointed to the fact that the French intended to fight in and around Amiens; on this basis Manteuffel, unaware of Farre's forward move, gave orders that the army should next day move up to the city, with the expectation of launching the decisive assault on November 28.[24] In a reminder of Manteuffel's continuing responsibilities elsewhere, Moltke telegraphed to him the welcome news of the fall of Thionville, coupled with the instruction that the troops made available should move at once to the siege of Montmèdy, in order to open the railway from Thionville to Sedan.[25] At 9.00 am on November 27 Bentheim moved forward from le Quesnel and Bouchoir up the main road to occupy the line of the Luce between Thezy and Démuin. By 11.00 it was clear that the French had moved south from Amiens to bar their progress, and had occupied Gentelles, Cachy and Marcelcave. On the other hand, there appeared for the moment to be no enemy troops to the west of the main road from Roye to Amiens, and Bentheim swung to his right to deal with the opposition immediately in his front. At the same time, Goeben's corps had moved forward in accordance with instructions between the Noye and the Celle, with the 15th Division moving on Forencamp and Sains, while the 16th Division marched up the Essertaux-Amiens road towards Hébecourt. The gradual divergence of the lines of march of the I and VIII Corps created a curious situation in the centre, between the Roye-Amiens road and the marshy valley of the Avre, where there developed as a result a considerable gap in the German line. It was to this point, at Thennes, that Manteuffel had ridden from Plessier with his headquarters staff; in order to plug the gap, or at any rate to conceal it he took up his position on the plateau north of the Luce, sending patrols from the headquarters escort squadron of hussars in all directions, and bringing up as well the escort battalion under Major Koppelow.[26]

Bentheim's advanced guard, led by the commander of the 2nd Division, Major General von Pritzelwitz, crossed the Luce and advanced on the Domart and Hangard woods, while the main body closed up to the river to the west of Hourges,

The Füsilier Battalion of the Prussian 70th Infantry Regiment storms the churchyard of Dury, at Amiens, by Röchling (Lindner)

with 8 batteries of artillery stationed at the crossroads just to the south. Domart wood was soon clear of the enemy; although halted briefly by Bentheim to allow the corps artillery to open fire, the 4th Regiment was soon able to push forward to Gentelles. The bulk of the enemy's forces were at Cachy, and these had meanwhile advanced on the Hangard Wood, the possession of which was bitterly contested by the 44th Regiment under Major Dallmer. Having occupied the eastern portion of the wood, Dallmer left one battalion to hold it, and pressed forward with his other two battalions to seize a redoubt which had been thrown up to the south of Villers Bretonneux. In spite of vigorous counter attacks, in the course of which Dallmer himself was wounded, he succeeded in hanging on to the redoubt.[27] Meanwhile at Cachy the French had been heavily reinforced, not least by several batteries; there ensued a prolonged duel with Bentheim's artillery, which he brought over the Luce to the east of Hangard Wood. The oncoming French reinforcements enabled them to reoccupy Gentelles, but any further advance was checked by two horse artillery batteries which Bentheim stationed north of Domart. For a while there was stalemate, neither side being able to improve its position. Then, at about 3.30 pm the leading troops of the 1st Division under Lieutenant Colonel Hullesheim began to arrive from Roye. This gave Bentheim immediate local superiority, and he ordered Hullesheim to occupy Domart and Thennes, while with the main body of the 2nd Division he advanced to the east of the Hangard wood. Joined by the troops there and in the redoubt, the whole Prussian line rushed forward with drums beating and loud cheers, and the French fell back. The Prussians charged on, taking Villers

Bretonneux at the point of the bayonet and capturing over 1,100 prisoners. The main body of the French, covered by a rearguard in Cachy, fell back partly towards Amiens and partly over the Somme at Corbie. By now night had fallen, and Bentheim, whose left wing was still held up to the south of Gentelles and Cachy, made no effort to pursue.[28]

Manteuffel, from his position in the centre, had been able to monitor the apparently successful progress of Goeben's advance on the left, but was far from clear what had been happening to Bentheim. Indeed, the French reinforcement of Gentelles meant that he had had to conduct a delaying action in the centre with only his headquarters troops at his disposal. By about noon he had been sufficiently concerned to send a message to Goeben asking him to lend some support to the I Corps by crossing the Avre at Fouencamps in the direction of Gentelles, a request which Goeben was obliged to refuse because by now the whole of the VIII Corps was engaged. The 29th Brigade had reached Sains and was advancing on St Fuscien, while the 30th Brigade had taken Paraclet and was advancing on Boves. Since it appeared that the 30th Brigade needed support, Bock swung the 29th Brigade to the right, and together the two brigades stormed the castle hill west of Boves and the village itself. Attempts by the French to mount counter attacks with the aid of fresh troops brought up by the railway from Amiens towards St Nicholas broke down under heavy artillery fire.[29]

Meanwhile Goeben's left wing, the 16th Division under Barnekow, had also made good progress. The 32nd Brigade had reached Rumigny without opposition before advancing against Hebecourt. By 11.00 the village had fallen, its defenders retreating rapidly to the woods to the north, although losing some 200 prisoners captured by a party of Prussian hussars. For a while, the French held out in the woods, but then retreated northwards to Dury in disorder. Here however they were able to take refuge behind a cemetery to the north of the village, where a line of entrenchments had been thrown up. Although driven out of the cemetery by the charge of a company of the 12th Regiment, the French were able to retreat behind the line of trenches, and there ensued until nightfall a prolonged artillery duel.[30] Manteuffel continued to conduct the battle in ignorance of events on his extreme right wing. The indications from his left, in the front of Goeben's corps, suggested that Farre intended to put up an obstinate defence of the city, and it seemed to Manteuffel that it would be necessary next day to bring his two corps closer together. He himself, after the charade he had conducted with his headquarters troops in front of Thennes, had retired to the windmill south of the village, from where at 5 pm he despatched orders to Bentheim with a view to his moving to his left next day. His immediate concern was that a French thrust might be directed through his centre towards Moreuil, and he prepared orders to Goeben to provide a garrison to hold that village. However just at this point came welcome news in the form of a telegram from Zglinitzki that La Fère had capitulated after a 28 hour bombardment by siege artillery, thus releasing his 4th Brigade for operations in the field, and orders went at once to him to march at once to Noyon with the bulk of his force. Manteuffel's staff was operating in very adverse conditions, as Wartensleben recorded: 'This telegram and other reports could only be read with difficulty, by the help of lucifer matches lighted under the shelter of the windmill, for the night was wet and windy.'[31] As the firing died down, Manteuffel rode back to Moreuil, and took up his quarters in the magnificent chateau of Count du Plessis, where he received the first reports of the success of the I Corps. It was not until the following day, however, that he was to learn of the full extent of this.

It had been a curious battle, fought in two entirely unrelated halves; pondering this, and the consequent lack of any central reserve, which had contributed to the gap that had opened up between the two corps, Wartensleben concluded that it was probably just as well that, no decisive battle being expected until the following day, troops had not been detached from the two corps to create a reserve. Certainly, a reduction in the strength of the already weak I Corps might seriously have jeopardised its position.[32] Total German losses were 1,270, of which 230 were killed and 1,140 wounded; Faidherbe puts the French losses at 266 killed, 1,117 wounded, about 1,000 missing and numerous gardes mobiles disbanded and scattered.

The French had, however, put up a spirited resistance, and Farre himself, who had gone to Corbie, had every intention of continuing the struggle next day. While there, however, he learned that a meeting had been held in Amiens between Lecointe, Derroja, Villenoisy and Charon. They had reached the conclusion that because of the impossibility of replenishing their ammunition, and the risk of further powerful German attacks, even from downstream, it was necessary to fall back covered by the force of gardes mobiles which occupied the citadel. In the face of this Farre had little choice but to order the retreat which, after prolonged reflection, he did at 3.am next morning.[33]

Still unaware of the extent of the victory, Manteuffel conferred with Goeben next morning; they concluded that it would be hazardous and potentially very expensive to launch assaults against the positions believed still to be held by the French, and Manteuffel directed that the army should hold its present positions until the missing units should have come up. However, the patrols operating in front of the army soon reported at all points that the French had retreated, and at midday Goeben rode into the ancient capital of Picardy at the head of the 40th Regiment and two batteries. In the citadel, however, immediately to the north of the river, the garrison of 400 men under Captain Vogel still held out; he was given until the following day to consider whether he would surrender. Next day, when the extension of time given him had expired, and he refused to do so, the garrison of the citadel were subjected to prolonged rifle fire, This, of course, was not much more than a gesture, and Manteuffel gave orders that eleven batteries should cross the Somme at Mortières, over a pontoon bridge west of city, during the night of 29/30 November, with a view to reducing the citadel next day. But the bombardment proved unnecessary; Vogel had been killed during the firing on November 29, and the garrison next morning hoisted a white flag. By 8.00 am there had been negotiated a surrender of the citadel with 400 prisoners and 30 guns.[34]

For Manteuffel, however, on November 28 the immediate and very pressing question was what he should do next. Farre's army had retreated northwards; all other things being equal, the correct course would be to pursue it, and finish it off. But Moltke's order of November 18 had explicitly identified Rouen as being the First Army's principal objective, and all the indications were that the French forces there under General Briand offered the most serious immediate threat. During the afternoon of November 28 Manteuffel considered the problem with Wartensleben, who recorded their conclusion:

> The main idea which had given rise to the operations against Amiens was to disturb the organisation of the enemy's armies. In order to follow up this idea it became a necessity, consistent both with the instructions of November 18, and with the general military situation, not to allow the army to be enticed to follow the enemy and entangle itself among the northern fortresses, thereby leaving the enemy in Normandy free scope, but rather now to turn against the latter. The march to Rouen was therefore decided on.[35]

On the basis of the information before them, it was probably the right decision; but they had by no means seen the last of the Army of the North.

Manteuffel attached one regiment of the 3rd Cavalry Division to each of the corps, and left von der Groeben with the rest of his division and the 3rd Brigade to occupy Amiens, and cover the rear of the army's march to Rouen. Von der Groeben was also to protect the railway from Amiens to Laon, which as a result of the capitulation of La Fère was now operational.

On December 1 the army set off on its march to Rouen, the VIII Corps taking the road through Poix and Formerie and the I Corps through Couty. The 4th Brigade rejoined the I Corps on December 2. By December 3 the advanced guards of both corps had reached the Epte without encountering opposition. Manteuffel had been temporarily assigned the Guard Dragoon Brigade, based on Beauvais, while Lippe's 12th Cavalry Division, at Gisors, had been ordered to co-operate with him. The latest intelligence suggested that Briand had about 44,000 men under arms, of which 11,000 were said to be troops of the line, with 94 guns. If true, this meant that the First Army was taking on a considerable adversary; its own infantry amounted to scarcely 30,000 men. The army was now entering very different country, which for some of the German soldiers would have seemed like home. 'Immediately beyond Gournay the landscape changes from the table –land and the mostly open plains of Picardy to the hilly and intricate country of Normandy, which greatly resembles the east part of Holstein. The pasture grounds, fenced in with hedgerows, abound with large herds of cattle.'[36] The French made no attempt to hold the line of the Epte; but beyond it lay the Andelle, and here on December 4 came the first contact with the enemy.

The I Corps did not on that day reach La Haye, its objective on the Andelle, but stopped about five miles short, at La Feuillie. Outposts pushed forward found Vascoeil occupied, and there was a brief encounter with hostile infantry near Lyons la Forêt, while a detachment of Lippe's cavalry reported enemy troops in front of Ecouis and that Les Andelys was occupied. It was however the VIII Corps that had the more significant encounters with the enemy. Goeben was moving in three columns; on the left Kummer with the 29th Brigade was on the Forges road, in the centre Barnekow with the 32nd Brigade was marching through Sommery to Buchy and on the right Colonel Mettler with the 31st Brigade through Neufchâtel to St Martin. Kummer met a force of some 6 battalions supported by a battery, which he drove back with heavy loss through Bosc-Bordel and Rozeron; due to turn south at Forgettes, he took that route, leaving Barnekow to take up the pursuit, which he did, although unable to overtake the enemy.

Mettler, with the right hand column, came through St Martin about noon, and found a force of about 6 battalions which withdrew southwest to Elteville, but not before Mettler had cut off part of the force, taking 235 prisoners. Meanwhile a detachment of the 31st Brigade, operating far out on the right, routed a force of about 1,200 men at Bosc le Hand, taking 100 prisoners.

Next day, December 5, reconnaissances were pushed forward towards Rouen, supported by the main body of the 16th Division. Goeben himself rode with the leading troops and was soon able to report back to Manteuffel from Quincapoix, about seven miles from Rouen, that the enemy had retreated and that he proposed to enter the city. This at about 2.30 pm he did, in the face of a population that was decidedly more hostile and resentful than that of Amiens. When Manteuffel heard the news, he ordered Goeben to pursue Briand next day down the right bank of the Seine, while Bentheim brought the I Corps into the city.[37] Briand, however, had moved too fast for Goeben to catch him, and the VIII Corps patrols reported that the French force had retreated in various directions, but principally on the left bank of the river. Manteuffel had taken the First Army as far as Moltke's orders had required; while awaiting a fresh directive, he sent out strong columns to ensure the enemy were kept at a safe distance, pushing out towards Dieppe, Le Havre, Pont Audemer, Bermany, Evreux and Vernon. He could feel considerable satisfaction that he had entirely carried out the mission allotted to him, driving back two armies that might seriously have embarrassed the investment of Paris. But, as Wartensleben pointed out, the responsibilities of the army were not at an end; they had merely changed in nature. 'This offensive task of the First Army was now at an end. The task of the army now became one of a defensive nature.'[38] It was to prove still more demanding.

17

Beaugency

Although the second battle of Orleans had not, as he had intended, resulted in the complete destruction of the Army of the Loire, the victory allowed Moltke to hope, once again, for an immediate advance on Bourges. Throughout the second phase of the war he had seen the capture of that city as the most effective means of putting paid to French operations to the west and south of Paris; and in the immediate aftermath of the victory, he had identified the line Bourges-Nevers-Chalon sur Saône as the proper objective of the Second Army, and of the corps of Zastrow and Werder. But Moltke was again to be disappointed. The pursuit to the south of the Loire had been assigned by Frederick Charles to the 6th Cavalry Division, reinforced by a detachment of infantry from the 18th Division. It took several days for the cavalry to catch up with the retreating 15th Corps, finally doing so on the evening of December 7 at Salbris, where the French had the best of a sharp rear-guard action before hastily retiring during the night. The cavalry now moved on Vierzon, reaching there at nightfall next day, where it proceeded to wreck the railway and seize large quantities of materiel in railway trucks there. But this was as far as it was meant to go; von der Groeben, commanding the 14th Cavalry Brigade, had orders to hold Vierzon and Salbris, but to advance no further. The hostile terrain that had so quickly discouraged von der Tann in October from advancing on Bourges soon made its influence felt; movement was only possible over the main roads, so icy that even these were barely passable, and the inhabitants displayed continuous hostility.

More so, in fact, than the enemy troops. The 15th Corps, shedding stragglers and equipment as it went, finally reached Bourges on December 15, in no better condition than the 18th and 20th Corps, which comprised the rest of what was now the 1st Army of the Loire under Bourbaki. Gambetta, desperate to make some offensive move towards Paris to aid the sortie there, was emphatic that Bourbaki should concentrate at Gien, and march north; but with the news of Ducrot's defeat and after having seen for himself the state of his troops he accepted the urgent protests of the generals, and allowed Bourbaki to give his troops a chance to restore themselves undisturbed for a short while at Bourges. However, he added ominously that once they were all collected there he reckoned that Bourbaki would be 'really ready for a decisive action.' This kind of thing proved too much for one of Bourbaki's commanders; Pallières, complaining 'of the military fantasies of the telegraph from Tours,' promptly resigned his command of the 15th Corps.[1] Moltke, meanwhile, mourned the lost opportunity; noting the scattered positions of Bourbaki's units when the 6th Cavalry Division took Vierzon, he wrote later that 'it can scarcely be doubted that if the 18th Division had followed the advance of the 6th Cavalry Division, possession would have been obtained of Bourges and of the vast military establishments there.'[2]

It was, however, the northern bank of the Loire that had particularly been occupying the attention of the Second Army headquarters. In the aftermath of the second battle of Orleans, the Second Army of the Loire had been formed out of the battered 16th and 17th Corps, together with the newly formed 21st Corps (Jaurès) and Camô's independent division.

Chanzy, whose energy and enthusiasm had never faltered, and who had profoundly impressed Gambetta and Freycinet, was put in command, while the redoubtable Jauréguiberry took over the 16th Corps and de Colomb the 17th Corps. Chanzy, whose units had been somewhat less knocked about in the recent fighting than those which had retreated southwards, at once gave an indication of his intentions, halting his retreat and taking up a position between the Loire and the Forest of Marchenoir. He there awaited the advance of the Detachment that had now, by Moltke's orders, been freed from the control of the Second Army; but the advance in the direction of Tours, which it had been ordered to undertake, was confirmed. Moltke explained his objective in a letter to the Grand Duke on December 7. 'It is important to compel the enemy government to abandon this location, which it has occupied up till now, and to disperse the troops around it, as also those which would be able to reach Le Mans.'[3]

The Detachment had been given a rest day after the taking of Orleans, with only cavalry riding westwards after the retreating French. These had soon encountered Chanzy's advanced posts, noting in particular a strong body of infantry behind Meung. This was Camô's Division; behind it stood Jauréguiberry's 16th Corps, while the 17th Corps was on its left at Crouat and the 21st Corps was on the extreme left at St Laurent on the edge of the forest. On December 7 the Detachment moved forward, the 17th Division advancing directly along the river road towards Meung, while the 1st Bavarian Division marched in the first instance in the direction of La Bourie; the 2nd Cavalry Division led the advance and provided a link between the two.

Tresckow's advanced guard quickly occupied Meung; but when his troops pushed on to the west of the village, they encountered heavy resistance, which led to a brisk artillery duel. The French had taken up a position at Foinard and La Bruère; a battalion from Tresckow's main body captured Langlochère, and checked troops advancing there from La Bourie. It was only after the German artillery had beaten down the French guns that further troops advancing along the river road through Baulle succeeded in throwing back the French right. Meanwhile the 1st Bavarian Brigade had also encountered stiff resistance around Le Mée and Grand Châtre; the latter place was taken and then retaken by the French as night fell. The 2nd Brigade, coming from some way back, moved up to support Tresckow; the 3rd Brigade came up on the right. Further north, the 22nd Division, following the 4th Cavalry Division, had reached Ouzouer. Cavalry patrols identified French forces in the forest, and after an exchange with enemy artillery, the German horse artillery broke off the action, since it was clear that the French were there in strength. By nightfall, there had been contacts along the whole of the Detachment's front, which was dangerously extended, being some 14 miles long; it was now clear to Stosch, as he got his troops into line, that he would next day have to fight a major battle against heavy numerical odds.[4]

Frederick Charles, trying to work out where the French had gone after the fall of Orleans, was impressed by intelligence reports suggesting that a large part of the enemy had fallen back through Gien (as was certainly true); and he ordered

Alvensleben with the III Corps to advance there on December 8. Manstein's IX Corps, led by the 25th Division, was to move up the left bank of the Loire, keeping abreast of the Detachment's advance on the other side of the river, while Voigts-Rhetz, with the X Corps, was ordered to support the operations of the 6th Cavalry Division, although he was not to move very far south.

Stosch concluded that the strength of the enemy resistance on December 7 made it necessary to shorten his line, and to concentrate on his left flank, on the river. Wittich was therefore ordered for the next day to bring the 22nd Division south towards Cravant, the 43rd Brigade through Mézières and the 44th Brigade through Château Coudray. The 17th Division was to be ready to move out from Baulle, while between them the Bavarians concentrating at Grand Châtre, would be covered by the 2nd Cavalry Division. The breadth of the Detachment's front of advance on December 7 suggests that the Germans did not for the moment expect any very serious opposition from Chanzy's army; but although this was a serious miscalculation, it may have stood them in good stead. The presence of Wittich as far north as Ouzouer on that day may well have discouraged Chanzy from attempting to outflank the German right on December 8, even though his enormous numerical superiority made this a possible option for him, particularly when the 22nd Division turned south to Cravant to shorten the German line. In fact, the French did not appreciate how weak the Detachment actually was. Freycinet, whose memoirs were usually inaccurate when it came to assessing enemy strength, was particularly wide of the mark in assessing the total of German infantry involved on December 7 at 50,000, exclusive of 'a strong reserve ... of fresh troops.'[5] The truth was very different. During the sustained campaign of the preceding eight weeks the Bavarian strength had been steadily eroded; after the detachment of five battalions on various duties, von der Tann went into this battle with twenty two battalions containing a total of 9,994 infantry. Both Tresckow and Wittich's divisions had also been much reduced; the Detachment cannot have had more than about 27,000 infantry in total at its disposal. The Bavarians had perhaps suffered from a somewhat lower standard of discipline than their Prussian allies; one staff officer, reflecting the low opinion of the Bavarian troops held by some but not all Prussian observers, noted their tendency to straggle.[6] This may not unreasonably be ascribed to their long and hard campaign and the high level of casualties they had suffered; it was not surprising that they were coming to the end of their tether. Their official historian conceded that although 'their courage and discipline had as yet in no degree suffered from their continuous fatigues, battles, and losses,' the effect had inevitably been that they were by now exhausted.

> Under fire, and during the active operations of the day, the feeling of military honour, the example of the officers, and a certain unquenchable lust of battle, all contributed to support the weary soldiers. Away from the field of battle, behind the scenes as it were, there were unmistakable signs of such a considerable falling off in physical strength, as must inevitably be followed by a loss of morale.[7]

Chanzy, therefore, also moved to his right; and as a result, the battle would begin with the adversaries facing each other across the shallow valley through which the Châteaudun-Beaugency road ran, the battle line running north west-south east. Behind the German lines, the country was mainly arable; behind the French position the country was densely covered with vineyards. During the night, which was again bitterly cold, it snowed again; next morning the frozen ground had a thin covering of snow and there was a dense fog.[8]

As the 43rd Brigade moved south, it came under fire from near Poisly; two battalions deployed west of Villermain towards the main road and halted the advance of swarms of French skirmishers that emerged from the thick fog. The eastern column, consisting of the 44th Brigade, pushed on, reaching the wood at Montsouris. At 11.00 am Wittich was ordered to close up on Cravant, to gain touch with the right wing of the Bavarians, which he succeeded in doing by 1.00 pm. By this move, Stosch had virtually halved the length of his front; the advance of the 22nd Division was the signal for the rest of the Detachment to begin its attack. On the left, the 17th Division was to move directly on Beaugency, while in the centre the 2nd Bavarian Division was to advance on Villechaumont. The 1st Bavarian Division and the 2nd Cavalry Division were for the moment held in reserve. The Bavarian advance soon collided with the advancing columns of de Roquebrune's 1st Division of the 17th Corps, supported by the 1st Division of the 16th Corps, which pushed forward from Villechaumont and by weight of numbers forced back the Bavarians towards Beaumont, although one battalion still held the line at Le Mée.[9]

The success of the French advance was, however, short-lived; Stosch deployed five batteries of his reserve artillery between Cravant and Beaumont, a move which brought them into action against the French masses at very close range; and under heavy artillery and rifle fire the French fell back again across the high road. Meanwhile to the northwest of Cravant, one battalion of the 44th Brigade had driven the French out of their advanced positions at Beaumont while the main body occupied Cravant itself. Behind it, Wittich brought up the whole of his artillery to form a powerful gun line at Beaumont, protected by the 8th Cavalry Brigade. In spite of this the French, advancing across the high road, briefly took Layes, only half a mile from Wittich's guns, before being driven back by the 43rd Brigade.[10]

The Bavarians, meanwhile, had been suffering considerable losses. Given the weakness of their battalion strengths, it is small wonder that facing the large numbers that Chanzy was able to throw at them they faltered under pressure. Their artillery, in action at close range, had suffered particularly and five batteries were pulled back out of range of the French guns, and also out of range of the chassepôts that had also done a lot of damage. Von der Tann's call for reinforcements was quickly answered by Stosch; three more batteries came into line on the left of the Bavarian guns. At the same time, at about 4.00 pm, the 1st Brigade joined the line along the high road, which surged forward to storm the heights opposite. It was, however, a foolhardy advance; the ensuing counter attack drove back the attenuated ranks of the Bavarian battalions, which retreated to Beaumont under the cover of a sustained barrage from the gun line along the crest. Against this the French infantry could make no headway, and as darkness fell they retreated across the road and up to the other side of the heights that formed their original position.

Meanwhile the 17th Division had been in action on the German left. Tresckow had spent the morning consolidating his position opposite Beaugency, pushing forward outposts towards Les Vallées and Villeneuve. At 12.30 he received orders to advance on Beaugency; with his advanced guard he moved down the main road, while with two battalions of the 75th Regiment he launched an attack towards Messas. The struggle for this village lasted all afternoon; it was only as darkness fell that it was finally taken, with some 150 prisoners. At Beaugency under cover of strong artillery support a battalion of the 90th Regiment stormed a height north east of the town, while the 14th Rifle Battalion worked its way forward into the town from the riverside. Stiff resistance was encountered at the railway embankment, and Beaugency was only securely in German hands after two more battalions had come up. In the confusion a retreating French battery, unaware the town had fallen, drove into Beaugency, and was captured. Before night fell, the 75th Regiment had advanced to Vernon, surprising the garrison and taking 200 prisoners.[11]

Although the French had put up a brave struggle along the whole of the front, they had been beaten all down the line, and Stosch and the Grand Duke may perhaps be forgiven for concluding that Chanzy would next day pull back to the west. Their orders reflected this conviction; Tresckow was directed on Tours, while Wittich relieved the battered 1st Bavarian Corps. Meanwhile Frederick Charles, in his orders for December 9, stuck to his intention to pursue the French troops that had disappeared towards Gien with the III Corps, while the IX Corps on the left bank of the Loire kept abreast of the Detachment as far as Blois, and the X Corps concentrated at Orleans before advancing to Salbris. As a result, the proceedings planned for the Second Army consisted of quite a lot of not very much, and provided little in the way of support to the Detachment, upon which most of the real work was falling. Frederick Charles, who was profoundly sceptical about the suggestion that the Grand Duke faced any substantial opposition, did go

The Bavarians at Beaugency, by Knötel (Pflugk-Harttung)

so far as to provide for Voigts-Rhetz to collect the 20th Division at Orleans in case the Detachment turned out to need any immediate support.[12]

Stosch, however, had not been content to rely on getting help from the Second Army, and after the fighting at Meung on December 7 had sent a full report direct to Moltke both by telegram and by letter; noting the political importance of an advance on Tours, he made clear that, in his existing situation, he could not guarantee success. Such a comment from such a reliable source prompted Moltke's immediate intervention, and he despatched a peremptory telegram, which reached the Second Army at 10.00 am on December 9:

> From a report from the Grand Duke, it appears that the bulk of the enemy are in his front. His Majesty orders that, in order to allow the particularly important operation against Tours to continue energetically the Detachment must, as quickly as possible, be supported on the right bank of the Loire by at least one division; in addition, you are free to bring effective strength to bear on the left bank.[13]

He added that Frederick Charles should again have the overall direction of all the operations on the Loire, the Detachment's independence proving to be short lived.

In the face of Moltke's insistence, Frederick Charles responded at once, giving up all thought of pursuing any advance into the Sologne in the direction of Bourges. By 10.30 am orders had gone to Voigts-Rhetz to bring forward all those troops he had concentrated in and and around Orleans, while Alvensleben was called back with the whole of the III Corps and the 1st Cavalry Division, apart from a small detachment left at Gien. The 6th Cavalry Division was, when it had finished wrecking the railway at Vierzon, to join the IX Corps on the left bank. It was as well that these dispositions were made; far from intending to retreat on December 9, Chanzy was planning to stand and fight, as Stosch and the Grand Duke found out from documents captured during the night. As a result the orders for the Detachment were changed; the 17th Division was to concentrate at Messas and the 22nd Division at Beaumont, its right covered by the 4th Cavalry Division. The I Bavarian Corps and the 2nd Cavalry Division were to be in reserve. The Detachment would, in spite of Moltke's intervention, still have to fight alone on December 9; and, even before the new orders could be carried out, it found itself obliged to resist a series of powerful assaults.

Between 7.00 and 8.00 am dense swarms of French skirmishers moved on Vernon, supported by artillery; when the latter was silenced, the infantry quickly retreated. To the left, strong columns of infantry advanced on the Bavarian position at Le Mée; this advance was also broken up by the German artillery. The 3rd Brigade advanced to a counter attack, which carried Villorceau by 10.30 am; French attempts to recapture the village were beaten off.

In the meantime the 4th Brigade at Villechaumont broke up attempts by the French to advance at this point, and succeeded in holding this village in spite of the French success in forcing their artillery support to pull back. By now Wittich had begun to move south from Launay in support of the Bavarians; when the French retreated on Cernay, Wittich followed them up, and a battalion of the 95th Regiment stormed the village capturing 200 prisoners.[14]

Meanwhile at Cravant the 44th Brigade had come under heavy attack. The French gained an immediate advantage when the farms of Beaumont and Layes were evacuated by mistake by the 83rd Regiment; Wittich, when he heard of this, ordered that they be retaken at once which, with the support of Orff's 2nd Bavarian Brigade, the 83rd Regiment was able to achieve. Wittich assembled a strong force of artillery to support the troops that occupied the farms, as it was evident that there were large French forces massing nearby. Soon afterwards, cavalry patrols also reported dense columns moving out of the forest towards Cravant.

With activity all down his line, Stosch was having to make the maximum use of the limited forces at his disposal; to counter the obvious threat to Cravant, he ordered Tresckow to move forwards to Villevent and Villorceau. Tresckow at once advanced from Messas to Grand Bonvalet with his main body, and on his right strengthened his advanced guard at Pierre Couverte. Only a weak detachment was left in Beaugency. As the 76th Regiment moved to relieve the Bavarians still hanging on to Loynes and Villorceau, it faced a fresh assault from the direction of Villejouan; once again, however, the tireless German artillery broke up the attack with heavy loss.[15] While this was going on, the rest of Tresckow's main body had overcome heavy artillery and mitrailleuse fire to advance as far as de Feularde Farm, a success which seriously threatened Chanzy's right flank.

When the threatened attack on Cravant failed to materialise, Stosch had pulled back out of the firing line as many units of the 22nd and 2nd Bavarian Divisions as he could; what he desperately needed was a reserve to counter the next threat. It was fortunate that he did so; the struggle of the 17th Division demonstrated the need to take Villejouan, and he put together a force of three battalions, six squadrons and fourteen guns to support Tresckow's advance. After a short struggle, this force was able to take Villejouan before the end of the afternoon.

Throughout the day the Detachment had been able to derive only long range artillery support from the IX Corps which was pushing on westwards on the other side of the river. Manstein had encountered little opposition; although the Château of Chambord was defended, it was taken at the charge by a party of fifty Hessian infantry, which captured 200 prisoners and five guns. Behind the Detachment the X Corps was coming up; its leading infantry only reached Meung that evening but Voigts-Rhetz sent forward a cavalry regiment and eight batteries, which arrived at Grand Châtre in mid afternoon.[16] Considering its exposed position, the Detachment had done extremely well: with the arrival of the X Corps, Von der Tann's battered corps could be withdrawn to refit, and the Bavarians were pulled out of the line to garrison Orleans. The Detachment's cavalry would next day reconnoitre towards Morée and Mer, while Voigts-Rhetz concentrated at Beaugency.

Although Chanzy had made no impression on the position of the Detachment, the mood at French headquarters was not downcast. Gambetta, who arrived there at 6.00 pm, sent a distinctly upbeat message to Freycinet: 'I have found everything perfectly in order here, thanks to the strength of will and indomitable energy of General Chanzy. Not only has he held his position from three days, but he has repelled the advancing masses of Prince Frederick Charles, and inflicted cruel losses on them.'[17] It was not a particularly accurate account of the day's fighting, but it reflected the temporary optimism engendered by Chanzy's attitude. But his determination to hold on to his position at Beaugency had been based on the hope that relief might come from Bourbaki's troops in the Sologne; without this he could not reckon to withstand the whole of the German forces at Orleans, and if it was not forth coming he would have to retreat. He was under no illusions as to what that would do to his army.

The loss of Villejouan, and then Origny, late on the afternoon of December 9 had caused Chanzy particular concern, and he ordered Guépratte, with the 2nd Division of the 17th Corps to recapture Origny before daybreak. This Guépratte succeeded in doing by 6.00 am on December 10, surprising the German defenders, and taking the village with one hundred and fifty prisoners. Encouraged by this success, Colonel Jouffroy, commanding the 3rd Division, launched a successful assault on Villejouan, causing the 22nd Division to retreat to a position near Villechaumont Mill. These assaults appeared to be the precursor to a major French advance in the centre, and Wittich applied to Stosch for reinforcements. The only troops immediately available were the Bavarians. For all von der Tann's units except the 1st Brigade, which was to move off to Orleans, December 10 had been prescribed as a rest day. But there was nothing for it; it was essential to shore up the German lines, and Orff's 2nd Brigade, which had been reinforced by a draft of newly arrived ersatz troops, moved up to Beaumont and Layes on Wittich's right. The 4th Brigade moved forward to Villechaumont.[18] By 10.30 am however, a new threat seemed about to materialise; Stosch received a report from cavalry patrols on his extreme right that the French were massing for an attack towards Villermain, and Orff was ordered to extend his position towards Château Coudray, while seven batteries were moved up to the front line.

Once again it was to be the artillery that effectively held the position on the northern part of the German line. With nineteen batteries in the front line, the German artillery gradually gained the upper hand during the day, and by 3.00 pm most of the French guns had been withdrawn. Only a number of isolated infantry attacks were made, which the 22nd Division and the two Bavarian brigades repulsed without difficulty. Further south, however, Tresckow was engaged in a more serious contest. His most advanced positions were around Villemarceau and Villorceau, while he also strongly held Loynes and Les Grolles. The capture of Villejouan had exposed his right, and Tresckow resolved to retake it, launching an assault about noon by the fusilier battalion of the 76th Regiment under cover of heavy artillery fire. The French defenders of the village put up a fierce resistance in the bitter house to house fighting that ensued; it was only after a battle lasting nearly four hours that the Germans were again possession of the village.[19] Even now, the French were not done with; reinforced by the 2nd Battalion of the 76th Regiment, and supported by the whole of the 17th Division's artillery, the Germans in Villejouan had to beat off another fierce assault from the direction of Origny and Ourcelle.

With the defeat of this attack, the offensive power of the 2nd Army of the Loire was finally exhausted. There was no sign whatever of any forward movement from Bourbaki in the south, on which Chanzy had been counting. On the evening of December 10 Chanzy spelled out his view of the position in a telegram to Gambetta, which he copied to Bourbaki:

> The movement which is possible and indispensable to enable us, whatever the cost, to restore our situation is as follows: march from Bourges on Vierzon; push the bulk of the 1st Army through Romorantin on Blois; take post between the Loire and the Cher to intercept enemy communications between Orleans and his army advancing on Tours, in this way cutting the latter off from its base.

Gambetta's doleful response was that the 1st Army was in no state to undertake any significant operations and Chanzy was left with no choice but to retreat next day to Vendôme.[20] Manstein's movement along the left bank of the Loire was increasingly threatening; having reached Montivault, one and a half miles from Blois, on December 9, he occupied Vienne next day, immediately opposite Blois.

Throughout the battle of Beaugency, Chanzy had fought energetically and had displayed an inspiring leadership that had earned Gambetta's praise; and his performance had brought the best out of his troops, as Helvig noted.

> Although the French had the advantage of superior numbers and a better firearm, it cannot be denied that at some points they fought with remarkable bravery and great devotion. It must at any rate be allowed that the tenacity and endurance with which the enemy's troops made their stand for four days, is a proof of the conspicuous energy and inspiriting activity of their leader, General Chanzy.[21]

Since the French had a fourfold numerical advantage, the German victory reflected particular credit on Stosch, and the way he had made the best use of his limited resources. Hönig, the most perceptive of the German historians of this phase of the war, attributed the success to Stosch's 'strong will and iron firmness. Up to this point, he had only proved himself to be an excellent chief of staff; from then on he showed himself a hero in his bearing thoughts and actions.' And in his obituary of Stosch, Hönig described his performance at the battle of Beaugency as 'perhaps the greatest performance with insufficient resources in the entire history of modern warfare.'[22] Moltke, on reading Stosch's report of the battle, was generous in his praise of the German soldiers who had fought so well: 'Victory after victory: our brave troops have only to be led to the right spot and then you can sleep in peace! You can't help taking off your hat even to the very driver of the transport!'[23] The victory had cost the Germans a total of about 3400 casualties; of these, 1986 had been sustained by the 1st Bavarian Corps, upon which the bulk of the fighting had fallen. In his report of the battle, Chanzy referred to significant losses, but an accurate total of French casualties during the three days battle is more difficult to arrive at.[24] They must, however, have been at least three times as great as the losses of their antagonists; the French infantry were committed during the battle to a series of assaults that were broken up with heavy losses, and the Germans took over 5,000 prisoners during the battle.

In his orders for the retreat, Chanzy directed the 16th Corps on Vendôme, while the 17th Corps marched towards Oucques and the 21st Corps to Fréteval. In the early morning of December 11 it was not immediately apparent to the German troops that the French were in fact retiring, and they prepared themselves to face another assault. By noon, however, the signs of a retreat were unmistakable; the pursuit was assigned to the relatively fresh troops of the X Corps, and Voigts-Rhetz pushed his 19th Division towards Josnes, with the 20th Division advancing to the south. Cautious as ever, Frederick Charles concluded that although there was no likelihood of Chanzy launching a fresh offensive, he would put up a stiff defence in the positions he took up. With this in mind, he moved very circumspectly, bringing Alvensleben's III Corps into the front line, and extending his front to the north by pushing the Detachment to Morée, with a view to preventing any retreat in the direction of Chartres. Throughout December 11, the direction of Chanzy's retreat was still unclear, and Voigts-Rhetz was ordered next day to move on Mer, while the Grand Duke advanced to the north.

Movement was hampered by a further change in the weather; the bitterly cold weather had been followed by a thaw and rain. Difficult as this made the task of their German pursuers, Chanzy's men suffered to an even greater extent. As the Germans advanced, the signs of the disintegration of the 2nd Army of the Loire became clearer:

> In the country to the south of Marchenoir Forest several thousand stragglers were picked up by the Germans, the roads were strewn with quantities of fire-arms which had been thrown away, and a mass of abandoned wagons; in the fields lay the unburied corpses of men and horses, in the villages were thousands of untended wounded.[25]

But it was not until the morning of December 13 that the full extent of the French disorganisation became apparent; cavalry patrols reported the abandonment of Blois and that, to the north of the Marchenoir Forest, Chanzy was in full retreat to the Loir. With this confirmation to hand, Frederick Charles ordered the Detachment to pursue Chanzy, the left wing moving on Oucques and the right wing on Morée.

Moltke, meanwhile, had written a lengthy letter to Stiehle, which arrived on the afternoon of December 13. Intended as an overall review of the situation of the various German armies, Moltke nonetheless did not fail to remind Stiehle of the continuing need for activity on the part of the Second Army. The letter noted that in the last days of November and in early December various attempts to raise the siege of Paris had been repulsed; the task was now,

> by an energetic pursuit, to put out of action for a long time the disorganised masses which the enemy have had in the field. This requirement still exists, in my opinion, in respect of the enemy corps which have in recent days been engaged with the Grand Duke's Detachment; it is necessary that they are pursued with sufficient force and, as far as possible, dispersed.

But Moltke did not want to see the whole of the Second Army set off in a long chase across France; the troops needed rest, and until Paris fell the limits of the advance should be to a line through Tours, Bourges and Nevers, with the main body held at Orleans. The Detachment could, Moltke thought, cover any threat from the west by taking up a position at Chartres. But Moltke had not lost sight of the threat from the south; 'it is necessary to pay particular attention to a close and permanent watch on the 18th and 20th Corps which under the orders of General Bourbaki have retired through Gien etc in the direction of Bourges and Nevers.' If Bourbaki did advance, the Second Army could count on support from Zastrow at Châtillon sur Seine. Meanwhile, in order to threaten Chanzy's left flank and rear,

Moltke sent orders that the 5th Cavalry Division, currently at and around Chartres, should move west through Nogent le Rotrou and La Ferté Bernard.[26]

During December 13 the Second Army continued its advance towards the Loir, and by nightfall had reached the line Oucques-Conan-Blois without encountering much opposition. Next day the Germans pushed on; the Grand Duke's Detachment moved somewhat to its right, heading for the Loir at Fréteval and Morée. At both places strong resistance was encountered, and in each case it was necessary for the artillery to come into action before the day's objectives could be reached. Further north, cavalry reports indicated that the French were in position at Cloyes; while the leading patrols of the X Corps, probing along the Loire, indicated a French concentration at Vendôme. All the available intelligence pointed to a French stand on the Loir, and Frederick Charles gave orders for a concentration of all his available troops in order to attack the French position. Alvensleben was ordered to push the III Corps forward into the gap between the X Corps and the Detachment; hurrying after the rest of the Second Army, over the poor roads and in foul weather, the III Corps made slow progress. The main body of the X Corps, pushing towards Vendôme, encountered particularly strong opposition there on December 15, which it was unable to overcome before darkness fell, and Voigts-Rhetz pulled back to await the rest of the army. Manstein, meanwhile, had had the bridge at Blois repaired, and by the afternoon of December 15 had begun to move the IX Corps to the right bank of the Loire, leaving only a mixed brigade on the south side of the river. It was evident to Frederick Charles and Stiehle that the attack on Chanzy would, in order to get the whole of their available force into position and to give the troops some rest, have to be postponed until dawn on December 17.

However, during December 16 the picture changed dramatically. An intelligent telegraph clerk at Blois succeeded in intercepting despatches going from Le Mans through Vendôme to Tours, from which it was learned that the 2nd Army of the Loire was now in retreat towards Le Mans and the camp of Conlie. Confirmation of this came during the afternoon, with news of the evacuation of Vendôme. Further north, the evident exhaustion of the 17th Division made its immediate relief by the 22nd Division essential, and the day was spent in these two divisions changing places; during the day this process was delayed by a French advance at Morée, where a brisk action ensued. By the end of the day, however, the attackers, which came from the 21st Corps, were seen to be retreating westward. It had indeed been Chanzy's intention to make a stand in the angle of the Loir. However, during December 15 it became increasingly clear that the state of the army would make this very hazardous; without shelter or campfires, bivouacked in the mud and snow, the French troops had suffered terribly. 'It was evident', Chanzy wrote, 'that they were so exhausted that it would prevent them responding vigorously, if the struggle commenced again that day; the corps commanders did not conceal their apprehensions on the point.'[27] In the face of this, Chanzy hesitated; but his mind was made up for him when Jauréguiberry, on whose tenacity he especially relied, came to him during the afternoon to tell him that he could not see that any serious resistance was possible. Chanzy wasted no time; the orders for the retreat next day of the whole army were issued at once.

Just as the opportunity for a decisive blow had thus escaped the Second Army, Frederick Charles was obliged to consider a fresh threat. On December 15, von der Tann had reported from Orleans that the 14th Cavalry Brigade had been obliged to retreat from Vierzon and Salbris in the face of a strong enemy force; in the evening news came of an advance from Briare upon Gien, and it seemed that the threat from Bourbaki was beginning to materialise. When these reports were first received, the Second Army was getting into position to deal with Chanzy; once his retreat had begun, it was possible to pull back the bulk of the army, and set it in motion for Orleans. The X Corps was to hold the line of the Loire and to advance as far as Tours; the IX Corps and the III Corps were to return at once to Orleans, and the Detachment, which was to move to Châteaudun, had its independence restored, reporting thereafter directly to Versailles.[28] Frederick Charles himself made his way back to Orleans, arriving on December 18.

Moltke had, meanwhile, been engaged in a brisk correspondence. Following up his letter of December 12, he wrote again to Stiehle on December 14; he was still anxious not to see the Second Army too extended, although he was still willing to leave operational decisions to the man on the spot. How far, he wanted to know, must the III Corps follow the enemy, and for how long?

> It is for you to decide in the light of the resistance you encounter. For me, I do not believe that it is necessary, either for forcing General Chanzy to continue his retreat or for occupying Tours. Even today, moreover, this city must doubtless have been occupied by a division of the IX Corps, which has followed the left bank of the Loire, and is fully sufficient to ensure possession of this area. One must also imagine that the other half of the Army of the Loire has had time to assemble around Bourges; under the leadership of a general as able as Bourbaki it would easily be able within a few days to take the offensive on the left bank against Orleans or on the right bank through Gien. In these two cases, the Bavarian Corps will scarcely be able to hold this attack; particularly in the second case it will not be strong enough, even with the support of Hartmann's division, of which we do not know the exact position.[29]

Next day, before this letter had reached the Second Army headquarters, Stiehle's report of the position on December 14 reached Versailles, followed by another reporting the advance of the X Corps on Vendôme. He did not mention Tours, however, and Moltke sent off a telegram sharply enquiring the position, and giving detailed instructions about the destruction of the railway bridges there. His resolve not to interfere in operational matters was evidently weakening. On December 16, becoming uncomfortable about the newly reported threat from Bourbaki, Stiehle wanted to know Zastrow's position, and Moltke responded at once with reassurances that the VII Corps was on the move.[30]

Moltke's uneasiness that his local commanders might tend to lose sight of the overall picture led him, on December 17, to write to Frederick Charles and Manteuffel explaining the strategy that was henceforth to be pursued, and the reasons for it.

> The general situation requires that after a victory the enemy is pursued only as far as it is necessary to disperse the bulk of his forces and thus render it impossible for them to concentrate again for a considerable time. We cannot follow

> the French all the way to their last strongholds such as Lille, Le Havre and Bourges; we do not wish to occupy permanently distant provinces such as Normandy, Brittany and the Vendée; we must resolve to abandon certain points which we have taken, such as Dieppe and eventually Tours, in order to concentrate our principal forces at a small number of important points.

Flying columns were to chase franc-tireurs away from the immediate vicinity of such points; meanwhile the main German forces must wait until the enemy concentrated, in order to deliver a short sharp blow against him. In the west, the Detachment would be based on Chartres, with a strong force at Dreux. The Second Army would concentrate at Orleans, giving up the left bank of the Loire entirely; if Tours was not occupied, then a strong force should be posted at each of Blois and Gien.[31] It was a clear, well-considered strategy; for Moltke the problem would be to keep a close watch on the commanders of the First and Second Armies to ensure that they had the necessary self restraint to carry it out. In practice, it should ensure that offensive decisions would generally be taken only in accordance with Moltke's wishes, since the question of whether the enemy had concentrated to an extent sufficient to justify an attack was one which he alone must decide.

Meanwhile Stosch's eventful stint with the Detachment was coming to an end. As Moltke's personal representative he had exerted a considerable influence on the conduct of operations; but with the retreat of the Army of the Loire it was judged that it was no longer necessary for him to remain; in any case, there was much for him to do back at Versailles. His spell as the Grand Duke's Chief of Staff had not been without its personal problems. The response of some of his senior commanders to the Grand Duke's military pretensions required the exercise of all the considerable tact that Stosch could display. On one occasion on December 13, when Stosch was talking to Voigts-Rhetz, the Grand Duke suddenly interrupted, saying 'What are you doing there? That goes against the first rules of tactics.' Voigts-Rhetz' reaction was so contemptuous that Stosch felt obliged to alter the plans to suit his royal master. And on the following day Prince Albrecht, the King's brother, was similarly outspoken. Entering the room where Stosch and the Grand Duke were discussing the day's operations, he said: 'Well then, Stosch, what shall I do today?' The Grand Duke, quick to take offence, snapped: 'I command here.' The Prince was unmoved. 'We all know what the score is, and don't need to inconvenience ourselves; so, Stosch, what shall I do?'[32] Back at Versailles on December 21, his welcome there showed Stosch how much his success was appreciated; the King told him that he had fulfilled all his expectations and had done exactly what he wished. And Moltke, never one to wear his heart on his sleeve, was warm in his praise: 'We have always felt your strong hand there.'[33] It had been a telling example of Moltke's confidence that his overall intentions would be realised as a result of his ability to impress his approach on his subordinates.

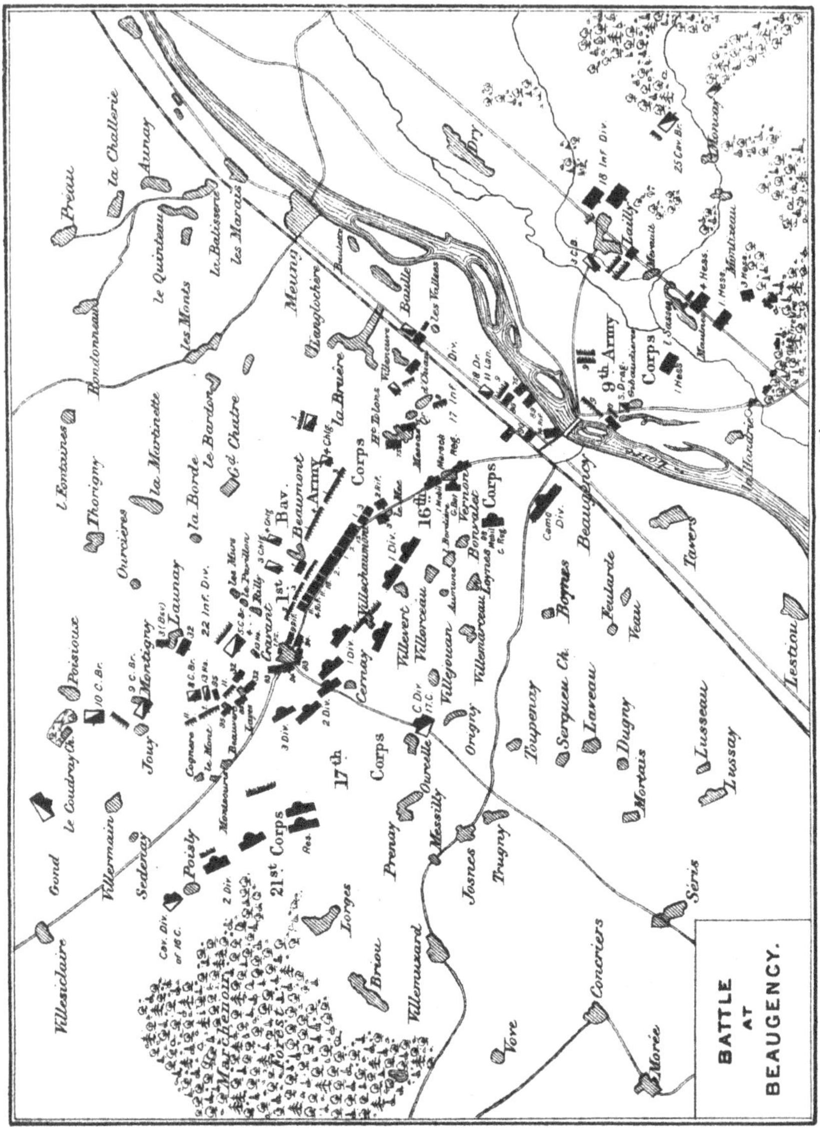

The actions of Beaugency, December 7-11 1870

18

Dijon and Belfort

The sixty three year old Giuseppe Garibaldi, had, at the outbreak of war, been in sympathy with Prussia and her German allies, speaking of the 'noble Germanic nation at last rewarding Napoleon for all his villainies;' but once his bête noire had received his comeuppance at Sedan, he transferred his support to the French Republic, believing that it was 'Italy's duty to fly to the assistance of France now that Napoleon no longer dishonours her.'[1] He at once offered his own services, arriving at Marseilles on October 8 and making his way to Tours three days later. This offer caused the French authorities a certain amount of embarrassment, since it was difficult at first to see how he could be usefully employed. However, in the course of his visit to Besancon in mid October Gambetta found the answer, appointing Garibaldi to the command of a multinational force of volunteers that was collecting in the Cote d'Or. This force would serve to block any German advance down the Upper Saône into the Rhone valley; based on Autun, it grew to a strength estimated by Bordone, who served as Garibaldi's Chief of Staff, as 16,600 men; the total was probably somewhat greater.[2] Many of the troops had military experience; among them were Italians, Polish, English, American, Spanish

Giuseppe Garibaldi, commander of the Army of the Vosges (Rousset/*Histoire*)

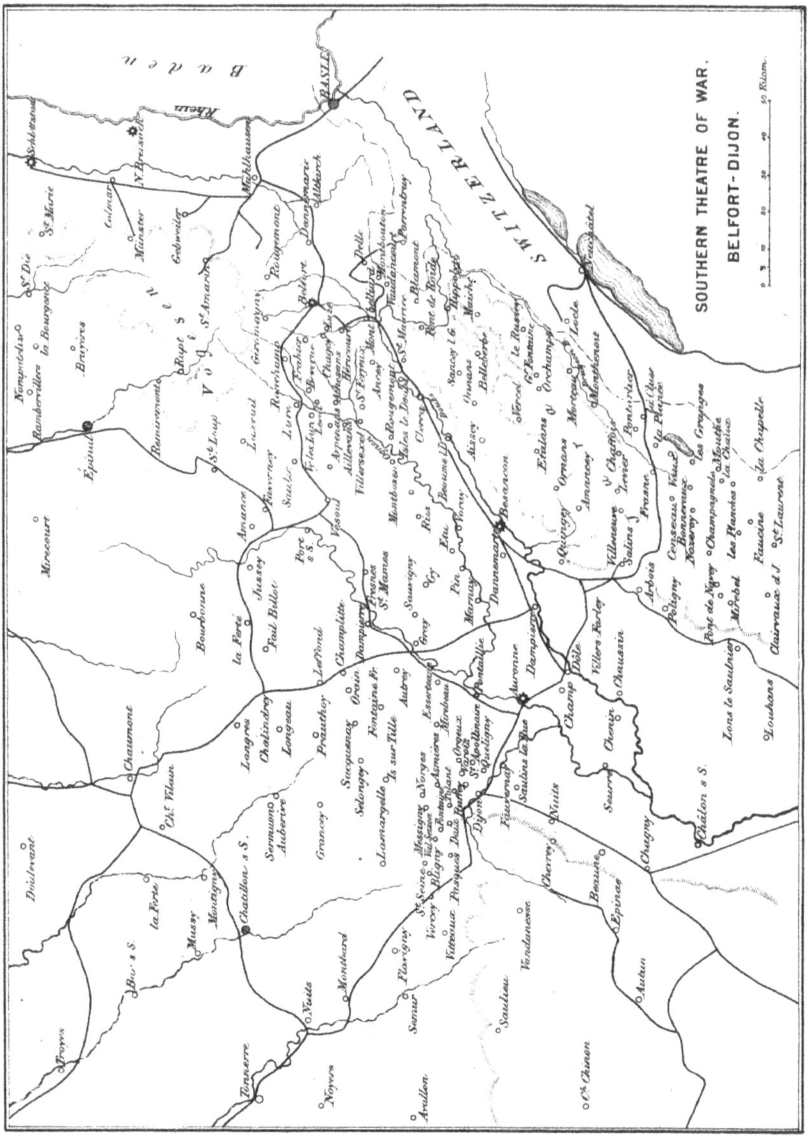

The Southern theatre of war - Belfort, Dijon

and Irish volunteers, as well as a considerable number of French. However, they remained a decidedly undisciplined force throughout the campaign. It was organised in four brigades, commanded by Bossack-Hauke, Delpech, Menotti Garibaldi and Ricciotti Garibaldi respectively. It was the latter's 4th Brigade which struck the first blow, surprising a force of some 500 Etappen troops at Châtillon sur Seine on November 19, a success which encouraged hopes of an advance to retake Dijon. There was available to support such an operation Cremer's division, about 25,000 strong, positioned on the roads heading south from the city. On November 21 the rest of Garibaldi's Corps advanced through Arnay le Duc, and by November 24 it had reached the Sombernon-Dijon road at Pont de Pany where it was rejoined by the 4th Brigade. The forward movement was unfortunately timed; Werder was beginning to concentrate the whole of the XIV Corps in and around Dijon, while Garibaldi's undisciplined force was certainly not ready to face experienced troops in the open field.

However, Garibaldi pushed on, across the Ouche to Pasques, and along the line of the river to Velars, and from these points on November 25 about two battalions advanced on Plombières. The attack was thrown back, with heavy loss, as was another assault to the south, on Corcelles les Monts; but for the moment, in part because of the remarkable mixture of units which made up Garibaldi's Corps, Werder could not for the moment work out his intentions.[3] He also had to take account of the indications of an advance by Cremer's Division from the south through Vougeot to Gevrey, from which it was evident that something serious was to be expected, as a sharp change in the attitude of the Dijon population also demonstrated.

On November 26 Degenfeld, who had moved out to the northwest, encountered Garibaldi's main body on the heights near Prenois; heavily outnumbered, having only three battalions with him, Degenfeld retreated slowly towards Hauteville, followed, also very slowly, by Garibaldi, who directed his movement towards Darois. Satisfied that in this way he had located the enemy's main body, Werder sent off reinforcements to Degenfeld, ordered Keller to the extreme right, at Messigny-Vantoux, and concentrated his other two brigades in Dijon. It was Werder's hope that next day he would be able to strike a major blow at Garibaldi with his whole force.

That night, however, as Degenfeld was getting his troops into position between Daix and Talart, preparing for the following day's attack, Garibaldi at 6.30 pm launched a night assault. It was pitch dark, and the rain was falling heavily. Achieving a complete surprise, the attack broke up the two leading companies; the situation was critical when the 1st Battalion, under Captain von Unger, arrived at the double, and deployed in four ranks across the road.

> There followed out of the intense darkness, accompanied by a tremendous noise, ringing of bells, shouting, blowing of various instruments, and the singing of the Garibaldi hymn, a furious attack of the Garibaldians, which recoiled faint and stricken from the volleys fired by the four ranks at 50 paces distant. A second, a third attack followed, delivered with as great bravery but with the same result; the dead lay thick up to within eight paces of the front.[4]

Silence fell, and the enemy disappeared into the enveloping night.

Francs-Tireurs, by Knötel (Pflugk-Harttung)

Werder's plan for the next day was to hold Garibaldi with his centre, while Keller came in on the enemy's left flank. Von der Goltz was to reinforce Degenfeld, while Prince William's brigade operated south of the Ouche sending forward a detachment of two battalions, one squadron and one battery, around Garibaldi's right. In heavy rain, it was not until 8.00 am that Werder's patrols found that Garibaldi had retreated under cover of darkness; with von der Goltz's brigade, Werder set off in pursuit, catching Garibaldi's rearguard near Prenois, and at once attacking. Meanwhile Colonel Renz, with the detachment from Prince William's brigade, had made good progress around the enemy right when he heard the sound of gunfire from the direction of Prenois. Wheeling north and rapidly pressing forward, he encountered the enemy retreating on Pasques; having at once brought up his guns he advanced to the attack. His troops soon linked with those of von der Goltz, and together they drove the enemy in confusion through Pasques. Just then, a Garibaldian counter attack from Lantenay came in on Renz's left; the German response amply illustrated their speed and effectiveness in meeting such an attack at close quarters.

> Immediately the fusilier battalion of the 2nd Regiment wheeled to the left flank, and a section of the battery galloped up to within 400 paces of the enemy. Decimated by the volleys of the infantry, some of which were delivered by them four deep, and by the case shot of the artillery the enemy turned; a thick line of killed and wounded marked the field.'[5] The enemy rearguard, which consisted of

Delpech's brigade, retreated in disorder through Lantenay; the main body had fallen back rapidly during the night in the direction of Autun. Total German casualties during the two days fighting amounted to seventy four; Garibaldi's losses amounted to about six hundred.

Werder had now to decide his next step. The news from Châtillon which was just to hand meant that he must despatch one brigade there, and on November 28 von der Goltz was sent off in that direction via St Seine and Baigneux les Juifs. Werder's inclination was to follow up Garibaldi, and to try to finish him off; but his troops were tired after the two days' fighting, and while he earmarked Keller's brigade for the task, he had not troops to spare to cover its left flank at Bligny. For the moment, therefore he deferred his advance. As it happened, on the morning of November 28 a feldjäger arrived with orders from Moltke which had been issued on November 24. Approving Werder's immediate intention to act against Garibaldi, he told him that in view of the formation of a 17th Corps at Le Mans and an 18th (under Bourbaki) at Tours, it would not be possible for the Second Army to detach sufficient troops to cover its lines of communication. Moltke went on:

> As soon as Your Excellency has succeeded in inflicting a decisive defeat on Garibaldi's bands, which will keep them quiet for a long while, the XIV Corps must detach flying columns between the Seine and the Loire to render it impossible for any significant enemy forces to operate from the south against the Second Army's lines of communication. This will thus indirectly provide the necessary support to this army. [6]

Werder's information was that Cremer was still in force at Gevrey, while Garibaldi, severely shaken, still held Ste. Marie and Sombernon. Attaching to Keller's force three battalions, two squadrons and two batteries under Colonel Wechmar to cover his left, he ordered Keller to advance against Garibaldi, leaving to him the decision as to how to conduct the operation. Hearing that the French had occupied Nuits in some force, Werder also ordered Renz to move against it with seven companies of infantry, supported by some cavalry and six guns. Renz advanced south on the morning of November 30, moving first on Gevrey, which was cleared of the enemy by 10.00 am, and pressed on to Nuits. Here too the French retreated rapidly; but while the advanced guard only of Renz's force was in the town, large forces of the enemy appeared from the hills to the west, firing from the heights into Nuits to such effect that it was immediately evident to Werder, who had accompanied Renz, that the place could not be held. Werder ordered Renz to move eastwards to Boncourt, an operation which, carried out under heavy fire, proved more difficult than might have been expected. Renz finally occupied Boncourt as night fell; but during the night, uncomfortably aware of how exposed was his position, he fell back to his start line at Marsannay and Longvic. Next day, his patrols found Nuits still to be occupied in strength; the French troops there were estimated to be some 12,000 strong, under Colonel Bourras.[7]

Keller, meanwhile, had advanced south in pursuit of Garibaldi; on November 29, reaching the line of the Ouche at Sombernon, and on the following day his advanced guard took Arnay le Duc after a brief skirmish. Wechmar, on his left, reached Veuvey sur Ouche, again encountering only isolated parties of the enemy, although gathering intelligence that suggested that Bligny was occupied in force.

This in fact proved not to be the case so, with his left flank now secure, Keller moved directly on Autun, reaching a position in front of the town just after 2.00 pm on December 1. He found the place to be strongly held by Garibaldi's infantry, supported by artillery on the height behind. Keller had at this point about 4,500 men in hand; he decided to attack, and began with a heavy artillery bombardment of the enemy positions which, by 4.00 pm had silenced the enemy guns. At this point part of the enemy infantry could be seen retreating, but substantial forces remained in Autun itself, and Keller deferred a direct assault until the following day. As darkness fell, however, he received unexpected instructions from Werder: 'The enemy showed himself in such force yesterday, at Nuits, that any further advance on your part at Autun is not advisable. I, therefore, wish you, if circumstances permit of it, to begin your retreat on Dijon today; in any case, I shall expect you in Dijon on the 3rd.'[8] Keller at once complied, pulling back to Dracy St Loup; by next day he had retraced his steps as far as Rouvres sous Meilly, while Wechmar marched back on Sombernon. Here he received fresh orders from Werder, directing him on Velars while Wechmar was ordered to Plombières.

Thus far Keller's retreat had been unmolested, and he expected to reach his objective on December 3 without difficulty; however, unobserved, Cremer had pushed forward strong forces on Bligny and from there had advanced on Châteauneuf with about 8,000 men and about 10 guns. This seriously threatened Keller's line of retreat; under cover of his artillery, his infantry were obliged to storm the French positions and to drive the enemy back before continuing their

German outpost near Belfort, by Knötel (Pflugk-Harttung)

Menotti Garibaldi, commander of the 3rd Brigade, Army of the Vosges (Rousset/*Histoire*)

march to Sombernon and Velars, which he reached by nightfall, while Wechmar, whose force had preceded him, entered Dijon that night. The abortive expedition towards Autun had cost Keller a total of 157 casualties, a number of the wounded with their attendant doctors having to be left behind.

Werder's decision to recall Keller to Dijon had arisen from his increasing unease at his position in the city. The despatch of both Keller and von der Goltz had left the XIV Corps very thin on the ground, and the restlessness of the population contributed to his discomfort. He strengthened the troops there by bringing up what there was immediately available of Schmeling's 4th Reserve Division, about three and a half battalions with two squadrons and two batteries, retaining them until von der Goltz returned on December 6 from his expedition to Châtillon, which had achieved very little. The units of the 4th Reserve Division now pushed eastwards to ascertain what French troops might be in the Dôle area, and to cover the lines of communication. No enemy was to be found; in the worsening weather movement became increasingly difficult both in terms of any military operations and of the bringing up of supplies. Fortunately however the enemy, for the moment similarly handicapped, made no movement to disturb the well earned rest of the XIV Corps. From December 6 until December 10, it snowed constantly, and it was bitterly cold. Secure for the moment in Dijon, Werder's troops suffered much less from the weather than their opponents.[9]

When it stopped snowing, the French embarked on a series of raids, in which they were assisted by remarkably comprehensive intelligence. One such raid might have captured the temporary commander of the Baden Division, General Beyer; the French, however, moved a day too soon, and alerted by an attack on a convoy on December 12, Beyer delayed his movement, waiting a day at Gray before safely resuming his journey.

Although these attacks on his lines of communication put further pressure on his over stretched forces, Werder was at least able to report to Versailles on December 12 that his reconnaissances to the south encountered no French opposition. It was possible, he added, that the enemy had withdrawn from the valley of the Saône. This message, however, crossed with one from Moltke, outlining what he saw as the tasks for the XIV Corps in the immediate future. Dated December 8, it only reached Werder on December 13. It brought the news of the defeats of the Army of the Loire and of the sortie from Paris, and defined Werder's task as being 'to cover the siege of Belfort, which he was to aid by all means possible, to isolate Langres and in conjunction with General von Zastrow to protect the communications of the Second and Third Armies and to complete the pacification of the southern part of the Goverments-General of Lorraine and Reims.' Zastrow was to be based on Châtillon sur Seine. The tasks assigned to Werder and Zastrow would, Moltke suggested, 'not be best performed by long periods of inactivity; on the contrary, it is necessary, with sufficient forces, to undertake vigorous offensives against enemy concentrations.' Werder was also required to bring to an end French operations from Langres, while his attention was also drawn to the area between Dôle and Senans, already once occupied by the XIV Corps, which would have the effect of cutting off Besancon from its rail links to the south west.[10]

The Baden Grenadiers at Nuits, painting by Becker (Rousset/*Histoire*)

With the limited forces actually available to Werder, all of this was rather a tall order; and Moltke's rather patronising tone must have conveyed an unmistakeable hint of criticism to the hard pressed commander of a corps with a huge area to protect against an unknown, but certainly rapidly strengthening adversary. However, Werder did his best to comply, sending von der Goltz off on December 14 to conduct an operation to isolate Langres, and detaching further units from the already attenuated 4th Reserve Division to reinforce the troops besieging Belfort. That day, too, he confirmed to Moltke his belief that the French had now left the Saône valley 'probably by rail westwards;' the effect of this report was only to increase his responsibilities still further, Moltke ordering Zastrow towards the Loire as far as Auxerre while Werder took over from the VII Corps part of its duties of protecting the lines of communication in the area of Nuits sous Rancières and Semur.[11]

Events, however, were soon to change the situation dramatically. By the middle of December a sharp thaw set in, giving the French the opportunity to move back into their more advanced positions in the Côte d'Or and the Saône valley; within days Werder was receiving alarming reports that Cremer with 30,000 men and Garibaldi with 20,000 men were getting ready to move against him. With the detachments he had made, and after including the fresh drafts that had recently joined him, Werder had 16,000 men and 54 guns to meet them. To hold Dijon against odds of maybe three to one, his best bet was to defeat the enemy in detail, and he resolved to begin with an assault on Cremer in the Saône valley, ordering Glümer with the Baden Division to move south on December 18. He briefed Glümer personally; the division was to clear the enemy from the triangle Dijon- Bouillard- Beaune, taking the latter town if possible.

In spite of the disparity of force the German plan for the advance on Nuits displayed all the confidence which had now become habitual. On the right flank, Degenfeld was to advance through the mountains against Villars Fontaine, and come in on Nuits from the west. A battalion under Major von Unger was to move down the main road, while the main body, largely comprising Prince William's brigade, was to move to the east of the road on Boncourt. The position they were attack was naturally extremely strong. 'The slopes of these chalk hills are very steep, much furrowed and broken up into terraces, the lower ones being covered with vineyards, the upper ones bare or wooded. The road is, therefore, only useful for operations to the force which holds these hills.' [12]In addition, a ridge to the south of Nuits commanded the town and the ground in front of it, while the Chaux Hill to the west covered it from an attack from that direction. The flat ground to the east and north of the town was cut by the railway, running first through a cutting some ten feet deep and then, further north, along a high embankment. Cremer had posted four and half battalions on his right, in Boncourt and the walled farm of La Berchère, and in the railway cutting; four battalions held Nuits and Vosne, and the slope of Chaux Hill; two more battalions held the west slope of the hill.

Early on the morning of December 18, Cremer took two battalions north up the Dijon road towards Gevrey. At about 11.00 am he encountered Unger's battalion coming south, and hastily retreated to Nuits, followed at a distance by Unger's troops. Meanwhile Glümer with the main body had set off to the east of the road, preceded by the advanced guard under Willisen which encountered only

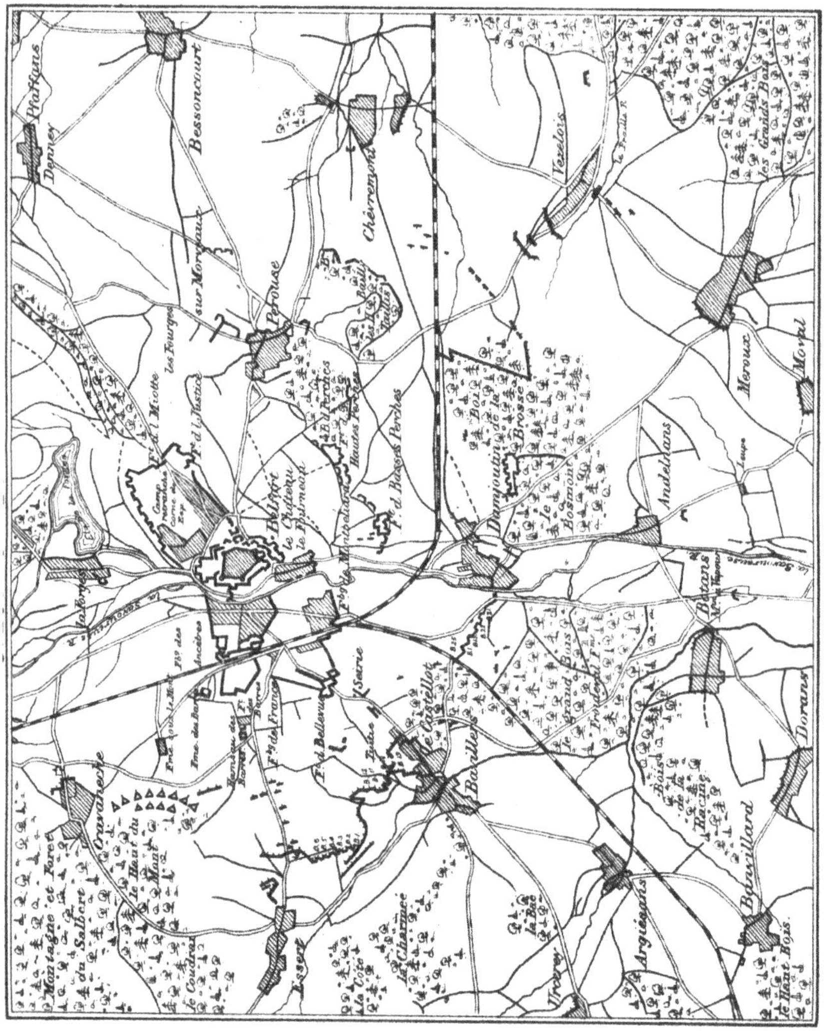

Siege of Belfort

a screen of pickets as it advanced towards Boncourt. There, however, it met stiff opposition from Graziani's troops occupying the village. Werder watched as Holtz's battery opened fire on the village from the other side of a wood, having only the church spire to aim at. Soon, the village caught fire; Wechmar, who was commanding the infantry of the advanced guard at this point, launched three battalions in an assault which carried the village without much loss, the French retreating to La Berchère at 12.30pm. The farm buildings there were well adapted to the defence and the garrison put up a stiff fight before Wechmar's leading battalion stormed the farm, albeit with heavy loss. By 1.45 Wechmar was able to switch his attention to his extreme left, where another battalion took Agencourt at about 1.45 pm.

Neither here, however, nor at La Berchère were the Germans for the moment able to make any further progress towards the heavily defended line of the railway, although the artillery was able to shell at long range the battalions which had fallen back in the face of Unger's advance on the main road. On the other side of the battlefield, Degenfeld's brigade had been held up by a strong position at Villers Fontaine, and in spite of making a determined assault was able to make no progress. Degenfeld had also lost touch with Arnold's battalion advancing on Concoeur, and also with Unger's battalion on the high road, and was thus unable to influence the main battle in and around Nuits. After fruitlessly banging his head against the impassable rock plateau that confronted him, Degenfeld retreated later in the day to Perrigny, on the main Dijon road, with nothing to show for his efforts.

By 2 pm Glümer had arrived with the main body west of Nuits, and launched a general attack on the railway line. On the left the 1st Battalion of the Guards Grenadiers encountered two French positions well in advance of the railway, and took each of them at the point of the bayonet, although suffering heavy losses, before moving on to the line of the railway. Behind the 1st Battalion came Wolff's Fusilier Battalion, which now advanced on the railway station, to the south east of Nuits, which was heavily defended and held out until 4 pm.

In the centre, Wechmar led two and half battalions forward towards the railway from La Berchère, in the face of heavy rifle fire and of artillery fire from Chaux Hill. Casualties were mounting; both Glümer and Prince William were wounded, and Renz, who took over from Prince William, was killed when he was hit by three bullets. Wechmar, too, was wounded, but he continued in action as his infantry jumped up to the line of the railway; by 4 pm, just as the troops on the left took the station, the rest of the cutting and embankment was in German hands.

Meanwhile, to the north of Nuits, Unger had taken Vosne and pushed on down the main road towards the town, while Arnold's battalion also at last made its way down the mountain slopes on the extreme right. It was just as well. Werder, who had taken over direct command when Glümer was hit, was thinking of calling a halt in the gathering gloom, when the news came that all along the line the German troops were advancing on Nuits itself, and in places had already penetrated into the suburbs. The enemy were not, however, yet done with; their artillery was still extremely effective in its commanding position on the heights above the town, while reinforcements had arrived on the railway and launched an immediate attack on Wolff's battalion in the southern suburbs of Nuits. This attack was beaten off in disorder as was a last counter attack on the northern edge of Nuits, and the Germans pressed on, although even now still encountering stiff resistance in the streets of the town. By 5.30 pm, however, Wechmar was able to report that it was entirely in German hands, and that the French were retreating southwards in the direction of Beaune.

Casualties on both sides had been heavy. The French lost a total of some 1,700 men, which included about 630 unwounded prisoners; the Germans suffered a total loss of 945, the bulk of which was sustained by the Grenadier battalions that had attacked Nuits from the east. That night Werder not unreasonably felt justified in issuing an order of the day congratulating his men on 'a most brilliant victory.' He did not, however, follow up the retreating enemy to Beaune; his troops were too exhausted for this and, in fact, such a move was for the moment unnecessary as Cremer's force had been badly shaken by the encounter, and although it was reinforced at Beaune by Ricciotti Garibaldi's brigade it was in no state to move forward again.[13]

In any case, Werder's principal task was, in accordance with Moltke's instructions, to support the siege of Belfort, and in considering his next move he was very mindful of the fact that hanging on to Dijon meant leaving a large part of his force a long way away from the key operations being conducted by Tresckow. Von der Goltz, too, was a long way off. Although he successfully fought a sharp little action at Longueau on December 18, and then invested Langres at a safe distance, thus bringing to an end the raids out of there which had been so disruptive of the main German lines of communication, this task also was subordinate to the operations against Belfort, which on both sides were now the focus of attention in south eastern France. If the French made an effort to raise the siege, it was there that the XIV Corps must go.

Belfort had, since the middle ages, been a fortress of considerable importance with a castle built on the rocky height on its southern edge towering over the town. Down the years, it had been extensively fortified, first to the designs of Vauban and later to take into account more modern developments. The castle was enlarged into a citadel, which commanded a wide field of fire. Around the main works a number of outlying forts had been constructed. To the north east lay a fortified camp, based on Forts La Miotte and La Justice. About to the south of the chateau rose the heights of Hautes and Basses Perches, which had not originally been fortified, a serious weakness which the new commandant of Belfort, Colonel Denfert Rochereau who was appointed in October, at once began to rectify. Covering the suburbs the west of the River Savoureuse, there had been constructed the Forts of des Barres and Bellevue. Denfert, who had commanded the engineers at Belfort for six years, knew the ground very well, and he further strengthened the defences by fortifying the outlying villages of Danjoutin, to the south, and Pérouse to the east.

The garrison included three line battalions, nine battalions of gardes mobiles, and a number of other troops drawn from various sources, and was some 17,000 strong. There were 341 guns and, with the exception of shells for the heavier artillery the fortress was extremely well provided with munitions. It was clearly going to be a tough nut to crack. 'The rocky soil could not fail to offer impediment to all earthworks; the inclement season was approaching, and the strength of the garrison foreshadowed a stubborn resistance, even though the quality of the troops might not be of the stoutest.'[14] It seemed to Tresckow, pondering the options open to him once the siege commenced, that an advance from the south on the forts on the Perches offered the best chance of success. It also seemed to him that he would require at least 15,000 men and 120 siege guns to prosecute the siege, and he reported his views to Moltke on November 23. Tresckow realised that, even before a preliminary bombardment, he must first tighten the cordon around the fortress, and between November 22 and 28 he succeeded in occupying the villages of Essert and Bavilliers on the western side of Belfort, as well as the important height of the Haut du Mont. By now reinforcements had reached him, bringing his total strength to 20 battalions, five squadrons and four field batteries.

At Versailles, Moltke was taking a keen interest in the arrangements to besiege Belfort, and he wrote on November 27 to tell Tresckow that he would have the required force. He was also to be given priority for his other needs:

> Above all, you must seek from Strasbourg artillery materiel and the necessary personnel. In case the resources there are not sufficient, you should address requests for what you need direct to the Bavarian War Minister at Munich. Headquarters has asked the Minister to deal at once with your proposals.[15]

With this encouragement, Tresckow was able to proceed and by the night of December 2 construction could be commenced of six batteries south east of Essert, with a further battery to the north of the road into Belfort, linked by trenches. Next day the bombardment began, and was vigorously answered by the garrison, which was able to bring artillery to bear on the siege batteries from all parts of the fortress. The guns in the château were particularly effective. The bombardment continued on the following days, although hampered by the weather: 'Severe cold, and especially an icy east wind, impeded work in the assailant's batteries; mist and snowstorms frequently hid the objects from view.'[16]

The garrison made a number of sorties on the west side of the fortress, which were driven back; then on the evening of December 13 a force led by Colonel von Ostrowski, about two battalions strong, captured the village of Andelnans, to the south, as well as the heights of Le Bosmont, thereby taking an important step forward. A further attempt by the garrison, towards Bavilliers, was beaten off on December 14, and during the rest of the month Tresckow was able to make progress with the construction of further batteries in and around that village, and also along the edge of the Bois de la Brosse, to the south. The work was hampered first by a sudden thaw and heavy rain, and then by the return of a heavy frost, and it was not until the last days of December that the new batteries could open fire. The fortress responded vigorously, and the duel continued during the first week of January. It was only by then that the continually reinforced German siege artillery began to get the upper hand.[17]

On the night of January 7/8, a surprise attack by about two battalions, under Captain von Manstein, was launched towards Danjoutin. Avoiding the heavily fortified southern end of the village, part of Manstein's force moved through the wood, towards the railway line, seizing the signalman's house to the north of the village, while other troops entered Danjoutin from the east. Reinforcing the troops on the railway line, Manstein was able to throw back French troops advancing from Belfort to the relief of Danjoutin, where a fierce house to house struggle was taking place. The French garrison, which still held the southern part of the village, was based on a strongly defended factory, and resisted all attempts to overrun the positions held. On the west bank of the river, a force from Bavilliers took the isolated houses there, a move which meant that Danjoutin's defenders were effectively cut off. In spite of this they continued to resist until 11.30 am on January 8, when 20 officers and 700 men surrendered. The operation had cost the Prussians in all some 90 casualties; its success meant that Tresckow could now push his front line forward to within striking distance of the two Perches forts.[18]

Meanwhile, however, the indications of a French advance from Besancon were becoming unmistakable. Tresckow's cavalry patrols, operating from Montbéliard, sent in a stream of reports of French activity on the roads leading to Belfort, and it was evident to him that he must be prepared for an early attempt to raise the siege. At Montbéliard itself he posted one battalion with one squadron and four guns, and he reinforced the strong château there. Ostrowski had two battalions strung out in a cordon from the Doubs valley to the Swiss frontier, while Colonel von Zglinicki, with three battalions and six guns, reinforced the battalion already posted at Arcey, covering any advance from L'Isle sur le Doubs.Tresckow was prepared if necessary merely to continue investing Belfort with ten battalions, and to use the rest of his force to resist any advance. But it was very clear to him that to prevent the relief of Belfort, the Prussians must rely on the prompt arrival of Werder and the XIV Corps.

19

The Battle on the Hallue

The switch from an offensive to a defensive role was not the only changed circumstance to which the First Army had to adapt after the battle of Amiens and the taking of Rouen. As early as December 1 the frost set in, at first mildly; but as the month wore on the cold steadily became more intense. After the first week of December, at the end of which there was a heavy snowfall, there was a prolonged period of alternate frost and thaw, turning the muddy country roads to a quagmire. An even more significant development, however, was the arrival of a new commander for the Army of the North. General Louis Faidherbe had been appointed to take over when Bourbaki was relieved, but at the time he had been in Algeria, and he did not arrive to take up his post until December 3. He had enjoyed a successful career in the French colonies, both as a soldier and as Governor of Senegal, but his health had been badly affected there, and the fever which was a legacy of his service in Africa meant that every day he was utterly worn out by the early evening.[1] Faidherbe soon proved himself an able and clear headed leader, who commanded the confidence not only of his soldiers, but also of the local administration, and with Farre's aid he at once set about the task of rebuilding the Army of the North and restoring its morale after the defeat at Amiens.

Meanwhile the immediate problem which Manteuffel faced was the need to operate against two separated enemy forces of unknown strength. For the moment all he knew about the Army of the North was that, having been conclusively beaten at Amiens, it had disappeared in the direction of Arras, evidently in considerable disorder. On the other hand Briand's army, by all accounts quite as large, had not stopped to fight but had retreated precipitately over the Seine. Experience had, however, already shown the ability of the armies of the Government of National Defence quickly to regroup and to be reinforced with fresh units. Manteuffel could not therefore safely assume that neither army would become an immediate threat, and he commissioned his artillery commander, Lieutenant General von Schwartz, and Major General Biehler, commanding his engineers, to report on the defensive capabilities of Rouen. Since Briand had made no attempt to defend the city, these had not been tested; its size and importance meant that it would be an inviting target for any French counter offensive.

Rouen is overlooked by the neighbouring heights on the right bank of the Seine, while another significant factor was the presence in the city of 100,000 decidedly hostile and excitable inhabitants. Schwartz and Biehler concluded that the defensive perimeter around Rouen would have to be nearly thirteen miles in length, based on fifteen redoubts, and would require at least one whole corps for its defence.[2] Even then, it would not be a strong position; and to lock up what would effectively be half of his field troops in this way would seriously inhibit Manteuffel's freedom of decision. The series of radial movements from Rouen which he had ordered immediately after the occupation of the city, which had had the effect of driving back any organised bodies of French troops around which any

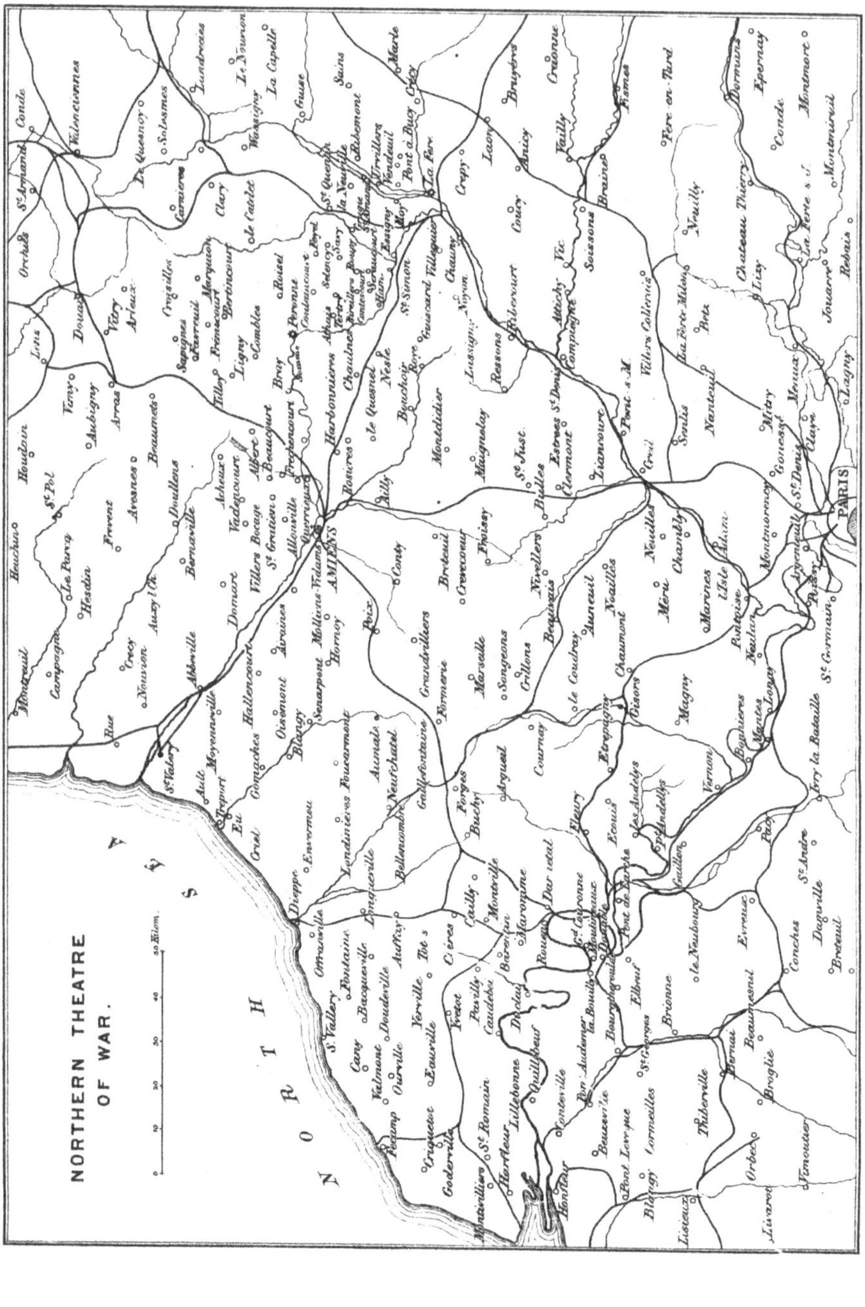

The Northern theatre of war

assault could be based, was, he reasoned, a more effective way of defending the city.

One of the most important of these movements was the despatch of a force to Dieppe, with the object of cutting land communication between the armies of Briand and Faidherbe. Led by the commander of the 7th Cavalry Brigade, Major General zu Dohna, it consisted of two cavalry regiments, two battalions of infantry and a horse artillery battery. Assembling his force on December 7, Dohna occupied Dieppe without resistance two days later, breaking up the coastal telegraph system and spiking 27 guns in the coastal batteries before withdrawing to Auffay en route to rejoin the main body of the army.[3] The French forces in front of Dohna's column, as in the case of those encountered by the other columns sent out from Rouen, rapidly fell back. In some instances, the French units which were met dispersed on first contact, and no significant engagements resulted.

At Versailles Moltke was keeping a sharp eye on developments in the north. At 9.30 pm on December 6, soon after receiving news of the occupation of Rouen, he despatched a telegram ordering Manteuffel to commence the pursuit towards Le Havre, while firmly holding Rouen, and promising further instructions next day. Moltke's concern that the capture of Rouen be actively followed up was such, however, that his letter of December 7 with detailed orders for the future was preceded by another telegram reiterating that the pursuit to Le Havre was to be 'as energetic as possible.' Moltke's evident anxiety that Manteuffel might be inclined to rest upon his laurels after his recent success was shown in his letter, in which he repeated yet again his instruction that there should be a vigorous pursuit to Le Havre. It is noticeable that the letter did not suggest that the First Army should assume a defensive stance, but required that its main body should

> continue its offensive against the enemy troops still in the field in the north west of France. His Majesty regards it as immediately essential to pursue vigorously the troops of General Briand, which have fallen back on Le Havre ... The Commander in Chief will decide on the spot whether to attempt a coup de main against this place.

Moltke went on to summarise the essence of the strategy that Manteuffel was to pursue.

> His Majesty does not wish to see the First Army undertake any prolonged operation against Le Havre. It should on the contrary always have as its principal aim the dispersal of any enemy troops that again take the field, and from this point of view a renewal of operations against the troops beaten at Amiens should not be neglected if they advance from their present points of concentration around Arras etc.[4]

As soon as he received these instructions, Manteuffel issued the necessary orders, which had the effect of dividing the First Army into two distinct battle groups. Bentheim, with the I Corps and the Guard Dragoon Brigade, was to be on the line of the Seine, watching Briand, while Goeben with the VIII Corps and the 3rd Cavalry Division was to take the line of the Somme. Manteuffel's intention was that, based on interior lines between the two rivers, the army would be able 'to form quickly to the front in either of these main directions.'[5] The positions to be taken up by the two parts of the army were to be based on Rouen and Amiens respectively, the retention of which Manteuffel regarded as both politically and militarily essential. Goeben's march to Amiens was to be by way of Le Havre, so that he could form a view as to the feasibility of taking it by a coup de main; if this was not practicable, he was to move up the coast before turning southeast to Amiens. Meanwhile Bentheim, while holding himself ready to meet Briand in the open field if the latter should advance, was to pursue an energetic policy by continuing to send flying columns over the Seine.

Any temporary sense of security which Manteuffel might have felt was soon to be dispelled. Von der Groeben, at Amiens, had sent out a number of reconnaissances during the first days of December; while not all of these had made contact with the enemy, there were clear signs from some of the reports that the Army of the North was beginning to prepare for an advance. From these, and from reports in English newspapers, von der Groeben came to the conclusion that an assault was to be expected from Arras through Péronne, in the villages around which French infantry were seen to be entrenching. With the limited forces under his command, von der Groeben decided against any advance, and contented himself with provisioning the citadel of Amiens, which he strengthened with guns brought up from La Fère, and meanwhile awaiting events.

He did not have to wait long. At Ham, about forty miles down the line from Amiens to La Fère, a number of railway engineers, escorted by a company of infantry, were engaged in repairing the railway. On the night of 9 December, in pitch darkness and a heavy snowstorm, they were surprised by a neatly executed attack on the town from all sides; although part of the German infantry managed to gain the shelter of the castle of Ham (where Louis Napoleon had been imprisoned after his second unsuccessful attempt at a coup d'etat at Boulogne) they were soon forced to capitulate. It was an excellent start to the Army of the North's campaign under its new leader, and the news caused consternation at the various German headquarters. Faidherbe followed up the seizure of Ham by moving his whole corps on the following day down to the line of the Somme there, ready to turn west towards Amiens, or east to La Fère or, if the opportunity arose, to march southwest towards Paris. It was the hope of executing the latter movement that had prompted Faidherbe's move; he had been ordered on December 7 by Gambetta to 'direct his army corps with a view to a possible junction with General Ducrot's Army, which would break out via St Denis and march north-east.'[6]

After reconnoitring the fortress of La Fère on December 12 and 13, Faidherbe came to the conclusion that it was too strongly held to justify an assault, and he had neither the time nor the resources to be able to consider a formal siege of the place. A thrust over the Somme in the direction was always going to be hazardous in the extreme, and he decided to move instead on Amiens. There, von der Groeben had, immediately after reporting the capture of Ham to the headquarters of the First Army, received orders to rertake the place at once. In the hope that the German troops might still be holding out in the castle of Ham, he sent off on the evening of December 10 a force under Captain Luckowtz. Consisting only of one battalion, one squadron and four guns, it was far too weak to push past the strong French forces now surrounding Ham; Luckowitz got within six miles of the town before he ran into heavy opposition at Eppeville on December 12 and was obliged to fall back, retracing his steps to Amiens.

The Army of the North occupies Ham, by Pallandre (Rousset/*Combattants*)

Manteuffel was far from pleased when the news reached him on December 13 of the check of Luckowitz' force, and he peremptorily ordered von der Groeben to retake Ham at all costs, and by pushing forward patrols beyond Péronne to find out what Faidherbe was up to. He was still more displeased when he got von der Groeben's response, to the effect that he would not be able to begin his march on Ham before December 16, but he reluctantly accepted this, while insisting that von der Groeben should leave sufficient troops to guarantee the security of Amiens, and should establish contact with Kummer's 15th Division, which was expected to reach Montdidier by December 17 or 18. This was the nearest limit of the VII Corps, the presence of which on the Somme had clearly now become an urgent necessity.

Goeben, setting off from Rouen in the direction of Le Havre on December 10, had soon after his departure received news of French activity west of Amiens, and he had directed the 30th Brigade of Kummer's Division to move in that direction, followed by the 29th Brigade from Pont Audemer. With the rest of the corps, Goeben probed the defences of Le Havre, which his patrols soon reported was held in considerable strength. Subsequent French accounts showed the French to have some 40,000 troops there, in positions supported by heavily armed redoubts, and Goeben's immediate conclusion, that a coup de main was impossible, was quite unavoidable. Instead, he set off towards Abbeville, from where he intended to march to Amiens.[7]

Moltke had meanwhile been watching with some considerable concern the ineffectual response of both von der Groeben and Manteuffel to Faidherbe's advance to Ham. On December 12, sending the message via the Army of the

Meuse because the direct telegraph line to Amiens had been cut, he telegraphed von der Groeben that 'the appearance of enemy troops near La Fère makes it necessary that you intervene.'[8] Dissatisfied with the lack of progress, and with what seemed to be a confusion of thought at the headquarters of the First Army, he issued orders on December 13 to Manteuffel with the intention of imposing some orders on his army's proceedings. In the event, these orders were not carried out, due to the immediate pressure of events; but they offered a better solution than Manteuffel's original deployment. Stressing that it was not his intention to occupy the whole of the north west of France, Moltke explained that the role of the First Army was to break up any force that threatened the investment of Paris. For this purpose, the First Army should be kept together and he designated Beauvais as the point of concentration.

> The main body of the First Army being concentrated around Beauvais, it will have the opportunity promptly to support Rouen and Amiens, and also to take the offensive against any hostile forces that emerge from the line of fortresses on the Belgian frontier. The events of the last few days show in a remarkable manner all the signs of an operation of this kind against our communications.

If the French moved rapidly on Soissons, the investing armies might have to detach troops to deal with them; for the moment, he repeated, the First Army's role was to cover their rear. Finally, he suggested that von der Groeben should be asked to explain the movements he intended to make towards Péronne and La Fère.[9]

Moltke found von der Groeben's next report even less satisfactory. The latter now insisted that it would jeopardise the safety of Amiens if he despatched a force larger than two battalions strong to retake Ham, which was patently inadequate. Manteuffel was obliged to depend to a greater extent upon the contribution of 15th Division. Kummer reported that his leading unit, Strübberg's 30th Brigade, would be at Bréteuil by December 16, and at Montdidier on the following day. Bock's 29th Brigade, worn out by exhausting marches, needed a rest day, and would follow one day's march behind. Goeben, marching with the 16th Division towards Abbeville, expected to be there by December 17 and be in a position to operate on the Somme by December 19.[10] With Moltke's order of December 13 in mind, Manteuffel issued instructions that von der Groeben should leave three battalions of the 3rd Brigade, with two batteries and a cavalry regiment, and set off to Raye with the rest of his force; Kummer was to continue to Montdidier, and take control of von der Groeben's force, but the 16th Division was to go to Beauvais. Notwithstanding Moltke's clear instructions, however, Manteuffel did not make any major change in the disposition of the I Corps; whether because he thought Goeben could take care of the Army of the North on his own, or because he rated the threat from Briand more highly than Moltke did, is unclear. It was, of course, the case that Bentheim had pressed forward towards the Rille in contact with part of Briand's army, while in his rear the Army of the Meuse had moved Lippe's division nearer to Beauvais. At all events, things now seemed to be falling into place to enable him to block any further advance by Faidherbe.

Or so Manteuffel must have thought; but on the evening of December 16 he received a very nasty shock when First Lieutenant Sulzer, who was serving as Prefect of Amiens, appeared at the Rouen headquarters of the First Army. He brought with him a letter evidently written before receipt of the latest orders, with the startling news that von der Groeben had decided to abandon Amiens, save for the garrison he left in the citadel, and march with his whole force towards a junction with Kummer in Montdidier. Manteuffel was incandescent with rage. Wartensleben noted, in moderate language, that he had 'set great store on maintaining the occupation of Amiens,' and that to give it up without cogent military reasons 'might easily, at least in the eyes of our adversaries, appear like an involuntary evacuation of the place, caused by the general state of affairs. We know how apt the French were to draw conclusions of this kind, and how easily they were, under such circumstances, excited and morally buoyed up.'[11] Moltke, for his part, was also dismayed to learn of von der Groeben's intention to go to Montdidier, although his response was somewhat more measured; he telegraphed von der Groeben with the news that the French had pulled back from La Fère, and pointed out that 'an offensive by the whole of your detachment in the direction of St Quentin will have at this time more effect than the movement to Montdidier.'[12] At Rouen, Manteuffel decided at once to take action to reverse the effect of von der Groeben's decision; within the hour two mounted orderly officers rode away with orders for the immediate reoccupation of Amiens, if possible before Faidherbe got there first.

Next day Manteuffel rode off himself, although not before despatching a telegram to Moltke explaining that notwithstanding Moltke's order of December 13, he was now concentrating on the Bréteuil-Montdidier line, as affairs at Amiens had become the more pressing. To Goeben he sent instructions that the 16th Division was, after all not to go to Beauvais, but to head for Bréteuil instead. Manteuffel himself reached Marseille by nightfall on December 18, and Bréteuil next day, where he received the anxiously awaited news from Amiens that Mirus, with the 3rd Brigade, had re-entered the city on December 18 without opposition. During the interregunum the population, discouraged by threats from Captain Hubert the commander of the citadel that he would open fire if there was any offensive addition, had remained largely quiet. Indeed, the publication by the French authorities of placards insisting that the German hospitals in the city be respected made a strong impression, and Manteuffel in recognition of this remitted a contribution imposed on the city by Captain Hubert. Mirus had reoccupied Amiens just in time; that day Faidherbe, accompanied only by his chief of staff Farre had ridden forward to the Faubourg Noyan to reconnoitre the city.[13]

Although Faidherbe had just missed, therefore, the quite unlooked for bonus of the recapture of Amiens, he was still resolved to give battle, and he took up an extremely strong position, facing west along the line of the Hallue, a small river which flowed south through water meadows into the Somme at Daours, about seven miles from Amiens. His left flank was covered by the Somme, behind which on the right bank, overlooking Corbie and Sailly, ran a series of heights which dominated any approach from the south. On the eastern slopes of the Hallue valley a series of villages provided billets for his troops as well as a line of outposts which ran northwards, while behind them on the hills that rose above them his main position was one of considerable strength. Behind this line, a substantial number of troops were quartered in Corbie, where Faidherbe established his headquarters.[14] His army was now organised in two corps, the 22nd and 23rd Corps commanded

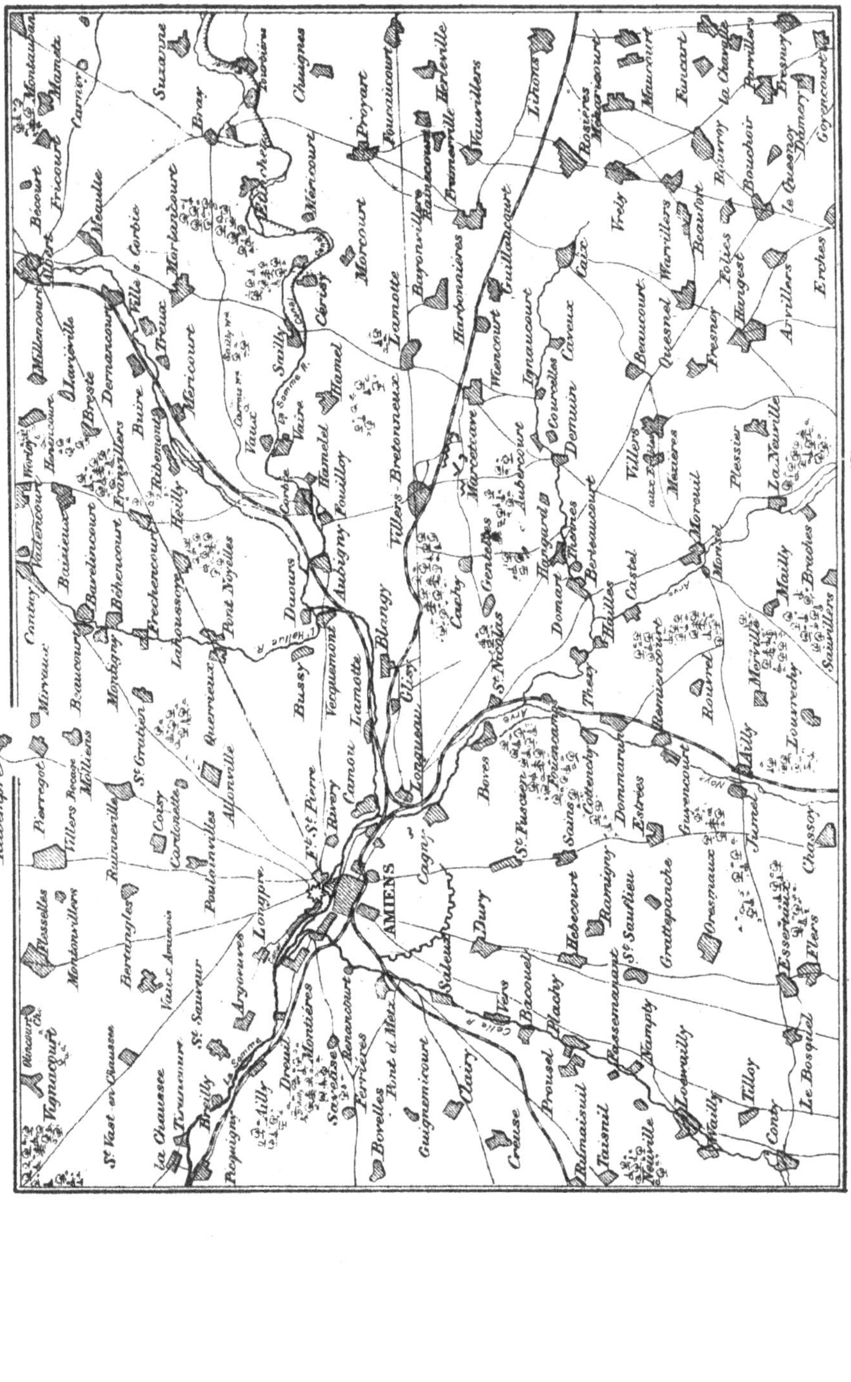

The Battle on the Hallue, December 23-24 1870

by Lecointe and Paulze d'Ivoy respectively. Faiderbe was a realist; he probable had little hope of winning an overwhelming victory over Manteuffel, but in the right position, with a heavy numerical advantage, there was every chance that he could fight a successful defensive battle. In the line of the Hallue he had found just such a position.

Reflecting on the operations of the armies of Frederick Charles after the recapture of Orleans and of Manteuffel after the battle of Amiens, Moltke concluded that a somewhat different strategy must be pursued. The circumference of the circle around Paris, from which an advance to threaten the investment might come at any point, was enormous. It could not possibly be covered by an extended line of German troops holding, or even watching, every key point. It would be very much easier, and more effective to keep the covering forces concentrated, as Moltke had already indicated to Manteuffel. On December 17 he despatched to each of Frederick Charles and Manteuffel the letter previously referred to, which set out the strategy that was in future to be followed. For the First Army, Beauvais was prescribed as the central point, with Rouen, Amiens and St Quentin being held; Moltke also made clear that it was unnecessary for Dieppe to be held.[15]

At Amiens Manteuffel was in little doubt that the spirit of Moltke's orders justified an assault on the Army of the North in the position it had taken up on the Hallue. To strengthen the available forces, Manteuffel could have recourse only to the I Corps, which had its hands full watching a long line from which Briand's forces made no significant forward move, but along which they were constantly active. Nonetheless, as Wartensleben noted, 'the momentary state of affairs at Amiens and the tenor of the instructions of December 17 justified the determination, already formed on December 21, to reinforce the troops at Amiens by bringing up six battalions per rail from Amiens.'[16] This would leave Bentheim with only thirteen battalions to watch the line of the Seine; now that he no longer had to operate on the left bank of the river, this would probably suffice, although if he was forced to retreat, he was to fall back on Beauvais rather than Paris. From the east, the 3rd Reserve Division (Schuler von Senden) was on its way to reinforce the First Army; Manteuffel had hoped that he would be allowed the 14th Division, but Moltke decreed that this should remain to besiege Mézières.

Mauteuffel had a pretty clear idea of Faidherbe's dispositions at the southern end of his line, not least after a sharp encounter at Querrieux, on the west of the Hallue, on December 20, when a battalion strength reconnaissance in force encountered stiff resistance from a French force of some four battalions. He was less well informed, however, about the northern end of the French position, and this was to cause him considerable difficulty. The decision to launch an assault was taken at a meeting on the morning of December 22, to which Manteuffel called Goeben, Sperling and Wartensleben. The possibility of standing passively on the defensive at Amiens was thoroughly explored, but it was concluded that to do so would lift French morale and depress that of the German troops. Leaving the French time to organise and launch further attacks could not be wise, and might have a knock-on effect on the Seine. Nor was it wise even to await the arrival of the 3rd Reserve Division; the detachment of six battalions from the Seine should be for as short a time as possible. Looking at the French position, the meeting reached the same conclusion as Faidherbe; any attack from the south across the Somme would be attended with great difficulty. To move along the river to the east, hoping to pick up the 3rd Reserve Division on the way, offered possibilities but meant again abandoning Amiens for the time being; and after much discussion it was agreed that the best plan would be to attack the position on the Hallue, holding Faidherbe in front with the 15th Division while the 16th Division executed a left hook around his northern flank.[17] Faidherbe had posted his better corps, the 22nd Corps, in the front line, with Derroja's division in position between Vadencourt and Belencourt, and du Bessol's division holding the rest of the line down to the Somme at Daours. The 23rd Corps was posted in close reserve, with Robin's division to the east of Belencourt and Admiral Moulac's division around Corbie. Faidherbe's total strength was of the order of 43,000 men, with 82 guns, so that on paper he outnumbered Manteuffel by more than two to one.[18]

It was a cold clear frosty morning on December 23 as the leading troops of Kummer's 15th division filed over the Somme bridges at La Neuville and Camor. Their mission was to drive the French back over the Hallue, and to get a firm footing on the eastern side of the river, and then to wait until the effect of Barnekow's turning movement was felt. The most advanced French posts had fallen back to Querrieux, so no opposition was encountered until Bock's 29th Brigade, leading the advance up the Albert road, had reached the eastern edge of the Querrieux wood, where the infantry came under fire from French troops in and around the village and from artillery on the other side of the Hallue. By 11.15 the German artillery was in action; by noon Bock judged that there had been sufficient preparation, and launched two battalions in an assault on Querrieux. It was imme-

The French assault on Pont Noyelles, by Pallandre (Rousset/*Combattants*)

diately successful; following up the retreating enemy, one battalion of the 65th Regiment crossed the Hallue and seized Pont Noyelles, taking a large number of prisoners. Stung by this, the French artillery opened a heavy fire on Pont Noyelles, which Bock at once reinforced by a battalion of the 33rd Regiment.

Meanwhile to the south, another battalion of the 65th Regiment advanced on Bussy les Daours, which was also assaulted from its southern edge by the 1st Battalion of the East Prussian Fusiliers; the defenders of Bussy speedily retreated over the Hallue, and by 1.00 pm the place was in German hands. Still further south, however, a better struggle was developing for the possession of Daours. On the direct road from Amiens to Corbie, Daours marked the southern end of Faidherbe's position; the bridge here had not been destroyed by the French, and its defenders had early that morning been reinforced by marines from Moulac's division. The attackers were led by Colonel von Löe, the commander of the 7th Hussars, who brought up the 8th Rifle Battalion from south of the river to join troops from the 33rd and 65th Regiments that had moved down from Bussy. By 1pm Goeben was becoming anxious about the lack of progress at Daours, and sent Colonel Witzendorff, his chief of staff, to Manteuffel to seek reinforcements. To provide these Manteuffel could choose between his general reserve, consisting of the 3rd Brigade under Mirus, which might be needed further north; and the group of battalions still in course of arriving from Rouen which had been ordered to concentrate by the river crossing at La Motte-Brebière. The latter troops were nearest; but since their commander, moving with the last of the battalions coming up from Rouen, was not yet on the Seine, Manteuffel ordered one of his staff officers, Major von Lewinski, to lead the two battalions already arrived to Vecquement and join the assault on Daours. This move soon brought success; between 3 and 4.00 pm Lewinski and Löe, after a fierce house to house struggle, finally took the village. Even then the French were able to keep the place under a constant fire from the heights immediately north of the village, so at 4.40 pm Lewinski attempted to advance out of Daours to clear the enemy from the hills, but the position was too strong and he fell back into the village.[19]

Meanwhile at Port Noyelles the fighting had increased in intensity, the French massing on the hills above the village; to drive them back, at about 3.30pm an assault was led by Lieutenant Colonel Henning with one and a half battalions, which initially gained a footing on the heights before being obliged to retreat in the force of heavy French reinforcements. This attack had been launched in the belief that the 30th Brigade, which Kummer had moved up the road to Querrieux, was to launch an attack on the northern slope of the heights above Pont Noyelles. However, as the leading troops of the 28th Regiment emerged from Querrieux on the Fréchencourt road, they were met with such heavy fire from the direction of Fréchencourt itself that they were obliged to turn towards the enemy there. This was a strong force descending from the hills with the aim of taking the village. Strübberg, with the 68th Regiment, coming up close behind, at once advanced at the run towards Fréchencourt, and succeeded in occupying the village after a brief struggle. Although able to repulse an immediate and heavy French counter attack, Strübberg was unable to make any impression on the French defences on the heights about the village, so much the same position now obtained there as at Pont Noyelles and Daours.

While the 15th Division was thus engaged in its holding attack on Faidherbe's front, for a long time nothing had been heard from Barnekow and the 16th Division. The 32nd Brigade (von Rex) had marched out of Amiens on the Rainneville road and the 31st Brigade (von Gneisenau) on the road to Poulainville. Making good progress as the morning wore on, Barnekow's leading troops had reached the vicinity of Renbeupre from which point their orders were to turn towards the French line and move on Beaucourt and Contay. This brought them not upon Faidherbe's flank, but directly into a frontal assault upon Derroja's division. Barnekow directed the 32nd Brigade on Beaucourt and the 31st Brigade on St Gratien. At St Gratien, Dohna, with six squadrons from the 3rd Cavalry Division, had been observing the French. As Gneisenau's troops moved forward, Dohna's horse artillery engaged in a brisk duel with the French artillery on the heights opposite. Dohna had, however, failed to locate the extreme northern end of Faidherbe's position and Gneisenau, in accordance with the orders received from corps headquarters, pushed forward towards Montigny. Here the leading troops of the brigade ran into stiff opposition from a large enemy force pushed forward from Behancourt. Although Gneisenau's men soon drove the enemy back into that village they were for the moment unable to pursue them, the bridges over the Hallue there having been broken. Under heavy rifle fire, the fusilier battalion of the 29th Regiment threw foot bridges over the river, and with the support of elements of Rex's brigade which came up at about 4.00 pm, succeeded in taking Behencourt. As had been the case to the south, however, Barnekow could make no impression on the heights above.[20]

By now Goeben and Manteuffel were together on the windmill hill at Querrieux. It was clear to them that the outflanking movement had failed; indeed, since the French line continued beyond Contay and Vadencourt, Faidherbe was in a position to outflank the Germans, if he had been minded to launch a major assault from these positions. On the other hand, the line of the Hallue itself was now firmly held, and any French advance on Amiens frustrated, not that Faidherbe had entertained any serious intention of marching on the city. For the moment, therefore, it was necessary only for the First Army to maintain its position. However, just as it seemed the fighting was over, the French suddenly launched a series of major assaults. By now, their artillery had set all the villages along the Hallue ablaze, giving them an excellent target. The first attack was launched between Daours and Querrieux; with horns blaring, the cheering French infantry stormed forward in an advance that was sufficiently threatening to cause Manteuffel to commit a battalion for the reserve to meet it. As darkness fell, another assault, on Daours itself, was beaten off by Löe and Lewinski only after it had got to within thirty yards of the village. At Pont Noyelles another assault was repulsed with the aid of two more battalions from the reserve, the 29th Brigade having run out of ammunition. Another assault, on Fréchencourt, was also kept at bay by the 30th Brigade. The defeat of the French attacks was complete by 6.00 pm. Manteuffel ordered his troops to dig in and around the villages they held which for the most part gave some cover for the night, a luxury that the French, out in the open in their positions along the hills, were not able to enjoy. To Faidherbe, for his troops to be able to remain their positions was important; 'it made them understand that in war sleeping on the battlefield established the victory.'[21] No doubt it was worth it, but the price of a night in the open in 7 or 8 degrees of frost was a heavy one to pay. And in truth, neither side could claim any clear tactical victory; for both, the expectation was that the renewal of fighting next day would decide the outcome.

Both sides expected the other to open the proceedings on December 24 by a further assault but in the event, apart from some desultory exchanges of artillery fire, and an abortive French advance from Contay, there was little activity. For the Germans, this was certainly not a matter for regret; an icy north east wind blew in their faces all day. As the afternoon wore on, Manteuffel received more and more reports which seemed to indicate that the French were preparing to retreat. For Christmas Day, therefore, he planned that if indeed Faidherbe did retreat, Goeben should closely pursue him; if on the other hand Faidherbe maintained his position on the heights along the Hallue valley, Manteuffel proposed to attack his flank and rear through Corbie, a move that would require the hazardous crossing of the Somme that had previously been rejected. Mirus was ordered to take the reserve south of the Somme and to be prepared to attack Corbie at dawn next day under the heaviest possible artillery barrage. He would be followed if necessary by one division of the VIII Corps. As night fell, however, the signs that the French were pulling out became overwhelming; Witzendorff, who had gone forward to Daours to reconnoitre, reported emphatically that the French were in retreat.

Next day, so it proved. Faidherbe's troops had abandoned their positions, and retired so quickly that by dawn on Christmas Day they had completely disappeared. Goeben pushed the 15th Division up the road in pursuit as far as Albert, but no contact with the retreating enemy was made, although several hundred stragglers were picked up; it was not even clear whether the French had fallen back on Arras or Cambrai, and for the moment Goeben moved forward on a broad front to Bapaume, Achiet le Grand and Bucquoy, in a limited advance that was in accordance with Moltke's instructions of December 15. Tactically, the battle had been drawn; but in a strategic sense Wartensleben was right in claiming it as a victory:

> the primary object which the Prussian leaders had in view in the battle of the Hallue was to secure their position of Amiens, and to dislodge the enemy from positions which he occupied in dangerous proximity to the town, thereby at the same time fulfilling the task assigned to the First Army, viz. the protection of the rear of the Army of the Meuse. Both objects were achieved in every sense of the word.[22]

Faidherbe estimated his losses at 141 killed and 905 wounded, several hundred prisoners and another thousand missing. This was certainly an underestimate; the Germans buried some 291 French dead on the battlefield, and took 1120 unwounded prisoners. Their own losses were 157 killed, 691 wounded and 52 missing. It had been a tough battle, leaving Manteuffel and Goeben in no doubt that in Faidherbe they faced a formidable enemy, of whom they had certainly not seen the last.

20

Moltke at Versailles

The location of the Royal Headquarters at Versailles had been necessitated by the requirement for sufficient facilities not only for Moltke and his staff, but also for the King and his entourage, as well as for Bismarck and the considerable administrative team that he brought with him. In addition there were the very many royal personages and their hangers on who felt it necessary to follow the King wherever he went. Although it was perhaps rather closer to the lines of investment than would have been ideal, and being to the west of Paris, made direct communication with Germany somewhat more difficult, Versailles did possess the necessary accommodation. It had originally been the first choice for the headquarters of the Third Army, which remained there; Blumenthal continued to note querulously in his diary the undesirable effect of the proximity of the Royal Headquarters to his own. The alternative site which had been considered, St Germain en Laye, would have been roughly equidistant from the respective sectors of the Third Army and the Army of the Meuse; but it was even further to the west, and almost as close to the lines of investment, while providing rather less suitable accommodation.

Their immediate surroundings were certainly agreeable to Moltke's staff; Verdy noted that 'Versailles is sometimes called the Parisian Potsdam, a comparison which is in many respects not inappropriate. Its propinquity to the capital, its

A German conference of commanders at Versailles, painting by von Werner (Scheibert)

palaces, its parks with their fountains, the villa-like character of a part of the town, make such a comparison plausible in many respects.'[1] But notwithstanding the quality of the amenities Moltke and his staff were obliged to work in a perpetually stressful atmosphere, as a result both of the close proximity of so much of Prussia's government and Germany's court life, as well as the steady build up of foreign representatives, military correspondence and casual visitors. Moltke was fighting a war that made enormous military and logistical demands on the resources at his disposal, and he wished only to be allowed to get on with the job without disturbance. But the King must, in the Prussian scheme of things, be at the Royal Headquarters and where he went Bismarck must also go; and behind them must follow all the rest of the huge retinues that moved into Versailles. With them they brought pressures to which even the imperturbable Moltke was sometimes not immune; and the longer the war went on the more volatile became the personal relationships of those working in such a hot house atmosphere. Given their huge responsibilities and the intricate nature of the problems which they had to face, it is no surprise that Moltke and Bismarck and their respective staff should become increasingly anxious and irritable.

Potentially serious difficulties arising from both policy and personalities were, as always, exacerbated by practical problems. As early as October 13 the Crown Prince was noting:

> Generals von Moltke and von Roon on the one side, Count Bismarck on the other, are often at loggerheads, the gist of their mutual reproaches being that the departments are kept separated by too hard and fast a line and not enough reciprocal interchange of information practised.[2]

Moltke was surrounded by a fiercely protective staff, who were always suspicious of civilian influences in general and that of Bismarck in particular. Some of them began early on to make insulting remarks about the Chancellor, and not only in conversation among themselves; their dislike was warmly reciprocated by Bismarck, who suspected them of intriguing against him on various questions and in particular over the issue of the bombardment of Paris. He expressed his feelings on the subject with characteristic intemperance in a letter to his wife on November 12.

> The plot, if it exists, has ramifications in the general staff, whom I don't like on the whole, with the exception of good old sensible Moltke. They are mad with imperialism; the success has affected them in their heads, and I am often afraid that this presumptuous self-conceit will be visited upon us. Some of them conceal themselves behind Moltke's name, for he is old and lets things pass. The regiments it was who pulled us through – not the generals.[3]

To his staff Moltke remained entirely unaffected by the ceaseless pressure. Writing a few weeks before the end of the fighting, Verdy expressed the devotion they all felt for him.

> Concerning Moltke, he lives entirely with his staff, and is as kind as ever to every one of us. No one has ever heard a single harsh word from him during the whole campaign. With us he is even merry, in his simple cheerful and modest way. We all feel happy in his company, and absolutely love and worship him. But outside

Lt Col Paul Bronsart von Schellendorf, Department Head in the German General Staff, and key member of Moltke's circle (a post-war photograph, from the collection of Duncan Rogers)

> of our small circle, also, there is only one feeling, and that is admiration towards him; everyone says that he is a truly ideal character.[4]

Moltke's routine soon became well established. The most important fixed point of his day was the regular conference with the King, attended also by Roon and Podbielski: the King was accompanied by Boyen and Tresckow, while the Crown Prince would also from time to time be in attendance.[5] Moltke lived in the same building in which were housed all the officers of his staff; from the moment he arrived at Versailles until the war's end there was no rest from his ceaseless work, and the only breaks came when he chose to go out to the lines of investment to see for himself the French positions or to witness the repulse of a French sortie. At 6.30pm Moltke would lead his staff over to the Hotel des Reservoirs, where a mess had been established, and where the great and the good regularly dined. There, he was always the centre of attention, as Verdy noted:

> As soon as Moltke enters at our head, walking rapidly to our table in the rear of the hall, the hum of conversation stops, everyone rising to salute him respectfully; even the numerous dogs belonging to officers stay their noisy game of chasing one another, astonished by the sudden silence, and eye us attentively.[6]

Dinner would often be punctuated by the arrival of telegrams;

> Then there is always a certain hush in the hall, everybody watches the generals and whichever of us opens the despatch and reads it out to them in an under-

General von Podbielski, Quartermaster General of the German armies (Rousset/*Histoire*)

> tone; everyone wishes to discover from our faces what impression the telegram is producing. But not much is to be gained in this way, they never alter, whatever may be the news.[7]

Then, after dinner, his solicitous staff would ensure that Moltke could indulge his favourite pastime and sit down in his study for a game of whist.

Throughout the seemingly unending winter of the struggle against the Government of National Defence, even in the unfamiliar environment of a People's War, Moltke continued to bring his calm and rigorously intellectual approach to the military problems confronting him. Bismarck, for his part, faced a set of enormously intricate diplomatic and political problems in which he was convinced that time was not on his side, and as the war dragged on his impatience grew and his sympathy with the military point of view drained away. Like Moltke, Bismarck was surrounded by a devoted staff, who also kept personal diaries and records of their time at Versailles. Unlike the General Staff, however, they were provided with plenty of copy: Bismarck was as voluble as Moltke was taciturn and his table talk was a good deal more entertaining. As the weeks went by, Bismarck expressed himself extremely forcefully on a wide range of subjects. In one respect his views accorded with those of the military: he preferred to see those Princes

> who loaf around here at Pückler's expense, and who are mere spectators of the man hunt, anywhere rather than at headquarters. It is all the more unpleasant to me to have them here, as they storm me with questions and force wise counsels

> upon me respecting matters that are in course of development and which are now being worked out.

And later he dismissed the royal tourists as being 'like a flight of vultures'.[8] But it was, of course, the issue of the bombardment of Paris that was most divisive. Military prudence had led Moltke to order the assembly of siege artillery and ammunition soon after the investment began; but the work proceeded slowly and Moltke, who never had much faith that bombardment was likely to be effective, and who absolutely set his mind against an infantry assault on the French lines, remained sure that starvation was the most effective weapon to bring about the city's surrender. Indeed, he had been hopeful that this would happen when the inhabitants ran out of fresh milk; disappointed in this, he still remained determined not to waste the lives of his men in a pointless assault.

And without an assault, a bombardment would by itself be fruitless. It was certainly true in any case that there were substantial difficulties to be overcome before any bombardment could take place. Villacoublay, where the siege park was established, was eleven miles from Nanteuil sur Marne, the nearest railhead to which the guns, equipment and ammunition could be delivered. Although an extension of the line to Cholles was completed by November 23, by then the bulk of the ammunition had been unloaded at Nanteuil. An additional factor which delayed progress in collecting the ammunition at Villacoublay was the priority on which Stosch insisted for the movement of supplies. Part of the road journey was itself very difficult, and the round trip took a wagon eight days, even in good weather conditions; snow and ice sometimes prolonged the journey considerably. The amount of materiel required was enormous; a minimum of 250 guns was regarded as essential for a bombardment, with 500 rounds per gun. Apart from the transport required to move the guns themselves, it was estimated that a total of 5000 wagon loads of ammunition and supplies would be required. The task of requisitioning the necessary transport was assigned to the Third Army, but in spite of considerable efforts the results were disappointing. The added burden of this responsibility did little to improve Blumenthal's temper, nor did it soften his view about the usefulness of the whole exercise. By the end of October, 235 guns had arrived, and the stockpile inexorably grew at the bottleneck of Nanteuil. Work had, however, begun on the preparation of siege batteries on the heights of Meudon, Clermont and Moulin de la Tour.[9]

Writing in December, Verdy put the General Staff case. Acknowledging that siege artillery was being concentrated for a good reason, he limited its use to silencing some forts and perhaps also a

> possibility of pushing forward a few batteries near enough, if not for a regular bombardment, at least to harass some limited part of the town. But in the beginning of an investment the latter proceeding would be useless. That we have seen plainly enough by the utterly fruitless bombardments of Strasbourg, Thionville, Montmèdy and Toul, which have taught us a lesson in this respect .... It will only be when the hope of relief from the provinces vanishes that a bombardment may possibly produce an effect; that moment will arrive, I should think, soon after the New Year.[10]

Prussian officers outside a camp hut ingeniously constructed from the remains of a French balloon, 1870 (Rousset/*Histoire*)

Bismarck's view was absolutely to the contrary. As early as September, in an early example of the art of political spin doctoring, he had been promoting articles by Moritz Busch for the press, refuting the suggestion that to bombard Paris would be a crime against civilisation with the argument that Paris was a fortress and that its character was not changed by filling it with art treasures or beautiful buildings. As time went by, and no progress was made with preparations for a bombardment, his after dinner outbursts on the subject became more strident. He was especially annoyed on November 4 that some sections of the Berlin press held him responsible for the delay.

> Nonsense! They will ultimately make me responsible for our losses during the siege, which are certainly already considerable, as we have probably lost more men in these small engagements than a general attack would have cost us. I wanted the city to be stormed at once, and have all along desired that to be done – or it would have been still better to have left Paris on one side and continued our march.[11]

Warming to his theme a few days later, he complained that a great deal of his time was taken up 'in dispelling the scruples and excessive circumspection of the military people. It appears that the artillery are constantly requiring more time for preparation and particularly a larger supply of ammunition.'[12]

Bismarck continued to press his views on the subject, which cropped up regularly at his dinner table. On November 19, he said: 'I told the King again yesterday that it was time to begin, and he had no objection to make. He replied that he had given orders to begin, but that the generals said they could not. I know exactly how it is. It is Stosch, Tresckow, and Podbielski.' When asked about Hindersin's views, Bismarck said that he too was against it, but that he thought Podbielski could be brought round. The others, he hinted, were influenced by thoughts of their own future when the Crown Prince became King; he saw Queen Victoria at the back of the opposition to bombardment, her influence being wielded through the Crown Princess, her daughter.[13] However, although in this he was almost alone among senior military figures, Roon supported Bismarck over the issue, as he had done from the outset; but as Bismarck told his wife, 'good old Roon is quite ill with vexation at our passive attitude and his waning attempts to bring us to attack; resignation has now made him better, but still no one can speak of the matter for he then becomes ill with bitterness.'[14]

Bismarck had two principal concerns. The first was to bring about peace on terms acceptable to Prussia and her German allies with as little delay as possible, in order to eliminate the possibility of foreign intervention. Secondly, he had to bring to a successful conclusion the tortuous negotiations with the southern states in order to complete the unification of Germany. Now, if ever, was the moment to do this; the German successes in the war meant that German public opinion was extremely favourable and Bismarck was determined to strike while the iron was hot. But it was the fear of interference that particularly fuelled his desire for a speedy end to the war, and hence his demands for the bombardment became increasingly aggressive, repeatedly emphasising the effect elsewhere.

> Here we have now collected this enormous mass of siege artillery. The whole world is waiting for us to begin, and yet the guns remain idle up to the present. That has certainly damaged us with the neutral Powers. The effect of our success at Sedan is very seriously diminished thereby, and when one thinks on what grounds'[15]

His military opponents were unimpressed, as Blumenthal noted on November 30:

> A written communication addressed by Bismarck to the King has just been communicated to the Crown Prince. It says that a bombardment of the forts has become a political necessity, as otherwise the neutrals will take it as a sign of weakness, and so create difficulties. He presses his point with Bismarckian energy, but his arguments are not conclusive.[16]

Inevitably the Berlin press soon picked up the rumours of disputes at the Royal Headquarters. Abeken, who was always anxious to play down stories of this kind, wrote somewhat disingenuously to his wife on October 31:

> Don't believe what the papers say about differences between Moltke and Bismarck in regard to peace and the way of obtaining it. It is absolutely untrue that Bismarck, for diplomatic reasons, and the King for the sake of humanity, have been opposed to the bombardment ... Divers people here think there is no need to bombard, and that, with patience everything will be accomplished without it, but the King and Bismarck belong to this set as little as I do.[17]

Speculation in the newspapers continued; on November 17 Verdy noted that they were now predicting that the bombardment would begin on November 25, but commented only that it would begin when they were ready, which was not yet the case.

Bismarck's memorandum to the King had followed close on the heels of the report which the latter had received from two of his most senior advisers, the Inspectors General of Artillery and Engineers, Hindersin and Kleist; from this he learned to his dismay that the bombardment could not be expected to start before the beginning of January. He passed on Bismarck's submission to Moltke, recording the 'astonishment' with which he had heard some of the things he had been told: 'This delay causes me the most serious anxieties, both from a military point of view and a political point of view.' He concluded with four pointed questions to which he required a response at least orally, on December 1; and the report to be given on that day was to demonstrate the way in which Moltke proposed 'to put in hand at once the work that will show the greatest activity in preparing the attack on the southern forts.'[18]

Moltke, when he sat down on November 30 to write his response to all this, was, beneath his outward calm, extremely angry. He opened with a curt statement which summarised all his feelings about the respective roles of the military and the politicians.

> The date at which the artillery attack on Paris should or can begin can only be decided on the basis of military considerations. Political questions can only be taken into account so far as they do not require anything, which from a military point of view is inadmissible or impossible. It will be inadmissible for politics to demand the commencement of the bombardment before the necessary means for it have been assembled; it will be to ask an impossibility to demand that the necessary material be put in place more quickly.

In a pointed side swipe at those soldiers, including Roon, who sympathised with Bismarck's position, he remarked that those members of the military

> who, following the report of the Federal Chancellor, support these political demands, appear certainly to have forgotten that the government of Paris can for this operation dispose of a large number of railroads, while the leaders of the Prussian Army are at the mercy of a single line, interrupted several times by sabotage and which, until the last few days, ended fourteen or fifteen miles from the siege park.

He attached reports from Colonel Rieff in charge of preparing for the bombardment, and from the Crown Prince, which clearly demonstrated the difficulties of assembling the necessary munitions. Finally, after repeating his view that a bombardment of Paris should be treated as the last resort, and that hunger was the most effective weapon, he added that 'it is not here that the outcome of the war will be decided; it is on the battlefields where we shall beat the fresh armies of the enemy which take the field.'[19]

Moltke's memorandum was handed to the King on December 1, and there, for a few days the matter of the bombardment rested. Bismarck was entirely unimpressed with the explanations for delay, remarking to his staff on the evening of December 1 that he had been told by Roon that he had several hundred carts at Nanteuil that could be used, and that the six horses used to draw wagons could be reduced to four. He also doubted the truth of the army's comments about the number of guns available: 'We have already 318 guns here, but they want forty more and Roon says he could have them also brought up. The others however won't hear of it.'[20]

Bismarck continued to apply pressure by any means open to him; but on December 10 he somewhat overreached himself, as Blumenthal gleefully recorded in his diary:

> As an indication of the determination with which Bismarck is pressing his point in the bombardment question, the following will serve. He is laid up with a bad leg, and so sent the Secretary of Legation, Abeken, to an audience with the King, with instructions to inform His Majesty that the excitement in Berlin on account of the delay in bombardment is so intense that they are in fear of insurrections. The King at once telegraphed to the Governor of Berlin, General von Canstein, to take immediate steps to suppress every sign of disorder and riot. Bismarck had not expected this action on the part of the King, and sent word at once to him, before the telegram had started, that there was some misunderstanding; it was not as bad as all that, but what he meant was that the people were beginning to get impatient of the delay, and moreover military men were calling out for bombardment.[21]

The original message had not surprisingly, made a considerable impression on William. The unfortunate Abeken, who was sent back a third time to retrieve the situation, recorded his experience: 'I went in fear and trembling, for I had been sent off on the second occasion, in the greatest disgrace, at least, the King had retired to his bedroom in great excitement and displeasure ... It was not a pleasant duty.'[22]

It turned out however to be easier than Abeken had anticipated. The King was easily persuaded not to send the embarrassing telegram; Abeken thought perhaps it was as well that he was able to 'act as intermediary, and soften some things, and be silent about others.' Bismarck may perhaps have been cheered up a couple of days later when Busch was able to show him a letter in the London 'Times' of November 18, from Thomas Carlyle, who wrote that Bismarck

> in fact seems to me to be striving with strong faculty, by patient, grand and successful steps, towards an object beneficial to Germany and to all other men. That noble, patient, deep, and solid Germany should at length be welded into a nation and become Queen of the Continent, instead of vapouring, vainglorious, gesticulating, quarrelsome, restless and oversensitive France, seems to me the hopefullest public fact that has occurred in my time.[23]

As the bombardment dispute continued to rage, Bismarck was able to count on the unyielding support of Roon. The latter had been subjected by Moltke to continuous pressure to bring forward further reinforcements from Germany, particularly in a very strong memorandum of December 8, and this further influenced the views of the choleric Roon. After a discussion of the issue in the course of Moltke's daily report to the King on December 11, the War Minister could contain himself no longer, and wrote an angry letter to Moltke on the subject:

> The declarations made by Your Excellency at today's report suggested to me reflections which I did not wish to express at the time, in order to avoid all controversy in His Majesty's presence, but which I am not however able to leave unspoken. Several months ago, Your Excellency issued His Majesty's order as to the bombardment of several forts: the Third Army was charged with its execu-

> tion for this limited objective. At that time Your Excellency did not appear to doubt the possibility of carrying this out. However subsequently the strangely long delay required by the technical services for commencing the attack has become longer and longer.

He went on to observe that if Moltke was relying solely on hunger to end the resistance of the garrison of Paris, the assembly of guns and shells would have been purposeless; and he felt obliged to express his surprise

> at hearing Your Excellency, at today's report, declare that the projected attack was absolutely impracticable and pointless.[24]

Moltke replied next day to set the record straight:

> The bombardment of the Paris forts, their capture and the formal siege of the place has always been considered from the beginning of the investment as a last resort: I have never intended to abandon this project and still today have not lost sight of it. At the request of His Majesty I spoke neither of the impossibility nor the pointlessness of this enterprise: I demonstrated all the difficulties, and that I was resolutely opposed to the idea, which I consider inopportune, that it should be commenced now.

His reasons for opposing it were, Moltke said, too well known to justify setting them out; but he added that reinforcements would in any case be required before any infantry attack could be mounted.[25]

In fact, although he was too annoyed with Roon to say so in his letter, Moltke was turning over in his mind the possibility of some limited artillery operation. Blumenthal, who thought that 'the rage there is for a bombardment is quite laughable,' recorded a conversation with him on December 8, in the course of which Moltke agreed

> that it would be better to apply our heavy artillery to strengthening our positions rather than to commence a bombardment with insufficient ammunition. In order, however, to meet halfway those who press for a bombardment, he is going to put the case to some of the artillerists as to whether a partial cannonading of Paris might not be possible without opening regular parallels. I imagine he overestimates the range of our weapons, and the moral effect that such a cannonading would have.[26]

It was against a background, therefore, of pressure from all sides that a special meeting was convened on December 17, to discuss a proposal for an artillery assault on the Third Army's front. Moltke could at least draw some satisfaction from the fact that this was strictly a military discussion, which Bismarck did not attend. However, the Chancellor's assiduous work on the mind of the King had been very successful, and it was soon evident that William had come to the meeting with a firm view that something must be done to get the bombardment under way. To Blumenthal's disgust, 'certain of the members were willing to compromise when they thought that the King was in favour of bombardment. How seldom it is that men in such circumstances speak their minds truly and honestly, without regard to consequences! I, at least, have always tried to do so.'[27] Roon, of course, was strongly in favour, but most of the rest remained opposed, and Blumenthal observed that 'the War Minister glared at us most angrily and resentfully.' The upshot, however, was that it was agreed that a bombardment of the southern forts should begin as soon as a ten day stockpile of ammunition had been built up. In the meantime, it was also agreed to begin the bombardment of Mont Avron as trial run: this was an operation which had been planned since December 4.[28]

Putting the best possible face on things, the Crown Prince regarded the outcome as a victory for the opponents of bombardment.

> Thank God, the opinion was expressed that we should rest satisfied with a blockade, only the forts to be bombarded. True, this will not do much to alter the present state of things, but in this way we shall be spared the fearful losses that would be involved in a bombardment of the city and the storming of the fortifications that must necessarily go with it.[29]

Bismarck, on the other hand, was delighted, and had no doubt of the reason for the military's reluctant change of heart, writing to his wife on December 24:

> at last there is a prospect of the bombardment of Paris, we hope before New Year. What Roon and myself with months of work could not achieve, the noise of the Berlin newspapers, and the echo of it which the Reichstag brought here has succeeded in bringing about. Even Moltke is said to be converted since he received newspaper poems which point out that his system of action- as if the matter did not concern him- found no mercy in the public opinion.[30]

The question of the bombardment was by no means the only issue which aroused deep personal feelings at Versailles during the long drawn out investment of Paris. The anxiety to miss no opportunity to hasten the war's end led to constant stress between individuals who, as a rule, felt a great deal of professional confidence in each other. Just as Moltke and Roon found themselves deeply at odds over the performance of the War Ministry as well as the bombardment issue, so there were strong words between the Crown Prince and Blumenthal; the latter recorded a sharp exchange on December 2 with the Crown Prince,

> who was very much put out that I had not had him called, as he said he ought to be informed of all orders as soon as they arrive. I said to him that I could not think of waking him for such details; moreover, that it came into my province, and not into his, to issue the subsequent orders ... my position could not be reduced to that of an adjutancy .... he does not grasp the exact relationship in which I stand to him.[31]

And in addition there were strong feelings held by Moltke and his immediate staff about the leadership of the Army of the Meuse by the Crown Prince of Saxony.

As for Bismarck, he might have got his own way, partially at any rate, but he made no secret of his continuing resentment. After dinner on December 19, he sat down beside Blumenthal to lecture him on the question of the military- political dispute, saying that 'War could not be carried on without a consideration of political results, and that politics must play their part in it.' He went on, however to complain bitterly of 'the treatment he was receiving at the hands of the King and of Moltke, who had left him for some time now without any information regarding the course of events; in fact, they had both been quite discourteous, even rude to him.'[32] The King's annoyance with Bismarck had nothing to do with the military situation or the bombardment issue; what was causing him to burn on a short fuse was the growing certainty that, however much he disliked it, he would shortly become Emperor. It was a prospect which thoroughly depressed him. On December 16 the deputation with the address from the Reichstag arrived; the Crown Prince noted that his father's outlook was ' of the blackest.' The painstaking negotiations by Bismarck with the Prussian political leaders and with the south German States, which had finally led to the treaties by which the German Empire was to come into being, had been a further source of continual strain for the Chancellor; but by the end of December the tortuous process was practically complete. What had particularly troubled Bismarck, however, and was the principal cause of his impatience to see the war brought to an end, was the unsettled international situation, which he feared increased the risk of foreign intervention. The Russian démarche of October 29, denouncing the Black Sea clauses of the Treaty of Paris of 1856, had been well timed. Russia's two principal adversaries in the Crimean War were not in a good position to do much about it, France because she was in the grip of a war for her existence and Britain because she had no effective continental allies on which she could count. Nonetheless Lord Granville made an effort to assert Britain's power, seeking Bismarck's support for an effort to persuade Russia to retract, and warning that if this did not happen, Britain would have to go to war over the issue. That was the last thing that Bismarck wanted, and he put forward the suggestion of a conference, to which he agreed that France might send a representative; after some prolonged negotiation the conference was fixed for January 3.

Bismarck's impatience was understandable; but in truth the war could not yet be said to have been a long one, as Moltke pointed out in a letter to his brother on December 22.

> The general desire for the conclusion of this dreadful war makes our people at home forget that it is only five months since it began. Everything is expected from a bombardment of Paris; and that this has not already been proceeded with is ascribed to considerations of delicacy for the Parisians or to the influence of some high personages, whereas as a matter of fact, all that is really kept in view here is military practicability and possibility.

And he reiterated his confidence in his own troops.

> Of course we assume that we shall conquer in the field of battle all the armies which continue to be raised against us. Only the terrorism of the lawyer government makes it possible to provide such armies; they send them out to face the rough weather badly organised and without proper means of transport, without even ambulances or surgeons. These unfortunates, with all their bravery and all their patriotism, are quite unable to withstand our well drilled troops.[33]

21

Le Bourget and Mont Avron

In spite of the failure of the great sortie towards the south east, Trochu had not abandoned his efforts to force a way through the German lines of investment. His aim remained to link hands with one or more of the armies raised by Gambetta; the defeat sustained by the Army of the Loire at Orleans meant that, for the moment at any rate, co-operation from that quarter was unlikely. With the morale of his troops remaining reasonably high, Trochu began to make plans for another attempt, this time in a northerly direction. The recent activity of Faidherbe suggested that this might be the most promising opportunity. The sector chosen for the advance was, once more, that of Le Bourget. The intention was to advance on the village from both the west, from St Denis, and from the south east, from Bondy. In preparation for the assault. earthworks were begun as early as December 13 between Bondy and Corneuve; the position at Mont Avron was fortified and crowned with batteries, while the artillery of the northern forts was reinforced.

These activities had of course not gone unnoticed. The investing armies had by now developed a thorough and reliable intelligence gathering operation that meant that no major operation could be undertaken by Trochu with any element of surprise at all. French security was, in any case, extremely poor. Labouchère, observing on December 20 the preparations for the latest offensive, noted that the French made little attempt to conceal their intentions.

> If the Prussians do not know when we are about to attack, they cannot complain that it is our fault. The "Après vous, Messieurs les Anglais," still forms the chivalrous but somewhat naïf tactics of the Gauls. On Sunday, as a first step to military operations, the gates of the city were closed to all those unprovided with passes. On Monday a grand council of generals and admirals took place at the Palais Royal. Yesterday and all last night drums were beating, trumpets were blowing, and troops were marching through the streets. The war battalions of the National Guard, in their new uniforms, spick and span, were greeted with shouts, to which they replied by singing a song.[1]

Public optimism within the city was high; a message from Gambetta had been published on December 18 announcing that 'The Prussian retreat is a movement about which there can be no mistake', and claiming that they had suffered 'enormous losses' and were experiencing extreme supply difficulties. Enthusiastic leader writers in the newspapers called for immediate action, and it was just as well that Trochu had already put in hand his plans for the northern offensive. On December 18 he published one of his familiar personal addresses to the army. Praising the 'heroic sacrifices' and 'indomitable energy of the resistance' of the Army of the Loire, he went on:

> May these noble encouragements sustain you! May the grand spectacle of the citizens of Paris-soldiers like new, fighting with you in the close union of peril and danger- elevate you to the height of every duty and every danger! May your General infuse into your souls the hopes, the sentiments, and the firm resolutions with which his own is filled![2]

On the left the attack from the west was to be made by the corps under Admiral de la Roncière; the follow up attack from the right was to be undertaken by the 2nd Army under Ducrot's command, which was not to advance until Le Bourget was in French hands, and then move on Le Blanc Mesnil and Aulnay. Ninety rounds of ammunition were issued to each infantryman, with six days rations. The attack, originally planned for December 19, was postponed until December 21: the postponement enabled the Prussians to pinpoint its target with even greater accuracy, as deserters came in with news of the planned sortie. On the morning of December 21, the 2nd Guard Division stood to in the tolerably certain knowledge that the attack would come that day. Preparations were made for an immediate counter punch. Six battalions of infantry, with seven batteries, were assembled at Gonesse; six more battalions of Saxon troops, with six batteries, stood at Sevran. Le Bourget itself, where the defensive positions had been greatly strengthened since Bellemare's abortive offensive in October, was held by the 1st battalion of the 3rd Grenadier Regiment, with a company of Guard Jägers, under the command of Captain von Altrock.[3]

After a preliminary barrage of thirty minutes, opening at 7.45 am, the first wave of de la Roncière's troops advanced on the cemetery of Le Bourget, where they were held up by the effective rifle fire of the Guards infantry posted there. On the left, however, a marine detachment got into the northern end of the village, and advanced on the church, taking the defenders in the rear and driving them back into the southern part of the village. Pushing on, the marines attacked the glass factory but were beaten back by a company of guardsmen there; seven battalions of Ducrot's troops had been sent forward up the main road in support, and now attacked the glass factory from the south east; but these assaults were also thrown back both here and at the railway station. Another five battalions, advancing from St Denis, also failed to break into the village. Altrock's men had been fighting against extremely heavy odds for three quarters of an hour before the first reinforcements came up, but at 9.00 am these began to arrive from Le Blanc Mesnil and Pont Iblon, and a bitter house to house struggle began. By 11.30 the last of the French attackers had been driven out of the village; and the fifteen companies of the Guards that were now in Le Bourget took up position to resist the further assault which was regarded as inevitable.[4]

The German artillery had come into action as soon as the French assault commenced, inflicting heavy losses on the enemy infantry advancing over the open plain around Le Bourget. The French artillery replied vigorously; it seemed to Archibald Forbes that 'the French fire was quite furious, half a dozen guns flashing out at once; but it seemed wild. The German was regular as the beats of the pendulum of a clock.'[5]

The assault had been supported by an armoured mitrailleuse train, but although moved rapidly back and forth its fire had little effect. With the defeat of the infantry assault the French concentrated on trying to reduce Le Bourget by artillery alone; but by mid morning the German gun line on either side of the main road behind Le Bourget was gaining the upper hand. In its search for fresh targets, it now turned on the main body of Ducrot's infantry, still waiting in their jumping off positions for the signal to advance. By noon it was apparent to the dispirited Trochu that the attack on Le Bourget had completely failed, and he ordered Ducrot to give up all thought of his advance on that day.

The battle had been fought in conditions of the most bitter cold; the hapless French infantry, who had been ordered to remain the positions taken up after their retreat, with a view to embarking on regular siege operations against Le Bourget, were obliged to spend the night in the most appalling state. D'Herisson, in attendance on Trochu throughout the day, described their suffering and the inevitable effect on morale.

> The night was terrible; I do not ever remember having been so cold as I was during the rides I was obliged to take that night. The men were literally frozen in the ditches and hastily dug trenches, in the huts and houses open to every wind. The cold sent them to sleep, and very many of them never awoke again. For the first time I heard men say openly that night, "We have had enough of this."[6]

Resilient though the Army of Paris had been despite its earlier defeats, the destruction of the high hopes with which this battle had begun had inflicted irreversible damage to morale. Casualties at Le Bourget had been considerable, although not excessively so – the German losses were about 400, while French losses totalled 983; it was the numbing disappointment of the complete failure that broke their spirit. And, of course, the abominable cold; out in the open some 900 cases of frostbite were reported.

It was December 24 before Trochu, very mindful of the response of the Paris population to news of the defeat, finally abandoned the pretence of conducting siege operations against Le Bourget. In the frozen ground and under the remorseless fire of the German artillery, it was an entirely pointless public relations exercise. Meanwhile further setbacks had been experienced by Vinoy, whose troops had launched a diversionary attack on December 21 to the east. At first all had gone well; driving back the Saxon outposts, his leading troops had by noon taken Ville Evraut and Maison Blanche, whose defenders fell back to prepared positions at Le Chenay. When the Saxon counter attack went in that night it soon retook the farmstead of Maison Blanche; at Ville Evraut the difficulty of controlling the night attack led to it being broken off until the next day, and the Saxon withdrew with some 600 prisoners. On December 22 heavy artillery fire sufficed to drive the French occupants out of Ville Evraut, and the Saxons took up their previous positions.[7]

With the morale of their army thus at rock bottom, and with supplies dwindling to the point where, if nothing happened to raise the investment the end could not be indefinitely delayed, the population of Paris prepared for a cheerless Christmas. A balloon message to Tours warned Gambetta that the food would finally run out by January 20. The bitter cold continued, and the Government authorised the cutting down of six acres of timber in the Bois de Boulogne for firewood as well as trees on the streets themselves; there was however a good deal of

French Fusilier Marines at Le Bourget, painting by Couturier (Rousset/*Histoire*)

unauthorised woodcutting as well, and observers felt a growing sense that official control of the situation was paper thin. Trochu and Ducrot had declined considerably in popular esteem; the Governor, it was thought, was 'not the right man in the right place. He is a respectable literary man, utterly unfit to cope with the situation ... The officers all swear by Vinoy, and hold the military capacity of Trochu and Ducrot very cheap.'[8]

At Versailles, Moltke and his staff had been unmoved by the assault on Le Bourget; Verdy noted that 'yesterday's sortie was repulsed successfully at all points, and what is more, apparently without any great loss on our side. Only we are not quite certain whether the French have not a yet greater sortie in view for today or tomorrow; for what they did yesterday was not energetic enough.'[9] Verdy could thus devote some attention to his own preparations for Christmas, which were a good deal more lavish than those of the enemy. On Christmas evening he entertained the staff in his own apartments, where 'so many gifts have come for us all, and especially for myself, that the boxes piled up in the ante-room of our office scarcely leave room to pass ... Cigars, various wines, caviar and preserves have arrived in plenty.' His soirée was a great success; Moltke, one of his guests, relaxed for once and asked him why he did not entertain more often, remarking that 'it does one a world of good, after all, to rest for once from all business.'[10]

The business which immediately concerned Moltke and his staff was the planned artillery assault on Mont Avron.Overall responsibility for the artillery attack on Paris, for which this was a useful trial run, had been entrusted on December 23 to Kameke, in charge of engineering operations, and Hohenlohe, the Guard artillery commander who was to take overall charge of the artillery. On the front of the Third Army, Rieff remained as the commander of the siege artillery and Schulz was in command of the engineers, while on the northern front Colonels Bartsch and Oppermann were their opposite numbers. Blumenthal received the news of the new appointments with some anxiety:

> So we are again to have new brooms and new oars. Who knows that I shall not now be turned out? In spite of all intrigues, they will not find it easy to do so. I have a good conscience, and feel that I have not only done my duty thoroughly, but that I have recognised such things as were necessary here.[11]

The attack on Mont Avron was therefore under Bartsch's immediate command. For this operation he had seventy six guns; two groups of these were on the plateaux of Raincy and Montfermeil, while two were on the slopes of the left bank of the Marne at Noisy le Grand. In addition Bartsch had sixty mortars.

Hindersin, the Inspector General of Artillery, had from the outset been a passionate advocate of bombardment as a means of reducing Paris. The dour Hindersin carried a lot of weight at Royal Headquarters; he was devoted to William, who respected him enormously for the huge improvement in the German artillery that he had achieved since being appointed Inspector General of artillery in 1864. This was just after he had successfully commanded the artillery in the siege of Düppel, in which the most important of the key lessons learned, on which the reform of the Prussian artillery was based, was the need to introduce rifled guns. Although Hindersin's first concern had been the improvement of the field artillery he had turned his attention to the development of the siege artillery, introducing annual exercises. Hohenlohe, who devoted a chapter of his 'Letters on Artillery' to Hindersin, recording the enormous complexity of his task, had the deepest admiration for him, in spite of his daunting personality. 'He was peppery and very violent, and his hot temper was increased by his impatience to get things done.' But there was no doubt that it was Hindersin who had forced through the necessary reforms that had made the Prussian artillery the most effective in the world, and a decisive influence on the outcome of the war of 1870–71. 'Hindersin led the transformation and directed it; he brought – and this was the principal point – all the many and frequently very divergent ideas on the subject to one conclusion, and it was he who hastened the matter … It was he who forged and sharpened the sword, while the highest authorities taught how it was to be used.'[12]

Reviewing the artillery available for the attack on Mont Avron, Hindersin wrote to the King on December 18:

> The number of weapons – 76 guns and 60 mortars – put at the disposal of Colonel Bartsch appears to be too great for the bombardment of Mont Avron; on the other hand, it seems too weak if, after the taking of this work, it is desired to undertake an attack on Forts Rosny and Nogent, on the eastern front.

He went on to say that even if this attack succeeded, he did not believe that a bombardment of Paris could be successfully conducted as planned. He suggested that, since success depended on a simultaneous bombardment on the eastern and south western fronts, only that number of guns absolutely necessary to reduce Mont Avron should be left there, and the rest moved from the eastern front to the south and used against Bicêtre and Villejuif. This would support the main attack from the southwest and, after the taking of Forts Bicêtre and Montrouge, would

General von Schlotheim, Chief of Staff of the German Army of the Meuse (Pflugk-Harttung)

enable positions to be taken up for the effective bombardment of the city. William passed this on to the Crown Prince, to Roon and to Moltke; on December 22, the latter wrote a careful and patient reply to the King commenting on Hindersin's proposals, with which he respectfully disagreed. He objected in particular to a change of plan at this stage, and pointed out that Hindersin's proposal would take a good deal longer to carry out than the existing scheme which was already completely prepared. He firmly requested the King to make up his mind; if that was what was wanted, the bombardment could begin accordance with the existing plan as early as December 28; if Hindersin's proposals were accepted, a postponement was unavoidable.[13]

The threat of a further postponement was, as Moltke well knew, the highest card he could play, and he did not hesitate to employ it. It put paid to Hindersin's attempt to take over the central policy making role on the subject of the bombardment of Paris; and on December 26 formal approval was given to the Army of the Meuse for the commencement of the artillery attack on Mont Avron. Although the abandonment by Trochu of his purported siege of Le Bourget made it academic, Moltke also authorised a withdrawal from that place if the siege operations necessitated it, as the local commanders feared. In a further demonstration of his intention to keep matters under his own control, Moltke followed this up on December 29 with an instruction that Bartsch should report to him at least daily and whenever anything occurred that justified more frequent reports.[14]

Burying the dead following the second battle at Le Bourget, a sketch by Knötel (Pflugk-Harttung)

That was, however, after the bombardment of Mont Avron had taken place. At 8.30 am on December 27 Bartsch's 76 guns opened fire on the French positions in a heavy snowstorm which hampered visibility and prevented any clear observation of the effects. The French had of course noted the preparations being made, and had transferred the troops camped in the open on the east side of the plateau to the western slope. They did nothing, however, to construct any shelter for either men or guns; and the German barrage caused heavy casualties to the men of Hugues' Division which constituted Mont Avron's garrison. The French artillery there and at Forts Rosny and Nogent replied at once to the bombardment, which continued throughout December 27. The poor visibility, and the heavy return fire which caused the Germans batteries a number of casualties both in artillery men and guns, led a rather pessimistic view to be taken of the effectiveness of the attack. However, on the following day, in clearer weather, the shelling was resumed, and it became more apparent that the German gunners were hitting their targets to great effect. In the face of this the French guns on Mont Avron soon fell silent, and the return fire from the forts dwindled. Trochu came to see for himself, and had no difficulty in reaching the conclusion that Mont Avron was untenable and must be abandoned, and he gave immediate orders to this effect to Colonel Stoffel, who was now in command there. Stoffel's skill and energy in pulling out his men and guns later that day and during the night of December 28/29 meant that by the following morning the evacuation was complete.[15]

It was a success so rapid and so comprehensive that not only Moltke and his staff, but even the most passionate supporters of bombardment as the decisive weapon in reducing Paris, were taken by surprise. The German casualties were 11 killed and 22 wounded; French losses were about 100. On December 30 the Army of the Meuse pushed forward patrols to take possession of Mont Avron; it was not intended to occupy it on a permanent basis, but merely to patrol it. So successful had been Stoffel's withdrawal that they found only one wrecked gun, and a quantity of ammunition. Bartsch was able thereafter to switch the fire of his guns to Forts Rosny and Nogent; it was not long before he gained the upper hand, and the forts fell silent.

There was no longer any room for argument about the wisdom of commencing the bombardment of the city. Not surprisingly, one or two of the former opponents were rather grudging in their acknowledgement of the success. Blumenthal noted in his diary:

> It is, I must say, much more than I expected, and a proof that it was not so strongly armed as we thought, and, moreover, that the French are no longer making a serious stand. At the same time we must not deceive ourselves into the idea that the defence on the south front will be so paltry. The conditions here are quite otherwise.[16]

A few days later the Crown Prince, who like Blumenthal remained profoundly sceptical about the bombardment, reflected rather sanctimoniously that it would grieve him if the bombardment damaged historic buildings, 'for all that is in question is to punish that section of the population whose wickedness was the guilty course of the war. But, unfortunately, in a bombardment we can, of cause, make ourselves responsible for nothing.' However, he was more hopeful than he had been: 'if we are favoured with the same good luck as heretofore, the bombardment may lead to important results.'[17]

Bismarck was, of course exultant; he wrote to his wife on New Year's Day to tell her the news, adding that 'those hitherto opposed to the bombardment are converted and look somewhat sour on account of the rapid success of the artillery, for everyone says to himself in private that we could have done this two months ago if a dozen people of influence had not prevented it for several reasons.'[18] However, in spite of the rapid success gained at Mont Avron, most of the soldiers shared Blumenthal's professional caution; the bombardment of the city itself, over a wide front, at maximum range, in a contest with the heavily armed forts, was likely to be a very different proposition.

22

The Le Mans Campaign

The threatening advance of a force of unknown strength from Briare on Gien, which had appeared to validate Moltke's insistence that the Second Army concentrate around Orleans, quickly evaporated. It had brought Frederick Charles and the bulk of his army hurrying back to Orleans; but it soon became apparent that, rather than the advanced guard of a major assault by Bourbaki, it was a small and detached force that only briefly occupied Gien before retreating. This gave the weary troops of Second Army the opportunity to rest and recover from their exertions of the past few weeks. Only Voigts-Rhetz, with the X Corps, remained in action; Kraatz, with the 20th Division and a cavalry brigade, was posted at Vendôme to keep an eye on the 2nd Army of the Loire, now a safe distance away at Le Mans, while with the rest of the corps Voigts-Rhetz marched on Tours. On December 19 he encountered opposition just beyond Monnaie, about fifteen miles north west of the city; after a brisk action he dispersed the enemy, sustaining about 100 casualties in the process; the French losses were estimated between three and four hundred.[1] Next day he pushed a column forward to Tours itself; but reckoning that he had not sufficient troops available both to carry out Moltke's orders to blow up the railway bridges and to occupy the city, completed his work of destruction and then retired to Blois. With the completion of this operation, the X Corps was also able to enjoy a period of rest.

This welcome respite, however, was not to be prolonged. It seemed increasingly likely to Moltke, as the year drew to a close, that some desperate attempt might be mounted to relieve Paris, since it must be evident to the Government of National Defence that there was little time left in which to do so. For the moment, there seemed no likelihood that Faidherbe could get past the First Army to offer any threat to the investing forces; but there was continuing uncertainty about Bourbaki's intentions, while the recuperative powers of the 2nd Army of the Loire under such an energetic leader as Chanzy could not be ignored. Indeed, before Moltke reached a conclusion as to the strategy he should now pursue, there were clear indications that Chanzy was ready to resume active operations.

On December 26 Kraatz had pushed forward a reconnaissance in force down the Loire to explore the strength of French forces which had appeared at Montoire. In command of the detachment was Lieutenant Colonel von Boltenstern, who had two battalions, a squadron of uhlans and two guns. Boltenstern reached Montoire without opposition, and next day pressed on to Sougé; here, however, his force encountered such stiff resistance that Boltenstern soon was obliged to retreat, only to find that he had run into an ambush, and was completely surrounded. Boltenstern resolved to break out; he

> first caused the guns to fire independently for a short time; then the five companies dashed forward with a cheer in skirmishing order, without firing a shot. After an embittered hand-to-hand struggle, on which the French artillery

Prince Frederick Charles during the Le Mans Campaign, by Speyer (Bork)

> poured a regardless shell fire, they succeeded in forcing back the enemy's right wing to the heights and through the gap thus created effected their retreat.[2]

Boltenstern had escaped with the whole of his force, at a cost of some 150 casualties; the French force, which was part of the 3rd Division of the 17th Corps supported by cavalry, suffered losses of about 450. The Crown Prince noted of Boltenstern's achievement that it was 'glorious news'; and 'a noble example for the Army, over which General Count Moltke, altogether against his wont, came very near breaking down.'[3]

Jouffroy, the Commander of the 3rd Division, had moved swiftly to intercept Boltenstern's force; emboldened by his near success, Chanzy authorised him to launch an attack on Vendôme. Collecting considerable reinforcements, he had by December 31 put together a force of about two divisions, with which he advanced from Azay and Mazange towards Vendôme. The build up of French forces in the area had not gone unnoticed by the German cavalry, and Kraatz was reinforced at Vendôme; the detachments on the Loire at Fréteval and Morée joined him, being relieved by the 1st Cavalry Brigade. By December 30 he had assembled a force of eleven battalions, with three regiments of cavalry and six batteries, and felt strong enough next day to send forward von Diringshofen with four battalions, two squadrons, and ten guns to test the enemy strength. He also ordered Luderitz to advance from Fréteval to Épuisay with the 1st Cavalry Brigade. It was soon clear to Kraatz, who accompanied Diringshofen's column, that they were running into strong French forces, and he ordered a retreat to Vendôme, from where he launched a number of spoiling attacks to break up Jouffroy's advancing columns. By early afternoon a serious engagement had begun, in which for a time it appeared that the French might get the upper hand; but as darkness fell, the French withdrew, closely pursued by three battalions ordered by Kraatz to occupy a number of farmsteads as an advanced defensive position.[4] Meanwhile Luderitz had carried out a successful raid on Épuisay, returning with 3 guns and 53 prisoners; his troopers had, however, encountered sufficient resistance to confirm that Jouffroy's advance had been made in considerable strength.

Although Moltke was still unsure of the direction Bourbaki would take – there were signs that he was moving east to the relief of Belfort, but Moltke thought an advance with Chanzy towards Paris was more likely – he was discontented at leaving the initiative with the enemy, and came to the conclusion that action must be taken without delay. Of all the potential threats to the investment of Paris, that posed by Chanzy was the most serious. It was against him that a blow must be directed; with any luck, and if it was launched with great speed, it might catch the French off balance. And it was important, too, to strike before the two armies of the Loire were reunited, if that was what was intended. Accordingly, on January 1 Moltke sent a telegram with the necessary orders to Stiehle. He followed it up with a letter explaining his intentions in more detail. Noting that until a few days previously at any rate Bourbaki was said still to be at Bourges, he predicted an early advance in conjunction with the enemy movement on Vendôme.

> It would be hazardous to await the approach to each other of these two groups, which are as yet separated by a considerable interval; it rather appears necessary to assume the offensive with superior forces as rapidly as possible against the nearest group, so as to defeat that ere the other can arrive sufficiently close to cooperate. His Majesty the King therefore orders the Second Army to take the offensive forthwith against the forces advancing from the west.

Moltke went on to restore the Detachment (now designated the XIII Corps) together with the 2nd and 4th Cavalry Divisions to the control of the Second Army. The XIII Corps now had a new Chief of Staff; after Stosch's return to Versailles, Moltke was not prepared to leave Krenski in the post, and to his great delight Waldersee was appointed to take over the task of keeping the Grand Duke in order. The immediate objective was to concentrate the army on the line of the Loire as quickly as possible. Frederick Charles also remained responsible for the defence of Orleans; but in order to support him in this, Fransecky's II Corps was to be pulled out of the lines of investment around Paris and moved to Montargis, while Zastrow with the VIII Corps was also to move west. Frederick Charles could hardly complain, therefore, that he was not being given the wherewithal to finish the job, which was to make an end of Chanzy once and for all.[5] In answer to an anxious enquiry from Stiehle as to the date of the II Corps' arrival at Montargis, Moltke was quick to confirm that Fransecky's leading troops would be there on January 5.

Moltke's instinctive conclusion that the Second Army should strike at once at Chanzy was entirely correct. On the other side of the hill there had been a lot of verbal activity in the closing days of the year. On December 22, Commandant Boisdeffre, of Trochu's staff, had escaped from Paris by balloon, and made his way

German troops, including Bavarians on the right, wearing makeshift footwear, including French clogs, to combat the horrendous winter weather, by Röchling (Lindner)

at once to the headquarters of the 2nd Army of the Loire. What he had to say deeply impressed Chanzy, who sent off to Gambetta on the following day a detailed appreciation of the situation, calling for an immediate and coordinated move towards Paris. In reply he got the kind of highly coloured and thoroughly imprecise response to which he was becoming accustomed. It ended with a typical Gambetta flourish: 'You have decimated the Mecklenburgers: the Bavarians have ceased to exist; the rest of the army is already overcome by anxiety and lethargy. Persevere, and we shall drive these hordes from our soil with empty hands.'[6]

Chanzy was unimpressed by this sort of empty rhetoric, observing caustically: 'This letter did not appear to contain sufficient information or appreciations to enable the situation to be defined.' He despatched an urgent reply on December 30 insisting on properly co-ordinated action.

> Our best chance of success must reside in the combination of our movements, in the simultaneous co-operation of three armies towards the same end, in the same effort at the same moment. Without this, we expose ourselves to seeing our forces beaten in detail, when properly directed, they would have been able to triumph.

He went on to set out the role of his own army as he saw it, which was, he said, clearly defined by the situation.[7] He followed this up with another letter, dated January 2, which he sent by hand with Boisdeffre to Bordeaux, reiterating the urgency of the situation. The final crisis had, he said, arrived; and it was necessary that all the forces available should be employed in an effort to relieve Paris. In a wide ranging review of the overall situation (hampered, as he not unreasonably

General Chanzy's personal staff (Rousset/*Histoire*)

pointed out, by the lack of clear information from the centre), he put forward a plan for the immediate advance towards Paris by all the various armies; his own advance, 120.000 strong, would be on a broad front from the Loir and the Huisne.[9]

The remaining exchanges between Chanzy and his political masters, before he embarked on what was to be his final campaign, must have depressed him profoundly. Boisdeffre came back from Bordeaux with a reply from Gambetta which made it clear that for the moment he was putting all his money on Bourbaki's offensive in the east; the role of Chanzy's army was to be a supporting one. As Chanzy himself noted, this reply from Gambetta did at least contain a clear decision.

> However, General Bourbaki's operation in the east, undertaken in similar conditions, with untried troops, in a mountainous and snow covered terrain which was in any case extremely difficult, offered so belated a prospect of success that the general commanding believed that he should make a last effort to restrict this operation and bring the 1st Army of the Loire more directly to Paris.[10]

But although professing to have reconsidered Chanzy's appeal carefully, Freycinet was adamant, telegraphing him on January 7 to say that it was now too late to change the plan. Bourbaki was committed; and the planned operation was 'still the best, for it is the one which will most demoralise the German Army.' There was no more to be said; Chanzy continued his forward movement, hoping for the opportunity 'to attempt, after having ensured the security of his rear, a bold and rapid advance in the direction of Paris.'[11]

It was not an opportunity that Frederick Charles intended to permit him. The Second Army was facing odds of approximately two to one in its strike against Chanzy, but it was Frederick Charles' intention to attack all along his front. He had a total of three and a half corps and four cavalry divisions, comprising 57,737 infantry, 15,426 cavalry and 318 guns.[12] The reduced strength of his individual corps demonstrated all too clearly the effects of the long and hard campaigns in which they had been engaged: the largest was Alvensleben's III Corps with 17,235 infantry and 1,038 cavalry. But Moltke had come to regard odds of two to one as being entirely favourable, and in launching the Second Army on its offensive he did so in complete confidence that if the weather permitted a decisive result could be obtained: having given his orders he was content to let Frederick Charles and Stiehle get on with the job. If he had any anxieties at all, they were associated with the security of Orleans, which was garrisoned by the 25th (Hessian) Division. Detachments were posted at Blois and Gien, and on January 7 Moltke ordered Major General von Rantzau, who commanded two battalions, four squadrons and a battery at Gien, to report directly to him on a daily basis, and to send reconnaissance patrols south towards Nevers and Clamecy. His principal concern about the large number of troops raised by the Government of National Defence was not so much their combat effectiveness as the possibility that fresh forces could turn up almost anywhere on the perimeter occupied by the armies covering the investment of Paris.

Bearing in mind the appalling weather conditions which had been experienced, Frederick Charles decided to stick to the main roads for his advance: the side roads would probably be found to be impassable, and although this meant in effect that each of his corps had only one road for its march he wanted no delays in getting to grips with the enemy. In fact, a spell of relatively clear frosty weather meant that the advance of the army towards its jumping off point on the line of the Loir was accomplished without difficulty.

Even before the main body of the army moved forward on January 6, there had already been contact with Chanzy's most advanced troops. On the extreme left a detachment of three battalions, two cavalry regiments and two batteries under Baumgarth, the commander of the 2nd Cavalry Brigade, fought a brisk action at Villeporcher after advancing at noon from St Amand. Baumgarth's leading troops stormed the village, only to be driven out in their turn by a French counter attack. Fresh troops, which in readiness for the following day's advance had moved up from Blois, joined in the fighting and recaptured Villeporcher.[13] To the north, the XIII Corps had also been engaged. Although the main line of its advance was to be through Brou, the corps had also been made responsible from the occupation of Nogent le Rotrou, and the force told off for this duty, the 44th Brigade, when moving forward, identified strong French forces holding La Fourche, five miles north east of Nogent.

The intention was for Voigts-Rhetz, with the 1st and 6th Cavalry Divisions, to advance on January 6 from the line Vendôme-St Amand to Montoire. On his right, Alvensleben's III Corps was to march through Vendôme to the line of the Azay. Next, Manstein, with the IX Corps (less the 25th Division at Orleans) together with the 2nd Cavalry Division advancing from Cloyes, was to move forward to Morée. Finally, the Grand Duke was to direct the main body of the XIII Corps through Brou to come in on Chanzy's left. The extreme right of the army was covered by the 5th Cavalry Division.

The French units holding La Fourche opened fire with artillery on the leading units of the 44th Brigade as it moved forward. With the support of a horse artillery battery which ascended a steep ridge to the east of La Fourche, and of heavy artillery coming south through Coulonges, infantry of the 83rd and 94th Regiments stormed forward and took the position, together with three guns; an advance into Nogent le Rotrou itself, however, was impracticable before dark, and the brigade remained overnight at La Fourche. Meanwhile the main body of the corps had moved forward, the 22nd Division to Beaumont les Autels and the 17th Division to Unverre, about five miles west of Brou.[14]

Jouffroy, who until the advance of the Second Army had intended a fresh assault on Vendôme, had taken up a position to the west of Azay-Mazange. As reports came in of the advance of the Second Army, and especially of the III Corps immediately in his front, Jouffroy decided to launch an attack on Alvensleben's leading troops, in order to prevent the Germans turning with great force on de Curten's force at Château Renault. As a result, as soon as the leading troops of the 5th Division had passed through Vendôme at about 11.00 am they found that a vigorous firefight was going on between two battalions of the 17th Regiment, left by Voigts – Rhetz to cover the town, and Jouffroy's troops which were advancing through the woods. The engagement rapidly developed, and by mid afternoon practically the whole of the III Corps had become involved. Rothmaler, commanding the advanced guard of the 6th Division, launched an attack on Jouffroy's positions at Azay, which were strongly held; although the French were ultimately driven back, it was only after heavy fighting, in which the Germans sustained a considerable number of casualties, among whom was Rothmaler himself, wounded towards the end of the engagement. To the south the 5th Division had also encountered stiff opposition north of Villiers. Advancing under heavy artillery fire from French batteries which commanded the whole of the valley, the German infantry were for a while pinned down. Seeing this, the French launched a series of counter attacks which were only finally driven off when strong reinforcements reached the front line. As the afternoon ended, Mazange was taken by storm after being attacked on three sides. The total casualties sustained by the III Corps in the course of the days fighting amounted to 485; French losses, which included some 400 prisoners, were a good deal higher.[15]

It was, however, around St Amand that the most serious fighting occurred on January 6. Baumgarth's detachment was intended to cover the left flank of Voigts-Rhetz's advance by moving up to the Château Renault-Montoire road, while the road from Château Renault to Vendôme was to be held by the 6th Cavalry Division, (Duke William of Mecklenburg-Schwerin) supported by the 1st Cavalry Brigade at St Amand. Early on the morning of January 6, Duke William was ordered to move west, establishing touch with Baumgarth while maintaining contact with the 1st Cavalry Brigade. This was an extremely thin screen to cover a sector in which the French had shown so much activity on the previous day, as the Germans were about to find out.

As a result of the fighting on January 5, Baumgarth's detachment had been scattered over a line of outposts from Amblay, through Vilthiou on the Château Renault road, as far as Villeporcher, about a mile north east of the Forest of Château Renault. The key point was really the cross roads at La Noue, about a mile north west of St Amand, where the fusilier battalion of the 57th Regiment was posted with a squadron of cuirassiers and a battery of horse artillery. The westward movement of the bulk of Baumgarth's force was delayed when at 9.30am, before the 6th Cavalry Division had taken up its position, the French attacked Villeporcher and drove its defenders about a mile north-eastwards to Pias. One battalion strong, these endeavoured to hold a position between Pias and Les Haies, just east of the railway line to St Amand. It was the existence of this line which made the French attack the more threatening; it enabled the advance to be swiftly reinforced. The arrival of Duke William at St Gourgon with the 15th Cavalry Brigade for the moment stabilised the situation; but further French troops pushed on up the road to Vendôme, and the Germans fell back behind the line of the little River Brenne, while the 57th Regiment reassembled at Neuve St Amand on the main road about a mile and half south west of La Noue. The 14th Cavalry Brigade had moved west to St Arnoult and Prunay; the 15th Cavalry Brigade took up a position on the right of the main road, while to the left Luderitz stood with the 1st Cavalry Brigade of four cavalry regiments. These dispositions seemed to have secured the position for the day; but due to a misunderstanding the six companies of the 16th Regiment, which had been posted at St Amand, abandoned the village and fell back along the railway line, uncovering the position at Neuve St Amande. Duke William had no choice but to order the troops there to fall back, which they did as far as Huisseau where the main body of the 38th Brigade had arrived.[16]

Duke William made his way that night to the Second Army headquarters at Vendôme to report in person to Frederick Charles. The latter had spent the day watching the fighting at Azay-Mazange and in general felt well satisfied with what had been achieved. The one sector with which he was profoundly discontented was of course at St Amand; and Duke William was curtly told to restore the situation next day by retaking the village.[17] The bulk of the X Corps had reached its objectives by crossing the Loir and taking up a position at Montoire after brushing aside opposition from Barry's division. Frederick Charles did not want now to lose the momentum of the advance of his left wing. On the other hand, de Curten's advance to St Amand was a deep thrust into the Second Army's flank, and the orthodox, and more cautious response might have been to turn south to deal with this threat before pressing forward. For once, however, Frederick Charles eschewed caution; only the 38th Brigade, supported by the 1st Cavalry Division and the 15th Cavalry Brigade, was left to deal with de Curten, and Voigts-Rhetz was ordered to continue his advance westwards with the rest of his corps. Voigts-Rhetz, however, was more circumspect, sending back from Montoire the rest of the 19th Division to St Amand.

During the night news arrived that the lingering doubts as to Bourbaki's intentions had finally been set at rest by the receipt of definite information that he had moved eastward. Meanwhile intelligence had also been received at Versailles that Chanzy's intention was to advance by way of Nogent le Rotrou; if true, he would run straight into the XIII Corps while the rest of the Second Army came down on his right flank. It necessitated no change in the orders already issued for January 7; the Grand Duke was to reach Montmirail, and on the two following days to push on as far as he could towards Le Mans. Manstein, maintaining contact with the XIII Corps with the 2nd Cavalry Division, was to advance through Épuisay, and seize a crossing over the Braye; Alvensleben was also to move up to the line of the Braye.[18] Frederick Charles accompanied the centre of his advance, riding forward towards Épuisay. Here, Alvensleben had directed three of his brigades towards the village, hoping to get around the left flank of the forces opposed to him, while the 9th Brigade and the corps artillery held the line of the Azay at Mazange. During the night, however, Jouffroy's advanced troops had slipped away, and the III Corps continued its westward movement. It was detained briefly by resistance at Épuisay itself, which required an attack by seven companies before it could be shifted at 1.30 pm; thereafter the 6th Division pressed on along the St Calais road, with the 5th Division on its left moving towards Savigny. An attempt to reach the latter place by the 14th Cavalry Brigade, advancing north from Montoire, was checked, and the brigade took up a position at La Richardière. Manstein, meanwhile followed closely behind the 6th Division while the 2nd Cavalry Division scouted north through Mondoubleau before ultimately making contact with the left wing of the XIII Corps advancing on Montmirail.[19]

The Grand Duke had prepared to meet stiff resistance at Nogent le Rotrou, and had directed the whole of the 22nd Division and the 4th Cavalry Division to take part in its capture. Tresckow was to get as far forward towards Montmirail as he could with the 17th Division. In fact, however, Nogent le Rotrou had been abandoned during the night although the Grand Duke only learned of this at 1pm on January 7. Preparations for the attack had delayed the advance, and the advanced guard of the 22nd Division got only as far as Le Gibet about five miles south west of Nogent le Rotrou before night fell, where it met stiff resistance which was only overcome by 6.30pm.

A similar situation had developed at the other end of the line. Concerned about the threat from St Amand, Voigts-Rhetz had sent Hartmann back with substantial reinforcements to ensure that de Curten's troops were thrown back, evidently doubting Duke William's ability to deal with the situation with the troops he already had. Hartmann and the reinforcements had already left by the time that news came of the French retreat from St Amand. This did not, however, mean the end of the fighting in this sector; Hartmann, who now took overall command, ordered the 38th Brigade to advance south through Vilthiou along the main road. At Villechauve, strong resistance was encountered at La Garionnière Farm, which was only taken at noon, after an assault by three companies which suffered considerable casualties. At 2.00pm the French put in an assault towards Villechauve, the object of which was to prevent the Germans from interfering with the retreat westward of the main body of de Curten's division. In this they succeeded; by the time the German counter attack had cleared the French out of the positions they had taken up, de Curten's troops were out of reach.[20] Chanzy blamed Jouffroy for de Curten's retreat which had, he said, been caused by the failure sufficiently to coordinate the movements of the French troops on this part of the front.[21] De Curten had, however, achieved an important success in that he had imposed the delay on the advance of the X Corps that Frederick Charles had hoped to avoid; Voigts-Rhetz did not make any effective advance beyond Montoire all day, while he waited for Hartmann to clear up the situation in his rear.

The terrain into which the Second Army was advancing was not conducive to rapid progress; in particular it seriously impaired the effectiveness of cavalry and the deployment of large masses of artillery. The district

> consists partly of small plateaux, partly of a labyrinth of ridges, which not infrequently attain a relative height of 200 feet or more. Well filled rivers flow with rapid course through valleys which are generally broad and with steep sides. The entire country is covered with the densest cultivation of long-standing growth, with vineyards, orchards and vegetable gardens. The villages consist mostly of a number of isolated and solidly constructed farmsteads, among which are interspersed châteaux, surrounded with extensive park enclosures and copses … Although the superior effect of the chassepôt here ceased to avail, the mitrailleuses were in their true element, and became a dangerous weapon in the narrow passes.'[22] These conditions put a special premium on the skill and courage of the leaders of smaller infantry units, since in this restricted countryside it was extremely difficult for the higher command to exert close control.

Another change in the weather retarded progress as well; there had been a thaw on January 7, but during the night there was another frost, and the roads were covered with black ice, making movement extremely difficult. In the north, the 22nd Division was particularly delayed in its march to La Ferté Bernard, which it reached at 4pm. The advanced guard of the 17th Division had by then already passed through the town; its main body was marching by roads somewhat to the south, while still further on the left of the advance of XIII Corps, a detachment under Rauch reached Vibraye after a short struggle around some farms on the outskirts of the town.[23] Contact with the IX Corps was maintained through the 2nd Cavalry Division, which headed for Conflans.

Manstein's corps, which had been marching on the right rear of the III Corps, reached St Calais on January 8; the 6th Division was already through the village and passed the night well to the west, its advanced guard having marched through the Bois des Loges. On its left the 5th Division encountered no opposition during the day. The 14th Cavalry Brigade, serving as the link between the III Corps and the X Corps, moved out of La Richardière, marching due west through Bessé. When the brigade reached Vancé, it came under heavy fire; but a horse artillery battery, at once brought to the front, soon dispersed the line of dismounted French cuirassiers, before later breaking up a long column of cavalry seen passing through Vancé.

Voigts-Rhetz, however, had not made such good progress. His advanced guard, moving through particularly close country, and finding the roads broken in many places, spent a large part of January 8 clearing a position taken up by the French near Ruillé; by nightfall the 20th Division had reached La Chartre. Of the 19th Division von Woyna, whose 37th Brigade had been sent back to St Amand on the previous day, only to be ordered west again by Hartmann, had reached Sougé. Around St Amand itself, not much had changed. Although the main body of de Curten's Division had marched westward, there remained strong rearguards close to Vilthiou, and at Villeporcher there was some desultory fighting before Hartmann received an order to march with his force to rejoin the rest of the corps at La Chartre. This order had been issued by Voigts-Rhetz in the mistaken belief that there was no longer any threat to be faced from Château Renault; although Hartmann deferred his move to the west until after dark, the later order from Voigts-Rhetz, telling him after all to stay put, did not arrive in time to prevent Hartmann setting off towards Montoire.[24]

At St Calais, Frederick Charles was irritated to discover that there remained uncertainty about the situation at St Amand, but he was determined not to allow it to delay any further his concentric advance on Le Mans. For January 9, the XIII Corps was to reach the Montfort heights, and seize a crossing over the Huisne; the III Corps was to reach Ardenay, the IX Corps following it to Bouloire, and the XII Corps Parigné l'Eveque. Voigts-Rhetz was to decide whether cavalry alone should cover the left flank threatened from Château Renault. When it was learned at Second Army Headquarters that Hartmann had already moved off to Montoire, the decision was taken that he should return to a position south of Vendôme with the 38th Brigade and the 1st Cavalry Division and strike hard at the French forces remaining in and around Château Renault. The immediate problem facing Frederick Charles was that the centre of his army was making quicker progress than either of the flanks; but notwithstanding this, he did not intend to put on the brakes, and hold up Alvensleben's march to let the others catch up.

The events of January 9 were, however, to increase the problem. A heavy snowstorm impeded progress all along the front. In the north, the 17th and 22nd Divisions were now advancing on a single road, so the advance was led by Tresckow's advance guard under Lieutenant Colonel von der Osten. In spite of encountering continuous resistance, von der Osten's men steadily pushed forward and by end of the day had progressed beyond Dureau. Tresckow had, however, also constituted a left flank detachment under Rauch, comprising three battalions, the 17th Cavalry Brigade and two batteries. Assembling at Dollon, Rauch marched on Connerré; en route, he learned of strong forces at Thorigné, to his left, and launched an attack on the place; ultimately successful in this, Rauch considered it now too late to advance beyond the village. During the night, however, the French pulled out of Connerré, and Rauch sent forward several companies of infantry to take possession of that village also.[25]

In the centre, the 6th Division, leading Alvensleben's corps, moved on Bouloire and took the place without difficulty. Further on down the road to Le Mans resistance was encountered on the heights southwest of Le Breil, but this too was brushed aside. It was at Ardenay that the most serious opposition was found, where Paris' Division of the 17th Corps had been sent forward by Chanzy to take the place of Jouffroy. After a prolonged artillery duel, the 64th Regiment stormed Château Ardenay at 4.00pm; to the north of the main road the advance was pushed forward at the point of the bayonet to La Butte and Ardenay, and a series of counter attacks beaten off. Paris concluded that it would be impossible to remain in the positions to which he had retreated; but he held on until nightfall before falling back to the plateau of Auvours.[26] The 5th Division, marching to the left rear of the 6th Division, had met with no resistance from the enemy, but had been much delayed by the condition of the roads. By nightfall however its advanced guard was over the Narais; patrols found the enemy still occupying Parigné l'Eveque. During the day, the III Corps had sustained casualties of about 160, but had in addition taken over 1000 prisoners.[27]

Voigts-Rhetz, with the X Corps, had made much less satisfactory progress, enduring a particularly uncomfortable day, as the Official History graphically records.

> To the inconvenience which snow and fog caused this day to all the troops of the Army, were added, in the case of the X Corps the extraordinary difficulties which were entailed at this time of the year in marching through hilly country full of steep slopes, ravines, and hollow roads. Cavalry and artillery had to dismount and lead their horses; every falling horse delayed the column.

Even Voigts-Rhetz was not exempt from the difficulties; he had to ride on a limber, while his staff had to march on foot.[28]

On the left of his advance, the 20th Division was held up by French troops occupying the Chahaignes heights; the advanced guard ran into heavy artillery and mitrailleuse fire. Three batteries of German artillery came into action but a heavy snowstorm at about 9.00am compelled them to cease fire. The enemy resistance appeared sufficiently determined for Voigts-Rhetz to order Woyna, advancing from Pont de Braye through Vancé, to swing to his left and march to the sound of the cannon. In fact, by the time he got near enough to be of any help, two battalions of the 92nd Regiment under Colonel Haberland had succeeded in throwing an improvised bridge over the little River Brives, and driving the French off the heights. This enabled the 20th Division to resume its march along the left bank of the river; at 3.30pm it ran into more opposition in the village of Brives, which could only be cleared away by a frontal attack. Mindful of the lost time, Kraatz ordered Valentini to push on after dark; advancing with four battalions, he drove the garrison out of St Vincent and occupied it for the night.[29] The rest of the division was echeloned back to La Chantre, while Wayne was around Vancé. Meanwhile Hartmann had succeeded in sorting out the position at Château Renault, on which he advanced with all the troops at his disposal. Meeting no opposition until he reached the outskirts of the town he put in a successful one battalion assault on a number of buildings on the outskirts which had been occupied by the evening; by 1.00pm he had entered the town. He was in fact pushing at an open door; de Curten was already in retreat westwards towards Château du Loir. What had seemed a potentially serious threat to the Second Army's flank had thus completely evaporated.

This left Frederick Charles free to concentrate all his forces for a decisive battle with Chanzy – if, that is to say, he could afford to take the time to do so. Any delay in launching his assault on Chanzy's defensive positions, which were assumed to be behind the Huisne, would give the French the opportunity to bring up their up their still widely scattered forces. Frederick Charles, who on the evening of January 9 was still not aware of how far the XIII and the X Corps had got, decided in any case not to wait until all his army was in position. The III Corps, still the furthest forward of his Corps, was to push on beyond Ardenay. On its right, the XIII Corps was to advance on St Mars la Bruyère; Manstein was ordered to send a detachment to support that advance, while the rest of the IX Corps closed up to Bouloire, still following the III Corps. Finally, with the support of Alvensleben's left wing, the X Corps was to continue its advance along the Parigné road. In giving his orders, Frederick Charles stressed the need for rapid marching by all corps; only in this way could full advantage be taken of the scattered positions of Chanzy's troops.[30] On this occasion at least Moltke could make no complaint that the Second Army was moving too deliberately; the plan was to inflict a crushing defeat on the enemy, and to do so with the minimum of delay.

As Frederick Charles had expected, the position taken up by Chanzy for the defence of Le Mans was principally based on the line of the Huisne. From the right it ran from Arnage on the River Sarthe along the Chemin des Boeufs up to the Huisne at Yvré railway station. From there, following the river, the position was carried along the Auvours heights as far as Montfort, where it turned north again as far as La Chapelle St Rémy. The overall length of this defensive position was over twenty miles, which meant that Chanzy's army was at some points along its length going to be stretched dangerously thin. On the other hand, the position had been well chosen and had considerable defensive potential; Chanzy's intention was to wait until the Germans, exhausted by their exertions over the last few days, failed to penetrate his defensive system and, recoiling, offered an opportunity for a decisive counter attack. That, at any rate, was the plan; it remained to be seen whether the shaken troops of the 2nd Army of the Loire could successfully resist the hammer blows of Frederick Charles' battle hardened veterans.

On January 8 Chanzy had taken one important step an effort to shore up his crumbling right wing when he placed Admiral Jauréguiberry in overall command of the divisions of Jouffroy, de Curten and Barry. Chanzy realised that for the moment these three divisions must continue their retreat; indeed the wide detour that de Curten especially must make could well have the effect of taking him off the board entirely for a couple of days. This in fact proved to be the case; and in addition only part of Barry's Division took part. The situation on the right wing was in fact very uncertain; Jauréguiberry was at 4.00pm on January 9 reporting that he had no news of de Curten and Barry, but that there were ominous reports from the civilian population of a strong German column moving through Chahaignes on Jupilles.[31] In the centre and on his left, however, Chanzy determined to launch on January 10 a pre-emptive strike at the leading troops of the Second Army; Jaurés with the 21st Corps was ordered to retake Connerré and Thorigné, while Paris' Division was directed towards Artenay. A stroke southwards between Champagné and Montfort which would have menaced Alvensleben's flank would have been extremely difficult to mount due to the flooded marshes along the river.

Alvensleben, advancing from Ardenay, made Changé the principal objective of the III Corps for January 10. The 9th Brigade (von Conta) was to advance from Gué-de-l'Aune and the 11th Brigade (von Flatow) from Ardenay while the left flank was covered by the 10th Brigade (Schwerin) advancing to Parigné. Meanwhile the 12th Brigade (von Bismarck) was to move straight along the main road. In fact, before the advance began, Alvensleben got news that Parigné had been abandoned, and was to be the objective for the day of Voigts-Rhetz and the X Corps, so the 10th Brigade was added to the force marching on Changé. The rather exposed position of the III Corps was soon illustrated, however, when a brigade

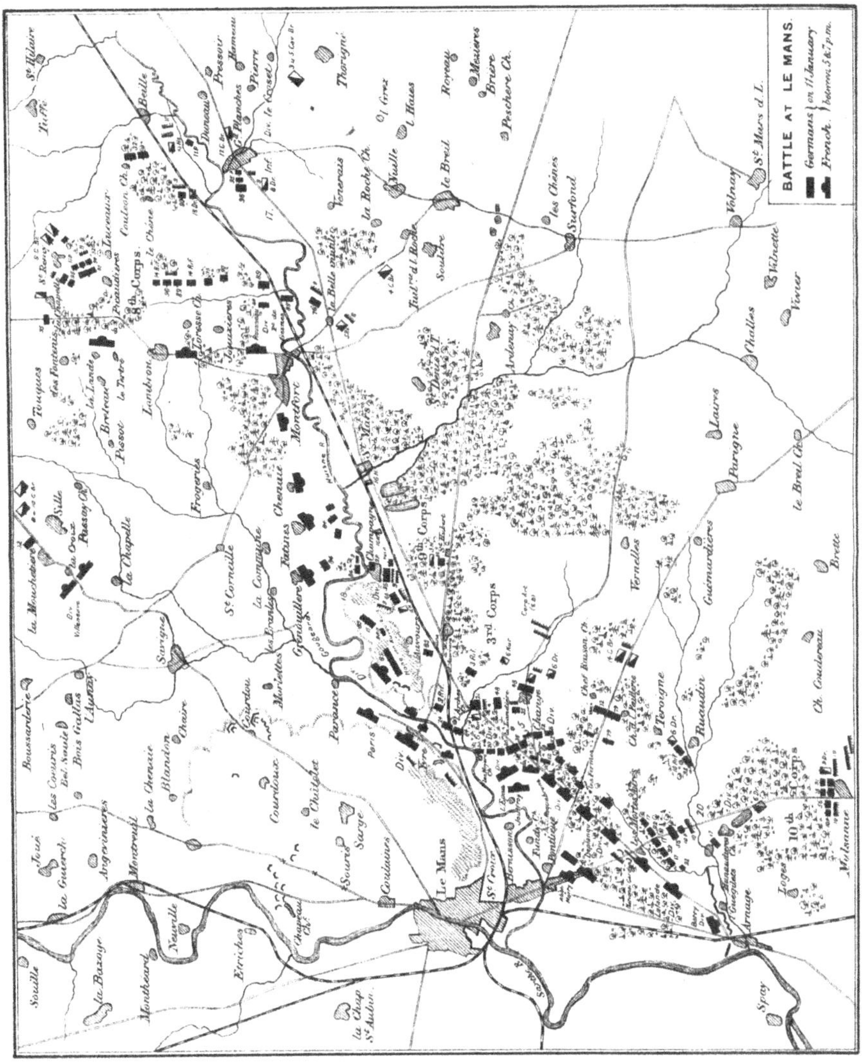

The Battle at Le Mans, January 11 1871

Vice-Admiral Jauréguiberry and his staff (Rousset/*Histoire*)

from Deplanque's Division moved up to reoccupy Parigné and from there attacked the left flank of Alvensleben's advance. Stülpnagel, the commander of the 5th Division, was anxious not to let Conta get too heavily embroiled in this action, preferring to leave it to Schwerin and the 10th Brigade. Conta in any case had had difficulty in deploying his artillery but Schwerin, coming from the southeast, was able to bring Parigné, which stands on rising ground, under the fire of his guns. At 12.30 he launched four battalions who charged forward with yells of 'Hurrah Brandenburg!' and soon swept the French defenders of Parigné aside; in all some 1,900 prisoners were taken. An attempted counter attack was broken up by the artillery, and Stülpnagel was able to turn his attention to the advance on Changé.[32] The other brigade directed towards Changé, Flatow's 10th Brigade, at first made good progress to the south of the road, but then had encountered considerable opposition. This was based on a position at Gué la Hart, and continued to frustrate Flatow throughout the early afternoon; Alvensleben, who was accompanying the brigade, ordered up fresh troops to right and left to attack the French flanks. With drums beating and bugles sounding these stormed the enemy position, taking over 1,000 prisoners. The delay, however meant that as darkness fell, Alvensleben still had not reached Changé; undaunted by this, he pushed forward a battalion of the 20th Regiment in a night attack and as it took and cleared away a barricade in front of the town, it found that after all it was in German hands. The 10th Brigade, advancing from Parigné, had advanced through La Girardrie and taken Changé bridge at 6.00pm, entering the town from the south east. After a bitter struggle, the French defenders of Changé were driven into the market place and made prisoners.

Meanwhile the 12th Brigade had pushed down the main road, meeting no resistance before it reached St Hubert-des-Rochers. The brigade was accompanied by Buddenbrock, the divisional commander who, learning that the French were in strength at Champagné and on the heights to the west, swung the brigade northwards. Here too considerable difficulty was experienced in deploying artillery; but two guns were brought into action, and these reduced the French artillery to silence before the infantry advanced to drive the French out of first their advanced positions and then Champagné itself.[33]

Alvensleben's advance had thus in the end been successful at all points; his own losses amounted to a total of 450 killed and wounded, but he had inflicted very much greater casualties on the enemy, and in addition had taken over 5,000 prisoners.[34] He was now directly in contact with Chanzy's main position; but the speed of his advance meant that he was no longer in touch with the corps of Voigts-Rhetz and Manstein, who were advancing on his left and right, nor with the XIII Corps which was still held up around Connerré and Thorigné. Indeed, it was clear that night to Alvensleben that even on the following day he could expect support only from Manstein's IX Corps; the other two could not be expected to reach their designated positions at all during January 11. Manstein was, at nightfall on January 10 still somewhat to the east of Ardenay, but at least he would next day have the advantage of being able to use the main road.

The resistance which had been met by the troops of the XIII Corps was based on the heights of Les Cohernières north of Connerré and a wood still further to the north. Tresckow's left flank detachment under Rauch, managed to penetrate into the wood, but failed to dislodge the enemy from the heights. The arrival of Wittich's 22nd Division, however, which crossed the river at Sceaux before marching on Beillé, brought welcome support. The French, though, were not done with; successive waves of counter attacks were launched, and Wittich was obliged to commit further troops on his right. These took the Couleon chateau; but here too the advance soon bogged down, and no further progress was possible here before night fell. On the extreme right of the XIII Corps, however the right flank detachment under Colonel von Beckedorff had done rather better, marching through Tuffé and then turning north west to Bonnétable where it met the expected advance from Belleme of the 4th Cavalry Division.[35]

Away to the south, Voigts Rhetz had only the elements to cope with; no contact was made with the enemy, but the appalling condition of the roads over which the X Corps was advancing meant that it was only able to reach Grand Lucé before taking up quarters for the night. Frederick Charles, who spent the day at the cross roads south of Le Breil, was thus by nightfall in what was a potentially hazardous position; the corps on his left and on his right were a long way behind his two centre corps, and would not be in a position to support Alvensleben and Manstein if the French launched an all out attack on them. However, it is doubtful if he was seriously concerned; Alvensleben was not unfamiliar with the experience of fighting unsupported, and Frederick Charles could feel justified confidence that he would be able to deal with whatever Chanzy could throw at him.

Chanzy was in the stance of a boxer who with his left, seeks to keep his enemy at arm's length while with his right hand he keeps his guard up. With the exception of de Curten's Division, and part of Barry's Division, which had not yet arrived, he

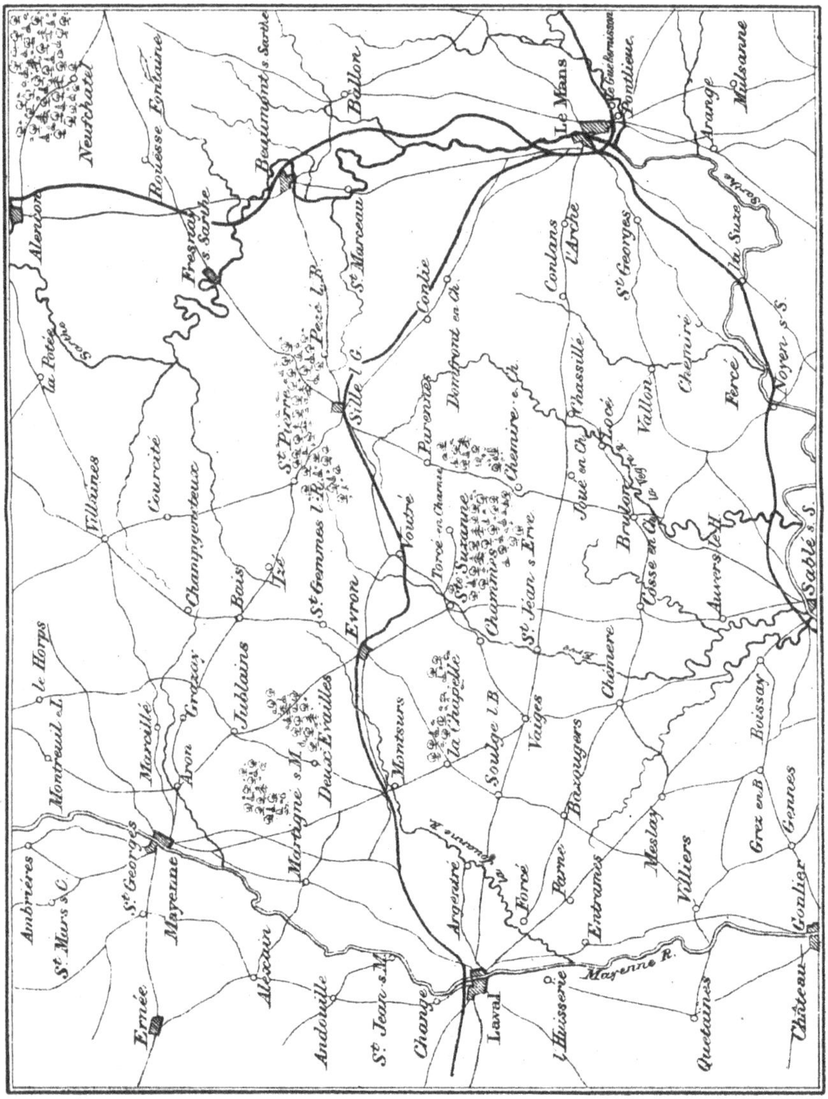

Westward of Le Mans, January 1871

now had had his whole army concentrated for the defence of Le Mans. Two detachments under Colonels Berard and Sobey were en route, and some further reinforcements had among reached him in the form of Lalande's 10,000 poorly armed Gardes Nationales from the camp of Conlie, together with nine more battalions from Laval. These represented the last resources available to Chanzy that could be considered as having some military usefulness, although in truth this was very slight; the rest of the troops that had been in training at Conlie, which it had not been possible to arm or equip, were sent back to Brittany. The newly arrived Gardes Nationales were posted on the right of Jauréguiberry's position, with only Barry's Division to the south of them. Chanzy's orders for 11 January, issued late the previous night, reflected his outrage at the performance of his subordinates.

> The explicit orders of the commanding general have not been carried out; he has explained his discontent to generals who, on their own responsibility, have taken on themselves not to obey. This failure to comply with orders which prescribed above all a vigorous offensive, because it was the only means of halting the enemy, has as a result caused practically a dissolution among our troops and leaves the enemy approaching our last positions in front of Le Mans ... The commanding general orders in the most formal manner, holding personally responsible the commanders of corps, divisions and brigades for what concerns them, that positions are taken up tomorrow morning first to throw back the enemy from positions he has occupied today and still directly threaten our lines, and to ensure the defence of the positions we must hold, whatever the cost and without any thought of retreat.[36]

Thorigné - a house pockmarcked by bullets fired during the action of 9 January 1871 (Rousset/*Histoire*)

Jauréguiberry, with five divisions plus another under Bouëdec cobbled together during January 11 from the detachments of Berard and Sobey, held the right; de Colomb, with two and a half divisions, was on the left facing the Grand Duke's XIII Corps. It was to de Colomb that Chanzy looked in particular for success; his was the key task of driving back Alvensleben and taking up a strong position along the main roads. It was soon evident to Alvensleben, contemplating the troops massed by de Colomb on the Auvours heights, that his flank would be threatened from this direction. To counter any such assault, the 12th Brigade had been posted in front of St Hubert; if Alvensleben was to advance westwards he needed the whole of his corps, and the support of the IX Corps was required to take over the protection of his flank. The position had been made rather more dangerous by the withdrawal by mistake of outposts from Champagné, which was promptly reoccupied by the French; Buddenbrock, the divisional commander, ordered a two battalion assault to recapture the village, which was stubbornly defended in bitter street fighting, and held out for most of the morning.

In Alvensleben's immediate front vigorous resistance was encountered; this led to fighting sufficiently severe to lead Frederick Charles, who had ridden up to St Hubert, to send an urgent message to Voigts-Rhetz to speed up his advance on Alvensleben's left. More immediate help was, however, at hand, with the arrival of the advanced guard of the IX Corps. Manstein was ordered at 1.00pm to take the Plateau d'Auvours, which was strongly held by de Colomb's troops, well supported by artillery and a group of four mitrailleuses behind Villiers. It was the latter that must first be silenced, before any assault could be mounted; and in a courageous charge across the snow covered ground a party of infantry from the fusilier battalion of the 11th Regiment succeeded in capturing three of the mitrailleuses after a brief hand to hand struggle.[37] Deprived of their support, the French pulled back out of Villiers; an attempt to retake the mitrailleuses was repulsed with the bayonet, and Manstein's infantry were able to tackle the French positions on the height between Villiers and Champagné. These were based on a number of farmhouses, and it was not until 5.30pm that the last of these were taken, and the Germans were able to clear the eastern end of the plateau of the enemy.

Meanwhile two battalions of the 85th Regiment, forming part of the main body of the IX Corps, advanced on the western part of the plateau. Here too the French were in strong positions in a number of farmhouses which had to be captured one by one, a process which occupied the rest of the day until the Germans held the northwestern edge of the plateau. As dusk fell de Colomb launched a strong counter attack from Yvré with part of Gourgeaud's Division; the first assault at 5.30pm was thrown back with heavy loss, but a further attack succeeded in retaking the farmhouses along the western edge of the plateau, which Gourgeaud held in considerable strength.

Manstein's assault, however, had achieved its objective, releasing the 12th Brigade and covering Alvensleben's right flank while he advanced on Jauréguiberry's positions. It soon became clear to Alvensleben that these were too strong for a direct assault and stretched too far south to be outflanked from that direction by the III Corps alone; he decided therefore to get round the left of Chanzy's position, where it rested on the Huisne, a task he entrusted to the 11th Brigade. The advance began at 11am, but part of the brigade had to face north to protect the advance from an apparent threat from the Auvours plateau, still at that time in enemy hands. The rest of the brigade pushed on along the Chemin des Boeufs, occupying the château of Les Noyers and the important bridge there over the Huisne. Three quarters of a mile south of the château, however, the advance ran into particularly stiff resistance around Les Granges, which was captured and then lost again; the 11th Brigade was heavily outnumbered, and obliged to fall back a little way although it was still able to hold La Landrière.

Meanwhile the 10th Brigade joined the attack, advancing from Changé, although not until 1.00pm; in the face of heavy odds, and a murderous infantry fire it was able to make only slow progress, being held up at Le Tertre all afternoon until Stülpnagel brought up reinforcements which took the farmhouse as night fell. To the north the 12th Brigade advanced along the railway line towards the Huisne, retaking the château of Les Arches which the French had reoccupied during the afternoon; an attempt to deploy 10 guns beside the château failed in the force of heavy artillery fire from the other side of the river, but the garrison held the château against a fierce counter attack from the direction of Yvré.

As night fell, Alvensleben's men stood to their arms in positions that were right up against those held by the enemy. Although not a great deal of ground had been gained, Alvensleben's corps had succeeded in breaking into the centre of Chanzy's position in the vital section along the Huisne, and now stood only two miles from the outskirts of Le Mans. Frederick Charles could, on the basis of the information immediately available to him, feel that the day had gone well although he was without any very significant news from the XIII Corps while from Voigts-Rhetz he had heard nothing at all. Whatever might be the position there, it was in the centre that the key to victory lay, and Manstein was ordered to keep open the river crossing at Champagné while holding on to the Auvours plateau.

The XIII Corps had delayed its forward march to enable the 22nd Division to recover from the vigorous fighting in which it had been engaged on the previous day. When the advance began, Tresckow's 17th Division soon occupied Haute Perche, west of Connerré, which was set on fire before its abandonment by the French, and pushed on through Les Cohernières and La Vallée westwards, the French retreating slowly before it. Meanwhile the 22nd Division took Le Chêre about a mile and half west of Beillé. Towards the end of the afternoon Rauch, with four battalions, advanced into the heart of Jauré's position to Lombron, although unable to clear it of the enemy before retreating for the night to La Vallée. Beckedorff's detachment, operating on the extreme right of the XIII Corps, took St Celerin after a brisk struggle before turning towards Chapelle St Remy. As the corps moved forward, Tresckow felt able to push forward his own advance along the river bank, reaching La Brosse before falling back to take up quarters for the night.

The movements of the XIII Corps were not therefore of a decisive character during the day; but at the other end of the Second Army's front more crucial developments had occurred. Advancing from Grand Lucé, the left flank of the X Corps had been covered by the 1st Battalion of the 12th Grenadier Regiment, from the 5th Division, which had seized the chateaux of Chef Raison and de la Paillerie; the battalion held on to these in the face of strong counter attacks until relieved by the arrival of the 14th Cavalry Brigade. The advanced guard of the 20th Division was still held up by the frozen and slippery roads, only reaching St Mars d'Outille by noon. Importantly, Voigts-Rhetz had chosen to come round further west before advancing on Le Mans from the south, rather than more directly through Parigné, in order to attack what he assumed to be the southern end of Chanzy's position, which he believed to be at Mulsanne. In fact, of course, Jauréguiberry's right was further north along the Chemin des Boeufs, so Voigts-Rhetz encountered only slight opposition and decided to go into quarters for the night. As the X Corps marched north, however, the sound of heavy gunfire could be heard ahead of it, and at 4.45pm Frederick Charles' hurry up order belatedly reached Voigts-Rhetz. In the face of this, the latter realised that however tired might be his troops, he must press forward up the Le Mans road. The advance was one of considerable difficulty; not only was he now running into Jauréguiberry's prepared positions, but the terrain was of great assistance to the defence, and 'presented extraordinary advantages to the adversary. Numerous ditches and banks offered cover to his skirmishers, while the separate copses and farmsteads formed points of support for the defence'.[38] In spite of this, the leading troops of the X Corps took Le Point du Jour before being held up at Les Mortes Aures. An advance to the west of the main road, however, led to the capture of this village, on the Chemin des Boeufs, and the X Corps pressed on up the road to take the key position of La Tuilerie. The attack had fallen on the luckless Breton Gardes Nationales, who were no match for the battle hardened veterans of the X Corps and who, having taken La Tuilerie, were quickly reinforced. Jauréguiberry could see that his whole front could be split wide open if he did not retake La Tuilerie, and ordered a night attack by Bouëdec, supported by Roquebrune. Heavy rifle fire proceded the assault; but when it came, it melted away in the face of the German infantry, and Bouëdec's disappointed troops did not merely return to their start lines; their spirit broken, they went on north towards Le Mans, deaf to the orders of their officers.

Chanzy had been greatly encouraged, earlier in the day, by the success of de Colomb in reoccupying part of the Plateau d'Auvours; and although as night fell he began to receive some very pessimistic reports from his commanders, they did nothing to weaken his belief that he could continue to hold his positions on the following day. The report he received from Jauréguiberry at 12.25am on January 12 changed all that. Reporting on the catastrophic events at La Tuilerie, Jauréguiberry was blunt in his advice. 'I am desolated to have to say that an immediate retreat seems to me to be imperative.' Perhaps only from Jauréguiberry would Chanzy accept such a doleful report; in the face of this, it was clear to him now that he could not hope to hold on to Le Mans. He wrote at once to the admiral to authorise the retreat: 'My heart bleeds; but when you, on whom I count the most, declare that the struggle is hopeless and the retreat unavoidable, I yield. Prepare, therefore, everything for the retreat, which should be as slow and as orderly as possible.'[39]

Frederick Charles and Stiehle, whose headquarters were now at Château Ardenay, received the reports from their subordinates with satisfaction. Although the III Corps had obviously had a hard struggle, and the progress of the XIII Corps was less than might have been hoped for, the advance of the X Corps showed as clearly to them as it did to Chanzy and Jauréguiberry that the battle for Le Mans was practically decided. For the following day the task of all four corps remained largely unaltered, except that Manstein was to send a brigade over the Huisne in support the Grand Duke's advance.

Next day the XIII Corps continued its advance, pressing steadily westwards, the 17th Division on either bank of the Huisne and the 22nd Division on its right. By nightfall, Tresckow's advance guard had reached Grand Houssaie, with his main body between Corneille and Pont- de-Gesnes. Wittich, with the main body of the 22nd Division came into action at La Croix in support of Beckedorff's detachment, which had been held up there by Villeneuve's Division. But what happened in this part of the field was no longer of much consequence; it was in the centre and on the left of the Second Army that the closing stages of the battle were to be fought out.

There, Manstein's leading troops, sent forward at dawn to clear the French from Lune d'Auvours, encountered little opposition, and patrols pushing on ahead found the country up to the Huisne to be clear of the enemy. On Manstein's right, the 35th Brigade advanced north to the support of the XIII Corps, finding little resistance before returning to Fatines. In Alvensleben's front, however, it soon became clear that the enemy had been reinforced, and preparations made for the defence of Pontlieue and the passages of the Huisne. Dense lines of skirmishers were seen, and numerous batteries on the heights. Contemplating this, and the appalling conditions under foot, Alvensleben concluded that there was no point in pushing forward to incur needless casualties; in discussion with him, Frederick Charles took the same view, and it was agreed that the III Corps should stand on the defensive, leaving the advance to Voigts-Rhetz and the X Corps.[40] During the morning a number of half hearted attacks were beaten off but by 11.00am the enemy could be seen to be falling back.

Voigts-Rhetz, leaving a detachment in Mulsanne to cover his rear, prepared to march directly into Le Mans. The 20th Division was concentrated at La Tuilerie, while the 14th Cavalry Brigade, followed by the corps artillery, moved on the road from Parigné. There was a brief French resistance at Les Epinettes, on the right of the advance; but the main body pressed on through Pontlieue and into the outskirts of Le Mans itself. Across the Huisne, Kraatz, with the leading troops of the 20th Division, was held up by a barricade, around which and in the adjoining houses the French put up a stiff resistance. As the X Corps penetrated further into the town, street fighting began to delay its progress. Nonetheless, after fierce house to house fighting, the victorious Germans by nightfall had reached the centre of the town, and the opposition petered out, thousands of prisoners being taken.

Chanzy's retreat had been skilfully executed. Although his casualties had been high -Frederick Charles had taken some 25,000 prisoners and it was estimated that twice as many as this had deserted from the 2nd Army of the Loire in the course of the campaign – he was able to take advantage of the shortness of the day, and the need for his adversary to seek quarters for the night, to get to get the bulk of his remaining troops away to the north, trudging to safety in the intense cold and through thick snow. That said, Chanzy's army had been smashed as an effective fighting force, and although he himself cherished hopes of being able to recruit his strength out of the reach of the enemy before making a fresh advance on Paris, it was a wildly optimistic assessment of the effective value of his army or its morale. Although on January 13 Frederick Charles sent forward troops briefly on pursuit

The staff of the French 2nd Army of the Loire, a contemporary photograph (Rousset/*Histoire*)

of Chanzy, he was soon content to let him go. And not even Moltke, usually so demanding of the relentless pursuit of a defeated enemy, found it necessary to follow Chanzy's shattered army. The evidence of the completeness of Frederick Charles' victory was everywhere. In addition to the prisoners taken, the Second Army had taken 17 guns, two colours, and a huge quantity of materiel. It had not achieved success without a high cost; total casualties were of the order of 3,400, and the army was utterly exhausted after a campaign fought in the most appalling conditions and which, as Michael Howard wrote, 'remained like a nightmare in the memories of all the participants, French and German alike'.[41] Nonetheless, of all the major battles in the second phase of the Franco-Prussian war, Le Mans was perhaps the most decisive. When Frederick Charles there broke the 2nd Army of the Loire, he destroyed the one army that had a chance, however remote, of inflicting a significant defeat on the German forces screening the investment of Paris. With an inspiring leader in Chanzy, who was supported by a number of other able and energetic commanders, the army's morale at the opening of the Le Mans campaign was, in spite of a string of previous defeats, reasonably high. It outnumbered its immediate adversary two to one and with the exception of the unfortunate Breton Mobiles, the troops were well equipped; their enthusiasm could not make up for their lack of training and experience but they were ready to go where they were led and to fight whoever they found there. But after Le Mans, all was changed; the comprehensiveness of the defeat, and the practical consequences of what was clear to everyone had been a military catastrophe, finally broke the army's will. The feeling was summed up by Roger de Mauni the day after the battle:

Streetfighting during the Battle of Le Mans, by Knötel (Pflugk-Harttung)

When I wrote the history of our retreat to Le Mans, I thought I should never again see a greater misfortune. I was mistaken. Our youth is destined to witness the most immense, the most overwhelming of disasters. France is sinking from one abyss to another, dragged down by the pitiless hand she has taken as her guide.[42]

23

The Lisaine

The first reaction of Werder's staff after the battle of Nuits had been to conclude that it would probably now be possible to hold on to Dijon until the fall of Paris, which it was believed could not be long delayed. Within days, however, intelligence reports came in which correctly indicated a rapid build up of the enemy in Lyons, coupled with information that these troops were moving north. This, in fact was incorrect; the enemy activity which had been noted was largely the movement eastwards of Bourbaki's troops. It was, however, clear that something was in the wind; intercepted letters referred to a French advance by Christmas, and the mercurial spirits of the population of Dijon again rose sharply. On December 21 Werder reported the information that he had received to Moltke, adding to his telegram: 'Is the corps to expect reinforcements? Dijon cannot be held with our present strength against attacks on all sides.'[1] In reply, Moltke next day could promise only one battalion by way of reinforcement; this, he said, was all that there was available. If a retreat was necessary, he suggested that Werder should take the direction of Chaumont, linking with von der Goltz and Zastrow. If the enemy moved on Belfort, the offensive could be resumed at once.[2] Meanwhile the Prussian ambassador at Berne had learned that the railway from Lyons to Besancon was reserved from December 23 for military purposes, which confirmed other intelli-

General von Werder at the Lisaine, painting by Becker (Rousset/*Histoire*)

gence suggesting a move towards Belfort. Two days later, Moltke's own news suggested that the threat to Werder was less than had been thought, and he telegraphed Werder to say that it was merely Gardes Nationales that were being moved to Besancon. This was, however, at odds with other information; Tresckow had now learned from Berne that a force of 25,000 men was marching to the relief of Belfort.

These conflicting reports caused considerable perplexity at Versailles, where attention was particularly focussed on the likely intentions for Bourbaki's army at Bourges and Nevers. As early as December 20 a rumour from Vienna that it that it might move eastwards was discounted on the basis that it was at Paris that the decision must come and that this was therefore the most likely objective. This view continued to be held for several days, and it was not until December 26, when Werder reported that Tresckow's estimate of the size of the relieving force was now 60,000, that Moltke began to accept that the French might after all, be determined on a stroke to the east. He approved Werder's intention to concentrate the forces of both Schmeling and von der Goltz at Vesoul and if necessary to evacuate Dijon, and told him that a further eight battalions of landwehr under Debschitz were on their way from Strasbourg to Belfort to reinforce him.[3] Moltke also notified both Werder and Zastrow that it now seemed likely that Bourbaki's army was being moved by rail from Nevers to Chalons sur Saône which if true would mean that some major operation in the east was intended, and would require the VII Corps to join the XIV Corps in order to thwart it. Blumenthal, who a few days earlier had been speculating that Bourbaki was marching on Paris, noted that it was now thought that he had gone to Lyons, with the intention not only to relieve Belfort but also to invade Germany. 'This last move would hardly be of any avail, and it is doubtful whether the invading troops would ever reach France again.'[4]

Next day the news that Gambetta was in Lyons, taken with all the other indications, confirmed to Moltke that the French were indeed preparing an offensive towards the east, and he set out the whole situation in a long letter to Zastrow, who he intended should take overall command of any operation against Bourbaki; Werder had, he wrote, a total of 53 battalions, 32 squadrons and 21 batteries including those actively besieging Belfort; Debschitz's force added another eight battalions, two squadrons and two batteries. As he marched south collecting his scattered forces Zastrow would have some 19 battalions, 12 squadrons and 10 batteries, so that the total force when he took overall command would be 80 battalions, 46 squadrons and 33 batteries.[5] It is difficult to resist the thought that this painstaking analysis was intended to hearten Zastrow in embarking on what might prove a distinctly difficult task, advancing over great distances through hostile territory to confront an enemy of unknown strength. Even now, however, Moltke was uncertain of the true situation. When he got news on December 30 that Bourbaki had perhaps not yet moved from Bourges and Nevers, he decided after all to leave Werder to operate independently for the moment, and halted the movement of the VII Corps. Telling Werder of this, he added that 'opposite you, at Besancon there are only disorganised units. Nothing more is known here.'[6] All in all, Werder could have been excused for thinking this not particularly helpful, as he raced to concentrate his troops in the area of Vesoul to meet the unknown but obviously developing threat from the south.

The evacuation of Dijon had begun on December 27; over 430 sick and wounded, with their attendant doctors and nurses had to be left behind in the city, where many of them were ill treated by the French when they arrived. The march eastwards was extremely difficult. 'The snow which had fallen heavily in the last few days had frozen hard, and had made the roads as slippery as glass; the horses slid about at every step, and made it most difficult for the baggage and the cavalry to travel.'[7] In spite of this, the XIV Corps made good time, Degenfeld reaching Vesoul on the evening of December 28 after marching 63 miles in two days. By December 30 the bulk of the corps had reached its intended positions. Keller was posted in Gray with five battalions, two squadrons and one battery; his task was to watch the enemy to see if he turned north through Dijon towards Langres, or continued eastwards through Dôle in the direction of Vesoul. Werder concentrated the rest of the corps around that town, pushing Schmeling with the 4th Reserve Division in the direction of Villersexel to watch for any French movement direct from Besancon or Belfort, which on the whole seemed the most likely course. However, on December 30 cavalry patrols reported that the French had blown up a bridge at l'Isle sur le Doubs, and further reports the following day confirmed that they had not crossed the Doubs, but had blown up other bridges.[8] Coupled with the erroneous news from Versailles that Bourbaki might still be at Bourges and Nevers, it began to look as if the French were after all not planning an immediate move on Belfort, and this led Moltke now to suggest to Werder that he should move back in a westerly and south westerly direction, re-establishing the investment of Langres and retaking Dijon if possible. Such a suggestion was, however, entirely inconsistent with the reality of the French position, as Werder was soon to discover.

After the defeat of the Army of the Loire, its enforced separation into two parts, and Bourbaki's assumption of command of the three corps around Bourges, there had been anguished debate about what next to do with them. At first, the immediate need had seemed to be an operation to relieve Chanzy; but his successful extrication of the 2nd Army of the Loire and its retreat westward made this unnecessary. Gambetta, who was at Bourges with Bourbaki, turned instead to the project of advancing through Gien and Montargis towards Paris. It was this that Moltke and his staff had thought most likely, and it was still being discussed on December 17 when Freycinet took a hand. Such a plan, he believed, could not succeed, since there was little prospect of a corresponding break out from Paris. In addition, the Germans would be on Bourbaki's flank at Orleans. Instead, he proposed taking advantage of the over stretched situation of Moltke's armies by moving Bourbaki, with two corps, to the east to combine with the troops already in the Saône valley and at Lyons. This army, 119,000 strong, could operate against Dijon, relieve Belfort and Langres and, if all went well, push on to the north. Gambetta and Bourbaki accepted the scheme without demur, even though its success depended on the doubtful ability of the French rail network to shift a lot of troops very quickly and keep them supplied as they advanced. Freycinet was now based at Bordeaux and he sent a young assistant, Auguste de Serres, to explain his scheme to Bourbaki. Almost at once the division of responsibility created a problem; Freycinet's idea had been for Bourbaki to take Dijon while Bressolles with the 24th Corps moved from Besancon to relieve Belfort, before the whole army marched north, but in the plan put to Bourbaki, the entire army was first to advance towards Belfort.

Freycinet and de Serres did not share Gambetta's belief that Bourbaki was the man to carry out such a bold scheme, and persuaded Gambetta that de Serres should remain at headquarters to oversee Bourbaki's conduct of operations. This was hardly likely to heighten the confidence of an already pessimistic commander, although in practice de Serres seems to have performed his mission with considerable tact.[9] The operation was intended to start on December 22, but disastrous and entirely predictable delays almost at once occurred, subjecting the unfortunate troops to a prolonged and nightmarish journey before they reached Chalons sur Saône. The situation was not improved by the fractured command structure, with Gambetta going to Lyons, Freycinet at Bordeaux and de Serres with Bourbaki. Although his enthusiasm worried Freycinet, it was thanks to de Serres that many of the logistic problems were overcome.

> The only hope of rescuing a campaign so fecklessly begun was a continuing genius for improvisation and unwearying energy, and this de Serres showed. He bull-dozed his way through obstructive railway officials, requisitioned labour to clear and mend the railway tracks, wheedled Garibaldi and charmed the generals. His task was impossible; but his efforts to perform it were Herculean.[10]

All these difficulties meant that Bourbaki was well behind schedule in getting his troops into positions from which they were more or less ready to advance; but he still had the not inconsiderable advantage that the Germans still had no idea that he was so close. By December 30 Bressolles, with the 24th Corps, was at Besancon; the 20th Corps, now commanded by Clinchant, was at Dôle and Billot with the 18th Corps was at Auxonne. Cremer meanwhile had moved into Dijon when Werder abandoned the city. Bourbaki's total strength was far greater than that of Werder, but characteristically he did not think it was enough, and he prevailed on Freycinet to let him have in addition the 15th Corps (Martineau), which had been left to cover Bourges. This unfortunate unit suffered even more severely at the hands of the French railway system than those which had preceded it, and it was not until January 8 that its leading units began to detrain at Clerval on the Doubs.

At Versailles, Moltke remained unconvinced that Werder was in any danger, and his prescription for preventing the relief of Belfort was still that the XIV Corps should take the offensive. Werder himself had been receiving a stream of intelligence about French movements, not all of which was consistent with the belief that the breaking of the bridges over the Doubs was a sign that no offensive was intended. His problem was to find out what was going on beyond that river, which since there were few crossing points was not easy. By January 3 the position was still unclear although von der Goltz, at Villersexel, reported that substantial enemy forces were expected at Rougemont, to which Werder responded by next day moving two brigades down the road from Vesoul towards Villersexel. The indications of enemy concentrations made it perfectly clear to Werder that Moltke's wish for an offensive to the west was out of the question, although ironically Moltke was still repeating the suggestion on January 4.[11]

On January 5 Werder planned to see for himself what the enemy was up to, intending to reconnoitre the Montbozon – Rioz road. Before he could set off, however, news came in that large forces had been seen behind Rioz; and later that there had been sharp encounters at Lévrecey and Echenoz le Sec, well to the west. Heavy snow storms made observation difficult, but by the afternoon units of both the 18th and 20th Corps were identified, leaving no doubt that Bourbaki's offensive had finally begun.[12] Werder had reported the first news to Moltke; at noon, he got a response that showed that his warnings were still not being taken seriously. Moltke recommended that he should concentrate all his forces for an immediate offensive. 'You will thus prevent the relief of Belfort, and your corps will thus be freed for another mission ... According to our information, Bourbaki is at Bourges.'[13] Moltke followed this with another telegram later that day; still holding to his belief that Bourbaki was at Bourges and Nevers, he suggested that the troops in front of Werder were those of Bressolles, Garibaldi and some Gardes Nationales. Werder was quick to correct the misapprehension at Versailles, with news that at least two of Bourbaki's corps had been identified; he had, as a result, abandoned any intention to move to the west, and proposed instead to attack the 20th Corps next day. This finally convinced Moltke; in a telegram of January 6, which Werder did not receive until the following day, he told him that if he was not successful, he should cover Belfort and hang on to the flank of any movement by Bourbaki towards Langres. More realistically, he added that the VII Corps would concentrate at Châtillon and would if necessary be reinforced by another corps.

Moltke's mind was now turning to a major reinforcement of his forces in the south east. The additional force which he had in mind was Fransecky's II Corps, currently at Montargis. He also decided that a new army command should be established to conduct the operations in the region, and chose Edwin von Manteuffel to lead it, ordering him to report as quickly as possible to receive instructions. Having failed for a number of days to appreciate the gravity of the situation, Moltke now acted with impressive speed. The 14th Division, which had been besieging Mézières, was at once ordered to rejoin Zastrow by marching to Châtillon; Fransecky was to move south east on a wide front through Joigny and Tonnerre.[14] If the French had, imprudently, decided to come out and fight, he did not intend to miss the opportunity of smashing them once and for all. For the moment, it was Werder upon whom the responsibility fell, and on the afternoon of January 7 Moltke sat down to write him a long letter reviewing the whole of the situation as he now saw it, which did not reach him until the evening of January 10. Although he had now accepted the true situation, Moltke's strategic views remained largely unchanged. Telling Werder of the formation of the new Army of the South, Moltke said that he should continue to report direct to Versailles until Manteuffel took over command. The priority remained the siege of Belfort, although Werder was to watch for any movement west of the Vosges. If he was obliged to retire, Werder must stay in close touch with Bourbaki to prevent him turning with his whole force on the II and VII Corps; Bourbaki would in any case be tied down to the railway and hence very susceptible to any threat to this.[15]

The general view at Versailles was that an advance by Bourbaki would ultimately expose him to complete defeat; on January 9 Blumenthal observed of the information that Bourbaki was heading for Nancy that it 'would indeed be the most foolish thing that he could do.'[16] By the time Werder read Moltke's letter his troops had been in action against Bourbaki for four days, and the situation was rapidly developing. Werder himself, with Glümer, Schmeling, and von der Goltz, had on January 5 settled on a number of alternative schemes to take account of widely differing situations that might develop. If Bourbaki marched on Nancy, which Werder regarded as the easiest threat to meet, a defensive position on the Durgeon brook near Vesoul had been identified. Werder very much hoped, however, that Bourbaki would not take the second option considered, which was to manoeuvre through Villersexel and try to cut off the XIV Corps from Belfort. In this case he intended to make use of his superior mobility to get to Belfort first. A third possibility, considered the least likely, was that Bourbaki might move direct on Belfort, covering his left along the Ognon. If he did so, Werder could attack his flank from Villersexel, a move which would certainly delay Bourbaki long enough for the XIV Corps to get to a defensive line covering Belfort along the Lisaine, which had already been identified as the best place to meet any attack on the besiegers.[17]

So far as the four generals could tell, the enemy movements on January 5 seemed to point to the first alternative being Bourbaki's intention; this was confirmed by interrogation of prisoners. Werder accordingly issued instructions to prepare to occupy the Durgeon position north of Vesoul to receive an attack next day. This involved withdrawing the bulk of his force behind Vesoul, with Schmeling in the town and Keller at its southern exit. No attack, however came: Bourbaki dared not risk a defeat at Vesoul, and did not believe his troops capable of a frontal assault. Instead, he stopped where he was, much to Werder's surprise; and to find out what the French were up to, the commander of the XIV Corps decided next day to push forward Glümer with the 2nd and 3rd Baden Infantry Brigades and the Baden Cavalry Brigade to probe the enemy's left. The weather was still appalling; heavy snow continued to fall, making movement down the roads extremely difficult. In the event, however, Bourbaki forestalled him, pulling back about several miles to Nordans, and Werder cancelled Glümer's advance, contenting himself with reconnaissance patrols. These suggested that Bourbaki was now moving to his right in the direction of Belfort, so Werder made preparations to move to the designated positions on the Lisaine to block the French advance.

There was no sign of enemy movement on January 7 and 8, and Werder remained unsure whether after all Bourbaki was heading for Belfort. He paused, therefore, to make certain of the French intentions, and in the absence of anything definite decided on January 9 to send forward Keller with the 3rd Brigade on a reconnaissance in force towards Rioz. On the night of January 8/9, however, his patrols were able in the bright moonlight to verify the eastward march of Bourbaki's army, and Werder, realising that there was no time to lose, put his whole force in motion. The Baden Division took the northern road to Athesans, while Schmeling was directed to Villersexel. Von der Goltz was held in reserve at Noroy le Bourg. A couple of battalions were left in Vesoul. Schmeling's advance guard, under Tresckow II, led the march on Villersexel, arriving opposite the town at 8.30am, finding it held by enemy troops in well prepared positions.[18]

Villersexel was going to be a tough nut to crack. Built on a hill, its key feature was a château in a walled park on the western edge of the town belonging to the Marquis de Gramont, who advised the defenders as to the best positions to take up.

A view of Villersexel photographed in 1871 (Rousset/*Histoire*)

There was one substantial bridge over the Ognon, which had been barricaded. The only other access was a rope bridge to the west, which an enterprising company of infantry crossed before pressing forward to the outskirts of the town. Early that morning, however, only some 200 French troops had reached Villersexel, and the energetic assault of the Germans had by 11.00 thrown them, and the first reinforcements to reach them, back and taken possession of the whole town. Riding up soon after with von der Goltz's brigade, Werder ordered it to occupy Marat, and then rode on to a hill where he had a good view of the country to the south. From here he could see heavy columns of French infantry to the east turning back towards Villersexel, while on the western side of the town the leading units of Billot's 18th Corps were getting in position to attack von der Goltz at Marat and Moimay. In spite of what was obviously a huge disparity of force, Werder was very satisfied. He ordered Schmeling and Tresckow II to hold Villersexel with as few men as possible, preferably pulling out the rest in the evening. The whole of the rest of his corps was to be ready to resume its eastwards march.[19] During the afternoon Bourbaki himself came up to the 20th Corps, whose troops were preparing to attack Villersexel for the south. Inspired by his presence, the French infantry stormed forward into the town just as the bulk of Schmeling's men were leaving the town. Fearing that this French success would seriously menace the movement of his division, Schmeling at once gave orders for the place to be retaken. The retreating Germans turned about and launched a furious bayonet charge upon their pursuers. As darkness fell they forced their way back into the town and a savage house to house battle began, the scene being lit by a bright moon and the flames of burning buildings. Werder, who had been supervising the march of the rest of his corps eastwards, called a hasty conference of his staff at a farm north of Marat, and issued orders for the following day. His intention was to disengage as many of his units as possible, in order to get them away to Belfort, while leaving enough support to Schmeling to hold Villersexel as long as necessary.

In fact however, something of a stalemate had developed in the town, and especially around the château, the ground floor of which was reoccupied by the

Streetfighting in Villersexel, by Zimmer (Pflugk-Harttung)

Germans while the French held the basement and the upper story. A bitter struggle ensued; in one room the Germans took 120 prisoners but elsewhere the French held out. Finally the building caught fire and partly collapsed on the combatants. It took until 2.00 am finally to clear the town of the French, which enabled Schmeling to pull back his troops in good order, and to follow the rest of the corps towards Aillerans. Von der Goltz, whose troops had held Moimay under strong pressure from the 18th Corps, was also now able to disengage and move on the prescribed route towards the Lisaine position. Total German casualties amounted to 579; the French losses exceeded this figure, and in addition they lost some 700 wounded prisoners. Each side claimed a victory, but in truth it had been a drawn battle.[20]

The French only cautiously followed up, entering Villersexel at dawn on January 10. By then Werder's troops were en route, moving down narrow roads as fast as they could. Anticipating the bottlenecks, staff officers had gone ahead to ensure that the troops moved through narrow places at the double.[21] As a result, the movement of the whole of the XIV Corps proceeded without disturbance by the

French infantry storming Villersexel, painting by de Neuville (Rousset/*Histoire*)

enemy. Werder himself paused for a brief rest in Lure before moving on through Ronchamps to Frahier, where he was met by a courier with Moltke's letter of January 7.

Next morning Werder met with Tresckow 1 at Argiesans to concert plans for the defence of the Lisaine position. A start had already been made on preparing the ground; batteries were being prepared, and trenches dug, and during the next couple of days the work of his troops proceeded apace.

> They brought up siege guns, dug trenches and mined the bridges; they cut paths through the thick woods behind their lines, laid a complex of telegraph wires, covered icy roads with sand and manure, lit fires to melt the worst patches of ice, and broke up the ice along the Lisaine.[22]

The work was carried out under the supervision of the able Colonel von Scheliha, who had been commanding the siege artillery at Belfort; the ultimate strength of the position in which Werder was to receive Bourbaki's assault owed a great deal to Scheliha's skill and energy.

The position into which the XIV Corps now marched was already naturally a strong one. It stood behind the shallow River Lisaine, which runs down from the Vosges to join the Doubs at Montbéliard. There, an old but still defensible castle stood over the town, in its turn commanded by the ruins of an old citadel to the west. On each side of the river northwards the wooded slopes of the valley rise steeply. No roads crossed the river south of Héricourt. The key to Montbéliard itself was a hill to the north of the town, la Grange Dame, where a heavy battery was located which also covered Bethoncourt to the north. At Bussurel a railway

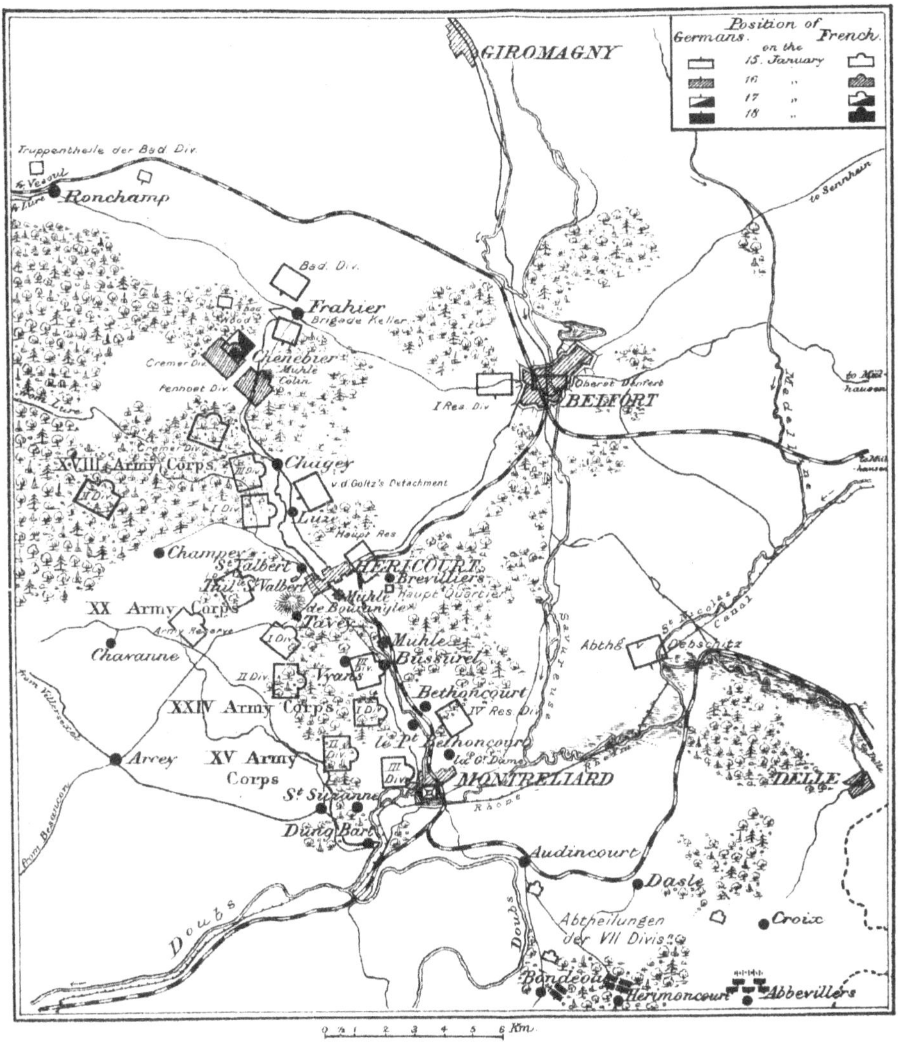

The actions on the Lisaine, January 1871

embankment provided a strong infantry position. South of Héricourt the valley widens; the marshy ground here was commanded by Mont Salamon. Héricourt bestrides the river, and a bridge head had been prepared to assist in the defence of the western half of the town based on the Mougnot Hill. North of Héricourt the heights were crowned by further batteries, overlooking the broader meadows here, where the slopes of the hills are shallower. Here a key point was Mont Vaudois, which was the principal point of support for the right of the position. Beyond this lay Chagey, a village that had been prepared for defence, although the impassable thick woodland west of the Lisaine here made an attack improbable.

Although this main position was a strong one, Werder had also to be concerned with his flanks. On his left eight miles of broken country separated Montbéliard from the Swiss frontier, in which a number of strong defensive positions were to be found. On his right Werder was at his weakest, between Etoben and Frahier, where a gap in the thick forests would allow an approach through the little villages clustered there. Behind them a useful defensive position on the heights of Rougeot provided a long stop in the event of the French making progress in this sector.

Werder and Tresckow had agreed that the forces containing Belfort must be pared down to a minimum to ensure the maximum possible strength in the Lisaine position. Debschitz, with eight battalions, was to cover the left flank reaching towards the Swiss border. Schmeling's division was to hold Montbéliard and the line up to Hericourt. Beyond this stood von der Goltz, with his main body in Chagey and Luze; Wechmar, with the 1st Baden Brigade, came next, around Mandevillars and Chalonvillars; and beyond him Degenfeld and Keller around Frahier. These were in touch with Willisen's outpost at Lure, which had orders to fall back if pressed on Ronchamp and then to Giromagny. Werder, who established his headquarters in Brévilliers, issued his detailed orders on the evening of January 11. Next day was spent all along the line in further strengthening the position, and deepening the river by excavations and damming; more guns were brought into line from the siege lines around Belfort, especially at Montbéliard Castle and on la Grange Dame. Further earthworks were thrown up on Mougnot Hill, and all along the front fields of fire were cleared. To the west, the French moved slowly forward; but there was little contact save with Willisen's force at Lure, which probed south as far as Athesans.[23]

On January 13 the French closed up to the advance guards which lightly held the line Saulnot – Chavanne – Arcey with orders to hold their positions as long as they could, but to fall back when strongly pressed. At midday Billot pushed forward through Saulnot and Corcelles with eight battalions, forcing Nachtigall, who commanded the advanced guard there to fall back on Champey, while further south Loos fell back from Sainte Marie to the line of the Rupt stream. These preliminary actions were sharply contested, costing the Germans nearly over 250 casualties.[24] They seemed, moreover, to suggest that the French intended to launch their main attack between Montbéliard and Héricourt, rather than further north, where there was little activity. As a result, Werder built up a strong reserve behind Hericourt around Brévillers to be ready for an attack which he expected on the following day.

Montbéliard, painting by Detaille (Rousset/*Histoire*)

It did not come; but in one respect January 14 brought a serious setback for Werder, a heavy frost causing the rivers and the canal to freeze hard to the point where they could be crossed not only by infantry, but also by cavalry, and he began to feel distinctly anxious. If the French could get over the Lisaine easily at any point, his thinly stretched line, nearly twelve miles in length from Montbéliard to Frahier, must become much more vulnerable. Reporting that evening to Moltke, he warned of the seriousness of his position.

> I urgently ask if I must remain for long before Belfort, in the face of superior forces which seek to surround me. I think I can protect Alsace, but not Belfort as well unless I am to put at risk the existence of my corps. The obligation to maintain the siege of Belfort deprives me of all freedom of movement. The frost allows all rivers to be crossed.[25]

This message reached Versailles just after midnight, and led to a pregnant moment at the daily report at the Royal Headquarters, as the Crown Prince noted in his diary:

> One must have seen General Count Moltke's face and known him too as well as I do to form a conception of the look with which he communicated this telegram to me in the King's antechamber, then read it out at the report, and with what an air of imperturbable, icy calm he added: " Your Majesty will, I trust, approve of this answer to General von Werder, that he has simply to stand firm

> and beat the enemy wherever he finds him." I cannot say how admirable beyond all praise I thought General Moltke at this moment; any other man would have launched out with reflections and exclamations – he in one second relieved the whole strain of the situation and, thank heaven, restored General von Werder's steadiness.[26]

Next day after the battle had begun, Moltke's implacable response arrived at Werder's headquarters: 'Await the enemy attack in the fortified position covering Belfort, and accept battle. The possession of the Lure – Belfort road is of the highest importance ... The march of General von Manteuffel will soon make its influence felt.'[27] Moltke himself, in his own history of the war, observed that Werder was in this way 'as was only fair, relieved of the moral responsibility of the consequences of a possibly disastrous issue.'[28]

Bourbaki may have made only painfully slow progress in his approach to Werder's position, but at least he had succeeded in deceiving his opponent as to his plan of attack. His intention was that the 20th, 24th and 15th Corps should act as a pivot, fixing the German line between Héricourt and Montbéliard while to the north Billot, with the 18th Corps and Cremer's division, turned the German right. He believed that Werder's prepared position went no further north than Héricourt; if so, Billot's turning movement through Chagey and Chenebier should encounter little opposition. In spite of his faulty intelligence, the plan was a good one; Werder's response to the preliminary clashes had been to concentrate further south, leaving the troops holding the right of the line dangerously weakened. Given that he had 111,000 men to Werder's 40,000, even the gloomy Bourbaki might reasonably hope for success.[29] He had plenty of troops, if they were not too inexperienced, too hungry and especially too cold. On the night January 15 there were eighteen degrees of frost; unlike Werder's men, many of whom were in billets, the French were obliged to bivouac in the open.[30]

Early on January 15 the French bugles sounded along the whole line, and the German troops stood to. By 8.30 the French artillery had opened up and under the cover of a general bombardment the infantry moved forward. Martineau's 15th Corps, opposite Montbéliard, drove back the German pickets from their advanced positions west of the Lisaine, although not without difficulty in the face of brisk local counter attacks. It was 1.00pm before the last German defenders retreated from Mont Chevis farm through Montbéliard. Colonel Zimmermann, commanding in this sector, fell back gradually through the town, taking up a position at Sochaux to the east; the castle however was firmly held, and the garrison, well supported by its own artillery and that on la Grange Dame, was able to command Montbéliard and prevent the French occupying it with more than skirmishers until after nightfall.[31]

The attack on Montbéliard had been carried out by the divisions of Rebillaud and Peytavin; to the north, d'Astughe's division advanced at the same time against Bethoncourt, coming under fire from the German batteries on la Grange Dame and heavy infantry fire from the defenders of the railway embankment. In spite of enormously outnumbering the defenders, and attacking with considerable élan, the assault broke down with heavy loss.

On the left of Martineau's Corps, Bressolles had the village of Bussurel as his principal objective. He was not able to get his troops forward through the narrow forest tracks and into position to attack until 2.00pm. The village itself, on the west bank of the Lisaine, had been abandoned by the Germans, who held the line of the river and the railway embankment, and also the mill buildings directly north of Bussurel. The initial French assault broke down with heavy loss; another attack at 4.00pm under the cover of a heavy artillery barrage, was directed on the mill. This threatened briefly to make ground but was finally broken up by artillery fire from a battery at Bethoncourt and from two batteries of the reserve which Werder had held around Brévilliers. Out in the open the long columns of advancing French infantry suffered heavily from the shellfire, and retreated with heavy losses.[32]

Clinchant's 20th Corps, opposite Héricourt, faced the strongest point of Werder's line, although the thick woods to the west gave him the opportunity to approach under cover close to the German position. The Mougnot, on the west side of the river, had been greatly strengthened by the energetic work of Werder's pioneers. 'The wood which partly covers it had been cut down, with the exception of a nearly impassable part at the south foot. Shelter trenches, two rows in places, crowned the summit, strong barricades closed the deep cutting of the high road, and the buildings of Marion Farm on the height to the south had been provided with loopholes. The town itself had been arranged for defence.'[33] Clinchant's orders were not to attack until Billot and Cremer had launched their outflanking movement to the north, and for the moment, having closed right up to the German position, he contented himself with artillery fire, and awaited developments on his left.

Here, however, things were not going well. Bourbaki's orders did not reach Billot until midnight, and although he passed them on at once to Cremer, the latter's troops were still some 14 miles from their first objective. Seriously hampered by the snow laden forest tracks, Cremer's forward march was held up still further when his leading columns collided in Lyoffans with the advancing troops of the 18th Corps, causing pronged delays to both units. These were made worse by orders to let the artillery pass through, and it was not until 2.00pm that Billot was able to deploy the whole of his corps in front of Luze and Chagey. The latter place was held only by one battalion under Major Lang, who earlier in the day had beaten off without difficulty a rather tentative assault by Billot's advance guard. Now, however, greatly outnumbered, he came under much stronger pressure, and by the middle of the afternoon the French forced their way into the village where fierce street fighting took pace. At this point, however, reinforcements in the shape of a battalion under Captain Weinzierl came up, sent by Werder from his reserve. The two battalions launched a counter attack, retaking the village by 5.00 pm and driving the French back into the shelter of the woods as night fell. As the fighting came to an end Werder was sufficiently anxious to send another battalion to Chagey, where he expected a fresh assault the following morning.[34]

Cremer, meanwhile, had still been plodding forward towards the intended start line for his assault on Chenebier on the far right of Werder's position. The delays imposed on his march by the confusion in the forest, and the distance he had to travel, meant that he got into position only as darkness tell, and he was able to do no more than move one brigade up to Etobon to cover his left while the rest of his division struggled forward, frequently halting for the engineers to make the roads passable. As a result, he arrived only as darkness fell; accidental contact with the German outposts caused some exchanges of fire, leading Cremer to order his troops to stand to arms throughout the bitterly cold night which followed.[35]

By the end of the first day's fighting Werder could feel pretty satisfied. Nowhere had Bourbaki broken through, and his attacks had been thrown back with heavy losses, which must have damaged the morale of the inexperienced French troops. Even more importantly, the German artillery had maintained its customary superiority, which augured well for the rest of the battle. On the other hand, the delay in the advance of Bourbaki's right wing, and signs of reinforcement of the enemy's forces between Héricourt and Montbéliard, confirmed Werder's belief that this continued to be the danger point, and the minor changes he made in his dispositions reflected this. He now put Glümer in overall command of the section between Héricourt and Montbéliard, and von der Goltz in command of all the troops in Chagey. Anxious to keep as large a reserve in hand as possible he added to it a battery from Schmeling's division and withdrew a battalion that had moved up to support the defenders of Chagey.

For his part, Bourbaki felt that things had not gone too badly. His troops had fought well, and he hoped that when his movement around the German right took effect he might get into a winning position. He had waited all day for news of this, finally sending at 5.00pm a senior staff officer to Billot to find out what was going on. Billot pointed out that Mont Vaudois was not, as had been thought, the northern end of the German position, and that the movement of the left must be correspondingly extended. Bourbaki put Werder's strength at between 80,000 and 100,000 men, believing him to have been substantially reinforced; but he nonetheless sent off an optimistic telegram reporting that he hoped to open the road to Belfort next day.[36]

When dawn broke on January 16, a thick mist covered the valley, limiting visibility until noon and preventing the effective use of artillery. The French made an early start, Clinchant's troops coming forward in separate attacks on the Mougnot and St Valbert at 8.00 am. Both failed, as did a third attack on the eastern side of the Mougnot. Just to the south of Héricourt, Bourangles mill which stood alone on the road to Montbéliard had been fortified and garrisoned by one company; at about noon this was subjected to a heavy assault, which was however with the clearing of the mist broken up by the German artillery. Opposite Bussurel, too, the French were observed to be concentrating for an attack, but Keller had plenty of time to get two battalions supported by a heavy battery into position; when the attack came in at about 11.00 am under a heavy French artillery barrage there were signs that the spirit of the infantry was beginning to flag. As they tried to get across the Lisaine, 'only the heads of the columns went on; the attacking troops quailed and broke under the heavy and well aimed shell and rifle fire, and sought shelter in the numerous gullies from which they had issued.'[37] In Montbéliard, possession of the castle prevented any effective French advance. Although they moved up to it, pouring a heavy rifle fire on the castle from behind the walls and roofs of houses in the town, they were able to make little impression.

At 3.00 pm, after a preliminary barrage that had continued for some three hours, Bressolles launched a brigade at the double towards Bethoncourt. Under heavy rifle fire, as well as artillery fire from la Grange Dame, the attack got no further than the banks of the Lisaine before breaking, the French infantry falling back into the woods opposite. Two further attacks, each of brigade strength, broke down before reaching the river. By 5.00pm, as night began to fall, the firing on this part of the line died down.[38] At Héricourt, Clinchant's troops had been keeping their heads down since the failure of the morning's attacks. At 7.00pm however, his artillery opened fire on the Mougnot, and the barrage gradually extended to the south where Bressolles' artillery joined in. Not much could be seen; the German artillery responded by aiming at the flashes of the enemy guns. Löhlein, at headquarters at Brévillers, recorded that Werder was extremely apprehensive as to what this assault portended; he 'sent staff officers to various points along the line, and listened in anxious expectation of the result. No one who spent these hours with him will ever forget them.'[39] Infantry attacks followed all along the line, but Werder was at the last reassured as news came that all the assaults had been driven back, in some cases at the point of the bayonet.

It was not, however, at Héricourt or Bethoncourt that the crucial engagements took place on January 16, but to the north, where Cremer and Billot were finally ready to launch the outflanking movement. Werder, still completely unaware of Bourbaki's intentions, had ordered Degenfeld at Frahier to be ready to take the offensive; but it was soon evident that this was out of the question, as strong bodies of French infantry moved up the road towards Chenebier, and French artillery opened fire on Degenfeld's positions, which extended from Courchamp through Chenebier and the woods to the north. The advancing enemy consisted of Cremer's Division supported on its left by Penhoët with the 1st Division of the 18th Corps, a force which heavily outnumbered Degenfeld, who had only two battalions, one squadron and two batteries with which to hold the position. After some hours of skirmishing, Colonel Poullet, Cremer's chief of staff, led two regiments forward to the south of Chenebier, while Penhoët launched two regiments towards the western end of the straggling village and two more battalions around to the north. In the face of these attacks, Degenfeld was unable to hold Chenebier, and was driven back towards Echevanne and Frahier. No defensible position was to be found there, and Degenfeld moved further back to the last position on the Belfort road, at Rougeot Mill, where he dug in on the higher ground to await the inevitable further assault.[40]

Repeated requests to Werder during the afternoon for support had been denied, but at last at 6.00pm Colonel Bayer arrived with two battalions from the reserve. Even so, the position was hazardous in the extreme. Cremer and Penhoët still had overwhelming numerical superiority, and if they broke through at Rougeot Mill the right of Werder's position would be turned, and Chagey and Luze would have to be abandoned; the whole line might at this point be rolled up. Werder sent a staff officer to Keller, by now at Mandrevillars, to see what he could do to launch a night attack to retake Chenebier, and reinforced him to a total strength of eight battalions four squadrons and four batteries. It was a desperate expedient; but it was in fact unnecessary. Exhausted by the day's fighting, Cremer's troops were in no state to advance further, and Bourbaki was in any case getting cold feet about the outflanking movement which was taking him further away from the crucial railway line from Besancon. As a result he told Billot not to push the attack any further.[41]

None of this was known to Werder, of course; deeply anxious at his exposed position, he applied to Tresckow for help from the besieging troops. The indefatigable Scheliha hurried to Essert and, using troops to pull the guns over the narrow roads, brought up three 24 pounders from the siege batteries and by dawn on January 17 had them in position at Rougeot Mill. Meanwhile, relieved by the defeat of the night attacks at Héricourt and Bethoncourt, Werder reassembled his reserve at Brévilliers, calling up troops from Glümer and Schmeling to put together a force of five battalions and two batteries while strengthening the front line with two battalions from Debschitz.[42]

Werder had reported the potentially threatening situation to Versailles and the steps he was taking to deal with it. Among some of those at Royal Headquarters there was a considerable nervousness. The Crown Prince observed that

> it is in no little suspense we look for the arrival of the next news, for, although the occurrence mentioned is in itself no real disadvantage, yet we have grounds for supposing that it is just at this point the enemy's main force will concentrate; thus even so small a success will no doubt duly set aflame the French spirit of enterprise.

The King was convinced that at the very moment of his installation as Emperor he would receive 'the very worst news' from the Vosges; but Moltke was unruffled. 'All he said to it was: "The good God will not allow us to suffer reverses," but otherwise went on unshaken in his usual calm composure.'[43] And Blumenthal, whose confidence in his own prognostications was not by any means always justified, had the day before recorded an entirely accurate prophecy: 'I can see clearly that Bourbaki's Army will be annihilated; whatever is left of it will be thrown over the Swiss frontier, unless it takes flight in the direction of Nancy, when it will be nicely caught on the flank.'[44]

Keller, who had spent the night collecting together his force, wasted no time next morning. The assault on Chenebier was to be undertaken by two columns; the right column of two and a half battalions was to advance through Echevanne against the northern edge of Chenebier, while Degenfeld with the 4th Regiment moved against the southern part of the village. The troops set off at 4.30 am in pitch darkness. At 5.00pm the right column surprised a French picket; the outbreak of rifle fire which followed this had alerted the French, and Keller ordered Degenfeld to advance at the run into Chenebier. In the first confusion Courchamp was also taken; but in parts of Chenebier the French pulled themselves together and put up a stout defence. Meanwhile the right column under Major Jacobi was pinned down in the Bois des Evauts, where a furious hand to hand combat ensued.

As day broke, Cremer reacted to the surprise attack, bringing up heavy reinforcements. It was soon evident that in the face of these the southern and eastern parts of Chenebier could not be held, and the Germans fell slowly back. To the north, however, an additional battalion sent up by Degenfeld enabled the wood to be taken, and an attempt on this side of the village was made. In the face of some unusually successful employment of mitrailleuses, however, the advance was beaten back with heavy loss.[45] Further south, meanwhile, von der Goltz had sent Major Lang forward from Chagey with one and a half battalions to support the attack on Chenebier; but he soon encountered strong French forces barring his way. Ultimately he managed to get round their right, and made his way towards Chenebier, arriving at the edge of the village at 4.00 pm. Here, however, the fighting had died down, but Lang's arrival meant that Keller could disengage his left.

Meanwhile the weather changed completely; the day had begun with a further heavy snowfall, but by noon this had changed to rain, and as a result the rapidly melting snow made off-road movement extremely difficult. Apart from the fighting at Chenebier and to the north of Chagey, there was however little activity along the rest of the front. At Héricourt an artillery exchange was followed by a halfhearted attack on the railway embankment; at Bussurel too there was some activity but at Bethoncourt there was no action. At Montbéliard, the batteries on la Grange Dame shelled the town, until a municipal deputation arrived to ask them to desist, assuring the Germans that the French infantry had all now pulled out. As a result contact was re established with the courageous defenders of the castle who had held their position so effectively. On the other side of the Lisaine Martineau's troops confined their activity to skirmishing parties pushed forward rather ineffectually towards the old citadel and the river.[46]

These were clear indications that the Army of the East had shot its bolt, and on the French side the realisation of defeat was widespread. At noon, Bourbaki 'rode over the battlefields, to hear the opinions of the generals in command. They assured him that, with soldiers worn out, ill-fed, and suffering from cold, the German lines could not be forced.'[47] Later that afternoon, at a conference with his senior officers, Bourbaki considered the possibility of making a further effort to outflank Werder's right; but his continued anxiety for his crucial supply line from Besancon, and the state of his troops, led him to conclude that no more should be attempted, and he gave the order to retreat. Reporting this to Freycinet, he put on it the best face he could:

> On the advice of my corps commanders I have decided, to my great regret, that the army should take up new positions some miles behind those in which we have fought … If the enemy decides to follow us I will be delighted; perhaps that will offer us the chance to fight again much more favourable circumstances.[49]

On his side Werder had been cautiously reaching the conclusion that the battle was won, but he intended to wait until the French pulled back from Héricourt before taking any steps to follow them up. That evening, as he made preparations to do so, he realised that an immediate advance would be extremely dangerous. If the French faced him in a strong defensive position, of which the broken country provided plenty, the boot would be entirely on the other foot, and he must risk extremely heavy casualties. His troops were hungry and exhausted; supplying an advance would be extremely difficult; and many of his units, especially the artillery, had almost exhausted their ammunition. As a result, his orders for January 18 were for reconnaissance only along the whole of the front, which soon established that strong rearguards were covering the French withdrawal.[50]

It is understandable that Löhlein, always a partisan historian, should thus defend the decision not immediately to pursue, but in all the circumstances it was clearly right. Werder's object had been to prevent the relief of Belfort, and he had succeeded in this, as well as inflicting a most damaging defeat on the Army of the East. If there was more fighting to come, as seemed very likely, it was better not to hazard the XIV Corps until the rest of the Army of the South began to arrive on the scene. As it was, he and his men richly deserved the praise which was heaped upon them. It had been a remarkable victory, fought in the most appalling conditions. The total French loss is uncertain, but their own estimates put it above 8,000 men. The Germans sustained total casualties of 1,595. In his message of congratulations William wrote to Werder: 'Your heroic three days defence of your position with a besieged fortress in your rear, is one of the greatest feats of arms of all times;' and he conferred on him the Order of the Red Eagle with Swords.[51] After the scarcely veiled criticism to which he had been subjected for many weeks, Werder must have found this recognition especially rewarding. The full fruits of the victory over Bourbaki's army were of course yet to be gathered, as Howard observed: 'The approach of Manteuffel turned the repulse into a retreat which was to end in one of the greatest disasters that has ever overtaken a European army.'[52]

24

Bapaume and Péronne

On the western side of the First Army's area of operations, Bentheim had had much less to contend with than had Goeben, who was facing a considerably more active opponent in Faidherbe. Unclear as to the position of Briand's forces, Bentheim on December 16 launched Gayl's 1st Division in a reconnaissance in force on the left bank of the Seine as far as the Rille. Gayl encountered no opposition, and reported that the only substantial body of troops in this direction seemed to be to the west of Brionne. These troops Bentheim watched thereafter with the 1st Brigade (von Böcking) at Elbeuf, until the time came to detach a substantial part of the corps to Amiens to reinforce Goeben before the battle on the Hallue. Thereafter, Böcking was pulled back to Grand Couronne, the French cautiously following and pushing forward outposts to Bourgtheroulde and La Bouille. Meanwhile, on the right back of the Seine, patrols from Pritzelwitz's 2nd Division towards Yvetot and Caudebec reported little enemy activity, although the French were making use of the river to bring steamers loaded with troops up stream as far as Duclair. These incursions Bentheim curtailed by sinking a number of colliers to block the river; a number of these vessels were British, which led to an energetic but fruitless protest by the British government.[1]

On December 23 there were signs of increased activity in the area of Bolbec; Bentheim despatched a force of four companies and three squadrons under Lieutenant Colonel von Ploetz to investigate. Although the French retired from Bolbec after some brief skirmishes, the troops there fell back on a force that Ploetz estimated as 7,000 strong, and the indication which this gave of an early advance in force on Rouen could not be ignored. Bentheim sent urgent requests to Manteuffel for reinforcement, to which the latter responded by ordering the return to Rouen of those troops from the I Corps that had gone to Amiens to support Goeben. Between December 25 and 30 their arrival enabled Bentheim first to strengthen his defences and then to prepare for an offensive to break up the threatening concentration.

With the threat from Faidherbe having for the moment disappeared, Manteuffel was able to consider what should be his next steps to secure his position. The most pressing need was now to secure Péronne, and as soon as the Army of the North had begun to retreat from the Hallue, he ordered the investment of this fortress, which Goeben was to cover from his position at Bapaume. The ancient town of Péronne of some 4,000 inhabitants was situated at the junction of the little Cologne river with the Somme. Surrounded by a bastioned wall, with mediaeval towers, there was a sixteenth century castle on its north west front. It was, however so much overlooked by higher ground that it seemed unlikely that it could sustain a prolonged siege, although little was known about the strength of the fortifications. The Somme at that point was not a very substantial obstacle, being about ten yards wide and five feet deep, but the canal that ran parallel to it was much wider and deeper. In spite of the cold weather, there was insufficient ice in the wet ditches to bear a man's weight; and in the clear moonlit nights, any attempt at a coup de main was unlikely to succeed over the snow covered ground and flooded areas around the fortress. Attempts to compel its surrender by field artillery bombardment had proved ineffective. Péronne had hitherto been a decided nuisance in the hands of the French, serving as a base for small scale attacks on the German lines of communications; more seriously, its possession gave Faidherbe a useful defensive cover for any large scale offensive he might have in mind. And all the time the French held on to it, they hampered German command of the line of the Somme between La Fère and Amiens. The commandant of the fortress, Major Garnier, had a garrison of about 3,600 men, with forty nine guns.[2]

German experience thus far in the war had shown that the French fortresses were largely impervious to attack by field artillery; but that when a siege train could be assembled and brought up, usually only a couple of days' bombardment was necessary to bring about a capitulation. There was no siege train immediately available; but the officer commanding the artillery in the Amiens citadel suggested that ten suitable siege guns could be found from there, and Manteuffel ordered him to go ahead and prepare for a siege of Péronne.[3] This improvised siege train could not leave Amiens before December 28, so for the moment the investment of the fortress proceeded with the support only of field artillery. Manteuffel put Schuler von Senden in overall command of the operation, which was to be carried out by Barnekow's 16th Division together with the 3rd Reserve Division. On December 28, the garrison of Péronne was summoned to surrender; this brought no response, and at 3.00pm the field artillery opened fire on the fortress from all sides.[4]

Since the operations at Péronne were clearly going to take some time, and Faidherbe was for the moment out of range, Manteuffel decided to return to Rouen, where the indications of an imminent French offensive continued to mount. Before leaving, he held a meeting with Goeben at his headquarters at Combles on the morning of December 28, where they agreed on the policy to be pursued. Goeben was, with the troops at his disposal, to prosecute the siege of Péronne, covering it to the north, and sending forward flying columns to break up enemy communications north of the Somme and, if possible, beyond Arras. Bentheim, to whom the 3rd Brigade had been restored, would have the unchanged task of holding Rouen and watching Le Havre. Manteuffel wrote to Goeben and Bentheim setting out these intentions, and also sought Moltke's approval for the attack on Péronne. This Moltke was quick to grant on December 29; he also modified his previous instruction about Beauvais, since the railway link between Amiens and Rouen was now in full working order. Thanks to this, reinforcements could reach Rouen from Amiens extremely quickly if the need arose, making it no longer necessary to hold a large reserve at Beauvais.[5]

On December 31 Manteuffel was able to check for himself the efficiency of the rail link; that morning he travelled the 67 miles from Amiens to Rouen in just over two hours, accompanied by part of his headquarters staff and an infantry escort, followed by a battalion of the 2nd Brigade that was returning to the I Corps.[7] There he found Bentheim still expecting the French to launch their offensive that day and, indeed, there was a forward move by a force from Moulineaux towards Grand Couronne, which was easily halted by artillery fire. Counter-attacking, a column led by Lieutenant Colonel von Hüllessem found that a number of French soldiers were occupying the ruined castle of Robert le Diable perched on a steep hill; two companies of the 41st Regiment stormed the ruins, taking two officers and eighty men prisoners. Other German columns encountered substantial French forces before returning to their original position. All the signs were that the French were in sufficient force to embark on a full scale advance if they chose. The immediate commander of the French forces was known to be General Roye.[8]

In spite of these indications of an early attack, Manteuffel told Bentheim that the return of his troops from Amiens was only be regarded as a temporary measure; if the French did not advance, then Bentheim should himself attack, in order to clear his lines and allow troops to go back to Amiens, where more serious operations were to be expected. Having given these instructions, Manteuffel returned to Amiens on the afternoon of January 1. Bentheim accordingly assembled a force of some twelve and half battalions, two squadrons and four batteries under his artillery commander Major General von Bergmann for an advance on Moulineax from Grand Couronne. Before day break on January 4 Hüllessem, with six companies, again led the advance, moving through the forest to the south of the river road while two and a half battalions on his right marched along the road towards Moulineaux. Colonel von Legat, with two more battalions, one squadron and two batteries, followed, and behind him was another column led by Colonel von Busse consisting of four battalions, one squadron and two batteries. Hüllessem fell on the French outposts in the moonlight and drove them back over familiar ground on to the heights of Château Robert le Diable. As soon as his supports came up, Hüllessem stormed the heights and made prisoner those French troops that attempted to defend themselves in the castle ruins. The taking of the heights effectively cleared the way for the further troops advancing up the river road, and the Germans pushed forward until they encountered a strong French force at the cross roads at Maison Brulet; a turning movement by Legat drove them back Bourgachard, with Legat's men in pursuit, while Hüllessem turned south through the forest of La Lande. Coming up behind, Busse's force took Bourgtheroulde, driving the French back towards Brionne.[9] Legat, advancing towards Bourgachard, met stiff resistance at St Ouen, which broke only when a Prussian battery dshed up and unlimbered within 300 yards of the French positions. After taking Bourgachard, Legat put Major Preinitzer and a company of infantry on carts, and with half a squadron and two guns sent him in pursuit of the retreating enemy, surprising them about six miles west of Bourgachard.[10]

Next day it was found that the French had retreated well out of reach, Bergmann's patrols finding the country up to the Rille clear of the enemy. The fighting on January 4 had cost Bergmann a total of 172 men killed and wounded; Roye's casualties were about the same, but in addition some 300 French prisoners and four guns were taken.[11] Considering the size of the forces involved, it was an insubstantial encounter; but it was the largest single engagement fought by the I Corps against Briand's forces, and it had the effect of causing General Peletingeas, commanding the French on the right bank of the Seine, and who had moved forward towards Rouen, to scurry hastily back to Le Havre. It was the last really significant threat which Bentheim had to face, and in consequence troops could safely be sent back again to Amiens, where they were urgently required to help deal with another advance by Faidherbe and the Army of the North.

At Péronne there had been a change of command. The 14th Division, which was besieging Mézières, had hitherto been commanded by Lieutenant General von Kameke, but he was now required to take charge of the engineering works for the bombardment of Paris, and Moltke appointed Schuler von Senden to succeed him. The conduct of the siege of Péronne was taken over by Barnekow. The 3rd Reserve Division was combined with the Guard Cavalry Brigade and the command was assumed by Prince Albrecht (junior).[12] Schmidt's siege train from Amiens had arrived on December 30 and by 10.00am on January 2 was in position to open fire, supported by twelve field guns. This brought an immediate response, Garnier sending to Barnekow under a flag of truce an enquiry as to whether the civil population might be permitted to leave the fortress; the request was refused, and the bombardment, by the siege guns alone, continued. The German policy of shelling towns in the course of such operations attracted considerable criticism from French writers after the war; Wartensleben retorted that these were

> astonishing and somewhat sentimental expressions of opinion ... Setting aside the fact that this mode of attack is perfectly justified by the usages of war, we find the conduct of the French themselves inconsistent with this opinion ... If, therefore, from good military reasons, the French General Faidherbe bombarded and burnt the French village of Pont Noyelles, the German general was surely justified in bombarding a hostile town defended by fortifications and troops, the possession of which was of military importance to him.

In any case, he pointed out, a short bombardment caused less civilian casualties than the hunger and sickness of a long siege.[13]

On January 1 Mézières capitulated to the 14th Division. Since it formed part of his army, Manteuffel had been looking forward to this division becoming available to him for operations in the north of France, but in this he was to be disappointed. Moltke ordered Major General von Woyna, temporarily commanding the division pending the arrival of Schuler von Senden, to make an immediate attack on Rocroi; thereafter, the 14th Division was required to reinforce the troops investing Paris. Moltke wrote on January 2 to explain the need for this to Manteuffel. He began his letter, however, with a tactful recognition of the First Army's successes: 'It is with a full heart that I send to Your Excellency not only my best wishes for the New Year, but also all my congratulations on the two important victories that you have won near Amiens. I believe that it will be extremely difficult for General Faidherbe again to get across the line of the Somme if you succeed in occupying Péronne.'[14] Goeben would, therefore, have to deal with any French advance with the troops he had got.

After the battle on the Hallue, Faidherbe had withdrawn his army behind the River Scarpe, between Arras and Douai, taking up a strong position in which he could hope to fight a successful defensive battle; but as he noted in his own account of the campaign, the enemy had no intention of going there to look for him, and if he was to make any impact on events in order to give some indirect help to Paris, he must again move forward.[15] The immediate objective must be the relief of Péronne; if something was not done at once, it would certainly fall, and the political consequences of that would be even greater than the military. An additional reason for taking action was that the German cavalry were daily growing bolder in carrying out raids into French held territory, and it would be necessary to advance to put a stop to them. Accordingly, on New Year's Day the Army of the North pulled out of its cantonments behind the Scarpe, and began to march in four columns towards the beleaguered town of Péronne.

Standing in their way was the screen posted by Goeben to cover the siege which stretched from Bienvillers-au- Bois, about fourteen miles north east of Bapaume, to St Quentin. The length of this line meant that the Germans were stretched extremely thin, and Goeben was perfectly aware that his forces were not strong enough to resist a really determined and concentrated attack, as he candidly reported to Manteuffel on December 31:

> With regard to the enemy's army, a change has in so far taken place, as it now occupies the villages in the immediate neighbourhood of the fortresses, and displays, on the whole, a greater degree of activity. It is said that considerable transport of troops from Douai to Cambrai took place yesterday, and that up to yesterday evening 15,000 men were assembled there. Our patrols have observed a great many trains passing from Douai. It seems, therefore, that an advance will be made for the purpose of relieving Péronne and I do not deceive myself as to the fact that, if such an attempt should be made on a large scale, I shall – as two infantry brigades must be left at Péronne – not remain strong enough to resist it with the prospect of success.[16]

For the moment, however, all he could do was to await Faidherbe's move in his existing position, and take advantage of the situation as it developed. On the left of his line was von der Groeben, who had Mirus' detachment at Bienvillers and the 7th Cavalry Brigade at Bucquoy. Next came the 32nd Brigade (Rex) between Bucquoy and Achiet le Grand, while the 30th Brigade (Strübberg) was posted at Bapaume. The 29th Brigade (Bock) was behind Bertincourt, with the Guards Cavalry Brigade on its right at Fins. Finally, on the road from Cambrai to St Quentin was posted the 12th Cavalry Division (Lippe), which had a detachment under Senfft at St Quentin itself. On the basis of the information derived from the reconnaissances which he reported to Manteuffel, Goeben believed that the greater threat to his line was probably from Cambrai rather than Arras and his dispositions were made accordingly with the 32nd Brigade moving to its right from Achiet le Grand to Fins.[17]

As it turned out, however, it was from Arras that the attack came. As Faidherbe came south, the 22nd Corps marched to the west of the Arras – Albert railway on Bucquoy, while the 23rd Corps, on its left was moving on the main Arras – Bapaume road. In front of Derroja's Division of the 22nd Corps, von der Groeben steadily fell back from Bucquoy, and by the evening of January 1 he had reached Miraumont. At Achiet le Grand, filling the gap left by the march eastwards of the 32nd Brigade, Strübberg had posted the Fusilier Battalion of the 28th Regiment while the 1st Battalion held Béhagnies to the east which, lying in a hollow, was scarcely defensible.[18] It was upon the latter that the first blow fell, an attack being launched by Payen's Division of the 23rd Corps. The defenders of Béhagnies fell back to Sapignies, where they were supported from Achiet le Grand and by the 2nd Battalion moving up from Bapaume. Behind this unit, Strübberg brought up the 68th Regiment. In spite of this reinforcement, the French advance continued

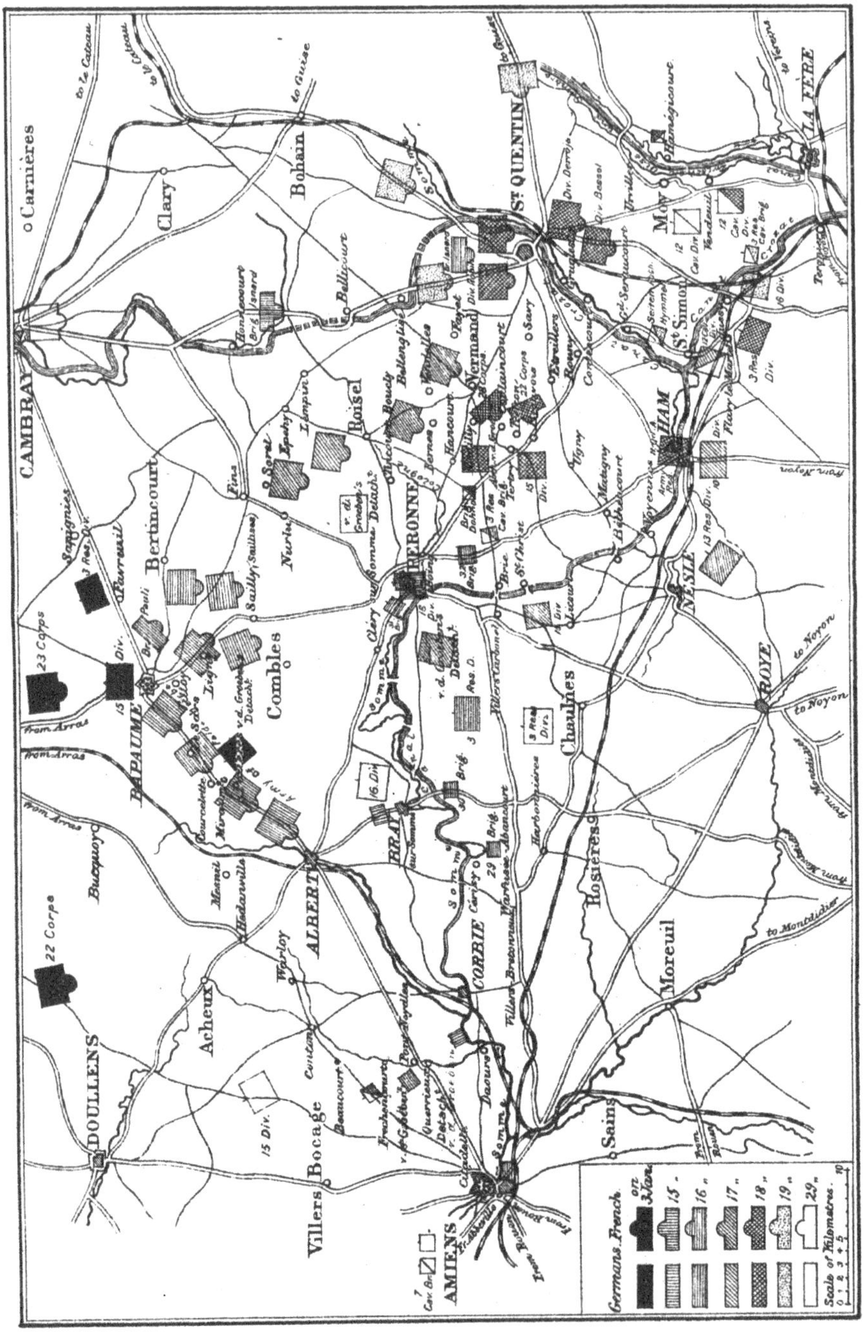

The battles around Bapaume and Saint-Quentin, January 1871

towards Sapignies, until it was checked by a sudden attack by a half squadron of the 7th Hussars Regiment, which, charging over the hard frozen ground, broke in to the left of the French skirmishers and drove them back. Kummer, who was accompanying Strübberg, ordered an immediate attack to retake Béhagnies, and by 2pm the village was again German hands, 250 prisoners being taken. East of Béhagnies, Robin's division reached Mory, but was then held up by a fusilier company and a squadron of the 7th Hussars; this tiny force succeeded in deceiving the French as to their strength, and although Robin's men marched and counter marched, and brought up artillery, they made no effort to dislodge their immediate adversaries.[19]. Meanwhile, at Achiet le Grand two companies of the 28th Regiment held up Bessol's division for the best part of an hour and a half before falling back through Brefvillers to Avesnes-les-Bapaume. Although he had made rather less progress than might have seemed possible, given the weakness of the forces opposed to him, by nightfall Faidherbe was in a position from which he could attack directly the line taken up by Goeben to cover Péronne, and for the following day he planned a concentric advance on Bapaume.[20]

Payen's losses were, according to Faidherbe, particularly severe; the total casualties sustained by the Germans during the day's fighting amounted to 108 killed, wounded and missing. Strübberg, with about 2,000 infantry, 279 cavalry and twelve guns, had successfully held up the advance of the entire Army of the North.[22] As the reports of the day's fighting reached Kummer, he soon became convinced that he was indeed facing the whole of Faidherbe's army, and he resolved to concentrate in Bapaume, and hold that town. Goeben reported the outcome early next morning by telegraph to Manteuffel. 'Whole division now in position at Bapaume. I am on the point of riding to Le Transloy; shall assemble

An episode from the combat at Sapignies, painting by Leclercq (Rousset/*Histoire*)

reserves there and at Bertincourt. Lieut-Col Pestel destroyed railway and telegraph between Abbeville and Boulogne.'[23]

Goeben may have had his doubts before the fighting began about the prospect of success, but he certainly did not draw up his plans for January 3 in any negative spirit. Kummer was ordered to put up an obstinate defence in and around Bapaume while Prince Albrecht from Fins through Bertincourt, and on his left von der Groeben, were ordered to attack the enemy's flank and rear. Such an operation, which was entirely in accordance with Moltke's military teaching, was facilitated by close concentration by Faidherbe of his forces preparatory to his attack on Bapaume. At this stage Goeben was not prepared to lift the siege of Péronne, but he did order Barnekow to send off three battalions and four batteries to Sailly-Saillisel to act as a reserve.[24]

On Faidherbe's right Lecointe's 22nd Corps was to attack Grevillers with the 1st Division (Derroja) and Biefvillers with the 2nd Division (Bessol) while on the left Paulze d'Ivoy pushed the 1st Division (Payen) of the 23rd Corps through Sapignies. Robin, with the 2nd Division, was on the left, east of Favreuil. Faidherbe himself accompanied Bessol. The whole army moved forward at 8.00 am, in the bitter cold under an overcast sky. Bessol gained an early success, when Foerster's Brigade of his division drove a company of the 33rd Regiment out of Biefvillers, a move which seriously jeopardised the German position on the Arras road. An immediate counter attack by the 1st Battalion of the 33rd Regiment, led by Captain von Fischer, successfully re-entered Biefvillers before engaging in a bitter hand to hand fight in the centre of the village. As the struggle reached its height, with heavy casualties on both sides, Lecointe switched Aynè's Brigade of Derroja's Division from its advance towards Grevillers into Biefvillers. Against such overwhelming odds, the 33rd Regiment was obliged to fall back not only from Biefvillers but also from Grevillers, where for a long time one company held up the advancing troops of Pittié's Brigade.[25] The further advance of the French towards Bapaume was, however, checked at Avesnes les Bapaume and the ravine in front of the village by the concentrated fire of the two batteries which Bock, whose brigade held this sector, had moved up to the outskirts of Bapaume.

The loss of Biefvillers exposed the left of the 30th Brigade fighting around Favreuil; Strübberg swung the 1st Battalion to face westward, to link with the defenders of Avesnes.

Meanwhile Robin's Division launched an assault on Strübberg's right; this quickly broke down in the face of heavy fire from two horse artillery batteries, in such disorder that Robin pulled back to Mory, allowing the horse artillery and a fusilier battalion to be brought back to Bapaume at about 10.30. As the morning wore on however, the overwhelming pressure from the French advance, increasingly supported by artillery, left Kummer no choice but to pull back his troops all along the line from the higher ground north of Bapaume into and on either side of the town itself. Faidherbe watched as his artillery engaged in a fierce and prolonged exchange with the German guns in Bapaume and examined the position taken up by the German infantry in the houses of the town. 'To dislodge them, it would be necessary to destroy with artillery fire the shelters in which they had established themselves, a cruel extremity when it was a matter of a French town, and to which the commander in chief could not resign himself, not holding it essential to the possession of Bapaume.'[26]

By noon, however, the movement by Prince Albrecht on Faidherbe's left flank was beginning to have an effect. Colonel Hertzberg's detachment of two battalions, two squadrons and a battery, marching first from Bertincourt, reached the Cambrai high road between Bapaume and Frémicourt, and leaving one battalion at Frémicourt advanced on Favreuil. Only recently abandoned as a result of Kummer's order to pull back into Bapaume, the village was already occupied by Payen's troops, which were also advancing to the west of the village. Hertzberg's advance carried him into Favreuil, but it was soon evident to Albrecht that in the face of the large enemy force the village could not be held, and at about 2.30 he pulled back to the Cambrai road.

Meanwhile Faidherbe's principal thrust had been continuing from Avesnes and Biefvillers through the Faubourg Arras under the cover of his fierce artillery bombardment. By 2.00 pm Bock's front line was along the edge of Bapaume itself, with the 65th Regiment holding the north of the town and the 33rd Regiment in position in the ancient fortifications facing west. In spite of the heavy and continuous bombardment, Bock held on; for the moment Lecointe refrained from launching his infantry in an assault. To the east of the town, Strübberg was holding St Aubin with the Fusilier Battalion of the 68th Regiment, while his main body and the bulk of Kummer's artillery was posted on the windmill hill southeast of Bapaume. A French assault on St Aubin took the place; reinforcements arriving from Prince Albrecht launched a counter attack at 2.45 pm and after a hand to hand struggle which lasted for three quarters of an hour, the Germans again took possession of St Aubin, taking 122 prisoners. For the next two hours there was a prolonged struggle, frequently at close quarters, on the Beugnâtre road, as the French again tried to seize St Aubin, but by 6.00 pm the fighting died out here, with St Aubin still in German hands.[27]

To the west and southwest of Bapaume, the fighting was by now concentrated around Ligny and Tilloy. Earlier in the day Mirus had been posted by von der Groeben some five miles to the west of Bapaume at Petit Miraumont, with three companies, two and a half squadrons and four guns. Undisturbed there, he could hear the heavy gunfire at Bapaume; by early afternoon he could stand the inaction no longer, and set off to the sound of the guns, arriving at Ligny at 4.00 to reinforce the garrison there. It was a timely moment; Derroja had launched an attack on Tilloy which had succeeded in taking that village notwithstanding the concentrated fire of 24 German guns from the heights behind. Soon after, further reinforcements arrived, Goeben sending one battalion of the 33rd Regiment which he had been holding in reserve at Beaulencourt, and Strübberg bringing two and half battalions from Bapaume. Confronted by those forces, and fearing in particular that Mirus' advance threatened his right flank, Derroja pulled out of Tilloy without waiting for the attack to develop; retreating to Grevillers he was closely followed up, and a substantial number of prisoners taken. Further north, Bessol broke off his attack on Bock's positions, and fell back from Avesnes les Bapaume and the Faubourg Arras to Bihucourt and Achiet le Grand. Elsewhere on the battlefield, Payen remained at Favreuil and Béhagnies, while Robin's Division, which had not made any very effective contribution, was echelonned back from

Beugnâtre to Vaulx. Desultory firing on the north side of Bapaume continued until 9.00pm; Goeben's men passed the night in the positions they occupied at the end of the fighting.[28]

The two day's fighting had cost Goeben a total of 750 casualties, of which 124 were killed and 558 wounded. Faidherbe's losses were very much greater, amounting to a total of 2,119 men, of whom 183 were killed, 1136 wounded and 800 missing.[29] Payen's division had been hardest hit, especially during the fighting around Béhagnies. For both Faidherbe and Goeben it had been a tough battle and each of them prepared to take a pessimistic view of its outcome. Goeben's forces had used up practically all their ammunition, and there was little available to replenish it, and his troops were in urgent need of rest. With a total infantry strength of not much more than 10,000 men, they had successfully resisted the attack of the Army of the North, which was four times as strong. During the afternoon, Goeben had issued a precautionary instruction to Barnekow to be ready to lift the siege of Péronne; when he got this order, issued at 2.00pm, Barnekow at once started shifting his siege train and equipment to the south of the river, keeping up the bombardment from only three guns, while he made the necessary preparation to move the rest to La Fère and Nesle early on the following morning. The successful defence of Bapaume had, though, made the immediate raising of the siege unnecessary, and Barnekow continued the bombardment. Goeben did not however, consider himself yet entirely out of the wood, taking into account in particular the ammunition problem, and he decided that it would be wisest to pull back the bulk of his covering force to the line of the Somme, leaving only the cavalry in touch with the enemy.

Faidherbe, meanwhile, had also been reviewing his position, which caused him great concern. Having set his face against what would probably have amounted to the complete destruction of Bapaume by his artillery he knew that he would face heavy casualties if he committed his infantry to a fresh assault on Goeben's unbroken positions. His troops, too, were exhausted by their efforts during the two day battle, and the weather continued bitterly cold. These factors, coupled with the fact that many of the villages were encumbered with dead and wounded, he gave as his reasons for orders retreat northwards. It was a difficult decision but probably militarily correct; for although if he had continued the attack, he might have taken Bapaume next day and been able to claim a victory, he would no doubt soon have faced a vigorous counter attack, which with his troops in desperate need of rest would have been hard to resist. 'As it was, the French and Germans withdrew north and south like exhausted boxers to their corners at the end of an inconclusive round.'[30] As Wartensleben pointed out, it was another tactical draw, but 'the strategical victory, however, consisted in the attempt to raise the siege of Peronne having been frustrated, and was therefore decidedly on the side of the Prussians.'[31] By nightfall on January 4, Kummer was in and around Bray, most of his troops being to the south of the Somme while Barnekow and Prince Albrecht continued the siege of Péronne.

Although his main body had returned to Albert, von der Groeben continued to hold Bapaume, his cavalry patrols monitoring the French withdrawal. Manteuffel, who had remained in Amiens, had by early on January 4 not yet received Goeben's report of the battle, and anxiously enquired the position. From his headquarters, now at Becquincourt, Goeben laconically reported the outcome. 'Division Kummer, most effectually supported by a combined detachment under Prince Albrecht junior, gloriously held its ground at Bapaume yesterday in a nine hours struggle against two Army Corps. The fight ended in the evening by our retaking St Aubin and Tilloy at the point of the bayonet. Our loss is heavy, that of the enemy extraordinarily high.' He added that in the face of such superior forces, and due to the fatigue of his men and the lack of ammunition, he had decided to retreat to the south bank of the Somme.[32] Later in the day, as news of the complete retreat of the French retreat became clearer he reported that he intended to leave von der Groeben in Bapaume. Manteuffel, however, was not entirely satisfied, at 5.15pm on January 4 demanding that von der Groeben should 'complete the victory you have gained by pursuing the enemy energetically, especially with cavalry. I also now expect that the siege of Péronne will be continued with all available and procurable means.'[33] For his part Moltke was quick to send a telegram of congratulation to Manteuffel on the successes of the last few days, although he noted that if the instructions given about not operating on the left bank of the Seine had been complied with it would have allowed the First Army to be stronger on the Somme.[34]

Goeben did not pay a great deal of attention to Manteuffel's demand for a close pursuit of the Army of the North, but he had no difficulty in agreeing with the need to take Péronne as soon as possible. Once in his hands, it would enable him effectively to command the line of the Somme and to take up a position to frustrate any move south which Faidherbe might make. Bapaume had demonstrated that the Army of the North was both numerically strong and increasing in effectiveness, and that it would no doubt very soon be in a position to make another attempt to raise the siege. Although some of the siege train employed at Mézières was required at Paris to support the planned bombardment, eighteen guns, with eleven captured French mortars were available for the use of the First Army, but it would be a week or more before these could arrive at Péronne. In the meantime, the siege train there could be strengthened by bringing another eleven captured French guns from La Fère. Schwartz, the First Army's artillery commander, was doubtful if even with the guns en route from Mézières Barnekow would have enough to reduce Péronne, and Manteuffel repeated, successfully, his request to Moltke for additional reinforcements to bring about a speedy end to the siege.[35]

Goeben's recognition of the need for haste was sharpened by rumours that Faidherbe was already getting ready to make another move, perhaps in the direction of Amiens. Although he had moved his forces back to the right bank of the Somme, so that Kummer was between Bray and Albert, and von der Groeben was at Bapaume, Goeben was in no doubt that to give himself the maximum room for manoeuvre, he should be prepared to meet any further advance by Faidherbe from a position south of the river. Manteuffel agreed; with the mounting indications that an early advance by the French was on the cards, he ordered the despatch on January 7 of three battalions from Rouen, and reported this to Goeben, with the promise of three more next day. He confirmed that, while closely watching the enemy, Goeben should assemble the bulk of his forces on the left bank of the river between Bray and Péronne. At 10.15 am however, Goeben sent an urgent telegram warning Manteuffel that the latest reports indicated that Faidherbe was concentrating at Hamelincourt. He would, he said, in consequence assemble his own forces behind the Somme; if Faidherbe marched on Péronne, he would raise the siege.[36]

For the moment, while awaiting confirmation of Faidherbe's movements, he left his troops where they were. Barnekow was left to continue the siege with the resources available, although Goeben took the precaution of ordering that the siege guns should be posted on the south side of the river, just in case it became necessary to raise the siege. On the evening of January 6 the reinforcements from La Fère had arrived, while news also came that the guns from Mézières were on their way. Goeben, however, decided not to wait. The threat posed by a further advance by Faidherbe from Arras seemed too pressing, and he ordered Barnekow to proceed at once to a formal attack on Péronne.Engineering works at once began under cover of a desultory bombardment of the fortress. The garrison, seeing those preparations, responded energetically, keeping up a brisk fire.

Throughout January 7 Goeben continued to update Manteuffel with news of Faidherbe's activity, as it reached him from his assiduous cavalry patrols. French intentions still seemed unclear; until the position was resolved, he deferred his retirement behind the Somme for the time being. Meanwhile something of the anxiety felt by Goeben and Manteuffel had communicated itself to Versailles, where Moltke was watching developments with mounting concern. It was a troubling time for him; events in the south east of France were reaching a climax and he now arrived at his conclusion that it would be necessary to reinforce the units already engaged there, and place them under the orders of a new army command, to be known as the South Army. On the morning of January 7 he decided that the new commander of this army should be Manteuffel, to whom he sent a telegram at 12.30 ordering him to report at once to Versailles for detailed instructions, after transferring command of the First Army to Goeben. To ensure continuity, Moltke ordered that although the rest of Manteuffel's staff should make their way to Châtillon sur Seine, Sperling was to remain as Chief of Staff with the First Army.[37] Later that afternoon, perhaps fearing some loss of concentration at the First Army headquarters, where Manteuffel and the staff were preparing for their departure, Moltke sent an anxious enquiry to Manteuffel: 'Have reinforcements been ordered up from Rouen for General Goeben?' To this, Manteuffel was able promptly to reply with the information that a total of nine battalions and two batteries of the I Corps were now in motion to reinforce Goeben, and that for the moment Faidherbe appeared to have advanced no further south.[38] Moltke, however, had became impatient while waiting for Manteuffel's response and took direct action himself; at 11.39 pm that night he despatched a telegram to Amiens:

> As no answer has yet arrived, whether General Goeben has been reinforced at the Somme, a brigade of the Army of the Meuse will hold itself in readiness early tomorrow morning to be conveyed per rail from Gonesse to Amiens. Materials of transport must, however, be sent from there to Gonesse, unless they are required between Rouen and Amiens. The First Army will communicate direct with the Army of the Meuse on this subject.[39]

Manteuffel replied at once to reiterate that no further French advance had taken place and that the rolling stock was committed to the transfer of troops from Rouen.

Moltke's ongoing concern about the likelihood of Faidherbe launching a fresh offensive was shown by another despatch to the First Army headquarters, reporting the news that a substantial number of troops appeared to have been transferred by sea from Le Havre and Cherbourg to Dunkirk and Calais, presumably to reinforce the Army of the North; he repeated that, if necessary Goeben could look for reinforcement to the Army of the Meuse.[40] The day passed, however, without further movement by Faidherbe, as Goeben duly reported. Moltke nonetheless remained extremely anxious and at 6.45 pm fired off a sharply worded telegram to Manteuffel demanding up to date information:

> French telegrams affirm that we have evacuated Bapaume. Where do the troops of the First Army stand, and what news has been received of the enemy's movements? It is absolutely necessary to be acquainted with the state of affairs there, of which we know nothing here. Has the Army of the Meuse been asked to send off a brigade? Are further reinforcements necessary?[41]

Late that night, Manteuffel sent a soothing reply to the effect that the French had still not moved further towards Bapaume, but had if anything pulled back towards Arras. The reinforcements from Rouen were still using up all the available rolling stock, so no request for help had been made to the Army of the Meuse.

At Péronne, during January 8, only a slow deliberate fire had been maintained on the fortress, but by that evening, in spite of transport problems on the overstretched railway system, sufficient supplies of ammunition had reached Barnekow for him to consider opening the formal attack. He announced this in a message to Garnier, pointing out the futility of further resistance. Following a brief pause for reflection, the French commander accepted this and at 11.00 am on January 9, after a general cease fire, negotiations began. By 11.45 that night terms for capitulation had been agreed, and at 2.00pm on the following day Barnekow entered the captured fortress.[42] 'The French garrison marched out with its arms, drums beating, and in good order, on the road to Eterpigny, where it then laid down its arms preparatory to being led off as prisoners of war.'[43] The Gardes Nationales in the garrison were released; about 3,000 prisoners in all were taken, together with forty seven guns.

By then Goeben had assumed command of the First Army, reporting this on January 9 to Moltke, and suggesting that for the moment at any rate he did not need to call on the Army of the Meuse for help. During the day he had been kept regularly informed by Barnekow of the tortuous progress of the negotiations at Péronne, and was greatly relieved to learn at 11.15 pm that night that terms had been provisionally agreed and, four hours later, that these had been ratified. There was a final alarm early on January 10, when reports were received of a French advance on Péronne, about which Goeben told Barnekow: 'Nothing can be of any effect today. If it is not possible for you to arrest his progress until you have taken possession of the fortress, my previous orders remain force. Therefore, position behind the Somme.'[44] Fortunately, it turned out to be a false alarm; and with Péronne having been secured, Goeben could now prepare to deploy his whole force to meet Faidherbe's advance, whenever and wherever it might come.

25

The Bombardment of Paris

Although on the subject of the bombardment of Paris Blumenthal is not necessarily the most reliable witness, it seems that those charged with the task of organising the artillery assault shared his doubts. On December 27 he recorded a conversation with Hohenlohe.

> He told me he did not believe that the bombardment could commence before the 6th or 7th of January, as the necessary ammunition could not be up till that date. He also seems to think, after having made a careful reconnaissance, that the whole affair is idiotic, and only finds his excuse for taking part in it in the fact that the King now appears to desire it.[1]

Blumenthal also took satisfaction two days later from a discussion with Kameke, newly arrived from the siege of Mézières who, he said, 'appears to agree with me in my view of the state of affairs. He likewise considers that we have not half enough materiel for a siege, and that we shall have to confine ourselves to a bombardment of the two forts which the King now desires to be fired at.' The continuing concern of Blumenthal and his fellow opponents of bombardment was one of professional pride over the problem that would arise if it produced no success. 'People will not see what contempt we bring ourselves into if we embark on a project, and then have to confess that we are unable to carry it through.'[2]

No one thought that a formal siege was practicable; but even the more limited aims of a bombardment would tax the resources of the artillery to the limit. Verdy, awaiting the outcome of the deliberations of Kameke and Hohenlohe, was still doubtful. 'It will not be an easy piece of work, and it is still questionable whether we shall be able to send our shot far enough into the town to produce any considerable moral effect.'[3] The effect of public opinion on strategy disturbed him, spoilt as it had become by the brilliant victories in the first months of the war. 'Everyone can easily imagine that all this urging from outside, and the observations that we hear of, are not without their influence on the enthusiasm with which the heavy tasks which are yet before us, must after all be carried through.'[4]

For his part Moltke was cooperating to the full in making preparations for the bombardment, whatever his views may have been about its usefulness. One of Hohenlohe's first requests was that steps be taken to ensure that, if necessary, further supplies of ammunition could be brought from Germany to bring the stocks up to one thousand rounds per gun. Notifying Roon of this on December 29, Moltke asked if Hohenlohe might directly access the depots where the ammunition was stored in order to reduce delay. In addition, to ensure that the batteries were at all times kept up to strength, Hohenlohe had asked that any lightly wounded men should be replaced at once even if still able to be counted as part of a unit's effective strength.[5] And in a detailed order to Blumenthal about the arrangements for the bombardment and the targets on which it should be concentrated, he made it clear that Kameke and Hohenlohe were to have the fullest powers to carry

Prince Kraft zu Hohenlohe-Ingelfingen (Hohenlohe-Ingelfingen)

out the operation: 'In anything which concerns the matters over which Lieutenant General von Kameke and Major General Prince Hohenlohe henceforth exercise their authority, His Majesty has ordered that these two general officers will be considered as attached to the General Staff.' In addition, although their proposals would be considered by the General Staff before giving orders to the Third Army, Kameke and Hohenlohe were to have the power to give orders direct to Schulz and Rieff who would be directly carrying out the operations.[6]

Moltke's task was not made easier by the outspoken response of some of his colleagues. Blumenthal's reaction to the decision to bombard Paris was typically intemperate.

> I shall offer no objection if Paris is regularly and properly besieged; in fact, I now hope it may come to that, as it seems to be the only means of bringing their inflamed passions to order. Whatever takes place, however, must be carried out properly. A few casual shells dropped in among them will not frighten even the gamins of Paris. The Parisians must be made to feel that we have them in the hollow of our hand, otherwise they will not give in.

Moltke soothingly promised to pass on Blumenthal's views to the King.[7] Keeping Blumenthal calm was difficult; he usually burned on a short fuse, and the frustration and anxiety he shared with Moltke was becoming very evident. On January 4 he was greatly annoyed by a suggestion made by the Crown Prince of

Saxony that his aversion to the bombardment was as a result of the influence of the Crown Princess, which he indignantly denied, recounting in his diary that 'Versailles is now a hotbed of gossip – a five o'clock tea-party, only much worse, and more harmful in its results.'[8]

Kameke and Hohenlohe duly presented their findings on December 31, at a prolonged session of Moltke's daily report to the King; all the arguments for and against bombardment were again rehearsed at length, but there was never any doubt about the outcome, and at the end of the conference it was ordered that the assault should begin as soon as possible. At a later meeting at the Third Army headquarters attended by Kameke, Hohenlohe and Schulz, Hohenlohe disclosed that the bombardment might be more effective than had been at first thought, as Blumenthal rather dubiously noted.

> Hohenlohe maintains that we can range 9,200 paces, and that this was told him by a specialist – an artillery officer – who knows more about the matter than Rieff. This is something new if it is the case, which I greatly doubt; but if so, we shall be able to fire as far as the Prussian Embassy, and place a large portion of the city in jeopardy.[9]

Next day the decision was taken to commence the bombardment on January 4 and, as the Crown Prince put it, 'thereby Count Bismarck's and the Berliners' wishes are fulfilled.' His gloomy expectation was that 'at the sound of the first shot the spirit of resistance will flare up again more hotly than ever.'[10] The hope was, however, that the reverse would be the case. Hohenlohe's orders made it clear that the primary objective was the morale of the 'Paris mob'; the bombardment was intended to make it 'more inclined to capitulate and accept peace by instilling in them a sense of fear ... since the hardships produced by the investment were not sufficient in themselves'[11]

On the southern front seventeen batteries had been prepared to undertake the initial bombardment. Four of these were located on the steep slopes in the park west of Château Meudon. In the centre, on the plateau of Moulin de la Tour, a further nine batteries were located while on the right three more batteries were on a lower site between Fontenay-aux-Roses and Bagneux. A detached battery was sited on the spur north of Sévres in the park of St Cloud. A total of 94 guns were installed in these batteries. On the front of the VI Corps two more batteries were established on the road between Chevilly and La Rue in order to prevent the right flank of the main batteries being enfiladed from Montrouge, Les Hautes Bruyères and Villejuif. The exercise of arming the batteries was itself a tricky operation, and during the process large movements of troops of the Army of the Meuse, and artillery operations on the eastern front, were conducted in order to distract the defenders. The outpost line on the southern front was moved forward with the support of five pioneer companies.[12] For those batteries out of sight of the enemy, the work was completed during the morning of January 3, while the rest of the batteries were armed that night, ready for action next day. They faced powerful opposition; apart from an estimated 300 guns in the works around the city, there were another 300 on Mont Valérien and in the forts of Issy, Vanves and Montrouge, 34 in the intermediate batteries and 40–50 guns in the works at Villejuif.

Prussian siege batteries bombard Paris, by Pallandre (Rousset/*Combattants*)

January 4 provided an anti-climax, as the Crown Prince recorded: 'The eager anticipation with which from daybreak on we watched for the first shot was frustrated by an impenetrable fog, that refused to clear even for one instant, so that there was no real daylight whatever. At the same time an icy wind was blowing that covered the whole landscape with hoar-frost.'[13] Next day, however dawned fine and clear; at 8.30 am the first signal gun was fired from Battery No 8 on the Moulin de la Tour Plateau, and the rest of the central batteries followed suit. The lower batteries to the right and left, waiting for the mists to clear, were unable to join until later in the morning. The French at once replied, supported by gun boats which appeared at Point du Jour. The artillery duel continued all morning; by 1.30 Fort Issy, which had taken the brunt of the German fire, fell silent, while as the day wore on the fire from Fort Vanves and the intermediate batteries gradually slackened. Only Fort Montrouge was able to keep up the counter battery work all day.

Operations were, however, still hampered by bad weather, which on some days altogether prevented any bombardment at all, and on others reduced the volume considerably, allowing the French to make good to some extent the damage to the forts. In spite of this, their defensive power had been so far reduced that the French were obliged to evacuate their positions in advance of the forts, allowing the Germans in their turn to fortify their own positions between Le Val, Notre Dame de Clamart and Châtillon. This took their line some 800 yards nearer the city, and the positions of some of the batteries were changed accordingly.[14] These moves caused increasing concern to the French who, after a series of reconnaissances towards the redoubt of Notre Dame de Clamart, pushed forward a

General von Kameke, commander of the German 14th Infantry Division (Rousset/*Histoire*)

detachment on the morning of January 10 and, after a brief hand to hand struggle, overpowered the small party of Bavarian infantry holding it. The redoubt was soon reoccupied; and to prevent a repetition of this occurrence it was strongly garrisoned with two companies, with three battalions in Clamart itself; on the night of January 12/13 a shelter trench, 1,300 yards long, was dug to connect Clamart with Châtillon.

It was a wise precaution; on the following night the French sent forward 500 Marines, supported by several battalions of Gardes Nationales, in an attack on Clamart. For an hour there was a vigorous exchange of rifle fire before a charge by a company of infantry from the 15th Regiment drove the French back in disorder to their start line.

Although the German siege batteries were certainly getting the best of the exchanges with the forts the French counter battery work was not without its effect. As the Official History notes, the isolated Battery No 1, at St Cloud, suffered particularly from the fire of several French batteries and from Mont Valérien. 'The rocky slopes in front and rear of the battery offered such facilities for the enemy to watch the shot and obtain the range, that the crest of the parapet was at times completely honeycombed. It was only by an extreme effort that the struggle could be continued at this point.'[15] Other batteries also suffered considerably; and the casualties sustained by the Germans included a number of senior officers, among them Rieff, who was wounded.

The fort at Montrouge, following the bombardment of Paris, a contemporary photograph (Rousset/*Histoire*)

So far as the forts were concerned, the Germans could see with the naked eye the extent of the damage caused by the bombardment, especially at Fort Issy; but the effect of the bombardment of the city itself was less clear. This was being undertaken by twelve 15cm guns, firing at maximum elevation and at times attaining ranges of upwards of 8.650 yards. Every day some 300–400 shells were fired into the city, and hits were observed on a number of prominent landmarks, although the extent of the damage was unknown. After the first few days the shelling of the city was confined to the hours of darkness, usually beginning around 10pm and continuing for four or five hours. The more prominent targets at which they were directed included the domes of the Pantheon and the Invalides, so that it was around buildings such as these that most damage was sustained. No shells actually reached the right bank of the Seine, and in fact civilian casualties were remarkably low, considering the volume of the bombardment. In the three weeks of the bombardment 97 were killed and 278 wounded; some 1,400 buildings were hit. But the firing caused about 20,000 inhabitants of the Left Bank to be driven from their homes, and there was widespread indignation throughout the city, a feeling reflected by neutral commentators. One British observer expressed surprise that the 'God-fearing and laws of war respecting Prussians' had not given notice in advance of the bombardment, while another remarked that 'it kindled ire and resentment in my breast.'[16] Labouchère found it difficult to realise the importance of the events that he was witnessing: 'When shells burst in restaurants and maim the waiters; when the trenches are in tea gardens; and when one is invited for a sou to look through a telescope at the enemy firing off their guns, there is a homely domestic air about the whole thing which is quite inconsistent with "the pomp and pride of glorious war."'[17] Not all commentators, however, took the line of outrage at the bombardment; Felix Whitehurst remarked that 'like a door, a city must be ouvert or fermée. If it is an open city, the law of nations says you must not fire on it, only summon it, and then take it by an attack. If it is a fortified city, behind forts, you may bombard it when and how you can.'[18]

The United States Minister to France, Edward Washburne, who sent regular and detailed reports to the Secretary of State of the situation inside Paris, wrote on January 16 to describe the effect of the first twelve days of shelling.

> When the length of time is considered that the bombardment has been going on, and the enormous quantity of material that has been expended, the small number of killed and wounded and the small amount of actual damage is surprising. The bombardment so far has not had the effect of hastening the surrender of the city. On the other hand, it has apparently made that people more firm and determined. In the presence of a common danger the feeling of hostility to the government, which was so openly manifested some two weeks ago, has been greatly modified.[19]

The ineffectiveness of the bombardment was gradually becoming apparent at Versailles as Verdy accurately noted as early as January 12: 'A few houses have been destroyed, small conflagrations break out every day; but still the bombardment has no decisive effect. The majority of the Parisians look upon it only as a spectacle.'[20] The strengthening of public morale led in its turn to a growing call for a sortie; the bombardment was only one of the factors that made it increasingly evident to the government that some decisive action was absolutely necessary. During the course of January the store of provisions, although carefully husbanded, was clearly running low, bringing nearer the date when surrender would become inevitable. The underlying unrest of the extremists was a constant source of anxiety to the government, bearing in mind the political unreliability of the Gardes Nationales. D'Herisson put the matter bluntly. 'Gradually there entered into the minds of the leaders that cruel, impious and yet logical idea, that the mob would not keep quiet until a certain amount of slaughter was allowed, and that, in order to cure Paris of her fever and reduce her excitement, some pints of blood must be taken from her.'[21] A member of the government was recorded as saying, less metaphorically, that 'when there are 10,000 Gardes Nationales lying on the ground, opinion will calm down.' And as a final spur to action there had arrived on January 9 a despatch from Gambetta dated December 22 announcing the plans for Bourbaki to march eastwards to cut the German lines of communication.

The pressure to mount an offensive was, therefore, irresistible; and although neither Trochu or Ducrot, nor any other senior officer, believed that a sortie could possibly succeed, they embarked on the planning process for an attack on the western side of the city. Based on Mont Valérien, the attackers were to assault the German positions at Bougival on the Gennevilliers peninsula with the aim of breaking through to Versailles. Trochu, indeed, made an effort to postpone the sortie until the Germans had been obliged by Bourbaki's advance to weaken the lines of investment to send forces to deal with it; but the rest of the Government would not hear of a delay, and at a meeting on January 15 the attack was finally authorised.[22] Vinoy, on the left, was to advance on Montretout; three divisions under de Bellemare were directed on Buzenval; and, on the right, Ducrot's advance was to extend to Celle St Cloud. Trochu was to command in person and the assault was to take place on January 19.

Before, then, however, Versailles was to witness a very different event. Throughout the autumn and winter Bismarck had been putting in place all the building blocks for German unification, and the proclamation of the German Empire; finally, by somewhat dubious means, he obtained the approval of the King of Bavaria, prevailing upon him to sign a formal letter of invitation to William to accept the Imperial Crown. Bismarck had been enthusiastically supported throughout by the Crown Prince; William, however, became increasingly depressed and fretful at his approaching elevation. At the last, a major stumbling block appeared; William wanted to be proclaimed as 'Emperor of Germany,' whereas in all the negotiations Bismarck had, in order to reach agreement, promised that the title should be 'German Emperor.' The King was furious, complaining that he was to be no more than 'President.' Greatly agitated, on the night before, he told Bismarck and the Crown Prince of his despair that 'he must bid farewell to the old Prussia, to which alone he clung and would always cling. At this point sobs and tears interrupted his words.'[23] Next morning Moltke arrived, and cheered the King with news of Bourbaki's retreat in front of Werder; and William's mood further improved when the guard of honour led by its band marched past his window, the Crown Prince having arranged the event with this in mind.

The magnificent ceremony took place in the Salle des Glaces in the Palace of Versailles at noon. It was a striking spectacle – an eighteenth century pageant staged against the background of a war that foreshadowed the twentieth century in its length, modernity and ferocity. Surrounded by most of the royal Princes, Grand Dukes and greater nobility of Germany, and by the senior officers and representatives of his army that was winning him the war, William was proclaimed Emperor by his Chancellor, whose feelings were evident to the Crown Prince. 'After His Majesty had read aloud in the familiar fashion a short address to the German sovereigns Count Bismarck came forward, looking in the grimmest of humours, and read out in an expressionless, business like way and without any trace of warmth or feeling for the occasion, the address "to the German People." The difficulty over the title was sidestepped when, by arrangement with Bismarck, the Grand Duke of Baden cried 'Long live His Imperial Majesty the Emperor William!' For the Crown Prince, 'the moment was extraordinarily affecting, indeed overwhelming, and was in every way wonderfully fine.'[24] In at least one observer, however, particularist feeling died hard; after witnessing the extinction of his country's independence, Prince Otto of Bavaria moaned in a letter to his brother: 'I cannot begin to describe to you how infinitely and agonisingly painful I found the scene .... It was all so cold, so proud, so glossy, so strutting and boastful and heartless and empty.'[25] Bismarck, writing to his wife three days after the ceremony in characteristically sardonic vein, observed that

> this Emperor parturition was a difficult one, and Kings have their peculiar fancies just like women before they give up to the world what they cannot keep from it. As the midwife I had often a violent desire to turn into a bomb and

> explode, so that the whole building might be blown to pieces. Necessary business grieves one but little, it is the unnecessary that annoys me.[26]

Fresh from the ceremony in the Salle des Glaces, Moltke turned back to the business of the war. Comprehensive intelligence of the forthcoming French assault had ensured that the Germans were ready for it when it came; the evident preparations for the attack confirmed the point at which the blow would fall, which was on the front of Kirchbach's V Corps. The advance had been timed to begin at 6.00 am; but both a sudden rapid thaw which turned the roads to mud, and obstructions which allowed only a narrow passage towards the two bridges to be used by the columns moving up to their jumping off points, meant that none of them could be ready at the appointed time. A total of 90,000 men had been committed to the assault of which a considerable number were Gardes Nationales. Even Trochu, on his way to Mont Valérien, could not get there in time, while Ducrot's troops, with the furthest to travel, were still a long way out of position when the signal gun was fired at 7.00am to trigger the assault. Nonetheless, with the advantage of the dense morning mist, de Bellemare and Vinoy achieved an initial surprise, falling on the lightly held Montretout redoubt with overwhelming forces. Its garrison of 89 men held out until 9.45 am, after which the French swept forward towards St Cloud and the Montretout Park.

When news was received of the French attack Moltke and Verdy were joined by William at the water tower at Marly, from where as the mist cleared they watched the developing situation. On the other side of the river, Trochu had an even better view, as d'Herisson observed. 'On the terrace like roofs of the highest portion of Mont Valérien the Governor took up his position. It was a unique position, which permitted him to follow with eye and glass the movements of his army – a superb pedestal such as probably no commander in chief, no conqueror had ever had.'[27] His troops continued for a while to push forward, pushing the German outposts out of Garches, and by 9.00am breaking into Buzenval park, before the first of the German supports could come into position. When they did, they retook Garches, and prepared themselves for the main French assault.

It was not long in coming. De Bellemare, at 9.30 am launched his troops in an attack not only upon Garches but towards the Porte Jaune and also the most advanced German position at La Bergerie. There, a small garrison faced an attack by five battalions led by a section of engineers who tried to blow up the surrounding wall; but the dynamite was frozen and would not explode.[28] Meanwhile behind the leading positions the German field artillery was getting into position, coming into action to shell the advancing columns at close range from the Porte Jaune and the Hospice Brezin. The French artillery, bogged down as they tried to come forward across the muddy fields, was no match for the German batteries, which soon achieved their customary dominance of the battlefield. From the Marly water tower Verdy watched as the French infantry tried to get forward.

> We could follow as clearly as possible the movements of the enemy, and as we stood at right angles to the attack, we saw them from the flank and rear. Stray French forces made repeated attempts to force their way up the slope in front of them to the park wall. But each time, when they reached the edge of the ascent, they were received with such a murderous fire, that they were thrown back again.[29]

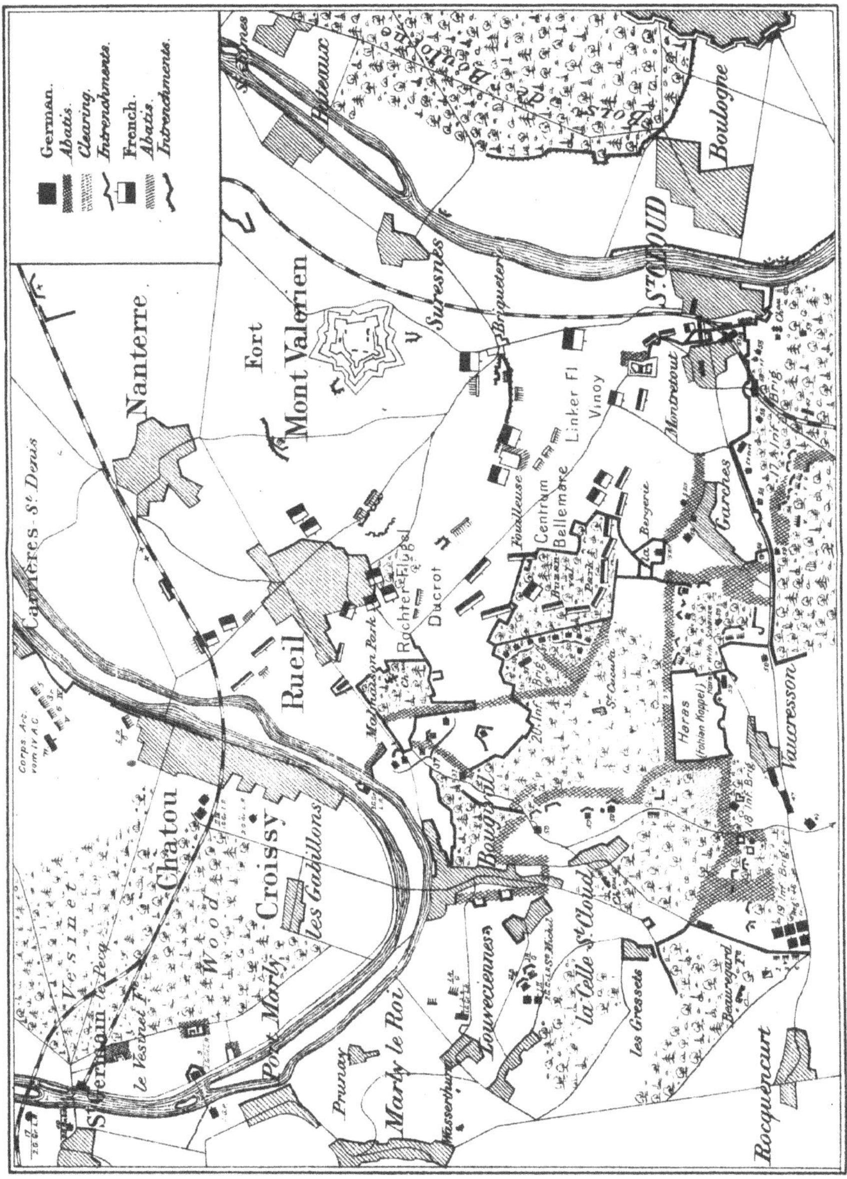

The battle at Mont Valérien/Buzenval, January 19 1871

French skirmish line at Buzenval, painting by Berne-Bellecour (Rousset/*Histoire*)

On the right, Ducrot had at last succeeded in getting into position to attack by 10.30am; although, with the support of his numerous artillery, his men made some progress to La Malmaison, by noon they were pinned down by the deadly rifle fire of the German infantry. As the day wore on, further German reinforcements came into line, followed by several more batteries from the V Corps and four from the IV Corps which had been sent round from the Army of the Meuse to strengthen the German position.[30] At 2.00 Ducrot made a final effort, launching the brigades of Miribel and Bôcher against the positions of the 10th Division at the Porte de Longbuyan and the park wall supported by elements of Faron's Division, under cover of a heavy artillery barrage. The French infantry got to within two hundred yards of the German position before they were halted by the withering German fire. By 3.00 pm it was clear to the Germans that the attack here had failed, and numbers of French troops were seen to be in retreat.

On the left Vinoy and de Bellemare were also making no impression on the positions of the 9th Division. Here, Sandrart had brought up his reserves to strengthen his front line, and as the French advance halted, he judged that the moment had come for a counter attack. This was directed at the French inside Buzenval park; but the first assault broke down with considerable losses and it seemed for a while that the French might capitalise on this success by making a further advance here and from Montretout. However, an advance from La Bergerie took the French in flank, and they fell back to Fouilleuse.

An attack by five companies to retake Montretout, however, also broke down in the face of fierce resistance from the French troops which had barricaded the houses in the northern part of the village. The French possession of Montretout caused Kirchbach some concern, and he ordered Sandrart to carry out a night attack. Eleven companies, in three columns, advanced to the assault at 8.00 pm; the redoubt itself was soon retaken, but the column advancing on the right encountered stiff opposition at St Cloud, and was unable to evict the French from the houses they had occupied, and the Germans were obliged merely to invest them and wait until morning. Meanwhile, Trochu, who had ridden forward in person in support of his troops fighting for the Garches heights, had concluded that the struggle was hopeless, and at 5.30 pm had given orders for a general withdrawal. These orders, however, did not reach the defenders of St Cloud; they held out until the following afternoon, only surrendering after lengthy negotiations and after two guns had been brought up. After the battle, the pessimism of the French became very apparent. Blumenthal took the opportunity to speak to a number of French officers taken prisoner during the battle, who said almost universally that they had no hope of victory; they fought partly for honour and partly because they were hounded on by the Parisians.[31] What was to prove the last sortie by the Army of Paris had failed, as Trochu had known it would. The battle of Buzenval had cost the Germans a total of 610 casualties; the French losses were 4,070. It was only after the thick mist had lifted on the following morning that the Germans appreciated the full extent of the assault and of the casualties inflicted on the attackers; the ground in front of the V Corps position was covered with French dead.[32]

The Francs-Tireurs of Ternes at Montretout, January 1871, drawing by Couturier (Rousset/*Histoire*)

Another casualty was Trochu's position as Governor of Paris. Favre's first reaction to Trochu's open defeatism on January 20 was to call for his dismissal, and for another general to lead a fresh assault. News of Chanzy's crushing defeat at Le Mans, however soon caused him to change his mind, and at a meeting with the mayors of the arrondissements he tried, unsuccessfully, to persuade them to his later view. They demanded however that the Governor resign, a demand that Trochu rejected as dishonourable. Faced by this, the Government on January 21 abolished the post of Governor, although leaving Trochu as President of the Council; and after Ducrot had refused the overall command, offered it to Vinoy, who accepted. Next day, not unexpectedly, there was an abortive rising, soon suppressed when a detachment of Gardes Nationales loyal to the government opened fire on the insurgents. With that out of the way, the members of the Government settled down to discuss what next to do. The information that there was enough flour to provide bread for only about two days concentrated their mind; the decision to open negotiations for the capitulation of the city was inevitable.

26

St Quentin

In many ways, the final stage of the campaign of the First Army against the Army of the North was typical of the field operations of the second phase of the Franco Prussian war. The battle of St Quentin was however to be fought between two of the ablest commanders of the war in Goeben and Faidherbe. Goeben had taken command of the First Army in time to demonstrate just why it was that Moltke had such a high regard for him. He and Faidherbe both possessed a clear understanding not only of their true objectives, but also of the reality of the strength of the resources available to them. Moltke's opinion that Goeben was an outstanding commander was shared by the officers and men of the First Army, as the *Daily News* correspondent accompanying the army observed.

> Very many officers of this army attribute to Manteuffel's slowness the fact of Faidherbe not having been beaten in a more decided manner on previous occasions. The confidence of the ordinary soldier in Goeben's talent is striking. On the march through snow and mud, from morning till evening, you can often hear these tired fellows say, "Well, Goeben knows that all this is necessary," and continue as jolly as ever.[1]

General von Goeben, commander of the German VIII Corps (Rousset/*Histoire*)

General Faidherbe, commander of the French Army of the North, painting by Rignot-Dubaux (Rousset/*Histoire*)

As with other armies brought into existence by the Government of National Defence, Faidherbe had the advantage of substantial overall numerical superiority, but this was solely in infantry, and inexperienced and untrained infantry at that. Goeben, on the other hand, had the inestimable benefit of the superb German artillery, which in battle after battle had been of decisive influence. And because the numerous cavalry which had so effectively led Moltke's advancing armies into France now had little to do around Paris, a large number could be spared for the provinces. As a result Goeben enjoyed a huge superiority in mounted troops, of which Faidherbe had virtually none. The French cavalry had been almost completely destroyed in the first phase of the war and by the surrender of the Army of the Rhine at Metz; while large bodies of infantry could be rapidly improvised, it was simply not possible to do the same for cavalry. Since Goeben's principal object was the frustration of whatever project Faidherbe might embark on, this gave him a crucial advantage. The First Army's cavalry was tough and experienced, and on the one hand was able almost with impunity closely to monitor and promptly report the enemy's movements, while on the other hand comprehensively screening Goeben's intentions from Faidherbe.

Although the Germans, even including Moltke, had become decidedly jittery during the closing stages of the siege of Péronne about an imminent thrust southwards by the French, Faidherbe had in fact never made any movement out of the position he had taken up after his retreat from the outside of Bapaume. It was certainly true that he had, after that battle, retreated no farther than Arras; but his troops were desperately in need of rest, and much though he would have liked to make another effort to raise the siege, he realised that this was simply not practicable.

Péronne was, as had been pointed out in the anguished discussions at the council of war convened within the fortress to discuss possible capitulation, the key to the line of the Somme. Its loss had seriously limited Faidherbe's options. Before the surrender he had strongly urged Garnier 'not to imitate the examples of weakness shown by the commanders of several other fortresses, pointing out that so long as the Army of the North was in the field, it must count on his support.'[2] However, with or without that support it was absolutely clear to Faidherbe that to do nothing was not an option, as he knew that the garrison of Paris was on the point of making a supreme effort. Freycinet had telegraphed him from Bordeaux to say that he must bring down on the Army of the North as large a part as possible of the German forces investing Paris. This, however, was the problem. Crossing the Somme below Amiens was, in his view, out of the question while a force as strong as the First Army was poised on his flank; in any case, the range of the guns in the citadel of Amiens would compel him to make a wide detour around the city. While engaged on such an operation he would be extremely vulnerable, since Goeben could with ease pounce on his flank and rear.

Forcing the line of the Somme between Amiens and Péronne would be even more hazardous, given Goeben's freedom of action to move south of the river to any threatened point. All that Goeben needed to ensure that he got maximum notice of the actual line taken by the French advance was to deploy a screen of cavalry patrols to the north of the river, behind which his army would have the opportunity of a well earned rest. That left available the option of a movement eastwards, and Faidherbe recorded his own conclusion that his best bet lay 'in slipping away from the army before him by several forced marches to the east and south east, and in this way rapidly arriving to the south of St Quentin, thus threatening the line of La Fère, Chauny, Noyon and Compiegne.'[3] He was under no illusion about the dangers of such a move, realising that he would very soon be confronted by strong enemy forces; but given the need to strike towards the armies investing Paris, it was the best he could do.

Goeben, of course, was able to make exactly the same analysis of the situation as Faidherbe. It was his practice to report fully and regularly to Moltke, and on January 10 he set out his own view of the position and the steps he proposed to take to meet whichever of the three movements – west, south, or east – that Faidherbe selected.[4] Immediately after the fall of Péronne, while waiting to see what Faidherbe's next move would be, he had posted a force, two battalions strong, on the Hallue to cover Amiens. These troops were drawn from the units detached from the I Corps, which now amounted to a total of nine battalions and four batteries, and which were placed under the command of Memerty. He was intended to operate in support of von der Groeben's 3rd Cavalry Division, which was watching Faidherbe, and generally to cover the First Army's left flank. Once again Daours, at the right angle of the junction of the Hallue and the Somme, was one of the key points, and Memerty posted three battalions on the Somme at Corbie. Meanwhile, Kummer, with the 15th Division was at Bray and Prince

Albrecht with the 3rd Reserve Division at Chaulnes. Barnekow, at Péronne with the 16th Division, was on stand by in case the Army of the North made a sudden lunge southwards, maintaining touch with Lippe's 12th Cavalry Division, at and to the north of St Quentin. Lippe had been told by the Crown Prince of Saxony to remain there and to cooperate with the First Army, although still remaining part of the Army of the Meuse, to which Goeben told him he must apply for support if he was seriously threatened.[5]

The First Army did not have long to wait. At 10.30am on January 11 came the news that on the previous night the French had begun to move, tentatively pushing forward to Sapignies, before retreating in the face of German infantry moving out of Bapaume. By 1pm, however, clearer indications that the French intended a serious offensive came with the news that a strong force was advancing on Bapaume, with von der Groeben's troopers falling back before them. By 3.00pm the French had occupied Bapaume, although news of this did not reach Goeben until 9.00am next day, when he at once issued orders to all units to prepare for action, although at pains to emphasise that troop movements should be minimised to avoid disrupting the process of replenishing the army's ammunition and supplies. Prince Albrecht's 3rd Reserve Division was now placed under Barnekow's command, and ordered to concentrate on the left back of the Somme, west of Péronne, while the 16th Division stood south of the line Péronne-Roisel. The 15th Division was to remain at Bray, covering the bridges over the Somme there and at Cappy, while the 3rd Cavalry Division was to halt at Albert. Memerty remained responsible for the line of the Somme to Daours. Strung out though this meant his forces were, Goeben could be reasonably confident of concentrating on either wing, or in the centre, as soon as the ultimate direction of the Army of the North could be confirmed. His only other concern was with the weakened I Corps, telling Bentheim that if he was attacked by superior forces he should, 'in case of extreme need, evacuate Rouen, and retreat straight towards Paris, in order to oppose the enemy's further advance on Paris in a suitable position. In this case the Army Corps will apply direct to the Paris blockade army for support!! ....'[6] On the basis of information he had received from Moltke, Goeben's view was that Faidherbe was probably going to move eastward to try and get around the First Army's right flank.

During the day, however, there seemed to be some indication that Faidherbe might be taking an opposite direction, as reports came in of significant French movements down the Albert road from Bapaume. Goeben, ordering the 3rd Cavalry Division to be ready to retreat to Contay if the French were in superior force, put Memerty on the alert to defend the Somme crossings, and ordered Bentheim to be ready to send three more battalions from Rouen. Later in the afternoon of January 12, however, it appeared to be a false alarm, the French troops which had advanced to Le Sars on the Albert road retreating to Warlencourt; to the south of Bapaume the French outposts had not moved further than Beaulencourt. In the light of this, Goeben ordered Memerty to push forward the advance guard to make contact with the enemy. Von der Groeben had during the day pulled back from Albert, which meant Memerty's forces reoccupying that town. Goeben was heartened by a report from Barnekow on the steps taken to prepare Péronne to face an attack: 'Péronne is in a good state of defence, and storm-free. High masonry works well preserved. Wet ditches. Platforms well protected by traverses. The guns used in the bombardment will be brought in today, with their ammunition.'[7] One anxiety, however, was the effect of the weather, which continued bitterly cold, raising fears that the Somme might freeze over to the point where the ice might be strong enough to bear the passage of troops.

On January 13 Goeben reached the conclusion that regardless of the consequences for the defence of Rouen, Memerty should be reinforced to division strength by the transfer from the I Corps of a complete regiment, with two batteries and other supporting troops, with a view to the move being completed by January 18. Reports from Bentheim spoke only of minor skirmishes by reconnaissance patrols, so the risk of denuding the defence positions around Rouen was clearly one worth taking. Much to Goeben's surprise, however, the French made no further forward move during the day, most of the excitement coming when a reconnaissance patrol of the 8th Cuirassier Regiment took five French dragoons prisoner at Puisieux. One of them turned out to be an orderly attached to Faidherbe who had lost his way with one of his General's horses; the standards of military courtesy remained high, however, Goeben sending both orderly and horse back to Faidherbe's headquarters, with a polite covering note.[8]

These early moves may have served to leave Goeben in a state of uncertainty as to Faidherbe's true intentions; what was certain, however was that if the Army of the North was to give its adversary the slip, it would have to move with very great rapidity indeed. On January 14 Faidherbe again advanced in echelon down the Albert road, causing Memerty's detachment to fall back to Querrieux on the Hallue. This time, Faidherbe was moving in strength, Bessol reaching Albert before nightfall with Derroja at Pozières and Payen at Courcelette; Robin remained in reserve at Bapaume.[9] The fact that at least a substantial part of the Army of the North was put in motion in this direction suggested that Faidherbe must be tinkering with the possibility of a thrust at Amiens, and this was something that Goeben could not ignore. He had tidied up his command structure that morning by putting Memerty under von der Groeben's orders, who would now have overall responsibility for the Army's left wing. Throughout the day, the German cavalry had closely watched the head of Faidherbe's advance, so that Goeben was pretty well informed; however, he thought it wise to see what might be happening behind the leading troops of the Army of the North, and ordered Barnekow to probe from Péronne the position and intentions of the French troops around Bapaume and to the east. Responding to Barnekow's enquiry as to whether Kummer would be supporting the more westerly of his reconnaissances, Goeben emphasised the limited scope of his intentions. 'I remark that it is not my intention to bring on an engagement on January 15, but only to ascertain whether any considerable force of the enemy is between Albert and Bapaume, especially at the latter place, in order in that case to arrange a combined attack for January 16.' Barnekow was ordered to reconnoitre the evening only with small patrols, and report his findings by telegraph.[10] One possibility was that instead of following Bessol down the Albert road, the rest of the Army of the North was already setting off eastwards, where increased activity was noted on the road south from Cambrai. A brigade under Colonel Isnard, not forming part of either the 22nd or 23rd Corps, had been identified at Masnières, south of Cambrai, a French prisoner stating that the total force there was some 10,000 strong.

On January 15 Goeben sent a detailed report to Moltke. In his view, Bentheim's force, even though now reduced to thirteen battalions, sixteen squadrons, and eight batteries, was sufficient to hold Rouen and cover Evreux and Dreux, so that the rest of the I Corps could safely be shifted eastwards, which would give him on the Somme a total of forty seven battalions, fifty two squadrons and 161 guns to deal with Faidherbe. Goeben told Moltke that Faidherbe appeared not yet to have made up his mind as to the direction of his advance; the next day would show if his movements were a mere demonstration or a real thrust at Amiens.

> If the latter is the case, I shall assume the offensive and attack the flanks of his line of march; if, on the other hand, he is concentrating at Cambrai in order to march from there either upon Paris or against our communications in the direction of the Moselle, I still hope to be always able to overtake him in time to fall upon his flank during his march, and thus to place him in a very disadvantageous strategical situation.[11]

During January 16 Goeben remained in considerable doubt as to Faidherbe's intentions. Barnekow's first reports showed little movement southwards from Bapaume, while von der Groeben reported during the day that his cavalry had spotted strong columns moving northwards from Albert towards Hedanville. Von der Groeben, always a decidedly cautious commander, at least when he had infantry under his command, believed that his left flank might be threatened, and if necessary planned to withdraw from Bresle to the line of the Hallue. On the other hand, Kummer's patrols operating from Maricourt towards Albert saw some eastward movement of French forces from there. To clear up the position, Goeben sent firm instructions to von der Groeben to attack Albert on January 17; he was to be supported by a brigade from the 15th Division; Kummer would take overall charge of the attack.

Faidherbe, however, had already begun his attempt to slip away to the east. His feint towards Amiens, if that was what it was, had had the effect of pushing back the left wing of the First Army under von der Groeben, but that had been the only effect. The rest of Goeben's forces remained exactly where their commander wanted them, poised to move once Faidherbe's intentions were clear. The movements of the Army of the North could not long be concealed; Lecointe with the 22nd Corps was marching on Combles, and Paulze d'Ivoy with the 23rd Corps on Sailly-Sallisel, a movement which kept them in close touch but which meant passing very close to the leading units of Barnekow's force. These were the positions which had been reached by nightfall on January 16, and by next morning a stream of reports reaching Goeben made the position perfectly clear to him. On the left, von der Groeben had found Albert to have been abandoned by the enemy, while Barnekow's patrols were accurately reporting the movement of Lecointe's troops in and towards Combles. This was enough for Goeben, and he immediately ordered von der Groeben to transfer his headquarters to Péronne, and to move at once in pursuit of the French; he was to reach a position between Combles and Péronne before dark. Intelligence reports suggested that Faidherbe had himself been at Albert on the evening of January 15, so the latest moves appeared to confirm the previous suggestions that St Quentin and the German lines of communication to the east were now the objective.[12] On the basis of the information pouring into his headquarters during the day, Goeben had no doubt that he should proceed on the basis that St Quentin was the enemy's objective, and he made his dispositions accordingly. Kummer, moving to the south of the Somme, was directed towards Villiers Carbonnel and Licant, due south of Péronne, while Barnekow's 16th Division was ordered to Ham, and Prince Albrecht 's 3rd Reserve Division to Nesle. Goeben himself moved his headquarters from Amiens to Nesle, so that he should be well up with his leading troops in the race to head off Faidherbe's move to the east. By nightfall on January 17 he had assembled in the sector Nesle-Ham-Brie some twenty six battalions, while the rest of his force followed his eastwards march. His most easterly unit, south of the Crouzat Canal at Flavy Le Mantel, was the 12th Cavalry Division, well placed to monitor any thrust for St Quentin.

Before he left Amiens, Goeben telegraphed a full report of all of this to Moltke, who had been watching attentively from Versailles.[13] Moltke had already, at 1pm, put an additional infantry brigade at Goeben's disposal, sending it by rail through Gonesse to Tergnier, and was also reassuring about the obligation to protect Rouen; the XIII Corps was en route there from Alençon and could take care of any threat to the city.[14] Later in the day, he received Goeben's full report of January 15, as a result of which he wrote him a lengthy reply. From the information reaching Royal Headquarters, it seemed to Moltke that Faidherbe was moving on La Fère or Laon. He entirely agreed with the plans that Goeben had proposed to follow, and he was content to leave him a free hand. Meanwhile, Moltke added, 'at Paris things are approaching a crisis. We await each day a desperate sortie en masse, perhaps the last. However, if it becomes necessary, it will still be possible to send you a second brigade by way of reinforcement.'[15] Moltke intended to spare no effort to ensure that Goeben had sufficient resources for the coming battle with Faidherbe; as the Grand Duke of Mecklenburg-Schwerin reached the Seine with the XIII Corps and asked if he could count on the cooperation of Bentheim's troops at Rouen, he was firmly told that he could not. Moltke was perfectly prepared to accept the abandonment of Rouen if the need arose, although in fact it did not. In spite of the assembly of probably more than 30,000 men at the mouth of the Seine, the French made no forward move from the strong position they held at Le Havre. Bentheim was, however, reminded on January 17 by Goeben of what he should do if the enemy did advance in overwhelming strength on Rouen. 'If in any case this town has to be abandoned, the march of the enemy on Paris must be checked on the right bank of the river. Only quite exceptional circumstances would justify the corps in crossing to the left bank of the Seine.'[16]

Goeben, travelling by train to the location of his new headquarters at Nesle, was delayed and did not get there until 8pm. When he arrived he found a report from Löe awaiting him, with news of Faidherbe's eastward march across the front of the First Army. Barnekow had been able to give Löe details of the skirmishes of the advanced units he had pushed forward with the intention of delaying Faidherbe's progress. A force of two battalions with two squadrons and four guns under Lieutenant Colonel Reinecke had taken up a position on the Cologne at Tincourt, where it was soon attacked by a very large force, which turned out to be the 2nd Brigade of Derroja's division. Heavily outnumbered, Reinecke succeeded in extricating his force, and fell back slowly towards Ham. Another detachment, under Major Holleben, had been at Vermand, and held on there until the late afternoon before also making its way to Ham. Meanwhile it was known from cavalry reports that some three or four thousand French troops were already in St Quentin, to which the whole of the Army of the North was moving. Goeben was not, however, entirely sure how far to the east Faidherbe had really got, and whether he intended to stand and fight at St Quentin or alternatively to continue eastwards, towards Reims. Anxious at all costs to avoid giving the enemy a start, Goeben's orders issued at 11.00pm were based on the cautious assumption that Faidherbe had made greater progress that was in fact the case. In fact, the French troops which had reoccupied St Quentin on January 15 came not from the main body of the Army of the North, but from the additional brigade of Colonel Isnard, which had advanced south from Cambrai.

Kummer, with the 15th Division, was directed towards St Quentin, by way of Tertry and Etreillers. Von der Groeben, whose force was furthest in arrears of the German units, had Vermand as his target; when he got there he was to pass under Kummer's orders. Barnekow, whose mission would be to head off the Army of the North if it tried to march beyond St Quentin, was directed towards Jussy, with Prince Albrecht following in reserve to Ham. Lippe, with the 12th Cavalry Division, was to move south east of St Quentin and report on French movements in that direction.[17] With Moltke's encouragement to treat the coming battle as his first priority, Goeben also ordered Bentheim that night to forward one more regiment and one battery to Amiens. Late that night Goeben telegraphed Moltke with a short summary of the position, adding that he 'intended the day after tomorrow either to make a concentric attack with the whole force at St Quentin, or, if the enemy marches on Reims, to march on a parallel line with him.'[18]

Concerned to be as close as he could to the critical point, whatever Faidherbe did, Goeben rode next morning with his headquarters to Ham. For some time the reports reaching him suggested that his more pessimistic view of Faidherbe's progress was probably correct. Barnekow, in a message arriving at 10.15am reported that Roupy had been found unoccupied, but that outposts had been encountered at L'Epine de Dallon. Holleben had reported that before retreating behind Beauvois a large column of French infantry had been seen clearly heading for St.Quentin. Lippe, whose 12th Cavalry Division was scouting towards La Fère, had found no enemy troops in that direction. Löe, in a further report from Brie, which arrived at 10.30 am, reported heavy columns of the enemy marching from Templeux, Hesbécourt and Jeancourt, all clearly bound for St Quentin. The next news came in a despatch from Barnekow of 10.00 am, which was in Goeben's hands within the hour, and which confirmed the progress of the French towards St. Quentin; importantly, however, Vermand was found still to be occupied.

It was still bitterly cold. In spite of the temporary thaw, the ice over the Crouzat Canal south of St Quentin was still strong enough to bear the weight of infantry. Slipping and sliding on the frozen roads, Faidherbe's troops had made slow progress on January 17, and by 8.00am on the morning of the next day the rear of Bessol's Division was being harassed by the leading cavalry of von der Groeben's detachment.[19] As the morning wore on the advance of the 15th Division also brought it into contact with Bessol's division. The 29th Brigade (Bock) had

French Garde Mobile on the march, January 1871, by Knötel (Pflugk-Harttung)

marched from St Christ on the line of the Somme Canal through Devize towards Tertry while on its left and somewhat to the rear the 30th Brigade moved from Brie towards Estrées and Chaussée. Kummer's intention was to concentrate at Tertry before continuing his advance. Bock's leading troops reached Tertry by 10.00 am, and at once reported that strong columns of the enemy were passing in front of them. Bock, anxious to slow them down at all costs, first opened fire with a four-pounder battery and then ordered up Captain Rudolphi, with two squadrons of the 7th Hussars. The First Army's historian graphically described the outcome. 'In spite of the soft ground, he charged the enemy vigorously between Trefcon and the high road, rode down the rearmost troops of the 1st Brigade of General Du Bessol's Division, overthrew several wagons, and forced others to turn back and fly.'[20] Pressing on, Rudolphi ran into heavy infantry fire from a battalion of gardes mobiles under Colonel Brouard. The attack, however, was already beginning to achieve its purpose; Bessol, who had already reached Roupy with his 2nd Brigade, felt obliged to turn back to disengage his rear. Having done so, however, he found that his movement had been unnecessary; Payen's division, marching from Vermand towards the sound of the gunfire, had already arrived to support the 1st Brigade.[21] Payen had been leading the march of the 23rd Corps; now he deployed his 1st Brigade towards Trefcon and Caulaincourt and the 2nd Brigade to Poeuilly, throwing out skirmishers to cover the continued march towards Vermand of the rest of the 23rd Corps. Further north, meanwhile, Memerty was pressing forward in pursuit of the French; when he heard the sound of the guns from the direction of

Tertry, he too changed direction towards them, in accordance with an order from von der Groeben at about 11.45am. The latter, however, soon realised that his attack would be more effective if directed towards Vermand, and he ordered Memerty to move in that direction.[22] The advance was, though, almost at once held up by French troops occupying Poeuilly; it took a heavy bombardment from four batteries, and a charge by the 4th Regiment, before the village fell, with a large number of prisoners. Memerty's troops pressed forward, obliging Paulze d'Ivoy to deploy the whole of both of his divisions, Payen in front of Vermand and Robin northwest between Soyécourt and Vendelles. Memerty had imposed the delay on the French march that he set out to achieve, and he now went on the defensive; in the ensuring exchange of rifle fire he was himself seriously wounded.

Bock's advance, meanwhile, had also delayed Bessol at Beauvois, where the French had got drawn into a sharp artillery exchange; further north Strübberg was getting into the action. The key to the struggle now became the village of Caulaincourt, which just before 4pm fell to a combined assault by troops from Memerty's detachment and from the 30th Brigade. The strength of the enemy forces at Vermand and to the north was, however, such that von der Groeben felt unable to resume his advance from Poeuilly, although it was 5.00 pm before the fighting finally subsided here. During the night Payen and Robin resumed their march towards the positions designated for them, although it was only early on the following morning that the last of Robin's troops moved down the Roman road from Vermand towards Fayet. Meanwhile Lecointe with the 22nd Corps had taken up a position to the south of St Quentin; Isnard's Brigade was now attached to this corps. Finally, moving south down the road from Lepine towards St Quentin, the detached brigade of Colonel Pauly, which had so far played no part in the operations of the Army of the North, was preparing to take up a position on the extreme right of the army. Total German casualties amounted to 19 killed, 199 wounded and one missing; French casualties were much higher, Faidherbe putting his loss in killed and wounded at 500, while over 400 unwounded prisoners were taken. But far more important was the fact that the eastward movement of the Army of the North had been significantly retarded.

At his headquarters at Ham, however, Goeben was as yet aware of this. At 3.00pm he reported to Moltke: 'The Army is concentrated westwards of St Quentin on the line Ham-Vendeuil, in readiness to attack the enemy tomorrow. The enemy had occupied St Quentin in force at midday, and was moving southwards; whether eastwards also has not yet been reported.'[23] In fact Faidherbe had already decided what he must do, as he recorded in his own account of the campaign.

> What had occurred on January 18 proved that the concentration of the Prussian forces was already too far advanced for it to be possible to attempt a march to the north, in order to be able to take a position under the guns of the fortresses; we were obliged to accept battle around St Quentin. By a happy coincidence, it was the same day that the Army of Paris fought the battle of Montretout.[24]

The positions taken up by Faidherbe were, as he described them, 'excellent,' based on the heights which ran in a semi circle about two and a half miles west and south of St Quentin. The position was divided by the Somme and the Crouzat

Canal; for the French, however, rapid communication between its two halves was possible via the bridges of St Quentin itself. It was well suited to Faidherbe's purpose of fighting a defensive battle, as the Official History noted. 'The heights in front presented an open range for fire, secured full effect for the artillery as well as for the infantry, and offered a covered position for the reserves.'[25] Their late arrival in the position, however, meant that the French had no time to strengthen it by any significant field works, although the main streets of St Quentin were barricaded, and some of the houses on the edge of town were prepared for defence. The principal weakness of Faidherbe's position was that both of his flanks were in the air, while his decision to stand on the defensive meant that he surrendered the initiative entirely to Goeben. According to his own account, Faidherbe had about 40,000 men, although this figure seems not to include the brigades of Pauly and Isnard, which brought the total to about 50,000; the maximum number at Goeben's disposal for the battle is put by the Official History at 32,580 of which 5580 were cavalry. Schell's account of the campaign puts the total at about 23,400 infantry and 6,200 cavalry. Goeben's artillery consisted of 161 guns.[26]

South of St Quentin, on the left bank of the Somme, Faidherbe posted Lecointe's 22nd Corps. This held the villages of Grugis and Gauchy, and initially occupied a position extending on its left to the La Fère road. On the right bank, facing westwards, stood Paulze d'Ivoy's 23rd Corps, to which the Brigade Isnard had been attached. Paulze d'Ivoy deployed between the Cambrai and Ham.roads from Fayet to Rocourt Mill. Mindful of the need to cover a possible retreat, Faidherbe left the Brigade Pauly, which was still somewhat behind the rest of the army, in position at Bellicourt on the Cambrai road.

By the evening of January 18 Goeben was still unclear as to the position of the enemy, and had still not received full reports of all the events of that day. Kummer's account of the fighting at Vermand arrived at 7.30 pm, while earlier Barnekow had reported his intention to move as far as Lizerolles to head off what seemed to be an intended advance towards Montescourt from Essigny Le Grand. To the west of this movement, French activity around Grand Seraucourt and Happecourt was also noted, while Lippe reported that Urvillers was occupied by the enemy, and that three regiments were in the south east suburbs of St Quentin. All of this information confirmed Goeben's belief that Faidherbe was already solidly established in the city, and he concluded that the units which had fought at Vermand were merely a rear guard rather than, as was the fact, the main body of the Army of the North.[27] In any event he had already made up his mind to attack next day and, having at 8.00pm confirmed to Moltke his intention to do so, he issued an hour later his orders for the First Army to move to a concentric attack on the enemy. Kummer was to open the attack at 8.00am advancing eastwards on St Quentin along the roads from Vermand and Etreillers, with von der Groeben on his left extending to the Cambrai road, while Barnekow was to advance from the south along the railway and through Essigny le Grand. Lippe, with the 12th Cavalry Division and whatever units of the 16th Brigade had by then reached him from the Army of the Meuse, was to advance on St Quentin up the La Fère road with the object of turning the French left. Goeben was already anxious that his prey might escape, and he added a rider about this: 'If the enemy should not await our attack, we must strain every nerve to pursue him energetically, for experience has shown that it is not so much in the battle itself as in the vigorous pursuit afterwards that the greatest results are obtained against such loosely organised forces.'[28]

Not only was the battlefield divided into two distinct segments by the canalised River Somme; the southern front of the Army of the North was further subdivided by the railway line, which ran northwards into St Quentin. The line crossed the heights on its route in cuttings some thirty to fifty feet deep, and the steep banks and quickset hedges made it an obstacle impassable for infantry, so that communication from one side to another was confined to a few road crossings. Anticipating that the attack would come from the direction of Grand Seraucourt, between the river and the railway, Lecointe had concentrated the bulk of his forward troops (Bessol's division) at Grugis, with pickets as far forward as Contescourt. Provided Barnekow stuck to the script, and attacked only to the west of the railway, the line would help shield Lecointe's left flank. In fact, however, the principal direction of Barnekow's advance was to be to the east of the railway, through Essigny Le Grand. It would still however have to traverse three successive ranges of hills, the western ends of which were at Contescourt, Giffecourt and Gauchy. And it was soon clear to Barnekow that if he was to move on St Quentin by the Essigny Le Grand road, he would have to take Grugis, the key to the French position.[29]

At 9.45am Barnekow therefore ordered Hymmen, commanding the detachment at Grand Seraucourt that acted as a link with Kummer's forces, to move forward towards Grugis in support of the advance of Rosenzweig's 31st Brigade from Essigny Le Grand. Rosenzweig's leading unit, the 2nd Battalion of the 69th Regiment, attempted to storm the French positions at and around the railway line where it passed the sugar factory on the heights south of Grugis. Four times the infantry charged over open ground towards their objective, but each time the attack broke down. At 10.30am three battalions of Hertzberg's 32nd Brigade moved forward to the valley in which Rosenzweig's men were taking cover while a spirited artillery duel went on over their heads. This was taking place between the French gun line on the windmill hill half a mile southeast of Giffecourt and four German batteries north and northwest of a farm called La Manufacture. At 11.15am six battalions of French infantry advanced against Rosenzweig's troops and gained some ground before being driven back at the point of the bayonet. An attempt to follow up this successful counter attack by seizing the sugar factory was, however, repulsed. Meanwhile, Hymmen had advanced on Contescourt and reached a height southeast of the village before being pinned down. To the east, on the right wing of Barnekow's advance, Lippe had at 10.00am advanced up the road from Cerizy; he had thus far received only one battalion of the expected reinforcements from the Army of the Meuse. By 11.00 am his advanced guard under Colonel von Carlowitz had reached Cornet d'Or, and was exchanging artillery fire with French batteries on a hill southwest of Neuville St Amand, while his infantry pushed on up the road.[30]

The remainder of the First Army was coming in from the west. On the immediate left of Barnekow's advance, Kummer had chosen Bock's brigade to lead the advance from Beauvois through Etreillers, followed by Strübberg. Paulze d'Ivoy had posted Robin between Fayet and Francilly, with Payen to the south. The latter's brigade under Lagrange extended with its left to the Ham road, while

Faidherbe's command post at the windmill that gave the Windmill Heights their name, during the Battle of St Quentin, 19 January 1871, by Knötel (Scheibert)

Michelet's Brigade was held in reserve to the west of St Quentin itself. The gap between the two divisions of the 23rd Corps was filled by Isnard's Brigade, to the east of Savy and hence directly in the path of Kummer's line of advance. To the north of this, von der Groeben's main thrust was coming down the Roman road, along which Massow led eight battalions, covered by seven squadrons and supported by 21 guns. This line led directly towards the position occupied by Robin, whose troops remained the least reliable in Faidherbe's army. Having encountered no opposition as he marched through Vermand, it was not until he reached Holnon that Massow first ran into Robin's Division; here some advanced companies of infantry had moved forward through the town to occupy the woods immediately to the west. They were soon driven back through Seleucy, and Massow moved on the Windmill Heights west of Fayet.

Bock meanwhile had reached Etreillers with the 29th Brigade at 10.00am and pressed on through Savy. East of the village the *Daily News* correspondent witnessed a ruthlessly efficient attack by the 4th Squadron of the 7th Hussars under Captain Rudolphi, which he thought 'one of the finest and most gallant cavalry attacks' he had ever seen.

> Immediately behind Savy several squadrons of French dragoons were drawn up in line against about an equal number of the King's Hussars. The former were extremely nice and clean; their horses well tended; saddles and bridles apparently a few days only in use; their white cloaks as if put on for the occasion. The

> hussars, on the other hand, as well as their horses, were covered with mud; their uniforms, usually so neat and shiny, were all soiled from the long and toilsome marches of the last few days. I was just instituting the comparison, when the hussars, like lightning dashed forward against the enemy, and overrode him in a pitiful manner. The first shock dismounted half of the French dragoons; their white cloaks covered the ground or were trodden into the earth; whilst those who remained on their horses fell under the heavy strokes of the hussars' sharp sabres, or were made prisoners.

The outcome was hardly surprising; some of the dragoons taken prisoner later said that they had had barely three weeks training.[31]

Bock's advanced guard under Dörnberg, on emerging from Savy, turned northeast towards the woods south of Francilly, which were strongly occupied by troops from Isnard's Brigade. A brisk artillery duel also ensued between three Prussian batteries that unlimbered to the east of Savy, and two French batteries that opened fire from a gap between the two sections of the wood. Dörnberg's infantry pressed on into the woods; but although by noon they had succeeded in taking the southern section, they were for the moment unable to overcome the stiff resistance of Isnard's troops in the northern part. Lagrange, on Isnard's left, sought to relieve the pressure by attempting to outflank the woods to the south, a move which Bock forestalled by bringing up a battalion of his 23rd Regiment on Dörnberg's right. Strübberg had in the meantime concentrated his brigade in a hollow just south of Savy, and was held there by Kummer in reserve.[32]

To the north Massow had successfully stormed the Windmill Heights, and strongly held Seleucy, and by 12.00 noon was ready to launch an attack on Fayet. Just at this moment Major General von Gayl, the intended commander of von der Groeben's infantry, arrived after a ride of eighteen miles from the station at Ham. He at once realised that there was no sense in his taking over in the middle of the battle, and left Massow to conduct the operations on the left, while he took charge of the right wing. By 1.00 pm, six companies from the Windmill Heights had driven the French out of Fayet; but the obvious threat which this posed to the line of any French retreat northwards towards Cambrai obliged Paulze d'Ivoy to do something about it. He now committed Michelet, his only reserve, in a powerful attack on Fayet and the Windmill Heights. The latter position was much more defensible, and Massow pulled his troops back from Fayet to the heights, from which Michelet was unable to dislodge them.[33]

In the meantime Goeben had felt obliged to commit the only reserve which he had. This was a force consisting of the 41st Regiment, with three squadrons and two batteries under Colonel von Böcking, and which had come forward to Roupy from Ham. In anticipation that this move would in due course become necessary, he had previously detached three battalions and one battery from Strübberg's 30th Brigade, sending this force under Major von Bronikowsky in the direction of Roupy to take Böcking's place. Bronikowsky reached Roupy at 11.30am, after an exhausting march through knee deep mud. At 11.00am Goeben had ordered Böcking 'to proceed forthwith to Grand Seraucourt and to join energetically in the action of the 16th Infantry Division wherever circumstances might demand it' and to put himself at Barnekow's disposal.[34] Goeben has been criticised for this move on the basis that it was strange that he should reinforce his right which had made relatively little progress, rather than his left, which had been advancing more swiftly.[35] However at Roupy Böcking was closer to the troops under Hymmen on Barnekow's left, and at the time he took the decision Massow was not yet in possession of the Windmill Heights. Böcking wasted no time.

> Hastening ahead with the cavalry, he next caused his batteries to come into action against the hostile position at Contescourt. The fire of the artillery speedily dislodged the adversary from the hollow road east of the village, which was then occupied by the 1st Battalion of the 19th Regiment. Immediately after its arrival, the 41st Regiment moved to the attack of the village position.[36]

Contescourt was soon cleared of the enemy, and Böcking pressed on to take Castres, forcing the French to fall back on the heights south of Grugis. Lecointe, whose right might be turned if this advance continued, reinforced the troops there with the rest of Gislain's Brigade, as well as two battalions from the brigade of Rettié and four from that of Ayrès. Soon after 1.30 pm, there were a total of 30 guns in position east of Contescourt, and this concentration of fire gradually wore down the French artillery. Seeing that some elements of the French infantry were beginning to retire, Böcking at 2.15 pm launched the 41st Regiment (von Hüllessem) in an assault on the French right which threw the French back into Grugis.

Böcking's energetic thrust had an immediate effect on the rest of the fighting south of St Quentin. At the sugar factory, Rosenzweig had still been able to make no impression, and the heavy concentration of French infantry there had obliged him to fall back. In spite of reinforcements reaching him from Hertzberg's 32nd Brigade, which momentarily allowed him to attack again and to retake the hill west of the sugar factory, the French pressure was too great, and Rosenzweig pulled back his exhausted troops, whose ammunition was running low, to the heights east of Essigny Le Grand. Barnekow, not realising that Böcking had been personally ordered by Goeben to go into action as soon as he arrived, had assumed that for the moment he could only depend upon Hymmen's detachment for action on his extreme left to relieve the position of Rosenzweig and the 31st Brigade, and had issued orders accordingly. Hertzberg launched an attack in battalion strength towards the railway and the sugar factory, which was at first successful but which soon broke down in the face of overwhelming French counter attacks, and at 2.00 pm the battalion fell back to its start line. Soon, however, the effect of Böcking's advance began to be felt here, in the centre of the 16th Division's position, and on the extreme right, where Lippe had only two battalions, about which Barnekow had been decidedly nervous. There was, however, no further danger in that quarter; by 3pm Lecointe, whose corps had suffered considerably in the course of the fierce fighting, occupied a position from Grugis, to the sugar factory and thence northeast towards St Lazare Ferme. The sugar factory thus formed a salient jutting out into the German line. In spite of its remarkably successful defence throughout the day, Lecointe's overall position was becoming decidedly vulnerable.

Meanwhile, on Kummer's front there had been further significant activity. He had responded to a build up of French troops between Francilly and Dallon by strengthening his gun line south east of Savy, while Bronikowsky, with the newly

The charge of the Prussian 70th Infantry Regiment at Saint-Quentin (Rousset/*Histoire*)

formed army reserve, was on Goeben's orders moving towards L'Epine de Dallon on the Roupy – St Quentin road, in order to clear away large numbers of skirmishers threatening Kummer's right wing. The increasing French pressure had compelled the troops holding the smaller of the two woods there to evacuate it; but although the French infantry moved in, they were ejected in their turn by a charge of the 1st Battalion of the 65th Regiment. It was against this wood that Lagrange and Isnard were directing their principal efforts, after the Fusilier Battalion had taken the larger wood to the north. Bock's men remained on the defensive; Kummer was content that von der Groeben and Bronikowsky should be responsible for the offensive operations necessary to drive back the 23rd Corps.

At 1.30pm Gayl with the right wing of von der Groeben's troops launched an assault with one and a half battalions from Seleucy against Francilly, and succeeded in taking the village with 2000 prisoners. Two more battalions took the height immediately to the south, enabling Bock to move up and Gayl to swing his troops eastwards facing St Quentin. More for the moment he could not do, as his troops were running short of ammunition; the pause in the attack allowed the French to slip back over the undulating ground out of sight of their attackers. Further north, efforts to retake Fayet stalled in the face of very substantial French forces from Michelet's Brigade, and Massow pulled his troops back to the Windmill Heights.

Lecointe, conscious that he had to do something to arrest the advance of Böcking's force and the right flank of the 16th Division, resolved on a final throw of the dice, a decision which coincided with Barnekow's determination to advance with his whole line. Lecointe's sudden and powerful assault led by Pittié's Brigade, supported by part of Foerster's Brigade, from the advanced position south of the sugar factory came as a considerable surprise to their adversaries. Preceded by a dense screen of skirmishers, firing from behind the piles of sugar beet that lay in the fields, the French came forward in a vigorous attack between the railway and the high road. Barnekow found himself riding between the front line of his own outposts and the advancing French skirmishers; turning, he led his weary infantry in an advance towards the heights, calling up the 3rd Reserve Cavalry Brigade (von Strantz) to charge forward over the crest of the hill. In the cover of a dip in the ground Strantz arrived at the right of the advancing French infantry and, wheeling into line, charged down both the skirmishers and their supports who fell back in disorder. Barnekow, who himself took part in the charge, had his horse wounded under him; but he did not mean to miss the opportunity which this success had given him, and he ordered Hertzberg and Strantz to follow up the enemy along the high road to St Quentin.[37] Meanwhile he had brought up the only uncommitted troops he had, five companies from the combined Infantry Brigade now led by Colonel von der Groeben advancing up the east side of the railway line towards Grugis. Böcking meanwhile had also launched an attack through Grugis, while those units of the 16th Division remaining west of the railway were also set in motion. While Barnekow was charging with Strantz's troopers to the east, the rest of the troops around the sugar factory stormed the position that had withstood them so long; with the loss of the key to the defence of his line gone, Lecointe had no choice but to pull back towards St Quentin, pursued all along the line by the advancing German troops. Böcking, now commanding all the troops west of the railway, brought down a hail of artillery fire on the retreating French troops, which were beginning to disintegrate under the German pressure, not least from the cavalry, which had a number of opportunities to ride down the fleeing infantry.[38] Meanwhile Hüllessem led four companies along the railway line and seized the station, fanning out into the southern suburbs of St Quentin. Out on the right Lippe's cavalry pressed forward hoping to cut off Lecointe's line of retreat; they were held up, however, by strong detachments in Harly and Homblierès, to the west of the town.

On the west of St Quentin, where the First Army headquarters was for the moment posted on a ridge between Savy and Fontaine Les Clercs, it had seemed to Goeben that although Barnekow appeared still to be held up, Kummer was in the presence of a beaten enemy force which should be followed up. The news of the taking of Francilly reached him about 2.30 pm, at which time he also learned of some progress being made to the south. At 3.00 pm he ordered Kummer 'to advance with his whole force on St Quentin,' which of course was what the 15th Division's commander was already doing.[39] Bronikowsky took L'Epine de Dallon at about 3.00 pm, and Kummer moved forward to the height between that village and Francilly. By now Paulze D'Ivoy's troops in the immediate front of the 15th Division were thoroughly demoralised, and were driven from position to position with comparative ease. As the German advance approached the outermost houses of St Quentin, however, darkness was beginning to set in, but Kummer, determined to enter the town that night, pushed forward one and a half battalions and one squadron, which encountered little opposition.

To the north, Paulze d'Ivoy had been apprehensive all day about von der Groeben's threat to his right flank, and hence to the Army of the North's line of retreat, and it was at Fayet that he had concentrated all his available troops to check the German advance. So strong were the French here that von der Groeben, expecting to march forward directly to St Quentin, was held up not only by

French Fusilier Marines, a drawing by Detaille (Rousset/*Histoire*)

Michelet's troops in Gricourt but also an advance from that direction by the troops of Pauly's Brigade. The French also pushed forward towards Seleucy, a move that was soon defeated by Gayl, who attacked them with the forces which he had concentrated at Francilly. Under the continuing hammer blows of the German artillery, the French attack soon broke down completely, and they retreated hastily towards their start line. Von der Groeben pursued them with the fire of his batteries, and with three battalions moved forward to take the village of Fayet, which was by now in flames.[40]

The French, now in retreat all along their line to the west of St Quentin, had endeavoured to cover their rearguard movement by the deployment of their artillery at Rocourt, but their effectiveness was soon ended by the concentration of the Prussian guns on their position there, and as darkness fell they retired with the French infantry into the suburb of St Martin. As the French gunfire slackened, Bronikowsky followed up the retreating enemy, storming Rocourt at the point of the bayonet at 5.00pm. The speed of his advance greatly alarmed Faidherbe, who had spent the morning with Lecointe before going for the rest of the day to the west side of St Quentin to watch the battle in Paulze d'Ivoy's front. He had believed, like Goeben, that to the south of the town the French line was holding out; now, fearful that the retreat of his whole army might be compromised by Kummer's advance, he ordered Paulze D'Ivoy to reinforce Lagrange and Isnard with troops from the right.

Going back into the town at about 4.30pm, he had a meeting with Lecointe, and learned from him that the front to the south of St Quentin had collapsed but that, since Paulze d'Ivoy was still holding out to the west, he would be able to get his troops through the town towards Le Cateau. Clear that the battle was lost, and that the important thing was to get as much of his army away as quickly as possible, Faidherbe confirmed to Lecointe that he should retreat towards Le Cateau as fast as he could, while Paulze d'Ivoy was ordered to fall back northwards in the direction of Cambrai. In fact it was not until 6.00pm that Paulze d'Ivoy heard the news that St Quentin was in German hands. Although Michelet and Pauly were already in retreat to Cambrai, the troops in the Faubourg St Martin were not so fortunate; unable to reach the road north, many of them were taken prisoner there. Faidherbe himself had a narrow escape which he only effected with the help of the local inhabitants.[41]

Goeben, staying close up behind his advancing troops, rode into Rocourt soon after it was occupied. On the way he received news of Barnekow's successful advance all along his line, which he could soon see for himself. A detailed report from Captain von Schell, later to be the First Army's historian of the campaign, reached him soon after 5.00pm, and gave him greater details of the 16th Division's progress. His complete victory was no longer in doubt, and Goeben rode back to establish his headquarters at L'Epine de Dallon, from where at 6.30pm he sent a terse report to Moltke:

> Have attacked the French Army of the North in its position in front of St Quentin, driven it from all its positions in a seven hours fight and forced it back upon St Quentin after an obstinate resistance. As yet ascertained, two guns taken fighting, above 4,000 unwounded prisoners. The operations which night has interrupted will be continued tomorrow.[42]

Meanwhile, through the dark streets of the town, the leading units of both the 15th and 16th Divisions were pushing forward to the north and northwest, collecting a considerable number of prisoners on the way. In fact Barnekow's forces had made the greater progress; when Schell, on his way to look for Goeben's headquarters, encountered Kummer's leading troops on the edge of town, he found them to be unaware that St Quentin was already in German hands.

As soon as Goeben received the news that St Quentin was safely in German hands, he sent a further telegram to Moltke to report it. Pleased though Moltke must have been at the brilliant success of his protegé, the response was characteristically terse and businesslike: 'His Majesty the Emperor congratulates your Excellency on your success, and recommends vigorous pursuit. The 16th Infantry Brigade is to be sent back here as soon as it can be spared.'[44] Understandably Faidherbe, not for the only time in his memoirs, played down the extent of the losses sustained by the Army of the North, suggesting that these amounted to about 3,000 in killed and wounded and about 7–8,000 prisoners. In fact, however, the total number of unwounded prisoners must have been over 10,000, while over 3,000 wounded prisoners were taken in St Quentin alone. The total loss of the French was somewhat in excess of 15,000. Total German losses were 2,400, of whom 450 were killed, 1,878 wounded and 72 missing. Although substantial, these casualty figures were, in the context of the victory gained, remarkably light.[45]

And it had been a striking victory. Although the subsequent pursuit failed to prevent the Army of the North reaching the safety of its fortresses, in spite of energetic measures to overtake them, Faidherbe's army had ceased to exist as an effective fighting force. Notwithstanding the appalling state of the roads, Goeben followed up the French line of retreat, uncertain for a long time as to the direction they had taken and the extent of their disorganisation. Gradually, however, it became evident that Faidherbe had sent a large part of his forces to Lille, Douai and Valenciennes, rather than retaining all of them around Arras, Cambrai and Le Cateau, the fortresses nearest to the Germans. From this it was clear that there was no longer any immediate likelihood of any further serious action being undertaken by the Army of the North, and Goeben, after giving his troops a well deserved break, brought them back to the line of the Somne by January 25. From here he could, in relative comfort and tranquillity, watch for any renewed French activity. Events at Paris, however, were soon to mean that no more would be required of the First Army.

27

Armistice

As the war neared its end, the growing conflict between Moltke and Bismarck also approached a climax. The Crown Prince had watched with increasing dismay the mounting hostility between the two men, and resolved to do what he could to effect a reconciliation. On January 10 he had a long talk with Bismarck, who agreed to a meeting with Moltke, in the Crown Prince's presence, to discuss 'the measures to be taken in case Paris capitulates and the preliminaries of peace that will follow in that event.' Bismarck was at pains, however, to make his position clear: 'He gave me to understand further that the hostility that exists between his Department and the High General Staff, and is growing more and more acute, would not be allowed to go on any longer.'[1]

The meeting took place on January 13. By now the news of Le Mans had been received, which ought to some extent have eased the pressure on all three men, since it was evident that Chanzy had ceased to be a threat; but on the other hand there was continuing anxiety about Werder's exposed position until Manteuffel arrived with the Army of the South. The Crown Prince recorded the discussion, which lasted an hour and a half and continued over dinner. It would, he gloomily concluded, need a good many more such meetings before they reached common ground.

> Both talked quite plainly to the other, and Moltke, generally so sparing of words, speaking in tones of reproach and quite eloquently, upbraided the Federal Chancellor, bringing forward all the grievances he had already confided to me on January 8; the other protested in return, and I had repeatedly to interfere to bring back the conversation into smoother water. The two were least of all in accord as to the consequences of an Armistice, inasmuch as Count Bismarck desires peace, but General Count Moltke a war of extermination. Then Count Bismarck attacked the General on his tenderest point, developing the theory that after the battle of Sedan we should have stayed on in Champagne to await further developments and ought never have gone to Paris. Under such circumstances agreement was clearly out of the question, and I could not even gain this much, that at any rate at coming reports at His Majesty's, mention might be avoided of the differences of opinion actually existing. It will rather come to this, that each separately for himself will lay his views before the King, and His Majesty must decide between them.[2]

The Crown Prince's disappointment was entirely understandable. While it was with Moltke that his personal sympathy lay, his hope was that the Chief of Staff's calm judgement and intellectual rigour would lead him to accept the desirability of an early end to the war. But by January 1871 even Moltke's icy detachment was coming under extreme stress. Now seventy years of age, he had endured a long period of ceaseless endeavour and vast responsibility in the course of which he had laboured tirelessly to reorganise the Prussian Army, making it the most effective military force on earth; and in six years he had fought three wars at a time of life that he had expected would be spent in peaceful retirement. For the past six months he had presided over the conduct of a war of enormous military, technological and political complexity which, in spite of the many brilliant victories he and his troops had won, still dragged on. For months he had been locked in a deeply stressful dispute with the Federal Chancellor. It is small wonder, therefore, that under the pressure of events he should, when invited to do so, have given expression to a number of extravagant views which caused the Crown Prince, his greatest admirer, the deepest anxiety. And yet to Moltke the ideas he was propounding were the product of a kind of remorseless logic. If, after the fall of Paris, the French did not at once completely capitulate, then the war must be fought out to the bitter end, not so much as a war of extermination, as the Crown Prince described it, but as a war to break French power for good. It was a response born of intense frustration and anxiety; calmer reflection might have told him that this was, in practical terms, impossible, but for the moment he could see no alternative that did not mean a failure to take proper advantage of all the achievements of the German armies. To the Crown Prince, longing above all things for the war to end, Moltke's language was particularly shocking.

He had not, however, in the slightest lost faith in Moltke; only two days later he was recording his admiration for Moltke's 'icy imperturbable calm' in dealing with Werder's suggestion that he might do better to abandon Belfort, and he certainly intended to continue his efforts at conciliation. But before he was able to take any further step in this direction, further developments occurred to sharpen the conflict between Moltke and Bismarck. First, as foreshadowed at their meeting with the Crown Prince, Moltke submitted a memorandum to the King setting out his views on the arrangements to be made for Paris in the event of the capitulation of the city. He suggested that the whole of the city should be surrendered and placed under martial law, and that its military garrison should be disarmed and sent as prisoners of war to Germany. Moltke claimed that in this paper he had limited himself to military issues; but his proposals so obviously affected other questions that were in Bismark's province that it was further grist to the latter's mill. In his own paper, on the same day, Bismarck emphasised the central significance of Paris to the ultimate peace negotiations; the need to embark on these quickly was, he contended, essential if the risk of intervention by the Great Powers was to be averted.[3]

Next, Moltke wrote a letter to Trochu on January 15 in reply to the latter's protest of January 11 about a large number of shells hitting various hospitals. Trochu had complained that the frequency with which this occurred meant that it could not be accidental. In his reply Moltke emphatically denied that this was so, pointing to the humanity with which the Germans had conducted the war, and coldly ending his letter: 'As soon as a clear atmosphere and short ranges permit the recognition of the domes and buildings which are indicated by white flags with the red cross, it will be possible to avoid even chance injuries.'[4] There was not much in the text of the response to which exception could be taken; but it presented Bismarck with a fresh opportunity to complain to the King that Moltke was interfering in questions that were solely political. This he put in a memorandum to William on January 18, obliging the newly proclaimed Emperor finally to make a

The proclamation of the German Empire at Versailles, 18 January 1871, painting by von Werner (Scheibert)

choice between the two enormously powerful adversaries. Bismarck in the meantime followed up his advantage by himself writing to Washburne requiring him to complain to Jules Favre about French artillery firing, on December 21, upon the hospital at Sévres, and the Dominican Convent, both bearing Red Cross flags, in which there were German sick and wounded. To make his point, he was careful to ensure that the content of his letter closely matched the exchange between Trochu and Moltke.[5]

On January 20, the day after Buzenval, d'Herisson arrived at Versailles on a mission from Trochu to ask for a forty eight hour truce to recover the wounded and bury the dead. This was reported to the Crown Prince while he was with his father; to both of them it seemed that this might be the beginning of the end. Significantly, they both felt that it was to Bismarck, and not Moltke, to whom the request must be taken, and they made their way to the former's quarters. The Crown Prince noted the text of the careful response: 'the outposts in the usual way would have to come to an understanding about looking after the wounded and disposing of the dead, but all other details could only be arranged in writing.'[6] When he went on to Moltke's quarters to tell him what had occurred, the latter was predictably unimpressed with the suggestion that there was any underlying significance in a request that was only to be expected after a major engagement.

The incident, however, led William to authorise Bismarck to conduct any armistice negotiations; and with this decision he effectively pronounced in the Chancellor's favour. To his credit, although he shared his son's personal sympathies with Moltke, the Emperor firmly accepted that it must be with Bismarck that ultimate authority lay. He finally put the matter beyond doubt when he issued, on January 25, two orders that spelt out clearly that he had adopted Bismarck's position in its entirety. First, he forbade Moltke from conducting any correspondence with Paris or Bordeaux without first obtaining his own approval. Secondly, he ordered that Bismarck should be kept informed about the future plans for the army, so that he might if he wished comment upon them.[7]

Moltke was profoundly shocked by this. He at once wrote, in obedience to the second order, a summary of the present military situation for Bismarck, to which the Emperor, evidently feeling that it was insufficiently informative, added some notes of his own.[8] Later that evening, still in the grip of strong emotion and feeling that his position had become untenable, Moltke drafted an intemperate response to the Emperor. In it, he denied that he had done anything which amounted to a political act or of having not kept the Chancellor informed of significant military operations, adding what amounted to his own resignation. Bismarck, he suggested, should thereafter be responsible for advising the Emperor on military questions. He did not, however, send it. Having slept on it, he wrote a fresh memorandum in which he toned down his indignation, and confined himself to a measured defence of his own position on the major issues that had arisen between him and Bismarck. He made no concession about the process of planning future military operations.

> To give information concerning operations planned or still in the course of being carried out to anyone except the generals charged with their execution, I would consider as a breach of duty … I believe it would be a good thing to settle my relationship with the Federal Chancellor definitively. Up till now I have considered that the Chief of the General Staff (especially in war) and the Federal Chancellor are two equally warranted and mutually independent agencies under the direct command of Your Royal Majesty, which have the duty of keeping each other reciprocally informed.[9]

Although William had a reply to this drafted, it appears never to have been sent.

This was no doubt because, before Paris, events were now beginning to move swiftly. Accompanied by his son in law, Martinez del Rio, and by d'Hérisson, Jules Favre set out on the evening of January 23 for an interview with Bismarck, taking the most elaborate pains to avoid being recognised en route by the French troops before embarking on a hazardous trip across the Seine in a leaking boat. Once on the German side of the river, d'Hérisson left him to make his way to Versailles, and went to Sévres to await his return. At Versailles, Bismarck gave Favre a very hard time, making it clear that if he stuck to his previous position about territorial integrity, he was wasting his time. In any case, he said, he was in touch with representatives of the Empress Eugénie, with whom he would be perfectly able to negotiate with a good deal more apparent legality than with Favre's government, a mere 'band of insurgents.'However, he was prepared to discuss the surrender of Paris and as to this showed himself to be much more accommodating than Moltke would have been. He would not insist on the French troops being sent to

Germany, and he would soften the army's demands both as to their disarmament, and also as to a triumphal entrance into Paris. He promised next morning to put his formal proposals in writing, after he had seen Moltke and the Emperor. These proved to be as moderate as he had foreshadowed. The 60 original battalions of Gardes Nationales would be allowed to keep their arms to preserve order in the city; an armistice could be agreed covering the whole of France; the forts were to be surrendered and the guns on the walls thrown into the ditches; Paris was to pay a war indemnity, and elections were to be held for a national assembly. Taken as a whole it was an offer that Favre could see at once was too good to refuse; and when he made his way back to Paris on the following evening his colleagues in the Government found no difficulty in agreeing with him.

On the morning of January 25 Favre returned to Versailles, this time accompanied by d'Hérisson, who, when Bismarck joined them, was struck by the physical contrast between the two men.

> Count Bismarck wore the uniform of the White Cuirassiers – white tunic, white cap, and yellow band. He looked like a giant. In his tight uniform, with his broad chest and square shoulders, and bursting with health and strength, his proximity overwhelmed the stooping, thin, tall, miserable looking lawyer, with his frock coat wrinkled all over, and his white hair falling over his collar.[10]

A long negotiation over the disarmament of the rest of the Gardes Nationales followed in which Favre insisted that all must retain their arms, together with three regular divisions. When this was put to Moltke, he was completely opposed; if it were to be conceded, only one regular division should, he thought remain under arms. At the end of this Bismarck finally gave way, although insisting on Moltke's demand that only one regular division should retain its arms. On the subject of the Gardes Nationales, Bismark remarked to Favre: ' So be it, but believe me, you are making a blunder. And sooner or later there will be a heavy reckoning for you with the rifles you are imprudently leaving in the hands of these enthusiasts.' As to the war indemnity, he asked for a billion francs; when Favre protested, Bismarck suggested that any less would be insulting to Paris. But in the end, he settled on two hundred million francs, unaware that Favre had authority to go to half a half a billion. Throughout the negotiations Bismack was extremely affable, later telling his staff that he liked Favre better than at Ferrières. Over dinner that evening he astounded d'Herisson by recalling the occasion of their previous meeting five years before; the chirpy Frenchman was greatly impressed by the Chancellor, who was, he thought, quite unlike French statesman in his lack of solemnity. 'He is downright gay, and in the middle of the most serious questions he voluntarily makes some little joke, some humorous remark, under which, however, the powerful lion's claw can be felt.'[11]

During January 25 and 26 the political outlines of the settlement were largely agreed; but a large number of military questions were still outstanding, for which Favre required military support. He and Bismarck were, however, able to agree upon a cease-fire to begin at midnight; Bismarck also allowed that the French should fire the last shot. On January 27 the negotiations continued. On this occasion Favre was accompanied by General Beaufort d'Hautpoul, who accepted the responsibility with the greatest reluctance, and after a prolonged emotional outburst; d'Herisson thought he had aged ten years on his journey to Versailles. He was still distressed when the talks began, although unkind German observers put it down to his being drunk. On the German side, Moltke joined the discussions, at which an armistice of twenty one days was agreed, and the lines of demarcation across France were settled; the eastern sector was however omitted from this, Bismarck suggesting that this be left until next day.

On January 28, Beaufort was replaced by General Valdan, Vinoy's Chief of Staff; for whatever reason, Beaufort's demeanour on the previous day had been acutely embarrassing to Favre. It is a matter of some doubt as to whether, in the course of the discussions, it was Beaufort who had persuaded Moltke to except Vincennes from the requirement that the forts be occupied, and to agree that the guns in the fortifications should merely be dismounted rather than be thrown into the ditches. This is what Beaufort later claimed; d'Herisson, who was a lively raconteur but possibly not an altogether reliable historian, claims that it was he who, entirely on his own initiative, persuaded Bismarck to agree to these concessions.[12]

D'Herisson, however, has left us with a graphic and entirely convincing picture of Moltke during these negotiations, throughout which he was icily correct and for the most part implacably unyielding, for which Bismarck occasionally chided him.

> With his clean shaven face, which bore evidence of suffering, and was, as it were, crackled with an infinity of small wrinkles, M. de Moltke did not in the least resemble a soldier such as we love to portray them in France. He rather resembled a Benedictine monk, or an ascetic, or an old actor. Each one of his words, clear, sharp, and precise, seemed to be produced by the vibration of a steel tongue. You could feel instinctively that he thoroughly enjoyed having under his hand the humble plenipotentiaries of humiliated France and conquered Paris. Dressed in a very simple uniform, he wore the ribbon of the Iron Cross knotted in his button hole and not sewn on his breast ... He had at his neck a cross in blue enamel resembling a Maltese cross.[13]

Once the details of the lines of demarcation had been settled, largely in accord with Moltke's wishes, there remained the question of the situation in the east. Favre, aware that Belfort was still holding out, and under the influence of Gambetta's optimistic predictions about the imminent success of Bourbaki's operation there, was reluctant to give up the chance that a victory for the Army of the East would provide a valuable negotiating point when the final peace negotiations got under way; and he was particularly anxious not to have to give up the fortress of Belfort. On the German side, also, there was little up to date information about the situation there, but Moltke had complete confidence that Manteuffel would be able to deal effectively with Bourbaki, and was perfectly ready to accept the exclusion from the armistice of the departments of Doubs, Jura and the Cote d'Or, and the fortress of Belfort.

Thus it was agreed; and on the evening of January 28 the armistice was signed. It was to come into effect within three days, and the news of it was sent out by the German staff to all their field armies. Favre reported the armistice to Gambetta by telegram immediately after it was signed; but, in an omission that was to have disastrous consequences for the Army of the East, he failed to tell Gambetta either of the three days allowed for the armistice to come into effect or of the exclusion of the eastern departments. Later, heavily criticised for this, Favre suggested that he had thought that only the lines of demarcation there remained outstanding, and that in any case that was Valdan's responsibility. However, another French observer, whose recollection accords with the material facts, recalled Bismarck as having said to Favre: 'A line of neutrality will be traced for the other armies, but since you do not want to give Belfort, operations will continue in the east.'[14] Favre's misjudgement condemned France to suffer a final crushing military humiliation.

28

Tragedy of an Army

Edwin von Manteuffel had wasted no time after receiving Moltke's orders that he was to take command of the newly formed South Army. Handing over command of the First Army to Goeben, he set off at once to Versailles, where he arrived on January 10 for a personal briefing from Moltke and William. The basic task of the South Army was easily explained, but the difficulties were considerable, and Manteuffel was given a wide latitude as to how he executed his mission. He was allowed to take with him as his Chief of Staff Colonel Hermann von Wartensleben, who had for long periods worked with him as acting Chief of Staff of the First Army, together with Major von Lewinsky as Quarter Master General. Part of the staff of the First Army also accompanied him; the rest of the army's administration had to be put together on an ad hoc basis as they travelled south.[1]

With his three corps widely scattered he was going to have to improvise; but the deeply held and instinctive understanding and tradition of cooperation among senior Prussian commanders stood him in good stead. In addition to Werder's XIV Corps, preparing to face Bourbaki in its critical confrontation before Belfort, he had the II and the VII Corps. The II Corps, led by the extremely capable Fransecky, had been pulled out of the investment lines around Paris and marched swiftly to Montargis, which was a considerable change from the static role it had been performing. The VII Corps, on the other hand, under the elderly Zastrow, had endured a difficult and frustrating time since the fall of Metz. Left behind by the First Army as it marched off to the north, it had been deprived of its 14th Division which had been detached to deal with the siege of Mézierès. Thereafter it had been involved in a series of frustrating marches and counter marches as it tried to deal with various threats to the German lines of communication, which came from all directions over a wide area. Even before he decided to form the South Army, Moltke had taken steps following the fall of Mézierès and Rocroi to restore the 14th Division to the VII Corps, ordering its commander Schuler von Senden on January 6 to transfer the division by rail to Châtillon sur Seine. This movement, expedited through the largely restored rail network, was carried out with great speed, its arrival at Châtillon being covered by Dannenberg's brigade. Zastrow and Fransecky were directed to the same place, Moltke ordering the latter to hasten his march so that the 3rd Division reached Nuits sur Armancon by January 12. If the South Army was to arrive in time to strike an effective blow at Bourbaki, speed was obviously essential.[2] The Official History noted that 'no halting days could be allowed during the last severe marches, and there was no prospect of any. The men's boots and the horses' shoes were in very bad order'.[3]

Manteuffel and Wartensleben arrived at Châtillon on the evening of January 12 to take up command. For the moment they did not have to concern themselves directly with Werder's operations; until the South Army was in touch with the XIV Corps, Werder was to continue reporting directly to Moltke. But they did have to take an immediate strategic decision which must have important consequences for

General Bourbaki, commander of the French Army of the East (Rousset/*Histoire*)

the South Army's future operations. The line of march of its main body could be either on Vesoul or Dijon. Wartensleben, in his history of the campaign, reviewed the alternatives.

> Very weighty and tempting reasons spoke for a march on Dijon. The principal and best roads from the neighbourhood of Montbard and Châtillon traverse the mountains in this direction, and converge towards Dijon. It was there that the two Prussian Corps d'Armee might expect to obtain a sure and easy success over Garibaldi's isolated corps; besides which the capture of the ancient capital of Burgundy was in itself a desirable object. For the return of the French troops to Dijon, after the evacuation of the town by the XIV Corps, had been turned to account by the French press in every possible way, both politically and morally. In addition, this route was further from the recently augmented garrison of Langres, and it would provide a rail link which when repaired would be the best line of communication.[4]

But the South Army's objective was solely Bourbaki's army, not the recapture of Dijon or the smashing of Garibaldi's Corps, and it was at Belfort where the crisis lay. The earlier that the effect of the South Army's approach was felt, the better in terms of bringing help to the hard pressed XIV Corps. On the morning of January 13 Manteuffel settled on the Vesoul route, in spite of the risks of abandoning much safer roads and instead passing between two strong enemy positions at Dijon and Langres, through the Cote d'Or where he would find no lateral roads enabling his columns to come to each other's aid. In addition, once he was out of the mountains, he would have to sever his line of communication to Châtillon; instead, he proposed to make Epinal the South Army's base.

The orders issued on January 13 reflected the need for flexibility in dealing with any situations which this hazardous march might produce. General instructions were given to the corps commanders as to how to deal with any opposition that might be encountered; because Manteuffel would 'for some days be unable to give many direct orders, all arrangements will therefore lie in the hands of the generals commanding the corps,' and they were given a wide freedom of action in pushing forward their march. Such had been the speed of the concentration at Châtillon that the movement was able to begin on January 14. The army faced the same fearful weather conditions that afflicted Werder.

> The landscape was veiled in mist and covered with snow; hard frost prevailed, the thermometer falling even to 14° below zero on the following morning. The roads were extremely slippery, so that cavalry, artillery and wagons could only make their way by dint of unspeakable exertions, the latter had often to be dragged up the hill sides by the men.[5]

Although patrols reported continual movements of enemy troops between Dijon and Langres, little effective opposition was encountered. By January 16 the main body of the army had reached the line Moloy-Prauthoy-Longeau, directly between Langres and Dijon. On each flank units were pushed forward to observe these places, from which some attempt to interfere with the army's progress was expected, but nothing of any consequence materialised, and the small parties of enemy troops that were encountered were easily brushed aside. The only incident that caused serious concern was the taking of a transport column south west of Langres, as a result of which Manteuffel ordered those units which had not yet caught up with the army to be rerouted through Epinal rather than across the Langres plateau.[6]

Werder and Manteuffel had been keeping each other well informed of their situation. By January 18, having received news of the outcome of the battle on the Lisaine, Manteuffel was able to report that by the following day his leading troops would have closed up to the Saône between Gray and Scey sur Sâone, while the main body would be between Fontaine-Francaise and Dampierre. The opportunity to retard the South Army's progress towards Bourbaki was largely gone. Freycinet was disgusted by the failure of Garibaldi's force to make any impression, writing angrily to Bordone (Garibaldi having been taken ill) on January 19: 'You have given Bourbaki's army no support, and your presence at Dijon has had no effect on the enemy march from west to east. In short fewer explanations and more action, that's what we want from you:'[7] Direct cooperation between the South Army and the XIV Corps would soon be possible, and since he expected to be over the Saône by January 20, Manteuffel, in response to Moltke's instructions, ordered Werder to 'endeavour as much as possible to keep firm hold of the enemy, so as to gain time for my flank movement.'[8]

However, although the South Army could now in only two marches join hands with the XIV Corps somewhere south of Villersexel, it seemed to Manteuffel and Wartensleben as they pondered the situation that this might not be the right course to follow. Although no doubt a further defeat might be inflicted on

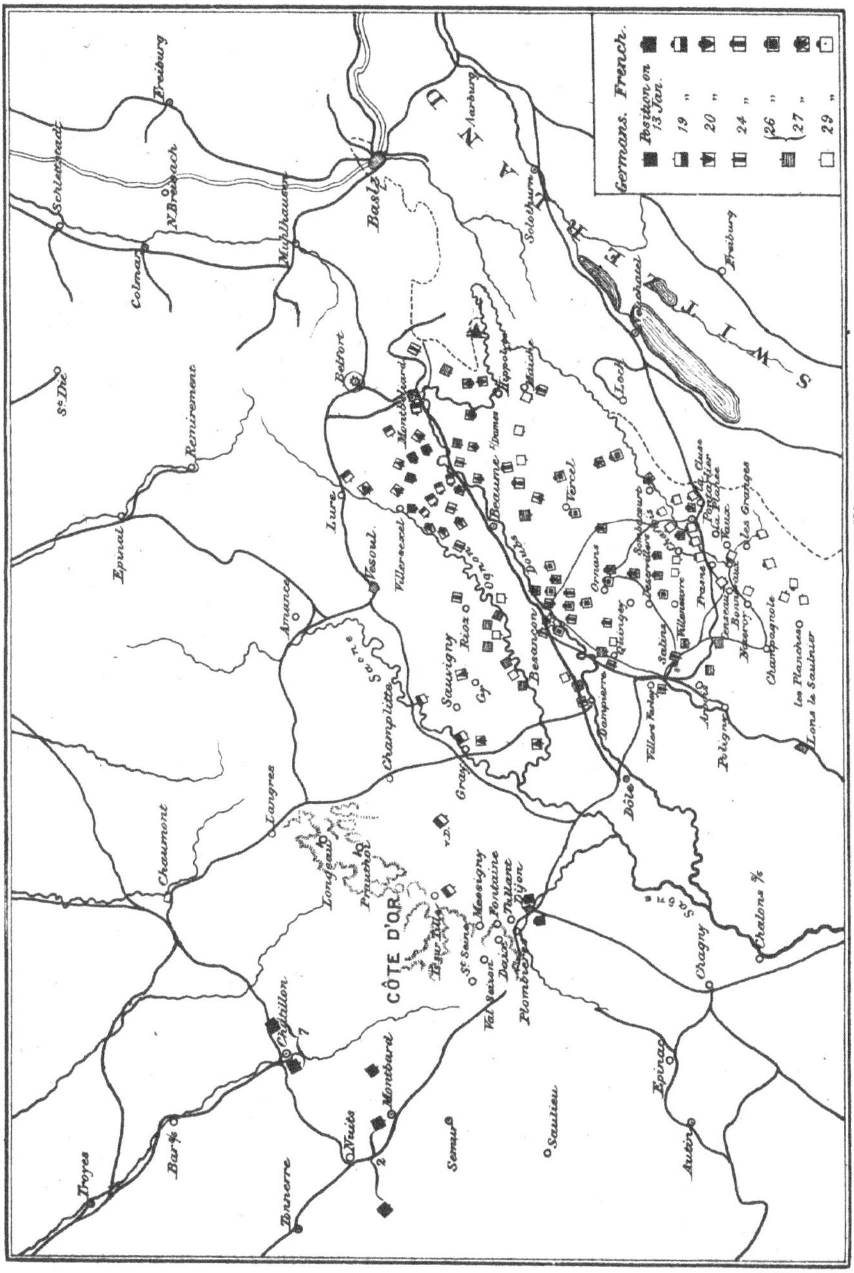

Operations of the Southern Army against Bourbaki

Bourbaki, 'he would only be weakened, not annihilated, as he would be thrown back on his natural line of retreat. With the restless energy which was characteristic of the French preparations, the same army, newly reinforced, would before many days have to be again encountered.'[9] A better if riskier course of action would be to march directly to cut Bourbaki's line of communications, down the Saône towards Lyons, which would oblige Bourbaki either to fight a decisive battle near Besancon, or to retreat through the forbidding mountains of the Jura. It would mean further rapid marching over rough country, with the possibility that supplies might run short, but it offered the chance of a truly decisive result. Back at Versailles, when he received news of Manteuffel's intention to take this course, Moltke entirely approved, remarking to the King: 'General von Manteuffel's movement is extremely bold, but it may lead to the greatest results. Should he suffer a check he ought not to be blamed, for in order to gain great successes, something must be risked.'[10] And he sent a telegram approving the plan. Moltke always responded better to those of his generals like Manteuffel or Goeben who proposed vigorous action; it was the extreme caution of Frederick Charles or the diffidence of Werder that tended to irritate him.

In spite of the condition of the roads, good progress continued to be made; the weather had changed, and a sharp thaw set in. For January 20, Fransecky was ordered to concentrate at Gray, with an advanced guard pushed forward to the south at Pesmes. On his left, Zastrow was to cross the Sâone and reach the area of Sauvigny-Cifrey, pushing forward his advanced guard towards Besancon and reconnoitring towards Rioz. The South Army was getting dangerously close to Bourbaki's lines of communication, and he would have to retreat a lot more quickly than he had advanced if he was to escape. It was no surprise, therefore, to learn from Werder on January 19 that the Army of the East had begun to pull back. Werder followed, rather slowly. His troops had not yet recovered from the exertions of their three day battle and Werder was anxious to avoid any risk of exposing them to a defeat at the hands of the strong rearguards covering Bourbaki's retirement. News that Bourbaki seemed to be wheeling to the left led Manteuffel on January 21 to spell out his plan to Werder:

> Your Excellency will have perceived that it is my intention to cut off the enemy's retreat, which may be expected to take place in the direction of Besancon and Lyons, with that part of the army which is now here ... I depend upon Your Excellency keeping at close quarters with the enemy; upon your following him in whichever direction his chief forces retreat, and upon your right wing opening and keeping up communication with me.[11]

Manteuffel was, however, suffering from a serious shortage of cavalry, and he ordered that Willisen's cavalry should be brought quickly around the rear of the VII Corps to join Fransecky's advanced guard at Pesmes. By the evening of January 20 Bourbaki was largely concentrated between Rougemont and the Doubs; only the 24th Corps was on the far side of the river. Werder himself was at Villersexel, the leading troops of his right wing approaching Rougemont and his left at L'Isle sur le Doubs; but he reported that he could not advance further next day because of the exhaustion of his troops and the lack of supplies. Zastrow, meanwhile, had closed up to the Ognon at Pin and Etuz, brushing aside attempts to bar his passage, and establishing bridgeheads on the far side. At the same time, Fransecky's advanced guard under Koblinski had pushed on to Dôle; the garrison was taken by surprise, and after a short struggle on the outskirts and within the town itself, occupied it and seized the vital bridge over the Doubs. Koblinski also seized large quantities of stores in 230 railway trucks, which came in handy in provisioning the South Army.[12]

Back at Dijon, there had been a brisk engagement. Major General von Kettler, with the 8th Brigade, had been left behind when the South Army plunged south east, his task being to mask Dijon and block any attempt by Garibaldi to interfere. He met little opposition as he neared the city and on January 21, even though outnumbered at least five to one, launched an assault which in spite of running into well prepared positions drove the defenders back into their last line of defence, between Fontaine and Talant. His immediate intention was to follow this up with a night attack; but he had sustained 336 casualties, and used up a lot of his ammunition, so he decided instead to draw back and resume his attack when he had been resupplied. He took with him some 500 prisoners, having inflicted in addition heavy losses on the enemy. Two days later he resolved to try again, moving around from the north west of the city to the plains on his left, and launched a vigorous assault either side of the Thil Chatel road towards Pouilly. In spite of the heroic efforts of his grossly outnumbered troops, he was unable to break through, and at nightfall he withdrew, having sustained further heavy casualties numbering 378 in all. The enemy also again suffered heavily, in addition to losing 150 prisoners; but, inspecting the battlefield after the fighting had ended, some of Garibaldi's men found under a heap of dead bodies the bloodstained colours of the 2nd Battalion of the 8th Regiment. This was the only regimental colour taken by the French throughout the war; and predictably much was made of it. The news of Kettler's repulse at Dijon was received with delight by Freycinet, who wrote effusively to Bordone: 'At last I discern again the brave Army of Garibaldi and his clever chief of staff.'[13] But Kettler's losses had bought a brilliant result; not only had he neutralised Garibaldi, but he had put up such a fight that the French became convinced that half of Manteuffel's army had been in action against Dijon.

While Kettler had been in action the South Army had been pushing on. On January 22, while the 14th Division masked Besancon, the 13th Division reached the Doubs at St Vit and Dampierre. Fanning out the advanced guard found, crucially, four unbroken bridges over the Doubs between Orchamps and Fraisans, and pushed forward a detachment to Quingey. On their night, the II Corps found additional evidence that the seizure of Dôle had completely surprised the French, locating bridges over the rivers to the south of Dôle unbroken, although preparations had been evidently made for their defence.[14]

Manteuffel was becoming impatient with Werder's lack of activity, ordering him to launch a vigorous offensive on January 23 in order to prevent a French corps, believed to be at Montbozon, from advancing towards Gray, since otherwise he would have to detach troops from Fransecky and Zastrow to cover their rear. At the same time the II Corps was to press on to Mont sous Vaudrey, to reconnoitre towards Salins and Arbois and break up the railway between Lons le Saulnier and Besancon, while the VII Corps occupied Quingey with the 13th Division and pushed the 14th Division towards Dannemarie, where its outposts were shelled from Besancon.

In the meantime Bourbaki had been directing his retreat towards Besancon, where he expected to find substantial reserve of supplies. Operating, from under the walls of this powerful fortress, he proposed to maintain himself along the line of the Doubs, and await further instructions.

These now came in the form of another ambitious scheme from the fertile brain of Freycinet, involving the removal of the army once more to the west, with the intention of cooperating with the newly formed 25th Corps in an advance towards Auxerre and Troyes. With the South Army in the vicinity, such a scheme was never really feasible, but the loss of Dôle completely put paid to it. Accordingly Bourbaki speeded up his movement on Besancon, and on January 22 moved the 1st Division of the 15th Corps through Besancon to secure the key town of Quingey. Only Minot's brigade, however, could be brought up on January 22 and during the following night; and a few shells from the artillery of Bothmer's approaching 13th Division were sufficient next morning to put Minot's men to flight. The divisional commander, d'Astugue, came up intending to launch a counter attack to retake Quingey; but such was the confusion that he soon abandoned it. An abortive advance in the direction of Dôle was also made by troops from Bonnet's Division on the right bank of the Doubs, but this also broke down swiftly. The morale of Bourbaki's men was visibly crumbling.

Manteuffel was as aware as Bourbaki of the importance of Quingey, and his orders for January 24 reflected this. The VII Corps was to secure the town from any assault from Besancon, if necessary preparing entrenched positions to do so. The II Corps was to continue its advance south east to the Besancon-Lons le Saulnier Road, its main body taking up a position at Vaudrey. These movements were carried out without difficulty, Koblinski with the advance guard occupying the road and rail junction after a brief skirmish. Zastrow's reconnaissances towards Besancon confirmed the presence there of the bulk of Bourbaki's army. Meanwhile Werder moved forward, his first objective being the enemy force in the town of Baume les Dames. His intended concentric advance there proved unnecessary, as the French pulled out after blowing the bridges over the Doubs. After these had been repaired, Werder moved Schmeling to the left bank of the river, to move on towards Besancon. Further east, Debschitz attacked the left of the rearguard at Blamont.

Reviewing his progress so far, and the position of Bourbaki's army, Manteuffel issued general instructions to each of his Corps commanders on January 24 setting out the various course of action which Bourbaki might, in his desperate situation, consider taking. He saw six possibilities. First, Bourbaki might try to go south, between Villars-Farley and Pontarlier. In that case, the II and VII Corps would fall on his flank. Secondly, he might try to break through by Quingey and Dampierre, where he would be met by the VII Corps in his front and the II Corps in his rear. Thirdly, he might head for Gray, in which case the 14th Division and Knesebeck's brigade would attack his left and the Baden Division his right, while the rest of the army came up. Next, he might turn back on the XIV Corps, in which case Fransecky and Zastrow would come on his rear. The fifth option would to be head for the Swiss frontier, when he would be pursued by the advanced guards of all three corps, compelling him to accept battle across the frontier. Finally, he might stay put around Besancon, in which case he would be blockaded there. Manteuffel went on to add, in accordance with the flexibility of his approach, that these instructions were given 'so that you may at any time be able to initiate operations in keeping with their spirit, without waiting for orders from me, in case circumstances should make it necessary to take a sudden resolution.'[15]

While Manteuffel was thus preparing for all possible eventualities, Bourbaki that day convened a council of war. When he had arrived at Besancon the previous day, he was appalled to discover that there were only five days provisions there for his army. (In fact, later enquiries showed that this was wrong, and that the supplies piled up in various places would have fed his men for six weeks). All his senior commanders were present with the exception of Martineau (with whom Borel, the army's Chief of Staff had had a meeting) and Bressolles, who was with part of his corps ineffectively probing at Debschitz's force, near Blamont. The reports of the corps commanders as to the state of their men were gloomy in the extreme; only about half the men were really effective. Analysing the options in much the same way as Manteuffel had done, Bourbaki narrowed them down to two. Either the army attempted to break out of the trap towards Auxonne, or it retreated to Pontarlier. His own view was for retreat; it was shared by all the others, except the ever optimistic Billot, who thought a break out possible. Bourbaki suggested that the 18th Corps should try it, and if it was successful he would follow with the rest of the army. No, said Billot, the whole of the army must attack. In that case, replied Bourbaki, Billot could take over the command. Billot declined the offer; only a commander like Bourbaki could carry it through. In the face of all this, it was generally agreed that the only option must be to retreat, and Bourbaki that afternoon telegraphed Freycinet with the decision.[16]

Before receiving Manteuffel's general instructions, Werder had been acting in accordance with his earlier orders of January 22. He now came to the conclusion that if, as now appeared, the French did not propose to attack towards Gray, he should concern himself in particular with covering the South Army's rear from any advance from Dijon, and he reported this to Manteuffel on January 25. His reluctance to move directly on Besancon was born of his previous experiences before the fortress; he was convinced that such an advance would be brought to a halt in the Chailuz Forest and at Châtillon le Duc where a defensive position had been prepared. He decided accordingly to march over the right bank of the Ognon to Etuz and Boult. Later on during the afternoon came Manteuffel's orders, for an advance on Besancon down both bank of the Doubs, as well as the general instructions. These messages crossed with Werder's report of January 25; when he got that, Manteuffel, who had no doubt in his brief sojourn at Versailles picked up some of Moltke's reservations about the XIV Corps commander's diffidence, irritably spelled out what Werder was to do: 'The course to be adopted in case the enemy try to break through towards Gray is not to stop him by standing across his path, but to attack him on the march by both flanks.'[17] Werder's move was at odds with the general instructions, but it was too late to do anything about it; rather than order a counter march Manteuffel instructed him to make not for Pesmes, as Werder had intended, but for Marnay, in order to come into direct contact with the VII Corps.[18]

Zastrow spent January 25 probing towards Besancon, picking up a number of prisoners in a series of isolated skirmishes. These suggested that the 20th Corps was already on the move to the south east, and was to be followed by the rest of the army. Fransecky meanwhile, had concentrated the 3rd Division at Mouchard and Villers-Farley; the 7th Brigade was at Vaudrey. Much the most important activity in the II Corps sector, however, were the reconnaissances towards Aubois and Salins; with these positions secure in German hands, Pontarlier would be the only way out. The information gleaned was important; Salins was held by some 2,000 French troops, and was dominated by two forts on the heights to the south and east.

Next morning Koblinski moved out of Mouchard with the advanced guard; encountering opposition at Pagnez, he duly brought up his artillery. For once it was not entirely effective; and an effort to silence the heavily armed Fort St André, beyond Salins, at long range had no effect at all. Koblinski had to rely, therefore, on his infantry; sending one company on a mountain path from Pagnoz to Salins, he pushed three more up the main road. Moving from point to point in short rushes, these cleared the mountain slopes either side of the road. By 2.15 the whole of the 2nd Grenadier Regiment came into line, and stormed into the town from the north and along the railway line from the west. Koblinski meanwhile had led the 42nd Regiment around in a wide flank march through St Thiebaud, reaching Salins from the east. Resistance soon ended in the town; at the request of the mayor, the commanders of the forts agreed not to shell the town, but negotiations for their surrender broke down, and they opened fire on any German troops that ventured within range.[19]

In his orders to Fransecky of the previous day, Manteuffel had remarked that it was still not clear whether Bourbaki intended to remain at Besancon to refit, or to continue his retreat, in the direction of Pontarlier through Ornans. Fransecky, was therefore, to push forward reconnaissances towards Pontarlier and Champagnole to see to what extent the French army had progressed in those directions. It was for this reason that Fransecky had decided to move up a substantial force to Salins. The effect however, was considerable. Not only did it shut off one more route of escape for the French; the discovery that the town was already in German hands finally broke Bourbaki's will. In deciding that the army must retreat to Pontarlier, he had given to Cremer the mission of protecting its flank, giving him the 3rd Division of the 20th Corps, the Army Reserve, and his own division to carry out this difficult task. Colonel Poullet, Cremer's Chief of Staff, took over his division and set off at 7.00 am on January 26 to Salins, the importance of which had belatedly become apparent. When he reached Nans sous Ste Anne he received news that Salins was already occupied, according to local inhabitants, by some 15,000 Prussian troops. The news was in fact a little premature, and of course Koblinski had only his brigade there; but in the face of this information Poullet felt unable to continue his advance, and he moved instead to Villeneuve d'Amont on the Salins-Pontarlier Road.[20]

Elsewhere on January 26 there was no good news for Bourbaki; Bressolles, with the 24th Corps, had been ordered to reoccupy the passages of the Doubs but an ineffective advance on Pont les Moulins to the south of Baume les Doubs soon broke down in front of Schmeling's outposts, and Bressolles fell back. Bourbaki was furious, and ordered him to make another attempt on January 26, supported by Billot's 18th Corps. Billot protested, again urging an attempt to break out to the west, but Bourbaki was adamant. In the event, it took all day for Billot's troops to get into position; Bressolles, who had advanced up the Baume les Doubs road from Vercel towards Passavant, awaited their arrival. When there was no sign of this, his officers convinced him that the state of the 24th Corps was such that to attack alone would mean its disintegration, and Bressolles again fell back to Vercel.[21]

During the day Werder's leading unit, Wechmar's brigade, had reached Marnay; but Werder himself, conscious that events might require von der Goltz to cross the Doubs at Baume les Dames to support Schmeling, remained at Rioz to keep in touch. On the west side of Besancon, meanwhile, Zastrow had closed up towards Besancon, pushing forward a series of vigorous reconnaissances, all of which suggested, correctly, that the French were now all to the south of the Doubs.

Bourbaki was now at the end of his tether. From his position between Manteuffel, remorselessly driving his army into the jagged mountains of the Jura, and Freycinet, bombarding him with wildly impractical orders, there seemed no escape. On the night of January 26 he went to his room, took his revolver, and shot himself in the head. But his aim was bad; the bullet only grazed his skull. In the meanwhile, however, Freycinet had heard enough; a telegram relieving Bourbaki, and appointing Clinchant in his place was already in transit. The inept Bressolles was also sacked, and replaced by General Comagny.[22]

Clinchant, reluctantly assuming the command, was in no doubt that it was a poisoned chalice. Had it not been for the fact that any major battle at that stage would have led to the complete disintegration of the army, his total strength and the positions he occupied would have suggested that the correct decision would have been to attack the encircling enemy with the maximum vigour. But looking again at the reality of the situation, he could see all too clearly that whatever Freycinet might suppose, the retreat on Pontarlier was the only hope. From now on, all that the Army of the East could do was to march, as fast as the daunting terrain and appalling weather would allow.

At Versailles, on the other hand, there remained some lingering if misplaced anxiety about the situation. Blumenthal recorded some personal doubts about the operations of the Army of the South, in spite of the progress made in surrounding Bourbaki's army:

> Manteuffel's troops are, however, so separated that he cannot prevent Bourbaki breaking through at any point if he attempts to do so in force. Manteuffel's manoeuvres do not appeal to me; but I do not know the country, and so cannot express any opinion that is of value. Doubtless there are many defiles which Manteuffel sees his way to defending easily.[23]

On January 27, Manteuffel tightened his grip. West of Besancon Wechmar reached the Doubs at St Vit, allowing Schuler von Senden's 14th Division to move entirely to the south bank. Bothmer with the 13th Division continued to move around Besancon to the south, occupying Courcelles and Chatillon, and pushing forward patrols towards Ornans. Fransecky, meanwhile, had received reports of Poullet's movement, and grasped at once that one of two of the possibilities contemplated by Manteuffel's general instructions had arisen;the French were trying to escape either direct on Champagnole, or through Pontarlier. He immediately pulled his troops out of Salins, occupying the pass to the west of the town, a move that confounded the garrison of the two forts, which had trained its guns to the east on the assumption that the Germans would march in that direction. Two battalions moved on to Pont d'Héry, where they were joined by the 7th Brigade from Arbois. The rest of the corps moved down to Arbois in support. When he received news of this Manteuffel, quickly appreciating Fransecky's grasp of the situation, ordered Zastrow to send troops south to relieve the troops watching Salins, releasing them to enable Fransecky to move further south towards Champagnole.[24]

Manteuffel was, however, much less pleased with events at the other end of his line, where Schmeling had halted in the face of improbable rumours that another attempt was to be made in the direction of Belfort through Blamont. Schmeling at first discounted this suggestion; but when what was apparently reliable confirmation was given by a peasant brought before him he felt unable to continue his advance, having only a total of 9 battalions with which to resist an attack. This somewhat timorous decision was contributed to by Tresckow's recall to the siege of Belfort of Debschitz's force: although four battalions of this were intended to reinforce Schmeling, he only received them on January 30 and 31.[25] It took a direct order from Manteuffel to get Schmeling on the move again, and it was January 30 before he reached Vercel.

The rapid progress made by the South Army led Manteuffel to decide that the time had come to deal with Dijon, and on January 27 he gave orders to General Hann von Weyhern, the commander of the 4th Division, to take command of a force comprising Kettler's 8th Brigade, Knesebeck's brigade, Willisen's detachment and a Baden Brigade, and march at once to take the city. Werder chose Degenfeld's brigade for inclusion in the force, which concentrated between Dôle and Gray on January 28 before commencing its march to join Kettler in front of Dijon.[26]

By the end of January 27 Fransecky was well established on the line Arbois – Pont d'Héry, while Zastrow had extended south to Salins. The bulk of the French army had left Besancon; and by every one of the available mountain roads was streaming towards Pontarlier. The leading units under Cremer seemed to be heading for Champagnole. Manteuffel and his staff could not know the extent of the collapse of morale among the French troops, although they could guess at it; on the other hand, as Wartensleben noted, the VII Corps had encountered well organised resistance; in Zastrow's front, 'the enemy had still shown perfect firmness and steadiness. We had to fight the compact heads of the army there; troops, moreover, that had not abandoned a single gun during their retreat.'[27] The Germans intended to take nothing for granted.

During January 28 Zastrow pushed the 14th Division through the mountains to Eternoz, while the bulk of the 13th Division was at La Chapelle. The progress of the II Corps had also been uninterrupted. Du Trossel with the 7th Brigade found Champagnole unoccupied; only a small number of enemy troops had got away to the south by this route.

The 6th Brigade was at Montrond, and the 5th Brigade, with the Corps II artillery, at Poligny. Fransecky's advance slammed the door on any escape down the Pontarlier – Lons le Saulnier road, which left only the road closest to the Swiss frontier still open, that which ran through Mouthe and Les Planches down toward St Laurent. News that French troops were in Les Planches reached Fransecky at 10.00 pm on January 28; he at once roused the 5th Brigade and the Corps artillery, and set off on a night march to Champagnoles, intending to attack Les Planches next day. Orders from Manteuffel, however, that he should move direct on Pontarlier, led him to reduce the force advancing on Les Planches to four battalions under Colonel Wedell, while the rest of the corps headed up the Pontarlier road towards Censean.

Manteuffel had also heard of Schmeling's failure to advance. Recognising that it would be some time before the 4th Reserve Division was able to influence events, he ordered Zastrow to cover his own left against Besancon and brought von der Goltz down to Mouchard to fill the gap opening between the VII and the II Corps. At 5.00pm on January 29 he received Moltke's telegram of the previous night that an armistice had come into force in Paris, and would be in general force on January 31; but that the departments of Cote d'Or, Doubs and Jura were for the moment excluded. He announced this at once to the army. The news that the end had come of course came as no surprise, but the exclusion of the South Army's theatre of operations was unexpected, and the immediate problem that was to arise was that although Moltke correctly recorded this, Clinchant's information from Bordeaux did not. Manteuffel, meanwhile, was beginning to lose touch with the progress of his army on an hour to hour basis; his troops were becoming widely scattered, and the condition of the roads made communication increasingly difficult.[28]

On January 29 Wedell reached Les Planches without encountering any resistance, and at once pushed detachments south to Saint Laurent and north east up the road to Mouthe. The last practicable escape route for the Army of the East was gone. Fransecky, had in the meantime headed up the road from Champagnole towards Pontarlier. Colonel du Trossel, whose 7th Brigade led the advance, met a battalion of Gardes Mobiles near Nozeroy, but this quickly withdrew.[29] To the north, the VII Corps had a busier day. The 14th Division was the furthest forward as the corps pushed towards Levier. Its advanced guard, under Colonel von Cosel, marched through Levier at noon, and carried on down the Pontarlier road. The first serious opposition was encountered at Chaffois which was taken by storm by the 53rd Regiment at 9.00 pm after a brief bombardment. Here, and at Sombacourt where a flanking advance had also been made, 4,000 prisoners were taken, together with Generals D'Astugue and Minot, and also twelve guns and seven mitrailleuses. By now news of the armistice had reached French units; about a thousand men surrendered voluntarily on the strength of it. General Thornton, the nearest divisional commander, sent Cosel a letter he had just received from Clinchant announcing the armistice, and calling for the release of those that had voluntarily surrendered. When Zastrow received a report of this, not yet having heard from Manteuffel, he ordered his troops to halt where they were, allowing the 1,000 men to go free, although retaining their arms.[30]

Back at Besancon, Werder had a largely uneventful day, confining himself to reconnaissances which showed that the fortress was still strongly held. Schmeling, at Savery le Grand, made no movement because he was awaiting support from Debschitz; Colonel Zimmermann, however, with four battalions got down the

Dismounted French Dragoons defend Les Planches, by Knötel (Pflugk-Harttung)

road in pursuit of the enemy as far as Maisle. It was as well that it was only part of the rapidly disintegrating 24th Corps that remained in his front; the German pursuit on this side of Besancon had been remarkably ineffectual.

So soon as Manteuffel heard of the proceedings at Chaffois, he sent out a general order confirming that the armistice did not apply to the South Army, and that the movement on Pontarlier should be pressed forward. Meanwhile the next German commander to have to tackle the situation was Fransecky; as his advanced guard moved on Frasne on January 30, a French officer arrived with the news of the armistice. Sent back to Fransecky's headquarters, he met another emissary forwarded there by Wedell. They produced a copy of Favre's report to Bordeaux of the armistice concluded with Bismarck, which was to be announced to 'the whole of France' but which disastrously omitted the exclusion of the south eastern departments. The French high command, and the individual officers who appeared before the German lines can hardly be blamed for feeling indignant at their enemy's reluctance to grant a cease fire. For his part Fransecky still had no news of the true situation, and allowed a truce till that evening on condition that the French pulled out of Frasne but otherwise halted. Later he got Manteufffel's message, and sent to let the French know that he would recommence operations the next day. At Besancon, Werder also received an approach for a cease fire from the commandant of the fortress which, having heard the full story direct from Versailles, he also declined.

At Arbois, Manteuffel was getting thoroughly frustrated; he rode forward to be nearer the front, aiming to transfer his headquarters to Villeneuve d'Amont, on the line of march of the VII Corps. En route he too received a message, this time direct from Clinchant. Courteously refusing the request for a ceasefire he suggested in his response that in order to avoid bloodshed, Clinchant might come to put forward proposals 'as are in conformity with the military situation prevailing here at this moment.'[31] By now, though, Manteuffel and Clinchant had reached an identical conclusion for different reasons; it would be better for the French army to pass over into Switzerland than be compelled to capitulate. For Clinchant, this was a matter of honour; for Manteuffel a matter of pragmatism, since in any future peace negotiations the maintenance of a French army of 100,000 men on neutral territory was preferable to their being sent as prisoners of war to Germany.[32]

Manteuffel's refusal of an armistice brought an angry telegram from Gambetta, and Clinchant sent another envoy, Colonel Chevals, to try to negotiate one. Arriving at 3.00 am on January 31 he too met with a polite refusal, in an interview with Manteuffel in the course of which he became extremely excited. Manteuffel calmly pointed out that Clinchant could either surrender or continue his retreat; Chevals blustered in reply that in that case General Clinchant would be delighted to continue with his operations. Later in the day yet another officer, Colonel Varaigne, arrived; in an interview with Wartensleben, the two men were obliged to agree to disagree, but drew up a record of what each regarded as the true position.[33] Manteuffel had in the meantime decided to draw the noose tighter by continuing his advance on Pontarlier, and he reported as much to Moltke. By the end of January 31 the villages around Pontarlier were in German hands, and Zastrow's VII Corps was in touch with Fransecky's troops coming up through Bulle. The advance guard meanwhile also closed up to the south at Narboz, while a detachment took Vaux and Grange – St Marie on the road to Jougne. Small parties of French troops had been trickling south over the mountain roads, and in the end several thousand got away in this direction including much of Cremer's cavalry; but the rest of the Army of the East was now penned into a narrow area around and to the east of Pontarlier.

Clinchant, who was still sending envoys to Manteuffel to persuade him to halt his advance, had also begun negotiations with the Swiss for the internment of his entire army. Although he had some 10,000 men in Pontarlier itself, it is not surprising that these made no effort to hold the town, which fell into German hands by noon on February 1. The French were now echelonned along the road to the frontier at Verrieres. A rearguard held two forts at La Cluse, which were armed with long range artillery and strengthened with mitrailleuses; and when du Trossel's 7th Brigade came up, it found itself facing obstinate resistance throughout the day. Fransecky, no doubt increasingly mindful of the need to avoid unnecessary casualties, sent the 5th Brigade around to the south through Jougne to take the position in rear. He need not have bothered; by nightfall du Trossel had taken La Cluse, albeit with some 400 casualties, and there and earlier at Pontarlier had taken a total of over 4,000 prisoners. The forts themselves remained untaken, and continued in action on the following day, firing promiscuously not only at the Germans, but also on some French ambulances and a German officer coming forward under a flag of truce.[34]

Clinchant had convened a final council of war on January 31; his generals were unanimous that they could no longer answer for the state of their troops, and later in the day Clinchant signed a convention with the Swiss General Herzog for the internment of his army. On February 1 the last doleful march of the Army of the East began, filing over the frontier along the roads through Verrieres, Les Fourgs and Hôpitaux.[35] Next day Manteuffel issued an order of the day congratulating his army:

> Soldiers of the South Army! Your marches and combats amidst the snow and ice of the High Jura have not been fruitless. 2 eagles, 12 cannons, 7 mitrailleuses, 15,000 prisoners including two generals and many officers, several hundreds of provision wagons, several thousands chassepôts are in your hands ... Bourbaki's army is hors de combat, and whatever still remains of it will soon succumb to your arms.[36]

The final act in the tragic debacle of the Army of the East was a series of old world and courtly exchanges between Clinchant and Manteuffel; and it is pleasant to record that Manteuffel, although contending that he would have been within his rights to retain the 1,000 rifles of the French infantry which had surrendered at Chaffois, responded to a request by Clinchant for their release by writing to his opponents:

> It is opposed to my feelings as a soldier, however, to withhold them from the brave troops who gave up the struggle under an erroneous supposition, and it affords especial satisfaction to return them as a proof my esteem for the brave resistance made by the French Army.

Clinchant thanked him with equally stately courtesy.[37]

Meanwhile Hann von Weyhern had dealt with the question of Dijon. Collecting up the scattered troops assigned to him, he marched swiftly on Dijon by way of Mirebeau and Essertenne. From here, he intended to move on Dijon itself, attacking from the south and southeast, or to cross the Burgundy Canal to the south and isolate it. On January 29 he too received envoys with news of the purported armistice; but soon after, he learned the true position from Werder, and on January 31 pressed on towards his target. As he approached Dijon at 3.30pm he found Garibaldi's men dug in a strong position, and resolved to defer his attack till the following day. During the night, however, the Germans could hear the sound of heavy rail traffic moving south; and when their patrols moved forward next morning, they found that the enemy was gone. Hann accordingly marched into the city without opposition.[38]

There remained only Belfort. The exclusion of the south east from the armistice continued of course to apply, and Tresckow's orders were to press on vigorously with the siege. Following the battle of the Lisaine, during which the garrison had kept remarkably quiet, Tresckow had on the night of January 20/21 launched an assault which succeeded in taking the village of La Perouse, at the cost of 186 casualties. He now constructed his first parallel; then, on the night of January 26/27, under cover of a heavy bombardment he attempted to storm the forts of Hautes and Basse Perches, which had been comprehensively strengthened by Denfert. After a savage battle around the perimeter of the forts, the attackers were obliged to retire, having suffered a total of 437 casualties. These seemingly pointless losses were incurred for largely political reasons; Belfort was the enemy's last point of resistance, and Bismarck and Moltke were anxious for it to fall before the peace negotiations were concluded. Tresckow now, however, largely confined himself to engineering operations, and to a selective bombardment by Scheliha's guns of key points in the fortifications. The siege works were steadily pushed forward; on February 9 Tresckow renewed the assault on the two Perches forts, and this time the attack was successful. From then on, the fall of the fortress was only a matter of a very short time, and after a few days Tresckow was empowered to allow the French to withdraw unimpeded from Belfort, and Denfert, not without difficulty, got authority from Bordeaux to give it up. By February 14 the guns finally fell silent, and on February 18 the Germans marched in to take possession of the fortress which had defied them for so long.

29

Peace

Although the conclusion of the armistice meant that the fearsome responsibilities which he had been facing for so long had for the moment been lifted, Moltke still had to deal with a hugely complex set of problems. Foremost among them, of course, was the fact that it was only an armistice which might prove to be temporary. It was by no means certain that the agreements reached at Paris would be accepted in the rest of France; Gambetta's personal reaction was thought likely to be hostile, as indeed it proved to be; and Moltke must therefore prepare for the possibility that a resumption of the fighting might be unavoidable. In the days following the ceasefire he worked on plans for the renewal of operations, and at the same time attended to the many questions that immediately arose. The magnitude of his task is demonstrated by his military correspondence for the period, which extends for several hundred pages after the conclusion of the armistice. In the meantime his personal feelings for his late adversaries had undergone little change, as he showed in a letter to his brother Adolph on February 4: 'Now that all the French armies have been defeated, and a third of the whole country is occupied by us, one might almost expect to find some sign of yielding. The French, however, are so overmastered by phrases that one cannot answer for anything.'[1] Moltke's discontent with the terms given to the French remained; but, as a letter he wrote to the Crown Prince of Saxony on the subject shows, his more extreme views were being moderated by an acceptance of the realities of the situation:

> The provisional government in Paris would have to put up with the most extreme conditions imposed by the victor, and Jules Favre had acknowledged this himself. But if the government wanted to stay in power it could not carry on like this ... it sincerely intended to bring about peace, and consequently we have a strong interest in keeping it in power.[2]

For many of Moltke's senior colleagues, however, it was increasingly a time for relaxation, and after the army had taken possession of the Paris forts, they hastened to inspect with close professional interest the extent of the damage done by their bombardment. Blumenthal, keen to be able to say 'I told you so,' noted that the first reports suggested that the forts 'were all in excellent condition, and so well armed that they could have held out against us for months – another proof that hunger alone has caused the capitulation.'[3] On January 31 he went to see for himself, finding that they were 'very much knocked about, especially in the interior, where many of the lofty barracks had been struck and burnt down.' However, although the effect of the shooting had been 'terrible', he found the counterscarps perfectly intact, and concluded that 'storming would have been impossible, and if the French had only fought well we should have been sent away with broken heads. I am convinced that these works, which really are in themselves complete fortresses, can only be taken after a formal siege, and for that service we had neither guns nor ammunition.'[4] Verdy too went on a tour of the forts, driving up to inspect

'Unter den Linden', Berlin, decorated with 'Battle and Victory' by von Werner, from a contemporary photograph (Pflugk-Harttung)

Mont Valérien with Brandenstein on February 4 through Sandrart's famous entrenchments. Looking back at them Verdy could see the enormous extent of the works that had been constructed in the course of the investment, and the inevitable destruction that had been caused.

> For thousands of yards the long slopes have been cleared of their trees, in order to obtain a clear field of fire for the different defensive positions lying behind each other. The villas in the way were levelled, many of the finest country houses burnt out; no staircases, no floors left, only the bare walls, so that the enemy should not find shelter in them. Enormous abattis, barricades and stockades, shelter casemates, trenches with capounières, newly constructed military roads etc., follow in endless succession.[5]

Some things did not change. Blumenthal remained as touchy and irritable as ever, noting the receipt on February 7 of a memorandum from Moltke 'which hands over to Prince Hohenlohe still greater power, and threatens to throw everything into confusion.' He rushed over to Moltke to protest; the latter, by now very used to dealing with these outbursts, made appropriately soothing noises. Two days later, however, Blumenthal was still getting excited, this time over the responsibility given by Moltke to deal with the captured weaponry.[6]

In considering the possibility that a resumption of hostilities might be necessary, Moltke's first concern was with Paris. On February 1 he prepared an outline of his plans for a formal attack on the city, which he circulated widely two days later.[7] The Third Army and the Army of the Meuse were required to submit their estimates of the number of troops that would be necessary to garrison the forts and embark on formal siege operations; and the possibility was taken sufficiently seriously for Blumenthal to convene a meeting with the senior siege experts on February 5, as a result of which 'everything was arranged so that at least the command is properly organised.' Blumenthal, who was still sensitive to his apparent loss of authority as a result of the powers given to Hohenlohe and Kameke, could not resist adding: 'It has struck me especially that it is here that everything has gone wrong, nobody knowing who was master and who was man.'[8]

Whether, on the French side, any renewal of the fighting was remotely possible was a matter of grave doubt. So that the government in Paris might know the views of the principal commanders in the field, Moltke on February 6 invited Chanzy, Faidherbe and two other generals to come to Paris to meet Favre and his colleagues.[9] The advice they gave was entirely characteristic; Chanzy was optimistic that by moving his army south of the Loire he could oblige the Germans to conduct a large scale and prolonged campaign to drive them back; Faidherbe, on the other hand, was pessimistic, suggesting that the best of his troops should be transferred to Brittany, and the process of moving them was in fact commenced later in the month.[10] Moltke meanwhile produced his own plan for continuing the war in the provinces. By now of course Bourbaki's army was off the board, freeing Manteuffel who should, Moltke proposed, advance southwest to deal with any opposition that might be found there. Meanwhile Frederick Charles, his flank and rear covered by troops released from the investment of Paris, would move due south from the Loire. In his orders of February 8 to the Second Army he spelt out his objective in familiar terms. It was not so much to occupy any particular point or area of territory; 'the object to be attained is the destruction of the enemy army, and this calls for a relentless pursuit.'[11]

Above all, however, this was for Moltke a time of deep anxiety about the forthcoming peace negotiations, in which he was determined to keep the Emperor and Bismarck up to the mark as to the terms to be obtained. His recent experiences had demonstrated the limits of his influence; but he was determined that the territorial demands that had been discussed during the war should not now be abandoned when peace was at hand. The negotiations could not of course begin until the elections to the National Assembly had been held, and for a moment it seemed that these might have to be delayed when Gambetta and his colleagues of the Delegation sought to exclude from the assembly all officials and official candidates of the Imperial regime; Gambetta also denounced the 'criminal carelessness' of the armistice terms and what he saw as Bismarck's intention to attain 'a shameful peace.'[12]

The crisis fizzled out on February 5, however, when the Government in Paris disavowed the Delegation's action; next day Gambetta resigned. The elections proceeded surprisingly smoothly, enabling the new Assembly to hold its first meeting in Bordeaux on February 12, although many of those elected could not get there by then. It met again on February 17, to hear a motion put forward on behalf of the people of Alsace and Lorraine that they should not leave French rule without their consent; although the proposal commanded huge emotional support, Thiers was obliged to speak against it, since it would have made the peace negotiations impossible. In the end a more anodyne resolution was carried, and Thiers was elected to lead the government and hence to represent France in the peace talks.

He presented his Cabinet (which retained Favre as Foreign Minister) to the Assembly on February 19, and it was duly accepted; a commission was named to carry on the peace negotiations; and on February 20 Thiers and Favre were back in Paris. Next day they set off to meet Bismarck in Versailles.

The bitter feelings that had characterised the relationship between Moltke and the Chancellor in the period before the armistice had somewhat subsided, due to a more generous approach from Bismarck, as Stosch noted: 'Bismarck tried to curb his earlier rudeness and was, during these days, endlessly obliging and amiable. The old proverb has again been proved true: "idleness is the root of all evil. The waiting has lasted too long."'[13] The negotiations for a preliminary peace treaty must address a number of weighty issues some of which were extremely complex and would in due course cause the discussions over the definitive treaty to be extremely protracted, but those that particularly concerned Moltke and the military leaders were clear enough. Foremost among these was the question of territorial acquisitions. There was no longer any doubt that the cession of Alsace must be included; but the transfer of parts of Lorraine as well – specifically the fortress of Metz and the area around it- was seen by the military as a strategic necessity. Thirty years before Moltke had adopted a nationalist stance on the subject of Alsace-Lorraine when he wrote an essay demonstrating their German nationality, observing that 'these fine provinces were severed like a sound limb from the living body of Germany.'[14] The passage of time had not moderated his views, which were reinforced by present and future military considerations, in particular in the light of his experiences during the first phase of the war. Bismarck, on the other hand, had even before Sedan, approached the question from a military rather than a nationalist viewpoint, promoting a press article that argued that

> the least, therefore, that we can demand and that the German people, and particularly our comrades across the Main, can accept is, the cession of the French gateways into Germany, namely Strasbourg and Metz ... What we require is increased security for our frontiers. This is only attainable, however, by changing the two fortresses that threaten us into bulwarks for our protection.[16]

Annexation should follow linguistic boundaries. But as the war went on he adopted the nationalist position, and sedulously encouraged the German press in its demands for annexation. The strength of public opinion on the question gave him an addition card in his hand to play during the peace talks.

The second issue on which the Emperor and most of the military had deep feelings was their desire to make a formal entry into the city of Paris. It was, they felt, essential to the honour of the German armies that they be able in this dramatic fashion to demonstrate their victory. This was one of the first points raised on February 21, when Thiers told Bismarck that it would be a catastrophe; but the Chancellor was adamant, offering the even less palatable alternative of a German occupation of the centre of Paris until a peace treaty was ratified. Bismarck moved on to the question of annexations, saying that Metz must be handed over on security grounds, although he would not press Roon's view that Nancy should be transferred as well. As to the war indemnity, he now put this at six billion francs.[17] Although, therefore, Bismarck was with Thiers following the hard line wished for by the military, he was privately not convinced of the need to acquire Metz, as he told his staff on February 22:

> if they were to give us another billion we might perhaps leave them Metz, and build a fortress a few miles further back, in the neighbourhood of Falkenberg or towards Saarbrûcken – there must be some suitable position there. I do not want so many Frenchmen in our house. It is the same with Belfort, which is entirely French. But the soldiers will not hear of giving up Metz, and perhaps they are right.[18]

Rumours of the possibility that Metz might have to be given back soon spread amongst the military, causing general outrage. To Blumenthal, it had the appearance of a defeat, which would 'arouse in Germany a terrific storm. I cannot bear to think that all the blood we have spilt round Metz is to avail us nothing. The good military frontier which we have made so many sacrifices to obtain is to be given up, merely that we may obtain peace.'[19]

During the second day's talks, which Thiers conducted on his own, a deadlock seemed to have been reached, both over Metz and the amount of the indemnity. In his heart, however, Thiers believed that Metz was lost, as he reported that night to the parliamentary commission, whose members took a realistic view of the situation, and gave Thiers a free hand both on that issue and on the indemnity. When he went back on February 24, accompanied by Favre, he found Bismarck, who had by now accepted military insistence on Metz, unyielding, saying: 'In Germany they accuse me of losing the battles Count Moltke has won. Do not ask me for impossibilities.' He was, however, now prepared to accept an indemnity of five billion, an offer which Thiers gratefully accepted.[20] A further sticking point then arose, when Bismarck said that Belfort too must be handed over. Thiers refused to give up Belfort and Metz, and continued to argue the matter until Bismarck agreed to put it to the Emperor, although saying that it would be hopeless unless Moltke could be persuaded. After some delay, he obtained the Emperor's agreement to give up Belfort if Moltke agreed. When he was able to get hold of Moltke, he discussed the matter with him; the upshot was that Bismarck was able to go back to Thiers and give him a choice – to give up Belfort or submit to a German entry into Paris, and give up four villages in Lorraine where some ten thousand Prussians were buried. Thiers did not hesitate to choose Belfort.

With this, the most emotive questions had been settled, and Bismarck's patience was running out. He wanted the deal done without further lengthy argument, saying to Thiers: 'you know that we will start shooting on Monday if we aren't through here by then. That language you would certainly understand. We have been sitting here today for seven hours already and are not finished yet. My health cannot stand such things.'[21] He wanted the preliminaries signed next day, February 25; but there were still disputes over the drafting which went on till 10pm that night. It was not until 4pm on February 26 that the documents were finally signed; these included a separate agreement between Moltke and Valdan which provided that up to 30,000 German troops should enter the city on March 1, and would leave it immediately the peace preliminaries were ratified by the National Assembly.

Moltke accompanies the Emperor, Bismarck and other dignitaries during the victory celebrations in Berlin, 1871, by Speyer (Bork)

Thiers went off to Bordeaux, arriving on February 28. There was an understandably emotional debate on that day and the following day, in the course of which Victor Hugo bitterly opposed the peace terms, but entirely failed to carry the assembly with him. A more realistic position was adopted by the aged General Changarnier, who said that France was paying for the crimes committed against Germany by Napoleon 1. When the vote was taken 546 members approved the treaty; 107 voted against, with twenty-three abstentions. Thiers swiftly telegraphed the news to Favre in Paris.

There, as agreed, the German troops had entered Paris on March 1 to be reviewed by the Emperor at Longchamp racecourse before marching into the city and through the Arc de Triomphe. Moltke and most of his staff took the opportunity to visit the city. On the following afternoon Favre presented the official documents to Bismarck at Versailles, and orders were given for the German troops in Paris to withdraw on the following morning. The speed of the ratification took the Germans by surprise; William was furious at being deprived of the opportunity of riding into Paris at the head of his troops, complaining that they were as good as being chased out of the city.[22] Suggestions were made that the Guard might nonetheless enter Paris; but Moltke, with Roon's support, insisted on the terms being punctiliously observed.

On the whole Moltke and the generals could feel satisfied with what they had got. Verdy thought that Belfort could only have been obtained at the cost of continuing the war, and it was not worth that. Blumenthal was overjoyed at the news that Metz was to be retained. 'I must really apologise to Bismarck from the bottom of my heart. Moltke must have had a word yesterday, and hung on to Metz.'[23] There still remained an immense amount of work to be day by Moltke and his staff; but by March 7 they were able to move first to Ferrières and thence to Nancy, before returning to Germany on March 15. From Ferrières, Moltke wrote to Adolph to record his ultimate satisfaction with what had been achieved, a letter which confirmed the restoration of his relationship with Bismarck. 'After the conference which was held today I consider all causes of difference with regard to the interpretation of the preliminaries of peace to be now removed, a thing which eases my mind considerably, as somehow, up to the present, I was unable to feel thoroughly satisfied with the affair.'[24]

30

Moltke as Military Commander

Like most legends, that of Moltke's infallibility has been the subject of extensive revisionism.

He has been accused by JFC Fuller of rigidity and an 'adherence to a somewhat static doctrine set in motion by directives rather than orders,' although it should be noted that the same commentator also suggested that he took inordinate chances, observing that 'his reckonings were wonderful, yet his risks against an able opponent might have proved damnable.'[1] Moltke shared with other great commanders an ability to judge just when he could afford to take a chance. He did not do so unthinkingly; it was never far from his mind that the line between victory and defeat was a very fine one. In fact, Moltke was far from rigid in the system which he employed. In an essay written soon after the war of 1870–71 he emphasised the importance of opportunism. 'Strategy,' he wrote,' is a system of expediencies. It is more than a science; it is the application of knowledge to practical life, the development of the original leading idea in conformity with ever changing circumstances; it is the art of acting under the pressure of the most trying circumstances.'[2] Nowhere is this more apparent than in the days after Gravelotte. Advancing on a broad front, he was obliged abruptly to change his direction and his formation, concentrating his forces as they wheeled to the right in pursuit of MacMahon. 'But also from this concentration a way was soon found again for a double turning movement, which at Sedan led to the most famous capture of an army in the open field known to history,'as a German commentator put it later in the century.[3]

Moltke's willingness to seek success by whatever expedient best served was illustrated in this freedom from dogmatic reliance on any one strategical system. His concentric advance into Bohemia in 1866, and his warnings against undue reliance on the inner line of operations, have been taken as a commitment to operate on exterior lines. But as Hajo Holborn pointed out, during the war of 1870–1871 'he used both concepts freely and successfully, depending chiefly on the actions of the enemy. Moltke's strategy was characterised by his openness of mind and by the elastic changes from one device to the other.'[4]

Writing two years after his death, a British biographer damned Moltke with faint praise:

> In the conduct of war he was able in the extreme, his conceptions were usually clear and just, his constancy and daring deserve the highest praise; but he was not original, or what may be called sublime; and he was often wanting in dexterity and art ... he had little imagination, sympathy or fiery passion.[5]

It may be said, however, that the author generally offered a very limited and one sided appraisal of Moltke's career.

Other contemporary criticism of Moltke is hard to come by. There are of course Blumenthal's ineffable diaries, although the occasional reproaches heaped on Moltke there proceeded more from the author's considerable vanity or temporary stress-induced irritation rather than any considered judgment. The view that the diaries give of Blumenthal is also misleading; he was extremely able and Moltke, who knew that he could rely on him absolutely, was untroubled by Blumenthal's occasional outbursts. Hönig's painstaking and detailed account of Moltke's strategy at Gravelotte did, however, contain a number of hard headed observations, principally arising from Moltke's failure to intervene more effectively to control the development of the battle.

After his death, a few more partisan writers commented adversely on Moltke's leadership, sometimes being prepared to stand facts on their head in an effort to belittle his achievement. A French writer, General Lewal, believed that Moltke lacked 'inspiration, boldness, the flash of genius,' describing him as 'a specialist, who brought the routine in the leading of troops to high perfection,' and who 'nipped in the bud with relentless vigour every tendency to independent thought in subordinate leaders.'[6]

In terms of the tactics employed by the German armies, there has been some well merited criticism of the use of the cavalry, particularly during the first days of the campaign. The battle of Spicheren was fought entirely unintentionally so far as Moltke was concerned, as a historian of the German cavalry noted: 'The battle may be characterised as a complete tactical surprise to the Germans. That this was so must be attributed absolutely to the improper use which already, on the days preceding, had been made of the numerous cavalry of the First and Second Armies.'[7] For this, Moltke must accept part of the responsibility. The mishandling of the German cavalry in 1866 had been one of the points particularly made by Moltke in his review of the campaign, and it is surprising that he allowed the army commanders again to misuse the cavalry in the advance up to and beyond the frontier. Thereafter, however, the use made of the cavalry was more effective. By August 13, in his orders to the First and Second Armies on that day, Moltke had taken firm control of the employment of the cavalry, emphasising that 'the cavalry of both armies will be pushed forward as far as possible, and must harass any possible retreat of the enemy on the road from Metz to Verdun.'[8] As these orders demonstrate, Moltke had clearly understood the situation of his opponent and the options open to him. And once the hunt for MacMahon had begun, the German cavalry began to exert a paralysing effect on their hapless adversaries.

The magnificent infantry had fewer lessons to learn from the campaign in Bohemia, and in France again performed outstandingly well, although their excessive enthusiasm frequently led to high casualties among their officers. The artillery, on the other hand, had learnt a lot from 1866; instead of being kept in rear, they were handled with great dash and enterprise, and played a decisive part in practically all the great battles of the campaign. Now completely equipped with steel breechloaders, the German gunners nullified the tactical advantage conferred on the French by the superior qualities of the chassepôt.

Moltke's day to day handling of the war against the French Empire was of course not flawless, even if some of his more enthusiastic disciples claimed that it was. In managing such a vast operation in the context of a new and untested technology, mistakes were bound to be made. Moltke's policy, as actual combat approached, of surrendering the initiative completely to his subordinates exposed him to the consequences of their individual blunders or eccentricities. Nowhere does this appear more clearly than in the opening stages of the campaign. His usually clear judgement in the selection of his officers was not sufficient to prevent him acquiescing in the appointment of Steinmetz to command the First Army. By 1870 he had sufficient clout to override the popular perception of the old man as a national hero, the 'lion of Nachod,' and sideline him in favour of a more dependable leader, but he failed to do so. At the least he could have give him a more effective chief of staff, who might have moderated the aged warrior's individualist view of his responsibilities. In general, though, Moltke's thorough training of his staff officers largely removed the scope for maverick commanders to wreck his plans, and his flexible system of strategy and of command usually enabled him to adjust to such errors as did occur.

Moltke's determination to let his army leaders lead also contributed to the appalling casualties sustained at Gravelotte. Having created the strategical conditions which, in the end, gave him the result he wanted, he chose a poor location for his headquarters and lost touch with developments on his left. But for this, he could have exercised more effective control of the battle, the unimaginative blundering of Steinmetz might have been avoided, and the true extent of the French position might have been appreciated much earlier.

When things went well, of course, his belief in letting his subordinates get on with it worked extremely well. Throughout September 1 at Sedan he was largely a spectator, as he watched the remorseless progress of his troops in the sure knowledge that it was unlikely that any significant intervention on his part was called for. For him, most of his work was done. He knew exactly what was required of his commanders and their superb troops, and so did they. The absorption by the Prussian Army of his military philosophy was demonstrable in all that it did, and on that he knew he could rely. Moltke's determination not 'to paralyse the fighting spirit of the army or to cripple the spontaneity of action and reaction on the part of subordinate commanders' was a consequence of his clear recognition that technological developments had enormously increased the responsibility of local commanders.[9] He was the first of modern military leaders to grasp this essential truth.

Another criticism of Moltke concerns the relative failure of the sophisticated supply system with which the Germans began the war. The speed with which Moltke concentrated on the Rhine was at the expense of the separation from each corps of its transport, so that as the troops moved forward to the frontier the trains had not caught up. As a result, the advancing troops had to be supplied by quartering and purchase.[10] Similar supply difficulties were experienced by the Third Army and the Army of the Meuse as they went in pursuit of MacMahon, and they too had to support themselves by living off the country and relying on iron rations as they outran their trains. But the strategic choices that Moltke had to make were exactly the kind of expedients that a fast moving situation called for; the disruption of the supply arrangements was an inevitable concomitant of the decisions that proved crucial to the German victory.

Given the command structure on which Moltke based his management philosophy an efficient staff system was a prerequisite of success. But as Gunther Rothenberg has noted, Moltke produced much more than an efficient adjunct to the leaders of his armies. 'To offset the evident constraints of the command system as he found it, Moltke transformed the Prussian general staff into a unique instrument combining flexibility and initiative at the local level with conformity to a common operational doctrine and the intentions of the high command.'[11] There were few failures on the part of his chosen staff officers, and their reliability gave Moltke the means to carry out his plans while preserving the flexibility that was the key to his strategic thinking. Of all the aspects of Moltke's contribution to the success of the Prussian Army, his reform and development of the Great General Staff was perhaps the most significant, and it was the most essential element of his success.

The patient application of the fundamental principles of his staff training was an instance of the thoroughness with which Moltke prepared his army for war. Another was his attention to detail in planning the mobilisation and deployment of that army. This he regarded as crucial to its success. If the army got off on the wrong foot, he knew that it would always thereafter be struggling to regain its balance, writing that 'a mistake in the original concentration of the army can hardly be rectified during the entire course of the campaign.'[12] There could hardly be a more telling comparison than that between the carefully planned and precisely executed mobilisation and deployment of the German armies and the casual last minute concentration of their opponents, apparently in pursuit of the chimerical Austrian alliance.

Throughout the war, and especially during the campaign of Sedan, the difference between the two sides could be measured in their ability to make the most of their chances. As General Bonnal put it, 'in the course of a war, luck more or less evens itself out between the two adversaries. When one is well commanded, and the other indifferently or badly, the first seizes every opportunity for victory, while the second lets them escape.'[13] Moltke's system, and his own clear eye for the strategical reality of the situation, ensured that the German army missed few of its opportunities.

In war, Moltke often remarked, nothing is certain. Although in comfortable retrospect the march of the Army of Châlons appears doomed from the outset, if the French had been better handled or had faced a lesser adversary things might have turned out differently. Palikao's gamble with the only field army left to France appears impossibly rash, but it was the only bet he could make by then which might save the dynasty, and on the basis of what he knew he was entitled to think it just might come off. The professional skill and dogged heroism displayed by the French army a few days later on September 1 suggests that properly led and fighting in decent positions it could have given a good account of itself, and as Hohenlohe pointed out, a breakout southwards from Metz on the right bank of the Moselle might have caused serious interruption to the German lines of communication at a critical stage of the Sedan campaign.[14]

As things stood, by August 25 MacMahon was, in the words of the Official History,

> in position with 150,000 men almost on the right flank of the German Army facing westward, whilst the latter continued to believe that the adversary was in their front in the direction of Paris. In the next few days the Army of Châlons might find an opportunity of advancing from the northward into the Argonnes,

> rolling up and beating in detail the troops of the Crown Prince of Saxony in that neighbourhood, but that very same evening the decisive course was adopted which at one stroke deprived the French of all their advantage of their present position.

Moltke was one of the last to be convinced that the French would play so comprehensively into his hands, but was careful to allow for the possibility. Once the likelihood that MacMahon had indeed embarked on a flank march became apparent. Moltke pondered deeply and then acted decisively. With subordinates on whom he could rely, his touch was sure, and from that point onwards MacMahon could have saved himself only by precipitate, if politically unacceptable, retreat.

Thereafter, Moltke maintained the strategic initiative. With a reliable flow of information restored to him by the indefatigable German cavalry, he could carry out with great precision the wheel to the right that would pin the unfortunate MacMahon to the ropes of the Belgian frontiers. This change of direction was itself an outstanding military achievement. A later British biographer of Moltke has written that 'it was, in fact, an extraordinarily brilliant feat of administration. To execute such an immense change of front at such short notice, necessitating the most exact arrangements for the huge columns in the woods and defiles of the Argonne, forms a striking proof the excellence of Prussian organisation.'[15] It was Moltke who had created that organisation and who wielded its power with such telling effect.

It was in real terms the culmination of all that had gone before. Commenting on the battles of Beaumont and Sedan, the Official History observes that

> the tactical decision in the two rapidly consecutive actions of the ten days' campaign against the Army of Châlons is already prepared to a certain extent by the strategical conditions under which the armies meet. This essential circumstance and the experiences of the struggles, which had occurred shortly before, are at times not without influence on the conduct and course of the action.[16]

Moltke's relentless pursuit of his enemy from the outset of the war created the conditions for what was ultimately one of the swiftest and most stunning victories over a Great Power in European military history. In the closing stages of the Sedan campaign, Moltke did not hesitate to take chances that in other circumstances would have been indefensible. After the capitulation Ducrot, in the course of one of his meetings with Blumenthal, commented that the German movements immediately before September 1 had been extremely rash. 'Rash? No,' replied Blumenthal: 'Audacious, yes. But in war, you know, General, that one must act in accordance with the morale of one's adversaries. We knew you were well beaten. We could thus be very bold.'[17]

The nature of the second phase of the war had been as unexpected to Moltke as it had been to everyone else in its duration, its ferocity and in the enemy's ability to create fresh armies with which to threaten his over extended forces. Moltke's military reputation had been securely established by brilliant Prussian victories over orthodox opponents in the previous wars of unification and in the first phase of the Franco-Prussian War. His response to the entirely novel problem posed by the Government of National Defence demonstrated above all his supreme ability to manage comprehensively the conduct of a very modern war. It was a period which demanded patience and a cool strategic insight rather than brilliance, and nobody else could have done so well. Some of the victories of his armies during this period were achieved entirely by the discipline and courage of the Prussian soldiers; often they prevailed after coming from a decidedly unpromising position. Moltke knew that he could rely on them absolutely; and for the most part he could also rely on the consistent and dependable judgement of those he had trained and to whom he gave the responsibility of dealing with the French armies in the field.

The extent of the French recovery following Sedan took almost everyone by surprise. After the surrender of the Army of Châlons there had been barely 40,000 regular troops in France outside Metz and Paris, with about the same number of Gardes Mobiles and Gardes Nationales. Less than 6,000 of the regulars were cavalry; the artillery had no more than 100 guns. In the ensuing five months, the Government of National Defence succeeded in raising and equipping over 600,000 fresh troops. Their training was, of course, not as comprehensive as was desirable, but in spite of this many of the new units fought bravely and well in the battles of the autumn and winter. They were generally well supported by the newly formed artillery units, which were equipped with over 1,400 guns of all calibres, and which on occasion put up some excellent performances. Raising and training new cavalry units was, however, more difficult, since the process necessarily took much longer; as a result, Faidherbe's Army of the North, for instance, had hardly any mounted troops at its disposal. Even so, over 30,000 cavalry were recruited and sent into action.

All this meant that the French enjoyed a pronounced numerical superiority in most of the major battles. However, even if every lucky chance had gone their way, the armies of the Government of National Defence could probably never have prevailed against these German armies and these leaders. Nonetheless, the strength of the French war effort during the second phase of the war required Moltke and his armies to put forward a mighty effort to overcome them.

During this phase of the war there were some in whom Moltke was able to put particular trust. These, such as Goeben, Stosch, Fransecky, Blumenthal and (most of the time) Manteuffel, were given considerable latitude and rarely let him down. Others, however, on whom great responsibilities devolved did not always give satisfaction. Frederick Charles and Stiehle, the Grand Duke and Krenski, and Werder, from time to time seriously disappointed Moltke, and they were in regular receipt of firm instructions from Versailles, usually to hurry up and get on with the operations they were undertaking. On occasion even Moltke's calm and analytical judgement gave way to impatience, sometimes not altogether with justification. He never, for instance, gave enough credit to Werder for coping with a wide range of responsibilities with a totally inadequate force, opposed to an enemy whose strength was growing all the time; his instructions often betrayed his conviction that the XIV Corps was being managed too diffidently. On the other hand, Moltke's discontent with the speed of operations of the Second Army was entirely justified. He was all too familiar with Frederick Charles' excessive caution, which he tried to overcome in his extensive and detailed correspondence with Stiehle. Stiehle was responsible for the management of the most important campaigns conducted outside Paris, and Moltke used their correspondence to give him a regularly updated appreciation of the overall strategic situation and the steps he planned to take.

As a military commander Moltke had a particular talent for making the best use of the mutual understanding of his subordinates, which in its turn owed much to the years of patient inculcation of the core principles of his strategic system. After Sedan Moltke did not usually find it necessary, nor was it practicable to give detailed orders; commanders of his widely separated armies would normally be given the widest latitude in carrying out his intentions. These were expressed in general 'Directiven'; Archibald Forbes, who translated Moltke's own account of the war, observed that these were

> messages of general suggestions as to the appropriate line of action to be pursued, leaving a wide discretion to the commanders to whom they were addressed, and refraining almost entirely from details. A collection of Moltke's "Directiven" would be perhaps in the finest tribute to his military genius.[18]

One of the best examples of these was the general directive issued on December 17, which demonstrated his comprehensive grasp of the overall strategic situation and on which the decisive campaigns of the next few weeks were based. This policy was not always successful, however. It was a system that put particular pressure on the Chiefs of Staff. One instance of this was the case of the Detachment and its operations to the west of Paris in November, when the problems caused by a lack of sound intelligence about the enemy's movements, combined with the task of managing a headstrong and not particularly capable commander, were altogether too much for the unlucky Krenski, its Chief of Staff, necessitating his replacement first by Stosch and later by Waldersee.

In the winter of 1870/71 the lack of reliable and comprehensive intelligence often severely hampered Moltke and all his commanders. The huge size of the country in which they were operating meant that even the intrusive and highly efficient cavalry patrols that probed ahead of the advancing German armies could not firmly locate the newly assembling French armies or form an accurate view of their size or intentions. The exaggerated concern at Versailles to meet the threat apparently posed by the so called Army of the West was one instance of this, and the later uncertainty about Bourbaki's movement at the end of December was another. The only way in which the difficulties caused by the lack of intelligence could be overcome was by retaining the initiative. Thus, when towards the end of December Moltke began to feel some concern that a further effort might be made to relieve Paris, he identified the various combinations that might be available to the army. As usual, he rated the probability of each of these being chosen in terms of their effectiveness as a threat to the investment. He concluded that much the best option for the French was for Bourbaki to join Chanzy at Le Mans for a joint advance on Paris. The other options looked much less likely; and of these an expedition to the east seemed least probable of all. The news that Bourbaki, far from moving westwards, was still at Bourges and Nevers at Christmas did throw him for a while, but his strategic instinct told him that in any case Chanzy's army was the most potentially dangerous opponent; that being so, it must be the target for his next offensive. In the result the French did surprise Moltke by sending Bourbaki on his ill fated march to the east, but that did not invalidate the move against Chanzy. His orders to Frederick Charles to advance against him were in terms that made it clear that this time he must finish off the 2nd Army of the Loire.[19]

The great size of the country in which his troops must operate presented Moltke with particular difficulty. As the German armies moved across France, first to Paris and then to the north, the west and the south, their lines of communication became more and more extended. As this process continued, more and more of Moltke's available resources were drawn into the protection of his communications, on which his armies depended for practically everything that kept them in the field. The extent of this can be shown by the number of troops engaged on these duties. At the outset, each of the German field armies had a number of battalions and squadrons, with supporting artillery and engineers, assigned to their respective 'etappen' inspections; the totals employed were 30 battalions, 13 squadrons, 3 batteries and three companies of engineers. By October 31 there were 85 battalions, 33 squadrons and 9 batteries employed permanently on communications duties, and these were supplemented from time to time by field units detached from the purpose. By March 31 1871 the numbers had increased still further; 114,093 infantry, 5686 cavalry and 68 guns were holding the lines of communication. Since the forces engaged in active operations at this time numbered 455,782 infantry, 57,779 cavalry and 1674 guns, it meant that for every four soldiers facing the French armies in the field another was employed in defending the lines of communication.[20] It was in order to deprive the franc tireurs, and others operating against the German communications, of potential bases that the decision was taken to reduce all the fortresses on the Meuse and the Moselle that still held out; this too required a considerable number of troops, but it was a policy that paid off in reducing the number of serious French raids. And the sheer expanse of France in which enemy armies might be assembling, equipping, training and deploying, far out of sight of German patrols, gave the Government of National Defence an opportunity to prepare undisturbed for their offensive moves towards Paris.

The supply lines depended on the French railway system, more and more of which was restored to operation as the war went on. Moltke had always been quick to exploit the use of the railways, both for the purposes of supplying his troops and also for their tactical employment. He would particularly have appreciated the comments of the correspondent of the *Daily News*, whose attention had been caught by Moltke's use of the railway to reinforce the First Army at short notice in January 1871; he thought that 'the whole war hardly affords a more striking example of the military genius of Moltke than the opportune railway trip he ordered for the 16th Brigade, forming part of the beleaguering army.'[21]

Moltke's acceptance of the military reality that the Germans were obliged to fight a war of attrition and his pursuit of that to its logical conclusion, raised the political questions that gradually brought about the fierce conflict with Bismarck. Neither conducted the bitter struggle solely out of desire for personal power; Bismarck was driven by his deep anxiety about foreign intervention if the war dragged on, while Moltke refused to adopt a policy that was militarily incorrect. In this he was wrong; in the last analysis, political considerations must prevail, as William recognised when he came down so firmly in Bismarck's favour. Nor did

Moltke bring any very subtle reflection to the peace terms to be demanded, as to which his thinking was extremely simplistic.

Commenting on Moltke's response to the threat posed by the Government of National Defence, a recent historian summarised his approach to political issues in these terms:

> In his military conduct, Moltke did not follow political principles; rather, he calculated as precisely as possible, using the concrete given realities, and repeatedly forced his imagination to be constrained by reason – that is what made him great. Moltke is indeed the ideal representative of the Prussian – German military state, a state in which the conduct of war remained the exclusive prerogative of the military.[22]

The effect on Moltke of the prolonged stress to which he had been subjected was not manifest in his military decisions but it had certainly affected his political and personal judgement. His day to day conduct of the war was based on the calm, analytical approach that was always characteristic of him. But in relation to the more emotional political issues he displayed strong personal feelings that brought him inevitably into conflict with Bismarck. His inability to recognise that the Chancellor was right was in part a product of his long held views about the French nation and in part a product of the extreme pressures to which all the German leaders were exposed as the war dragged on. From all directions came the expression of forceful opinions as to Germany's war aims and the basis on which peace should be negotiated. From the press and the general public, from family and friends, from colleagues on the staff and in the field, from foreign statesmen and commentators there was an endless flow of advice and opinion, to such an extent that it is not surprising that from time to time Moltke and others, bearing the responsibility of conducting a war of immense complexity, should lose touch with political reality.

But it was his military achievement that made Moltke the idol not only of the German people but of military commentators all over Europe. His success set the military fashion for decades to come, not only strategically and tactically, but even in the adoption by other armies of various features of the design of German uniforms. His success was above all due to his ability not to be thrown off balance or to take his eye off the ball. Although privately warm and humorous, and capable of the strong personal emotions that led him into political error, his outward reserve and modesty made Moltke a hard man to understand. Bismarck's summary of his professional character was typically succinct; Moltke was, he said, 'cold to the very heart.' There could be no more graphic expression of Moltke's personality as it applied to his conduct of war.

The outstanding historian of the Franco-Prussian war reviewed its outcome and the reasons for it in these terms:

> Unlike the victories of Napoleon, Moltke's successes were not due to any brilliant generalship, either on his own part or that of his commanders. There had been little in the way of manoeuvre; tactics, as often as not, were murderously clumsy; and strategic direction had been largely a matter of dour commonsense ... The German victories, as was universally recognised had been won by supe-

> rior organisation, superior military education and, in the initial stages of the war at least, superior man power.[23]

However, the freedom to manoeuvre was, in the early stages of the campaign, limited by the confined space in which it was fought and the size of the armies involved. Once his armies were well across the frontier, and he was able to make use of the developing options, Moltke did so deftly and precisely. He was certainly not a showy leader; his unhurried composure might seem unexciting when compared with Napoleon. But the 'dour commonsense' might have been more fairly described as a clear sighted grasp of the essential objectives and the way to achieve them, a grasp which he never relaxed. And for the superior organisation and military education, which enabled the German Armies to operate so efficiently in the campaign against the Army of Chalôns, and to fight most of the second phase of the war at a substantial numerical disadvantage, Moltke was very substantially responsible.

He combined a magisterial administrative ability with penetrating wisdom and strategic flair, and the results speak for themselves. In a month he had smashed the armies of what had hitherto been regarded as the strongest military power in the world, and in the following six months he was victorious in a struggle against the reviving French nation fought over a huge geographical area. Judged on these victories, and the manner of their achievement, he was more entitled than most successful military leaders to the uncritical adulation which he subsequently received, but to which he personally paid little regard. Detailed comparisons usually, in the end, lead into absurdity; but set in the context of his time, Helmuth von Moltke's place is secure as one of the truly great commanders of modern history.

Notes

Chapter 1: The Road to Paris

1 Prince O von Bismarck, *Letters to His Wife from the Seat of War 1870–71*, (London 1915), p 50
2 General J von Verdy du Vernois, *With the Royal Headquarters in 1870–71*, (London 1897), p 144
3 German Official Account, *The Franco-German War 1870–71*, (trans Capt. FCH Clarke) (London 1877), III, Appendix LIX
4 ibid, Appendix LXV
5 The 'Daily News' Correspondence, *The War between Germany and France, 1870–71*, (London 1871), pp 116–18
6 ibid, pp 120–1
7 Field Marshal Count K von Blumenthal, *Journals for 1866 and 1870–1871*, (London 1903), p 120
8 Verdy, pp 152–3
9 ibid, p 153
10 Field Marshal Count H von Moltke, *Letters to his Wife and Other Relatives*, (London 1896), II, pp 223–4
11 M Busch, *Bismarck in the Franco German War 1870–1871*, (London 1879), I, p 162
12 Daily News, pp 118–19
13 Blumenthal, pp 122–123
14 ibid, p 130
15 M Busch, *Bismarck: Some Secret Pages of his History*, (London 1898), I, p 174
16 Count d'Herisson, *Journal of a Staff-Officer in Paris during the Events of 1870 and 1871*, (London 1885), p 179
17 Busch, *Bismarck in the Franco-German War*, I, p 168
18 Moltke, *Correspondance Militaire*, (Paris), II, p 360
19 Official Account, III, p 15
20 ibid, p 11
21 ibid, p 59
22 ibid, p 193
23 ibid, p 59
24 Busch, *Secret Pages*, I, p 168

Chapter 2: Investment

1 Official Account, III, p 29
2 Ibid, p 30
3 d'Herisson, p 75
4 ibid, p 135
5 quoted M Howard, *The Franco-Prussian War: the German Invasion of France 1870–71*, (London 1962), p 322
6 Official Account, III, p 28
7 ibid, p 37

8 Blumenthal, p 125
9 Verdy, p 222
10 Official Account, III, p 43
11 ibid, p 47
12 ibid, p 51
13 EA Vizetelly, *My Days of Adventure: The Fall of France 1870–71*, (London, 1914), pp 102–3
14 Blumenthal, p 129
15 Crown Prince Frederick William, *The War Diary of the Emperor Frederick III 1870–71*, (trans AR Allinson) (London 1927), p 126
16 ibid, p 128

Chapter 3: Battle to the Last

1 Moltke, *Letters to His Mother and His Brothers*, (trans. C Bell and HW Fischer) (New York, 1893), p 193
2 Crown Prince, p 129
3 Verdy, p 177
4 quoted Col. Lonsdale Hale, *The 'People's War' in France, 1870–71*, (London, 1904), p 26
5 Verdy, p 161
6 Moltke, *Letters to His Wife*, II, p 228
7 ibid, p 227
8 Verdy, p 160
9 ibid, p 167
10 Hale, p 24
11 Howard, p 237
12 J P T Bury, *Gambetta and the National Defence: A Republican Dictatorship in France*, (London, 1936), p 112
13 Hale, p 22
14 quoted Howard, p 249
15 Roger de Mauni, *Eight Months on Duty*, (London 1872), p 62
16 Official Account, III, pp 83–5
17 Hale, p 31
18 Official Account, III, pp 175–6
19 GT Robinson, *The Fall of Metz*, (London 1871), p 189
20 Moltke, *Correspondance Militaire*, II, p 131
21 Official Account, III, pp 178–9
22 ibid, p 182
23 ibid, p 184

Chapter 4: The Key of our House

1 Busch, *Secret Pages*, I, p 212
2 Official Account, II, p 429
3 ibid, p 431
4 ibid, p 433
5 Moltke, *Correspondance Militaire*, I, pp 264–5
6 Official Account, II, p 445

7 ibid, p 446
8 Moltke, *Correspondance Militaire*, I, p 302
9 Official Account, II, p 349
10 ibid, p 451
11 Howard, p 275
12 Official Account, II, p 456
13 ibid, III, p 66
14 ibid, p 70
15 Moltke, *Correspondance Militaire*, I, p 348
16 ibid, II, p 359
17 ibid, p 360
18 Official Account, III, p 78
19 Moltke, *Correspondance Militaire*, II, p 387
20 ibid, p 389
21 Official Account, III, p 89
22 ibid, p 91

Chapter 5: Chevilly

1 Blumenthal, pp 141–2
2 ibid, p 158
3 Moltke, *Moltke as a Correspondent*, (trans M Herms) (London 1893), p 248
4 Official Account, III, pp 9
5 ibid, p 10
6 ibid, pp 107–8.
7 Blumenthal, p 14
8 d'Herisson, p 16
9 Offical Account, III, pp 110–11
10 d' Herisson, p 141
11 H Labouchere, *Diary of the Besieged Resident in Paris*, (London 1871), p 67
12 Official Account, III, pp 126–7
13 Moltke, *Correspondance Militaire*, II, p 406
14 Blumenthal, p 149
15 ibid, p 152
16 Field Marshal A von Waldersee, *A Field Marshal's Memoirs*, (trans F Whyte) (London 1924), p 75
17 Moltke, *Letters to his Wife*, II, p 230
18 Crown Prince, p 147
19 ibid, pp 137–8
20 Official Account, III, p 119–21
21 Blumenthal, p 158
22 Verdy, p 183
23 Blumenthal, p 165
24 Moltke, *Correspondance Militaire*, II, p 410
25 Busch, *Secret Pages*, I, p 255
26 Moltke, *Correspondance Militaire*, II, p 413
27 Official Account, III, pp 121–2
28 ibid, p 125

29 Verdy, p 190
30 Moltke, *Letters to His Wife*, II, p 230

Chapter 6: The Fall of Orleans

1 Official Account, III, p 148
2 Hale, p 32
3 Moltke, *Correspondance Militaire*, II, pp 409–11
4 Blumenthal, p 150
5 Moltke, *Correspondance Militaire*, II, p 413
6 Official Account, III, pp 154–6
7 Blumenthal, p 153
8 Official Account, III, p 158
9 H Helvig, *Operations of the I Bavarian Army Corps*, trans G Schwabe (London 1874), pp 154–5
10 Official Account, III, p 162
11 Bury, p 115
12 ibid, p 122
13 ibid, p 136
14 ibid, p 129
15 ibid, p 131
16 H Stannard, *Gambetta*, (London 1921), p 79
17 Hale, p 44
18 Stannard, p 82
19 Moltke, *Correspondance Militaire*, II, pp 415–16
20 Hale, p 36
21 Helvig, I, p 160
22 ibid, pp 161–2
23 Blumenthal, p 156
24 Hale, pp 38–9
25 Official Account, III, p 166
26 Hale, p 41
27 General L von Wittich, *Journal de Guerre*, (Paris 1902), p 99
28 Blumenthal, p 167
29 ibid, p 168
30 Moltke, *Correspondance Militaire*, II, pp 438–42
31 Blumenthal, p 162
32 Hale, p 55
33 Official Account, III, p 169

Chapter 7: Metz

1 P Guedalla: *The Two Marshals*, (London 1943), p 204
2 Howard, p 267
3 Moltke, *Correspondance Militaire*, II, p 391
4 G Craig: *The Politics of the Prussian Army*, (Oxford 1955), pp 207–8
5 Official Account, III, p 186
6 ibid, p 187n
7 ibid, p 188

8 Robinson, p 226
9 Official Account, III, p 188
10 Robinson, p 291
11 Official Account, III, p 191
12 ibid, p 193
13 ibid, p 196
14 A Bazaine: *Episodes de la Guerre de 1870*, (Madrid 1883), p 194
15 ibid, pp 196–206
16 ibid, pp 207–9
17 Crown Prince, pp 155–6
18 Bazaine, pp 209–10
19 ibid, pp 229–32
20 Moltke, *Correspondance Militaire*, II, p 445
21 Crown Prince, p 173
22 Verdy, p 194
23 Waldersee, p 80
24 Moltke, *Correspondance Militaire*, II, p 430
25 ibid, p 387
26 ibid, p 401
27 Official Account, III, p 233
28 ibid, p 236
29 ibid, pp 231–2
30 Moltke, *Correspondance Militaire*, II, pp 436–7
31 Official Account, III, p 238
32 ibid, p 240
33 Moltke, *Correspondance Militaire*, II, p 478
34 Official Account, III, pp 248–9
35 ibid, p 253
36 ibid, pp 254–5

Chapter 8: Coulmiers

1 V Cartier, *Le General Trochu*, (Paris 1914), p 298
2 Official Account, III, p 130
3 Cartier, p 298
4 Official Account, III, p 130
5 ibid, p 131
6 ibid, p 134
7 d'Herisson, p 188
8 Cartier, p 128
9 Moltke, *Moltke as a Correspondent*, p 237
10 Moltke, *Correspondance Militaire*, II, pp 454–8
11 Official Account, III, p 259
12 Moltke, *Correspondance Militaire*, II, p 469
13 ibid p 468
14 Stannard, p 89
15 General C d'Aurelle de Paladines, *La Première Armée de la Loire*, (Paris 1872), p 40

16 ibid, p 60
17 ibid, p 61
18 Moltke, *Correspondance Militaire*, II, pp 459–60
19 Blumenthal, p 179
20 Hale, p 81
21 Blumenthal, pp 180–1
22 Moltke, *Correspondance Militaire*, II, p 463
23 Blumenthal, p 183
24 Verdy, p 209
25 Blumenthal, p 184
26 Crown Prince, p 185
27 Moltke, *Correspondance Militaire*, II, pp 468–9
28 Crown Prince, p 183
29 Blumenthal, pp 184–5
30 Hale, p 73
31 Blumenthal, p 31
32 Helvig, p 171
33 ibid, p 174
34 ibid, p 178
35 Official Account, III, p 270
36 Helvig, p 187
37 Official Account, III, p 271
38 ibid, p 273
39 ibid, p 278
40 Helvig, p 208
41 d'Aurelle, p 111
42 Bury, p 180
43 Helvig, pp 213–4
44 Moltke, *Correspondance Militaire*, II, p 473
45 ibid, pp 476–7
46 Blumenthal, p 186
47 Crown Prince, p 184

Chapter 9: The March of the Detachment

1 d'Aurelle, p 130
2 C de Freycinet, *La Guerre en Province*, (Paris 1872), p 101
3 d'Aurelle, pp 133–4
4 Official Account, III, pp 281–2
5 ibid, p 282
6 Blumenthal, pp 188–9
7 Hale, p 90
8 Blumenthal, pp 189–90
9 Hale, p 92
10 Verdy, p 211
11 Moltke, *Correspondance Militaire*, II, pp 480–3; Hale, pp 95–7
12 Official Account, III, pp 282–3; Hale, pp 99–100; Helvig, p 219
13 Blumenthal, p 190

14 Moltke, *Correspondance Militaire*, II, pp 486–7; Hale, 100–1
15 Moltke, *Correspondance Militaire*, II, pp 487–8
16 Helvig, p 218
17 Official Account, III, p 294
18 Blumenthal, p 192
19 Helvig, p 219
20 Hale, p 101
21 ibid, p 116–7
22 Official Account, III, p 293
23 Hale, p 114–5
24 C von der Goltz, *Gambetta und seine Armeen*, quoted Hale, p 118
25 Hale, p 121
26 Official Account, III, pp 493–4
27 Blumenthal, p 193
28 Helvig, p 220
29 Crown Prince, p 193
30 Moltke, *Correspondance Militaire*, II, pp 491–2
31 Hale, p 109
32 Official Account, III, p 297
33 Helvig, p 224
34 ibid, p 224–5
35 ibid, p 225
36 Hale, p 112
37 Helvig, p 227
38 ibid, p 230
39 Official Account, III, p 299
40 Helvig, p 235
41 quoted Hale, p128
42 Hale, p 131
43 Hale, p 133
44 Hale, pp 133–4

Chapter 10: Stosch

1 Hale, p 124
2 Official Account, III, p 293
3 Hale, p 125
4 Official Account, III, p 293
5 Hale, pp 139–40
6 Moltke, *Correspondance Militaire*, II, p 500
7 ibid, p 499
8 Blumenthal, p 198
9 Moltke, *Letters to His Wife*, II, pp 232–4
10 Crown Prince, p 199
11 Blumenthal, p 200
12 Hale, p 163–4
13 ibid, p 165
14 Waldersee, pp 81–2

15 Blumenthal, p 199
16 Helvig, pp 239–40
17 Blumenthal, p 201
18 Hale, p 182
19 Moltke, *Correspondance Militaire*, II, p 505
20 F B M Hollyday *Bismarck's Rival*, (Durham, N Carolina 1960), pp 73–4
21 Hale, p 168
22 Helvig, p 243
23 Official Account, III, p 305
24 Hollyday, p 74; Hale, p 186; Blumenthal, p 202
25 Hale, pp 186–7
26 Hollyday, p 75
27 Hale, p 198
28 ibid, p 199
29 ibid, p 189
30 Official Account, III, pp 310–311
31 Freycinet, p 112
32 Freycinet, p 123
33 Official Account, III, pp 312–3

Chapter 11: Dead or Victorious

1 Official Account, III, pp 366–7
2 Bury, pp 184–5
3 quoted Howard, p 341
4 Cartier, p 300
5 Official Account, III, p 367
6 Crown Prince, p 196
7 Blumenthal, p 200
8 Moltke, *Correspondance Militaire*, II, p 514
9 Quoted R Baldick, *The Siege of Paris*, (London 1964), pp 131–2
10 Blumenthal, p 203
11 quoted A Horne, *The Fall of Paris*, (London 1965), p 149
12 d'Herisson, p 244; Baldick, p 135
13 Moltke, *Correspondance Mititaire*, II, pp 516–7
14 Official Account, III, p 369
15 Blumenthal, p 205
16 Official Account, III, p 373
17 ibid, p 378
18 ibid
19 ibid, p 380
20 Moltke, *Correspondance Militaire*, II, p 518
21 ibid pp 518–9
22 Verdy, p 219
23 ibid, p 221
24 Moltke, *Correspondance Militaire*, II, p 519
25 Blumenthal, p 211
26 Official Account, III, p 382; Moltke, *Correspondance Militaire*, II, p 521

27 Official Account, III, p 385
28 d'Herisson, p 259
29 Official Account, III, p 388
30 Moltke, *Correspondance Militaire*, II, p 524
31 ibid, pp 524–5
32 ibid, pp 526–7
33 quoted Howard, p 346
34 quoted Horne, p 160

Chapter 12: Werder

1 Moltke, *Correspondance Militaire*, II, pp 393–5
2 ibid, p 398
3 Official Account, III, p 207
4 L Löhlein, *The Operations of the Corps of General von Werder*, (trans T Maxwell) (Chatham n.d), p 4
5 Official Account, III, p 207
6 Löhlein, p 9
7 ibid, p 10
8 Official Account, III, p 210
9 Howard, p 290
10 Stannard, p 89
11 quoted Howard, p 290
12 Löhlein, p 16
13 ibid, p 18
14 ibid, p 19
15 Moltke, *Correspondance Militaire*, II, p 419
16 ibid, p 420
17 ibid, p 420; Löhlein, p 19
18 Moltke, *Correspondance Militaire*, II, pp 420–1
19 Löhlein, p 19
20 ibid, p 23
21 Moltke, *Correspondance Militaire*, II, pp 433–3
22 ibid, pp 434–6
23 Löhlein, pp 25–6
24 Official Account, III, p 216
25 ibid, p 218
26 Löhlein, p 32
27 ibid, p 34
28 ibid, p 39
29 Official Account, III, p 221; Löhlein, pp 39–40
30 Löhlein, p 41
31 ibid, p 43
32 Official Account, III, pp 233–4
33 Löhlein, p 44
34 ibid, Appendix VIII, pp xx-xviii
35 Moltke, *Correspondance Militaire*, II, p 446
36 Lohlein, p 44

37 Moltke, *Correspondance Militaire*, II, p 462
38 Official Account, III, p 225
39 ibid, p 226
40 Löhlein, pp 47–8
41 Moltke, *Correspondance Militaire*, II, pp 478–9

Chapter 13: Beaune La Rolande

1 d'Aurelle, pp 239–40
2 Official Account, III, p 313
3 ibid, p 315
4 ibid, p 316
5 ibid, p 318
6 Hale, pp 205–6
7 ibid, p 209
8 quoted Hale, pp 209–10
9 Official Account, III, p 320
10 ibid, p 321
11 Hale, p 203
12 Official Account, III, p 321
13 Hale, p 211
14 d'Aurelle, pp 245–6
15 ibid, pp 247–8
16 Helvig, p 245
17 Hale, p 214
18 Official Account, III, p 321
19 H von Kretschmann, *Kriegsbriefe aus dem Jahren 1870–71*, (Stuttgart 1904), p 300
20 Moltke, *Correspondance Militaire*, II, pp 513–5
21 Hale, p 219
22 Helvig, p 248
23 ibid, p 250
24 Hale, p 219
25 Official, III, pp 324–5
26 Hale, pp 222–3
27 Crown Prince, p 206
28 ibid, p 207
29 Hale, p 224
30 ibid, p 225
31 Official Account, III, p 327
32 d'Aurelle, pp 275–6; Freycinet pp 136–7
33 Helvig, p 253
34 Hale, pp 229–31
35 ibid, pp 231–2
36 Helvig, p 255
37 Official Account, III, p 327
38 Helvig, p 258
39 ibid, p 259

40 Official Account, III, p 329
41 Helvig, p 265
42 Hale, p 235
43 quoted Howard, p 310

Chapter 14: Loigny Poupry

1 Official Account, III, p 331
2 Hale, p 238
3 Moltke, *Correspondance Militaire*, II, p 593
4 Helvig, p 266
5 ibid, pp 267–9; Official Account, III, p 331
6 Helvig, p 268
7 Official Account, III, p 332
8 ibid, p 334
9 Helvig, pp 274–5
10 ibid, p 276
11 quoted E Rich, *A History of the Franco-German War*, (London 1884), p 309
12 ES May, *Field Artillery with the Other Arms*, (London 1898), p 250
13 Official Account, III, pp 335–6
14 May, p 257
15 Helvig, pp 277–8n
16 Official Account, III, p 339
17 General A Chanzy, *La Deuxième Armée de La Loire*, (Paris 1871), p 73
18 Helvig, p 280
19 Official Account, III, p 339
20 May, p 254
21 Baunard, *Le Général de Sonis*, (Paris 1903), p 336; Official Account, III, pp 339–40
22 Helvig, p 279
23 Official Account, III, p 340
24 Ibid
25 Ibid
26 d'Aurelle p 312
27 Official Account, III, p 340
28 ibid, p 341
29 d'Aurelle, p 313
30 Official Account, III, p 342n
31 d'Aurelle, p 312
32 Official Account, III, p 342
33 Helvig, p 281
34 Hale, p 237
35 ibid, p 239
36 quoted Hale, p 240
37 Moltke, *Correspondance Militaire*, II, pp 539–40
38 Hale, pp 242–3n
39 Blumenthal, p 212
40 Crown Prince, p 210

41 Hale, 248
42 Hale, pp 246–7
43 ibid, pp 249–50

Chapter 15: The Second Battle of Orleans

1 d'Aurelle, p 320
2 ibid, p 322
3 ibid, p 321
4 Official Account, III, p 345
5 ibid, p 344
6 Hale, p 251
7 ibid, p 252
8 quoted Hale, p 255
9 quoted Prince Krafft zu Hohenlohe, *Letters on Artillery*, (London 1890), p 105
10 ibid, p 107
11 Official Account, III, p 347
12 Ibid, p 107
13 Kretschmann, p 309
14 Hale, p 258
15 Official Account, III, p 348
16 ibid
17 ibid, pp 349–350
18 quoted Hale, p 260
19 Official Account, III, p 350
20 Helvig, p 284
21 Chanzy, p 82
22 Official Account, III, p 350
23 Hale, pp 261–2
24 d'Aurelle, p 326
25 Hale, p 264
26 Official Account, III, p 353
27 quoted Hale, pp 263–4
28 Hale, pp 259–60
29 d'Aurelle, p 333
30 ibid, pp 334–5
31 d'Aurelle, pp 339–40; Freycinet, pp 165–6
32 d'Aurelle, pp 341–2; Freycinet, pp 167–8
33 d'Aurelle, p 344; Freycinet, p 168
34 Official Account, III, p 354
35 quoted Hale, p 266
36 Hale, p 265
37 Official Account, III, p 355
38 Kretschmann, p 310
39 Hale, p 268; Official Account, III, p 355; Kretschmann p 310
40 Hale, p 270
41 Official Account, III, p 357
42 ibid, pp 367–8

43 Helvig, p 287
44 Official Account, III, p 358
45 Hale pp 271–2
46 Official Account, III, p 360
47 Hale, p 273
48 Lehautcourt, quoted Hale, p 273
49 Official Account, III, pp 361–2
50 Chanzy, p 92
51 Helvig, p 293
52 ibid, p 294
53 Official Account, III, p 362
54 d'Aurelle, p 344
55 ibid, p 347
56 Hale, pp 278–9
57 quoted Hale, p 28
58 Crown Prince, pp 214–217
59 Moltke, *Correspondance Militaire*, II, p 543
60 ibid, p 543–4
61 Official Account, III, p 364

Chapter 16: Amiens

1 General L Faidherbe, *Campagne de l'Armée du Nord,* (Paris 1871), p 10
2 ibid, p 12
3 Howard, pp 292–3
4 Faidherbe, pp 12–13
5 Moltke, *Correspondance Militaire*, II, pp 423–4
6 ibid, p 430
7 Colonel H von Wartensleben, *Operations of the First Army under General von Manteuffel,* (London 1873), p 11n
8 ibid, pp 8–9
9 Moltke, *Correspondance Militaire*, II, p 447
10 ibid, p 448
11 Wartensleben, p 18
12 Moltke, *Correspondance Militaire*, II, p 464
13 Wartensleben, p 22
14 ibid, p 31
15 Moltke, *Correspondance Militaire*, II, pp 473–5
16 Wartensleben, p 40
17 Moltke, *Correspondance Militaire*, II, pp 494–5
18 Wartensleben, p 48
19 ibid, pp 52–3
20 Official Account, IV, p 3
21 Wartensleben, p 57
22 Faidherbe, p 14
23 ibid
24 Official Account, IV, p 4
25 Moltke, *Correspondance Militaire*, II, p 508

26 Wartensleben, p 62
27 ibid, p 64
28 Official Account, IV, p 10
29 Wartensleben, p 69
30 Official Account, IV, p 15
31 Wartensleben, p 72
32 ibid, p 73
33 Faidherbe, p 22; Official Account, IV, p 16
34 Official Account, IV, pp 16–17; Wartensleben, p 82
35 Wartensleben, p 73
36 ibid, pp 92–3
37 ibid, p 101

Chapter 17: Beaugency

1 Howard, p 582
2 Field Marshal H von Moltke, *The Franco-German War of 1870–71*, (London 1908), p 235
3 Moltke, *Correspondance Militaire*, II, p 547
4 Official Account, IV, pp 43–4
5 Freycinet, p 191
6 Kretschmann, p 320
7 Helvig, p 344
8 ibid, pp 312–3
9 Official Account, IV, p 48
10 ibid, p 49
11 ibid, pp 50–1
12 ibid, pp 51–2
13 Moltke, *Correspondance Militaire*, II, p 564
14 Official Account, IV, p 54
15 ibid, p 56
16 Moltke, *Franco-German War*, p 240; Official Account, IV, p 57
17 Freycinet, p 195
18 Official Account, IV, p 59
19 ibid, p 61
20 Chanzy, pp 150–1
21 Helvig, p 352
22 quoted Hollyday, pp 77–8
23 Verdy, p 225
24 Official Account, IV, p 63
25 ibid, p 65
26 Moltke, *Correspondance Militaire*, II, pp 566–7
27 Chanzy, p 203
28 Official Account, IV, pp 75–6
29 Moltke, *Correspondance Militaire*, II, pp 591–2
30 ibid, pp 593–4
31 ibid, pp 594–5

32 General A von Stosch, *Denkwurdigkeiten*, (Berlin 1904), p 216; Hollyday pp 75–6
33 Verdy, p 227; Hollyday p 78

Chapter 18: Dijon and Belfort

1 quoted C Hibbert, *Garibaldi and his Enemies*, (London 1965), p 360
2 Official Account, IV, Appendix CIV; Löhlein, Appendix II
3 Löhlein, p 63
4 ibid, p 64
5 ibid, p 66
6 Moltke, *Correspondance Militaire*, II, p 504
7 Löhlein, p 71
8 ibid, p 72
9 ibid, p 75
10 Moltke, *Correspondance Militaire*, II, pp 559–61; Löhlein, pp 78–9
11 Moltke, *Correspondance Militaire*, II, pp 588–9
12 Löhlein, p 82
13 ibid, p 90
14 Official Account, IV, p 290
15 Moltke, *Correspondance Militaire*, II, pp 515–6
16 Official Account, IV, p 294
17 ibid, p 296
18 ibid, p 298

Chapter 19: The Battle on the Hallue

1 Howard, p 391
2 Wartensleben, pp 107–8
3 Official Account, IV, p 23
4 Moltke, *Correspondance Militaire*, II, pp 550–1
5 Wartensleben, p 115
6 quoted Howard, p 392
7 Official Account, IV, p 25
8 Moltke, *Correspondance Militaire*, II, p 578
9 ibid, pp 579–80
10 Wartensleben, p 130
11 ibid, p 136
12 Moltke, *Correspondance Militaire*, II, p 583
13 Faidherbe, p 34
14 ibid, p 35
15 Moltke, *Correspondance Militaire*, II, pp 594–5
16 Wartensleben, p 149
17 ibid, p 151
18 Official Account, IV, p 110
19 Wartensleben, p 158
20 Official Account, IV, p 114
21 Faidherbe, p 40

Chapter 20: Moltke at Versailles

1 Verdy, p 184
2 Crown Prince, pp 155–6
3 Bismarck, *Letters to his Wife*, p 83
4 Verdy, p 239
5 Crown Prince, p 180
6 Verdy, pp 201–2
7 Verdy, p 202
8 Busch, *Secret Pages*, I, pp 272 and 280
9 Official Account, IV, pp 128–9; W Blume: *The Operations of the German Armies in France*, (London 1872), pp 178–80
10 Verdy, p 160
11 Busch, *Secret Pages*, I, p 288
12 ibid, p 291
13 ibid, p 315
14 Bismarck, *Letters to his Wife*, p 87
15 Busch, *Secret Pages*, I, p 325
16 Blumenthal, p 207
17 H Abeken, *Bismarck's Pen*, (London 1911), p 303
18 Moltke, *Correspondance Militaire*, II, pp 531–3
19 ibid, pp 533–536
20 Busch, *Secret Pages*, I, p 349
21 Blumenthal, p 224
22 Abeken, pp 321–2
23 Busch, *Secret Pages*, I, pp 378–9
24 Moltke, *Correspondance Militaire*, II, p 571
25 ibid, p 572
26 Blumenthal, pp 218–9
27 ibid, pp 235–6
28 Official Account, IV, p 128
29 Crown Prince, p 225
30 Bismarck, *Letters to his Wife*, p 93
31 Blumenthal, p 217
32 ibid, p 240
33 Moltke, *Letters to his Wife*, III, pp 237–8

Chapter 21: Le Bourget and Mont Avron

1 *Diary of a Besieged Resident*, p 250
2 *Daily News*, p 351
3 Official Account, IV, p 131
4 ibid, p 133
5 A Forbes, *My Experiences of the War Between France and Germany*, (London 1871), II, p 200
6 d'Herisson p 266
7 Official Account, IV, p 135
8 *Diary of a Besieged Resident*, p 255
9 Verdy, p 227

10 ibid, p 228–9
11 Blumenthal, p 245
12 Hohenlohe, *Letters on Artillery*, pp 247–9
13 Moltke, *Correspondance Militaire*, II, pp 609–611
14 ibid, p 622
15 Official Account, IV, p 137
16 Blumenthal, p 254
17 Crown Prince, p 247
18 Bismarck, *Letters to his Wife*, pp 96–7

Chapter 22: The Le Mans Campaign

1 Official Account, IV, p 87
2 ibid, p 89
3 Crown Prince, p 287
4 Official Account, IV, p 91–3
5 Official Account, IV, Appendix CXX; Moltke, *Correspondance Militaire*, ii, pp 637–8
6 Chanzy, p 242
7 ibid, pp 243–4
8 ibid, pp 245–9
9 ibid, p 252
10 ibid, p 254–5
11 Blume, p 193
12 Official Account, IV, pp 141–2
13 ibid, pp 144–5
14 ibid, pp 147–9
15 ibid, p 154
16 ibid, pp 153–4
17 ibid, p 157
18 ibid, p 158
19 ibid, p 275
20 Chanzy, p 275
21 Official Account, IV, p 159
22 ibid, p 160
23 ibid, p 163
24 ibid, p 166
25 Chanzy, p 284
26 Official Account, IV, p 26
27 ibid, p 170
28 Ibid, p 171
29 ibid, p 172
30 Chanzy, p 559
31 Official Account, IV, pp 176–7
32 ibid, p 180
33 ibid
34 ibid, p 183
35 Chanzy, pp 307–8

36 Official Account, IV, p 187
37 ibid, p 198
38 Chanzy, pp 327–8
39 Official Account, IV, p 205
40 Howard, p 399
41 de Mauni, p 110

Chapter 23: The Lisaine

1 Löhlein, p 94
2 Moltke, *Correspondance zilitaire*, II, p 612
3 ibid, pp 627–8
4 Blumenthal, p 249
5 Moltke, *Correspondance Militaire*, II, p 632
6 ibid, p 633
7 Löhlein, p 96
8 Official Account, IV, p 105
9 Howard, p 413
10 ibid, p 415
11 Moltke, *Correspondance Militaire*, II, p 646
12 Löhlein, p 104
13 Moltke, *Correspondance Militaire*, II, p 649
14 ibid, pp 656–7; Official Account, IV, p 307
15 Moltke, *Correspondance Militaire*, II, p 657–60; Löhlein, pp 117–8
16 Blumenthal, p 269
17 Löhlein, pp 104–6
18 ibid, p 110
19 ibid, p 112
20 Official Account, IV, p 318
21 Löhlein, p 116
22 Howard, p 423
23 Löhlein, p 127
24 Official Account, IV, p 326
25 Löhlein, p 127
26 Crown Prince, pp 259–60
27 Moltke, *Correspondance Militaire*, II, p 669; Löhlein, p 131
28 Moltke, *Franco-German War*, p 337
29 Official Account, IV, p 328; Howard, pp 424–5
30 Howard, pp 424–5
31 Löhlein, p 133
32 Official Account, IV, p 335
33 ibid, p 336
34 Löhlein, p 136
35 Official Account, IV, p 341; Löhlein p 136n
36 Official Account, IV, p 342
37 Löhlein, p 137
38 ibid, p 138
39 Ibid

40 Official Account, IV, p 348–9
41 Howard, p 425
42 Löhlein, p 141
43 Crown Prince, pp 264–5
44 Blumenthal, p 276
45 Löhlein, p 142
46 ibid, p 144
47 Official Account, IV, p 357
48 ibid, p 358n
49 Löhlein, pp 145–7
50 ibid. p 148
51 Howard, p 426

Chapter 24: Bapaume and Péronne

1 Official Account, IV, p 121
2 ibid, p 248
3 Wartensleben, pp 175–6
4 ibid, p 180
5 ibid, pp 180–2
6 ibid, pp 188
7 Official Account, IV, pp 122–3
8 ibid, pp 243–4
9 Wartensleben, p 194
10 Official Account, IV, p 245
11 Wartensleben, p 195
12 ibid, p 176n
13 Moltke, *Correspondance Militaire*, II, p 640
14 Faidherbe, p 42
15 Major A von Schell *The Operations of the First Army under General von Goeben*, (London 1873), p 15
16 Official Account, IV, p 231
17 Schell, p 19
18 Official Account, IV, p 234
19 ibid, p 235
20 Schell, p 23
21 Ibid
22 ibid, p 24
23 Official Account, IV, pp 237–8
24 Faidherbe, p 46
25 Schell, p 31
26 Official Account, IV, p 240
27 ibid, p 241; Faidherbe p 48
28 Howard, p 397
29 Wartensleben, p 199n
30 Schell, p 43
31 ibid, pp 43–4
32 Moltke, *Correspondance Militaire*, II, pp 648

33 Schell, p 47; Moltke, *Correspondance Militaire*, II, pp 648–9
34 Schell, pp 54–5
35 Moltke, *Correspondance Militaire*, II, p 656
36 Schell, pp 59–60
37 ibid, p 60; Moltke, *Correspondance Militaire*, II, p 662–3
38 Moltke, *Correspondance Militaire*, II, p 663
39 ibid, p 664; Schell, p 61
40 Official Account, IV, p 254
41 Schell, p 67
42 ibid, p 66

Chapter 25: The Bombardment of Paris

1 Blumenthal, p 252
2 ibid, p 254
3 Verdy, p 235
4 Ibid
5 Moltke, *Correspondance Militaire*, II, p 623
6 ibid, pp 624–5
7 Blumenthal, pp 259–60
8 ibid, p 261
9 ibid, p 256
10 Crown Prince, p 244
11 Howard, p 357ns
12 Official Account, IV, pp 364–5
13 Crown Prince, p 247
14 Official Account, IV, p 367
15 ibid, p 369
16 Horne, p 214
17 *Diary of a Besieged Resident*, p 318
18 quoted Horne, p 215
19 E B Washburne, *Correspondence relating to the Franco-German War and Insurrection of the Commune*, (Washington 1878), p 123
20 Verdy, p 240
21 d'Herisson, p 270
22 Official Account, IV, p 372
23 Crown Prince, p 267
24 ibid, pp 272–3
25 quoted L Ball, Bismarck: *The White Revolutionary*, (London 1986), I, p 372
26 Bismarck, *Letters to his Wife from the Seat of War*, p 105
27 d'Herisson, p 271
28 Official Account, IV, p 378
29 Verdy, p 245
30 Official Account, IV, p 381
31 Blumenthal, p 284
32 Official Account, IV, p 385

Chapter 26: St Quentin

1 *Daily News* Correspondence, pp 503–4
2 Faidherbe, p 55
3 ibid, p 59
4 Schell, pp 69–70
5 ibid, p 71
6 ibid, p 73
7 ibid, pp 75–6
8 ibid, p 78
9 Official Account, IV, p 257
10 Schell, p 83
11 ibid, pp 85–6
12 ibid, pp 93–4
13 ibid, p 95
14 Moltke, *Correspondance Militaire*, II, p 676
15 ibid, p 95
16 Schell, p 98
17 ibid, pp 101–2; Faidherbe, p 111
18 Schell, p 104
19 Faidherbe, p 60
20 Schell, p 111
21 Faidherbe, p 60
22 Official Account, IV, p 262
23 Schell, p 108
24 Faidherbe, p 61
25 Official Account, IV, p 263
26 Faidherbe, p 62: Official Account, IV, p 264: Schell, p 172
27 Schell, p 124
28 ibid, pp 124–6
29 ibid, p 134
30 ibid, pp 136–7
31 *Daily News* Correspondence, p 505: Official Account, IV, p 268
32 Schell, pp 139–40
33 Official Account, IV, p 269
34 Schell, p 143
35 Howard, p 405
36 Official Account, IV, p 270
37 Schell, pp 165–6
38 Official Account, IV, p 273
39 Schell, p 159
40 ibid, p 161
41 Official Account, IV, pp 275–6
42 Schell, pp 164–5
43 ibid, p 171
44 iIbid
45 ibid, p 173: Official Account, IV, p 276

Chapter 27: Armistice

1 Crown Prince, p 255
2 ibid, p 257–8
3 Craig, pp 212–13
4 Official Account, IV, Appendix CXLVII
5 Washburne, p 126
6 Crown Prince, p 277
7 Craig, p 213
8 Moltke, *Correspondance Militaire*, II, pp 691–4
9 quoted Craig, p 214
10 d'Herisson, p 294
11 ibid, pp 295–98
12 R I Giesberg, *The Treaty of Frankfort* (Philadelphia 1966), p 93; d'Herisson pp 325–7
13 d'Herisson, p 313
14 Giesberg, p 95 n37

Chapter 28: Tragedy of an Army

1 Colonel H von Wartensleben, *Operations of the South Army*, (London 1872), p 5
2 Moltke, *Correspondance Militaire*, II, pp 656–7
3 Official Account, V, p 3
4 Wartensleben, *South Army*, p 10
5 ibid, p 17
6 Official Account, V, p9
7 quoted Howard, p 427
8 Wartensleben, *South Army*, p 26
9 Official Account, V, p 9
10 ibid, p 10
11 Wartensleben, *South Army*, p 34
12 ibid, pp 35–6
13 quoted Howard, p 427
14 Wartensleben, *South Army*, pp 40–1
15 ibid, pp 49–50
16 Official Account, V, p 48
17 Lohlein, p 162
18 Wartensleben, *South Army*, pp 52–3
19 ibid, pp 58–59; Official Account, V, p 45
20 Official Account, V, p 49
21 ibid, p 50
22 ibid, p 51
23 Blumenthal, p 292
24 Wartensleben, *South Army*, p 62
25 Löhlein, pp 164–6
26 Wartensleben, *South Army*, p 60
27 ibid, p 64
28 ibid, p 73

29 Official Account, V, p 58
30 Wartensleben, *South Army*, p 76
31 ibid, p 80
32 ibid, p 81
33 ibid, p 83
34 ibid, p 97
35 Official Account, V, p 71
36 Wartensleben, *South Army*, p 95
37 ibid, p 99
38 Official Account, V, p 78

Chapter 29: Peace

1 Moltke, *Letters to his Wife*, II, p 241
2 Howard, p 442 n3
3 Blumenthal, p 294
4 ibid, p 296
5 Verdy, p 251
6 Blumenthal, pp 302–4
7 Moltke, *Correspondance Militaire*, III, pp 729–31
8 Blumenthal, pp 300–301
9 Moltke, *Correspondance Militaire*, III, p 740
10 Howard, p 445
11 Moltke, *Correspondance Militaire*, III, p 744
12 Giesberg, p 100
13 Stosch, p 228
14 quoted Otto Pflanze, *Bismarck and the Development of Germany*, (Princeton NJ 1990), I, p 487
15 Busch, I, pp 124–125
16 Giesberg, p 108
17 Busch, I, pp 556–7
18 Blumenthal, p 316
19 Giesberg, p 111
20 ibid, p 112
21 ibid, p 123
22 Verdy, p 256; Blumenthal, p 318
23 Moltke, *Letters to His Wife*, II, p 242

Chapter 30: Moltke as Military Commander

1 Major General J F C Fuller, *The Decisive Battles of the Western World*, (London 1956), III, p 134
2 Lieutenant General von Caemmerer, *The Development of Strategical Science*, (London 1905), p 212
3 ibid, p 213
4 H Holborn, 'The Prusso-German School' in P Paret (ed): *Makers of Modern Strategy*, (Oxford 1994), p 295
5 O'Connor Morris, W, *Moltke*, (London 1893), pp 410–11
6 Caemmerer, p 229

7 Pelet-Narbonne, General von, *Cavalry on Service*, (London 1896), p 3
8 ibid, p 265
9 Holborn, p 291
10 Martin van Creveld, *Supplying War*, (Cambridge 1977), p 97
11 G Rothenburg, 'Moltke, Schlieffen and the Doctrine of Strategic Envelopment' in Paret: *Makers of Modern Strategy*, p 3
12 ibid, p 300
13 General H Bonnal, *La Manoeuvre de Saint Privat*, (Paris 1904), II, p 439
14 Prince Krafft von Hohenlohe, *Letters on Strategy*, (London 1898), II, p 439
15 Official Account, II, p 411
16 Lieutenant Colonel F E Whitton, *Moltke*, (London 1921), p 277
17 Official Account, II, p 414
18 General A Ducrot, *La Journée de Sedan*, (Paris 1872), p 26
19 Moltke, *Franco-German War*, p 243n
20 Blume, p 191
21 Colonel G A Furse, *The Organisation and Administration of Lines of Communication in War*, (London 1894), pp 115–16; Blume p 26
22 *Daily News* Correspondence, p 509
23 W Deist, 'Remarks on the Preconditions of Waging War in Prussia – Germany 1866–71', in S Forster and J Nagler (ed): *On the Road to Total War*, (Washington DC 1997), p 325
24 Howard, p 455

APPENDIX I

Order of Battle of the 13th French Corps (mid September 1870)

Commander:	General of Division Vinoy
Chief of Staff:	General of Brigade de Valdan

1st Division

Commander:	General of Brigade D'Exéa

1st Brigade (General Mattat)

5th Regiment de Marche
6th Regiment de Marche

2nd Brigade (General Daudel)

7th Regiment de Marche
8th Regiment de Marche

Divisional Artillery
3 4 pounder batteries

2nd Division

Commander:	General of Brigade Maud'huy

1st Brigade (General Guérin)

9th Regiment de Marche
10th Regiment de Marche

2nd Brigade (General Blaise)

11th Regiment de Marche
12th Regiment de Marche

Divisional Artillery
3 4 pounder batteries

3rd Division

Commander:	General of Brigade Blanchard

1st Brigade (General Baron Susbielle)

13th Regiment de Marche
14th Regiment de Marche

2nd Brigade (General Guilhem)

35th Line Infantry Regiment
42nd Line Infantry Regiment

Divisional Artillery
3 4 pounder batteries

Corps Artillery
6 4 pounder batteries

Corps Total:
25,000 men, 90 guns

APPENDIX II

Order of Battle of the 14th French Corps (31st August 1870)

Commander:	General of Division Renault
Chief of Staff:	General of Brigade Appert

1st Division

Commander:	General of Brigade Caussade

1st Brigade

15th Regiment de Marche
16th Regiment de Marche
1 Chasseur Battalion

2nd Brigade

1st Zouave Regiment de Marche
17th Regiment de Marche
18th Regiment de Marche

Divisional Artillery
2 4 pounder batteries
1 mitrailleuse battery

2nd Division

Commander:	General of Brigade d'Hugues

1st Brigade

19th Regiment de Marche
20th Regiment de Marche

2nd Brigade

21st Regiment de Marche
22nd Regiment de Marche
1 Chasseur Battalion

Divisional Artillery
2 4 pounder batteries
1 mitrailleuse battery

3rd Division

Commander: General of Brigade de Maussion

1st Brigade

23rd Regiment de Marche
24th Regiment de Marche

2nd Brigade

25th Regiment de Marche
26th Regiment de Marche

Divisional Artillery
2 4 pounder batteries
1 mitrailleuse battery

Corps Artillery

2 4 pounder artillery batteries
2 4 pounder horse artillery batteries
2 12 pounder batteries

Corps Total:
25,000 men, 72 guns, 18 mitrailleuses

Cavalry Division

Commander: General of Brigade Champeron

1st Brigade

1st Dragoon Regiment de Marche
2nd Dragoon Regiment de Marche

2nd Brigade

1st Chasseur Regiment
9th Chasseur Regiment

Divisional Total
5,000 men

APPENDIX III

Strength of the III Army and Army of the Meuse (31st October 1870)

III ARMY

A. Before Paris

Corps	*Infantry*	*Cavalry*	*Guns*
V Army Corps	19,713	1,156	84
VI Army Corps	22,762	1,279	84
XI (21st Infantry Division)	10,158	497	48
II Bavarian Army Corps	20,973	2,732	102
17th Infantry Division	10,111	1,166	36
Guard Landwehr Division	8,680	—	18
Württemberg Field Division	14,395	1,637	54
Total	106,792	8,467	426

B. Elsewhere

Corps	*Infantry*	*Cavalry*	*Guns*
1 Bavarian Army Corps	20,329	2,154	118
2nd Infantry Division	7,622	565	36
2nd Cavalry Division	3,063	12	—
4th Cavalry Division	2,725	12	—
5th Cavalry Division	4,736	12	—
6th Cavalry Division	2,711	6	—
Total	27,051	15,954	196

ARMY OF THE MEUSE

A. Before Paris

Corps	*Infantry*	*Cavalry*	*Guns*
Guard Corps	20,938	3,410	90
IV Army Corps	19,368	1,103	72
XII (Saxon) Army Corps	21,589	—	84
Total	61,895	4,513	246

B. Elsewhere

Corps	*Infantry*	*Cavalry*	*Guns*
Guard Corps	2,327	1,129	—
IV Army Corps	2,649	—	12
XII (Saxon) Army Corps	816	3,268	12
Total	5,792	4,397	24

Notes:

1. The II Bavarian Army Corps had been increased by a battery

2. The I Bavarian Army Corps had been strengthened by 2 battalions and 4 batteries. The strength given includes the 2 battalions attached to the 5th Cavalry Division, the battalion attached to the 6th Cavalry Division, the 3 batteries attached to the 22nd Infantry Division, and a company detached as escort to prisoners.

3. The 4th heavy and 6th light batteries joined the 22nd Division in the latter end of October.

APPENDIX IV

Order of Battle of the 15th French Corps (12th October 1870)

Commander:	General d'Aurelle de Paladines
Chief of Staff:	General Borel

1st Division

Commander:	General Martin des Pallières

1st Brigade (General de Chabron)

4th Battalion de Marche
38th Line Regiment
1st Zouaves
12th Gardes Mobiles
One battalion of Marine Infantry

2nd Brigade (General Bertrand)

Algerian Tirailleurs
29th Regiment de Marche
18th Gardes Mobiles

Artillery
One battery 13th Regiment
18th battery of the 2nd and 6th Regiments
Engineers
1st section, 19th company, 3rd Regiment

2nd Division

Commander:	General Martineau des Chenez

1st Brigade (General Dariés)

5th Rifle Battalion de Marche
39th Line Regiment
25th Gardes Mobiles
Foreign legion

2nd Brigade (General Rébillard)

2nd Zouaves
30th Regiment de Marche
29th Gardes Mobiles

Artillery
One battery of the 9th and 12th Regiments
14th Mixed battery of the horse artillery regiment of the former Imperial Guard
Engineers
2nd section, 19th company 3rd Regiment

3rd Division

Commander: General Peytavin

1st Brigade (General Peytavin)

6th Rifle Battalion de Marche
16th Line Regiment
33rd Regiment de Marche
32nd Gardes Mobiles

2nd Brigade (General Martinez)

27th Regiment de Marche
34th Regiment de Marche
69th Gardes Mobiles

Artillery
18th battery of the 7th, 10th and 14th Regiments
Engineers
1st Section 19th Company 2nd Regiment

Cavalry Division

Commander: General Reyau

1st Brigade (General Galand de Longuerue)

6th Dragoons
5th Hussars

2nd Brigade (General Brémond d'Ars)

9th Cuirassiers
1st Cuirassiers de Marche

Cavalry Brigade (General Michel)

2nd Lancers
5th Lancers
3rd Dragoons de Marche

Cavalry Brigade (Colonel d'Astugue)

1st Chasseurs de Marche
11th Chasseurs

Artillery
13th, 14th, 15th, 16th, batteries 3rd Regiment
19th battery 2nd Regiment
11th battery 6th Regiment
14th battery of the 18th and 19th Regiments

Mixed Division

Infantry Brigade (General Maurice)

2 companies of the 2nd and 17th Rifle battalions
31st Regiment de Marche
22nd Gardes Mobile

Cavalry Brigade (General Tripart)

1st Hussars de Marche
2nd mixed Regiment de Marche

Total of 15th Corps, 60½ battalions, 44 squadrons, 17 batteries with 102 guns, and 3 sections of Engineers

APPENDIX V

Order of Battle of the XIV Army Corps (beginning of October 1870)

Commander:	General of Infantry von Werder
Chief of Staff:	Lieutenant-Colonel von Leszczynski

Baden Field Division

Commander:	Lieutenant-General von Glümer (later Lieutenant-General von Beyer)

1st Infantry Brigade (Lieutenant-General du Jarrys Baron von la Roche)

1st Body Guard Grenadier Regiment
2nd Grenadier Regiment

2nd Infantry Brigade (Major-General Baron von Degenfeld)

3rd Regiment
4th Regiment

3rd Infantry Brigade (Major-General Keller)

5th Regiment
6th Regiment

Pontoon Company with light field bridge train

Cavalry Brigade (Major-General Baron von La Roche-Starkenfels)

1st Body guard Dragoons
2nd Dragoons
3rd Dragoons
H A battery

Divisional Artillery

1st and 2nd Light, 1st and 2nd Heavy Batteries

Corps Artillery

3rd and 4th Light, 3rd and 4th Heavy Batteries

Columns Division
1st, 2nd and 3rd Artillery Ammunition Columns
1st and 2nd Infantry Ammunition Columns Pontoon Column

Train Division

Combined Prussian Infantry Brigade (Major-General von Boswell)

30th Regiment
34th Fusilier Regiment

Combined Prussian Cavalry Brigade (Major-General Krug von Nidda)

2nd Reserve Dragoons
2nd Reserve Hussars

Prussian Artillery Division
Reserve Heavy battery, I Army Corps
1st Light Reserve Battery, III Army Corps
2nd Light Reserve Battery, III Army Corps

Total for the XIV Army Corps 23 battalions, 20 squadrons, 72 guns, 1 pioneer company

APPENDIX VI

Order of Battle of the 4th Reserve Division (beginning of October 1870)

Commander: Major-General von Schmeling

Combined Infantry Brigade (Colonel Knappe von Knappstädt)

25th Regiment
1st Battalion
2nd Battalion
Fusilier Battalion
1st Combined East Prussian Landwehr Regiment, No 4/5
Osterode Landwehr Battalion
Graudenz Landwehr Battalion
Thorn Landwehr Battalion

East Prussian Landwehr Brigade (Colonel von Zimmermann)

1st Combined East Prussian Landwehr Regiment, No. 1.3
Tilsit Landwehr Battalion
Wehlau Landwehr Battalion
Insterburg Landwehr Battalion
Gumbinnen Landwehr Battalion
3rd Combined East Prussian Landwehr Regiment No. 43/45
Loetzen Landwehr Battalion
Goldap Landwehr Battalion
Dantzig Landwehr Battalion
Marienburg Landwehr Battalion

4th Reserve Cavalry Brigade (Major-General von Tresckow II)

1st Reserve Lancers
3rd Reserve Lancers

Combined Artillery Division

1st, 2nd, 3rd, and 4th Light, and 2nd Heavy Batteries

Total for the 4th Reserve Division, 15 battalions, 8 squadrons, 36 guns, 1 pioneer company

APPENDIX VII

Order of Battle of the 16th French Corps (about the middle of November 1870)

General Commanding:	General Chanzy
Chief of Staff:	General Renault (later General Lallemant, then Colonel Vuillemot)

1st Infantry Division

Commander: Vice-Admiral Jauréguiberry

1st Brigade: (General Bourdillon)

39th Regiment de Marche
75th Gardes Mobiles
3rd Rifle Battalion de Marche

Artillery
3 batteries
Engineers
1st section, 20th company, 3rd Regiment

2nd Infantry Division

Commander: General Barry

1st Brigade (General Desmaisons)

31st Regiment de Marche
22nd Gardes Mobiles
7th Rifle Battalion de Marche

2nd Brigade (Colonel Bérard)

38th Regiment de Marche
66th Gardes Mobiles

Artillery
3 batteries
Engineers
2 sections, 20th company, 3rd Regiment

3rd Infantry Division

Commander: General Maurandy

1st Brigade (Colonel Marty)

36th Regiment de Marche
8th Gardes Mobiles
8th Rifle Battalion de Marche

2nd Brigade (None)

40th Regiment de Marche
71st Gardes Mobiles

Artillery
3 batteries
Engineers
1st section, 18th company, 1st Regiment

Cavalry Division

Commander: General Reffayre (after 10th November, General Michel)

1st Brigade (General Tripard)

1st Hussars de Marche

2nd Brigade (General Digard)

6th Lancers

3rd Brigade (General Abdelal) (later General de Tucé)

3rd Cuirassiers de Marche
4th Dragoons de Marche
4th Mixed Regiment de Marche (Light Cavalry)

Reserve Artillery
11 batteries
Park
3 companies of the Artillery Train
Engineer Reserve
2nd section of 18th Company, 1st Regiment
Train
3 companies

APPENDIX VIII

Order of Battle of the Second Army (15th November 1870)

Commander-in-chief:	General Field-Marshal H.R.H. Prince Frederick Charles of Prussia
Chief of Staff:	Major-General von Stiehle

Summary of Forces:
III Army Corps 25 battalions, 8 squadrons, 14 batteries (84 guns) 3 pioneer cos.
IX Army Corps 23 battalions 12 squadrons 15 batteries (90 guns) 3 pioneer cos.
X Army Corps 25 battalions 8 squadrons 14 batteries (84 guns) 3 pioneer cos.
1st Cavalry Division 24 squadrons 1 battery (6 guns)

Total 73 battalions 52 squadrons 44 batteries (264 guns) 9 pioneer cos.

III ARMY CORPS

Commander:	Lieutenant-General von Alvensleben II
Chief of Staff:	Colonel von Voigts-Rhetz

5th Infantry Division

Commander:	Lieutenant-General von Stülpnagel (owing to illness replaced by Major-General von Schwerin)

9th Infantry Brigade (Colonel von Conta)

8th B.G. Grenadiers
48th Regiment

10th Infantry Brigade (Major-General von Schwerin) (later Colonel von Wulffen)

12th Grenadiers
52nd Regiment

Divisional Troops

3rd Rifle Battalion
1st Field Division 3rd F.A. Regiment (1st and 2nd Heavy, 1st and 2nd Light Batteries
2nd Field Pioneer Company with Entrenching Tool Column

6th Infantry Division

Commander: Lieutenant-General Baron von Buddenbrock

11th Infantry Brigade (Major-General von Rothmaler)

20th Regiment
35th Fusiliers

12th Infantry Brigade (Colonel von Bismarck)

24th Regiment
64th Regiment

Divisional Troops

2nd Dragoons
3rd Field Division, 3rd F A Regr. (5th and 6th Heavy, 5th and 6th Light Batteries)
1st Field Pioneer Company, with Light Field Bridge Train

Corps Artillery (Colonel von Dresky)

H.A. Division 3rd F.A. Regt (1st and 3rd H.A. Batteries)
2nd Field Division 3rd F.A. Regt. (3rd and 4th Heavy, 3rd and 4th Light Batteries)
3rd Field Pioneer Company

Columns Division, 3rd F.A. Regt.

Artillery Ammunition Columns, Nos. 1 to 5: Infantry Ammunition Columns, Nos. 1 to 4: Pontoon Column

3rd Train Battalion

IX ARMY CORPS

Commander: General von Manstein
Chief of Staff: Major Bronsart von Schellendorff

18th Infantry Division

Commander: Lieutenant-General Baron von Wrangel

35th Infantry Brigade (Major-General von Blumenthal)

36th Fusiliers
84th Regiment

36th Infantry Brigade (Colonel Baron von Falkenhausen) (temp.)

11th Grenadiers
85th Regiment

Divisional Troops

9th Rifle Battalion
6th Dragoons

1st Field Division, 9th Field Artillery Regiment (1st and 2nd Heavy, 1st and 2nd Light Batteries)
2nd Field Pioneer Company, with Entrenching Tool Column,
3rd Field Pioneer Company

25th Grand Ducal Hessian Division

Commander: Lieutenant-General H.S.H. Prince Louis of Hesse

49th Infantry Brigade (Colonel von Winckler)

1st Regiment (Body Guard)
2nd Regiment
1st Rifle Battalion

50th Infantry Brigade (Colonel von Lyncker)

3rd Regiment
4th Regiment
2nd Rifle Battalion

25th Cavalry Brigade (Major-General von Rantzau)

1st Cavalry Regiment (Guard Chevauxlegers)
2nd Cavalry Regiment
Horse Artillery Battery

Division of Field Batteries (1st and 2nd Heavy, 1st 2nd and 3rd Light field Bridge Train

Corps Artillery (Colonel von Jagemann)

2nd Field Division, 9th Field Artillery Regiment (3rd and 4th Heavy, 3rd and 4th Light Batteries)
2nd Horse Artillery Battery, 9th Field Artillery Regiment

Part of Columns Division, Nos. 1 to 3: Infantry Ammunition Columns, Nos. 1 and 2

Grand Ducal Ammunition Column

Artillery Ammunition Columns, Nos.1 and 2; Infantry Ammunition Columns, Nos.1 and 2

Part of 9th Train Battalion

Grand Ducal Train Division

X ARMY CORPS

Commander: General von Voigts-Rhetz
Chief of Staff: Lieutenant-Colonel von Caprivi

19th Infantry Division

Commander: Lieutenant-General von Schwartzkoppen (later Major General von Woyna)

37th Infantry Brigade (Colonel Lehmann)

78th Regiment
91st Regiment

38th Infantry Brigade (Major-General von Wedell)

16th Regiment
57th Regiment

Divisional Troops

9th Dragoons
1st Field Division, 10th F.A. Regiment (1st and 2nd heavy 1st and 2nd light batteries)
1st Field Pioneer Company, with Light Field bridge Train
3rd Field Pioneer Company

20th Infantry Division

Commander: Major-General von Kraatz-Koschlau

39th Infantry Brigade (Major-General von Woyna) (later Colonel von Valentini)

6th Regiment
79th Regiment

40th Brigade (Major-General von Diringshofen)

17th Regiment
92nd Regiment

Divisional Troops

10th Rifle Battalion
16th Dragoons
2nd Field Division, 10th F.A. Regiment (3rd and 4th Heavy, 3rd and 4th Light Batteries)
2nd Field Pioneer Company

Corps Artillery (Colonel Baron von der Goltz)

H.A. Division F. Artillery Regiment (1st and 3rd H.A. Batteries)
3rd F. Division 10th F. Artillery Regiment (5th and 6th Heavy, 5th and 6th Light Batteries)

Columns Division 10th F.A. Regiment

Artillery Ammunition Columns Nos 1 to 5; Infantry Ammunition Columns Nos. 1 to 4

10th Train Battalion

1st Cavalry Division

Commander: Lieutenant-General von Hartmann

1st Cavalry Brigade (Major-General von Lüderitz)

2nd Cuirassiers
4th Lancers
9th Lancers

2nd Cavalry Brigade (Major-General Baumgarth)

3rd Cuirassiers
8th Lancers
12th Lancers

Divisional Troops

1st H.A. Battery

APPENDIX IX

Order of Battle of the Detachment under the command of The Grand Duke of Mecklenburg-Schwerin (15th November 1870)

Commander-in-chief:	General H.R.H. The Grand Duke Frederick Francis of Mecklenburg-Schwerin
Chief of Staff:	Colonel von Krenski

Summary of Forces:
I Bavn A.C. 27 battalions, 16 squadrons, 20 batteries (118 guns) 3 pioneer cos.
17th Inf. Divn. 13 battalions 12 squadrons 6 batteries (36 guns) 1 pioneer co.
22nd Inf Divn 12 battalions 4 squadrons 6 batteries (36 guns) 2 pioneer cos.
2nd Cav. Divn 24 squadrons 2 batteries (12 guns)
4th Cav. Divn. 24 squadrons 2 batteries (12 guns)
5th Cav. Divn. 34 squadrons 2 batteries (12 guns)
6th Cav.Divn. 20 squadrons 1 battery (6 guns)

Total 52 battalions 134 squadrons 39 batteries (232 guns) 6 pioneer cos.

I BAVARIAN ARMY CORPS

Commander:	General Baron von der Tann-Rathsamhausen
Chief of General Staff:	Colonel von Heinleth

1st Infantry Division

Commander:	Lieutenant-General von Stephan

1st Infantry Brigade (Major-General von Dietl)

Body Guard Regiment
1st Regiment
2nd Rifle Battalion

2nd Infantry Brigade (Major-General von Orff)

2nd Regiment
11th Regiment
4th Rifle Battalion

Divisional Troops

9th Rifle Battalion
3rd Chevauxlegers

Artillery Division (1st 4-pr, 3rd 4-pr, 5th 6-pr, 7th 6-pr batteries, 1st Artillery Regiment)
Ammunition Column (1st Artillery Regiment)

2nd Infantry Division

Commander: Lieutenant-General von Maillinger

3rd Infantry Brigade (Major-General Roth)

3rd Regiment
12th Regiment
1st Rifle Battalion

4th Infantry Brigade (Major-General Baron von der Tann-Rathsamhausen)

10th Regiment
13th Regiment
7th Rifle Battalion

Divisional Troops

4th Chevauxlegers
Artillery Division (2nd 4-pr, 4th 4-pr, 6th 6-pr, 8th 6-pr, 1st Artillery Regiment)
Ammunition Column (1st Artillery Regiment)

Cuirassier Brigade (Major-General von Tausch)

1st Cuirassiers
2nd Cuirassiers
1st H.A. Battery 3rd Artillery Regiment

Reserve Artillery Division (Colonel Bronzetti)

1st Division (2nd H.A. 3rd 6-pr, 4th 6-pr. 3rd Artillery Regiment)
2nd Division (5th and 6th 6-pr batteries 3rd Artillery Regiment)
3rd Division (7th 6 and 8th 6-pr batteries 3rd Artillery Regiment)
4th Division (9th 6-pr. Battery 1st Artillery Regiment, 10th 6-pr. Battery 4th Artillery Regiment
11th (mitrailleuse) battery 1st Artillery Regiment
12th 12-pr. Battery 3rd Artillery Regiment
Ammunition Column 1st Artillery Regiment

1st Field Engineer Division (3 Field Engineer Companies with 2 Pioneer equipments, 3 bridge equipments, and 1 field telegraph equipment)
Main Ammunition Column, 3rd Artillery Regiment

17th Infantry Division

Commander: Lieutenant-General von Schimmelmann (later Lieutenant-General von Tresckow)

33rd Infantry Brigade (Major-General Baron von Kottwitz)

75th Regiment
76th Regiment

34th Infantry Brigade (Grand Ducal Mecklenburg) (Colonel von Manteuffel)

89th Grenadiers
90th Fusiliers
14th Rifle Battalion

17th Cavalry Brigade (Major-General von Rauch)

17th Dragoons
18th Dragoons
11th Lancers

Divisional Troops

3rd Field Division (5th and 6th Heavy, 5th and 6th Light Batteries) and 1st and 3rd Horse Artillery Batteries, 9th Field Artillery Regiment
1st Field Pioneer Company with light field bridge train
Ammunition Columns Nos. 3 and 4 (from 9th F.A. Regiment)

22nd Infantry Division

Commander: Major-General von Wittich

43rd Infantry Brigade (Colonel von Kontzki)

32nd Regiment
95th Regiment

44th Infantry Brigade (Major-General von Schkopp) (later Colonel Marshall von Bieberstein)

83rd Regiment
94th Regiment

Divisional Troops

13th Hussars
2nd Field Division (3rd and 4th heavy, 3rd and 4th light batteries) 5th and 6th light batteries 11th F.A. Regiment
1st Field Pioneer Company, with light field bridge train
3rd Field Pioneer Company, 1st Lieutenant von Heemskerk
From the Columns Division of 11th F.A. Regiment
Artillery Ammunition Columns Nos. 2,3, and 5
Infantry Ammunition Columns Nos. 1 and 3

2nd Cavalry Division

Commander: Lieutenant-General Count zu Stolberg-Wernigerode

3rd Cavalry Brigade (Major-General von Colomb)

1st B.G. Cuirassiers
2nd Lancers

4th Cavalry Brigade (Major-General Baron von Barnekow)

1st Body Guard Hussars
5th Hussars

5th Cavalry Brigade (Major-General von Baumbach)

4th Hussars
6th Hussars

Divisional Troops

1st Horse Artillery Battery, II Army Corps
3rd Horse Artillery Battery, VI Army Corps

4th Cavalry Division

Commander: General H.R.H. Prince Albrecht of Prussia (senior)

8th Cavalry Brigade (Major-General von Hontheim)

5th Cuirassiers
10th Lancers

9th Cavalry Brigade (Major-General von Bernhardi)

1st Lancers
6th Lancers

10th Cavalry Brigade (Major-General von Krosigk)

5th Dragoons
2nd Body Guard Hussars

Divisional Troops

1st Horse Artillery Battery, V Army Corps
2nd Horse Artillery Battery, XI Army Corps

5th Cavalry Division

Commander: Lieutenant-General von Rheinbaben

11th Cavalry Brigade (Major-General von Barby)

4th Cuirassiers
13th Lancers
19th Dragoons

12th Cavalry Brigade (Major-General von Bredow)

7th Cuirassiers
16th Lancers
13th Dragoons

13th Cavalry Brigade (Major-General von Redern)

10th Hussars
11th Hussars
17th Hussars

Divisional Troops

1st Horse Artillery Battery
2nd Horse Artillery Battery

6th Cavalry Division

Commander:	Lieutenant-General H.S.H. Duke William of Mecklenburg-Schwerin (later Major-General von Schmidt)

14th Cavalry Brigade (Major-General von Schmidt)

6th Cuirassiers
3rd Lancers
15th Lancers

15th Cavalry Brigade (Major-General von Rauch)

3rd Hussars
16th Hussars

Divisional Troops

2nd Horse Artillery Battery

APPENDIX X

Order of Battle of the 17th French Corps (end of November 1870)

Commander:	General de Sonis, afterwards General Guepratte, then General de Colomb
Chief of Staff:	Colonel de Bouillé (later General Forgemol)

1st Infantry Division

Commander:	General de Roquebrune

1st Brigade (General Paris) (later General Bevard)

41st Regiment de Marche
74th Garde Mobile Regiment

2nd Brigade (General de Roquebrune) (later Colonel Faussemagne)

43rd Regiment de Marche
72nd Garde Mobile Regiment
11th Chasseurs de Marche

Artillery
3 batteries
Engineers
1 section

2nd Infantry Division

Commander:	General Dubois de Jancigny (later General Paris)

1st Brigade (Colonel Bonet) (later Colonel Koch)

48th Regiment de Marche
64th Regiment
80th Garde Mobile Regiment
10th Chasseurs de Marche

2nd Brigade (General Hainglaise) (later Lieutenant-Colonel Thibonville)

51st Regiment de Marche
85th Garde Mobile Regiment

Artillery
3 batteries
Engineers
1 section

3rd Infantry Division

Commander: General Dessandre (later General de Jouffroy d'Abbans)

1st Brigade (Colonel de Jouffroy d'Abbans) (later Colonel Didier)

45th Regiment de Marche
70th Garde Mobile Regiment
1st Chasseurs de Marche

2nd Brigade (Colonel Sautereau)

46th Regiment de Marche
76th Garde Mobile Regiment

Artillery
3 batteries
Engineers
1 section

Cavalry Division

Commander: General de Longuerue (later General Guépratte, (later General d'Espeuilles)

1st Brigade (General de Laudreville)

6th Light Cavalry (mixed)
4th Lanciers de Marche
5th Cavalry of the Line (mixed)

2nd Brigade (General Guépratte, later General Barbut)

4th Light Cavalry (mixed)
4th Cuirassiers de Marche
7th Cuirassiers de Marche

Reserve Artillery
8 batteries
Engineers
1 section
Train
1 company

APPENDIX XI

Order of Battle of the 18th French Corps (early in December 1870)

Commander:	General Bourbaki
Chief of Staff:	General Billot

1st Infantry Division

Commander:	General Feillet-Pilatrie

1st Brigade (General Robert)

42nd Regiment de Marche
19th Garde Mobile Regiment
9th Chasseurs de Marche

2nd Brigade (General Bonnet)

44th Regiment de Marche
73rd Garde Mobile Regiment

Artillery
3 batteries

Engineers
1 section

2nd Infantry Division

Commander:	Rear-Admiral Penhoet

1st Brigade (Colonel Perrin)

52nd Regiment de Marche
77th Garde Mobile Regiment
12th Chasseurs de Marche

2nd Brigade (General Perraux)

92nd Regiment of the Line
Light African Regiment de Marche
80th Garde Mobile Regiment

Artillery
3 batteries

Engineers
1 section

3rd Infantry Division

Commander:

1st Brigade

4th Zouaves de Marche
81st Garde Mobile Regiment

2nd Brigade (Colonel Marcq de Sainte-Hilaire)

53rd Regiment de Marche
82nd Garde Mobile Regiment

Artillery
3 batteries

Engineers
1 section

Cavalry Division

Commander: General de Bremond d'Ars

1st Brigade (General Charlemagne)

2nd Hussars de Marche
3rd Lanciers de Marche

2nd Brigade (General Guyon-Bernier)

5th Dragoons de Marche
5th Cuirassiers de Marche

Reserve Artillery
7 batteries

Engineers
Half a company

Train
A naval detachment

APPENDIX XII

Order of Battle of the 20th French Corps (end of November 1870)

Commander:	General Crouzat
Chief of Staff:	Colonel Varaigne

1st Infantry Division

Commander:	General de Polignac

1st Brigade (Colonel Boisson)

85th Regiment of the Line (probably the depot companies)
Garde Mobile of the Loire
Garde Mobile of the Jura

2nd Brigade (Colonel Brisac)

Garde Mobile of the Upper Loire
Garde Mobile of the Upper Garonne
Franctireurs of the Upper Rhine

Cavalry
2nd Lanciers de Marche
Artillery
2 batteries
Engineers
1 company

2nd Infantry Division

Commander:	General Thornton

1st Brigade (Captain de Vaisseau Aube)

Garde Mobile of Deux-Sèvres
Garde Mobile of Savoy
7th Mounted Chasseurs

2nd Brigade (Colonel Vivenot)

Garde Mobile of the Upper Rhine
3rd Zouaves de Marche

Artillery
2 batteries
Engineers
1 company
Franctireurs of Bordeaux

3rd Infantry Division

Commander: General Ségard

1st Brigade (Colonel Durochat)

47th Regiment de Marche
Garde Mobile of Corsica

2nd Brigade (Colonel Girard)

78th Regiment of the Line (probably depot companies)
Garde Mobile of the East Pyrenees
Garde Mobile of the Vosges
Garde Mobile of the Meurthe

Cavalry
Cuirassiers de Marche
Artillery
2 batteries
Engineers
1 company
Franctireurs of Doubs
Franctireurs of Nice

Reserve Artillery
3 batteries (including a mitrailleuse battery)

Engineers
1 company

Train
1 company

APPENDIX XIII

Order of Battle of the Third Army (30th November 1870)

Commander-in-Chief:	General Field-Marshal H.R.H. Crown Prince of Prussia
Chief of Staff:	Lieutenant-General von Blumenthal

General Summary of Forces:
II Army Corps 25 battalions, 8 squadrons, 14 batteries (84 guns) 3 pioneer cos. V Army Corps 25 battalions, 8 squadrons, 14 batteries (84 guns) 3 pioneer cos. VI Army Corps 25 battalions, 8 squadrons, 14 batteries (84 guns) 3 pioneer cos. XI Army Corps 13 battalions, 4 squadrons, 8 batteries (48 guns) 1 pioneer co II Bavarian Army Corps 25 battalions, 20 squadrons, 18 batteries (106guns) 3 pioneer cos. Guard Landwehr Division 12 battalions, 3 squadrons, 3 batteries (18 guns) 1 pioneer co.

Total 125 battalions 48 squadrons 71 batteries 424 guns 14 pioneer

II ARMY CORPS

Commander:	General von Fransecky
Chief of Staff:	Colonel von Wichmann

3rd Infantry Division

Commander:	Major-General von Hartmann

5th Infantry Brigade (Major-General von Koblinski)

2nd Grenadiers
42nd Regiment

6th Infantry Brigade (Colonel von der Decken: later Colonel von Wedell)

14th Regiment
54th Regiment

Divisional Troops

2nd Rifle Battalion
3rd Dragoons
1st Field Division, 2nd Field Artillery Regiment (1st and 2nd heavy, 1st and 2nd light batteries)
1st Field Pioneer Company, with Light Field Bridge Train

4th Infantry Division

Commander:	Lieutenant-General Hann von Weyhern

7th Infantry Brigade (Major-General du Trossel)

9th Grenadiers
49th Regiment

8th Infantry Brigade (Major-General von Kettler)

21st Regiment
61st Regiment

Divisional Troops

11th Dragoons
3rd Field Division, 2nd Field Artillery Regiment (5th and 6th Heavy, 5th and 6th Light Batteries)
2nd Field Pioneer Company with Entrenching-Tool Column
3rd Field Pioneer Company

Corps Artillery

H.A. Division 2nd Field Artillery Regiment (2nd and 3rd H.A. Batteries)
2nd F.Division 2nd F. Artillery Regiment (3rd and 4th Heavy, 3rd and 4th Light Batteries

Columns Division 2nd F. Artillery Regiment

Artillery Ammunition Columns Nos. 1 to 5
Infantry Ammunition Columns Nos. 1 to 4
Pontoon Column
2nd Train Battalion

V ARMY CORPS

Commander:	General von Kirchbach
Chief of Staff:	Colonel von der Esch

9th Infantry Division

Commander:	Major-General von Sandrart

17th Infantry Brigade (Colonel von Bothmer)

58th Regiment
59th Regiment

18th Infantry Brigade (Major-General von Voigts-Rhetz)

7th Grenadiers
47th Regiment

Divisional Troops

5th Rifle Battalion
4th Dragoons
1st Field Division, 5th F. Artillery Regiment (1st and 2nd Heavy 1st and 2nd Light Batteries)
1st Field Pioneer Company with Light Field Bridge Train

10th Infantry Division

Commander: Lieutenant-General von Schmidt

19th Infantry Brigade (Colonel von Henning auf Schönhoff)

6th Grenadiers
46th Regiment

20th Infantry Brigade (Major-General Walther von Monbary)

37th Fusiliers
50th Regiment

Divisional Troops

14th Dragoons
3rd Field Division, 5th F. Artillery Regiment (5th and 6th Heavy 5th and 6th Light Batteries)
2nd Field Pioneer Company with Entrenching Tool Column
3rd Field Pioneer Company

Corps Artillery

H.A. Division 5th Field Artillery Regiment (2nd and 3rd horse Artillery Batteries)
2nd Field Division 5th Field Artillery Regiment
3rd and 4th Heavy 3rd and 4th Light Batteries

Columns Division 5th F. Artillery Regiment

Artillery Ammunition Columns Nos. 1 to 5
Infantry Ammunition Columns Nos. 1 to 4
Pontoon Column

5th Train Battalion

VI ARMY CORPS

Commander: General von Tümpling
Chief of Staff: Colonel von Salviati

11th Infantry Division

Commander: Lieutenant-General von Gordon

21st Infantry Brigade (Major-General von Malachowski)

10th Grenadiers
18th Regiment

22nd Infantry Brigade (Major-General von Eckartsberg)

38th Fusiliers
51st Regiment

Divisional Troops

6th Rifle Battalion
8th Dragoons
1st Field Division 6th Field Artillery Regiment (1st and 2nd Heavy 1st and 2nd Light Batteries)
1st Field Pioneer Company with Light Field Bridge Train
2nd Field Pioneer Company with Entrenching Tool Column

12th Infantry Division

Commander: Lieutenant-General von Hoffmann

23rd Infantry Brigade (Colonel Gündell)

22nd Regiment
62nd Regiment

24th Infantry Brigade (Major-General von Fabeck)

23rd Regiment
63rd Regiment

Divisional Troops

15th Dragoons
3rd Field Division 6th F. Artillery Regiment (5th and 6th Heavy 5th and 6th Light Batteries)
3rd Field Pioneer Company

Corps Artillery

H.A. Division 6th F. Artillery Regiment (1st and 2nd H.A. Batteries)
2nd Field Division 6th F. Artillery Regiment (3rd and 4th Heavy 3rd and 4th Light Batteries)

Columns Division 6th F. Artillery Regiment

Artillery Ammunition Columns Nos. 1 to 5 Infantry Ammunition Column Nos. 1 to 5

XI ARMY CORPS*

Commander: Lieutenant-General von Bose (later Leiutenant-General von Schachtmeyer)
Chief of Staff: Major-General Stein von Kaminski

21st Infantry Division

Commander: Lieutenant-General von Schachtmeyer (later Major General von Schkopp)

41st Infantry Brigade (Colonel von Koblinski)

80th Fusiliers
87th Regiment

42nd Infantry Brigade (Major-General von Thile)

82nd Regiment
88th Regiment

Divisional Troops

11th Rifle Battalion
14th Hussars
1st Field Division 11th F. Artillery Regiment (1st and 2nd Heavy 1st and 2nd Light Batteries)
2nd Field Pioneer Company with Entrenching Tool Column

Corps Artillery

H.A. Division 11th F.A. regiment (1st and 3rd H.A. Batteries)
3rd F. Division 11th F.A. Regiment 5th and 6th Heavy Batteries)

Columns Division 11th F. Artillery Regiment

Artillery Ammunition Columns Nos. 1 and 4 Infantry Ammunition Columns Nos. 2 and 4
Pontoon Column

11th Train Battalion

*Except the 22nd Infantry Division which was attached to the Grand Duke of Mecklenburg's Detachment

II BAVARIAN ARMY CORPS

Commander:	General von Hartmann
Chief of Staff:	Major-General Baron von Horn

3rd Infantry Division

Commander:	Lieutenant-General von Walther

5th Infantry Brigade (Major-General von Schleich)

6th Regiment
7th Regiment
8th Rifle Battalion

6th Infantry Brigade (Major-General von Diehl)

14th Regiment
15th Regiment
3rd Rifle Battalion

1st Chevauxlegers

Artillery Division (3rd and 4th 4-pr 7th and 8th 6-pr Batteries 4th Regiment)
Ammunition Column (4th Regiment)

4th Infantry Division

Commander: Lieutenant-General Count von Bothmer

7th Infantry Brigade (Major-General Börries von Witzell)

5th Regiment
9th Regiment
6th Rifle Battalion

8th Infantry Brigade (Lieutenant-General von Maillinger: later Colonel Count von Leublsing)

3rd Battalion 1st Regiment
3rd Battalion 5th Regiment
1st Battalion 7th Regiment
3rd Battalion 14th Regiment
5th Rifle Battalion
10th Rifle Battalion

2nd Chevauxlegers

Artillery Division (1st and 2nd 4-pr 5th and 6th 6-pr Batteries 4th Artillery Regiment)
Ammunition Column (from 4th Artillery Regiment)

Lancer Brigade (Colonel Horadam)

2nd Lancers
5th Chevauxlegers
2nd H.A. Battery 2nd Artillery Regiment

Artillery Reserve Division

1st Division (1st H.A. 3rd and 4th 6-pr Batteries 2nd Artillery Regiment)
2nd Division (5th and 6th 6-pr Batteries 2nd Artillery Regiment and Mitrailleuse Battery 4th Artillery Regiment)
3rd Division (7th and 8th 6-pr 9th and 12th 12-pr Batteries 2nd Artillery Regiment)

Ammunition Column (from 4th Artillery Regiment)

2nd Field Engineer Division (3 Companies with 2 Pioneer 3 Bridge 1 Field Telegraph Equipments)

Main Ammunition Column (from 2nd Artillery Regiment)

Guard Landwehr Division

Commander: Lieutenant-General Baron von Löen

1st Guard Landwehr Brigade (Colonel Girodz von Gaudy)

1st Guard Landwehr Regiment
2nd Guard Landwehr Regiment

2nd Guard Landwehr Brigade (Colonel von Roehl)

1st Guard Grenadier Landwehr Regiment
2nd Guard Grenadier Landwehr Regiment

Combined Artillery Division (1st and 2nd Heavy and Light Reserve Battery of Guard Corps)
1st Fortress Pioneer Company X Army Corps
Pontoon Column with Escort Squadron

APPENDIX XIV

Order of Battle of the Army of the Meuse (30th November 1870)

Commander-in- Chief: General H.R.H. The Crown Prince of Saxony
Chief of Staff: Major-General Baron von Schlotheim

General Summary of Forces:
Guard Corps 29 battalions, 32 squadrons, 15 batteries (90 guns) 3 pioneer cos.
IV Army Corps 25 battalions, 8 squadrons, 14 batteries (84 guns) 3 pioneer cos.
XII Royal Saxon Army Corps 29 battalions, 24 squadrons, 16 batteries (96 guns) 3 pioneer cos.
Würt. Field Divn. 15 battalions, 10 squadrons, 9 batteries (54 guns) 2 pioneer cos.

Total Army of Meuse 98 battalions, 74 squadrons, 54 batteries (324 guns) 11 pioneer cos.

GUARD CORPS

Commander: General H.R.H. Prince Augustus of Wurttemberg
Chief of Staff: Major-General von Dannenberg

1st Guard Infantry Division

Commander: Major-General von Pape

1st Guard Infantry Brigade (Major-General von Kessel)

1st Foot Guards
3rd Foot Guards

2nd Guard Infantry Brigade (Major-General Baron von Medem)

2nd Foot Guards
Fusiliers of the Guard
4th Foot Guards

Divisional Troops

Guard Rifle Battalion
Guard Hussars
1st Field Division Guard F.A. Regiment (1st and 2nd Heavy 1st and 2nd Light Batteries
1st Field Pioneer Company with Light Field Bridge Train

2nd Guard Infantry Division

Commander: Lieutenant-General von Budritzki

3rd Guard Infantry Brigade (Colonel Knappe von Knappstadt: later Colonel Count von Kanitz)

1st Grenadiers of the Guard
3rd Grenadiers of the Guard

4th Guard Infantry Brigade (Major-General von Berger)

2nd Grenadiers of the Guard
4th Grenadiers of the Guard

Divisional Troops

Guard Sharpshooter Battalion
2nd Field Pioneer Company with Entrenching Tool Column
3rd Field Pioneer Company

Guard Cavalry Division

Commander: Lieutenant-General Count von der Goltz

1st Guard Cavalry Brigade (Major-General Count von Brandenburg)

Gardes du Corps Regiment
Guard Cuirassiers

2nd Guard Cavalry Brigade (Lieutenant-General H.R.H. Prince Albrecht of Prussia) (junior)

1st Lancers of the Guard
3rd Lancers of the Guard

3rd Guard Cavalry Brigade (Major-General Count von Brandenburg II)

1st Dragoons of the Guard
2nd Dragoons of the Guard

Corps Artillery

H.A. Division Guard F.A. Regiment (1st 2nd and 3rd H.A. Batteries)
2nd Field Division Guard F.A. Regiment (3rd and 4th Heavy 3rd and 4th Light Batteries)

Columns Divisions Guard F.A. Regiment

Artillery Ammunition Columns Nos. 1 to 5 Infantry Ammunition Columns Nos. 1 to 4 Pontoon Column

Guard Train Battalion

IV ARMY CORPS

Commander: General von Alvensleben I
Chief of Staff: Colonel von Thile

7th Infantry Division

Commander: Lieutenant-General von Schwarzhoff

13th Infantry Brigade (Major-General von Borries: later Colonel von Krosigk)

26th Regiment
66th Regiment

14th Infantry Brigade (Major-General von Zychlinski)

27th Regiment
93rd Regiment

Divisional Troops

4th Rifle Battalion
7th Dragoons
1st Field Division 4th F.A. Regiment (1st and 2nd Heavy 1st and 2nd Light Batteries)
2nd F. Pioneer Company

8th Infantry Division

Commander: Lieutenant-General von Schoeler

15th Infantry Brigade (Major-General von Kessler)

31st Regiment
71st Regiment

16th Infantry Brigade (Colonel von Scheffler)

86th Fusiliers
96th Regiment

Divisional Troops

12th Hussars
2nd Field Division 4th F.A. Regiment (3rd and 4th Heavy 3rd and 4th Light Batteries)
1st Field Pioneer Company with Light Field Bridge Train

Corps Artillery

H.A. Division 4th F.A. Regiment (2nd and 3rd H.A. Battteries)
3rd Field Division 4th F.A. Regiment (5th and 6th Heavy 5th and 6th Light Batteries)
Columns Division 4th F.A. Regiment

Artillery Ammunition Columns Nos. 1 to 5 infantry Ammunition Columns Nos.1 to 4 Pontoon Column

4th Train Battalion

XII (ROYAL SAXON) ARMY CORPS

Commander: Lieutenant-General H.R.H. Prince George of Saxony

Chief of Staff: Colonel von Zezschwitz (later Lieutenant-Colonel Schubert)

23rd Infantry Division

Commander: Major-General von Montbé (temp)

45th Infantry Brigade (Colonel Garten) (temp)

100th Grenadiers
101st Grenadiers
108th Sharpshooters

46th Infantry Brigade (Major-General von Montbé: later Colonel von Seydlitz-Gerstenberg)

102nd Regiment
103rd Regiment

Divisional Troops

1st Cavalry Regiment
1st Field Division, 12th F.A. Regiment (1st and 2nd Heavy, 1st and 2nd Light Batteries)
2nd Field Pioneer Company with Entrenching Tool Column
4th Field Pioneer Company

24th Infantry Division

Commander: Lieutenant-General Nehrhoff von Holderberg

47th Infantry Brigade (Major-General von Leonhardi: later Colonel von Elterlein)

104th Regiment
105th Regiment
12th Rifle Battalion

48th Infantry Brigade (Major-General von Schulz: later Colonel von Abendroth)

106th Regiment
107th Regiment
13th Rifle Battalion

Divisional Troops

2nd Cavalry Regiment
2nd Field Division 12th F.A. Regiment (3rd and 4th Heavy 3rd and 4th Light Batteries

3rd Field Pioneer Company with Light Field Bridge Train

12th Cavalry Division

Commander: Lieutenant-General Count zu Lippe

23rd Cavalry Brigade (Major-General Krug von Nidda)

Guard Cavalry Regiment
17th Lancers

24th Cavalry Brigade (Major-General Senfft von Pilsach)

3rd Cavalry Regiment
18th Lancers

Divisional Troops

1st H.A. Battery 12th F.A. Regiment

Corps Artillery

3rd Field Division 12th F.A. Regiment (5th and 6th Heavy 5th Light Battery)
4th Field Division 12th F.A. Regiment (7th and 8th Heavy 6th Light Battery and 2nd H.A. Battery

Columns Division 12th F.A. Regiment

Artillery Ammunition Columns Nos. 1 to 5 Infantry Ammunition Columns Nos. 1 to 4 Pontoon Columns

12th Train Battalion

Württemberg Field Division

Commander: Lieutenant-General von Obernitz

1st Field Brigade (Major-General von Reitzenstein)

1st Regiment
7th Regiment
2nd Rifle Battalion

2nd Field Brigade (Major-General von Starkloff)

2nd Regiment
5th Regiment
3rd Rifle Battalion

3rd Field Brigade (Major-General von Hügel: later Colonel von Mauch)

3rd Regiment
8th Regiment
1st Rifle Battalion

Cavalry Brigade (Major-General Count von Schéler)

1st Cavalry Regiment
3rd Cavalry Regiment
4th Cavalry Regiment

Artillery

1st F. Artillery Division (1st 6-pr 2nd and 3rd 4-pr Batteries
2nd F. Artillery Division (4th and 5th 4-pr 6th 6-pr Batteries
3rd F. Artillery Division (7th and 8th 4-pr 9th 6-pr Batteries
Pioneer Corps with Bridge Train and Entrenching tool Column
Horsed Ammunition Reserve (Columns Nos. 1,2 and 3)

APPENDIX XV

Order of Battle of the 2nd Paris Army (8th November 1870)

Commander-in-Chief: General Ducrot
Chief of Staff: General Appert

1st ARMY CORPS

Commander: General Blanchard
Chief of Staff: Colonel Filippi

1st Infantry Division

Commander: General de Malroy

1st Brigade (General Martenot)

1st,2nd,4th Ille and Vilaine Battalions
1st,2nd,3rd,4th Côte d'Or Battalions

2nd Brigade (General Paturel)

121st Regiment of the Line
122nd Regiment of the Line

Artillery
3 batteries

2nd Infantry Division

Commander: General de Maud'huy

1st Brigade (General Valentin)

109th Regiment of Line
110th Regiment of the Line
2nd 3rd,4th,5th Finistère Battalions

2nd Brigade (General Blaise)

111th Regiment of the Line
112th Regiment of the Line

3rd Infantry Division

Commander: General Faron

1st Brigade (Colonel Comte)

113th Regiment of the Line
114th Regiment of the Line
1st,2nd,3rd Vendée Battalions

2nd Brigade (General de la Mariouse)

35th Regiment of the Line
42nd Regiment of the Line

Artillery
3 batteries

Reserve Artillery
6 batteries

2nd ARMY CORPS

Commander:	General Baron Renault
Chief of Staff:	General Ferri-Pisani

1st Infantry Division

Commander: General Baron Susbielle

1st Brigade (General Ladreit de la Charrière)

115th Regiment of the Line
116th Regiment of the Line

2nd Brigade (General Lecomte)

117th Regiment of the Line
118th Regiment of the Line

Artillery
3 batteries

2nd Infantry Division

Commander: General Berthaut

1st Brigade (General Bôcher)

119th Regiment of the Line
120th Regiment of the Line

2nd Brigade (Colonel de Miribel)

2nd,3rd,4th,5th Loire Battalions
1st,4th,5th Lower Seine Battalions
2nd Drome Battalion

Artillery
3 batteries

3rd Infantry Division

Commander: General de Maussion

1st Brigade (General Courty)

123rd Regiment of the Line
124th Regiment of the Line

2nd Brigade (General Avril de l'Enclos)

125th Regiment of the Line
126th Regiment of the Line

Artillery
3 batteries
Reserve Artillery
5 batteries

3rd ARMY CORPS

Commander:	General d'Exéa
Chief of Staff:	Colonel de Belgaric

1st Infantry Division

Commander: General de Bellemare

1st Brigade (Colonel Fournès)

4th Zouaves
136th Regiment of the Line

2nd Brigade (Colonel Colonien)

1st, 2nd, 3rd, 4th Seine and Marne Battalions
1st, 2nd, 5th Morbihan Battalions

Artillery
3 batteries

2nd Infantry Division

Commander: General Mattat

1st Brigade (Colonel Bonnet)

105th Regiment of the Line
106th Regiment of the Line

2nd Brigade (General Daudel)

107th Regiment of the Line
108th Regiment of the Line

Garde Mobile Brigade (Colonel Reille)

1st, 2nd, 3rd Tarn Battalions
3rd Lower Seine Battalion

Artillery
3 batteries

Cavalry Division

Commander: General Count de Champéron

1st Brigade (General de Gerbrois)

1st Dragoons de Marche
2nd Dragoons de Marche

2nd Brigade (General Cousin)

1st Chasseurs
9th Chasseurs
1st Gens d'armes

Reserve Artillery
6 batteries

General Artillery Reserve of 2nd Army
10 batteries

APPENDIX XVI

Order of Battle of the First Army (15th November 1870)

Commander-in-Chief:	General Baron von Manteuffel
Chief of Staff:	Major-General von Sperling (later Colonel Count von Wartensleben)

Summary of Forces:
I Army Corps 25 battalions, 8 squadrons, 14 batteries (84 guns) 3 pioneer cos.
VII Army Corps 25 battalions, 8 squadrons, 14 batteries (84 guns) 3 pioneer cos.
VIII Army Corps 25 battalions, 8 squadrons, 15 batteries (90 guns) 3 pioneer cos.
3rd Res. Division 6 battalions, 8 squadrons, 3 batteries (18 guns)
3rd Cav.Division 16 squadrons, 1 batteries (6 guns)

Total 81 battalions, 48 squadrons, 47 batteries (282 guns) 9 pioneer cos.

I ARMY CORPS

Commander:	General Baron von Manteuffel (later Lieutenant General von Bentheim)
Chief of Staff:	Lieutenant-Colonel von der Burg

1st Infantry Division

Commander:	Lieutenant-General von Bentheim

1st Infantry Brigade (Major-General von Gayl: later Colonel von Boecking)

1st Grenadiers
41st Regiment

2nd Infantry Brigade (Major-General Baron von Falkenstein)

3rd Grenadiers
43rd Regiment

Divisional Troops

1st Rifle Battalion
1st Dragoons
1st Field Division 1st Field Artillery Regiment (1st and 2nd Heavy 1st and 2nd Light Batteries)
2nd Field Pioneer Company with Entrenching Tool Column
3rd Pioneer Company

2nd Infantry Division

Commander:	Major-General von Pritzelwitz

3rd Infantry Brigade (Major-General von Memerty: later Colonel von Busse)

4th Grenadiers
44th Regiment

4th Infantry Brigade (Major-General von Zglinitzki)

5th Grenadiers
45th Regiment

Divisional Troops

10th Dragoons
3rd Field Division 1st Field Artillery Regiment (5th and 6th Heavy 5th and 6th Light Batteries)
1st Field Pioneer Company with Light Field Bridge Train

Corps Artillery

H.A. Division 1st Field Artillery Regiment (2nd and 3rd H.A. Batteries)
2nd Field Division 1st Artillery Regiment (3rd and 4th Heavy 3rd and 4th Light Batteries)

Columns Division 1st Field Artillery Regiment

Artillery Ammunition Columns Nos. 1 to 5 Infantry Ammunition Columns Nos. 1 to 4 Pontoon Column

1st Train Battalion

VII ARMY CORPS

Commander:	General von Zastrow
Chief of Staff:	Colonel von Anger (later Major von Kaltenborn-Stachau)

13th Infantry Division

Commander:	Lieutenant-General von Bothmer

25th Infantry Brigade (Major-General Baron von der Osten-Sacken)

18th Regiment
73rd Fusiliers

26th Infantry Brigade (Major-General Baron von der Goltz: later Colonel von Barby)

15th Regiment
55th Regiment

Divisional Troops

15th Rifle Battalion
8th Hussars

3rd Field Division 7th Field Artillery Regiment (5th and 6th Heavy 5th and 6th Light Batteries)
2nd Field Pioneer Company with Entrenching Tool Column
3rd Field Pioneer Company

14th Infantry Division

Commander: Lieutenant-General von Kameke

27th Infantry Brigade (Colonel von Pannwitz)

39th Fusiliers
74th Regiment

28th Infantry Brigade (Major-General von Woyna II)

53rd Regiment
77th Regiment

Divisional Troops

15th Hussars
1st Field Division 7th Field Artillery regiment (1st and 2nd Heavy 1st and 2nd Light Batteries)
1st Field Pioneer Company with Light Field Bridge Train

Corps Artillery

Horse Artillery Division 7th Field Artillery regiment (2nd and 3rd Horse Artillery batteries)
2nd Field Division 7th Field Artillery Regiment (3rd and 4th Heavy 3rd and 4th Light Batteries)

Columns Division 7th Field Artillery Regiment

Artillery Ammunition Columns Nos.1 to 5 Infantry Ammunition Columns Nos. 1 to 4 Pontoon Column

7th Train Battalion

VIII ARMY CORPS

Commander: General von Goeben
Chief of Staff: Colonel von Witzendorff

15th Infantry Division

Commander: Lieutenant-General von Kummer

29th Infantry Brigade (Colonel von Bock)

33rd Fusiliers
65th Regiment

30th Infantry Brigade (Major-General von Strübberg)

28th Regiment
68th Regiment

Divisional Troops

7th Rifle Battalion
7th Hussars
1st Field Division 8th Field Artillery Regiment (1st and 2nd Heavy 1st and 2nd Light Batteries)
2nd Field Pioneer Company with Entrenching Tool Column

16th Infantry Division

Commander: Lieutenant-General Baron von Barnekow

31st Infantry Brigade (Major-General Count Neidhardt von Gneisenau)

29th Regiment
69th Regiment

32nd Infantry Brigade (Colonel von Rex)

40th Fusiliers
70th Regiment

Divisional Troops

9th Hussars
3rd Field Division 8th Field Artillery Regiment (5th and 6th Heavy 5th and 6th Light Batteries)
1st Field Pioneer Company with Light Field Bridge Train
3rd Field Pioneer Company

Corps Artillery

Horse Artillery Division 8th Field Artillery Regiment (1st,2nd,and 3rd Horse Artillery Batteries)
2nd Field Division 8th Field Artillery Regiment (3rd and 4th Heavy 3rd and 4th Light Batteries)

Columns Division 8th Field Artillery Regiment

Artillery Ammunition Columns Nos. 1 to 5 Infantry Ammunition Columns Nos 1 to 4 Pontoon Column

8th Train Battalion

3rd Reserve Division

Commander: Major-General Baron Schuler von Senden

Combined Line Infantry Brigade (Major-General von Blanckensee)

19th Regiment
81st Regiment

3rd Reserve Cavalry Brigade (Major-General von Strantz)

1st Reserve Dragoons
3rd Reserve Hussars

Combined Artillery division (1st and 2nd Heavy, Light Reserve Battery)

3rd Cavalry Division

Commander: Lieutenant-General Count von der Groeben

6th Cavalry Brigade (Major-General von Mirus)

8th Cuirassiers
7th Lancers

7th Cavalry Brigade (Major-General Count zu Dohna)

5th Lancers
14th Lancers

Divisional Troops

1st Horse Artillery Battery VII Army Corps

APPENDIX XVII

Order of Battle of the 21st French Corps

Commander:	General Jaurès
Chief of Staff:	General Loysel

1st Infantry Division

Commander:	General Rousseau

1st Brigade (Lieutenant-Colonel Roux)

58th Regiment de Marche
13th Foot Chasseurs
1st Battalion Garde Mobile of Deux-Sèvres
1st Battalion Garde Mobile of the Loire Inférieure
1st Battalion Garde Nationale of the Sarthe

2nd Brigade (Lieutenant-Colonel de Villars)

26th Regiment de Marche (3 companies)
94th Regiment de Marche (3 companies)
Garde Nationale of the Corrèze
49th Regiment de Marche (2 companies)
Garde Nationale of the Sarthe (1 battalion)

Artillery: 2 batteries
Engineers: 1 section
Franctireurs of the Dordogne
Phalanx from Nice
Eclaireurs of the Sarthe
Mounted Eclaireurs

2nd Infantry Division

Commander:	General Collin

1st Brigade (Lieutenant-Colonel de la Marlière)

10th Battalion Marine Infantry
63rd Garde Mobile
6th Battalion Garde Nationale of Ille and Vilaine
4th Battalion Garde Nationale of the Eure and Loire
56th Regiment de Marche

2nd Brigade (Lieutenant-Colonel des Moutis)

49th Garde Mobile Regiment
94th Regiment of the Line (2 companies, probably depôt troops)
59th Regiment de Marche (also shown in Camô's Division)
41st Regiment of the Line (1 battalion, probably depot troops)
9th Battalion Marine Infantry

Artillery: 2 batteries
Engineers: 1 section
Franctireurs of Gard
Guerillas of the Seine
Eclaireurs of Mamers
Franctireurs of the Sarthe and Argentan

3rd Infantry Division

Commander: General de Villeneuve

1st Brigade (Lieutenant-Colonel Stéphanie)

78th Garde Mobile Regiment
4th Battalion of Calvados
4th Battalion of Finistère
Battalion of the Loire Inférieure
15th Garde Mobile Regiment of Calvados
6th Battalion Marine Fusiliers

2nd Brigade (General du Temple)

1st,4th,5th Battalions
2nd and 3rd Battalions of the Manche
Battalion of Garde
Battalion of the Côtes du Nord
3rd Battalion Marine Fusiliers

Artillery: 2 batteries
Engineers: 1 company
Franctireurs of the Eure and Loire
Franctireurs of the Maritime Alps
Eclaireurs of La Ferté-Macé

4th Infantry Division (Brittany Corps)

Commander: General Gougeard, Captain French Navy

1st Brigade

3rd Battalion Garde Nationale of the Loire Inférieure
Garde Nationale of Ille and Vilaine (1 battalion)
62nd Regiment of the Line (1 battalion)
97th Regiment of the Line (1 battalion)
Detachments of the 25th and 86th Regiments of the Line

2nd Brigade

19th Regiment of the Line 1 battalion (probably depot troops)
Garde Nationale of the Mayenne (2 battalions)
Garde Nationale of Morbihan (1 battalion)
Garde Nationale of the Loire Inférieure (1 battalion)
Detachment of the Foreign Legion

Cavalry Division

Commander: General Guillon
8th Hussars
1st Hussars de Marche
3rd Mixed Regiment of Light Cavalry
8th Mixed Regiment of Light Cavalry
6th Dragoons de Marche
8th Cuirassiers de Marche

Reserve to the Army Corps

Collet's Brigade

Battalion of Garde Nationale of Deux-Sèvres
Battalion of Garde Nationale of Gard
9th Battalion Marine Infantry
Detachment of Marine Fusiliers

Reserve

Infantry:	5th Battalion Marine Fusillers
	Franctireurs of the East
Cavalry:	2 squadrons Gendarmerie de Marche
	2 squadrons 6th Dragoons (either detached from 15th Corps or Depôt troops)
	One squadron 5th Hussars (probably depot troops)
	Two squadrons of Hussars
Artillery:	4 batteries
Engineers:	1 company

Composition of Camô's Division (Beginning of December 1870)

Infantry

16th Foot Chasseurs de Marche
Regiment of Foot Gendarmerie de Marche
59th Regiment de Marche
27th Garde Mobile Regiment (Isère)
88th Garde Mobile Regiment (Indre et Loire)
Franctireurs of the Army (with the 59th Regiment de Marche)
Franctireurs of the Ain (with the 27th Garde Mobile Regiment)

Cavalry

4th Lancers de Marche
3rd Hussars de Marche
2nd Chasseurs de Marche
7th Cuirassiers de Marche
1st Regiment Mounted Gendarmerie

Artillery
5 batteries

APPENDIX XVIII

Order of Battle of the French Army of the North (23rd December 1870)

Commander-in-Chief:	General Faidherbe
Chief of Staff:	General Farre

22nd ARMY CORPS

Commander:	General Lecointe

1st Division

Commander:	General Derroja

1st Brigade (Lieutenant-Colonel Aynès, later)

2nd Chasseurs de Marche
67th Regiment de Marche
91st Garde Mobile Regiment

2nd Brigade (Colonel Pittié)

17th Chasseurs de Marche
69th Regiment de Marche
46th Garde Mobile Regiment

Artillery
3 batteries

2nd Division

Commanding:	General Dufaure du Bessol

1st Brigade (Colonel Foerster)

20th Chasseurs de Marche
69th Regiment de Marche
44th Garde Mobile Regiment

2nd Brigade (Colonel de Gislain)

18th Chasseurs de Marche
70th Regiment de Marche
Garde Mobile Regiment of the Somme and Marne

Artillery
3 batteries

23rd ARMY CORPS

Commander: General Paulze d'Ivoy
Chief of Staff: Lieutenant-Colonel Marchand

1st Division

Commander: Admiral Moulac

1st Brigade (Captain Payen, Navy)

19th Chasseurs de Marche
Regiment of Marine Fusiliers
48th Garde Mobile Regiment

2nd Brigade (Colonel de Legrange)

1st Battalion Garde Nationale of the Pas de Calais
47th Garde Mobile Regiment
48th (bis) Garde Mobile Regiment

Artillery
3 batteries

2nd Division

Commander: General Robin

1st Brigade (Colonel Brusley)

1st Voltigeur Battalion
1st Regiment Garde Nationale of the North
2nd Regiment Garde Nationale of the North

2nd Brigade (Colonel Amos)

4th Battalion of the 5th Legion
3rd Regiment Garde Nationale of the North
4th Regiment Garde Nationale of the North

Artillery
2 batteries

At Disposal of Headquarters

Cavalry
2 squadrons Gendarmerie
2 squadrons Dragoons

Artillery
2 batteries

Engineers
2 companies

APPENDIX XIX

Order of Battle of the 25th French Corps (end of January 1871)

Commander: General Pourcet
Chief of Staff: Colonel Fouchault

1st Infantry Division

Commander: General Bruat, Captain the Navy

1st Brigade (General De Bernard de Seigneurens)

74th Regiment de Marche
Two Battalions Marines

2nd Brigade (General Le Mordan de Langourian)

75th Regiment de Marche
Two Battalions Marine Fusiliers

Artillery
3 batteries
Engineers
1 section

2nd Infantry Division

Commander: General de Chabron

1st Brigade

77th Regiment de Marche
One Legion Garde Nationale of the Cher

2nd Brigade

7th Rifle Battalion de Marche
6th Battalion Garde Mobile of Puy de Dôme
One Legion Garde Nationale of the Indre

3rd Brigade

Two Legions Garde Nationale of the Gironde

Artillery
3 batteries
Engineers
1 section

3rd Infantry Division

Commander: General Ferri Pisani Jourdan, Comte de Saint-Anastase

1st Brigade (Lieutenant-Colonel Laurens)

78th Regiment de Marche
One Legion Garde Nationale of the Dordogne

2nd Brigade (Lieutenant-Colonel Blot)

79th Regiment de Marche
One Battalion Garde Nationale of the Côte d'Or
Three Legions Garde Nationale of the Departments des Landes

Artillery
3 batteries
Engineers
1 section

Cavalry Division

Commander: General Tripart

1st Brigade (General Delhorme)

9th Mixed Light Regiment
9th Dragoons de Marche
One Squadron Eclaireurs of Deux-Sèvres

2nd Brigade (General de Bruchard)

10th Mixed Light Regiment
One Regiment Garde Mobile of the Dordogne

Reserve Artillery
7 batteries
Engineers
1 section

APPENDIX XX

Order of Battle of the 19th French Corps (end of January 1871)

Commander:	General Dargent
Chief of Staff:	Colonel Colin

1st Infantry Division

Commander:	General Vardin

1st Brigade (General Ritter)

55th Regiment de Marche
66th Regiment de Marche
96th Garde Mobile Regiment

2nd Brigade (General Luzeux)

71st Regiment de Marche
Two Legions Garde Nationale of the Gironde

Artillery
3 batteries
Engineers
1 section

2nd Infantry Division

Commander:	General Girard

1st Brigade (General Robert)

22nd Rifle Battalion de Marche
64th Regiment de Marche
One Legion of Garde Nationale of the Lower Seine

2nd Brigade (Lieutenant-Colonel de Brême)

65th Regiment de Marche
70th Regiment de Marche
One Battalion Garde Mobile of the Lower Charente

Artillery
3 batteries
Engineers
1 section

3rd Infantry Division

Commander: General Saussier

1st Brigade (General Roy)

10,000 infantry

2nd Brigade

8,000 infantry

Cavalry
12th Chasseurs
Artillery
20 guns
Engineers
1 section

Cavalry Division

Commander: General Abdelal

1st Brigade (Colonel de Kerhué)

3rd Hussars
4th Hussars de Marche

2nd Brigade (General de Vouges de Chanteclair)

8th Dragoons de Marche
9th Cuirassiers de Marche

Reserve Artillery
6 batteries

Engineers
1 section

Train
1 company

APPENDIX XXI

Order of Battle of the French Eastern Army (commencement of January 1871)

Commander-in-Chief:	General Bourbaki
Chief of Staff:	General Borel

15th ARMY CORPS

Commander:	General Martineau des Chenez
Chief of Staff:	Colonel des Plas

1st Infantry Division

Commander:	General d'Astugue

1st Brigade (General Minot)

1st Zouaves de Marche
12th Gardes Mobiles Battalion

2nd Brigade (General Questel)

Algerian Tirailleurs
18th Gardes Mobiles (Charente)
4th Chasseurs de Marche

Artillery
3 batteries
Engineers
1 section

2nd Infantry Division

Commander:	General Rébillard

1st Brigade (General Le Camus)

39th Regiment of the Line
Foreign Legion
25th Gardes mobiles (Gironde)
5th Chasseurs de March

2nd Brigade (General Choppin Merey)

2nd Zouaves de Marche
30th Regiment de Marche
29th Gardes Mobiles (Maine et Loire)

Artillery
3 batteries

Engineers
1 section

3rd Infantry Division

Commander: General Peytavin

1st Brigade (General de Jacob de la Cottière)

16th Regiment of the Line
33rd Regiment de Marche
32nd Gardes Mobiles (Puy de Dôme)
6th Chasseurs de Marche

2nd Brigade (General Martinez)

27th Regiment de Marche
34th Regiment de Marche
69th Regiment de Marche

Artillery
2 batteries
Engineers
1 section

Cavalry Division

Commander: General Garland de Longuerne

1st Brigade

11th Chasseurs
6th Dragoons
6th Hussars

2nd Brigade (General de Boerio)

1st Chasseurs de Marche
2nd Lancers
9th Cuirassiers

3rd Brigade (General Tillon)

5th Lancers
1st Cuirassiers de Marche

Reserve Artillery
4 8-pr batteries
4 H.A. batteries
2 mitrailleuse batteries
2 mountain batteries

Total strength of the artillery of 15th Army Corps: 20 batteries with 114 guns

18th ARMY CORPS

Commander:	General Billot
Chief of Staff:	Colonel du Sachy de Fourdrinoy

1st Infantry Division

Commander:	General Feillet-Pilatrie

1st Brigade (Colonel Leclaire)

42nd Regiment de Marche
19th Gardes Mobiles (Cher)
9th Chasseurs de Marche

2nd Brigade (General Robert)

44th Regiment de Marche
73rd Gardes Mobiles (Loiret Isere)

Cavalry
1 sqn. 3rd Lancers de Marche
Artillery
3 batteries
Engineers
1 section

2nd Infantry Division

Commander:	Rear-Admiral Penhoat

1st Brigade (General Perrin)

52nd Regiment de Marche
77th Gardes Mobiles (Maine et Loire, Tarn, Allier)
12th Chasseurs de Marche

2nd Brigade (General Perreaux)

92nd Regiment of the Line
1 Regiment of African Light Infantry (2 battns)

Cavalry
1 sqn. 5th Dragoons de Marche
Artillery
3 batteries
Engineers
1 section

3rd Infantry Division

Commander: General Bonnet

1st Brigade (Colonel Goury)

4th Zouaves de Marche
82nd Gardes Mobiles (Vancluse, Drome, Var)

Cavalry
1 sqn. 3rd Lancers de Marche
Artillery
3 batteries
Engineers
1 section

Cavalry Division

Commander: General de Bremond d'Ars

1st Brigade (General Charlemagne)

2nd Hussars de Marche
3rd Lancers de Marche

2nd Brigade (General Guyon-Vernier)

5th Dragoons de Marche
5th Cuirassiers de Marche

Reserve Artillery
7 batteries

20th ARMY CORPS

Commander: General Clinchant
Chief of Staff: Colonel Varaigne

1st Infantry Division

Commander: General de Polignac

1st Brigade (General Godefroy)

Gardes Mobiles of the Loire
50th Regiment de Marche
55th Gardes Mobiles (Jura)

2nd Brigade (Colonel Brisac)

67th Gardes Mobiles (Haute Loire)
24th Gardes Mobiles (Haute Garonne)
4th Garde Mobile Battalion (Saône et Loire)
Franctireurs of the Upper Rhine

Cavalry
2nd Lancers de Marche

Artillery
2 batteries
Engineers
1 company

2nd Infantry Division

Commander: General Thornton

1st Brigade (General Bernard de Seigneurens)

34th Gardes Mobiles (Deux-Sèvres)
One Garde Mobile Battalion (Savoy)
25th Chasseurs

2nd Brigade (Colonel Vivenot)

3rd Zouaves de Marche
68th Gardes Mobiles (Haut Rhin)

Cavalry
7th Chasseurs
Artillery
2 batteries
Engineers
1 company

3rd Infantry Division

Commander: General Ségard

1st Brigade (General Durochat)

47th Regiment de Marche
Corsican Gardes Mobiles

2nd Brigade (General Simonin)

78th Regiment of the Line
58th Gardes Mobiles (Vosges)
2 battalions Garde Mobile (Eastern Pyrénées)
1 Garde Mobile Battalion (Meurthe)
Allier Franctireurs
Nice Franctireurs

Cavalry
6th Cuirassiers de Marche
Artillery
2 batteries
Engineers
1 company

Reserve Artillery
At least 3 batteries

24th ARMY CORPS

Commander: General de Bressolles
Chief of Staff: Colonel Tissier

1st Infantry Division

Commander: General d'Aries

63rd Regiment de Marche
15th Chasseurs de Marche
Garde Mobile Regiment (1 battalion each from Haute Garonne,Tarn et Garonne and Haut Rhin)
3rd Rhone Legion

Artillery
2 batteries
Engineers
2 sections

2nd Infantry Division

Commander: General Comagny

1st Brigade (General Irlande)

60th Regiment de Marche
61st Regiment de Marche
21st Chasseurs de Marche

1st Brigade (General Bramas)

14th Gardes Mobiles (Yonne)
87th Gardes Mobiles (Lozère,Tarn et Garonne)

Detachment of Engineers
Artillery
Unknown strength

3rd Infantry Division

Commander: General Carré de Busserolle

1st Rhône Legion
2nd Rhône Legion
89th Gardes Mobiles (Var)
1 Garde Mobile Battalion (Loire)

Artillery
3 batteries

Corps Cavalry

7th Mixed Cavalry Regiment de Marche
1 sqn. 6th Dragoons
1 sqn. 10th Dragoons

Reserve Artillery
Unknown strength

Crémer's Division

Commander:	General Crémer

1st Brigade (Colonel Millot)

1 Garde Mobile Battalion (Giroude)
32nd Regiment de Marche
57th Regiment de Marche

2nd Brigade (General Carot-Tevis: later Lieutenant-Colonel Reboulet)

La Vendée Franctireurs
83rd Gardes Mobiles (Ande, Gers)
86th Gardes Mobiles

Artillery
5 batteries with 32 guns
Engineers
1 company
Cavalry
1 detachment of Eclaireurs

Army Reserve

Commander:	General Pallas de la Barrière Captain the Navy
Infantry:	38th Regiment of the Line
	29th Regiment de Marche
	2nd Marine Infantry de Marche
Cavalry:	2nd Chasseurs d'Afrique de Marche
	3rd Dragoons de Marche
Artillery:	3 batteries
Engineers:	A detachment

Troops of the 7th Military Division (Besancon)

Commander:	General Rolland, Captain the Navy
Infantry:	3 Garde Mobile Battalions of Doubs (54th Regiment de Marche)
	1 Garde Mobile Battalion (Vosges)
	1 Garde Mobile Battalion (Upper Alps)
	Mobilised Gardes Nationales of the Haute Saône
	Miners of the Loire
	9 battalions Mobilised Gardes Nationales (Hérault, Vaucluse, Drôme)
Cavalry:	5th Lanciers de Marche
Artillery:	1 horsed battery

APPENDIX XXII

Staff of the Artillery and Engineer attack on Paris

Artillery Attack

Chief Director:	Major-General Prince Krafft of Hohenlohe-Ingelfingen
Chief of Staff:	Lieutenant-Colonel Heydenreich, XII Army Corps
Adjutants:	1st Lieutenant Braumüller 2nd Lieutenant Clauson von Kaas

Engineer Attack

Chief Director:	Lieutenant-General von Kameke
Adjutants:	Major Peters Captain von Fritze

APPENDIX XXIII

Order of Battle of the South Army

Commander-in Chief:	General Baron von Manteuffel
Chief of Staff:	Colonel Count von Wartensleben

Summary of Forces:
II Army Corps 25 battalions, 8 squadrons, 14 batteries (84 guns)
VII Army Corps 31 battalions, 12 squadrons, 14 batteries (84 guns)
XIV Army Corps 24 battalions, 20 squadrons, 13 batteries (78 guns)
4th Res. Division 15 battalions, 8 squadrons, 6 batteries (36 guns)
Siege Corps before Belfort (exclusive of the troops temporarily detached from the 4th Reserve Division, and also exclusive of technical troops)

Total 118 battalions, 54 squadrons, 53 batteries (316 guns)

II ARMY CORPS (11th January 1871)

Commander:	General von Fransecky
Chief of Staff:	Colonel von Wichmann

3rd Infantry Division

Commander:	Major-General von Hartmann

5th Infantry Brigade(Major-General von Koblinski)

2nd Grenadiers
42nd Regiment

6th Infantry Brigade (Colonel von Wedell)

14th Regiment
54th Regiment

Divisional Troops

2nd Rifle Battalion
3rd Dragoons
1st Foot Division 2nd field Artillery Regiment (1st and 2nd Heavy 1st and 2nd Light Battery)
1st Field Pioneer Company with Light Field Bridge

4th Infantry Division

Commander:	Lieutenant-General Hann von Weyhern

7th Infantry Brigade (Major-General du Trossel)

9th Grenadiers
49th Regiment

8th Infantry Brigade (Major-General von Kettler)

21st Regiment
61st Regiment

Divisional Troops

11th Dragoons
3rd Foot Division 2nd Field Artillery Regiment (5th and 6th Heavy 5th and 6th Light Battery)
2nd Field Pioneer Company with Entrenching Tool Column
3rd Pioneer Company

Corps Artillery

Horse Artillery Division 2nd Field Artillery Regiment (2nd and 3rd Horse Artillery Batteries)
2nd Foot Division 2nd Field Artillery Regiment (3rd and 4th Heavy 3rd and 4th Light Batteries)

Columns Division 2nd Field. Artillery Regiment, Artillery Ammunition Columns Nos. 1–5 Infantry Ammunition Columns Nos. 1–4 Pontoon Column.
2nd Train Battalion

VII ARMY CORPS (11th January 1871)

Commander:	General von Zastrow
Chief of Staff:	Colonel von Salviati

13th Infantry Division

Commander:	Lieutenant-General von Bothmer

25th Infantry Brigade (Major-General Baron von der Osten Sacken)

13th Regiment
73rd Fusiliers

26th Infantry Brigade (Colonel von Barby)

15th Regiment
55th Regiment

Divisional Troops

7th Rifle Battalion
8th Hussars
3rd Foot Division 7th Field Artillery Regiment (5th 3rd Foot Division 7th Field Artillery Regiment (5th and 6th Heavy 5th and 6th Light Batteries)
1st Pioneer Company with Light Field Bridge Train

14th Infantry Division

Commander:	Major-General Baron Schuler von Senden

27th Infantry Brigade (Major-General von Woyna II)

53rd Regiment
77th Regiment

Divisional Troops

15th Hussars
1st Foot Division 7th Field Artillery Regiment (1st and 2nd Heavy 1st and 2nd Light Batteries)
2nd Field Pioneer Company with Entrenching Tool Column
3rd Field Pioneer Company with Entrenching Tool Column

Corps Artillery

Horse Artillery Division 7th Field Artillery Regiment 2nd and 3rd Horse Artillery Batteries)
Columns Division 7th Field Artillery Regiment Artillery Ammunition Columns Nos. 1–5 Infantry Ammunition Columns Nos. 1–4 Pontoon Column 7th Train Battalion

Attached to the Corps
60th Regiment
72nd Regiment
5th Reserve Lancers

XIV ARMY CORPS (19th January 1871)

Commander:	General von Werder
Chief of Staff:	Lieutenant-Colonel Leszczynski

Prussian Troops

Commander:	Major-General Baron von der Goltz

Mixed Infantry Brigade (Colonel Wahlert)

30th Reserve Dragoons
2nd Reserve Hussars

Mixed Cavalry Brigade

2nd Reserve Dragoons
2nd Reserve Hussars

Combined Artillery Division (Heavy Reserve Battery 1 A.C. 1st and 2nd Light Reserve Battery III A.C.)

Baden Division

Commander:	Lieutenant-General von Glümer

1st Infantry Brigade (Colonel Baron von Wechmar)

B.G. Grenadier Regiment
2nd Grenadiers

2nd Infantry Brigade (Major-General Keller)

5th Regiment
6th Regiment

Divisional Troops

3rd Dragoons
Divisional Artillery (1st,2nd, and 5th Heavy 1st and 2nd Light Batteries)
Pontoon Company with Light Field Bridge Train

Cavalry Brigade (Colonel Baron von Willisen)

Body Guard Dragoon Regiment
2nd Dragoons
Horse Artillery Battery

Corps Artillery

Grand Duchy of Baden 3rd and 4th Heavy 3rd and 4th Light Batteries

Prussian Columns Division
Artillery Ammunition Columns Nos. 1–4
Infantry Ammunition Columns Nos. 1–3

Baden Columns division
Artillery Ammunition Columns Nox. 1–3
Infantry Ammunition Columns Nox. 1 and 2 Pontoon Column

5th Field Railway Detachment

4th Reserve Division (19th January 1871)

Commander: Major-General von Schmeling

Combined Infantry Brigade (Colonel Knappe von Knappstadt)

25th Regiment
2nd Combined East Prussian Landwehr (Nos. 4 and 5)
(Osterode, Ortelsburg, Graudenz, and Thorn Battalions)

East Prussian Landwehr Brigade (Colonel von Zimmermann)

Combined East Prussian Landwehr Regiments (Nos. 1–3)
(Tilsit, Wehlau, Insterburg, and Gumbinnen Battalions)
Combined East Prussian Landwehr Regiments (Nos. 43–45)
(Loetzen, Goldap, Danzig, and Marienburg Battalions)

4th Reserve Cavalry Brigade (Major-General von Tresckow II)

1st Reserve Lancers
3rd Reserve Lancers

Combined Artillery Division (1st and 2nd Heavy 1st,2nd, 3rd and 4th Light Batteries)
2nd Fortress Pioneer Company VII A.C.

Bibliography

ABBOTT, JSC, *Prussia and the Franco-Prussian War,* (London 1871)
ABEKEN, H, *Bismarck's Pen,* (London 1911)
ADDINGTON, LH, *The Blitzkrieg Era and the German General Staff 1865–1941,*
(New Brunswick, NJ 1971)
ADRIANCE, TJ, *The Last Gaiter Button,* (Westpoint, Connecticut 1987)
ALLNUTT, H, *Historical Diary of the War Between France and Germany 1870–71,*
(London 1871)
(ANON), *Papiers et Correspondance de la Famille Imperiale,* (Paris 1870)
(ANON), *Le Général Chanzy,* (Paris 1896)
ARONSON, T, *The Fall of the Third Napoleon,* (London 1970)
ASCOLI, D, *A Day of Battle: Mars la Tour 16 August 1870,* (London 1987)
AURELLE de PALADINES, General C d', *La Première Armée de la Loire,* (Paris 1871)
BALDICK, R, *The Siege of Paris,* (London 1964)
BARKER, AJ, *The Vainglorious War,* (London 1970)
BAUNARD, Monsignor, *Le Général de Sonis,* (Paris 1903)
BAZAINE, Marshal A, *Episodes de la Guerre de 1870,* (Madrid 1883)
BENEDETTI, V, *Ma Mission en Prusse,* (Paris 1871)
BIBESCO, Prince G, *Campagne de 1870: Belfort, Reims, Sedan,* (Paris 1872)
BIRD, Brevet-Major WD, *Lectures on the Strategy of the Franco-German War 1870,* (London 1909)
BISMARCK, Prince O von, *The Correspondence of William I and Bismarck,* (New York 1903)
BISMARCK, Prince O von, *Letters to his Wife from the Seat of War 1870–1871,* (London 1915)
BISMARCK, Prince O von, *Reflections and Reminiscences,* (London 1898)
BLUME, W, *The Operations of the German Armies in France,* (London 1872)
BLUMENTHAL, Field Marshal Count K von, *Journals for 1866 and 1870–71,* (London 1903)
BOGUSLAWSKI, A von, *Tactical Deductions from the War of 1870–71* (trans Colonel L Graham), (London 1872)
BONIE, Lieutenant Colonel, 'The French Cavalry in 1870' in: *Cavalry Studies from Two Great Wars,* (Kansas City 1896)
BONNAL, General H, *La Manoeuvre de Saint Privat,* (Paris 1904)
BONNIN, G (ed), *Bismarck and the Hohenzollern Candidature for the Spanish Throne,* (London 1957)
BORBSTAEDT, A and DWYER, F, *The Franco- German War to the Catastrophe of Sedan,* (London 1911)
BOWLES,TG, *The Defence of Paris,* (London 1871)
BRESLER, F, *Napoleon III: A Life,* (London 1999)
BROCKETT, LP, *The Franco-German War of 1870–71,* (New York 1871)

BRONSART von SCHELLENDORFF, General P, *The Duties of the General Staff,* (London 1905)
BUCHOLZ, A, *Moltke and the German Wars,* (New York 2001)
BUCHOLZ, A, *Moltke, Schlieffen and Prussian War Planning,* (New York 1991)
BURY, JPT, *Gambetta and the National Defence: A Republican Dictatorship in France,* (London 1964)
BURY, JPT and TOMBS, RP, *Thiers 1797–1877: A Political Life,* (London 1871)
BUSCH, M, *Bismarck in the Franco-German War 1870–71,* (London 1879)
BUSCH, M, *Bismarck: Some Secret Pages of his History,* (London 1898)
CAEMMERER, Lieutenant General von, *The Development of Strategical Science,* (London 1905)
CANE, Brigadier General JP du, *The Campaign in Alsace August 1870,* (London 1912)
CARR, W, *The Origins of the Wars of German Unification,* (London 1991)
CARTIER, V, *Le General Trochu,* (Paris 1914)
CHABOT, Colonel Jules de, *La Cavalerie Allemande pendant la Guerre de 1870–71,* (Paris 1899)
CHANZY, General A, *La Deuxième Armée de la Loire,* (Paris 1871)
CHAPELLE, Count de la, *The War of 1870,* (London 1870)
CHESNEY, Lieutenant Colonel C and REEVE, H, *The Military Resources of Prussia and France,* (London 1870)
COX, GP, *The Halt in the Mud,* (Oxford 1894)
CRAIG, GA, *The Battle of Königgrätz,* (London 1965)
CRAIG, GA, *The Politics of the Prussian Army,* (Oxford 1964)
CREVELD, M van, *Supplying War,* (Cambridge 1977)
'DAILY NEWS', *Correspondence of the War between Germany and France, 1870–71, (London 1871)*
DEMETER. K, *The German Officer Corps in Society and State 1650–1945,* (London 1965)
DUCROT, General A, *La Journée de Sedan,* (Paris 1872)
ELLIOT-WRIGHT P, *Gravelotte-St Privat 1870,* (Westport, Connecticut 2005)
FAIDHERBE, General L, *Campagne de l'Armée du Nord,* (Paris 1871)
FILON, A, *Recollections of the Empress Eugénie,* (London 1920)
FITZGEORGE, Captain, *The Battle of Sedan,* (London 1871)
FOERSTER, W, *Prinz Friedrich Karl von Preussen,* (Stuttgart 1910)
FORBES, A, *Memories and Studies of War and Peace,* (London 1895)
FORBES, A, *My Experiences of the War between France and Germany,* (London 1871)
FRANKLYN, HB, *The Great Battles of 1870 and Blockade of Metz,* (London 1887)
FREDERICK WILLIAM, Crown Prince *The War Diary of the Emperor Frederick III* (trans AR Allinson), (London 1927)
FRENCH GENERAL STAFF, *La Guerre de 1870–71,* (Paris 1901)
FREYCINET, C de, *La Guerre en Province,* (Paris 1872)
FRIEDRICH, O, *Blood and Iron,* (New York 1995)

FROSSARD, General, *Rapport sur les Opérations de Deuxième Corps,* (Paris 1872)
FULFORD, R (ed) *Your Dear Letter: Private Correspondence Of Queen Victoria and the Crown Princess Of Prussia 1865–71,* (London 1981)
FULLER, Major General JFC, *Decisive Battles of the Western World,* (London 1956)
FURSE, Colonel GA, *The Organisation and Administration of Lines of Communication in War,* (London 1894)
GALL, L, *Bismarck: The White Revolutionary,* (London 1896)
GERMAN GENERAL STAFF, *Official Account of the Franco-German War 1870–1871* (trans Capt FCH Clarke), London 1874)
GHEUSI, PB, *Gambetta: Life and Letters,* (London 1910)
GHIO, A (ed), *Procés de Maréchal Bazaine,* (Paris 1874)
GIESBERG, RI, *The Treaty of Frankfort,* (Philadelphia 1966)
GOLTZ, C von der, *Leon Gambetta und Seine Armeen,* (Berlin 1877)
GÖRLITZ, W, *The German General Staff,* (London 1953)
GUEDALLA, P, *The Two Marshals,* (London 1943)
HALE, Colonel LONSDALE, *The 'People's War' in France 1870–71,* (London 1904)
HATZFELDT, Count P, *Letters to his Wife 1870–71,* (London 1905)
HELMS, M, *Moltke, his Life and Character,* (London 1892)
HELVIG, H, *Operations of the I Bavarian Corps under General Von der Tann,* (trans G Schwabe), (London 1874)
HENDERSON, Colonel GFR, *The Battle of Spicheren,* (London n.d)
HENDERSON, Colonel GFR, *The Battle of Wörth, (Yorktown Surrey 1899)*
HERISSON, Count d', *Journal of a Staff Officer in Paris during The Events of 1870 and 1871,* (London 1885)
HEYDE, E and FROESE, A, *Geschichte der Belagerung von Paris im Jahre 1870/71,* (Berlin 1874)
HIBBERT, C, *Garibaldi and his Enemies,* (London 1965)
HOFFBAUER, Captain E, *The German Artillery in the Battles Near Metz,* (London 1874)
HOHENLOHE-INGELFINGEN, Prince Kraft zu, *Letters on Artillery,* (trans NL Walford), (London 1890)
HOHENLOHE-INGELFINGEN, Prince Kraft zu, *Letters on Cavalry,* (trans NL Walford), (London 1889)
HOHENLOHE-INGELFINGEN, Prince Kraft zu, *Letters on Infantry,* (trans NL Walford), (London 1892)
HOHENLOHE-INGELFINGEN, Prince Kraft zu, *Letters on Strategy,* (London 1898)
HOLLYDAY, FBM, *Bismarck's Rival,* (Durham, N Carolina 1960)
HOLMES, R, *The Road to Sedan,* (London 1984)
HOLSTEIN, F von, *Memoirs,* Cambridge 1955)
HÖNIG, F, *Inquiries concerning the Tactics of the Future,* (trans Captain HM Bowes), (London 1899)
HÖNIG, F, *Twenty Four Hours of Moltke's Strategy,* (trans NL Walford), (Woolwich 1895)

HOOPER, G, *The Campaign of Sedan,* (London 1908)
HORNE, A, *The Fall of Paris,* (London 1965)
HOWARD, M, *The Franco-Prussian War,* (London 1962)
HOWES, Colonel P, *The Catalytic Wars,* (London 1998)
HOZIER, Captain HM (ed), *The Franco-Prussian War: Its Causes Incidents and Consequences,* (London n.d)
HUGHES, DJ, *Moltke on the Art of War,* (Novato, California 1993)
JOHN, K, *The Prince Imperial,* (London 1939)
JOUBERT, L, *La Bataille de Sedan,* (Paris 1873)
KOEHLER, Major, 'The German Cavalry in the Battle of Vionville-Mars-la-Tour' in: *Cavalry Studies from two Great Wars,* (Kansas City 1896)
KRETSCHMANN H von, *Kriegsbriefe aus dem Jahren 1870–71,* (Stuttgart 1904)
LABOUCHÈRE, H, *Diary of the Besieged Resident in Paris,* (London 1871)
LÖHLEIN, L, *The Operations of the Corps of General von Werder,* (Chatham n.d)
LONLAY, Dick de, *Francais et Allemands, (Paris 1890)*
LORD, RH, *The Origins of the War of 1870,* (Harvard 1924)
MAGUIRE, TM, *The Franco-German War July 15-August 18, 1870,* (London 1909)
MAUNI, R de, *Eight Months on Duty,* (London 1872)
MAURICE, Major General (ed), *The Franco-German War 1870–71,* (London 1900)
MAY, Major ES, *Field Artillery with the Other Arms,* (London 1898)
MAY, Major ES, *Guns and Cavalry,* (London 1896)
McCABE, JD, *History of the War between Germany and France, (New York 1871)*
McELWEE, W, *The Art of War from Waterloo to Mons,* (London 1974)
MILLMAN, R, *British Foreign Policy and the Coming of the Franco-Prussian War,* (Oxford 1965)
MOLTKE, Field Marshal H von, *Correspondance Militaire de Maréchal de Moltke,* (Paris n.d)
MOLTKE, Field Marshal H von, *Letters to his Mother and his Brothers,* (trans C Bell & H Fischer) (London 1891)
MOLTKE, Field Marshal H von, *Letters to his Wife,* (London 1896)
MOLTKE, Field Marshal H von, *Military Correspondence 1870–71,* (ed. S Wilkinson) (Oxford 1923)
MOLTKE, Field Marshal H von, *Military Correspondence 1870–71,* (trans. H Bell), (Fort Leavenworth, Kansas n.d)
MOLTKE, Field Marshal H von, *Moltke as a Correspondent,* (ed. M Herms), (London 1893)
MOLTKE, Field Marshal H von, *The Franco- German War of 1870–71,* (London 1907)
MOLTKE, Field Marshal H von, *Strategy: Its Theory and Application,*(Westport, Connecticut 1971)
MORRIS, W O'Connor, *Moltke,* (London 1893)
NASO, E von, *Moltke,* (Hamburg 1937)

NEWDIGATE, Colonel E (trans), *The Army of the North German Confederation,* (London 1872)
OLLIER, E, *Cassell's Illustrated History of the War between France and Germany,* (London n.d)
OLLIVIER, E, *The Franco-Prussian War and its Hidden Causes,* (London 1913)
ORTHOLAN, Henri, *L'Armée de la Loire,* (Paris 2005)
PARET, P (ed), *Makers of Modern Strategy,* (Oxford 1994)
PATRY, L, *The Reality of War* (trans D Fermer), (London 2001)
PELET-NARBONNE, General von, *Cavalry on Service,* (London 1906)
PFLANZE, O, *Bismarck and the Development of Germany,*(Princeton, New Jersey 1990)
POTTINGER, EA, *Napoleon III and the German Crisis,* (Cambridge, Massachusetts 1968)
PRATT, Lieutenant Colonel SC, *Saarbrück to Paris 1870,* (London 1914)
RICH, E, *A History of the Franco-German War,* (London 1884)
RIDLEY, J, *Napoleon III and Eugènie,* (London 1979)
RIEZ, MG Martiny de, *La Guerre de 1870–71,* (Laon 1871)
RODD, R, *Frederick: Crown Prince and Emperor,* (London 1888)
ROBINSON, GT, *The Fall of Metz,* (London 1871)
ROSINSKI, H, *The German Army,* (London 1939)
SARAZIN, Doctor, *Récits de la Dernière Guerre, Franco-Allemand,*(Paris 1887)
RUSSELL, WH, *My Diary during the Last Great War,* (London 1874)
RÜSTOW, W, *The War for the Rhine Frontier 1870,* (London 1871–2)
SCHEIBERT, J, *Franco-German War 1870–71,* (trans JA Ferrier), (Chatham 1891)
SCHELL, Major A von, *The Operations of the First Army under General von Goeben,* (London 1873)
SCHELL, Major A von, *The Operations of the First Army under General von Steinmetz,* (London 1873)
SENCOURT, R, *Napoleon III: The Modern Emperor,* (London 1933)
SHERIDAN, General P, *Personal Memoirs,* (London 1888)
SHOWALTER, D, *Railroads and Rifles: Soldiers, Technology and the Unification of Germany,* (Hamden, Connecticut 1975)
SHOWALTER, D, *The Wars of German Unification,* (London 2004)
STADELMANN, R, *Moltke und der Staat,* (Krefeld 1950)
STANNARD, H, *Gambetta,* (London 1921)
STOFFEL, E, *Military Reports addressed to the French War Minister,* (London 1872)
STONE, D, *First Reich,* (London 2002)
STONE, Captain FG, *Tactical Studies from the Franco-German War of 1870–71,* (London 1886)
STOSCH, General A von, *Denkwurdigkeiten,* (Berlin 1904)
STRAUSS. GLM, *Men who have made the New German Empire,* (London 1875)
TAYLOR, AJP, *Bismarck,* (London 1955)
TAYLOR, AJP, *From Napoleon to the Second International,* (London 1993)
'THE TIMES', *The Campaign of 1870–71,* (London 1871)
THOMPSON, JM, *Louis Napoleon and the Second Empire,* (Oxford 1954)

TIEDEMANN, Colonel B von, *The Siege Operations in the Campaign against France 1870–71,* (trans. Major Tyler) (London 1877)
TOVEY, Lieutenant Colonel, *The Elements of Strategy,* (London 1904)
TURNBULL, P, *The Birth of a Nation,* (London 1985)
VERDY du VERNOIS, General J von, *With the Royal Headquarters in 1870–71,* (London 1924)
VIDAL, Commandant P, *Campagne de Sedan,* (Paris 1910)
VIZETELLY, EA, *My Days of Adventure: The Fall of France 1870–1871,* (London 1914)
WALDERSEE, Field Marshal, Count A von, *A Field Marshal's Memoirs* (trans F Whyte), (London 1924)
WARTENSLEBEN, Colonel H von, *Operations of the First Army under General von Manteuffel,* (London 1873)
WARTENSLEBEN, Colonel H von, *Operations of the South Army,* (London 1872)
WASHBURNE, EB, *Correspondence relating to the Franco-German War and Insurrection of the Commune,* (Washington DC 1878)
WAWRO, G, *The Franco- Prussian War,* (Cambridge 2003)
WELLESLEY, Sir V and SENCOURT, R, *Conversations with Napoleon III,* (London 1934)
WETZEL, D, *A Duel of Giants,* (Madison, Wisconsin 2001)
WHITTON, Lieutenant Colonel FE, *Moltke,* (London 1921)
WIEGLER, P, *William the First: his Life and Times,* (London 1929)
WILKINSON, Spencer, *The Brain of An Army,* (London 1895)
WILMOT, S Eardley, *Life of Vice Admiral Lord Lyons,* (London 1898)
WILSON, R, *The Franco- German War,* (Edinburgh 1881)
WIMPFFEN, General EF de, *Sedan,* (Paris 1871)
WITTICH, General L von, *Journal de Guerre,* (Paris 1902)
WOOD, Field Marshal Sir E, *Achievements of Cavalry,* (London 1897)

Index

BOOKS IN THIS SERIES:

1. *The Battle of Majuba Hill The Transvaal Campaign 1880–1881* John Laband (ISBN 978-1-911512-38-7)
2. *For Queen and Company Vignettes of the Irish Soldier in the Indian Mutiny* David Truesdale (ISBN 978-1-911512-79-0)
3. *The Furthest Garrison Imperial Regiments in New Zealand 1840–1870* Adam Davis (ISBN 978-1-911628-29-3)
4. *Victory Over Disease Resolving the Medical Crisis in the Crimean War, 1854–1856* Michael Hinton (ISBN 978-1-911628-31-6)
5. *Journey Through the Wilderness Garnet Wolseley's Canadian Red River Expedition of 1870* Paul McNicholls (ISBN 978-1-911628-30-9)
6. *Kitchener The Man Not The Myth* Anne Samson (ISBN 978-1-912866-45-8)
7. *The British and the Sikhs Discovery, Warfare and Friendship c1700–1900* Gurinder Singh Mann (ISBN 978-1-911628-24-8)
8. *Bazaine 1870 Scapegoat for a Nation* Quintin Barry (ISBN 978-1-913336-08-0)
9. *Redcoats in the Classroom The British Army's Schools For Soldiers and Their Children During the 19th Century* Howard R. Clarke (ISBN 978-1-912866-47-2)
10. *The Rescue They Called a Raid The Jameson Raid 1895–96* David Snape (ISBN 978-1-913118-77-8)
11. *Hungary 1848 The Winter Campaign* Christopher Pringle (ISBN 978-1-913118-78-5)
12. *The War of the Two Brothers The Portuguese Civil War 1828-1834* Sérgio Veludo Coelho (ISBN 978-1-914059-26-1)
14. *Forgotten Victorian Generals Studies in the Exercise of Command and Control in the British Army 1837–1901* Christopher Brice (editor) (ISBN 978-1-910777-20-6)
15. *The German War of 1866 The Bohemian and Moravian Campaign* Theodore Fontane (ISBN 978-1-914059-29-2)
16. *Dust of Glory The First Anglo-Afghan War 1839–1842, its Causes and Course* Bill Whitburn (ISBN 978-1-914059-33-9)
17. *Saarbruck to Sedan The Franco-German War 1870–1871 Volume 1* Ralph Weaver (ISBN 978-1-914059-88-9)
18. *The Battle of Lissa 1866 How the Industrial Revolution Changed the Face of Naval Warfare* Quintin Barry (ISBN 978-1-914059-92-6)
19. *The Zulu Kingdom and the Boer Invasion of 1837–1840* John Laband (ISBN 978-1-914059-89-6)
20. *The Fire of Venture Was in His Veins* Major Allan Wilson and the Shangani Patrol 1893 David Snape (ISBN 978-1-914059-90-2)
21. *From the Atacama to the Andes Battles of the War of the Pacific 1879–1883* Alan Curtis (ISBN 978-1-914059-90-2)
22. *The Rise of the Sikh Soldier The Sikh Warrior Through the Ages, c1700–1900* Gurinder Singh Mann (ISBN 978-1-915070-52-4)
23. *Victorian Crusaders British and Irish Volunteers in the Papal Army 1860–70* Nicholas Schofield (ISBN 978-1-915070-53-1)
24. *The Battle for the Swiepwald Austria's Fatal Blunder at Königgrätz, the climactic battle of the Austro-Prussian War, 3 July 1866* Ernst Heidrich (ISBN 978-1-915070-49-4)
25. *British Military Panoramas Battle in The Round, 1800–1914* Ian F.W. Beckett (ISBN 978-1-915113-84-9)
26. *Onwards to Omdurman The Anglo-Egyptian Campaign to Reconquer the Sudan, 1896–1898* Keith Surridge (ISBN 978-1-915070-51-7)
27. *Hungary 1849 The Summer Campaign* Wilhelm Ramming, Christopher Pringle (editor) (ISBN 978-1-915113-80-1)
28. *Line in the Sand French Foreign Legion Forts and Fortifications in Morocco 1900–1926* Richard Jeynes (ISBN 978-1-915113-83-2)
29. *The Republic Fights Back The Franco-German War 1870-1871 Volume 2* Ralph Weaver (ISBN 978-1-915070-50-0)
30. *Controlling the Frontier Southern Africa 1806–1828, The Cape Frontier Wars and The Fetcani Alarm* Hugh Driver (ISBN 978-1-915113-78-8)
31. *The Battle of Magersfontein Victory and defeat on the South African veld, 10–12 December 1899* Garth Benneyworth (ISBN 978-1-915113-79-5)
32. *Too Little Too Late The Campaign in West and South Germany June–July 1866* Michael Embree (ISBN 978-1-804513-77-4)
33. *The Destruction of the Imperial Army* Volume 1: The Opening Engagements of the Franco-German War 1870–71 Grenville Bird (ISBN 978-1-915113-81-8)
34. *Kitchener* The Man Not the Myth Anne Samson (ISBN 978-1-804513-84-2)
35. *From Ironclads to Dreadnoughts* The Development of the German Battleship, 1864–1918 Dirk Nottelmann & David M. Sullivan (ISBN 978-1-804511-84-8)
36. *The Destruction of the Imperial Army* Volume 2: The Battles around Metz Grenville Bird (ISBN 978-1-804511-85-5)
37. *More Work Than Glory* Buffalo Soldiers in the United States Army, 1866–1916 John P Langellier (ISBN 978-1-804513-34-7)
38. *The Spioenkop Campaign* The Battles to Relieve Ladysmith 17–27 January 1900 Robert Davidson (ISBN 978-1-804513-31-6)
39. *The Destruction of the Imperial Army* Volume 3: *The Sedan Campaign 1870* Grenville Bird (ISBN 978-1-804513-32-3)
40. *The Destruction of the Imperial Army* Volume 4: *Sedan, Strasbourg and Metz* 1870 Grenville Bird (ISBN 978-1-804514-59-7)
41. *Memorandum on the Prussian Army in Relation to the Campaign of 1866* Lieutenant Colonel W.E.M Reilly (ISBN 978-1-804516-27-0)
42. *Black Week: The British Army and Defeat in Anglo-Boer War 1899-1900* Quintin Barry (ISBN 978-1-804511-86-2)
43. *War in the East. A Military History of the Russo-Turkish War 1877-78* Quintin Barry (ISBN 978-1-804517-30-7)
44. *The First Schleswig-Holstein War 1848-50* Nick Svendsen (ISBN 978-1-804517-36-9)
45. *The Hundred Thousand Sons of St Louis* Ralph Weaver (ISBN 978-1-804517-37-6)
46. *Bismarck's First War: The Campaign in Schleswig and Jutland 1864* Michael Embree (ISBN 978-1-804517-38-3)
47. *The Honvéd War. Armies of the Hungarian War of Independence 1848-49* Nigel James Smith (ISBN 978-1-804514-60-3)
48. *Radestzky's Marches. The Campaigns of 1848 and 1849 in Upper Italy* Michael Embree (ISBN 978-1-804517-42-0)
49. *The Campaign on the Loire 1870-71: Orléans and Le Mans* Quintin Barry (ISBN 978-1-804517-82-6)
50. *The British Empire's Regulars 1880-1914: Soldiers of Britain, India and Africa* Wendell Scholander (ISBN 978-1-804515-62-4)
51. *The Last Throw of the Dice: Bourbaki and Werder in Eastern France 1870-71* Quintin Barry (ISBN 978-1-804517-78-9)
52. *Three Weeks in November. A Military History of the Swiss Civil War of 1847* Ralph Weaver (ISBN 978-1-804518-49-6)
53. *The Battle of Wörth August 6th 1870* Lieut.-Col. G.F.R. Henderson (ISBN 978-1-804517-90-1)
54. *The Battle of Spicheren August 6th 1870* Lieut.-Col. G.F.R. Henderson (ISBN 978-1-804518-50-2)
55. *The Serbian Army in the Wars for Independence against Turkey 1876-1878* Dusan M. Babac (ISBN 978-1-804518-69-4)
56. *The Campaign in Alsace August 1870* Brigadier-General J.P. Du Cane, C.B. (ISBN 978-1-804518-82-3)
57. *The Franco-Prussian War 1870-71 Volume 1* Quintin Barry (ISBN 978-1-806721-04-7)
58. *The Franco-Prussian War 1870-71 Volume 2* Quintin Barry (ISBN 978-1-806721-05-4)